Developmental Psychopathology

Developmental Psychopathology

AMANDA VENTA
CARLA SHARP
JACK M. FLETCHER AND
PETER FONAGY
EDITORS

WILEY Blackwell

This edition first published 2021

Registered Office(s)
John Wiley & Sons, Inc., 111 River Street, Hoboken, NJ 07030, USA
John Wiley & Sons Ltd, The Atrium, Southern Gate, Chichester, West Sussex, PO19 8SQ, UK

Editorial Office
The Atrium, Southern Gate, Chichester, West Sussex, PO19 8SQ, UK

For details of our global editorial offices, customer services, and more information about Wiley products visit us at www.wiley.com.

Wiley also publishes its books in a variety of electronic formats and by print-on-demand. Some content that appears in standard print versions of this book may not be available in other formats.

Library of Congress Cataloging-in-Publication Data

Names: Venta, Amanda, 1987– editor.
Title: Developmental psychopathology / edited by Amanda Venta, Ph.D. Associate Professor Department of Psychology University of Houston [and three others].
Description: First edition. | Hoboken, NJ : Wiley, 2021. | Includes bibliographical references and index.
Identifiers: LCCN 2020043391 (print) | LCCN 2020043392 (ebook) | ISBN 9781118686485 (paperback) | ISBN 9781118686218 (adobe pdf) | ISBN 9781118686447 (epub)
Subjects: LCSH: Child psychopathology. | Child development. | Child mental health.
Classification: LCC RJ499 .D4828 2021 (print) | LCC RJ499 (ebook) | DDC 618.92/89–dc23
LC record available at https://lccn.loc.gov/2020043391
LC ebook record available at https://lccn.loc.gov/2020043392

Cover Design: Wiley
Cover Image: © sarayut /iStock /Getty Images Plus/Getty Images

Set in 10.5/12pt Times by Straive, Pondicherry, India
Printed and bound by CPI Group (UK) Ltd, Croydon, CR0 4YY

C076566_030621

This book is dedicated to the many youth and families who, by volunteering to participate in research, have taught us so much about developmental psychopathology.

Contents

Preface

Developmental Psychopathology is an interdisciplinary field that emerged in the late 1970s and early 1980s and is defined as "an evolving scientific discipline whose predominant focus is elucidating the interplay among the biological, psychological, and social contextual aspects of normal and abnormal development across the life span" (Cicchetti, 2006, p. 1). While this definition certainly highlights the enormous undertaking that a developmental psychopathology perspective demands, a number of principles help to guide us:

- Interweaving studies of *normal development and pathological* functioning into a true synthesis
- Examining developmental *continuities and discontinuities* of traits, behaviors, emotional responses, and disorders
- Evaluating evidence across *multiple levels of analysis* to include the biological, individual, family, social, and cultural levels
- Incorporating *distinct perspectives*: clinical, developmental psychology, child/adolescent psychiatry, genetics, neurology, public health, and philosophy of science into multidisciplinary effort
- Exploring *both risk and protective* factors and their interplay in order to delineate pathways of risk and resilience
- Involving *reciprocal, transactional models* of influence in the field's causal models (e.g., gene–environment interaction)

These principles highlight how the developmental psychopathology approach differs from the traditional descriptive psychiatric approaches represented in most child psychology textbooks. The developmental psychopathology approach goes beyond the "what" of psychopathology to include the "how" of psychopathology. How does normal development go awry? What factors determine the multiple pathways that lead to psychopathology in one child, but not another? Because of the focus on "how," the developmental psychopathology approach has, over the last 30 years, become the guiding framework for understanding psychopathology in youth. Courses both at the undergraduate and graduate levels are being renamed from "Abnormal Child Psychology" to "Developmental Psychopathology." Yet, few textbooks have been created to guide teaching of developmental psychopathology courses at the upper undergraduate level.

There are two major challenges in writing a developmental psychopathology textbook: (1) finding organizing principles that can structure a complex, dense, and multidisciplinary field into manageable chapters and (2) not digressing back to a descriptive psychiatric approach of providing information on the "what" of disorders, but rather staying true to the "how" of psychopathology. In addressing these challenges, the organization of the textbook is as follows:

- In Part I, three introductory chapters lay the foundation. First, we want to present how psychology has typically classified and understood psychopathology, highlighting both the benefits and problems of the traditional approach. Building on that background, we then describe how the developmental psychopathology approach can address some of the limitations of the traditional approach. We will use the principles of developmental psychopathology throughout the rest of this book. In Part I, we also provide a summary of normal development, which is key to the developmental psychopathology approach—that is, we understand that normal and abnormal development are both components of understanding disorder. In this section you will also find a chapter on insecure attachment—a way of describing relationships between children and their caregivers—because, when disrupted, those relationships often relate to various forms of psychopathology.
- To showcase the fact that our approach is "developmental," disorders are organized not following the usual organization in psychopathology textbooks (e.g., mood disorders), but rather how they appear through development. Accordingly, Part II of this book focuses on the problems that first emerge in childhood: attention deficit hyperactivity disorder, autism spectrum disorders, antisocial behavior, and fear and anxiety. In Part III, we shift our focus further down the developmental course in order to focus on adolescents, with chapters covering depression and suicide, eating disorders, substance use disorders, schizophrenia, and emerging personality disorders. It is important to note that the problems described in Part II also affect teenagers, and that the problems described in Parts II and III also affect adults. We have arranged sections by the stage of development where problems are typically first noticed by individuals and their loved ones, but every chapter reviews psychopathology that exists, in some form, across the whole lifespan. Finally, in Part IV of the book we talk about important topics in developmental psychopathology that were not covered elsewhere, like maltreatment and divorce, separation, and loss. We close with a chapter asking "quo vadis?" or "where do we go from here?" which looks to the future.
- Disorder chapters will be organized similarly: (1) *defining the disorder* according to the DSM, (2) presenting the most empirically validated developmental psychopathology *model* for that disorder, reflecting the interplay between risk and protective factors across multiple levels of analyses—to include the biological, individual, social, and cultural factors, (3) discussing the empirical evidence in support of each of the *etiological factors* in the model, including studies that have tested

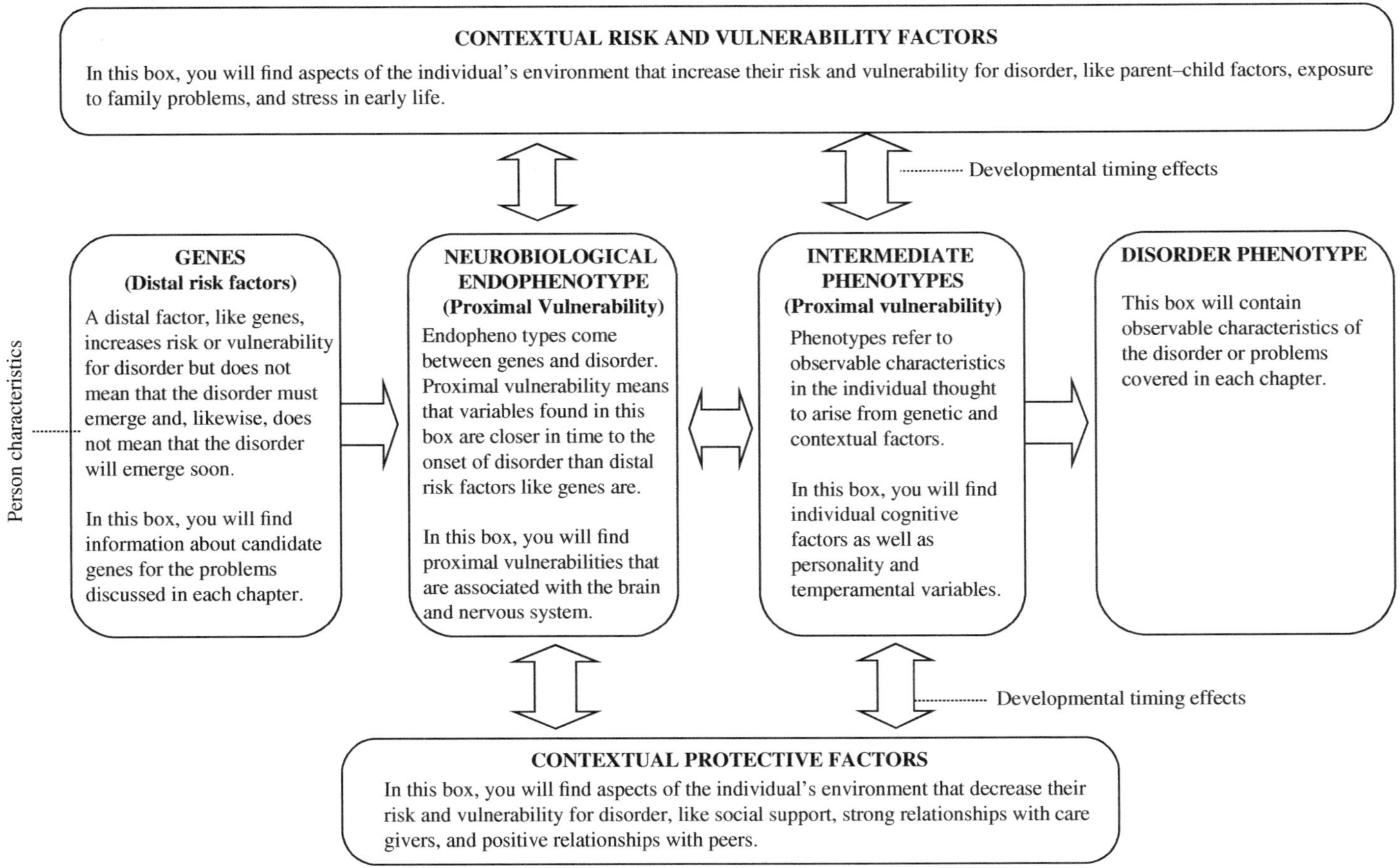

FIGURE 1 Developmental Psychopathology Framework

interactions between factors (e.g., gene–environment studies), (4) presenting *assessment and intervention* implications, and (5) highlighting areas for *future research*.
- Each chapter will contain a figure capturing the developmental psychopathology approach visually. Your first introduction to that figure is in this preface, where each of the terms is defined (see Figure 1). You will also see this framework through the remainder of the book and we encourage you to refer back here when you need a reminder of what each component represents.

It is our hope that this textbook will provide you with a rich understanding of psychopathology that moves beyond simple characterizations of mental health disorder as something you either do or do not have—something that was absent one day and emerged the next. The developmental psychopathology approach instead paints a more complicated, flexible picture of psychopathology. We will review research in each of the areas described above, showing that psychopathology emerges through the combination of many factors that shift across time—some of which are deeply buried in our biology and some of which exist in our outside environments. This approach is not only consistent with the most cutting-edge science, but it can help combat stereotypes and stigma about mental illness head-on by showing that all of us are shaped by small and large forces across our lives, many of which are out of our control.

Reference

Cicchetti, Dante (2006). Theory and method. In Dante Cicchetti & D. J. Cohen (Eds.), *Development and psychopathology* (2nd ed., pp). New York, NY: John Wiley & Sons, Inc.

The Editors

Amanda Venta, PhD
Associate Professor
Department of Psychology
University of Houston

Carla Sharp, PhD
Professor
Department of Psychology
University of Houston

Jack M. Fletcher, PhD
Hugh Roy and Lillie Cranz Cullen Distinguished Professor
Associate Vice President for Research Administration
Associate Chair, Department of Psychology
University of Houston

Peter Fonagy, FMedSci FBA
Head of the Division of Psychology and Language Sciences, University College London
Chief Executive, Anna Freud National Centre for Children & Families
Director, UCLPartners Integrated Mental Health & Behaviour Change ProgrammeSenior Clinical Advisor on Children's Mental Health, NHS England

Library of Congress Information

Amanda Cristina Venta, Date of Birth: March 20, 1987
Carla Sharp, Date of Birth: October 9, 1971
Jack McFarlin Fletcher, Date of Birth: May 12, 1952
Peter Fonagy, Date of Birth: August 14, 1952

About the Editors

Amanda Venta, PhD, is an Associate Professor of Psychology serving the APA Accredited Clinical Psychology doctoral program at the University of Houston. She received her BA from Rice University and her MA and PhD in Clinical Psychology from the University of Houston. She completed her pre-doctoral internship at DePelchin Children's Center through the Menninger Department of Psychiatry and Behavioral Sciences at Baylor College of Medicine, where she remains Adjunct Faculty. Dr. Venta's clinical training focused on children, adolescents, and families, with practicum placements at DePelchin Children's Center and Texas Children's Hospital. She also provided psychological services within the University of Houston's Psychology Research and Services Center and in several Houston-area schools. Her primary research interests are the development of psychopathology in youth and the protective effect of attachment security, with additional interests in emotion dysregulation and social cognition. She has recently focused on the psychological functioning of recently immigrated adolescents from Central America, with related research and clinical work. Her published work includes more than 90 manuscripts and chapters as well as two books in press besides the current edited volume, including *Cultural competency in psychological assessment: Working effectively with Latinos* with Oxford University Press and an edited collection entitled *Serving Refugee Children: Listening to Stories of Detention in the USA* with Peter Lang. She has received research funding from the National Institute of Minority Health and Health Disparities, the National Institutes of Mental Health, and the American Psychological Foundation.

Carla Sharp, PhD, trained as a clinical psychologist (University of Stellenbosch, South Africa) from 1994 to 1997, after which she completed a PhD in Developmental Psychopathology at Cambridge University, UK, 1997–2000. In 2001, she obtained full licensure as a Clinical Psychologist in the UK through a Statement of Equivalence with the British Psychological Society. From 2001 to 2004 she was appointed as a Research Postdoctoral Fellow in Developmental Psychopathology, Cambridge University. In 2004, she moved to the United States to take up an appointment as Assistant Professor in the Menninger Department of Psychiatry at Baylor College of Medicine. She obtained provisional licensure as a Clinical Psychologist in Texas in 2008. In 2009, she was appointed as Associate Professor in the Department of Psychology at the University of Houston. In 2014 Dr. Sharp was promoted to Full Professor. Her published work includes over 270 peer-reviewed publications and numerous chapters reflecting her interests in the social-cognitive basis of psychiatric problems and problems of behavioral health, and the application of this work in developing diagnostic tools and interventions in youth. She has co-authored three books: An edited volume with Springer titled *The handbook of borderline personality disorder in children and adolescents*, an edited volume with Oxford University Press titled *Social cognition and developmental psychopathology*, and a book with MIT Press titled *Midbrain mutiny: Behavioral economics and neuroeconomics of gambling addiction as a basic reward system disorder*. Her work has been continuously funded since 2009 by the National Institutes of Health and various foundations.

Jack M. Fletcher, PhD, is a Hugh Roy and Lillie Cranz Cullen Distinguished Professor of Psychology at the University of Houston. He received a BA degree from Davidson College in 1973 and a PhD in clinical psychology from the University of Florida in 1978. Dr. Fletcher has been affiliated with The University of Houston since 1979, first as an adjunct assistant professor (1979–1985), then as a tenured Associate Professor (1985–1989), adjunct Professor (1989–2006), and beginning his current tenured appointment in 2006. From 1978 to 1985, Dr. Fletcher was the Acting Director of the Mental Retardation/Developmental Disabilities Research Section at the Texas Research Institute of Mental Sciences; from 1989 to 2006, Dr. Fletcher was a tenured Professor in the Division of Developmental Pediatrics in the Department of Pediatrics at The University of Texas Medical School, Houston. For the past 40 years, Dr. Fletcher, a board-certified child neuropsychologist, has worked on issues related to child neuropsychology, including studies of children with spina bifida, traumatic brain injury, and other acquired disorders. In the area of developmental learning and attention disorders, Dr. Fletcher has addressed issues related to definition and classification, neurobiological correlates, and, most recently, intervention. Dr. Fletcher directs a Learning Disability Research Center grant funded by the National Institute of Child Health and Human Development. He served on the Eunice Kennedy Shriver National Institute of Child Health and Human Development National Advisory Council, the Rand Reading Study Group, the National Research Council Committee on Scientific Principles in Education Research, and the President's Commission on Excellence in Special Education. The author of three books and over 400 papers, Dr. Fletcher was the recipient of the Samuel T. Orton award from the International Dyslexia Association in 2003 and a co-recipient of the Albert J. Harris award from the International Reading Association in 2006. He was President of the International Neuropsychological Society in 2008–2009.

Peter Fonagy, PhD, is Head of the Division of Psychology and Language Sciences at UCL; Chief Executive of the Anna Freud National Centre for Children and Families, London; Consultant to the Child and Family Programme at the Menninger Department of Psychiatry and Behavioural Sciences at Baylor College of Medicine; and holds visiting professorships at Yale and Harvard Medical Schools. He has occupied a number of key leadership positions including Chair of the Outcomes Measurement Reference Group at the UK Department of Health, Chair of two NICE Guideline Development Groups, Chair of the Strategy Group for National Occupational Standards for Psychological Therapies, and co-chaired the UK Department of Health's Expert Reference Group on Vulnerable Children. His clinical interests centre on issues of early attachment relationships, social cognition, borderline personality disorder and violence. He has published over 550 scientific papers, 260 chapters, and has authored or co-authored 20 books. He is a Fellow of the British Academy, the Academy of Medical Sciences, the Academy of Social Sciences, and the American Association for Psychological Science, and was elected to Honorary Fellowship by the American College of Psychiatrists. He has received Lifetime Achievement Awards from several national and international professional associations, including the British Psychological Society, the International Society for the Study of Personality Disorder, the British and Irish Group for the Study of Personality Disorder, the World Association for Infant Mental Health, and was in 2015 the first UK recipient of the Wiley Prize of the British Academy for Outstanding Achievements in Psychology by an international scholar.

List of Contributors

Anna Abate, MA
Sam Houston State University
Huntsville, TX

Brian Allen, PhD
Penn State College of Medicine
Hershey, PA

Emma Anderson-White, MA
Sam Houston State University
Huntsville, TX

Sarah Barksdale, BA
Sam Houston State University
Huntsville, TX

Bailey A. Barnes, BA
Sam Houston State University
Huntsville, TX

Katherine Bergez BS
University of Houston
Houston, TX

Johanna Bick, PhD
University of Houston
Houston, TX

Caitlin H. Child, BS
Sam Houston State University
Huntsville, TX

Maxwell R. Christensen, MA
Sam Houston State University
Huntsville, TX

Haley E. Conroy, BA
University of Houston
Houston, TX

Michelle P. Desir, PhD
Penn State College of Medicine
Hershey, PA

Rachel H. Fein, PhD
Texas Children's Hospital
Houston, TX

Jack M. Fletcher, PhD
University of Houston
Houston, TX

Peter Fonagy, PhD
University College London
London, UK

Jessica R. Hart, PhD
Northwest Forensic Institute
Portland, OR

Craig E. Henderson, PhD
Sam Houston State University
Huntsville, TX

Sophie Kerr
University of Houston
Houston, TX

Beata A. Krembuszewski, MA
Sam Houston State University
Huntsville, TX

Hillary A. Langley, PhD
Sam Houston State University
Huntsville, TX

Rebecca Lipschutz, MS
University of Houston
Houston, TX

Allison C. Meinert
University of Houston
Houston, TX

Deborah Michel, PhD, CED-S, FAED
Eating Recovery Center
Houston, TX

Sarah S. Mire, PhD
University of Houston
Houston, TX

Francesca Penner, MA
University of Houston
Houston, TX

Elizabeth M. Raines, MA
University of Houston
Houston, TX

Mayra B. Ramos, MA
Sam Houston State University
Huntsville, TX

Mia M. Ricardo, MA
Sam Houston State University
Huntsville, TX

Matthew T. Roberts
Sam Houston State University
Huntsville, TX

Lauren J. Ryan, MA
Sam Houston State University
Huntsville, TX

Carla Sharp, PhD
University of Houston
Houston, TX

Chad E. Shenk, PhD
Penn State College of Medicine
Hershey, PA

Eric Sumlin, BA
University of Houston
Houston, TX

Cody Sze, BA
Sam Houston State University
Huntsville, TX

Erika S. Trent, MA
University of Houston
Houston, TX

Amanda Venta, PhD
University of Houston
Houston, TX

Andres G. Viana, PhD
University of Houston
Houston, TX

Jesse Walker, BA
University of Houston
Houston, TX

Kiana Wall, MA
University of Houston
Houston, TX

Part I

Background

In these first four chapters, we provide the background you will need for the rest of the book. You will learn first about the ways that mental health practitioners and researchers have thought about and defined psychopathology traditionally (Chapter 1) and also about an alternative approach (Chapter 2) that solves some of the problems identified in the traditional approaches. The approach covered in Chapter 2—called developmental psychopathology—will carry us through the remaining chapters in this book. Throughout this entire book, we will highlight how studying psychopathology goes hand-in-hand with studying normal development, or the absence of psychopathology. For that reason, in this introductory part of the book we also include a chapter on normal development (Chapter 3) and a chapter highlighting the essential role of caregiving relationships (Chapter 4), for context. Specifically, in this part of the book, we will cover the following topics:

Chapter 1

Traditional Approaches to Child Psychopathology

KIANA WALL, ERIC SUMLIN, AND CARLA SHARP

Chapter Overview

What is psychopathology? How do we know when a child or adolescent has clinically significant symptoms of a psychological or behavioral disorder? How do we ensure that medical and mental health professionals, patients, and other stakeholders assess for, and communicate about, mental illness in a consistent way? Formal diagnostic systems and other approaches to the classification of psychopathology allow us to answer these questions to varying degrees. In this chapter, we will discuss different approaches to understanding, classifying, and diagnosing psychopathology in children and adolescents. We conclude with a summary of the limitations of each approach and introduce the benefit of a developmental psychopathology approach to conceptualizing psychopathology.

Diagnosis and Classification

Psychopathology is the study of mental disorders. *Mental, or psychological, disorders* are characterized by behavioral patterns and cognitive, emotional, and physical symptoms that deviate from a normative developmental trajectory and are not typical of individuals living in the same cultural context. "Mental disorders are usually associated with significant distress or disability in social, occupational, or other important activities" (American Psychiatric Association, 2013, p. 20) because symptoms of mental illness can have serious negative impacts on people's physical health, education, employment, relationships, and

Developmental Psychopathology, First Edition. Edited by Amanda Venta, Carla Sharp, Jack M. Fletcher, and Peter Fonagy.

well-being. Unsurprisingly, then, scientists, philosophers, doctors, and other scholars have taken an interest in psychopathology since ancient times. Historically, how have we decided what psychological symptoms or behaviors are considered *abnormal*? How do we keep track of this knowledge or information to ensure that everyone with an interest in mental health or a role in treating mental health concerns is educated and "on the same page" when it comes to psychopathology? In the modern era, we have facilitated communication about mental health and tried to understand and organize knowledge about psychopathology using classification systems.

Classification is the act of categorizing things according to a set of criteria. Things in the same category tend to share similar characteristics or features. For example, biologists interested in *taxonomy*, the science of classification, might classify sea creatures according to dimensions such as size, diet, or gestation process. Classification systems for psychopathology aim to organize the observed symptoms of psychological disorders. The most commonly used and well-known classification system for mental disorders in the United States (US) is the Diagnostic and Statistical Manual of Mental Disorders (DSM). The most recent version of the DSM, the DSM-5, contains 22 classes of disorders. Within each class, specific diagnoses are listed and most of these diagnoses list a set of criteria and number of symptoms that must be met for an individual's functioning to be considered abnormal and for a diagnosis to be given. The diagnoses in each class share similar features. For example, one class of disorders in the DSM-5 is the anxiety disorders. These disorders "share features of excessive fear and anxiety and related behavioral disturbances" (APA, 2013, p. 189). Diagnoses *within* the anxiety disorder class differ from one another in the types of situations and objects that cause fear, anxiety, and avoidance behavior, and all the diagnoses within the anxiety disorder class differ from diagnoses in the *other* classes in important ways. According to the DSM-5, the organization of symptoms into disorders and disorders into classes based on their shared features is "a historically determined cognitive schema imposed on clinical and scientific information to increase its comprehensibility and utility" (APA, 2013, p. 10). In other words, historical scientific research and clinical wisdom was utilized to organize and classify symptoms in a way that would allow for easier communication between mental health providers, patients, and other stakeholders.

How do classification systems for psychopathology improve our understanding of an individual's mental illness and communicate about it more easily? Once mental health providers assess for the presence of psychopathological symptoms or observe certain behaviors in their patients, they can use a classification and diagnostic system to organize their findings and come to a *differential diagnosis*. The process of diagnosing an individual gives mental health providers a starting point, including guidance about the cause of this person's difficulties, the likely course their symptoms might take, and the outcomes they might experience without intervention. These considerations can have important implications for treatment planning. Classification and diagnostic systems also act as a "shorthand" between providers, with insurance companies, and with government agencies. Rather than describe all the symptoms an individual is experiencing one by one, which could be a time-consuming process that potentially violates an individual's right to privacy, mental health providers and other involved agencies can quickly communicate the overall "gist" of a person's presenting problems by using a classification system to give them a diagnostic label.

It is important to note that although individuals with the same diagnosis experience some of the same symptoms, they often present with very *heterogeneous* symptom profiles. Additionally, there is no one *etiology* underlying the symptoms of these disorders. Therefore, a psychological disorder diagnosis, as described in the DSM-5, is only a list and description of symptoms that appear to occur together, resulting in a *phenotype* or set of observable characteristics. This phenotype is often associated with specific outcomes, suggesting that intervention on the phenotype is necessary. But why should we use a classification and diagnostic system, like the DSM-5, if there are sometimes large differences between individuals with the same diagnosis or uncertainty regarding the cause of diagnoses? In short, it is because diagnoses are useful to us (Frances & Widiger, 2012). They help us do all the things already discussed in this chapter, such as communicate with other professionals and patients, conceptualize patient problems, and identify the most effective interventions possible.

Psychopathology classification and diagnostic systems are, however, not infallible (Frances & Widiger, 2012) nor definitive. They are simply our best attempt to describe and organize the psychological, behavioral, and emotional *phenomena* that clinicians and researchers observe in their practices, laboratories, and in the real world. We will now review the history and content of two of the most well-known and widely used psychological disorder classification and diagnostic systems – the DSM and the International Classification of Diseases (ICD).

The Diagnostic and Statistical Manual of Mental Disorders (DSM)

The DSM is the most well-known and widely used classification and diagnostic system for psychological disorders in the US. The DSM was born out of the American Psychiatric Association's (APA) desire to create a coherent system of communication in the field of psychiatry, and the first edition was published in 1952. The DSM-I contained 128 diagnoses organized into different classes of disorders (Blashfield et al., 2014). The distinct disorders were derived from the clinical experiences of APA members and not through research, as available studies at that time were extremely limited. Each category and diagnosis contained a brief description of that class and the disorders' symptoms, *traits*, and behaviors (Blashfield et al., 2014). Of significant note, the DSM-I contained few references to children or adolescents, or how psychopathology would present itself in these periods of development.

The DSM would go on to be substantively revised five times (DSM-II, III, III-R, IV, and 5), with the number of diagnoses listed increasingly steadily since 1952 (see Figure 1.1). Whereas the DSM-I contained 128 diagnoses, the DSM-5 contains 541 diagnoses organized into 22 diagnostic categories. Between the publication of DSM-I in 1952 and the publication of DSM-II in 1963, studies examining the *reliability* of psychiatric diagnoses and the clinical utility of categories of diagnoses increased (Blashfield et al., 2014). This provided the APA with some empirical evidence for drafting DSM-II and began the shift that would lead the DSM from being a descriptive, clinically based classification system to an *empirically supported* one.

The publication of DSM-III was significant because it aimed to bring psychiatry in line with the rest of medicine by ensuring that more information was provided in the text about the symptomology, demographics, etiology, and course of each disorder, basing this information on available empirical evidence. Importantly, it provided specific symptom thresholds for determining whether the disorder was present (e.g., at least three of seven symptoms must be present), and exclusion criteria for determining when an individual should not be diagnosed with a disorder. DSM-III was also *atheoretical*, which means that it did not adhere to any one theory about psychopathology (e.g., psychoanalytic, behavioral).

These changes initiated a period of rapid, systematic empirical research. For the first time, researchers at different institutions were able to reliably assess and report on disorders because of the newly *operationalized* symptoms, and the provision of exclusion criteria allowed studies to examine specific disorders one at a time. *Structured interviews* were also created, and these further increased the reliability of assessment. However, almost immediately after publication of DSM-III, several studies suggested that the diagnostic criteria published had a number of flaws (Blashfield et al., 2014). Therefore, in 1987, DSM-III-R was published with new diagnoses and diagnostic categories, updated diagnostic criteria for many of the disorders, and a section containing unofficial disorders for further research and consideration. Reliance on empirical evidence for revising the DSM continued to increase such that prior to the publication of DSM-IV, *workgroups* were assigned to each diagnostic category to conduct thorough literature reviews and analyses of existing databases so that empirical evidence could be used to revise the diagnostic criteria and organization of the DSM.

Iteration of the DSM	Schizoid personality description or criteria
DSM-I	"Inherent traits in such personalities are (1) avoidance of close relations with others, (2) inability to express directly hostility or even ordinary aggressive feelings, and (3) autistic thinking. These qualities result early in coldness, aloofness, emotional detachment, fearfulness, avoidance of competition, and day dreams revolving around the need for omnipotence. As children, they are usually quiet, shy, obedient, sensitive, and retiring. At puberty, they frequently become more withdrawn, then manifesting the aggregate of personality traits known as introversion, namely, quietness, seclusiveness, 'shut-in-ness,' and unsociability, often with eccentricity." (APA, 1952, p. 35)
DSM-II	"This behavior pattern manifests shyness, over-sensitivity, seclusiveness, avoidance of close or competitive relationships, and often eccentricity. Autistic thinking without loss of capacity to recognize reality is common, as is daydreaming and the inability to express hostility and ordinary aggressive feelings. These patients react to disturbing experiences and conflicts with apparent detachment." (APA, 1968, p. 42)
DSM-III	**A.** "Emotional coldness and aloofness, and absence of warm, tender feelings for others. **B.** Indifference to praise or criticism or to the feelings of others. **C.** Close friendships with no more than one or two persons, including family members **D.** No eccentricities of speech, behavior, or thought characteristic of Schizotypal Personality Disorder. **E.** Not due to a psychotic disorder such as Schizophrenia or Paranoid Disorder. **F.** If under 18, does not meet the criteria for Schizoid Disorder of Childhood or Adolescence." (APA, 1980, p. 311)
DSM-III-R	**A.** "A pervasive pattern of indifference to social relationships and a restricted range of emotional experience and expression, beginning by early adulthood and present in a variety of contexts, as indicated by at least four of the following: **1.** Neither desires nor enjoys close relationships, including being part of a family. **2.** Almost always chooses solitary activities. **3.** Rarely, if ever, claims or appears to experience strong emotions, such as anger and joy. **4.** Indicates little if any desire to have sexual experiences with another person (age being taken into account) **5.** Is indifferent to the praise and criticism of others. **6.** Has no close friends or confidants (or only one) other than first-degree relatives. **7.** Displays constricted affect, e.g., is aloof, cold, rarely reciprocates gestures or facial expressions, such as smiles or nods. **B.** Occurrence not exclusively during the course of Schizophrenia or a Delusional Disorder." (APA, 1987, p. 340)
DSM-IV	**A.** "A pervasive pattern of detachment from social relationships and a restricted range of expression of emotions in interpersonal settings beginning by early adulthood and present in a variety of contexts, as indicated by four (or more) of the following: **1.** Neither desires nor enjoys close relationships, including being part of a family. **2.** Almost always chooses solitary activities. **3.** Has little, if any, interest in having sexual experiences with another person. **4.** Takes pleasure in few, if any, activities. **5.** Lacks close friends or confidants other than first-degree relatives. **6.** Appears indifferent to the praise or criticism of others. **7.** Shows emotional coldness, detachment, or flattened affectivity. **B.** Does not occur exclusively during the course of Schizophrenia, a Mood Disorder with Psychotic Features, another Psychotic Disorder, or a Pervasive Developmental Disorder and is not due to the direct physiological effects of a general medical condition." (APA, 2000, p. 641)
DSM-5	**A.** Identical to criteria A of DSM-IV. **B.** "Does not occur exclusively during the course of schizophrenia, a bipolar disorder or depressive disorder with psychotic features, another psychotic disorder, or autism spectrum disorder and is not attributable to the physiological effects of another medical condition." (APA, 2013, pp. 652–653) General personality disorder (PD) criteria that must also be met: **1.** Symptoms must be inflexible and pervasive across multiple contexts (e.g., the symptoms do not occur only at home or during certain times). **2.** Symptoms must result in significant distress or impairment in functioning. **3.** Symptoms or patterns of behavior are stable across time and their onset can be traced back to adolescence or early adulthood. (APA, 2013)
DSM-5-AMPD	Criteria for schizoid personality disorder are not listed.

FIGURE 1.1 Schizoid Personality as Defined by DSM-I Through DSM-5 and the AMPD of DSM-5

Leading up to the publication of DSM-5, many researchers pushed for the inclusion of more *dimensional* representations of psychopathology. A dimensional approach suggests that symptoms and traits exist on *continuums*. Rather than putting people into yes–no categories based on whether or not they have a certain number of symptoms, researchers who advocate for a dimensional approach place people on a dimension of symptom severity ranging from not present or not severe to very severe, for example. This is in contrast to a *categorical* representation of psychopathology (the majority of the DSM) where symptoms are assessed and a clinician makes a *dichotomous* (yes/no) decision about the presence of a diagnosis. Some studies have found that these distinct, diagnostic categories are supported by empirical data, but most studies have found that they are not.

Subsequently, a number of dimensional components were integrated into the DSM-5 (Regier, Kuhl, & Kupfer, 2013). For example, an alternative dimensional model for personality disorders was introduced to Section III of the DSM for "Emerging Measures and Models" for future research. Additionally, the diagnoses of autistic disorder, Asperger's disorder, and pervasive developmental disorder were combined into one autism spectrum disorder. This reflects an understanding that these disorders do not differ in "kind" of symptoms or problems, but in "degree" (of severity). Finally, and importantly to the topic of developmental psychopathology, the DSM-5 had several revisions that improved the assessment of psychopathology in children and adolescents. Specifically, the DSM-5 added a heading entitled "Development and Course" to each disorder section to describe the typical development of an individual with that disorder across the lifespan and how the individual might present during each developmental stage. The text of many disorders now also expands upon individual variables or characteristics important to the etiology of that disorder, including culture and gender.

The International Classification of Diseases (ICD)

While the DSM is the standard diagnostic manual used in the US, the ICD is the classification system of mental disorders used most widely in the world (Reed et al., 2019). Published by the World Health Organization (WHO), the ICD system was developed in order to catalog and track diseases across populations. The primogenitor of the ICD, the *International List of Causes of Death*, was published in 1883 and revised four times throughout the following half-century until the newly formed WHO assumed the responsibility for disease classification in 1948 (ICD-6; Hirsch et al., 2016). Of note, the ICD-6 was the first edition to include psychiatric disorders in a compilation of diseases that had previously been more traditionally medical.

Until recently, the ICD-10, published in 1992 and now named the *International Statistical Classification of Diseases and Related Health Problems*, was the latest iteration of the ICD currently in use. The eleventh iteration of the ICD will come into effect on January 1, 2022 (WHO, 2019) and makes several changes over the ICD-10 while maintaining the goal of prioritizing clinical utility (Reed et al., 2019). Taxonomically, the boundary between disorders usually associated with childhood and adolescence versus adults was removed, reflecting a similar shift to a lifespan approach that we saw in the DSM. Also, similarly to the DSM-5, the ICD-11 includes more dimensional approaches to psychopathology. Dimensional qualifiers have been added to describe the symptom presentation of psychotic disorder, and the conceptualization of personality disorders has been overhauled and resembles the Alternative Model of Personality Disorders (AMPD) found in Section III of the DSM-5.

Quantitative Classification Approaches

The histories of the DSM and the ICD are rooted in psychiatry and a largely categorical approach to classification and diagnosis. The ICD and DSM can also be thought of as "top down" approaches because they rely on the authoritative opinion and clinical experience of psychiatrists to organize symptoms or behaviors into groups or categories. However, there have also been individuals who have suggested that "bottom up" approaches to defining types of psychopathology are ideal. "Bottom up" approaches to the classification of psychopathology often take a statistical or factor analytic approach to organizing symptoms. One of the first articles using "bottom up" analyses to investigate the statistical covariation of symptoms was by Moore (1930). More recently, the well-known Achenbach System of Empirically Based Assessment (ASEBA), the Research Domain Criteria (RDoC), and the Hierarchical Taxonomy of Psychopathology (HiTOP) have been developed.

The Achenbach Sysyem of Empirically Based Assessment (ASEBA)

The ASEBA was developed by Dr. Thomas Achenbach in the 1960s in order to provide clinicians with a tool for assessing psychopathology in children and adolescents (Achenbach, Rescorla, & Maruish, 2004). At that time, the DSM provided very little information about mental illness in childhood. To develop the ASEBA, he first developed *self-report questionnaires* that asked about *all* types of psychopathological symptoms. Using *factor analysis*, Dr. Achenbach was able to determine which symptoms co-occurred with one another and seemed to "hang together."

This allowed him to identify different psychological *syndromes*, similar to how groups of symptoms are listed under a disorder in the DSM. Today, when a clinician or researcher uses one of the measures of the ASEBA, they can use computer software to score the questionnaire and create a symptom profile displaying their score on each syndrome. Using *norms* established by studying large pools of people of the same age and gender, these profiles indicate how severe a person's symptoms are compared to others like them. The ASEBA is a "bottom up" approach to understanding and classifying psychopathology and the scales are dimensional because they do not create distinct categories (e.g., those with depression and those without).

The Research Domain Criteria (RDoC) Initiative

In 2009, the National Institute of Mental Health (NIMH) launched the RDoC initiative (Insel et al., 2010). This was part of the Institute's strategic plan to begin developing a dimensional system of psychopathology, ultimately aiming to revamp the traditional categorical models used in the field (i.e., DSM and ICD). The RDoC initiative is not a classification system per se. It is a systematic framework or template for guiding and conducting psychopathological research from a "bottom up" dimensional approach (Kozak & Cuthbert, 2016). Thus, much of the research conducted as part of RDoC examines *transdiagnostic* symptoms or causal factors shared across many forms of psychopathology. For example, research conducted as part of the RDoC initiative might not look at the symptom or surface level differences between different anxiety disorders defined by the DSM. Instead, studies might look at a certain symptom typically associated with anxiety disorders, such as fear, and study the neurobiological *mechanisms*, and *endophenotypes*, underlying fear so that we can better understand how or why a person might develop this specific symptom (see Figure 1.2).

The Hierarchical Taxonomy of The Psychopathology (HiTOP) System

Building on the Achenbach system of classification, the HiTOP system (Kotov et al., 2017; Krueger et al., 2018) was developed to address limitations of categorical systems. HiTOP derived its psychopathology syndromes or disorders using statistical analyses, and is therefore a quantitative, "bottom up" approach to psychopathology. Behaviors and symptoms that mental health professionals typically assess were analyzed to identify which covaried, co-occurred, or clustered together to form syndromes. The "H" in HiTOP (hierarchical)

<table>
<tr><td colspan="3">One domain of functioning described in the RDoC framework is Negative Valence Systems (how we respond to negative situations).</td></tr>
<tr><td colspan="3">One construct that might be studied under the domain of "Negative Valence Systems" is "Acute Threat" or the experience of fear in response to something. Acute Threat can be studied at any unit of analysis or "level" of the body.</td></tr>
<tr><td></td><td>Unit of Analysis</td><td>Examples of how the Acute Threat construct can be studied at each level of analysis</td></tr>
<tr><td>TOP</td><td>Paradigms</td><td>Use experimental social stress or stranger tests to induce stress in participants in the laboratory and observe their behavior.</td></tr>
<tr><td></td><td>Self-Report</td><td>Self-report measures such as the fear survey schedule (Wolpe & Lang, 1974).</td></tr>
<tr><td></td><td>Behavior</td><td>Measurement of response inhibition, or stopping oneself from acting, in response to anxiety or fear-provoking stimuli in an experimental task.</td></tr>
<tr><td rowspan="2">Level of Abstraction</td><td>Physiology</td><td>Measurement of blood pressure and heart rate during an experimental task, as indicators of when the sympathetic nervous system, which helps us respond to dangerous or stressful stimuli, is activated.</td></tr>
<tr><td>Circuits</td><td>Use functional imaging techniques to gauge the activity of the insular cortex, a key area of the brain proposed to be involved in fear, in response to certain stimuli.</td></tr>
<tr><td></td><td>Cells</td><td>Study the activity of glia cells in the brain, which help to regulate the fear responses so that it does not last too long or become too extreme.</td></tr>
<tr><td></td><td>Molecules</td><td>Study the neurotransmitter dopamine, which is associated with processing of fear in the brain.</td></tr>
<tr><td>DOWN</td><td>Genes</td><td>At the time of publication of this textbook, the RDoC framework does not propose which specific genes may be associated with acute threat because of the lack of available evidence from genome-wide association studies.</td></tr>
</table>

FIGURE 1.2 Illustration of How the Research Domain Criteria (RDoC) Matrix Guides Research

indicates that this system of classification is based on a *hierarchical statistical model*. After syndromes were statistically identified, they were then organized under *higher-order factors* that describe the similarities of the disorders in that factor. For example, HiTOP lists the disorders major depressive disorder (MDD), dysthymia, general anxiety disorder (GAD), post-traumatic stress disorder (PTSD), and borderline personality disorder (BPD) under a higher-order "distress" factor based on statistical findings that the symptoms of all of these disorders covary. In all, there are currently seven higher-order factors in the HiTOP system. These factors were then organized under spectra, or groups of factors that correlate with each other. For example, the substance abuse and antisocial behavior factors correlate, and this correlation is explained by an underlying disinhibited externalizing spectra (dimension), suggesting that both substance use problems and antisocial behaviors are both characterized by problems with self-control of behaviors. Importantly, the HiTOP system is a dimensional classification system for psychopathology (Krueger et al., 2018).

The Limitations of Traditional Approaches to Diagnosis and Classification

Most of this chapter has been dedicated to reviewing major approaches to classifying and diagnosing psychopathology. At the beginning of this chapter, we noted that these systems are not perfect. The table in Figure 1.3 compares the limitations of each approach.

System(s)	Approach	Limitations/Criticisms
DSM/ICD	Categorical; Top-Down	• Currently defined diagnostic categories have limited validity. Research does not support discreet categories. o High rates of comorbidity (meeting criteria for multiple disorders) imply that categories may not be well-defined (Kessler, Chiu, Demler, & Walters, 2005). o High heterogeneity (where two individuals with the same diagnosis may present differently) suggests that a particular category may include multiple, qualitatively distinct disorders (Clark, Watson, & Reynolds, 1995; Lilienfeld & Treadway, 2016). • Do not account for subthreshold symptoms, which may still be impairing (Kotov et al., 2017; Lilienfeld & Treadway, 2016). o Clinical thresholds were arbitrarily defined. Thus, someone just below the clinical cut-off number of criteria may be as impaired as someone above it. • Do not comprehensively account for development across the lifespan.
RDoC	Dimensional; Bottom-Up	• Emphasizes biological phenomena at the expense of psychological experience (Franklin et al., 2015). o Useful for research, but difficult to translate to clinical practice (Franklin et al., 2015; Insel et al., 2010; Lilienfeld & Treadway, 2016). • Does not systematically operationalize how the course of psychopathology should be studied across the lifespan.
ASEBA/ HiTOP	Quantitative; Dimensional; Bottom-Up	• Lack considerations of development across the lifespan. o Purely continuous approach neglects the concept of developmental discontinuities (e.g., developmental changes that are abrupt or discrete, rather than continuous; Rutter, 2011) • HiTOP is inextricably linked to DSM-based systems and therefore shares many of their limitations. • Quantitatively derived models may not hold over time (Wittchen, et al., 2009; Wittchen & Beesdo-Baum, 2018).

FIGURE 1.3 Limitations of Approaches to Diagnosis and Classification of Psychopathology

The Value of a Developmental Psychopathology Approach

We hope it is now evident that the major approaches to classification and diagnosis across history serve important purposes but also suffer from substantial weaknesses. In the next chapter, we will describe the *developmental psychopathology* approach to conceptualizing psychopathology. Developmental psychopathology (DP) means exactly what its name suggests: it is the study of psychological or mental disorders (psychopathology) from a developmental or lifespan perspective. Many features of the DP approach make it a superior alternative to understanding mental illness, particularly in children and adolescents. Briefly, it heavily emphasizes understanding normal development in order to better understand abnormal functioning, making it a dimensional approach to understanding psychopathology. It is also not a classification or diagnostic system per se. Therefore, similar to RDoC, it is not constrained by diagnostic labels or categories but can be used to study these constructs if desired. Also, like the RDoC initiative, and unlike statistical models of psychopathology like HiTOP, a DP approach to studying mental illness examines mechanisms underlying symptomology, rather than the phenotype alone. Finally, unlike all the models and approaches previously described, the DP approach emphasizes and systematically investigates developmental, individual, and environmental risk and protective factors in the etiology of all mental illness. This is particularly critical to understanding childhood and adolescent psychopathology.

Chapter Summary

This introductory chapter was meant to provide you with an understanding of traditional approaches to diagnosing and classifying psychopathology. We reviewed five diagnostic or classification systems and the limitations of these approaches. Finally, we gave you a preview of how a developmental psychopathology approach to conceptualizing psychopathology in children and adolescents can address the limitations of previous diagnostic systems.

Further Reading

Clark, L. A., Cuthbert, B., Lewis-Fernández, R., Narrow, W. E., & Reed, G. M. (2017). Three approaches to understanding and classifying mental disorder: ICD-11, DSM-5, and the National Institute of Mental Health's Research Domain Criteria (RDoC). *Psychological Science in the Public Interest*, *18*(2), 72–145. doi: 10.1177/1529100617727266.

Insel, T., Cuthbert, B., Garvey, M., Heinssen, R., Pine, D. S., Quinn, K., Sanislow, C., & Wang, P. (2010). Research domain criteria (RDoC): Toward a new classification framework for research on mental disorders. Available at: https://pubmed.ncbi.nlm.nih.gov/20595427/.

Kotov, R., Krueger, R. F., Watson, D., Achenbach, T. M., Althoff, R. R., Bagby, R. M., & Eaton, N. R. (2017). The Hierarchical Taxonomy of Psychopathology (HiTOP): A dimensional alternative to traditional nosologies. *Journal of Abnormal Psychology*, *126*(4), 454.

Regier, D. A., Kuhl, E. A., & Kupfer, D. J. (2013). The DSM-5: Classification and criteria changes. *World Psychiatry*, *12*(2), 92–98.

Discussion/Essay Questions

1. Discuss at least three purposes of classification and diagnostic systems for psychopathology.
2. Compare and contrast the categorical approach to classifying psychopathology of the DSM-5 with at least one of the dimensional approaches to classifying psychopathology. Make a list of advantages and disadvantages for each approach.
3. Are dimensional approaches to thinking about psychopathology superior to categorical approaches? Provide evidence for your answer.

Glossary

Abnormal, in the context of psychopathology, can be defined as behaviors, emotions, and cognitions that deviate from the norm (culturally or developmentally) and cause distress, impairment in functioning, or endanger an individual or those around them.

Alternative Model for Personality Disorders (AMPD) is a hybrid (categorical and dimensional) model for diagnosing personality disorders found in Section III of the DSM-5.

Categorical refers to an approach to classification of psychopathology that distinguishes between different forms of psychopathology by grouping symptoms to create distinct categories of diagnoses.

Classification is the act of categorizing things according to a set of criteria.

Continuum refers to a way of thinking about a phenomenon as existing on a scale ranging from normal to abnormal.

Developmental psychopathology is the study of psychological or mental disorders (psychopathology) from a developmental or lifespan perspective.

Dichotomous refers to any two-option choice (most often "yes" or "no") that an individual or clinician could make about the presence of a symptom of psychopathology or the presence of a diagnosis, overall.

Differential diagnosis is the process of deciding between two or more diagnoses that share similar features.

Dimensional refers to an approach to classification of psychopathology that conceptualizes psychological phenomenon as existing on continuums, ranging from abnormal to normal, and typically avoids categorizing symptoms or disorders according to traditional methods.

Empirically supported refers to something (a measure, a classification system, or a psychological intervention) that has research-based, scientific evidence in support of its validity.

Endophenotype refers to a measurable construct that, although not observable, links an individual's genotype and phenotype.

Etiology refers to the cause of a symptom or a disorder.

Factor analysis is a form of statistical analysis that tries to explain the covariation of observable phenomenon by revealing underlying common factors.

Heterogeneous means diverse, dissimilar, or not the same.

Higher-order factors refer to constructs or factors in a hierarchical statistical or classification model that are "above" other factors at a lower level.

Mechanisms refer to processes or characteristics that underlie or cause a psychological symptom.

Mental (psychological) disorders are characterized by behavioral patterns, and cognitive, emotional, and physical symptoms that deviate from a normative developmental trajectory and are not typical of individuals living in the same cultural context.

Norms are standardized comparison values for the interpretation of an individual's results on some psychological measure, relative to other people of the same age, gender, etc.

Operationalize means to define what a phenomena, symptom, or construct is and how it should be measured.

Phenomena are characteristics, circumstances, facts, or events (e.g., a psychological symptom) observed through the senses.

Phenotype is a set of observable characteristics (e.g., a group of psychological symptoms).

Psychopathology is the study of mental disorders.

Reliability refers to the consistency of a measure, or the measurement of a symptom or diagnosis, in different instances or under different circumstances.

Self-report questionnaire is a method of measuring psychological symptoms where individuals complete a survey about their thoughts, feelings, behaviors, and experiences.

Structured interviews are interviews used by clinicians and researchers to diagnose a psychological disorder. These interviews consist of standard instructions, questions, and scoring procedures that must be administered in the same way every time to ensure reliability.

Syndrome is a cluster of symptoms and behaviors that often present together.

Taxonomy is an area of scientific study that aims to systematically classify objects, organisms, or phenomena.

Traits are characteristics of an individual that are relatively stable across time and context.

Transdiagnostic means that a specific symptom or cause of a symptom is not unique to one disorder category but cuts across multiple diagnoses.

Workgroup is a group of individuals with expertise in a given area, assigned to collaborate in order to propose updates for the next DSM.

References

Achenbach, T. M., Rescorla, L. A., & Maruish, M. E. (2004). The Achenbach system of empirically based assessment (ASEBA) for ages 1.5 to 18 years. *The use of psychological testing for treatment planning and outcomes assessment* (vol. 2, pp. 179–213). Mahwah, NJ: Lawrence Erlbaum, Associates.

American Psychiatric Association (1952). *Diagnostic and statistical manual of mental disorders* (1st ed.). Washington, DC: American Psychiatric Association.

American Psychiatric Association (1968). *Diagnostic and statistical manual of mental disorders* (2nd ed.). Washington, DC: American Psychiatric Association.

American Psychiatric Association (1980). *Diagnostic and statistical manual of mental disorders* (3rd ed.). Arlington, VA: American Psychiatric Association.

American Psychiatric Association (1987). *Diagnostic and statistical manual of mental disorders* (3rd ed., rev.). Arlington, VA: American Psychiatric Association.

American Psychiatric Association (2000). *Diagnostic and statistical manual of mental disorders* (4th ed., text rev.). Washington, DC: APA.

American Psychiatric Association (2013). *Diagnostic and statistical manual of mental disorders (DSM-5®)*. Washington, DC: APA.

Blashfield, R. K., Keeley, J. W., Flanagan, E. H., & Miles, S. R. (2014). The cycle of classification: DSM-I through DSM-5. *Annual Review of Clinical Psychology*, *10*, 25–51. doi: 10.1146/annurev-clinpsy-032813-153639.

Clark, L. A., Watson, D., & Reynolds, S. (1995). Diagnosis and classification of psychopathology: Challenges to the current system and future directions. *Annual Review of Psychology*, *46*(1), 121–153.

Frances, A. J., & Widiger, T. (2012). Psychiatric diagnosis: Lessons from the DSM-IV past and cautions for the DSM-5 future. *Annual Review of Clinical Psychology*, *8*, 109–130. doi: 10.1146/annurev-clinpsy-032511-143102.

Franklin, J. C., Jamieson, J. P., Glenn, C. R., & Nock, M. K. (2015). How developmental psychopathology theory and research can inform the research domain criteria (RDoC) project. *Journal of Clinical Child Adolescent Psychology*, *44*(2), 280–290. doi: 10.1080/15374416.2013.873981.

Hirsch, J. A., Nicola, G., McGinty, G., Liu, R. W., Barr, R. M., Chittle, M. D., & Manchikanti, L. (2016). ICD-10: History and context. *AJNR American Journal of Neuroradiology*, *37*(4), 596–599. doi: 10.3174/ajnr.A4696.

Insel, T., Cuthbert, B., Garvey, M., Heinssen, R., Pine, D. S., Quinn, K., & Wang, P. (2010). Research domain criteria (RDoC): Toward a new classification framework for research on mental disorders. *American Journal of Psychiatry*, *167*(7), 748–751.

Kessler, R. C., Chiu, W. T., Demler, O., & Walters, E. E. (2005). Prevalence, severity, and comorbidity of 12-month DSM-IV disorders in the National Comorbidity Survey Replication. *Archives of General Psychiatry*, *62*(6), 617–627.

Kotov, R., Krueger, R. F., Watson, D., Achenbach, T. M., Althoff, R. R., Bagby, R. M., Zimmerman, M. (2017). The hierarchical taxonomy of psychopathology (HiTOP): A dimensional alternative to traditional nosologies. *Journal of Abnormal Psychology*, *126*(4), 454–477. doi: 10.1037/abn0000258.

Kozak, M. J., & Cuthbert, B. N. (2016). The NIMH Research Domain Criteria Initiative: Background, issues, and pragmatics. *Psychophysiology*, *53*(3), 286–297. doi: 10.1111/psyp.12518.

Krueger, R. F., Kotov, R., Watson, D., Forbes, M. K., Eaton, N. R., Ruggero, C. J., & Zimmermann, J. (2018). Progress in achieving quantitative classification of psychopathology. *World Psychiatry*, *17*, 282–293.

Lilienfeld, S. O., & Treadway, M. T. (2016). Clashing diagnostic approaches: DSM-ICD versus RDoC. *Annual Reviews on Clinical Psychology*, *12*, 435–463. doi: 10.1146/annurev-clinpsy-021815-093122.

Moore, T. V. (1930). The empirical determination of certain syndromes underlying praecox and manic-depressive psychoses. *American Journal of Psychiatry*, *86*(4), 719–738.

Reed, G. M., First, M. B., Kogan, C. S., Hyman, S. E., Gureje, O., Gaebel, W., & Saxena, S. (2019). Innovations and changes in the ICD-11 classification of mental, behavioural and neurodevelopmental disorders. *World Psychiatry*, *18*(1), 3–19.

Regier, D. A., Kuhl, E. A., & Kupfer, D. J. (2013). The DSM-5: Classification and criteria changes. *World Psychiatry*, *12*(2), 92–98.

Rutter, M. (2011). Research review: Child psychiatric diagnosis and classification: Concepts, findings, challenges and potential. *Journal of Child Psychology and Psychiatry*, *52*(6), 647–660. doi: 10.1111/j.1469-7610.2011.02367.x.

Wittchen, H. U., & Beesdo-Baum, K. (2018). "Throwing out the baby with the bathwater"? Conceptual and methodological limitations of the HiTOP approach. *World Psychiatry*, *17*(3), 296–298. doi: 10.1002/wps.20560.

Wittchen, H. U., Beesdo-Baum, K., Gloster, A. T., Hofler, M., Klotsche, J., Lieb, R., & Kessler, R. C. (2009). The structure of mental disorders re-examined: Is it developmentally stable and robust against additions? *International Journal of Methods in Psychiatric Research*, *18*(4), 189–203. doi: 10.1002/mpr.298.

World Health Organization (2019). World Health Assembly Update. Retrieved from: https://www.who.int/news-room/detail/25-05-2019-world-health-assembly-update.

Chapter 2

Developmental Psychopathology

Rebecca Lipschutz and Johanna Bick

Chapter Overview

The developmental psychopathology approach helps us to understand why some individuals develop mental disorders and other individuals follow a different path. *Developmental psychopathology* is the study of the origins and course of individual patterns of behavior (Sroufe & Rutter, 1984). This approach to studying mental disorders in childhood and adolescence stresses the importance of developmental processes or how one changes and adapts throughout childhood. It takes into account individual factors about the child (temperament, biological risk) and their context (family, neighborhood, community) as influences on child development. In addition to understanding risk for psychopathology, the developmental psychopathology approach also seeks to understand resiliency. This approach links different fields or disciplines of science together to study normal development and *psychopathology* (mental disorders).

In summary, an overarching objective of the developmental psychopathology framework is to better understand why some individuals develop psychopathology whereas others do not. This can be broken down into several more questions:

1. How does psychopathology look the same or different across different phases of child development?
2. Are there underlying traits or biological factors that help explain individual risk?
3. What role does the environment (parents, neighborhood, culture) play in increasing or decreasing risk for an individual?

Developmental Psychopathology, First Edition. Edited by Amanda Venta, Carla Sharp, Jack M. Fletcher, and Peter Fonagy.

4. How can we understand the interplay of timing (i.e., stage of development), nature (i.e., genetic susceptibility), and nurture (i.e., environmental influence) to explain risk and resiliency?
5. Can answers to the above questions help prevent or ameliorate psychopathology at different phases of life?

The History of the Developmental Psychopathology Approach

The field of developmental psychopathology emerged from a synthesis of theories across several disciplines, including embryology, genetics, the neurosciences, psychoanalysis, and clinical, developmental, and experimental psychology (Cicchetti, 1990). Influential theorists across these disciplines came to a mutual conclusion: learning about what it means to "function normally" was reliant on understanding the non-normal or pathological. Likewise, a complete understanding of abnormal depends on accurate understanding of normal behavior, development, and functioning (Cicchetti, 2006). Implicit in this thinking was that psychopathology and normal behavior were opposite ends of a continuum, and that behavior described as "psychopathological" was merely an exaggerated case of the normal. Building from this logic, the field of developmental psychopathology pushed a new way of studying abnormal behavior by examining the entire continuum of behavior, rather than focusing on the extreme, atypical cases (Cicchetti, 2006).

Some of the early applications of the developmental psychopathology model took place in the 1970s. One group of researchers followed children at high and low risk for developing schizophrenia over time (Wall et al., 1984). This prospective, longitudinal study allowed for a comparison of typical and atypical developmental trajectories. A goal of this work was to understand better the developmental origins of a serious mental illness that is typically not diagnosed until late adolescence or early adulthood.

Over the past four decades, the field of developmental psychopathology has grown substantially. It is now considered an integrative framework that links different scientific disciplines, theories, and research strategies to understand better how individuals adapt and develop risk for psychopathology. Importantly, the developmental psychopathology approach is not a specific theory in its own right. It is better considered as a guide or framework for how to best understand psychopathology, in terms of its roots, development, and persistence or remittance over the lifespan.

By bringing together ideas from separate disciplines and fields, studying developmental change, and comparing normal to abnormal, this approach offers a promising framework for furthering knowledge on etiology, developmental change, course, and pathways to resilience. In summary, this reflects the overall mission of developmental psychopathology, which is to "prevent or ameliorate behavioral problems and disorders and promote positive development" (Masten, 2006).

The Definitional Principles of Developmental Psychopathology

There are several core principles of developmental psychopathology that comprise an overarching framework.

1. Interplay between normal development and pathological functioning
2. Studying developmental continuities and discontinuities of traits, behaviors, emotions, and disorders
3. Evaluating evidence across multiple levels of analyses to include the biological, individual, family, social, and cultural levels
4. Incorporating distinct perspectives: clinical, developmental psychology, child/adolescent psychiatry, genetics, neurology, public health, philosophy of science into a multidisciplinary effort
5. Examining both risk and protective factors to delineate pathways of risk and resilience
6. Involving reciprocal, transactional models of influence in the field's causal models

Interplay Between Normal Development and "Abnormal" or Pathological Functioning

The common, unifying principle of developmental psychopathology is the integration of understanding "normal" and "abnormal" behavior, traits, and processes. Developmental psychopathology models highlight that all phenomena occur along a continuum of normal developmental processes and pathways. Psychopathology is judged in relation to what is "normal" in a given time and society for a person of a specific gender or age (Masten, 2006). Developmental psychopathologists look at developmental processes and how they function by looking at the extremes, which may indicate psychopathology. The level of psychopathology an individual exhibits may change over time and at one point in the lifespan it may be classified as a mental disorder whereas at another point it would not be. It is also common for individuals to move between pathological and nonpathological forms of functioning (Cicchetti, 1993). Therefore, manifestations of psychopathology may be non-linear or transient.

Let us consider examples of psychopathology defined as abnormal functioning or symptoms outside of a normative range. *For example, think about when you were in high school*: it might be considered "normal" to feel sad some days, get upset, and want to sleep in late. However, if someone was staying in bed for two weeks at a time to sleep, feeling sad or depressed most of the time, and not having fun with activities they used to enjoy, that could indicate "abnormal" functioning, such as signs of a depressive disorder. Developmental psychopathology allows us to compare and measure psychopathology across a continuum of normal to abnormal.

Other examples of the interplay between normal and abnormal may include individuals who fail to meet developmental expectations due to psychopathology. Across the lifespan, there are established *developmental milestones*, or indicators for how an individual has adapted and is functioning in their environmental context. At different stages of development, there are expected milestones and behaviors that are considered normal or abnormal for that stage.

Think about a toddler: they are learning to feed themselves, walk independently, regulate their own emotions or needs, and form attachments to their caregiver. If a toddler were to be separated from their caregiver, it would be considered normal for them to cry and become upset. However, if an eight-year-old demonstrates similar behavior, such as throwing a tantrum, screaming, and crying every time they are separated from their parent, this would be considered abnormal, and potentially indicative of psychopathology. Thus, understanding variation in normal/abnormal behaviors across development may improve understanding of those at risk for mental health problems.

STUDYING DEVELOPMENTAL CONTINUITIES AND DISCONTINUITIES OF TRAITS, BEHAVIORS, EMOTIONS, AND DISORDERS

The next principle is that developmental psychopathology models examine developmental continuities and discontinuities of traits, behaviors, emotions, and disorders. *Homotypic continuity* is defined as stability in the same or similar behavioral responses over time; that is, the same disorder predicts itself over time (e.g., earlier depression predicting later depression). *Heterotypic continuity* is defined as stability of an underlying construct that is exhibited differentially across development (Sroufe & Rutter, 1984); that is, different disorders predict one another over time (e.g., anxiety predicting later depression).

Consider externalizing or antisocial behaviors, which have established stability across the lifespan. What does this mean? Rank order stays the same across time, so individuals that are more aggressive early in life are also more aggressive than others later in life. However, the specific externalizing behaviors exhibited may look different over time. For example, during early childhood, children may show extreme temper tantrums but are not likely to display the same behavior during adolescence. As shown in Figure 2.1, the nature of externalizing or antisocial behavior changes

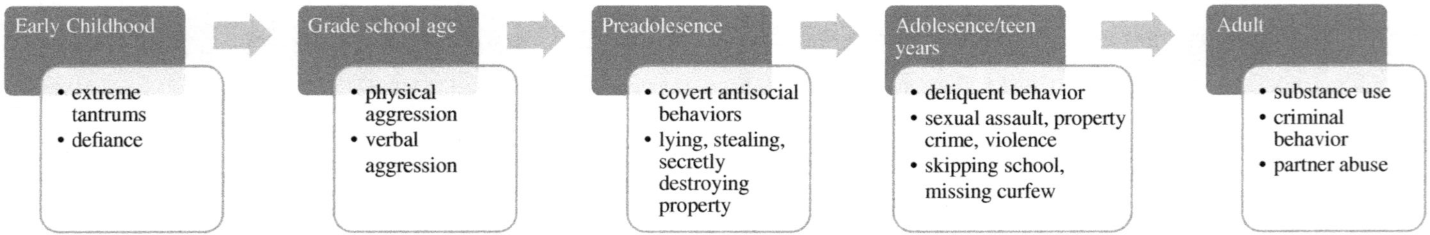

FIGURE 2.1 Example of Heterotypic Continuity. The Nature of Externalizing or Antisocial Behavior Changes as Children Get Older and Become Adults

as children get older and become adults. This demonstrates *heterotypic continuity*, as the form or manifestation of the trait changes with development.

Another important concept in developmental psychopathology is *pathways*, or how individuals change and adapt over time and reach different outcomes or pathologies. *Equifinality* refers to the idea that many different pathways or early experiences may lead to the same outcome or condition (see Figure 2.2b).

For example, conduct disorder could occur due to early child abuse, heritable tendency toward externalizing behaviors, familial factors such as harsh parenting interactions or attachment disruption, environmental factors such as prenatal risk factors, or exposure to trauma. It is more likely that a combination or interaction of these multiple vulnerability and risk factors contributes to the development of psychopathology. Correspondingly, *multifinality* refers to how similar early experiences or risk factors can lead to different outcomes (Cicchetti & Rogosch, 1996) (See Figure 2.2a). For example, early maltreatment may lead to the development of psychopathology or not, depending on a variety of other factors.

Individuals or subgroups may have different pathways or trajectories across development that affect these patterns of continuity. In our previous example of children who start off highly aggressive in preschool, some children may "return to normal" behavior by adolescence, whereas others may maintain high rates of externalizing behaviors. Additionally, other groups of children do not display externalizing problems in early childhood, but their problems emerge in adolescence (Moffitt, 2003). This variety demonstrates the different pathways, patterns, and subgroups of individuals and how they change over time, which is a key principle of developmental psychopathology. Developmental psychopathology aims to understand these behaviors and problems over time and determine how we can predict these different trajectories.

EVALUATING EVIDENCE ACROSS MULTIPLE LEVELS OF ANALYSES TO INCLUDE THE BIOLOGICAL, INDIVIDUAL, FAMILY, SOCIAL, AND CULTURAL LEVELS

The next principle of developmental psychopathology is that research should examine multiple levels of analyses to include biological, individual, familial, social, and cultural levels. Developmental psychopathologists have learned that to answer their overarching questions about processes of psychopathology and development, they need to incorporate scientists from different fields and use different levels and methods of analysis. Key models that have influenced the multilevel principle include Bronfenbrenner's (1979) ecological model, Sameroff's (1989) model of

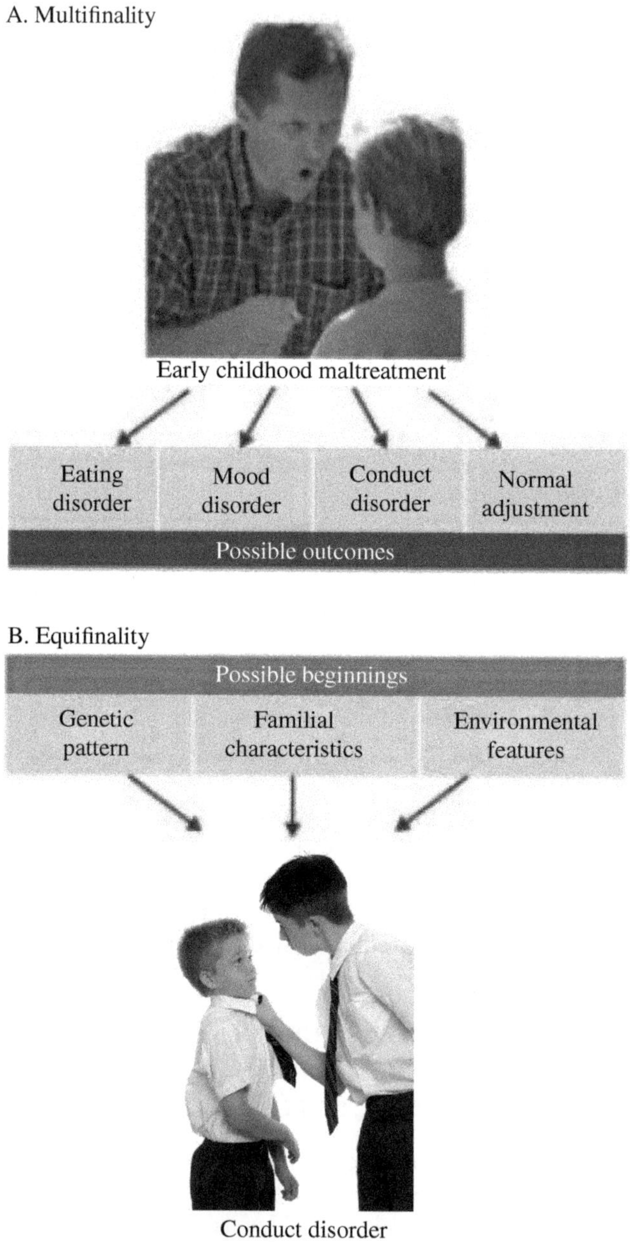

FIGURE 2.2 A. Multifinality: Similar Early Experiences Lead to Different Outcomes. B. Equifinality: Different Early Experiences Lead to a Similar Outcome. Reproduced with permission of Getty Images. Sources: (a) SW Productions/Photodisc/Getty Images. (b) Yellowsarah/iStock/Getty Images.

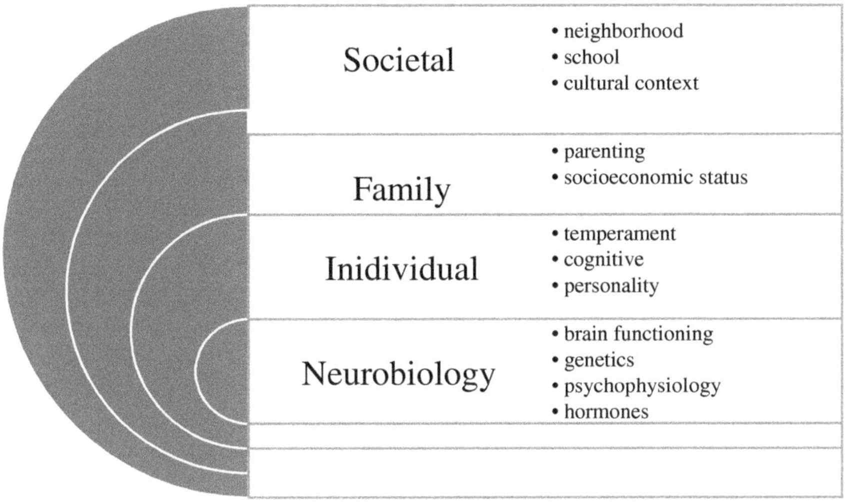

FIGURE 2.3 Multiple Levels of Analyses

gene and environment interactions, and Gottlieb, Wahlsten, and Lickliter's (2007) model of four levels (environment, behavior, neural activity, genetics) and how these levels influence one another. The takeaway from these different models is that we should study processes and systems at multiple levels and how they interact across levels to better understand psychopathology and the risk for disorders.

Figure 2.3 shows commonly studied levels of analyses in developmental psychopathology studies. As discussed above, pathways to psychopathology can vary, so it is important to consider contextual factors. There are factors or levels that we can study *across* individuals (e.g., high and low socioeconomic status) or *within* individuals (e.g., temperament, genetics, brain activity). Developmental psychopathology brings together these micro and macro levels to study how the individual functions in their larger context.

INCORPORATING DISTINCT PERSPECTIVES ACROSS CLINICAL, DEVELOPMENTAL PSYCHOLOGY, CHILD/ ADOLESCENT PSYCHIATRY, GENETICS, NEUROLOGY, PUBLIC HEALTH, AND PHILOSOPHY OF SCIENCE INTO A MULTIDISCIPLINARY EFFORT

Given the emphasis on multiple levels of analyses, developmental psychopathology is well poised to integrate knowledge across diverse scientific disciplines into a multidisciplinary effort. Many scientists may only study one of these systems; thus, developmental psychopathology encourages collaboration and interdisciplinary research to study how these systems interact and influence one another.

EXPLORING BOTH RISK AND PROTECTIVE FACTORS TO DELINEATE PATHWAYS OF RISK AND RESILIENCE

Another key principle of developmental psychopathology is examining both risk and protective factors to understand pathways of risk and resilience. *Risk factors* increase the likelihood of a negative outcome, whereas *protective factors* buffer against risk, decrease the likelihood of adverse outcomes, and promote successful outcomes. The remaining chapters in this book will include discussions of risk and protective factors for various forms of psychopathology. Risk factors can be acute stressful events, such as experiencing a trauma, exposure to violence, family divorce, or chronic adversity, such as living in poverty, negative parenting behavior, or parent mental illness. It is important to note that risk factors are *not deterministic* as not all individuals at risk develop psychopathology, but they *increase the probability* for adverse outcomes. *Resilience* refers to the capacity to avoid adverse outcomes and adapt successfully and competently, despite being at risk or experiencing adversity (Masten, 2007). This connects with our previously mentioned concept of multifinality, which suggests that a variety of outcomes (both adaptive and maladaptive) can emanate from common risk factors (see Figure 2.4). The study of protective factors is important for understanding family and child strengths that can reduce the impact of risk factors and lead to positive developmental outcomes. Ultimately, developmental

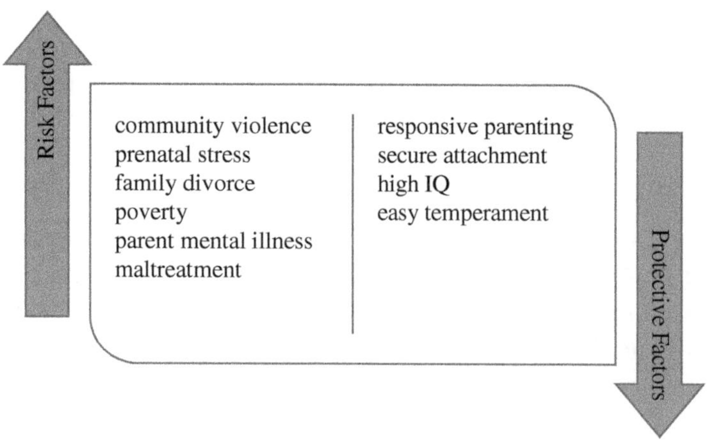

FIGURE 2.4 Common Risk and Protective Factors in Child Outcomes. Risk Factors Increase the Likelihood of a Negative Outcome, Whereas Protective Factors Buffer Against Risk, Decrease the Likelihood of Adverse Outcomes, and Promote Successful Outcomes

psychopathologists hope to understand and identify at-risk individuals and what factors may mitigate this risk to improve prevention and intervention efforts.

INVOLVING RECIPROCAL, TRANSACTIONAL MODELS OF INFLUENCE IN THE FIELD'S CAUSAL MODELS

Lastly, developmental psychopathology involves *reciprocal transactional models of influence*. What does that mean? For a long time, researchers believed in a linear model of development, such as early brain injury causing child development of cognitive, social, or emotional problems. However, this belief ignores children with brain injuries that develop normally and children with developmental problems without evidence of a brain injury.

Additionally, the "nature or nurture" debate assumed that developmental outcomes were a product of either nature (genetics, biology) *or* nurture (parenting, environment) alone. Later on, theorists began to adopt a more transactional model of development (Sameroff & Chandler, 1975). It is now accepted that concepts of nature and nurture are not as easily separated as once thought.

On the nature side, the field of epigenetics has demonstrated that even when individuals have the same genetic "code," the environment can influence the expression of genes or which genes "turn on." On the nurture side, research has shown that children's inherent individual personality, temperament, or other traits can influence how their parent responds to them. Thus, in the transactional model, a child's outcomes are a product of the continuous, dynamic, reciprocal interactions of the child and experiences provided by their family and social context (Sameroff & Mackenzie, 2003). The remaining chapters in this book will give concrete examples of gene–environment interactions that have been discovered.

Compare a linear model with a transactional model for understanding developmental problems. Figure 2.5 shows that birth complications predict poor language and social skills in childhood. In a transactional model, a normally non-anxious mother may have increased anxiety after experiencing adverse birth complications, and then interact with her infant in an apprehensive and inconsistent manner. Due to these parenting practices, the infant may exhibit difficulties with self-regulation and temperament, which decreases the mother's engagement with her child. This lack of social or verbal interaction with her infant may contribute to the child's slower development (Sameroff & Mackenzie, 2003).

Think about your family. Do you and your siblings have the same personality? Do your parents interact with each of you in exactly the same way? Even though we might share similar genes and environments with

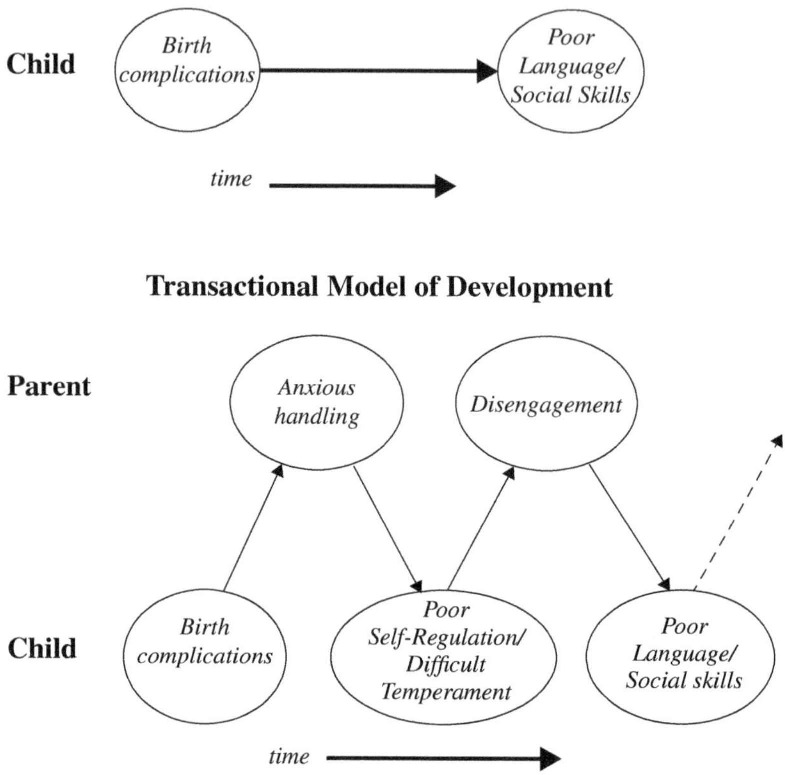

FIGURE 2.5 Contrasting Linear and Transactional Models for Explaining Developmental Problems

our siblings, many complex interactions explain why we have different personalities, behaviors, and interactions with our parents and friends.

Developmental Psychopathology Research Methodology

The complex nature of the developmental psychopathology requires a variety of advanced methods to study its questions. This section will provide a brief overview of the methods used to study developmental psychopathology; these methods will be discussed further in subsequent chapters. The key principles of developmental psychopathology directly inform the methods used to study it. Developmental psychopathology research is often longitudinal, examines risk and protective factors, maps trajectories of traits or behaviors, and incorporates multiple levels of analyses across disciplines. Thus, the field must utilize research designs and statistical methods that can appropriately address these types of research questions.

RESEARCH DESIGNS

Longitudinal

The developmental psychopathology perspective emphasizes the significance of *prospective longitudinal* research designs that follow a sample of individuals across time for multiple time points. If a researcher wants to investigate the association between childhood maltreatment and development of depression in adolescence, they could design a prospective longitudinal study that first examines a sample of young children and asks parents about maltreatment experiences and depression symptoms. Then, researchers would follow up during adolescence for another report of depression symptoms. This method allows researchers to study how depression symptoms develop from early childhood to adolescence and ask about current maltreatment experiences in early childhood.

Cross-sectional

A *cross-sectional* design occurs when researchers do not sample variables over time. Researchers may assess development in children over different ages, rather than following the same children over time. An advantage is that the study may be more feasible in that participants do not have to be followed over time.

Retrospective research methodologies are also widely used in developmental studies. Retrospective studies ask subjects to report on prior experiences, such as exposure to life stress, maltreatment, or other life experiences that occurred prior to the current point in time. An important note is that there are often differing results from studies that use retrospective versus prospective designs (Baldwin et al., 2019).

Correlations versus causation?

A central methodological challenge in developmental psychopathology concerns establishing causal relationships. One way to establish causation is through a *randomized controlled trial (RCT)* in which individuals are randomly assigned to a condition/treatment or a control. Because individuals were assigned at random, there should be no other factor that explains group differences beyond the experimental manipulation. RCT's are considered the "gold standard" in understanding causality; however, there are ethical and logistical concerns to designing experiments. To study the effects of living in poverty on developmental outcomes, it would not be ethical to take one child and randomly assign them to live in poverty and assign another to live in a wealthy home; thus, researchers must sample from different populations to compare effects, a method that does not truly assess causation. Similarly, researchers cannot intentionally design experiments to expose children to adverse experiences. However, researchers have utilized "experiments of nature" to understand how early adversity shapes developmental and neurobiological outcomes.

Person-centered designs

Person-centered research designs are used to examine the effects of risk/protective factors on subgroups of a sample, such as genotypes, personality, neighborhood, or other grouping factors and their developmental trajectories (Bergman & Magnusson, 1997). Advanced statistical strategies (growth mixture modeling, group-based trajectory modeling) are used to study continuities and trajectories of behaviors as well as examine subgroups and how they change over time.

RESEARCH METHODOLOGIES

In this chapter, we have discussed how developmental psychopathology encompasses a wide range of disciplines and methods to answer our big questions. Improvements in brain imaging techniques and genetics have advanced research in these areas and development of psychopathology as a result. This section will briefly explain some of the methods discussed in later chapters.

Examining genetic factors

There are three main types of genetic studies that have increased our understanding of relationships between genes and behavior. The first is *behavioral genetics*, which separates variability in behavioral traits (e.g., aggression, anxiety) into heritability, environment, and Gene × Environment mechanisms. The second method of studying genetics is *molecular genetics*, which examines specific alleles, genetic markers, and gene expression patterns that are associated with psychopathology. Lastly, *epigenetics* refers to changes in gene expression due to environmental influences.

Neuroimaging

There are many available tools for capturing information about brain function and structure in children. Investigating brain function and structure helps us understand the neurobiological factors that contribute to current or later psychopathology risk. (e.g., Pinkham et al., 2008). *Magnetic resonance imaging* (MRI) is a technique that is widely used because it is non-invasive and can capture properties about brain structure and function at all ages, even prenatally (Peterson, 2003). *Structural MRI* studies inform about brain anatomy and are used to examine the volume and shape of brain regions. *Functional MRI* (fMRI) studies provide information about activation in the brain, often in key regions, during rest or during specific tasks that require basic cognitive or emotional functioning.

Electroencephalography (EEG) and magnoencephalography (MEG) are techniques that allow for the non-invasive assessment of brain function. EEG and MEG provide highly accurate measurements of the timing of neural responses, but there is less spatial precision. Each neuroimaging technique offers specific advantages and disadvantages for studying neurobiological functioning across development.

Chapter Summary

This chapter provided an introduction to the developmental psychopathology framework. We first discussed the history of the developmental psychopathology model and discussed how it provided a new model for better understanding changes and individual differences in psychopathology across the lifespan. We provided an overview of several key tenets of the framework. Finally, we outlined various research designs and methodologies that have been employed to shed light on DP questions. An emphasis of this chapter is how the application of this framework to the study of psychopathology can be leveraged to support improved detection, diagnosis, prevention, and treatment.

Further Reading

Beauchaine, T. P., & Hinshaw, S. P. (Eds.) (2017). *Child and adolescent psychopathology*. Hoboken, NJ: John Wiley & Sons, Inc.

Cicchetti, D. (Ed.) (2016). *Developmental psychopathology (vols 1–4)*. Hoboken, NJ: John Wiley & Sons, Inc.

Pollak, S. D. (2015). Developmental psychopathology: Recent advances and future challenges. *World Psychiatry*, *14*(3), 262–269.

Sroufe, L. A. (2013). The promise of developmental psychopathology: Past and present. *Development and Psychopathology*, *25*(4 pt. 2), 1215–1224.

Toth, S. L., & Cicchetti, D. (2010). The historical origins and developmental pathways of the discipline of developmental psychopathology. *The Israel Journal of Psychiatry and Related Sciences*, *47*(2), 95–104.

Discussion/Essay Questions

1. How does studying normal and abnormal behavior inform understanding of developmental psychopathology?
2. Discuss how risk/resilience factors relate to psychopathology and provide an example of each.
3. Explain at least three levels of analyses that researchers study and how you would research a psychological disorder/concept at each level.

4. Discuss three research methods and at least one advantage and limitation of each method.
5. Discuss the nature vs. nurture debate and provide evidence for each side.

Glossary

Behavioral genetics separates variability in behavioral traits (e.g., aggression, anxiety) into heritability, environment.

Cross-sectional design occurs when researchers do not sample variables over time. Data are collected at one time point.

Developmental milestones are indicators for how an individual has adapted and is functioning in their environmental context.

Developmental psychopathology is the study of the origins and course of individual patterns of behavior.

Epigenetics refers to changes in gene expression due to environmental influences.

Equifinality refers to the idea that many different pathways or early experiences may lead to the same outcome or condition.

Gene–environment interactions occur when both genes and the environment predict behavior or other outcomes. In a statistical model, GxE refers to when the effect of a gene depends on an environmental factor or the effect of the environment depends on genotype.

Heterotypic continuity is defined as stability of an underlying construct that is exhibited differentially across development; that is, different disorders predict one another over time (e.g., anxiety predicting later depression).

Homotypic continuity is defined as stability in the same or similar behavioral responses over time; that is, the same disorder predicts itself over time (e.g., earlier depression predicting later depression).

Macro factors such as family environment, school, peer interactions, community, and cultural context.

Magnetic resonance imaging (MRI) is a neuroimaging technique that is widely used because it is non-invasive and can capture properties about brain structure and function.

Micro factors include neurobiological factors such as genetics, psychophysiology, brain functioning, as well as individual differences in temperament, cognition, and emotional responses.

Molecular genetics examines specific alleles or genetic markers that are associated with psychopathology.

Multifinality refers to how similar early experiences or risk factors lead to different outcomes with multiple levels of analyses.

Pathways refer to how individuals change and adapt over time and reach different outcomes or pathologies.

Person-centered research designs examine the effects of risk/protective factors on subgroups of a sample.

Prospective longitudinal research designs follow a sample of individuals across time for multiple time points.

Protective factors buffer against risk, decrease the likelihood of adverse outcomes, and promote successful outcomes.

Psychopathology refers to mental disorders.

Randomized controlled trials are experimental designs where participants are randomized to treatment or control groups.

Reciprocal, transactional models propose that a child's outcomes are a product of the bidirectional, continuous, dynamic interactions of the child and experiences provided by his or her family and social context.

Resilience refers to the capacity to avoid adverse outcomes and adapt successfully and competently, despite being at risk or experiencing adversity.

Retrospective design involves retrospective studies where subjects are asked to report on prior experiences, such as exposure to life stress, maltreatment, or other life experiences that occurred prior to the current point in time.

Risk factors increase the likelihood of a negative outcome.

References

Bergman, Lars R., & Magnusson, D. (1997). A person-oriented approach in research on developmental psychopathology. *Development and Psychopathology*, *9*(2), 291–319. https://doi.org/10.1017/S095457949700206X.

Bronfenbrenner, U. (1979). Contexts of child rearing: Problems and prospects. In *American Psychologist*. https://doi.org/10.1037/0003-066X.34.10.844.

Cicchetti, Dante (1990). A historical perspective on the discipline of developmental psychopathology. In *Risk and protective factors in the development of psychopathology* (pp. 2–28). New York, NY: Cambridge University Press. https://doi.org/10.1017/CBO9780511752872.003.

Cicchetti, Dante (1993). Developmental psychopathology: Reactions, reflections, projections. *Developmental Review*, *13*(4), 471–502. https://doi.org/10.1006/drev.1993.1021.

Cicchetti, Dante (2006). Theory and method. In Dante Cicchetti & D. J. Cohen (Eds.), *Development and psychopathology* (2nd ed., pp. 1–23). New York, NY: John Wiley & Sons, Inc.

Cicchetti, Dante, & Rogosch, F. A. (1996). Equifinality and multifinality in developmental psychopathology. *Development and Psychopathology*, *8*(4), 597–600. https://doi.org/10.1017/S0954579400007318.

Gottlieb, G., Wahlsten, D., & Lickliter, R. (2007). The significance of biology for human development: A developmental psychobiological systems view. In *Handbook of child psychology*. Hoboken, NJ: John Wiley & Sons, Inc. https://doi.org/10.1002/9780470147658.chpsy0105.

Masten, A. S. (2006). Developmental psychopathology: Pathways to the future. *International Journal of Behavioral Development*, *30*(1), 47–54. https://doi.org/10.1177/0165025406059974.

Masten, A. S. (2007). Resilience in developing systems: Progress and promise as the fourth wave rises. *Development and Psychopathology*, *19*(3), 921–930. https://doi.org/10.1017/S0954579407000442.

Moffitt, T. E. (2003). Life-course-persistent and adolescence-limited antisocial behavior: A 10-year research review and a research agenda. In B. B. Lahey, T. E. Moffit, & A. Caspi (Eds.), *Causes of conduct disorder and juvenile delinquency*. New York, NY: Guilford.

Peterson, B. (2003). Conceptual, methodological, and statistical challenges in brain imaging studies of developmentally based psychopathologies. *Development and Psychopathology*, *15*(3), 811–832. https://doi.org/10.1017/S0954579403000385.

Pinkham, A. E., Hopfinger, J. B., Pelphrey, K. A., Piven, J., & Penn, D. L. (2008). Neural bases for impaired social cognition in schizophrenia and autism spectrum disorders. *Schizophrenia Research*, *99*, 164–175. https://doi.org/10.1016/j.schres.2007.10.024

Sameroff, Arnold J. (1989). Models of developmental regulation: The environtype. In D. Cicchetti (Ed.), *The emergence of a discipline: Rochester Symposium on Developmental Psychopathology* (vol. *1*). Hillsdale, NJ: Lawrence Erlbaum Associates, Inc.

Sameroff, A.J., & Chandler, M. J. (1975). Reproductive risk and the continuum of caretaking casualty. *Review of Child Development Research*, *4*, 187–244.

Sameroff, A., & Mackenzie, M. J. (2003). Research strategies for capturing transactional models of development: The limits of the possible. *Development and Psychopathology*, *15*(3), 613–640. https://doi.org/10.1017/S0954579403000312.

Sroufe, L. A., & Rutter, M. (1984). The domain of developmental psychopathology. *Child Development*, *55*(1), 17–29. https://doi.org/10.1111/j.1467-8624.1984.tb00271.x.

Wall, N. F., Anthony, E. J., Wynne, L. C., & Rolf, J. E. (1984). *Children at risk for schizophrenia: A longitudinal perspective*. New York, NY: Cambridge University Press.

Chapter 3

Normal Development: What Is Actually Normal?

Hillary A. Langley, Sarah Barksdale, Bailey A. Barnes, Caitlin H. Child, Matthew T. Roberts, and Mayra B. Ramos

Chapter Overview

In this chapter, we focus on "normal development," although we recognize that this term is misleading as no two people are exactly alike and there are a range of outcomes that may all be considered "normal." Even so, it is important to examine developmental milestones and the developmental progression of skills that are thought to be within the normal range, so as to better understand and identify what might *not* be normal. As you learned in Chapter 2, a fundamental principle of developmental psychopathology is that normal and abnormal development inform one another. We learn about how developmental trajectories move towards psychopathology, in part, by studying normal development.

It is critical to begin this chapter with the acknowledgment that human development is an incredibly complex topic to study, as there are a myriad of potential influences and outcomes to consider. In fact, there are too many to count! Researchers have spent over a century studying biological and environmental contributions to human development. In each of the sections below, we highlight how both biology *and* family, society, culture, and other contextual factors influence various aspects of human development. For example, in normal development, we see a fairly universal pattern of physical development and some cognitive skills, regardless of context, while other aspects of cognition seem to be heavily influenced by our environment. When it comes to social, emotional, and moral development, research indicates that there may be underlying biological determinants of behavior, but that our experiences and culture play a role as well. In developmental psychopathology, we

Developmental Psychopathology, First Edition. Edited by Amanda Venta, Carla Sharp, Jack M. Fletcher, and Peter Fonagy.

appreciate that all of these factors interact in complex manners to predict an individual's likelihood of a developmental trajectory that includes psychopathology.

In the first section of this chapter, we discuss the family as a context for development and how aspects of the home affect infants' and children's development. In subsequent sections, we focus on specific aspects of development, including physical, cognitive, social-emotional, moral, and sex-role identity development across the infancy, childhood, and adolescent years.

The Family Context and Life Cycle Theory

In this section, we highlight how the family context and individual differences play an important role in predicting the development of psychopathology in children and adolescents. The family development theory classifies family and individual development according to developmental stages that encompass roles and tasks within the family dynamic over time. Duvall (1957) identified eight stages in this family life cycle: (1) beginning families, (2) childbearing families, (3) families with preschool children, (4) families with school children, (5) families with teenagers, (6) families as launching centers, (7) families in the middle years, and (8) aging families. There are other theories that classify the patterns of families based on different criteria; however, it is Duvall's theory that has emerged as the most significant.

A major criticism of the family development theories is the assumption of universality, as they focused primarily on mid-twentieth century, middle-class, heterosexual, white families. Subsequent theories have attempted to address the complex challenges of parenting in a heterosexist society, and the unique experiences and perspectives of sexual minority parents. Further research within the field should attempt to address the increasingly diverse nature of individuals who comprise the family cycle.

ATTACHMENT

As we narrow our focus away from the general concept of the family life cycle, we begin to address the impact that specific aspects of the family—such as parenting—have on the developing child. We start by examining attachment: the quality of the bonds developed between parents (or caretakers) and infants. Though covered more thoroughly in the next chapter of this volume, Ainsworth, Bowlby, and others determined that attachment can be broadly categorized in two ways: secure and insecure. Research consistently suggests that parents who are affectionate, responsive, predictable, and sensitive when caring for their child are likely to have securely attached infants who develop better social competence, higher levels of psychological well-being, and lower levels of behavior problems years later (Belsky, 2006). Securely attached children, adolescents, and adults are more likely to have more positive perceptions of their attachment figures, may communicate more effectively with others, and demonstrate more interpersonal flexibility (Lamb et al., 1999).

TEMPERAMENT

Until the late 1950s, there was a tendency to attribute children's maladjustment to poor parenting; specifically, poor mothering (Thomas & Chess, 1977). Born out of research investigating this assumption was the theory of *temperament*: the individual differences in behavioral styles, emotions, and characteristic ways of responding. Features of temperament can be observed even in early infancy and include rhythmicity of biological function, approach or withdrawal from new stimuli, adaptability, distractibility, activity level, quality of mood, persistence threshold or attention span, intensity of reaction, and sensory threshold of responsiveness. Such characteristics appear to be strongly heritable, emerge early in life, are relatively consistent across time and situations, and derive from interactions between genetic predispositions, environment, maturation, and individual experiences (Thompson, 1999).

In devising ways to classify children's temperament and identify long-term outcomes, Thomas and Chess (1977) identified four basic temperament styles. First, children with *easy temperaments* are generally of positive moods, adaptable, and persistent. Children who are *slow-to-warm-up* take longer to adjust to changing circumstances but can adjust, especially if their temperament traits are respected. Children with *difficult temperaments* are irritable, react adversely, or withdraw when presented with changes in routine. Finally, children with *average temperaments* do not notably fall into any of these categories. Children with difficult temperaments are more likely to have internalizing and externalizing behavior problems (Lamb et al., 1999).

Another way to classify temperament comes from research by Rothbart and colleagues, who conceptualize temperament in terms of reactivity and self-regulation. Reactivity reflects how easily a person is aroused by stimuli, measured by the speed of escalation, onset, persistence, and intensity of emotional reactions. Self-regulation is how reactivity is modulated, including the child's approach–withdrawal tendencies, soothability, emotion regulation, and adaptability (Rothbart & Bates, 1998; Thompson, 1999).

GOODNESS OF FIT

Thomas and Chess (1977) determined that the *goodness of fit*, or compatibility between the environment and a child's temperament, plays a significant role in their adjustment and the likelihood of eventual psychopathology. Poorness of fit occurs when the child's temperament is not respected or accommodated in their environment. Children's temperament not only influences the way in which they interact with others, but it also elicits certain reactions from people around them. In addition, parents' own temperaments affect how they interact with their children. For instance, parents with easy temperaments may better accommodate their child with a difficult temperament, which may mitigate the child's predisposition for psychopathology. Conversely, parents with difficult temperaments may not be able to adjust to the needs of children who are slow-to-warm-up, and thus perpetuate the poorness of fit between the child's temperament and their environment (Lamb et al., 1999).

PARENTING STYLES

It is clear from decades of research that parents and children shape one another's behavior (Patterson, 1982), though the bulk of the research is focused on where parents fall on two primary domains: warmth–coldness and restrictiveness–permissiveness (Baumrind, 1989). Parents high in warmth are generally caring, supportive, and engage in behavior that demonstrates they enjoy spending time with their children, while parents low in warmth express few feelings of affection for their children and are more likely to physically discipline their children. Children of warm parents are more likely to develop internalized standards of conduct (i.e., a moral sense of conscience) and are more likely to have better social and emotional well-being (Lau et al., 2006) than their peers with parents low in warmth. Parents also fall somewhere on the restrictiveness–permissiveness spectrum. Indeed, even the most well-behaved children misbehave at times, and parents have to decide how they will respond to their children's (mis)behavior and to what extent they will enforce boundaries or rules with their children. Parents who are restrictive tend to watch their children more closely and impose more rules than permissive parents.

Decades ago, Baumrind identified four styles of parenting (Baumrind & Black, 1967). *Authoritative* parents maintain consistent boundaries, use reasoning, and offer consistent affection and support for their child; this parenting style is associated with children who have the most favorable outcomes. *Authoritarian* parents value obedience, impose a forceful imposition of their will on their child, and offer little affection. *Permissive* parents are high in warmth, non-intrusive, and lax, but are available as resources to their child when needed. Finally, *neglectful* or *nonconformist* parents are generally low on warmth and control, and tend to be uninvolved parents (Baumrind, 1975). Baumrind argued that authoritative parents—the ideal parenting style—instill values that contribute to their children's sense of social responsibility by communicating realistic and fair expectations of their children. Importantly, Baumrind's findings may be culture-specific, as deleterious outcomes in children with authoritarian parents in cultures in which this is the norm (e.g., China) have not always been found.

Physical Development

From the moment of conception, physical development in humans occurs quickly and continues into adulthood. These processes develop fairly similarly across individuals, with the exception of a few differences. In this section, we discuss brain and motor development, along with puberty and problems in physical development.

PRENATAL DEVELOPMENT

The process of physical development begins before birth. Soon after conception, the single cell formed by the union of the sperm and egg begins to multiply at a fast pace. Over the course of the following weeks, tissues, organs, and structures begin to form, and the developing fetus takes the shape of a human being. Prenatal development occurs during three phases: the *germinal stage* (the first two weeks), the *embryonic stage* (second to eighth week gestation), and the *fetal stage* (ninth week to birth). Physical development occurs rapidly during the embryonic stage, when most organ systems are rapidly established and a neural tube begins to form, as well as during the fetal stage, during which the remaining organs and extremities continue to mature until birth. During the fetal stage, the fetus begins to move and the sensory systems begin to develop. Around seven months gestation, a fetus is able to respond to sound and light, and by birth, other sensory abilities become fully functional.

BRAIN DEVELOPMENT

Over the course of the first few months and years of life, various skills and competencies improve at an impressively rapid rate. Many of the changes that we observe in human development happen in response to changes in the brain. Even before we are born, the brain and central nervous system support basic sensory and motor functions. Once born, rapid brain development occurs and continues well into adolescence.

At birth, the brain contains most of the information-transmitting cells—also known as *neurons*—that it will ever have. Yet, the brain becomes four times larger by adulthood, with much of that growth occurring during the first few years of life (Groeschel et al., 2010).

Processes that account for such growth in the size of the brain include *synaptogenesis* (the process of synapse formation between neurons) and *myelination* (the formation of myelin sheaths that allow for the increase in speed of electrical transmissions between neurons).

Additionally, certain areas of the *cerebral cortex*—the brain's outermost layer and most complex system—are specialized for certain functions. For example, the *occipital lobe* is primarily involved in visual processing; memory, visual recognition, and emotional/auditory processing occurs in the *temporal lobe*; spatial awareness and sensory processing are associated with the *parietal lobe*; and, the *frontal lobe* of the brain is responsible for humans' ability to organize and plan ahead. As the brain continues to develop, connections between neurons become more efficient, and repeated stimulation enables the development and adjustment of humans' physical and cognitive capacities.

MOTOR DEVELOPMENT

At one time it was presumed that our brain had a predetermined sequence of motor development that would enable certain physical abilities to activate according to a predetermined timeline. However, this belief is now considered to be too simple. Instead, Thelen (2005) introduced the dynamic systems theory (DST), which supports the idea that motor development is influenced by an individual's interaction with their environment, thereby suggesting that there are multiple factors involved in the speed and sequence of motor development. Developmental norms have been established to understand large samples, but individual differences are present and are important to consider when attempting to determine what is normal versus abnormal motor development.

Much of the research on motor development has focused on the development of *fine motor skills*, which involve the development and coordination of the small muscles of the body, and *gross motor skills*, which involve the large muscles of the body and allow for locomotion to occur. As infants and children grow, both their fine and gross motor skills are fine-tuned through various experiences in a predictable progression, although the timing of these skills varies.

PUBERTY

Puberty, which occurs during adolescence, is one of the most significant changes in a human's physical development. This biological process signifies a human's physical and sexual maturation, as individuals become capable of reproduction during this developmental period. Puberty begins with a chemical signal from the hypothalamus, which directs the pituitary gland to start producing more growth hormones.

Testosterone and estrogen play an important role in the development of sex characteristics in males and females, respectively. This maturation process can vary by individual and generally takes three to four years to complete. Increases in both height and weight occur in both sexes during the growth spurt. *Primary sex characteristics* include the reproductive organs (e.g., sperm-producing testes in males and egg-producing ovaries in females), while *secondary sex characteristics* include the outward physiological indicators or traits of sex (e.g., breasts and facial hair) that distinguish males from females, but are not involved in sexual reproduction. Puberty is thought to cause social reorientation in adolescents, as well as engagement in high-risk behaviors.

Cognitive Development

AN OVERVIEW OF COGNITIVE DEVELOPMENT ACROSS DOMAINS

Huge changes occur in humans' cognitive capabilities over the course of infancy, childhood, and adolescence. However, cognitive—or intellectual—development does not proceed in the same way or at the same pace for everyone. While an individual's cognitive abilities can confer risk or protection for psychopathology, as you will see in the subsequent chapters, it is important to note that the abilities described below interact with the child's environment, demonstrating how individual and contextual factors interact in developmental psychopathology.

Memory

A huge literature is devoted to characterizing children's memory development and mnemonic capabilities. Research suggests that even very young children are able to perform quite well on a variety of memory tasks, but that there are also many age-related differences in children's memory abilities, including in short-term, working, and long-term memory. These age-related differences are frequently attributed to the maturation of basic processes in the brain that are involved in the encoding, storage, retrieval, and reporting of information, as well as other contextual factors such as level of prior knowledge and the way in which parents structure conversations with their children (Ornstein & Haden, 2001).

Language

Humans appear to be born with a brain for language, as newborns are able to distinguish between phonemes from all the world's languages at birth (although this ability becomes extinct by the end of the first year of life), and there are special structures in the brain that, when damaged, severely affect language production (Broca's area) and language comprehension

(Wernike's area). Despite our biological and genetic predisposition to learn language, there are also environmental influences of language learning. The environmental key to language is best illustrated when examining language development in children raised in language-impoverished environments (e.g., extreme neglect).

Generally, language acquisition proceeds through four universal stages. In the *phonological stage* infants learn how to segment strings of speech into meaningful units. During *semantic development*, infants and children learn the meanings of words and word combinations; children's first words usually develop by 12 months and at 18 months many infants undergo a vocabulary spurt in which they rapidly learn the meaning of many new words. In the third stage, known as the stage of *grammar development*, young children learn the rules of a particular language for sequencing words in a sentence and word parts within words. Finally, in the fourth and final stage of language development, called *pragmatic development*, preschool-aged children learn the social and cultural conventions of language use in particular contexts; that is, they learn what is (and is not) appropriate to say across different settings.

Executive function

A key component of cognitive development in early and middle childhood involves children's abilities to control and monitor their own thinking and behavior in order to make plans, solve problems, and pursue goals. *Executive function* abilities refer to these higher-order cognitive processes (such as planning and problem solving) that involve supervising and controlling lower-level cognitive processes (such as attention and memory). Generally, executive function involves cognitive flexibility, attention, memory (particularly working memory), and inhibitory control (similar to self-regulation; Zelazo & Müller, 2011).

Theory of mind

Theory of mind refers to the ability to attribute mental states (beliefs, intentions, desires, emotions, and knowledge) to oneself and others. Development of theory of mind is required in order to reflect on and understand that others have thoughts, feelings, beliefs, and knowledge that is different from your own. This ability to perspective-take, which typically develops during early childhood, is vital for a range of both cognitive and social skills in childhood and adolescence. You will see that it appears again and again in the chapters to come because it is an important factor in developmental psychopathology.

PIAGET'S CONSTRUCTIVIST THEORY

One of the most influential theories in all of developmental psychology is Piaget's constructivist theory of cognitive development. Piaget argued that children have an innate motivation to learn and explore and that brain development aids in cognitive advancements (i.e., nature), while children's own experiences and sensorimotor skills also play a pivotal role in their intellectual development (i.e., nurture). According to his theory, children acquire knowledge and advance in their cognitive skills by actively striving to master their environments, and advance through a series of stages of cognitive development, each stage reflecting a unique way of understanding or making sense of reality.

VYGOTSKY'S SOCIOCULTURAL THEORY

Around the same time that Piaget developed his constructivist theory of development, Vygotsky was also in the process of creating his sociocultural theory of cognitive development. Vygotsky agreed with Piaget's claim that both biological (i.e., nature) and social (i.e., nurture) factors influence children's development, and that children play an active role in constructing their own reality through their interactions with the environment. According to Vygotsky (1978), however, nature and nurture shape development, not by interacting directly, but by interacting with the culture. One of the most important contributions to understanding children's development is Vygotsky's theory of the *zone of proximal development*, which is defined as the gap between what children can do independently and what they can accomplish when they are interacting with more capable peers or adults. Essentially, as children begin to participate in activities that are somewhat beyond their capabilities, adults scaffold children by offering the necessary structure for accomplishing the task. As children participate in adult-guided activities over time, they begin to incorporate new skills.

INFORMATION-PROCESSING THEORIES

Information-processing theories describe humans' mental functioning as analogous to the workings of a computer. These theories distinguish between the "hardware" and "software" of intellectual functioning, in which the "hardware" refers to certain brain structures and neural features (with the recognition that there are limits on information processing in humans, including storage capacity and speed of processing) and the "software" refers to problem-solving strategies and methods that individuals use to help them process and remember information (such as memory strategies and study skills). In general, from an information-processing approach, young children's cognitive difficulties are due to general cognitive factors, such as limited knowledge, memory, attentional control, and speed of processing information, as well as by limited strategies for acquiring and using information (Thompson & Siegler, 2010). As children grow older, their performance improves and its unevenness decreases because the cognitive limitations are gradually being reduced through maturation of the brain ("hardware") and the development of more effective information-processing strategies ("software").

Social–Emotional Development

From infancy to adulthood, big changes occur in our abilities to experience, express, and regulate emotions; form relationships with family and friends; and engage in ways that are socially acceptable. Indeed, the ability to respond to others socially and emotionally is critical for human development to proceed normally and for individuals to be resilient to life stressors and psychopathology.

EMOTIONS

It is generally agreed that there are a number of universal basic emotions expressed in similar ways across all cultures, including joy, fear, anger, surprise, sadness, and disgust. Moreover, these basic emotions are expressed beginning in early infancy. Indeed, infants have the ability to communicate their emotions through smiling, crying, and the use of facial expressions, and these basic expressions are remarkably similar all over the world. Given that infants are fully dependent on their caregivers for survival, crying is believed to be an evolutionarily adaptive way of communicating their needs.

Sometime during the toddler and preschool years, children start to experience new emotions, called *self-conscious emotions*, which include embarrassment, pride, shame, guilt, and envy (Reddy, 2005). Self-conscious emotions depend on children's newly acquired abilities to recognize and think about themselves in relation to other people and the goals they desire (Lewis, 2007). Unlike basic emotions, which occur in response to events that elicit them, self-conscious emotions involve a complex combination of cognition and emotion. As their sense of self evolves, their self-conscious emotions become deeper and more complex.

SELF-REGULATION

The ability to control one's thoughts, emotions, and behaviors, called *self-regulation*, begins in infancy and evolves during early childhood. You will see that deficits in self-regulation act as risk factors for various forms of psychopathology in the chapters that follow. Infants and young children require help with regulation, such as soothing by caregivers and guidance of emotional expressions. One important aspect of self-regulation is the ability to inhibit an action that is already underway, known as *effortful control*. Children high in effortful control show an ability to keep their arousal from getting too intense by developing strategies for soothing themselves; children low in effortful control are often unable to control their arousal and become easily agitated and highly emotional.

Emotion regulation

In addition to controlling one's thoughts and actions, children must learn to control their emotions and express their feelings in a socially appropriate way. Between two and six years, children develop a number of strategies to help them keep their emotions under control. This emerging ability is highly beneficial for young children in coping with disappointments, frustrations, and hurt feelings often experienced at this point in development. As children get older, the ability to regulate emotions becomes increasingly important. Research indicates that good emotion regulation skills predict academic performance, resilience, and well-being (Graziano et al., 2007). Additionally, difficulties in emotion regulation are believed to underlie most forms of psychopathology.

DEVELOPMENT OF AGGRESSION

Aggression begins to develop early in life. In fact, there are two types of aggression easily identified during early childhood, hostile aggression and instrumental aggression (Berkowitz, 2003). *Hostile aggression* is characterized by the intent to harm or injure the victim, whereas *instrumental aggression* is directed at achieving a particular goal (e.g., hitting or threatening another child in order to obtain a toy or gain peer approval). Children who have not successfully developed age-appropriate strategies for regulating aggressive behavior are at high risk for engaging in chronic aggressive and antisocial behavior.

DEVELOPMENT OF PROSOCIAL EMOTIONS AND BEHAVIORS

Young children can be remarkably sensitive to the emotional needs of others. Beginning in early childhood, many children begin to develop *prosocial behaviors*, or voluntary actions intended to benefit others (e.g., sharing, helping, and showing compassion). The two biggest aspects of prosocial behavior are *empathy* (the sharing of another person's emotions and feelings) and *sympathy* (feelings of sorrow or concern for another person). Empathy is believed to provide the essential foundations for prosocial behavior (Eisenberg, Fabes, & Spinrad, 2006).

PEER RELATIONSHIPS

Peers play a powerful role in the lives of children and adolescents (Bukowski, Laursen, & Rubin, 2018). Peers have the power to influence and shape each other's behaviors, attitudes, and beliefs, especially in adolescence.

Peer pressure and conformity

Young adolescents conform more to peer standards than children do. *Conformity* refers to the degree to which friends are similar to each other in their behavior, interests, style, and goals and aspirations for the future. Around the time of high school, conformity to peers—especially to their antisocial standards—peaks (Brown & Larson, 2009). At this point, adolescents are most likely to go along with a peer to skip class, paint graffiti, or steal items from a store. Adolescents tend to select friends that seem similar to them and share their same views. However, when adolescents are uncertain about their social identity or are in the presence of someone that they perceive to have a higher status than they do, they are much more likely to conform to peers (Prinstein & Giletta, 2016).

Dating and romantic relationships

Adolescents spend a considerable amount of time dating or thinking about dating (Furman, 2018). Romantic relationships are central to adolescents' sense of belonging and group status (Collins, 2003). Research indicates that engaging in romantic relationships is associated with both positive (higher levels of social acceptance, friendship competence, and romantic competence) and negative outcomes (substance use, delinquency, and sexual behavior; Furman, Low, & Ho, 2009). Additionally, early dating has been linked to depression in adolescent girls, higher risk of teenage pregnancy, and problems at home and school (Starr et al., 2012).

Moral Development

Have you ever encountered a situation in which you were expected to choose between right and wrong? This distinction was likely influenced by your personal morals. Many of us are presented with issues of morality beginning in our early childhood years. *Morality* is defined as principles that determine how people treat one another in regard to justice, the welfare of others, and human rights (Turiel, 1983). Moral development is a process through which individuals decide whether or not to establish a moral identity (Hardy & Carlo, 2011).

PIAGET'S THEORY OF MORAL DEVELOPMENT

In addition to Piaget's theory of cognitive development, he is also known for his theory of moral development, which focused on the degree to which a child's awareness and understanding of the world translates to their progression through stages of morality (Piaget, 1932). The first stage of his theory, *heteronomous morality*, typically includes children under the age of 7 as they become aware of rules and view them as fixed and sacred. Children in this stage deem actions as "good" or "bad" based on their consistency with rules set by authority figures and believe that a child's violation of rules makes one deserving of a punishment regardless of intentions or motives (Nobes & Pawson, 2003). Interacting with peers, learning that rules are not permanent, and considering the perspectives of others all prepare children for the second stage—*autonomous morality*. Around the age of 11, children begin to realize that people cooperate in order to set rules, determine "fit" punishments for violating rules, no longer blindly obey rules, and consider a person's intentions when evaluating their actions.

KOHLBERG'S THEORY OF MORAL DEVELOPMENT

Kohlberg (1958, 1963) contributed to research on moral development by constructing six stages. *Preconventional morality* is behavior that is influenced by external forces (e.g., rewards and punishments). This level includes stage 1, *obedience and punishment*, and stage 2, *instrumentalism*. Stage 1 is marked by blind obedience to authority, avoidance of punishment, and behavior guided by *egocentrism*, a child's inability to take another person's perspective. During stage 2, a child begins to understand that cooperation with others can result in mutual benefit, but the child still maintains a sense of self-interest. *Conventional morality* is the second level of Kohlberg's theory where youth start to comply with social rules and develop a conscience. Egocentrism has begun to dissipate, allowing consideration of other perspectives. Stage 3 of this level is often referred to as *"good boy, good girl,"* in which people's actions are motivated by social approval. Stage 4, or *"law and order"* is when people find importance in "doing one's duty" and maintaining a sense of order. Those in this stage accept society's rules in order to prevent chaos and many people demonstrate conventional morality throughout their entire lives. The last level of Kohlberg's theory, *postconventional morality*, focuses on personal moral principles instead of relying on conventional standards in society. *Social contract* and *universal ethical principles* are stages 5 and 6 and people may not reach these stages of morality in their lifetime. It is possible that people achieve postconventional morality in adolescence, but this level is more commonly seen in adulthood (Kohlberg, 1973).

Kohlberg's theory has limitations: while he developed his theory with intentions of making it universal, evidence has indicated there are differences in moral reasoning between individualistic and collectivistic cultures. For example, postconventional morality appears to reflect values of Western intellectuals; therefore, it is difficult for non-Westerners to progress through later stages (Snarey, 1985).

GILLIGAN'S THEORY OF MORAL DEVELOPMENT

Gilligan's (1982) contribution to the study of moral development stems from a flaw in Kohlberg's research—the lack of consideration of gender differences. Gilligan disagreed on generalizing Kohlberg's findings to both males and females, given that his initial research was solely conducted with male participants. Gilligan focused on the different standards women have for making moral decisions. She also concluded that while men are more concerned with the *morality of justice*, women are more concerned with the *morality of care*, which results in women being placed lower on Kohlberg's moral hierarchy. While influential, Gilligan's theory has limitations. She has been criticized for stereotyping gender while research has concluded that gender differences regarding moral reasoning are small (Jaffee & Hyde, 2000).

SOCIAL DOMAIN THEORY

The Social Domain Theory suggests that children make judgments that are influenced by three social domains—moral, conventional, and personal (Turiel, 1998). Children may consider the *moral domain* by judging norms pertaining to human rights, fairness, and justice. The *conventional domain* consists of judging norms associated with social conventions and rules to ensure social organization (e.g., making appropriate decisions about table manners and dress). Lastly, children consider the *personal domain*, which includes focusing on individual preferences and how certain decisions will affect the self. Research concludes that differences in culture, religion, and socioeconomic status are likely to influence whether people perceive decisions as moral, conventional, or personal (Nucci, 1997).

PARENTAL, PEER, AND CULTURAL INFLUENCES

Parents, peers, and culture are far more influential in the development of moral reasoning than originally proposed. Parents who promote a supportive environment, encourage children to question and actively develop moral reasoning, and who maintain high-quality relationships with children are likely to raise adolescents with higher levels of moral reasoning (e.g., Malti & Latzko, 2010). A child's interaction with peers can also increase their moral reasoning through discussing moral conflict (Eisenberg & Morris, 2004). Additionally, culture plays a role in moral development; those in individualistic cultures typically base moral reasoning on justice, while those from collectivist cultures usually focus on group harmony.

Roots of Moral Development

Socialization and internalization are two processes that contribute to moral development in early childhood. *Socialization* is when children learn to behave in a socially acceptable way by developing habits, skills, values, and motives deemed appropriate by society. Socialization occurs when children have internalized society's standards and held them as their own—they no longer blindly obey rules (Grusec & Goodnow, 1994).

The development of a conscience stems from an individual's internal standards of conduct and begins early in childhood (Thompson, 2014). Individuals learn how to abstain from certain behaviors and, if unable, may experience emotional discomfort. Parenting is highly involved and parents may notice their children need additional guidance. However, children may have already internalized their parents' standards and act in a way that meets these standards without assistance (Kochanska, Coy, & Murray, 2001). When toddlers have mutually responsive relationships with their mothers, they are more likely to show moral emotions (e.g., guilt, empathy), moral conduct, and moral cognition in their early school years. Overall, one's conscience can influence moral development by restricting destructive tendencies, promoting compliance with society's standards, and encouraging prosocial behavior (Eisenberg, 2000).

Prosocial Moral Reasoning

Prosocial behavior can be defined as behavior that is voluntarily performed in order to benefit another person. The urge to engage in this behavior is associated with a person's morality and many people use prosocial moral reasoning to aid decision-making. This reasoning may be useful when an individual has to decide between helping another person or meeting the needs of oneself. *Altruism* is at the center of prosocial behavior and can be referred to as the motivation to help other people, even if it comes at a cost. Altruism is seen in infants as young as 14 months old, but children may differ in their readiness and reasons for engaging in prosocial behavior (Warneken & Tomasello, 2009). Some research shows humans may be biologically predisposed to act in prosocial ways while other research focuses more on parental and societal influences. Parents who are warm, sympathetic, and demonstrate prosocial behavior are more likely to instill prosocial behavior in children. Child peer groups that model prosocial behavior also result in a greater likelihood of increasing this behavior among other children (Hoorn et al., 2016).

Sex-Role Development

Sex Versus Gender

A person's *sex* is assigned at birth based on outward physical characteristics/genitalia. In contrast, *gender identity* refers to how a person feels inside; it is one's personal conception, or feeling, as male or female (or, sometimes, both or neither). Gender does not depend on the outward physiological indicators or internal reproductive organs that determine our biological sex. While most people's gender identities align with their biological sex, it is not uncommon for people to identify with a gender that does not align with their assigned sex.

Development of Gender Identity

In the short span of just a few years, children begin to identify as a girl or a boy, and act in ways that are characteristic of their gender. By the preschool years, girls and boys start to differ in forms of play. Boys tend to be more active, independent, "rough-and-tumble," and less compliant than girls, whereas girls tend to be more verbal and nurturing. This developmental period is also when girls and boys generally start to play with same-sex individuals, a phenomenon referred to as *gender segregation* (Fenson et al., 1994).

By early elementary school, children gravitate towards activities, such as sports, that are historically associated with their gender. Over time, through continued exposure and interaction with members of the same gender, children align their behavior with gender-role norms through the process of general socialization of gender norms, through which children acquire the standards, values, and knowledge of their society as it pertains to gender.

Expression of Gender Identity

Once gender identity is established, children tend to engage in activities associated with their identified gender through a process called identification. *Identification* is a psychological process in which children try to look, act, feel, and be like significant people in their social environment, such as peers and adults. Adults often provide certain expectations for children that serve as a framework for how children should or should not behave. When individuals identify as a gender other than the gender aligned with their assigned biological sex, they identify as *transgender*. Research suggests that gender identity in transgender children is just as strong as it is in *cisgender* children (Gülgöz et al., 2019). Additionally, societal expectations have little to no impact on a transgender child's sense of gender identity. While the child may risk social rejection, they are likely still to seek environmental cues that support their gender identity.

SEX-ROLE IDENTITY

Cultural stereotypes of males and females involve broad expectations of behavior that we call gender or sex-roles. In Western cultures, the feminine sex-role stereotype includes traits such as gentleness, helpfulness, dependence, warmth, emotionality, and submissiveness, while the masculine sex-role stereotype includes independence, self-confidence, competitiveness, and aggressiveness. There are four major views on the process of sex-role identification in children. While not always substantiated by evidence, the first is the psychodynamic view, conceptualized by Freud. This view uses Freud's psychosexual stages of development and assumes young children are caught in hidden conflicts between their fears and desires. According to this view, early stages of psychosexual development, such as the phallic stage, mark the period during which children look to their parents for ways in which they ought to behave. Through the process of identification, children look for cues on how to be similar to their same sex parent.

The second major view of sex-role identity is called the social learning view, which emphasizes two processes—modeling and differential reinforcement. *Modeling* is the process by which children observe and imitate individuals of their own gender. Movies, television shows, books, and magazines tend to portray male and female characters differently; this can play a significant role in how boys and girls decide how they should behave. *Differential reinforcement* occurs when girls and boys are differentially rewarded for engaging in gender-appropriate behavior (boys may be praised for engaging in aggressive behavior while girls may be punished).

The third and fourth major views are the cognitive-developmental view and the gender schema view, respectively, which focus on the idea that a child's own conceptions are central to the formation of sex-role identity. Three stages proposed by Kohlberg are highlighted in the cognitive-developmental view. The first stage is *basic sex-role identity* where a child labels oneself as a boy or a girl. The second stage is *sex-role stability* in which the child starts understanding the stability of the sex-role over time.

The third stage is *sex-role constancy* in which the child understands that sex remains the same no matter the situation. The gender schema view, in contrast, states that the environment affects a child's understanding of gender through schemas, or mental frameworks, which guide them to act in gender appropriate ways. A *gender schema* is a mental model containing information about males and females that is used to process gender-relevant information (Martin & Ruble, 2004).

Chapter Summary

In this chapter, we focused on theories of normal development that developmental psychopathologists study in order to understand better how deviations in development might result in risk for psychopathology. In particular, we focused on individual factors—like a child's temperament, physical development, cognitive development, social-emotional development, moral development, and sex-role development. We also emphasized that the child's context, which includes their parents, siblings, peers, and societies, play a role in these developmental processes, particularly though attachment experiences, parenting styles, socialization, and goodness of fit. Across the chapter, we highlighted multiple levels of analysis, which you learned about in Chapter 2 as a guiding principle of developmental psychopathology, by reviewing how bodies, hormones, cognitions, emotions, and context all interact with one another during the course of healthy development.

Further Reading

Bronfenbrenner, U., & Morris, P. A. (2006). The bioecological model of human development. In R. M. Lerner & W. Damon (Eds.), *Handbook of child psychology: Theoretical models of human development* (vol. 1, 6th ed., pp. 793–828). Hoboken, NJ, USA: John Wiley & Sons Inc.

Eisenberg, N., Cumberland, A., & Spinrad, T. L. (1998). Parental socialization of emotion. *Psychological Inquiry*, *9*(4), 241–273.

Rothbart, M. K., & Bates, J. E. (2006). Temperament. In W. Damon and N. Eisenberg (Eds.), *Handbook of child psychology*, vol. 3: Social, emotional, and personality development (pp. 105–176). New York, NY: John Wiley & Sons, Inc. doi: 10.1002/9780470147.

Vygotsky, L. (1978). Interaction between learning and development. *Readings on the Development of Children*, *23*(3), 34–41.

Discussion/Essay Questions

1. Explain how one of the guiding principles that you learned about in Chapter 2 relates to the theories and research reviewed in this chapter. That is, how do the developmental theories reviewed in this chapter fit, or fail to fit, with a developmental psychopathology approach? Pick one example to support your answer.

2. Use the goodness-of-fit concept described in this chapter to explain how infant temperament and parenting style might interact. Which parenting style would you expect would fit best with which child temperament style? Do a quick literature search to see if scientists have proven your hypothesis to be correct.
3. Think of an example of child behavior from your own life—either your behavior or the behavior of a child you know. Describe the example, including the age of the child, and how it fits into the various theories of moral development included in this chapter.

Glossary

Altruism is the motivation to help other people, even if it comes at a cost.

Authoritarian style of parenting in which parents value obedience, impose a forceful imposition of their will on their child, and offer little warmth or affection.

Authoritative style of parenting in which parents maintain consistent boundaries, use reasoning, and control their children within reasonable limits while also offering consistent affection and support for their child.

Conformity refers to the degree to which friends are similar to each other in their behavior, interests, style, and goals and aspirations for the future.

Effortful control is the ability to inhibit an action that is already underway.

Egocentrism is a child's inability to take another person's perspective.

Empathy is the sharing of another person's emotions and feelings.

Executive function involves cognitive flexibility, attention, memory, and inhibitory control.

Fine motor skills involve the development and coordination of the small muscles of the body.

Gender identity refers to how a person feels inside; it is one's personal conception, or feeling, as male or female (or sometimes, both, or neither).

Gender segregation is the phenomenon characterized by girls generally preferring to play with other girls and boys tending to play with other boys.

Goodness of fit is the compatibility between the environment and a child's temperament.

Gross motor skills involve the large muscles of the body and allow for locomotion to occur.

Hostile aggression is characterized by the intent to harm or injure the victim.

Identification is a psychological process in which children try to look, act, feel, and be like significant people in their social environment, such as peers and adults.

Instrumental aggression is directed at achieving a particular goal.

Morality is defined as principles that determine how people treat one another in regard to justice, the welfare of others, and human rights.

Myelination is the formation of myelin sheaths that allow for the increase in speed of electrical transmissions between neurons.

Neglectful or non-conformist style of parenting in which parents are generally low on warmth and control, and tend to be uninvolved parents.

Neurons are specialized nerve cells found in the brain.

Permissive style of parenting in which parents are non-intrusive and lax but are available as resources to their child when needed and offer high levels of warmth.

Primary sex characteristics include the reproductive organs or gonads (e.g., sperm-producing testes in males and egg-producing ovaries in females).

Prosocial behaviors are voluntary actions intended to benefit others.

Puberty is the biological process in both males and females that signifies a human's physical and sexual maturation, as individuals become capable of reproduction.

Secondary sex characteristics include the outward physiological indicators or traits of sex (e.g., breasts and facial hair) that distinguish males from females; these are not involved in sexual reproduction.

Self-regulation is the ability to control one's thoughts, emotions, and behaviors.

Sex (male or female) is a label that is assigned at birth based on outward physical characteristics.

Socialization is the process by which children learn to behave in a way that is socially acceptable by developing habits, skills, values, and motives that are deemed appropriate by society's standards.

Sympathy is the emotional component of empathy and involves feeling sorrow or concern for another person.

Synaptogenesis is the process of synapse formation between neurons.

Temperament is a term used to describe individual differences in behavioral styles, emotions, and characteristic ways of responding.

References

Baumrind, D. (1975). *Early socialization and the discipline controversy.* Morristown, NJ: General Learning.

Baumrind, D. (1989). Rearing competent children. In W. Damon (Ed.), *Child development today and tomorrow.* San Francisco, CA: Jossey-Bass.

Baumrind, D., & Black, A. E. (1967). Socialization practices associated with dimensions of competence in preschool boys and girls. *Child Development, 38,* 291–327.

Belsky, J. (2006). Determinants and consequences of infant-parent attachment. In L. Balter & C. S. Tamis-LeMonda (Eds.), *Child psychology: A handbook of contemporary issues* (2nd ed., pp. 53–77). New York, NY: Psychology Press.

Berkowitz, L. (2003). Affect, aggression, and antisocial behavior. In R. J. Davidson, K. R. Scherer, & H. H. Goldsmith (Eds.), Series in affective science, *Handbook of affective sciences* (pp. 804–823). New York, NY: Oxford University Press.

Brown, B. B., & Larson, J. (2009). Peer relationships in adolescence. In R. M. Lerner & L. Steinberg (Eds.), *Handbook of adolescent development* (3rd ed.). New York, NY: John Wiley & Sons, Inc.

Bukowski, W. M., Laursen, B., & Rubin, K. H. (Eds.) (2018). *Handbook of peer interactions, relationships, and groups* (2nd ed.). New York, NY: Guildford.

Duvall, E. M. (1957). *Family development.* Philadelphia, PA: Lippincott.

Eisenberg, N. (2000). Emotion, regulation, and moral development. *Annual Review of Psychology, 51,* 665–697.

Eisenberg, N., & Morris, A. D. (2004). Moral cognitions and prosocial responding in adolescence. In R. M. Lerner & L. Steinberg (Eds.), *Handbook of adolescent psychology* (2nd ed., pp. 155188). Hoboken, NJ: John Wiley & Sons, Inc.

Eisenberg, N., Fabes, R. A., & Spinrad, T. L. (2006). Prosocial development. In N. Eisenberg, W. Damon, & R. M. Lerner (Eds.), *Handbook of child psychology: Social, emotional, and personality development* (pp. 646–718). Hoboken, NJ: John Wiley & Sons, Inc.

Fenson, L., Dale, P. S., Reznick, J. S., Bates, E., Thal, D. J., Pethick, S. J., & Stiles, J. (1994). Variability in early communicative development. *Monographs of the Society for Research in Child Development, 59*(5), v-173. https://doi-org.ezproxy.shsu.edu/10.2307/1166093.

Furman, W. (2018). The romantic relationships of youth. In W. M. Bukowski et al. (Eds.), *Handbook of peer interactions, relationships, and groups* (2nd ed.). New York, NY: Guildford.

Furman, W., Low, S., & Ho, M. J. (2009). Romantic experience and psychosocial adjustment in middle adolescence. *Journal of Clinical Child and Adolescent Psychology, 38,* 7590.

Gilligan, C. (1982). *In a different voice: Psychological theory and women's development.* Cambridge, MA: Harvard University Press.

Graziano, P. A., Reavis, R. D., Keane, S. P., & Calkins, S. D. (2007). The role of emotion regulation in children's early academic success. *Journal of School Psychology,* 3–19.

Groeschel, S., Vollmer, B., King, M. D., & Connelly, A. (2010). Developmental changes in cerebral grey and white matter volume from infancy to adulthood. *International Journal of Developmental Neuroscience, 28*(6), 481–489. https://doi-org.ezproxy.shsu.edu/10.1016/j.ijdevneu.2010.06.004.

Grusec, J. E., & Goodnow, J. J. (1994). Impact of parental discipline methods on the child's internalization of values: A reconceptualization of current points of view. *Developmental Psychology, 30,* 419.

Gülgöz, S., Glazier, J. J., Enright, E. A., Alonso, D. J., Durwood, L. J., Fast, A. A., & Olson, K. R. (2019). Similarity in transgender and cisgender children's gender development.

Proceedings of the National Academy of Sciences of the United States of America, 116(49), 24480–24485. https://doi-org.ezproxy.shsu.edu/10.1073/pnas.1909367116.

Hardy, S. A., & Carlo, G. (2011). Moral identity: What is it, how does it develop, and is it linked to moral action? *Child Development Perspectives, 5*, 212–218.

Hoorn, J., Dijk, E., Meuwese, R., Rieffe, C., & Crone, E. A. (2016). Peer influence on prosocial behavior in adolescence. *Journal of Research on Adolescence, 26*, 90–100.

Jaffee, S., & Hyde, J. S. (2000). Gender differences in moral orientation: A meta-analysis. *Psychological Bulletin, 126*, 703–726.

Kochanska, G., Coy, K. C., & Murray, K. T. (2001). The development of self-regulation in the first four years of life. *Child Development, 72*, 1091–1111.

Kohlberg, L. (1958). The development of modes of thinking and choices in years ten to sixteen. In J. Fleming (Ed.), *Psychological perspectives on human development* (pp. 152–161). Prescott, AZ: Southwest Psychometrics and Psychology Resources.

Kohlberg, L. (1963). The development of children's orientations toward a moral order: I. Sequence in the development of moral thought. In J. Fleming (Ed.), *Psychological perspectives on human development* (pp. 152–161). Prescott, AZ: Southwest Psychometrics and Psychology Resources.

Kohlberg, L. (1973). Continuities in childhood and adult moral development revisited. In P. Baltes & K. W. Schaie (Eds.), *Life-span developmental psychology: Personality and socialization* (pp. 180–207). New York, NY: Academic Press.

Lamb, M. E., Hwang, C. P., Ketterlinus, R. D., & Fracasso, M. P. (1999). Parent–child relationships: Development in the context of the family. In *Developmental psychology: an advanced textbook* (4th ed., pp. 411–436). Mahwah, NJ: Erlbaum.

Lau, A. S., Litrownik, A. J., Newton, R. R., Black, M. M., & Everson, M. D. (2006). Factors affecting the link between physical discipline and child externalizing problems in Black and White families. *Journal of Community Psychology, 34*(1), 89–103.

Lewis, M. (2007). Self-conscious emotional development. In J. L. Tracy, R. W. Robins, & J. P. Tangney (Eds.), *The self-conscious emotions: Theory and research* (pp. 134–149). New York, NY: Guilford Press.

Malti, T., & Latzko, B. (2010). Children's moral emotions and moral cognition: Towards an integrative perspective. *New Directions for Child & Adolescent Development, 2010*, 1–10.

Martin, C. L., & Ruble, D. (2004). Children's search for gender cues: Cognitive perspectives on gender development. *Current Directions in Psychological Science, 13*(2), 67–70. https://doi-org.ezproxy.shsu.edu/10.1111/j.0963-7214.2004.00276.x.

Nobes, G., & Pawson, C. (2003). Children's understanding of social rules and social status. *Merrill-Palmer Quarterly, 49*, 77–99.

Nucci, L. (1997). Cultures, universals, and the personal. In H. D. Saltzstein (Ed.), *Culture as a context for moral development: New perspectives on the particular and the universal* (pp. 5–22). San Francisco, CA: Jossey-Bass.

Ornstein, P. A. & Haden, C. A. (2001). Memory development or the development of memory? *Current Directions in Psychological Science, 10*, 202–205.

Patterson, G. R. (1982). *Coercive family processes* (vol. 3). Castalia Publishing Company.

Piaget, J. (1932). *The moral judgment of the child.* New York, NY: Harcourt Brace.

Prinstein, M. J., & Giletta, M. (2016). Peer relations and developmental psychopathology. In D. Cicchetti (Ed.), *Developmental psychopathology* (3rd ed.). New York, NY: John Wiley & Sons, Inc.

Reddy, V. (2004). Feeling shy and showing-off: Self-conscious emotions must regulate self-awareness. In J. Nadel & D. Muir (Eds.), *Emotional development: Recent research advances* (pp. 183–204). New York, NY: Oxford University Press.

Rothbart, M. K., & Bates, J. E. (1998). *Temperament.* In W. Damon & N. Eisenberg (Eds.), *Handbook of child psychology: Social, emotional, and personality development* (pp. 105–176). Hoboken, NJ: John Wiley & Sons, Inc.

Snarey, J. R. (1985). Cross-cultural universality of social-moral development: A critical review of Kohlbergian research. *Psychological Bulletin*, *97*, 202–232.

Starr, L. R., Davila, J., Stroud, C. B., Li, P. C. C., Yoneda, A., Hershenberg, R., & Miller, M. R. (2012). Love hurts (in more ways than one): Specificity of psychological symptoms as predictors and consequences of romantic activity among early adolescent girls. *Journal of Clinical Psychology*, *68*, 373–381.

Thelen, E. (2005). Dynamic systems theory and the complexity of change. *Psychoanalytic Dialogues*, *15*(2), 255–283. https://doi-org.ezproxy.shsu.edu/10.1080/10481881509348831.

Thomas, A., & Chess, S. (1977). *Temperament and development*. New York, NY: Brunner/Mazel.

Thompson, C. A., & Siegler, R. S. (2010). Linear numerical-magnitude representations aid children's memory for numbers. *Psychological Science*, *21*(9), 1274–1281. https://doi-org.ezproxy.shsu.edu/10.1177/0956797610378309.

Thompson, R. A. (1999). The individual child: Temperament, emotion, self, and personality. In *Developmental psychology: an advanced textbook* (4th ed., pp. 377–403). Mahwah, NJ: Erlbaum.

Thompson, R. A. (2014). Conscience development in early childhood. In M. Killen & J. G. Smetana (Eds.), *Handbook of moral development* (2nd ed., pp. 73–92). New York, NY: Psychology Press.

Turiel, E. (1998). *The development of morality*. In W. Damon (Ed.), *Handbook of child psychology* (pp. 863–932). New York, NY: John Wiley & Sons, Inc.

Warneken, F., & Tomasello, M. (2009). The roots of human altruism. *British Journal of Psychology*, *100*(3), 455–471.

Vygotsky, L. (1978). Interaction between learning and development. *Readings on the Development of Children*, *23*(3), 34–41.

Zelazo, P. D., & Müller, U. (2011). Executive function in typical and atypical development. In U. Goswami (Ed.), *The Wiley-Blackwell handbook of childhood cognitive development* (pp. 574–603). Malden, MA: Wiley-Blackwell.

Chapter 4

Insecure Attachment and Related Difficulties

Amanda Venta and Anna Abate

Chapter Overview

We will begin by introducing *attachment theory* in order to provide a lens through which to think about the other topics covered in this book. *Attachment* refers to a biologically based instinct to seek a caregiver when in need of safety, security, and/or comfort (Bowlby, 1960). Attachment theory is heavily influential in research related to child development, psychopathology, and treatment and is not exclusively related to one psychological disorder. Thus, in this chapter we will use the term *attachment styles* to describe categories of attachment behavior and avoid confusing them with specific disorders. After defining attachment styles, we will focus on how psychopathology relates to attachment styles and on the development of insecure attachments. Often, attachment issues and emerging psychopathology go hand-in-hand, making attachment theory a critical piece of developmental psychopathology.

Case study in attachment issues and behavioral difficulties

Ivan is a six-year-old Hispanic boy who lives with his grandparents. He first lived with his young mother who regularly used narcotics, left Ivan alone for long periods of time, and struggled to provide adequate food, water, and shelter for the family. Ivan was removed from the home by child welfare when he was three years old. His mother's parental rights were terminated and his grandparents adopted him. Ivan currently has no contact with his mother.

Developmental Psychopathology, First Edition. Edited by Amanda Venta, Carla Sharp, Jack M. Fletcher, and Peter Fonagy.

His grandparents have struggled with how to manage Ivan's behavioral difficulties since they adopted him; he cries, yells loudly, breaks things when he is frustrated and behaves aggressively when they try to comfort him. Ivan's grandparents also worry about his social development, noting that he has behavioral issues at school (e.g., tantrums) and tends to be rude and physically aggressive towards peers.

As the clinician seeing this family, what diagnoses would you consider? Discuss how Ivan's early experiences with his mother might underlie his current difficulties and use this information to guide how you might intervene to treat Ivan's behaviors.

Definition and Theoretical Underpinnings

John Bowlby originally put forth the idea that early in development, the emotional and physical needs of a baby, and whether those needs are consistently met by caregivers, inform the development of an *internal working model* (Bowlby, 1969, 1973)—a template we carry with us to make sense of ourselves and others. *Attachment security* emerges when the child's needs are consistently met; his or her internal working model is one of him- or herself as worthy of care and others as reliable caregivers (Bretherton & Munholland, 2008). *Attachment insecurity*, on the other hand, is characterized by an internal working model of the self as unworthy of care and others as unreliable caregivers. Attachment behavior differs depending upon the caregiver's behavior (see Figure 4.1) and development (see Figure 4.2).

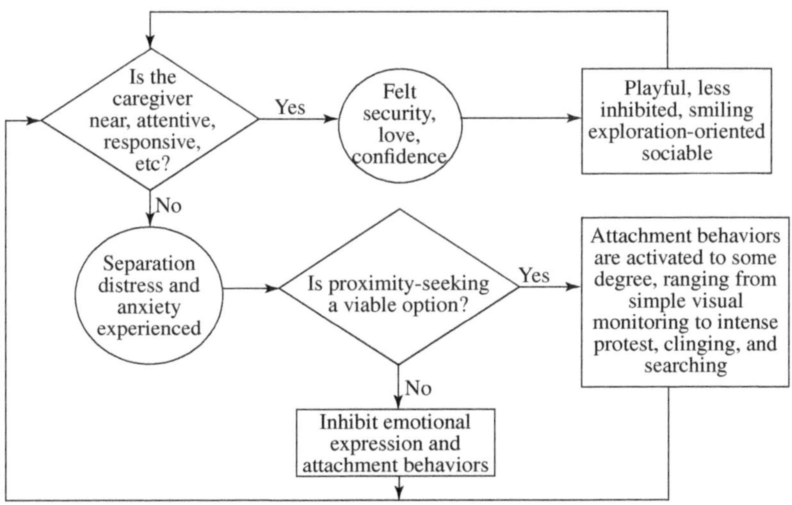

FIGURE 4.1 Control Systems Model of the Attachment Behavioral System .Source: Fraley and Speiker (2003a). Reproduced with permissions of American Psychological Association.

Latent Dimension	Infancy	Childhood	Adulthood
Proximity-Seeking	• When distressed, child crawls toward attachment figure upon reunion • Infant successfully established and maintains contact with caregiver	• When hurt or frightened, child verbally expresses and clearly signals his or her negative feelings to the attachment figures	• Adult contacts attachment figure to seek emotional support during times of distress • Adult is willing and able to provide care for ageing attachment figure if necessary
		VERSUS	
Withdrawal	• Infant withdraws gaze from attachment figure • Infant crawls past attachment figure during reunion episode	• Conversations with caregiver are polite and cool, with little affective content	• Adult minimizes the importance of relationship with caregiver in his or her life
Angry and Resistant	• Infant arches back or cries more loudly and persistently when held by attachment figure • Infant is not easily soothed, despite the attachment figure's provision of comfort	• Child uses a variety of exaggerated or escalating affective displays to influence caregiver response, including anger, coyness, helplessness and fear	• Adult accuses attachment figure of never having been available, sensitive, or responsive to his or her needs • Adult is resentful over having to care for aging attachment figure • Adult has difficulties setting boundaries and limits with attachment figures
		VERSUS	
Emotional Confidence	• Infant quickly returns to play after being comforted and reassured by attachment figure	• Child is comfortable exploring new hobbies and friendships without requiring the constant presence or assistance of caregivers	• Adult is able to develop an independent emotional, relational life

FIGURE 4.2 Ways in Which Attachment Manifests Behaviorally Across Development. Source: Fraley and Speiker (2003a). Reproduced with permissions of American Psychological Association.

Mary Ainsworth, a student of John Bowlby, made a major contribution to attachment theory by developing the Strange Situation Paradigm (Ainsworth, Blehar, Waters, & Wall, 1978). In this paradigm, an infant (ages 12–20 months) and caregiver are together in an unfamiliar playroom and guided through separations and reunions. You can watch the Strange Situation in videos created by researchers (https://www.youtube.com/watch?feature=player_embedded&v=QTsewNrHUHU). By using this procedure, Ainsworth discovered four patterns of behavior, known as *attachment styles* (Ainsworth et al., 1978). A child with a *secure attachment* will use the caregiver as a safe base to explore but return to when distressed. This pattern of behaviors is thought to arise from consistent, sensitive caregiving. A child with an *anxious-resistant (or ambivalent) insecure attachment* may demonstrate clingy behavior but will reject the attachment figure when they try to engage. This behavior is likely a response to unpredictable caregiving; the behavior of the child may be a strategy for maintaining the attention of the caregiver (e.g., Crittenden, 1999). A child with an *anxious-avoidant insecure attachment* tends to be independent and ignore the caregiver during both separations and reunifications. This behavior is thought to emerge as a self-protective strategy when attachment behavior has been rejected by the caregiver in the past. The fourth category, called *disorganized attachment*, refers to children that cannot be classified into one of the aforementioned categories. Behaviors commonly observed in this group are contradictory; incongruent with affect; stereotypic, jerky; and freezing (Main & Solomon, 1990). Disorganized attachments often emerge in the context of a caregiver who is at times frighten*ing* and also frighten*ed* (Main & Hesse, 1992).

This foundational work in attachment theory was later extended to attachment in older children and adults. Across development, our attachments become less about physical proximity and more about emotional availability. Therefore, Mary Main and her colleagues (George, Kaplan, & Main, 1985) developed the Adult Attachment Interview, which focuses on *how* individuals talk about their early childhood experiences (you can find a full interview at http://www.psychology.sunysb.edu/attachment/measures/content/aai_interview.pdf). Critically, the interview bases attachment styles on the *way* in which caregiving experiences are described. Respondents are assigned to four groups that mirror those identified in the Strange Situation Paradigm. An *autonomous* (i.e., securely attached) adult is one who values attachment relationships and talks about caregiving experiences in a way that is balanced, coherent, and open. A *preoccupied* adult will dominate the interview with excessive attention towards caregivers and anger. A *dismissing* adult, on the other hand, will tend to de-emphasize the impact of caregiving experiences. Finally, a *disorganized* adult's interview will contain evidence of prior difficult caregiving experiences (like abuse or loss) that are unresolved in adulthood. Extensions of this interview have now been developed and used with school-age children (Shmueli-Goetz, Target, Fonagy, & Datta, 2008) and adolescents (Venta, Shmueli-Goetz, & Sharp, 2014).

While most early research has focused on categorical attachment styles (e.g., secure), more recent research measuring attachment with self-report questionnaires demonstrated that people's attachment may vary

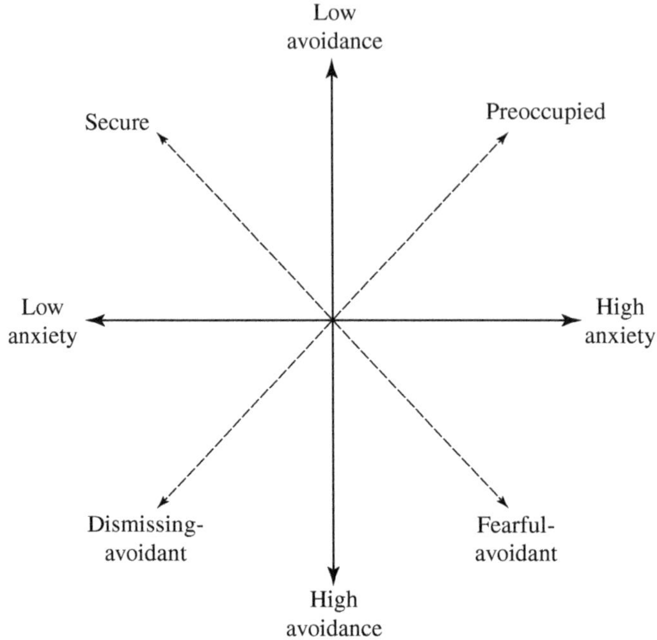

FIGURE 4.3 Two-Dimensional Model of Attachment. Source: Fraley et al. (2015). Reproduced with permissions of American Psychological Association.

continuously (Brennan, Clark, & Shaver, 1998; Fraley & Waller, 1998). In the continuous model (Figure 4.3), people are assumed to vary regarding avoidance and anxiety. The combination of an individual's location on each dimension maps on to the categorical notion of attachment styles (Fraley, Hudson, Heffernan, & Segal, 2015). Whether attachment is categorical or dimensional remains quite controversial.

Factors Affecting the Distribution of Attachment Styles in the General Population

The distribution of attachment styles in the general population depends somewhat on the assessment used, whether a dimensional or categorical approach was considered, and the developmental stage. Overall, about 60% of people tend to be classified as securely attached, with the remaining 40% divided among the insecure and disorganized classifications. Estimates are also affected by age, gender, socioeconomic status, and race/ethnicity, as described in the following sections. It should be noted, however, that the attachment classification estimates provided are based on community samples—that is, based upon studies that did *not* seek out participants with psychopathology where, as a general rule, attachment security is less common.

GENDER AND AGE

Regarding age, rates of attachment security are similar across development, though adolescents tend to be overrepresented in the dismissing group and very young children are more often rated as disorganized. Indeed, in a sample of fifteen-month-old children, 60.0% were classified as secure, 13.3% avoidant, 4.2% resistant (i.e., ambivalent), and 15% disorganized (Fraley & Spieker, 2003b), whereas in childhood, 66% were classified as secure, 28% dismissing, 3% preoccupied, and 4% disorganized (Shmueli-Goetz, Target, Fonagy, & Data, 2008); in adolescence, approximately 52% were classified as secure (with 34.44% dismissing, 5.38% preoccupied, and 2.87% disorganized; Fearon, Shmueli-Goetz, Viding, Fonagy, & Plomin, 2014); and in adults, 58% were rated as secure, 24% dismissing, and 18% as preoccupied (van IJzendoorn & Bakermans-Kranenburg, 1996). In terms of gender differences, Shmueli-Goetz et al. (2008) reported a non-significant association between attachment and gender in middle childhood and van IJzendoor and Bakermans-Kranenburg (1996) reported comparable attachment classifications between mothers and fathers. However, age and gender differences have been more pronounced in studies of continuously rated attachment (Fraley et al., 2011).

SOCIOECONOMIC STATUS (SES), RACE, AND ETHNICITY

There are mixed findings regarding relations between attachment, SES, race, and ethnicity, which are further complicated by interactions between these variables. For example, Bakermans-Kranenburg and colleagues (2004) found that African American children had significantly lower scores on a measure of attachment security than White children but that this relation was explained by income—African American ethnicity was associated with low-income status, which affected the quality of maternal sensitivity and therefore attachment security. Thus, in this study, it was poverty, not race/ethnicity that was truly linked to decreased attachment security. This study echoes a broader link between low income and attachment insecurity (van IJzendoorn & Bakermans-Kranenburg, 2010).

There have been concerns that the measurement of attachment is biased against non-Western cultures. Some studies have demonstrated the overrepresentation of insecurity among children from parts of Africa, Japan, Indonesia, and Israel (see van IJzendoorn & Bakermans-Kranenburg, 2010; van IJzendoorn & Sagi-Schwartz, 2008). However, most evidence suggests that secure attachments are readily detected across varied cultures (van IJzendoorn & Sagi, 1999), intracultural differences are larger than intercultural differences (van IJzendoorn & Sagi-Schwartz, 2008), and attachment styles are similar across studies conducted with many cultures and languages (van IJzendoorn & Bakermans-Kranenburg, 2010).

Attachment and Psychopathology

Many studies conducted in children, adolescents, and adults document a link between insecure attachment and psychopathology with, generally, attachment insecurity in infants and young children relating most to behavior problems, with the links between attachment insecurity and psychopathology becoming more diffuse across development.

INFANCY

Research with high-risk samples of infants shows significant relations between psychopathology and attachment. For example, avoidant attachment was longitudinally associated with *externalizing symptoms* like non-compliance and hostility at age 4 (Erikson, Sroufe, & Egeland, 1985) and in elementary school (Renken, Egeland, Marvinney, Mengelsdorf, & Sroufe, 1989). Disorganized attachment in infancy has been linked to the later emergence of hostile and aggressive behavior (e.g., Lyons-Ruth, Alpern, & Repacholi, 1993) and to *dissociative symptoms* across a 19-year *longitudinal study* (Ogawa, Sroufe, Weinfield, Carlson, & Egeland, 1997). Specific links between early attachment styles and other forms of psychopathology have been more difficult to establish. For example, *internalizing symptoms* have been associated with resistant (Warren, Huston, Egeland, & Sroufe, 1997), disorganized (Shaw, Keenan, Vondra, Delliquandri, & Giovannelli, 1997), and avoidant (Lyons-Ruth, Easterbrooks, & Cibelli, 1997) attachments.

PRESCHOOL AND SCHOOL-AGED CHILDREN

In preschool and school-aged children, a link between attachment insecurity and behavior problems remains with studies among preschoolers linking behavior problems to resistant-like attachment behaviors (DeVito & Hopkins, 2001) and disorganized attachment (Vondra et al., 2001). Similarly, a *meta-analytic study* conducted by Fearon and colleagues (2010) found a significant relation between attachment insecurity and externalizing symptoms across studies. A complimentary meta-analytic study conducted by Groh et al. (2012) found a significant link between attachment insecurity, particularly avoidance, and internalizing symptoms. This conclusion agrees with many other studies linking avoidant attachments to increased anxiety symptoms in school-aged children (Warren, Emde, & Sroufe, 2000; Shamir-Essakow, Ungerer, & Rapee, 2005). Importantly, these findings suggest that while attachment relates to various forms of psychopathology, the relation to externalizing problems is strongest.

ADOLESCENCE

Among adolescents, research has linked insecure attachment to higher symptoms of both internalizing and externalizing disorders in *clinical samples* (Lacasa, Mitjavila, Ochoa, & Balluerka, 2015; Venta, Shmueli-Goetz, & Sharp, 2014), as well as elevated trauma symptoms (Jardin, Venta, Newlin, Ibarra, & Sharp, 2015), suicidal ideation (Venta, Mellick, Shatte, & Sharp, 2014), and *borderline personality disorder* (covered later in Chapter 13) traits. While these studies point to non-specific relations between attachment insecurity and psychopathology, the picture becomes a bit clearer when looking just at studies that explore *subtypes* of insecure attachment. For example, preoccupied attachments have been linked to depression, social problems, aggression, and thought problems (e.g., Lacasa et al., 2015) as well as suicidal ideation (Adam, Sheldon-Keller, & West, 1996) and eating disorders (Miljkovitch, Pierrehumbert, Karmaniola, Bader, & Halfon, 2005). In contrast, avoidant attachments have generally been linked to externalizing behaviors like oppositional defiant behaviors, conduct problems, social problems, and substance use (Lacasa et al., 2015; Venta et al., 2014). The broad array of psychopathology associated with insecure attachment in adolescents is mirrored among adults, in which studies have linked nearly every form of psychopathology to attachment insecurity (see Mikulincer & Shaver, 2007).

Developmental Continuities and Discontinuities

Overall, research has been mixed regarding the continuity of attachment. For instance, some research suggests that attachment classifications at 15 months are not associated with attachment classifications at age 14 (Groh et al., 2014). However, other research shows greater stability in attachment security from 24 months to 18 years (Groh et al., 2014). One category that does seem stable is disorganization, in which significant links to adult disorganization are seen as early as 15 months.

Research has sought to understand discontinuities in attachment. Individuals who were reclassified from secure in early childhood to insecure at 18 years of age were likely to have experienced lower and declining maternal sensitivity; were less likely to be living with their fathers; and had mothers who reported increased negative life events, compared to individuals who remained securely attached across development (Booth-LaForce et al., 2014). Individuals who changed from early insecure attachments to secure attachments experienced higher maternal sensitivity during the timeframe in question. Continuous insecure attachment was associated with less maternal sensitivity and greater paternal depressive symptoms (Booth-LaForce et al., 2014). Thus, this research indicates that insecure attachment is not a fixed property of an individual but clearly malleable by the environment and experience.

A Developmental Psychopathology Model of the Etiology of Attachment Security

Figure 4.4 depicts a developmental psychopathology model of attachment security, laying out how risk and protective factors interact in the development of attachment security.

GENETIC FACTORS (DISTAL RISK FACTORS)

Family and twin studies

Most attachment research has focused exclusively on environmental predictors of attachment security like caregiving, which have been supported by several twin studies. Bokhorst and colleagues (2003) found that more than half of the variance in attachment security was attributed to twins' shared environment, with 48% being attributed to the non-shared environment. However, Fearon and colleagues (2014) documented a high rate of heritability among adolescents! The authors suggest that adolescence is a phase of reorganization during which attachment changes from predominantly behavioral to predominantly cognitive, and that genetic factors are particularly influential during this time. Similarly, research examining genetic links to *dimensions* of attachment anxiety and avoidance suggest that about 40% of the variability in attachment security is attributable to genes. Critically, several studies have noted that this genetic influence is strongest in relation to attachment anxiety (Picardi, Fagnani, Nistico, & Stazi, 2011).

Molecular genetic studies

There does not appear to be any one attachment gene (Fearon et al., 2014). Some evidence suggests a link between OXTR, the receptor that controls oxytocin—a neuropeptide that has been linked to social and attachment behaviors (Feldman, Weller, Zagoory-Sharon, & Levine, 2007)—and attachment styles and psychopathology (Costa et al., 2009). However, genes associated with dopamine receptors (i.e., DRD4 and DRD2), which are implicated in social behavior, have also been linked to attachment (disorganization, Lakatos et al., 2002; and anxiety, Gillath et al., 2008). Research has also suggested a genetic link between the serotonin receptor HTR2A and attachment (Gillath et al., 2008).

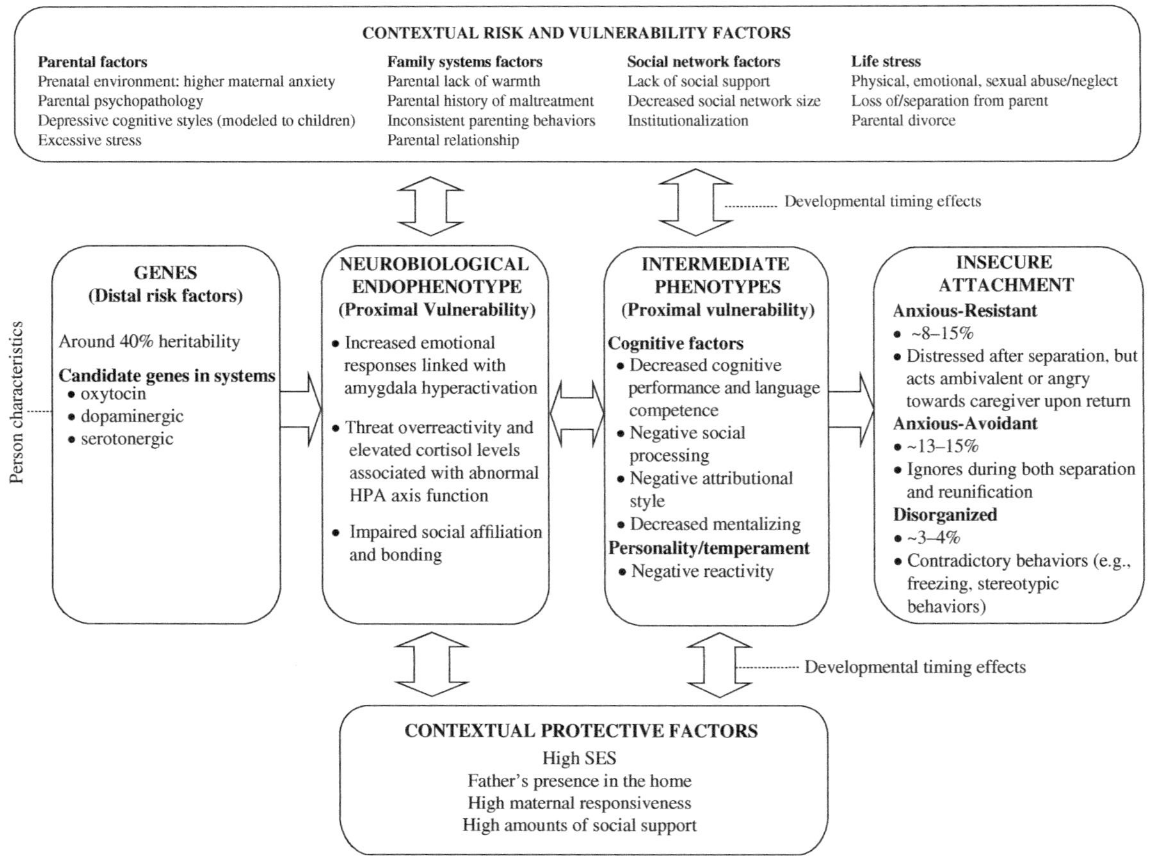

FIGURE 4.4 A Developmental Psychopathology Model of Insecure Attachment

NEUROBIOLOGICAL FACTORS (PROXIMAL VULNERABILITY FACTORS)

Structural and functional imaging findings

Like with genes, there is no "attachment circuit" explicitly defined in the brain. Attachment behaviors have complex relations to neuroanatomy, and, thus, many brain regions are implicated. Nonetheless, a few brain structures and circuits implicated in threat detection and regulating experienced emotions are particularly important, such as the amygdala, the hypothalamus, and other structures included in the hypothalamic–pituitary–adrenocortical (HPA) axis. Indeed, studies have linked greater activation in the amygdala to the telling of attachment stories that contain themes of loss, death, abuse, or abandonment (Buchheum et al., 2006) and anxious attachment (Vrtička, Anderson, Grandjean, Sander, & Vuilleumier, 2008). Further, the hypothalamus has been implicated in the soothing effect of attachment figures (see Coan, Schaefer, & Davidson, 2006). These studies suggest that neurobiological vulnerabilities underlie insecurely attached individuals' tendency to be over-reactive to threat and less equipped to regulate that threat response.

Neurotransmitters

As you may have guessed based on the genetic research linking attachment to DRD4 and DRD2, there is a consensus that the neurotransmitter dopamine, which regulates the brain's reward systems, plays a role in bonding between parents and children as well as between adults (Insel, 2003). For example, low maternal care has been linked to an elevated stress dopamine response (Pruessner, Champagne, Meaney, & Dagher, 2004). Strathearn and colleagues (2008) found that brain areas associated with dopamine-related reward processing displayed increased activation in response to the mother's own infant, when compared with an unknown infant. Further, Strathearn and colleagues (2009) found that secure mothers showed greater activation in areas of the brain associated with the dopaminergic reward system when viewing their babies than mothers with a dismissing attachment. You can see an example of the pictures used and the brain imaging data in Figure 4.5.

Genetic research has also implicated the neurotransmitter serotonin in attachment. Serotonin helps maintain stable mood and affect, and dysfunction is associated with depression and anxiety. With regard to romantic attachment, one study concluded that limited serotonin produces altered perceptions of relationships (Bilderbeck et al., 2011). Bartz (2011) posited that serotonin depletion has a similar effect to fearful attachments (i.e., preoccupied) and a temporary reduction in serotonin induces a temporary fearful attachment state.

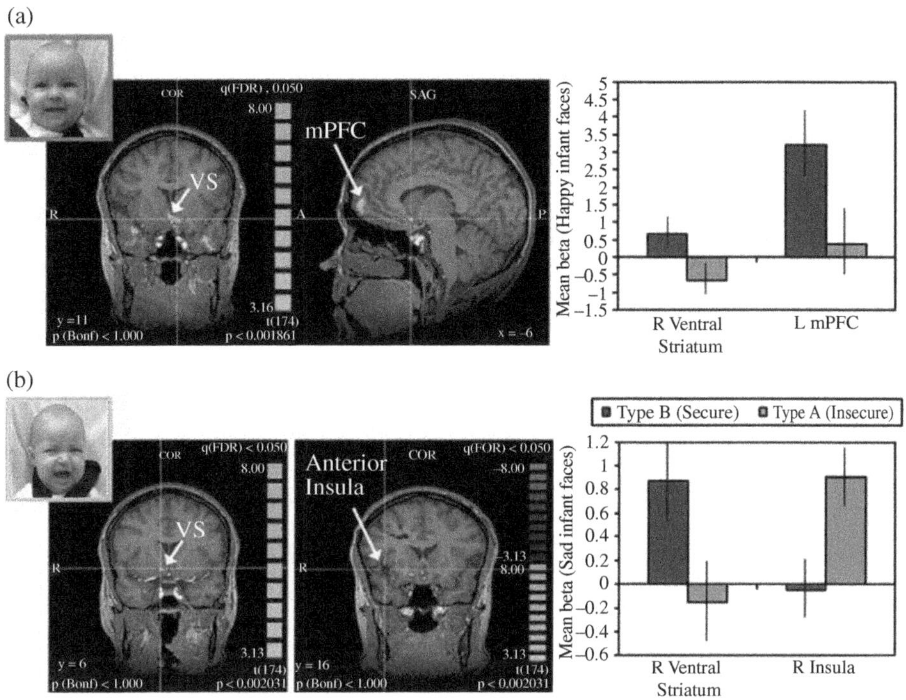

Brain responses to happy and sad own-infant faces, contrasting mothers with Type A (insecure/dismissing) and B (secure) attachment classifications (mean β values±SEM) (a) Type B mothers show greater activation of the ventral striatum (VS; t=3.1, P<0.005) and medial prefrontal cortex (mPFC; t;3,0, P<0.01) in response to own-happy infant faces. (b) Type B mothers show greater activation of the right ventral striatum (t=3.0, P<0.01) in response to own-sad infant faces. Type A mothers show greater activation of the right anterior insula (t;-3.9, P<0.0005).

FIGURE 4.5 Secure Mothers Showed Greater Activation in Areas of the Brain Associated with Reward. Source: Strathearn L., et al. (2009). Reproduced with permissions of Springer Nature.

Hormones

Attachment research has predominantly focused on two hormones: oxytocin and cortisol. Oxytocin is a critical hormone in lactation, nurturance, and trust. Higher oxytocin levels are associated with maternal sensitivity to infants (Feldman, Weller, Zagoory-Sharon, & Levine, 2007), quality of play and contact with infants (Feldman, Gordon, Schneiderman, Weisman, & Zagoory-Sharon, 2010), and maternal trust in adolescents (Venta et al., 2017). Further, cortisol, a hormone released by the HPA axis in response to stress, has been found to differ between secure, disorganized, and insecure children (Spangler & Grossman, 1993). Similarly, Schieche and Spangler (2005) found that securely attached and behaviorally inhibited infants experienced declines in cortisol after a challenging task, whereas avoidant infants experienced a decrease in cortisol early on, followed by an increase in cortisol after the task. While the design and findings of these studies are complex, they lend some support for a cortisol-coping hypothesis (Spangler & Grossman, 1993).

TEMPERAMENT

Vaughn, Bost, and Van IJzendoorn (2008) posit that while attachment and temperament domains overlap, they are discrete: attachment exists first in a caregiving relationship and is internalized later, whereas temperament is always an attribute of the individual. Indeed, secure versus insecure groups do not show statistically significant differences with regard to emotional reactivity (Marshall & Fox, 2005), behavioral inhibition (Stevenson-Hinde & Marshall, 1999; Burgess, Marshall, Rubin, & Fox, 2003), or negative emotionality (Pauli-Pott Haverkock, Pott, & Beckmann, 2007) in most studies though some have found reduced negative reactivity among securely attached children (Vaughn et al., 2008; van IJzendoorn et al., 2004). Further, some research suggests that the interaction between attachment and temperament is important in predicting behavior. For example, Bohlin, Hagekull, and Andersson (2005) reported that, for securely attached children, high behavioral inhibition was associated with higher social competence whereas, for insecurely attached children, high behavioral inhibition was associated with poorer social competence.

COGNITIVE FACTORS

Intelligence and language

Because secure attachments allow young children to venture out to explore their world, they underlie the capacity to interact with and learn from our environment. Indeed, a meta-analysis by van IJzendoorn and colleagues (1995) concluded that insecure attachment is associated with both lower cognitive performance and poorer language competence. Securely attached infants perform better than insecurely attached infants on tests of cognitive development (Egeland & Farber, 1984; van Bakel & Riksen-Walraven, 2004) and this pattern extends to intelligence testing in kindergarten (van IJzendoorn & Vliet-Visser, 1988). In third and fourth grades, children who were more securely attached had (among other things) parents who provided more encouragement and assistance with school and were able to form better relationships and be more cooperative and self-regulated in school (West, Matthews, & Kerns, 2013). Reciprocal models in which a child's cognitive ability influences their development of secure attachments have also been supported (e.g., Stievenart, Roskam, Meunier, & van de Moortele, 2011) suggesting the link between cognitive development and attachment is likely to be bidirectional.

Social cognition

Our early attachment relations shape the way that we see, remember, and interact with the social world later on. For instance, studies have shown that securely attached adolescents attend to positive feedback about the self and seek it out from non-attachment related targets (Cassidy, Ziv, Mehta, & Feeney, 2003); perceive attachment experiences and memories more favorably (Dykas, Woodhouse, Ehrlich, & Cassidy, 2010); and report more prosocial social-information processing (Granot & Mayseless, 2012). In contrast, insecure adolescents process social information in a negatively biased way (Dykas, Cassidy, & Woodhouse, 2009).

Attentive caregivers are likely to treat their children as psychological agents, implicitly guiding the child to develop mental state reasoning abilities (Fonagy & Allison, 2012). For securely attached children, this process results in accurate social cognition, or reasoning about others' underlying mental states (Dykas & Cassidy, 2011). This relation is evident into adolescence and beyond. For instance, Hünefeldt, Laghi, Ortu, and Belardinelli (2013) reported that attachment anxiety was associated with less accurate identification of mental states in the eyes of others. Likewise, attachment security has been associated with more frequent and more accurate social cognition (Ammaniti et al., 1999). Among adolescents with psychiatric diagnosis, Sharp and colleagues (2016) tied over-attribution of mental states to decreased attachment security, and Venta and Sharp (2015) documented associations between attachment disorganization and poor social cognition.

Contextual Risk Factors

Parental psychopathology

Attachment security is more likely among the children of parents who are psychologically healthy. For instance, higher prenatal anxiety (Del Carmen et al., 1993); higher maternal stress (Atkinson et al., 2000); lower maternal psychological adjustment (NICHD Early Child Care Network, 1997); higher paternal depression (Booth-LaForce et al., 2014); and higher parental depression, anxiety, and personality disorder (Hobson, Patrick, Crandell, Garcia-Perez, & Lee, 2005) have been linked to insecure child attachments. Still, this area of research has yielded inconsistent findings, suggesting that protective factors are at play. It is most likely that parental psychopathology predisposes parents to parenting practices that are less conducive to secure attachments for their children.

Parent behaviors and attachments

Maladaptive parent behaviors, like child maltreatment, have been consistently associated with attachment insecurity—particularly attachment disorganization—with rates of insecure attachment as high as 90% among infants who are the victims of maltreatment (Cicchetti, Rogosch, & Toth, 2006). Moderate to heavy alcohol (O'Connor, Sigman, & Brill, 1987) and drug use (Melnick, Finger, Hans, Patrick, & Lyons-Ruth, 2008) have been associated with high rates of infant insecure attachment as well. More generally, Main and Hesse (2006) suggested that "frightened or frightening" parental behaviors place a child at risk of disorganized attachment (Lyons-Ruth & Jacobvitz, 2008). Main and Hesse (1990) posit that these behaviors emerge from a parent's own traumatic experiences and create a conflict for the child about whether the parent is a source of distress or a solution to distress (Main & Hesse, 1990). Indeed, research suggests that a parent's own attachment history is a relevant, albeit distal, risk factor for insecure attachment. Indeed, this is a model known as the "transmission model," in which it is expected that parental attachment style affects parenting behaviors which, in turn, affect the child's attachment style (van IJzendoorn, 1995).

Parental relationship

At a basic level, the presence of both parents in the home appears to be associated with attachment security (Booth-LaForce et al., 2014); however, lower marital satisfaction (Howes & Markman, 1989), decreased marital harmony (Teti et al., 1995), and greater marital conflict (Owen & Cox, 1997) have been linked to greater attachment insecurity. Still, many studies have failed to replicate these results, suggesting a complex relation between parental marital functioning and a child's attachment.

CONTEXTUAL PROTECTIVE FACTORS

Maternal sensitivity

Many studies (see Belsky & Fearon, 2008) have documented a relation between a mother's sensitivity to the needs of her infant and the infant's attachment style. Specifically, a mother's rapid response when her child is in distress (e.g., Del Carmen, Pederson, Huffman, & Bryan, 1993), as well as her warmth and involvement with the child (e.g., Leyendecker, Lamb, Fracasso, Scholmerich, & Larson, 1997) have been repeatedly linked to secure attachment in the child including across cultures and SES (Belsky & Fearon, 2008). However, meta-analytic research on these relations reveals small effect sizes (De Wolff & van IJzendoorn, 1997; Belsky & Fearon, 2008). Two related concepts—maternal reflective functioning (Fonagy, Steel, & Steel, 1991) and maternal mind-mindedness (Bernier & Dozier, 2003)—have garnered attention within attachment research. Both of these concepts are centered upon a parent's ability to recognize their baby's underlying mental states and link these mental states to the baby's behavior. Research suggests that increases in this maternal capacity enhance attachment security in young children (Slade et al., 2005).

Social support

Research suggests that social support is associated with more sensitive parenting. Among low-income ethnic minority mothers, social network size (Burchinal, Follmer, & Bryant, 1996) and material support from social networks (Feiring, Fox, Jaskir, & Lewis, 1987) have been associated with more engaged and responsive caregiving. Moreover, child attachment security has been linked to the family's social support (e.g., Crnic, Greenberg, & Slough, 1986). However, research suggests that social support enhances caregiving, thus predicting attachment security, but it does not have a direct influence on attachment security (Belsky & Fearon, 2008).

GENE–ENVIRONMENT INTERPLAY

Gene–environment interactions

Several of the biological contributors to attachment that we have already discussed have been shown to impact attachment via interactions with environmental variables. Although researchers are careful to point out that gene–environment interaction studies in attachment are sparse, the prevailing view is that there are likely to be genetically based vulnerabilities that make children more or less susceptible to caregiving environments (Gervai, 2009). For example, a polymorphism of the serotonin transporter gene interacts with the caregiving environment to predict attachment insecurity (Spangler, Johann, Ronai, & Zimmerman, 2009). Similar findings have been noted with regard to a dopamine receptor gene; genetic vulnerability seems to increase the effects of difficult caregiving on attachment (van IJzendoorn & Bakermans-Kranenburg, 2006) but also enhances the effects of a positive environment (Bakermans-Kranenburg & van IJzendoorn, 2007), suggesting differential susceptibility to both favorable and unfavorable environments.

Gene–environment correlations

Caregiving environments are heavily affected by genetic influences (Kendler & Baker, 2007). Burt (2009) calls the gene → behavior → social consequence chain an evocative gene–environment correlation, in which an individual's genes evoke a particular environmental response through their behavior. Imagine, for example, a child with a disorganized attachment; this child, when upset and dysregulated, would evoke a different response from adults than a securely attached child. If we can tie the genes linked to disorganized attachment to those caregiver responses, we have identified an evocative gene–environment correlation with consequences for the study of attachment. Researchers have just recently begun to document these sorts of gene–environment correlations with regard to the serotonin transport and dopamine receptor genes we have discussed. For instance, the serotonin transport gene has been linked to peer popularity (Burt, 2008, 2009) such that genetic factors predict rule-breaking behavior which, in turn, results in peer popularity. The DRD2 dopamine receptor gene has been associated with unfavorable caregiving as well (Beaver,

Shutt, Vaughn, DeLisi, & Wright, 2012), although whether these links represent an evocative gene–environment correlation is not yet known.

DEVELOPMENTAL TIMING EFFECTS: SENSITIVE PERIODS

Most attachment research has traditionally pointed to early infancy as an influential time in the parent–child attachment. Separations from primary caregivers that occur near six months of age appear to have a particularly detrimental impact on children's attachment (Hazen et al., 2015). Still, it would be too simplistic to say that only the first six months of life are relevant for later attachment. Indeed, Fraley and Hefferman (2013) found that individuals who were younger (i.e., within the first few years of life) at the time that their parents divorced were more likely to have an insecure parental attachment in adulthood than individuals whose parents divorced later in childhood.

Interventions

Given links between attachment and psychopathology, numerous researchers have developed attachment intervention programs. Perhaps the best-known attachment intervention is Circle of Security (Hoffman, Marvin, Cooper, & Powell, 2006), a program for parents of young children that focuses on augmenting a parent's ability to serve as a secure attachment figure by providing comfort in times of threat and serving as a base from which to explore their environment (see Figure 4.6). This intervention decreases disorganized and insecure attachment styles (Cassidy, Woodhouse, Sherman, Stupica, & Lejuez, 2011; Hoffman et al., 2006).

Child–Parent Psychotherapy (CPP) is a manualized intervention for families with young children (less than five years of age; Lieberman & Van Horn, 2005) who have experienced trauma and helps parent resolve their own difficult childhood experiences. This program increases maternal empathy (Lieberman, Weston, & Pawl, 1991) and attachment security (Cicchetti, Rogosch, & Toth, 2006), and reduces psychopathology among children (Lieberman, Van Horn, & Ippen, 2005). Two other programs, the UCLA Family Development Project (e.g., Heinicke et al., 2006) and Minding the Baby (e.g., Slade et al., 2005), target mothers *before* the birth of their firstborn infants.

Chapter Summary

In this chapter, we introduced attachment theory and assessment. We summarized how behavioral difficulties and psychopathology relate to attachment security. We also presented complex findings regarding the

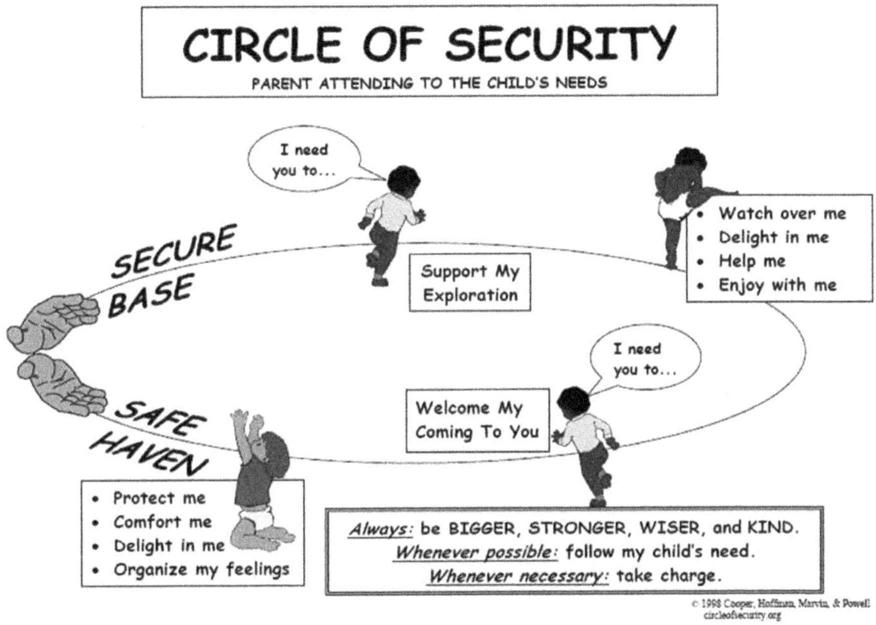

FIGURE 4.6 Circle of Security. Source: Cooper, Hoffman, Marvin, & Powell, CircleofSecurity. org. 1998.

interplay of genetic, neurobiological, cognitive, temperamental, and environmental factors that contribute to attachment insecurity and closed with several current interventions intended to address attachment insecurity and related problems.

Further Reading

Dykas, M. J., & Cassidy, J. (2011). Attachment and the processing of social information across the life span: Theory and evidence. *Psychological Bulletin*, *137*(1), 19–46. doi: 10.1037/a0021367.

Groh, A. M., Roisman, G. I., Booth-LaForce, C., Fraley, R. C., Owen, M. T., Cox, M. J., & Burchinal, M. R. (2014). The Adult Attachment Interview: Psychometrics, stability and change from infancy, and developmental origins: IV. Stability of attachment security from infancy to late adolescence. *Monographs of the Society for Research in Child Development*, *79*(3), 51–66. doi: 10.1111/mono.12113.

Discussion/Essay Questions

1. Attachment behaviors express themselves differently across development. The adolescent developmental stage was not included by Fraley and Speiker (2003a) in Figure 4.2. How would you expect attachment behaviors to express themselves during adolescence?

2. Are parents to blame if their children have an insecure attachment? Provide evidence for your answer.
3. Describe both the dimensional and categorical models of attachment.
4. Explain at least three ways in which research has shown that attachment impacts our everyday lives.

Glossary

Anxious-avoidant insecure attachment is seen in a child who will tend to ignore the caregiver during both separations and reunifications.

Anxious-resistant (or ambivalent) insecure attachment is seen in a child who will explore less than a child with a secure attachment when his caregiver is present.

Attachment insecurity develops when an internal working model of the self as unworthy of care and others as unreliable caregivers emerges.

Attachment security emerges when the needs of a young child are consistently met and his or her internal working model generally espouses a view of him- or herself as worthy of care and others as reliable caregivers.

Autonomous (i.e., securely attached) adult is one who values attachment relationships and is able to talk about caregiving experiences in a way that is balanced, coherent, consistent, and open.

Borderline personality disorder is a mental disorder characterized by instability in mood, behavior, and relationships.

Clinical samples are groups of research participants who are diagnosed with a mental disorder and receiving mental healthcare in, for example, an outpatient clinic or a psychiatric hospital.

Dismissing adults will tend to de-emphasize the impact of caregiving experiences (particularly negative ones) and will struggle to provide answers that thoroughly describe early caregiving.

Disorganized adults show evidence of prior difficult caregiving experiences (like abuse or loss) that are unresolved in adulthood.

Disorganized attachment refers to children that cannot be classified into one of the main attachment categories. Behaviors commonly observed among children with a disorganized attachment include contradictory behaviors; behaviors that are incongruent with affect; stereotypic, jerky movements; and freezing.

Dissociative symptoms are associated with disorganized attachment and can include temporary lapses in memory, sense of unreal-ness, and disconnection from those around you.

Externalizing symptoms are behavior problems including non-compliance and hostility.

Internal working model was developed by Bowlby and can be understood as a template that we carry with us, across development, and use to make sense of ourselves and our social world.

Internalizing symptoms are emotional in nature and include depressive and anxious symptoms.

Longitudinal study is a research design that collects data from the same group of people across time.

Meta-analytic studies combine the results from many previously published studies to give us a better picture of how research has accumulated across time.

Preoccupied adults will produce an interview that is dominated by excessive attention towards his or her caregivers and anger may dominate the interview.

Secure attachment is seen in a child who will be observed exploring the playroom while her caregiver is in the room but, when the caregiver leaves the room, the child will become upset.

References

Adam, K. S., Sheldon-Keller, A. E., & West, M. (1996). Attachment organization and history of suicidal behavior in clinical adolescents. *Journal of Consulting and Clinical Psychology*, *64*(2), 264–272. doi: 10.1037/0022-006X.64.2.264.

Ainsworth, M. S., Blehar, M. C., Waters, E., & Wall, S. (1978). *Patterns of attachment: A psychological study of the strange situation. Oxford*, England: Lawrence Erlbaum.

Ammaniti, M., Tambelli, R., Zavattini, G. C., Vismara, L., & Volpi, B. (1999). Attacamento e Funzione Riflessiva in Adolescenza (Attachment and reflective function in adolescence). *Psicologia Clinica Dello Sviluppo*, *3*(1), 155–175.

Atkinson, L., Niccols, A., Paglia, A., Coolbear, J., Parker, K. H., Poulton, L., & Sitarenios, G. (2000). A meta-analysis of time between maternal sensitivity and attachment assessments: Implications for internal working models in infancy/toddlerhood. *Journal of Social and Personal Relationships*, *17*(6), 791–810. doi: 10.1177/0265407500176005.

Bakermans-Kranenburg, M. J., & van IJzendoorn, M. H. (2007). Research review: Genetic vulnerability or differential susceptibility in child development: The case of attachment. *Journal of Child Psychology and Psychiatry*, *48*(12), 1160–1173. doi: 10.1111/j.1469-7610.2007.01801.x.

Bakermans-Kranenburg, M. J., van Uzendoorn, M. H., Bokhorst, C. L., & Schuengel, C. (2004). The importance of shared environment in infant–father attachment: A behavioral genetic study of the attachment Q-Sort. *Journal of Family Psychology*, *18*(3), 545–549. doi: 10.1037/0893-3200.18.3.545.

Bartz, J. A. (2011). Serotonin and the neurochemistry of intimacy. *Biological Psychiatry*, *69*(8), 716–717. doi: 10.1016/j.biopsych.2011.03.001.

Beaver, K. M., Shutt, J. E., Vaughn, M. G., DeLisi, M., & Wright, J. P. (2012). Genetic influences on measures of parental negativity and childhood maltreatment: An exploratory study testing for gene × environment correlations. *Journal of Contemporary Criminal Justice*, *28*(3), 273–292. doi: 10.1177/1043986212450220.

Belsky, J., & Fearon, R. P. (2008). Precursors of attachment security. In J. Cassidy, P. R. Shaver, J. Cassidy, & P. R. Shaver (Eds.), *Handbook of attachment: Theory, research, and clinical applications* (2nd ed., pp. 295–316). New York, NY: Guilford Press.

Bernier, A., & Dozier, M. (2003). Bridging the attachment transmission gap: The role of maternal mind-mindedness. *International Journal of Behavioral Development*, *27*(4), 355–365. doi: 10.1080/01650250244000399.

Bilderbeck, A. C., McCabe, C., Wakeley, J., McGlone, F., Harris, T., Cowen, P. J., & Rogers, R. D. (2011). Serotonergic activity influences the cognitive appraisal of close intimate relationships in healthy adults. *Biological Psychiatry*, *69*(8), 720–725. doi: 10.1016/j.biopsych.2010.12.038.

Bohlin, G., Hagekull, B., & Andersson, K. (2005). Behavioral inhibition as a precursor of peer social competence in early school age: The interplay with attachment and nonparental care. *Merrill-Palmer Quarterly*, *51*(1), 1–19. doi:10.1353/mpq.2005.0001

Bokhorst, C. L., Bakermans-Kranenburg, M. J., Fearon, R. P., van IJzendoorn, M. H., Fonagy, P., & Schuengel, C. (2003). The importance of shared environment in mother–infant attachment security: A behavioral genetic study. *Child Development*, *74*(6), 1769–1782. doi: 10.1046/j.1467-8624.2003.00637.x.

Booth-LaForce, C., Groh, A. M., Burchinal, M. R., Roisman, G. I., Owen, M. T., & Cox, M. J. (2014). The Adult Attachment Interview: Psychometrics, stability and change from infancy, and developmental origins: V. Caregiving and contextual sources of continuity and change in attachment security from infancy to late adolescence.

Monographs of the Society for Research in Child Development, 79(3), 67–84. doi: 10.1111/mono.12114.

Bowlby, J. (1960). Separation anxiety. *The International Journal of Psychoanalysis, 41*, 89–113.

Bowlby, J. (1969). Disruption of affectional bonds and its effects on behavior. *Canada's Mental Health Supplement, 59*, 12.

Bowlby, J. (1973). *Attachment and loss: Separation: Anxiety and anger (vol. 2).* New York, NY: Basic Books.

Bowlby, J. (1988). *A secure base: Parent–child attachment and healthy human development.* New York, NY: Basic Books.

Brennan, K. A., Clark, C. L., & Shaver, P. R. (1998). Self-report measurement of adult attachment: An integrative overview. In J. A. Simpson, W. S. Rholes, J. A. Simpson, & W. S. Rholes (Eds.), *Attachment theory and close relationships* (pp. 46–76). New York, NY: Guilford Press.

Bretherton, I., & Munholland, K. A. (2008). Internal working models in attachment relationships: Elaborating a central construct in attachment theory. In J. Cassidy, P. R. Shaver, J. Cassidy, & P. R. Shaver (Eds.), *Handbook of attachment: Theory, research, and clinical applications* (2nd ed., pp. 102–127). New York, NY: Guilford Press.

Buchheim, A., Erk, S., George, C., Kächele, H., Ruchsow, M., Spitzer, M., & Walter, H. (2006). Measuring attachment representation in an fMRI environment: A pilot study. *Psychopathology, 39*(3), 144–152. doi: 10.1159/000091800.

Burchinal, M. R., Follmer, A., & Bryant, D. M. (1996). The relations of maternal social support and family structure with maternal responsiveness and child outcomes among African American families. *Developmental Psychology, 32*(6), 1073–1083. doi: 10.1037/0012-1649.32.6.1073.

Burgess, K. B., Marshall, P. J., Rubin, K. H., & Fox, N. A. (2003). Infant attachment and temperament as predictors of subsequent externalizing problems and cardiac physiology. *Journal of Child Psychology and Psychiatry, 44*(6), 819–831. doi: 10.1111/1469-7610.00167.

Burt, S. A. (2008). Genes and popularity evidence of an evocative gene–environment correlation. *Psychological Science, 19*(2), 112–113.

Burt, A. (2009). A mechanistic explanation of popularity: Genes, rule breaking, and evocative gene–environment correlations. *Journal of Personality and Social Psychology, 96*(4), 783.

Cassidy, J., Woodhouse, S. S., Sherman, L. J., Stupica, B., & Lejuez, C. W. (2011). Enhancing infant attachment security: An examination of treatment efficacy and differential susceptibility. *Development and Psychopathology, 23*(1), 131–148. doi: 10.1017/S0954579410000696.

Cassidy, J., Ziv, Y., Mehta, T. G., & Feeney, B. C. (2003). Feedback seeking in children and adolescents: Associations with self-perceptions, attachment representations, and depression. *Child Development, 74*(2), 612–628. doi: 10.1111/1467-8624.7402019.

Cicchetti, D., Rogosch, F. A., & Toth, S. L. (2006). Fostering secure attachment in infants in maltreating families through preventive interventions. *Development and Psychopathology, 18*(3), 623–649. doi: 10.1017/S0954579406060329.

Coan, J. A., Schaefer, H. S., & Davidson, R. J. (2006). Lending a hand: Social regulation of the neural response to threat. *Psychological Science, 17*(12), 1032–1039.

Cooper, G., Hoffman, K., Marvin, R., & Powell, B. (1998). Circle of security. Available online at: circleofsecurity.org.

Costa, B., Pini, S., Gabelloni, P., Abelli, M., Lari, L., Cardini, A., & Martini, C. (2009). Oxytocin receptor polymorphisms and adult attachment style in patients with depression. *Psychoneuroendocrinology, 34*(10), 1506–1514. doi: 10.1016/j.psyneuen.2009.05.006.

Crittenden, P. M. (1999). Danger and development: The organization of self-protective strategies. *Monographs of the Society for Research in Child Development, 64*(3), 145–171. Retrieved from: http://www.jstor.org/stable/3181562.

Crnic, K. A., Greenberg, M. T., & Slough, N. M. (1986). Early stress and social support influences on mothers' and high-risk infants' functioning in late infancy. *Infant Mental Health Journal*, *7*(1), 19–33. doi: 10.1002/1097-0355(198621)7:1<19::AID-IMHJ2280070104>3.0.CO;2-1.

del Carmen, R., Pedersen, F. A., Huffman, L. C., & Bryan, Y. E. (1993). Dyadic distress management predicts subsequent security of attachment. *Infant Behavior & Development*, *16*(2), 131–147.

DeVito, C., & Hopkins, J. (2001). Attachment, parenting, and marital dissatisfaction as predictors of disruptive behavior in preschoolers. *Development and Psychopathology*, *13*(2), 215–231. doi: 10.1017/S0954579401002024.

De Wolff, M., & van IJzendoorn, M. H. (1997). Sensitivity and attachment: A meta-analysis on parental antecedents of infant attachment. *Child Development*, *68*(4), 571–591. doi: 10.2307/1132107.

Dykas, M. J., & Cassidy, J. (2011). Attachment and the processing of social information across the life span: Theory and evidence. *Psychological Bulletin*, *137*(1), 19–46. doi: 10.1037/a0021367.

Dykas, M. J., Cassidy, J., & Woodhouse, S. S. (2009). *Rejection sensitivity in adolescence: The role of attachment behavior and representation*. Denver, CO: Society for Research on Adolescence.

Dykas, M. J., Woodhouse, S. S., Ehrlich, K. B., & Cassidy, J. (2010). Do adolescents and parents reconstruct memories about their conflict as a function of adolescent attachment? *Child Development*, *81*(5), 1445–1459. doi: 10.1111/j.1467-8624.2010.01484.x.

Egeland, B., & Farber, E. A. (1984). Infant–mother attachment: Factors related to its development and changes over time. *Child Development*, *55*(3), 753–771. doi: 10.2307/1130127.

Erickson, M. F., Sroufe, L. A., & Egeland, B. (1985). The relationship between quality of attachment and behavior problems in preschool in a high-risk sample. *Monographs of the Society for Research in Child Development*, 147–166.

Fearon, R. P., Bakermans-Kranenburg, M. J., van IJzendoorn, M. H., Lapsley, A., & Roisman, G. I. (2010). The significance of insecure attachment and disorganization in the development of children's externalizing behavior: A meta-analytic study. *Child Development*, *81*(2), 435–456. doi: 10.1111/j.1467-8624.2009.01405.x.

Fearon, P., Shmueli-Goetz, Y., Viding, E., Fonagy, P., & Plomin, R. (2014). Genetic and environmental influences on adolescent attachment. *Journal of Child Psychology and Psychiatry*, *55*(9), 1033–1041. doi: 10.1111/jcpp.12171.

Feiring, C., Fox, N. A., Jaskir, J., & Lewis, M. (1987). The relation between social support, infant risk status and mother–infant interaction. *Developmental Psychology*, *23*(3), 400–405. doi: 10.1037/0012-1649.23.3.400.

Feldman, R., Gordon, I., Schneiderman, I., Weisman, O., & Zagoory-Sharon, O. (2010). Natural variations in maternal and paternal care are associated with systematic changes in oxytocin following parent–infant contact. *Psychoneuroendocrinology*, *35*(8), 1133–1141. doi: 10.1016/j.psyneuen.2010.01.013.

Feldman, R., Weller, A., Zagoory-Sharon, O., & Levine, A. (2007). Evidence for a neuroendocrinological foundation of human affiliation: Plasma oxytocin levels across pregnancy and the postpartum period predict mother–infant bonding. *Psychological Science*, *18*(11), 965–970. doi: 10.1111/j.1467-9280.2007.02010.x.

Fonagy, P., & Allison, E. (2012). What is mentalization? The concept and its foundations in developmental research. In N. Midgley, I. Vrouva, N. Midgley, & I. Vrouva (Eds.), *Minding the child: Mentalization-based interventions with children, young people and their families* (pp. 11–34). New York, NY: Routledge/Taylor & Francis Group.

Fonagy, P., Steele, H., & Steele, M. (1991). Maternal representations of attachment during pregnancy predict the organization of infant–mother attachment at one year of age. *Child Development*, *62*(5), 891–905. doi: 10.2307/1131141.

Fraley, R. C., & Heffernan, M. E. (2013). Attachment and parental divorce: A test of the diffusion and sensitive period hypotheses. *Personality and Social*

Psychology Bulletin, *39*(9), 1199–1213. doi: 10.1177/0146167213491503.

Fraley, R. C., & Spieker, S. J. (2003a). What are the differences between dimensional and categorical models of individual differences in attachment? Reply to Cassidy (2003), Cummings (2003), Sroufe (2003), and Waters and Beauchaine (2003). *Developmental Psychology*, *39*(3), 423–429. doi: 10.1037/0012-1649.39.3.423.

Fraley, R. C., & Spieker, S. J. (2003b). Are infant attachment patterns continuously or categorically distributed? A taxometric analysis of strange situation behavior. *Developmental Psychology*, *39*(3), 387–404. doi: 10.1037/0012-1649.39.3.387.

Fraley, R. C., & Waller, N. G. (1998). Adult attachment patterns: A test of the typological model. In J. A. Simpson, W. S. Rholes, J. A. Simpson, & W. S. Rholes (Eds.), *Attachment theory and close relationships* (pp. 77–114). New York, NY: Guilford Press.

Fraley, R. C., Heffernan, M. E., Vicary, A. M., & Brumbaugh, C. C. (2011). The experiences in close relationships—Relationship Structures Questionnaire: A method for assessing attachment orientations across relationships. *Psychological Assessment*, *23*(3), 615–625. doi: 10.1037/a0022898.

Fraley, R. C., Hudson, N. W., Heffernan, M. E., & Segal, N. (2015). Are adult attachment styles categorical or dimensional? A taxometric analysis of general and relationship-specific attachment orientations. *Journal of Personality and Social Psychology*, *109*(2), 354–368. doi: 10.1037/pspp0000027.

George, C., Kaplan, N., & Main, M. (1985). The Adult Attachment Interview. Unpublished manuscript, University of California at Berkeley, CA. Retrieved from: http://www.psychology.sunysb.edu/attachment/measures/content/aai_interview.pdf.

Gervai, J. (2009). Environmental and genetic influences on early attachment. *Child and Adolescent Psychiatry and Mental Health*, *3*(1), 25. doi: 10.1186/1753-2000-3-25.

Gillath, O., Shaver, P. R., Baek, J., & Chun, D. S. (2008). Genetic correlates of adult attachment style. *Personality and Social Psychology Bulletin*, *34*(10), 1396–1405. doi: 10.1177/0146167208321484.

Granot, D., & Mayseless, O. (2012). Representations of mother-child attachment relationships and social-information processing of peer relationships in early adolescence. *The Journal of Early Adolescence*, *32*(4), 537–564. doi: 10.1177/0272431611403482.

Groh, A. M., Roisman, G. I., Booth-LaForce, C., Fraley, R. C., Owen, M. T., Cox, M. J., & Burchinal, M. R. (2014). The Adult Attachment Interview: Psychometrics, stability and change from infancy, and developmental origins: IV. Stability of attachment security from infancy to late adolescence. *Monographs of the Society for Research in Child Development*, *79*(3), 51–66. doi: 10.1111/mono.12113.

Groh, A. M., Roisman, G. I., van IJzendoorn, M. H., Bakermans-Kranenburg, M. J., & Fearon, R. P. (2012). The significance of insecure and disorganized attachment for children's internalizing symptoms: A meta-analytic study. *Child Development*, *83*(2), 591–610.

Hansen, S., Bergvall, Å. H., & Nyiredi, S. (1993). Interaction with pups enhances dopamine release in the ventral striatum of maternal rats: A microdialysis study. *Pharmacology, Biochemistry and Behavior*, *45*(3), 673–676. doi: 10.1016/0091-3057(93)90523-V.

Hansen, S., Harthon, C., Wallin, E., Löfberg, L., & Svensson, K. (1991). Mesotelencephalic dopamine system and reproductive behavior in the female rat: Effects of ventral tegmental 6-hydroxydopamine lesions on maternal and sexual responsiveness. *Behavioral Neuroscience*, *105*(4), 588–598. doi: 10.1037/0735-7044.105.4.588.

Hazen, N. L., Allen, S. D., Christopher, C. H., Umemura, T., & Jacobvitz, D. B. (2015). Very extensive nonmaternal care predicts mother–infant attachment disorganization: Convergent evidence from two samples. *Development and Psychopathology*, *27*(3), 649–661.doi:10.1017/S0954579414000893.

Heinicke, C. M., Goorsky, M., Levine, M., Ponce, V., Ruth, G., Silverman, M., & Sotelo, C. (2006). Pre- and postnatal antecedents of a home-visiting intervention and family developmental outcome. *Infant Mental Health Journal*, *27*(1), 91–119. doi: 10.1002/imhj.20082.

Hobson, R. P., Patrick, M., Crandell, L., García-Pérez, R., & Lee, A. (2005). Personal relatedness and attachment in infants of mothers with borderline personality disorder. *Development and Psychopathology*, *17*(2), 329–347.doi:10.1017/S0954579405050169.

Hoffman, K. T., Marvin, R. S., Cooper, G., & Powell, B. (2006). Changing toddlers' and preschoolers' attachment classifications: The circle of security intervention. *Journal of Consulting and Clinical Psychology*, *74*(6), 1017–1026. doi: 10.1037/0022-006X.74.6.1017.

Howes, P., & Markman, H. J. (1989). Marital quality and child functioning: A longitudinal investigation. *Child Development*, *60*(5), 1044–1051. doi: 10.2307/1130778.

Hünefeldt, T., Laghi, F., Ortu, F., & Belardinelli, M. O. (2013). The relationship between "theory of mind" and attachment-related anxiety and avoidance in Italian adolescents. *Journal of Adolescence*, *36*(3), 613–621. doi: 10.1016/j.adolescence.2013.03.012.

Insel, T. R. (2003). Is social attachment an addictive disorder? *Physiology & Behavior*, *79*(3), 351–357. doi: 10.1016/S0031-9384(03)00148-3.

Jardin, C., Venta, A., Newlin, E., Ibarra, S., & Sharp, C. (2015). Secure attachment moderates the relation of sexual trauma with trauma symptoms among adolescents from an inpatient psychiatric facility. *Journal of Interpersonal Violence*, *32*(10), 1565–1585.

Kendler, K. S., & Baker, J. H. (2007). Genetic influences on measures of the environment: A systematic review. *Psychological Medicine*, *37*(5), 615–626. doi: 10.1017/S0033291706009524.

Lacasa, F., Mitjavila, M., Ochoa, S., & Balluerka, N. (2015). The relationship between attachment styles and internalizing or externalizing symptoms in clinical and nonclinical adolescents. *Anales De Psicología*, *31*(2), 422–432.

Lakatos, K., Nemoda, Z., Toth, I., Ronai, Z., Ney, K., Sasvari- Szekely, M., & Gervai, J. (2002). Further evidence for the role of the dopamine D4 receptor (DRD4) gene in attachment disorganization: Interaction of the exon III 48-bp repeat and the -521 C/T promoter polymorphisms. *Molecular Psychiatry*, *7*(1), 27–31. doi: 10.1038/sj/mp/4000986.

Leyendecker, B., Lamb, M. E., Fracasso, M. P., & Schölmerich, A. (1997). Playful interaction and the antecedents of attachment: A longitudinal study of Central American and Euro-American mothers and infants. *Merrill-Palmer Quarterly*, *43*(1), 24–47.

Lieberman, A. F., & Van Horn, P. (2005). *Don't hit my mommy! A manual for child–parent psychotherapy with young witnesses of family violence.* Washington, DC: Zero to Three.

Lieberman, A. F., Van Horn, P., & Ippen, C. G. (2005). Toward evidence-based treatment: Child–parent psychotherapy with preschoolers exposed to marital violence. *Journal of the American Academy of Child & Adolescent Psychiatry*, *44*(12), 1241–1248.

Lieberman, A. F., Weston, D. R., & Pawl, J. H. (1991). Preventive intervention and outcome with anxiously attached dyads. *Child Development*, *62*(1), 199–209. doi: 10.2307/1130715.

Lyons-Ruth, K., Alpern, L., & Repacholi, B. (1993). Disorganized infant attachment classification and maternal psychosocial problems as predictors of hostile-aggressive behavior in the preschool classroom. *Child Development*, *64*(2), 572–585. doi: 10.2307/1131270.

Lyons-Ruth, K., Easterbrooks, M., & Cibelli, C. D. (1997). Infant attachment strategies, infant mental lag, and maternal depressive symptoms: Predictors of internalizing and externalizing problems at age 7. *Developmental Psychology*, *33*(4), 681.

Lyons-Ruth, K., & Jacobvitz, D. (2008). Attachment disorganization: Genetic factors, parenting contexts, and developmental transformation from infancy to adulthood. In J. Cassidy, P. R. Shaver, J.

Cassidy, & P. R. Shaver (Eds.), *Handbook of attachment: Theory, research, and clinical applications* (2nd ed., pp. 666–697). New York, NY: Guilford Press.

Main, M., & Hesse, E. (1990). Parents' unresolved traumatic experiences are related to infant disorganized attachment status: Is frightened and/or frightening parental behavior the linking mechanism? In M. T. Greenberg, D. Cicchetti, E. M. Cummings, M. T. Greenberg, D. Cicchetti, & E. M. Cummings (Eds.), *Attachment in the preschool years: Theory, research, and intervention* (pp. 161–182). Chicago, IL: University of Chicago Press.

Main, M., & Hesse, E. (1992). *Frightening, frightened, dissociated, or disorganized behavior on the part of the parent: A coding system for parent–infant interactions* (4th ed.). University of California at Berkeley, CA; Unpublished manuscript.

Main, M., & Solomon, J. (1990). Procedures for identifying infants as disorganized/disoriented during the Ainsworth Strange Situation. In M. T. Greenberg, D. Cicchetti, E. M. Cummings, M. T. Greenberg, D. Cicchetti, and E. M. Cummings (Eds.), *Attachment in the preschool years: Theory, research, and intervention* (pp. 121–160). Chicago, IL: University of Chicago Press.

Marshall, P. J., & Fox, N. A. (2005). Relations between behavioral reactivity at 4 months and attachment classification at 14 months in a selected sample. *Infant Behavior & Development*, *28*(4), 492–502. doi: 10.1016/j.infbeh.2005.06.002.

Melnick, S., Finger, B., Hans, S., Patrick, M., & Lyons-Ruth, K. (2008). Hostile-helpless states of mind in the AAI: A proposed additional AAI category with implications for identifying disorganized infant attachment in high-risk samples. In H. Steele, M. Steele, H. Steele, & M. Steele (Eds.), *Clinical applications of the Adult Attachment Interview* (pp. 399–423). New York, NY: Guilford Press.

Mikulincer, M., & Shaver, P. R. (2007). Reflections on security dynamics: Core constructs, psychological mechanisms, relational contexts, and the need for an integrative theory. *Psychological Inquiry*, *18*(3), 197–209. doi: 10.1080/10478400701512893.

Miljkovitch, R., Pierrehumbert, B., Karmaniola, A., Bader, M., & Halfon, O. (2005). Assessing attachment cognitions and their associations with depression in youth with eating or drug misuse disorders. *Substance Use & Misuse*, *40*(5), 605–623. doi: 10.1081/JA-200055349.

NICHD Early Child Care Research Network (1997). The effects of infant child care on infant–mother attachment security: Results of the NICHD Study of Early Child Care. *Child Development*, 860–879.

O'Connor, M. J., Sigman, M., & Brill, N. (1987). Disorganization of attachment in relation to maternal alcohol consumption. *Journal of Consulting and Clinical Psychology*, *55*(6), 831–836. doi: 10.1037/0022-006X.55.6.831.

Ogawa, J. R., Sroufe, L. A., Weinfield, N. S., Carlson, E. A., & Egeland, B. (1997). Development and the fragmented self: Longitudinal study of dissociative symptomatology in a nonclinical sample. *Development and Psychopathology*, *9*(4), 855–879. doi: 10.1017/S0954579497001478.

Owen, M. T., & Cox, M. J. (1997). Marital conflict and the development of infant–parent attachment relationships. *Journal of Family Psychology*, *11*(2), 152–164. doi: 10.1037/0893-3200.11.2.152.

Pauli-Pott, U., Haverkock, A., Pott, W., & Beckmann, D. (2007). Negative emotionality, attachment quality, and behavior problems in early childhood. *Infant Mental Health Journal*, *28*(1), 39–53. doi: 10.1002/imhj.20121.

Picardi, A., Fagnani, C., Nisticò, L., & Stazi, M. A. (2011). A twin study of attachment style in young adults. *Journal of Personality*, *79*(5), 965–991. doi: 10.1111/j.1467-6494.2010.00707.x.

Pruessner, J. C., Champagne, F., Meaney, M. J., & Dagher, A. (2004). Dopamine release in response to a psychological stress in humans and its relationship to early life maternal care: A positron emission tomography study using [^{11}C] Raclopride. *The Journal of*

Neuroscience, *24*(11), 2825–2831. doi: 10.1523/JNEUROSCI.3422-03.2004.

Renken, B., Egeland, B., Marvinney, D., Mangelsdorf, S., & Sroufe, L. A. (1989). Early childhood antecedents of aggression and passive-withdrawal in early elementary school. *Journal of Personality*, *57*(2), 257–281. doi: 10.1111/j.1467-6494.1989.tb00483.x.

Schieche, M., & Spangler, G. (2005). Individual differences in biobehavioral organization during problem-solving in toddlers: The influence of maternal behavior, infant–mother attachment, and behavioral inhibition on the attachment-exploration balance. *Developmental Psychobiology*, *46*(4), 293–306.

Shamir-Essakow, G., Ungerer, J. A., & Rapee, R. M. (2005). Attachment, behavioral inhibition, and anxiety in preschool children. *Journal of Abnormal Child Psychology*, *33*(2), 131–143. doi: 10.1007/s10802-005-1822-2.

Sharp, C., Venta, A., Vanwoerden, S., Schramm, A., Ha, C., Newlin, E., & Fonagy, P. (2016). First empirical evaluation of the link between attachment, social cognition and borderline features in adolescents. *Comprehensive Psychiatry*, *64*, 4–11.

Shaw, D. S., Keenan, K., Vondra, J. I., Delliquadri, E., & Giovannelli, J. (1997). Antecedents of preschool children's internalizing problems: A longitudinal study of low-income families. *Journal of the American Academy of Child & Adolescent Psychiatry*, *36*(12), 1760–1767. doi: 10.1097/00004583-199712000-00025.

Shmueli-Goetz, Y., Target, M., Fonagy, P., & Datta, A. (2008). The Child Attachment Interview: A psychometric study of reliability and discriminant validity. *Developmental Psychology*, *44*(4), 939–956. doi: 10.1037/0012-1649.44.4.939.

Slade, A., Grienenberger, J., Bernbach, E., Levy, D., & Locker, A. (2005). Maternal reflective functioning, attachment, and the transmission gap: A preliminary study. *Attachment & Human Development*, *7*(3), 283–298. doi: 10.1080/14616730500245880.

Spangler, G., & Grossmann, K. E. (1993). Biobehavioral organization in securely and insecurely attached infants. *Child Development*, *64*(5), 1439–1450. doi: 10.2307/1131544.

Spangler, G., Johann, M., Ronai, Z., & Zimmermann, P. (2009). Genetic and environmental influence on attachment disorganization. *Journal of Child Psychology and Psychiatry*, *50*(8), 952–961.

Stevenson-Hinde, J., & Marshall, P. J. (1999). Behavioral inhibition, heart period, and respiratory sinus arrhythmia: An attachment perspective. *Child Development*, *70*(4), 805–816. doi: 10.1111/1467-8624.00058.

Stievenart, M., Roskam, I., Meunier, J. C., & van de Moortele, G. (2011). The reciprocal relation between children's attachment representations and their cognitive ability. *International Journal of Behavioral Development*, *35*(1), 58–66. doi: 10.1177/0165025410370790.

Strathearn, L., Fonagy, P., Amico, J., & Montague, P. R. (2009). Adult attachment predicts maternal brain and oxytocin response to infant cues. *Neuropsychopharmacology*, *34*(13), 2655–2666.

Strathearn, L., Li, J., Fonagy, P., & Montague, P. R. (2008). What's in a smile? Maternal brain responses to infant facial cues. *Pediatrics*, *122*, no. 1, 40–51.

Teti, D. M., Gelfand, D. M., Messinger, D. S., & Isabella, R. (1995). Maternal depression and the quality of early attachment: An examination of infants, preschoolers, and their mothers. *Developmental Psychology*, *31*(3), 364–376. doi: 10.1037/0012-1649.31.3.364.

van Bakel, H. A., & Riksen-Walraven, J. M. (2004). Stress reactivity in 15-month-old infants: Links with infant temperament, cognitive competence, and attachment security. *Developmental Psychobiology*, *44*(3), 157–167. doi: 10.1002/dev.20001.

van IJzendoorn, M. (1995). Adult attachment representations, parental responsiveness, and infant attachment: A meta-analysis on the predictive validity of the Adult Attachment Interview. *Psychological Bulletin*, *117*(3), 387–403. doi: 10.1037/0033-2909.117.3.387.

van IJzendoorn, M. H., & Bakermans-Kranenburg, M. J. (1996). Attachment representations in mothers, fathers, adolescents, and clinical groups: A meta-analytic search for normative data. *Journal of Consulting and Clinical Psychology*, *64*(1), 8–21. doi: 10.1037/0022-006X.64.1.8.

van IJzendoorn, M. H., & Bakermans-Kranenburg, M. J. (2006). DRD47-repeat polymorphism moderates the association between maternal unresolved loss or trauma and infant disorganization. *Attachment & Human Development*, *8*(4), 291–307. doi: 10.1080/14616730601048159.

van IJzendoorn, M. H., & Bakermans-Kranenburg, M. J. (2010). Invariance of adult attachment across gender, age, culture, and socioeconomic status? *Journal of Social and Personal Relationships*, *27*(2), 200–208.doi:10.1177/0265407509360908.

van IJzendoorn, M. H., Dijkstra, J., & Bus, A. G. (1995). Attachment, intelligence, and language: A meta-analysis. *Social Development*, *4*(2), 115–128. doi: 10.1111/j.1467-9507.1995.tb00055.x.

van IJzendoorn, M. H., & Sagi, A. (1999). Cross-cultural patterns of attachment: Universal and contextual dimensions. In J. Cassidy, P. R. Shaver, J. Cassidy, P. R. Shaver (Eds.), *Handbook of attachment: Theory, research, and clinical applications* (pp. 713–734). New York, NY: Guilford Press.

van IJzendoorn, M. H., & Sagi-Schwartz, A. (2008). Cross-cultural patterns of attachment: Universal and contextual dimensions. In J. Cassidy, P. R. Shaver, J. Cassidy, P. R. Shaver (Eds.), *Handbook of attachment: Theory, research, and clinical applications* (2nd ed., pp. 880–905). New York, NY: Guilford Press.

van IJzendoorn, M. H., & van Vliet-Visser, S. (1988). The relationship between quality of attachment in infancy and IQ in kindergarten. *The Journal of Genetic Psychology: Research and Theory on Human Development*, *149*(1), 23–28.

van Ijzendoorn, M. H., Vereijken, C. L., Bakermans-Kranenburg, M. J., & Riksen-Walraven, J. M. (2004). Assessing attachment security with the attachment Q Sort: Meta-analytic evidence for the validity of the observer AQS. *Child Development*, *75*(4), 1188–1213. doi: 10.1111/j.1467-8624.2004.00733.x.

Vaughn, B. E., Bost, K. K., & van IJzendoorn, M. H. (2008). Attachment and temperament: Additive and interactive influences on behavior, affect, and cognition during infancy and childhood. In J. Cassidy, P. R. Shaver, J. Cassidy, & P. R. Shaver (Eds.), *Handbook of attachment: Theory, research, and clinical applications* (2nd ed., pp. 192–216). New York, NY: Guilford Press.

Venta, A., Ha, C., Vanwoerden, S., Newlin, E., Strathearn, L., & Sharp, C. (2017). Paradoxical effects of intranasal oxytocin on trust in inpatient and community adolescents. *Journal of Clinical Child & Adolescent Psychology*, *48*(5), 706.

Venta, A., Mellick, W., Schatte, D., & Sharp, C. (2014). Preliminary evidence that thoughts of thwarted belongingness mediate the relations between level of attachment insecurity and depression and suicide-related thoughts in inpatient adolescents. *Journal of Social and Clinical Psychology*, *33*(5), 428–447. doi: 10.1521/jscp.2014.33.5.428.

Venta, A., & Sharp, C. (2015). Mentalizing mediates the relation between attachment and peer problems among inpatient adolescents. *Journal of Infant, Child and Adolescent Psychotherapy*, *14*(3), 323–340.doi:10.1080/15289168.2015.1071997.

Venta, A., Shmueli-Goetz, Y., & Sharp, C. (2014). Assessing attachment in adolescence: A psychometric study of the Child Attachment Interview. *Psychological Assessment*, *26*(1), 238–255. doi: 10.1037/a0034712.

Vondra, J. I., Shaw, D. S., Swearingen, L., Cohen, M., & Owens, E. B. (2001). Attachment stability and emotional and behavioral regulation from infancy to preschool age. *Development and*

Psychopathology, *13*(1), 13–33. doi: 10.1017/S095457940100102X.

Vrtička, P., Andersson, F., Grandjean, D., Sander, D., & Vuilleumier, P. (2008). Individual attachment style modulates human amygdala and striatum activation during social appraisal. *PLoS One*, *3*(8), e2868–e2868.

Warren, S. L., Emde, R. N., & Sroufe, L. A. (2000). Internal representations: Predicting anxiety from children's play narratives. *Journal of the American Academy of Child and Adolescent Psychiatry*, *39*(1), 100–107. doi: 10.1097/00004583-200001000-00022.

West, K. K., Mathews, B. L., & Kerns, K. A. (2013). Mother–child attachment and cognitive performance in middle childhood: An examination of mediating mechanisms. *Early Childhood Research Quarterly*, *28*(2), 259–270. doi: 10.1016/j.ecresq.2012.07.005.

Part II

Problems of Early and Middle Childhood

In Part I on this book we focused on the building blocks of the developmental psychopathology approach, by laying out some of the problems with traditional approaches to psychopathology and then reviewing the fundamental principles of developmental psychopathology, normal development, and attachment theory.

In Part II, we shift our focus to various forms of psychopathology, though you will see that each chapter also includes discussion of normal development—a hallmark of the developmental psychopathology approach. Each chapter will focus on a category of problems that typically emerges during early and middle childhood, including problems of development, behavior, and emotion. You will see that all of the chapters in this section tend to follow the same format; in fact, it was the format you were introduced to in Chapter 3 (insecure attachment). Consistent with the developmental psychopathology approach, each chapter will first describe the problem, giving you a sense of how many (and what kinds of) people in society it affects and how it changes across development. Then, we will focus on genetics, neurobiology, temperament, cognition, and context as risk and/or protective factors. Finally, chapters close with how practitioners are making use of the research described to craft and deliver treatments, or interventions, for people with psychopathology.

Towards the end of Part III, we hope that you will be comfortable with the developmental psychopathology approach and be accustomed to thinking of problems as emerging through the interaction of risk factors, protective factors, and development. In this part, we will practice these skills focusing on problems that emerge in childhood, specifically:

Chapter 5

Attention-Deficit/Hyperactivity Disorder (ADHD)

Jack M. Fletcher

Chapter Overview

Attention-Deficit/Hyperactivity Disorder (ADHD) is characterized by problems with the self-regulation of behavior, cognitive and motor skills, and inhibitory control. Although ADHD is persistent and occurs in adults, the focus of this chapter will be its presentation in children. In the DSM-5, ADHD is classified as a neurodevelopmental disorder, reflecting the common understanding that ADHD is a brain-based disorder. ADHD is partly maladaptive because of comorbid *disruptive behavior* that is often secondary to problems with impulse control and hyperactivity, which can lead to significant impairments at home, school, and the community.

Different iterations of the DSM varied in diagnostic and descriptive criteria before settling on Attention-Deficit Hyperactive Disorder (hyperactive-impulsive, inattentive, and combined subtypes) in the DSM-III. DSM-5 made few changes in diagnostic criteria but changed "types" to "presentation" because of the instability of the subtype distinctions. Despite these fluctuations in nomenclature, there is strong evidence for two primary behavioral dimensions, one involving hyperactivity/impulsivity and the other involving inattention, in children and adolescents (Haslam et al., 2006) and adults (Marcus, Norris, & Coccaro, 2012). ADHD is often presented as a categorical disorder, but its attributes are dimensional. DSM-4 and DSM-5 also added criteria for *age of onset* (age 12 in DSM-5), *pervasiveness* (that symptoms occur in more than one setting), and *adaptive impairment*. Below we present a case example from our clinical work.

Developmental Psychopathology, First Edition. Edited by Amanda Venta, Carla Sharp, Jack M. Fletcher, and Peter Fonagy.

Case study in ADHD

Keith is a seven-year-old boy who has been struggling in school. His behavior is often disruptive in the classroom: he blurts out answers, has trouble taking turns, and cannot keep his hands to himself, often annoying other children. His grades are lower than they should be because he does not complete assignments in class or at home. Other children avoid Keith because he gets upset during recess and loses his temper if he does not feel others are playing fairly. At times, these behaviors are so severe that he is sent to the principal's office, which he likes because of the attention.

His parents observed that Keith has a long history of disorganized and disruptive behavior. He was irritable and did not sleep well as an infant. He was highly active, had temper tantrums, and, in kindergarten, he could not sit at his desk. In first grade, he had an experienced teacher who was strict, but caring, and he seemed to do well. As school became more difficult in second grade, his behavior seemed to escalate. The parents consulted with their pediatrician when he was six, who indicated that Keith had ADHD and placed him on a trial of stimulant medication. The parents were not comfortable with the use of medication and quickly abandoned it. The school would not evaluate Keith because he was passing all of his classes. The parents then consulted a child clinical psychologist who collected a developmental history, conducted a structured interview, and collected *behavior rating scales* from the parents and teachers. The results of the assessment indicated that Keith met criteria for ADHD, Combined Type as well as for Oppositional-Defiant Disorder. In an academic skills assessment, Keith was average in reading and math, but struggled to write. The clinician observed that often children with ADHD needed medication dosage adjustments and may not respond to the first medication that was tried, referring back to the pediatrician. The clinician offered parent training focused on behavior management. The clinician also noted that ADHD was a category of eligibility in special education and that because he was in danger of suspension, there was clear evidence of educational need. The clinician suggested that the parents request that the pediatrician complete an "Other Health Impaired" form and ask that the child be considered for special education with development of a behavior plan.

As the clinician reviewing this case, which do you think is primary, ADHD or Oppositional-Defiant Disorder? How would you handle the parents' reluctance to use medication and the school's refusal to assess Keith?

Definition, Diagnosis, and Clinical Features

The evolution of diagnostic criteria for ADHD has led to a set of criteria that have a strong evidence base. Table 5.1 summarizes the DSM-5 and ICD-11 criteria and gives the items for the two ADHD scales in the Child Behavior Checklist (Achenbach & Rescorla, 2001) at different ages.

TABLE 5.1 ADHD as Defined by the DSM 5, ICD-11, and the Actuarial Child Behavior Checklist (CBCL) Scales

DSM-5	*ICD-11*	*CBCL Attention Problems Syndrome Scale*	*CBCL ADHD DSM Scale*
A. A persistent pattern of inattention and/or hyperactivity-impulsivity that interferes with functioning or development, as characterized by (1) and/or (2): 1. **Inattention:** Six (or more) of the following symptoms have persisted for at least 6 months to a degree that is inconsistent with developmental level and that negatively impacts directly on social and academic/occupational activities:	Attention deficit hyperactivity disorder is characterized by a persistent pattern (at least 6 months) of inattention and/or hyperactivity-impulsivity, with onset during the developmental period, typically early to mid-childhood.	**1.5–5-year-olds** Concentration difficulties Struggles to sit still Clumsy Quickly shifts activities Wanders	**1.5–5-year-olds** Concentration difficulties Struggles to sit still Can't wait turn DemandingGets into things Quickly shifts activities
Note: The symptoms are not solely a manifestation of oppositional behavior, defiance, hostility, or failure to understand tasks or instructions. For older adolescents and adults (age 17 and older), at least five symptoms are required. a. Often fails to give close attention to details or makes careless mistakes in schoolwork, at work, or during other activities (e.g., overlooks or misses details, work is inaccurate). b. Often has difficulty sustaining attention in tasks or play activities (e.g., has difficulty remaining focused during lectures, conversations, or lengthy reading).	The degree of inattention and hyperactivity-impulsivity is outside the limits of normal variation expected for age and level of intellectual functioning and significantly interferes with academic, occupational, or social functioning.	**6–18-year-olds** Acts young	**6–18-year-olds** Fails to finish tasks Concentration difficulties
c. Often does not seem to listen when spoken to directly (e.g., mind seems elsewhere, even in the absence of any obvious distraction).	Inattention refers to significant difficulty in sustaining attention to tasks that do not provide a high level of stimulation or frequent rewards, distractibility and problems with organization.	Fails to finish tasks Concentration difficulties Struggles to sit still Confused	Struggles to sit still Impulsive Inattentive Talks too much Loud

(*Continued*)

TABLE 5.1 (Continued)

DSM-5	*ICD-11*	*CBCL Attention Problems Syndrome Scale*	*CBCL ADHD DSM Scale*
d. Often does not follow through on instructions and fails to finish schoolwork, chores, or duties in the workplace (e.g., starts tasks but quickly loses focus and is easily sidetracked).	Hyperactivity refers to excessive motor activity and difficulties with remaining still, most evident in structured situations that require behavioral self-control. Impulsivity is a tendency to act in response to immediate stimuli, without deliberation or consideration of the risks and consequences. The relative balance and the specific manifestations of inattentive and hyperactive-impulsive characteristics varies across individuals, and may change over the course of development. In order for a diagnosis of disorder the behavior pattern must be clearly observable in more than one setting.	Daydreams	
		Impulsive	
e. Often has difficulty organizing tasks and activities (e.g., difficulty managing sequential tasks; difficulty keeping materials and belongings in order; messy, disorganized work; has poor time management; fails to meet deadlines).		Poor school performance	
		Inattentive	
		Stares	
f. Often avoids, dislikes, or is reluctant to engage in tasks that require sustained mental effort (e.g., schoolwork or homework; for older adolescents and adults, preparing reports, completing forms, reviewing lengthy papers).			
g. Often loses things necessary for tasks or activities (e.g., school materials, pencils, books, tools, wallets, keys, paperwork, eyeglasses, mobile telephones).			
h. Is often easily distracted by extraneous stimuli (for older adolescents and adults, may include unrelated thoughts).Is often forgetful in daily activities (e.g., doing chores, running errands; for older adolescents and adults, returning calls, paying bills, keeping appointments).			
i. **Hyperactivity and impulsivity:** Six (or more) of the following symptoms have persisted for at least 6 months to a degree that is inconsistent with developmental level and that negatively impacts directly on social and academic/occupational activities:			

Note: The symptoms are not solely a manifestation of oppositional behavior, defiance, hostility, or a failure to understand tasks or instructions. For older adolescents and adults (age 17 and older), at least five symptoms are required.

a. Often fidgets with or taps hands or feet or squirms in seat.
b. Often leaves seat in situations when remaining seated is expected (e.g., leaves his or her place in the classroom, in the office or other workplace, or in other situations that require remaining in place).
c. Often runs about or climbs in situations where it is inappropriate. (**Note:** In adolescents or adults, may be limited to feeling restless.)
d. Often unable to play or engage in leisure activities quietly.
e. Is often "on the go," acting as if "driven by a motor" (e.g., is unable to be or uncomfortable being still for extended time, as in restaurants, meetings; may be experienced by others as being restless or difficult to keep up with).
f. Often talks excessively.
g. Often blurts out an answer before a question has been completed (e.g., completes people's sentences; cannot wait for turn in conversation).
h. Often has difficulty waiting his or her turn (e.g., while waiting in line).

(Continued)

TABLE 5.1 (Continued)

DSM-5	*ICD-11*	*CBCL Attention Problems Syndrome Scale*	*CBCL ADHD DSM Scale*
i. Often interrupts or intrudes on others (e.g., butts into conversations, games, or activities; may start using other people's things without asking or receiving permission; for adolescents and adults, may intrude into or take over what others are doing).			
B. Several inattentive or hyperactive-impulsive symptoms were present prior to age 12 years.			
C. Several inattentive or hyperactive-impulsive symptoms are present in two or more settings (e.g., at home, school, or work; with friends or relatives; in other activities).			
D. There is clear evidence that the symptoms interfere with, or reduce the quality of, social, academic, or occupational functioning.			
E. The symptoms do not occur exclusively during the course of schizophrenia or another psychotic disorder and are not better explained by another mental disorder (e.g., mood disorder, anxiety disorder, dissociative disorder, personality disorder, substance intoxication or withdrawal).			

Sources: The DSM-5 (APA, 2013), ICD-11 (WHO, 2020), Child Behavior Checklist items (Achenbach & Rescorla, 2001).

The first core feature represents the two primary dimensions of ADHD in the DSM-V. The first dimension is inattention, which is identified by nine behaviors. The second dimension is hyperactivity and impulsivity, also assessed by nine behaviors. A cut point of six behaviors is identified for both dimensions. A person can be identified with a *combined presentation* if both dimensions are at the cut-point or either a *predominantly inattentive presentation* or *predominantly hyperactive and impulsive presentation* if the cut-off is achieved on just one dimension. It is important to recognize that the 18 criteria are behavioral, not cognitive. *ADHD is a behavioral disorder with cognitive consequences*. The 18 behaviors are both historical and concurrent because ADHD is a disorder that often starts early in development, necessitating a careful developmental history. In older adolescents and adults (age 17 years and up), the cut-off is five behaviors per dimension.

The second core feature is the age of onset, which, in DSM-5 must be prior to 12 years. This criterion is important because ADHD is a disorder that typically begins early in development and persists. However, in milder cases, or in females who are less likely to show hyperactivity, the onset may be later, especially given the need for evidence of adaptive impairment. Because of the latter issues, DSM 5 increased the age of onset from 7 to 12 years. Even now, the issue of age of onset is not completely settled among researchers and practitioners, and some adolescents and adults are formally identified after age 12. In these cases, evidence of adaptive impairment may not emerge until later in childhood or as an adult, but there is usually a history of the defining behavioral patterns earlier in development.

The third core feature is pervasiveness. The behavioral patterns we have been discussing should be present in two or more settings, like home, school, daycare, and different social and vocational settings. This criterion is important because contextual factors may drive the appearance of the behavior. For example, a child who is well behaved at school, but not at home, may show behaviors that look like ADHD, but that actually reflect environmental factors rather than true disorder.

The fourth criterion is evidence of problems with adaptation that interfere with social, academic, or vocational functioning. This means that the person should show evidence of difficulties managing behavior at school, home, or work. This could be manifested in difficulties with peers, teachers, parents, or spouses. Academic functioning may be impaired because the child is distractible and disorganized, leading to under-achievement and low grades. At work, the person may not be able to sit still, persist in completing assignments, or get along with their colleagues.

The final core feature is that the behavioral pattern associated with ADHD is not better explained by another disorder (e.g., substance-related disorder), by an acute psychotic episode, or by oppositional behavior, defiance, or failure to understand tasks and directions. A neurological disorder is not exclusionary and ADHD is commonly seen in relation to prematurity, congenital brain injuries, and traumatic brain injury.

You can access the recommendations for the diagnosis and treatment of ADHD from the American Academy of Pediatrics (AAP) (Wolraich et al., 2019; online https://pediatrics.aappublications.org/content/144/4/e20192528). These seven evidence-based recommendations, called Key Action Statements, were agreed upon through a literature review, committee consensus, and peer review. We will refer to these throughout different sections of this chapter. For now, we begin with the first two principles.

In identifying ADHD, it is important to use the DSM-5 behavioral descriptions and assess all five core features. Alternative explanations for the behavioral pattern observed should be considered. Many young children, like those under four years of age, show excessive motor activity and impulsivity. The difference between this age-appropriate behavior and ADHD is that the behavior persists and becomes maladaptive in children with ADHD. Many adults self-identifying with ADHD will complain about concentration problems, but the diagnostic questions centers on whether these problems significantly interfere with adaptation. Children may show behavior patterns resembling ADHD in just one setting, which means that contextual factors need to be examined.

The assessment of the five core features we have just discussed is completed using a number of approaches. The gold standard method is a structured interview that includes all five core features, such as the Structured Clinical Interview for DSM-5 (First, Williams, Karg, & Spitzer, 2016). While time consuming, the advantage of this approach is that it deals directly with all five core criteria. Additionally, the identification guidelines from the AAP (Wolraich et al., 2019) specifically recommend that practitioners, including pediatricians, collect multiple rating scales from parents and teachers. Most rating scales treat ADHD as a dimensional disorder and use cut points to identify a clinically significant elevation. There is strong evidence for thresholds in ADHD because of the consensus around definition and the number of studies using some variation of the DSM criteria. There can be disagreement across raters, such as two parents who disagree with one another about a child's behavior, especially if the child lives in more than one home or attends multiple classes. The *concordance* between parents and teachers can be relatively low and the clinician needs to review the other core criteria and consider the context and degree of impairment in adjudicating across different informants.

There is no evidence that medical tests, including blood work, electroencephalograms, or brain scans, are useful in the identification of ADHD unless the person presents with indicators unrelated to ADHD that would demonstrate a need for such tests (Wolraich et al., 2019).

There is also controversy over the use of cognitive tests for identification. Remember, ADHD is a behavioral disorder with cognitive consequences. Neuropsychological and other kinds of cognitive tests often show impairment in studies of ADHD. The relation between cognitive assessments and behavioral assessments is weak. For instance, many children with ADHD show much less inattention and impulsivity in a highly controlled, one-on-one assessment situation. There is no reason to give IQ tests unless there is concern about an intellectual disability. It is, however, important to give norm-referenced achievement tests to determine the child's academic development in general and to evaluate for specific learning disabilities (SLD) due to the comorbidity of ADHD and SLD and possibility for educational services.

Prevalence

Specific prevalence estimates depend on whether they are based on structured interviews, which give lower prevalence figures, or rating scales, which give higher prevalence figures. There is also variation in prevalence rates depending on whether the study formally assessed for ADHD behavior or simply asked the parent if the child had been diagnosed with ADHD.

A meta-analysis of 175 studies from around the world (Thomas et al., 2015) yielded a prevalence rate of 7.2% for ADHD. The estimates were based on multiple reporting methods, including rating scales, parent and teacher reports, and reports by others (e.g., clinicians). The samples were generally not population-based (about 20%), with the remainder community and clinical samples. There is regional variability in the frequency of diagnosis: Wolraich et al. (2019) reported community-based estimates in the United States of 8.7% to 15.5% depending on the community and the informant.

Studies based solely on counts, like the U.S. Centers for Disease Control National Survey of Children's Health, ask parents if a healthcare provider has ever identified their child with ADHD. Danielson et al. (2018) analyzed data from 2016 and found a cumulative prevalence of 9.4% for children aged 2–17 ever diagnosed with ADHD, with 8.4% currently diagnosed with ADHD. This estimate of prevalence is higher than in previous surveys, reflecting increases in the number of children diagnosed over time. Using the National Survey of Children's health data, Xu et al. (2018) reported an increase from about 6% in 1997 to the current figure of around 10%. These increases have been popularly interpreted as over-diagnosis, but, in fact, seem to reflect the number of children who need treatment for ADHD more realistically than previous estimates (Hinshaw & Scheffler, 2014).

PREVALENCE BY GENDER AND AGE

ADHD is male predominant in children and adolescents, but less so in adults. Willcutt (2012) reported that across studies male children were about 2–3 times more likely than females to meet criteria for ADHD. Using counts, Danielson et al. (2018) reported a ratio of about 2.3:1 in favor of males (12.9% versus 5.6%). There is evidence that sex differences are diminished by adulthood (Owens, Cardoos, & Hinshaw, 2015). One factor in the sex ratio is the increased presence of hyperactivity and externalizing behavior in boys, which makes identification more likely. Hyperactivity recedes with age (Weiss & Hechtmann, 1993), but the impulsivity and inattention continue to be apparent in males and females, which may account for the roughly equal representation of males and females in adult samples.

ADHD diagnoses also vary by age. The Centers for Disease Control National Survey of Children's Health found cumulative prevalence rates of 2.4% in children 2–5 years, 9.6% in children 6–11 years, and 13.6% in adolescents 12–17 years of age. Current diagnoses (i.e., counts) revealed a similar pattern. In adults, Kessler et al. (2006) found a prevalence of 4.4% using a population-based sample.

PREVALENCE BY SOCIOECONOMIC STATUS (SES), RACE, AND ETHNICITY

The prevalence of ADHD varies by race and ethnicity. Rates of ADHD are lower in Latinx and Asian samples. Black children are more likely than White children to be diagnosed with ADHD (Danielson et al., 2018), although this has not always been the case (Miller, Nigg, & Miller, 2009). Children who are Black are more likely to be rated as hyperactive and impulsive by their teachers compared to White children, but less likely to be identified and treated for ADHD (Miller et al., 2009). Kang and Harvey (2020) found that White teachers rated ADHD behavior more highly in Black boys than did their parents. These associations were stronger if the teachers identified with stereotypical racist views of Black students. These studies indicate a need for more research that addresses ADHD in minority populations in order to develop approaches to assessment and treatment that are more culturally sensitive.

Lower SES is associated with more frequent diagnoses of ADHD (Xu et al., 2018). Russell, Ford, and Russell (2015) examined the association of ADHD and SES in a United Kingdom population-based longitudinal study. They found that financial difficulties, lower income housing, and younger or single mothers were associated with an ADHD diagnosis. Rowland et al. (2018) found an interaction of parental income and SES in relation to ADHD. The influence of lower parental income was stronger in the absence of a family history of ADHD.

Comorbidity

The third key action statement from the AAP consensus report (Wolraich et al., 2019) is to initiate screening for another comorbid condition, including emotional and behavioral problems, other neurodevelopmental disorders, and relatively infrequent physical conditions. The Centers for Disease Control National Children's Health Survey (Centers for Disease Control, 2020) reported that about 64% of children with ADHD had been identified with another behavioral disorder. Of these children, 52% had a disruptive behavior problem (e.g., Oppositional-Defiant Disorder, Conduct Disorder); 33% had anxiety disorders; 17% had a mood disorder; and 14% had been identified with autism spectrum disorders.

Higher rates of comorbidity with other behavioral problems are evident in *clinical samples* than in community samples, perhaps because of the general problems children with ADHD experience with emotional regulation (Barkley, 2015a) and because the parents of children with ADHD and externalizing disorders have higher rates of psychopathology themselves. Many children with ADHD, both males and females, seem irritable and oppositional, often threatening and engaging in verbally defiant behavior as well as physical aggression, resulting in a diagnosis of an externalizing disorder. Relations with internalizing disorders are more complex. Females with ADHD seem more likely to develop problems with anxiety and mood, but this is consistent with normative expectations for females (Owens et al., 2015). Somewhat alarming are reports of high rates of self-harm behavior in adolescence among girls with ADHD (Hinshaw et al., 2012). The extent to which internalizing problems are secondary to the adaptive difficulties associated with ADHD is not clear.

Comorbidity is due in part to overlap in genes that are involved in multiple disorders. Faraone and Larssen (2019) summarized multiple studies showing that a shared genetic factor accounts for up to 45% of the variance in the phenotypic expression of ADHD and other behavioral disorders. Comorbidity is important because it should influence the development of a treatment plan. This need is reflected in the third key action statement from the AAP guidelines (Wolraich et al., 2019).

Developmental Continuities and Discontinuities (Course)

ADHD is a disorder that generally starts early in development and persists. Owens et al. (2015) reviewed over a dozen longitudinal studies that used some version of the DSM criteria to identify children with ADHD as preschool or school age children and then follow them into adolescence or adulthood. If parent reports were used, about half continued to meet full diagnostic criteria. If symptom inventories were used, persistence of the inattentive and impulsive behaviors was evident in an even higher percentage. Self-reports, however, were associated with much lower rates of persistence—likely underestimates. In a substantial minority of children, ADHD behaviors did not persist. These children were largely identified and treated, explaining why they did not continue to develop symptoms.

In keeping with the developmental psychopathology approach, it is important to consider normal development. The traits associated with ADHD improve over time across normal development. Motor overactivity in a young child is very different from the fidgety and restlessness of adolescents and adults. Similarly, there is improvement in behaviors related to distractibility and impulsivity, but adolescents and adults with a history of ADHD still show these behaviors more than those who are typically developing. Therefore, when considering the developmental course of ADHD, we see that the normal developmental progression may not occur to the same extent.

Academic and vocational outcomes are predictably poorer in relation to ADHD, even when comorbidity with SLDs and communication disorders is controlled. Social functioning is poorer in relation to ADHD and persists across development. There is elevated risk for substance abuse, but this may be moderated by a comorbid externalizing disorder. In samples that screen out aggression, ADHD is still a significant risk factor for externalizing disorders. Although most children with ADHD do not become juvenile offenders, criminals, or drug users, there is a higher risk for problems with juvenile detention, antisocial behavior, and substance abuse in both males and females (Satterfield et al., 2007).

Sex differences in the expression of ADHD across development are important, especially because of concerns about under-identification of ADHD in girls. Longitudinal studies show higher rates of hyperactivity in boys, but comparable rates of impulsivity and inattention across the sexes. On the whole, ADHD manifests similarly and has a similar developmental course in males and females, with differences reflecting how males and females develop in society and are therefore not specific to ADHD (Owens et al., 2015).

A Developmental Psychopathology Model of ADHD

Figure 5.1 displays a developmental psychopathology model of ADHD that includes many of the factors we will review in this section.

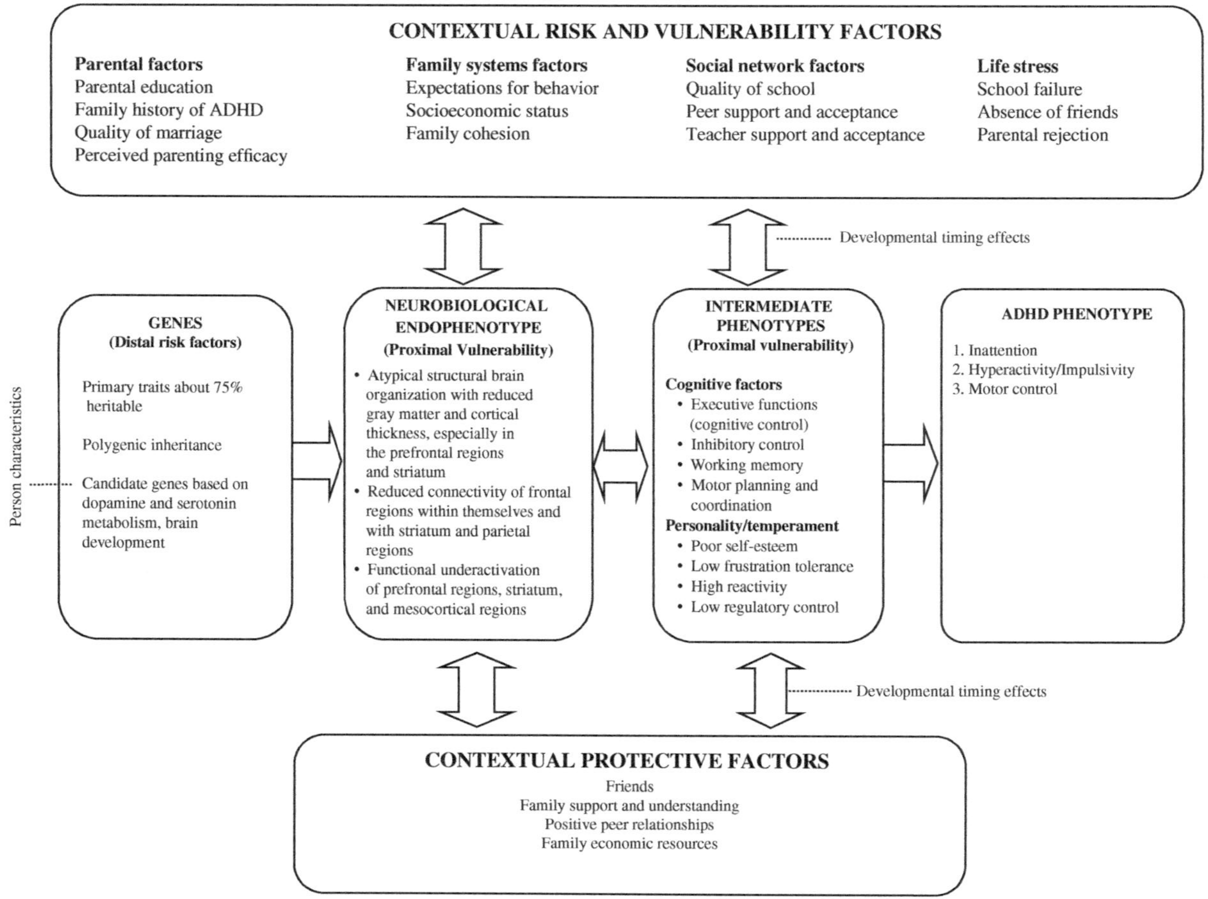

FIGURE 5.1 Developmental Psychopathology Model of ADHD

Genetic Factors

Family and twin studies

The familial nature of ADHD has been recognized from the earliest descriptions (e.g., Still, 1902). The traits associated with ADHD are highly heritable. Summarizing this research, Barkley (2015b) reported a rate of over 30% in siblings of individuals with ADHD, while Faraone and Larrsen (2019) cited studies showing a nine-fold increase in siblings compared to control samples. Parents of children with ADHD have elevated rates of multiple forms of psychopathology and are still two to eight times more likely to manifest ADHD than control parents (Barkley, 2015b). These findings are apparent across sex and racial groupings.

Studies of twins raised apart (adoption studies) show that the adopted children display behavior more like their biological parents than their adoptive parents (Barkley, 2015b; Faraone & Larrsen, 2019). Adoptive studies are important because of the tendency to cite environmental factors, such as television or other forms of screen exposure, and parenting, as causes of ADHD. Environmental factors are contributory and ADHD behavior is malleable, but the hereditary basis is strong.

Twin studies show much higher concordance for the two primary traits of ADHD in *monozygotic* twins who share the same genotype than among *dizygotic* twins who share 50% of a genotype. These studies show ranges of 55–98% heritability, with an average of over 70% for both dimensions (Barkley, 2015b; Faraone & Larssen, 2019). The influence of shared environmental factors (e.g., same school placement, SES) is small, with a larger contribution from non-shared environmental factors (e.g., different classroom placement, differences in parenting). Even if a categorical diagnosis is used, heritability estimates exceed 75%.

Molecular genetic studies

The molecular genetic component of ADHD is very complicated. In general, studies support the high heritability of traits associated with ADHD but have left an incomplete picture that is changing with the rapid advances in molecular genetic science. ADHD is a *polygenetic disorder* that likely involves many genes and where the genotypic manifestation into the ADHD phenotype is influenced by environmental factors that may interact with genetic factors. Barkley (2015b) reviewed evidence for a polygenetic susceptibility to ADHD that is influenced by the environment even though ADHD is highly heritable. This model, akin to the diathesis–stress model proposed by Meehl (1962), likely fits many of the disorders in this book and, indeed, you have read about it before. The importance of this conceptualization is the idea that the genetic manifestations are malleable and heredity is not destiny.

As genome-wide association studies became possible in the last decade, many genes have been statistically associated with ADHD. Surprisingly, few of the candidate genes related to the initial candidate genes emerged from the genome-wide studies (Gallo & Posner, 2016). Many of the genes emerging as statistically significant in the genome-wide association studies were related to brain development. Other genes identified were related to presumed drug mechanisms.

Genetic research will continue to grow along all these fronts. Genome-wide association studies support polygenetic modes of heritability, accounting for about a third of the heritability of ADHD (Faraone & Larssen, 2019). The genes that are involved are also involved in other neuropsychiatric disorders, including schizophrenia and autism spectrum disorder as well as with externalizing disorders.

NEUROBIOLOGICAL FACTORS

Neurobiological studies of ADHD employ multiple modalities. Most are based on *magnetic resonance imaging* (MRI), although psychophysiological and electrophysiological methods have been illuminating. The MRI studies of brain structure evaluate volumes of regions as well as white matter connectivity using methods such as *diffusion tensor imaging*. Functional studies are conducted without tasks (functional connectivity) and in relation to tasks (functional MRI). These studies consistently implicate neural networks involved in the allocation of cognitive resources (cognitive control) that include inhibitory control and response selection (Dennis, Sinopoli, Fletcher, & Schachar, 2008). In addition, circuits involved in motor control are implicated, as well as circuits involved in motivation and incentive processing (Gallo & Posner, 2016). Figure 5.2 provides a schema of brain regions involved in ADHD.

Brain structure

Structural MRI studies have shown volumetric reductions in the *basal ganglia*, a subcortical region involved in motor control, motivation, and goal-directed behavior (Gallo & Posner, 2016). At a cortical level, cortical thickness is reduced in the prefrontal and parietotemporal regions. For example, Fernández-Jaén et al. (2015) found reduced cortical thickness in the prefrontal region, especially the right lateral region. This reduction was related to the DAT 10R allele involved in dopamine regulation. In a large-scale study of thousands of adults and children, Hoogman et al. (2019) found reduced thickness in the frontal, temporal, and cingulate regions. These differences were not apparent in adolescents and adults, supporting a view of these differences as maturational in nature. Many structural MRI studies have found volumetric reductions

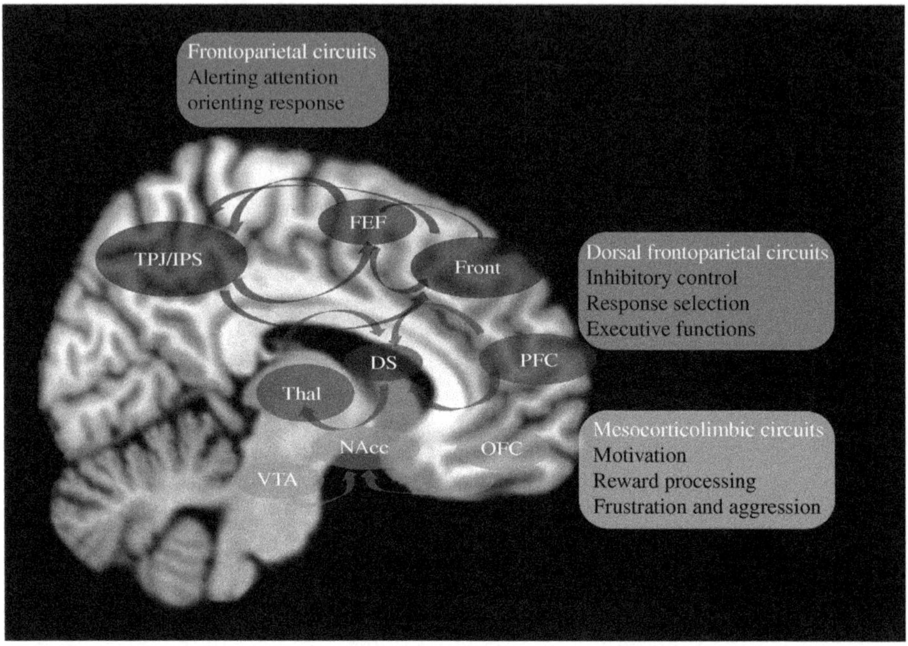

FIGURE 5.2 Neural Circuits Implicated in Attention-Deficit Hyperactivity Disorder Frontoparietal circuits encompass the frontal lobes (front), including the supplemental motor area and frontal eye fields (FEF), and the temporal parietal junction and inferior parietal sulcus (TPJ/IPS). These circuits underlie attentional processes including the altering and orienting of attentional resources. Dorsal frontostriatal circuits encompass the dorsolateral prefrontal cortex (PFC), dorsal striatum (DS), and the thalamus. These circuits underlie inhibitory control including response inhibition and interference control. Mesocorticolimbic circuits encompass the orbitofrontal cortex (OFC), ventral striatum and nucleus accumbens (NAcc), ventral tegmental area (VTA), and anterior hippocampus. These circuits underlie reward and emotional processes including motivation, frustration tolerance, and reward anticipation. *Source:* From Gallo & Posner (2026, p. 557). Reprinted from The Lancet, Vol. 3(6), Author links open overlay panel, Dr. Eduardo F. Gallo PhD, Jonathan Posner MD, Moving towards causality in attention-deficit hyperactivity disorder: overview of neural and genetic mechanisms, Pages 555–567, Copyright © 2016, with permission from Elsevier.

of gray matter in the prefrontal regions, especially the right lateral frontal region associated with cognitive control.

Diffusion tensor imaging studies measure the integrity of the white matter pathways that link different regions of the brain. These studies consistently implicate reduced integrity of the pathways that connect frontal regions with one another, with the striatum, and with parietal regions (Gallo & Posner, 2016).

There are both longitudinal and cross-sectional studies of brain structure using MRI (e.g., Hoogman et al., 2019). Supporting the view of ADHD as a dynamic disorder where features of the behavior pattern recede over time, these studies show attenuations of differences in brain structure with age, especially into adulthood. Such findings support the hypothesis that ADHD reflects a delay in brain maturation and the idea that stronger regulatory control is possible as children age (Barkley, 2015b). This finding speaks to the importance of treating ADHD early and aggressively in order to prevent the secondary, adverse outcomes associated with the adaptation difficulties in school, the family, and peers.

Brain function

Functional MRI (fMRI) studies have focused primarily on cognitive control, especially *response inhibition*. Imaging studies of response inhibition tasks show under-activation of prefrontal regions and connected parietal regions that are part of the circuitry involved in the regulation of attention and motor control. These regions include the bilateral inferior frontal gyrus, insula, right medial frontal gyrus, and right superior middle and frontal gyri (Janssen et al., 2015). Other studies evaluate the motivational and incentive-based systems by offering incentives, usually in the form of small amounts of money, for successful responding. Offering incentives to children with ADHD leads to improvement in performance, but under-activation of networks associated with motivational responses across multiple studies (see Figure 5.2; e.g., ventral striatum; Gallo & Posner, 2016).

Temperament

Temperament and ADHD are distinct, but overlapping constructs (Nigg, Goldsmith, & Sachek, 2004). Two temperamental dimensions, reactivity and regulatory, may be most related to ADHD. In evaluating reactivity, Nigg et al. (2004) distinguished a fearful and hostile-angry negative affect, contrasting it with an exuberant and content positive affect. Aspects of both negative affect and exuberance are related to ADHD. In regulation, a central dimension of ADHD, Nigg et al. (2004) noted that the concept was not unitary and encompassed a range of behaviors that accentuate, amplify, and maintain emotional response. They noted that the strongest relations in relation to ADHD were between effortful control in the regulatory domain and inattention and disorganization in ADHD. In addition, for those children who tend towards comorbid presentations of oppositionality or aggression, the negative affect is relevant.

In Barkley's (2015a) model identifying emotional regulation as a core problem in many individuals with ADHD, early difficulties with inhibiting negative emotional responses (which are associated with reactivity and regulation) predicted the severity of ADHD in older children and adults. While considering aspects of temperament, in their extreme manifestations these traits are important concepts for understanding ADHD, especially the disinhibition problem that pervades many components of both the inattention and hyperactivity/impulsivity components.

COGNITIVE FACTORS

Intelligence

IQ is not a prominent consideration among children with ADHD, as scores range from intellectually disabled to gifted within ADHD. Still, even in samples that exclude children with intellectual disability and autism spectrum disorder, IQ scores are about nine points lower among children with ADHD than children without ADHD (Weyandt & Gudmundsdottir, 2015), reflecting comorbidity with SLDs including impairment in language and reasoning skills assessed by IQ tests. Also, IQ tests measure skills such as working memory and attention persistence that are often impaired in children with ADHD. Finally, performance factors, such as persistence, motivation, and effort may affect performance. ADHD is also commonly identified in children with intellectual disabilities. Invoking intelligence to explain the cognitive problems of children and adults with ADHD, however, is not a compelling argument.

Executive functions

The most important cognitive construct for ADHD is *executive functions*, often referred to as cognitive control in neuroscience research, which describes the functions of the prefrontal cortex involved in regulating cognitive and affective behavior. As Figure 5.2 shows, neural networks involving frontal, parietal, and subcortical structures are linked to these regulatory skills.

There are many definitions of executive functions, a term that is often used too broadly to refer to any kind of problem with organization and regulation and to refer to the effects of damage to the frontal lobes in children and adults. Executive functions exercise "top-down," regulatory control on cognitive skills (and behavior) and are essential to goal-directed behavior, especially if involving on-line processing of immediate events or events in the future. Components of executive functions include *working memory*, or the ability to manipulate and maintain information in a short-term store; *shifting*, the ability to move attention from one task or strategy to another; planning; problem solving; as well as *response control* (and inhibitory control), which are prominent components of selective attention. The ability to write and generate words relies on internal speech and formulation skills that are often impaired in children with ADHD. *Metacognition* is an overarching awareness of the self in action.

All of these cognitive skills and constructs represent sources of impairment in children and adults with ADHD. They are not independent from one another but share common features, pointing to *bifactor models* that posit a common executive function factor, with several specific factors. For example, Cirino et al. (2018) analyzed 27 tasks of executive function taken from neuropsychological, cognitive, and educational perspectives in a large sample of children 8–11 years of age. The model that fit their data best was a bifactor model with a common executive function factor that reflected the overlap across measures and processes embedded in any executive function task.

Attention

Executive functions overlap considerably with cognitive models of attention. For example, Zelazo and Carson (2012) defined executive functions as the allocation of attentional resources. In Cirino et al. (2019), inhibitory control did not emerge as a specific executive function factor but was strongly related to the general factor. Dennis et al. (2008) proposed that *response control*, a component of *voluntary* or top-down, regulatory attention, was an endophenotype for ADHD and contrasted it to attention components that involved alerting and arousal, examples of involuntary or bottom-up attention, labeling it stimulus control. They reviewed literature from different studies showing that response control was generally impaired in ADHD and related it to the regulatory components of attention. In contrast, there was much less impairment of stimulus control, a bottom-up component of attention that often appears in relation to unexpected changes in the environment. This attention system operates primarily from the midbrain and parietal regions, but is linked with the frontal networks that regulate attention.

Motor control

Historically, children with ADHD have been described as clumsy, with poor fine motor coordination (Wender, 1987) manifested in difficulties with handwriting as well as other tasks involving motor learning, especially procedural learning (Duda et al., 2019). *Procedural learning* refers to the effects of repeated efforts to learn a task where there is incidental learning that occurs in the process of acquiring a skill and is different from the knowledge of skill that is acquired. Duda et al. (2019) found that children with ADHD did not show evidence of procedural learning on a multitrial motor learning task. Procedural learning is related to the striatum, which is volumetrically reduced in children with ADHD (see Figure 5.2). More generally, attention and movement are closely linked. We attend in order to act. Our attention is drawn to something startling (e.g., flash of light) in order to approach or avoid it. Movement itself reshapes attention by shifting the stimulus field in which the person is attending.

Contextual Risk and Protective Factors

Many risk and protective factors involve the family and are related to disruptive behavior (Johnston & Chronis-Tuscano, 2015). Children with ADHD are often born into families where there is a history of ADHD or other forms of psychopathology. Children with ADHD need structure and consistent discipline at home. Just as ADHD behavior makes parenting difficult, parents with ADHD have more trouble with parenting and are at higher risk for marital discord, the latter exacerbated by ADHD. Marital discord can lead to disagreements about parenting that make efforts at structure and discipline even more difficult to implement. In contrast, a strong marital relationship is usually associated with more effective parenting. Parents with a low sense of *efficacy* are less likely to be effective with children who have ADHD. Parental ADHD as well as depression, anxiety, and substance abuse, which are sometimes primary and sometimes secondary to the difficulties presented by a child with ADHD, are risk factors for children. Exposure to violence exacerbates disruptive behavior and is more likely to lead to aggressive behavior. Parents who are less conscientious and who do not monitor their children closely introduce risk factors that may be associated with the higher rate of accidental injuries in children with ADHD.

School risk and protective factors reflect the need for classrooms that are structured and organized. Pedagogical approaches that are less explicit exacerbate the inattentive and disorganized behavior of children with ADHD. Teachers who are structured, warm, and caring are protective factors. Having a best friend is a protective factor, while peer rejection is a risk factor. Children who understand their ADHD and maintain self-esteem do better than those who feel negatively about themselves and do not understand the basis of their difficulties. Any form of comorbidity is a risk factor.

Demographic risk factors include poverty, lower parental education, single parent status, and other forms of psychosocial adversity present in the neighborhood or school, which all can exacerbate ADHD symptoms.

Gene–Environment Interplay

Gene–environment correlations

As we have emphasized throughout this chapter, ADHD is highly heritable and children with ADHD are born into families where the rate of ADHD and other forms of psychopathology occur at higher rates than in the rest of the population. Thus, genetic risk is carried to the child and leads to an environment that is less structured and organized and less conducive to effective parenting. It is important to think about family history when treating ADHD. Imagine trying to help parents provide structure and consistent management when they themselves are disorganized and have trouble structuring their environment. In many families, parental ADHD has not been identified, but emerges as a concern as the assessment proceeds. It is not unusual to refer parents for treatment of ADHD themselves. The general picture of this gene–environment correlation is the intergenerational perpetuation of problems organizing and structuring the environment and engaging in effective parenting practices that could ameliorate ADHD behavior.

Gene–environment interactions

Interactions of genes and environments are important because genetic factors do not account for the full expression of the phenotype. In ADHD, gene–environment interactions typically look for interactions of a particular genetic marker with a characteristic of the environment. Low birth weight, exposure to environmental toxins, and SES may potentiate the genetic effects of ADHD (Nigg & Barkley, 2014). A recent review (Franke & Buitelaar, 2018) found a mixture of main effects for genetic and environmental factors. Parental education, parental involvement, and parental self-blame showed gene by environment interactions in twin studies, such that lower parental education, lower parental involvement, and higher parental self-blame, in combination with genetic vulnerability, led to worst outcomes for children. There have been inconsistent results for maternal smoking and pregnancy complications in studies involving candidate genes. Franke and Buitelaar (2018) concluded that research on gene–environment interactions was "patchy" because of excessive focus on candidate genes and single genetic markers. Nonetheless, the search for gene–environment interactions is important and will likely be facilitated by investigations of larger samples, clusters of genes, and explicit efforts at replication.

DEVELOPMENTAL TIMING EFFECTS

Two important issues involve developmental timing. The first is the persistence of ADHD behavior. While components such as hyperactivity are more apparent in younger children and recede in adolescents and adults, children and adults lag behind age-matched peers on dimensions associated with inattention and impulsivity. The manifestations of ADHD change with the developmental context, with adventurous, risk-seeking behavior apparent in young children and problems with driving and substance abuse in older children and adults. Social difficulties are constant, but also associated with impulsivity that manifests differently over time.

Second, at behavioral and brain levels, ADHD behavior improves normatively over time, with evidence of maturational delays in brain development. In many respects, treatment should try to prevent secondary effects of ADHD behavior on family and social relations as well as underachievement in school. Early, aggressive treatment is necessary to prevent ADHD impairment from growing across development.

Interventions

Interventions for children with ADHD involve a combination of medication treatment and psychosocial interventions addressing the child's behavioral difficulties at school and home. These latter interventions may include parent training as well as school-based programs and training in social skills. Key Action Statements 4–7 from the AAP guidelines (Wolraich et al., 2019) address treatment. The fourth statement simply affirms that ADHD is a chronic condition that may need treatment across the lifespan and should be managed like other chronic health conditions. Statements 5a–c break down treatment into evidence-based recommendations for different developmental phases. Noteworthy is the recommendation to avoid the diagnosis of ADHD in children under four years of age because of the difficulties discriminating ADHD behavior from behavior that is often characteristic of typically developing children and because the most effective intervention in young children, parent-based training, does not require a diagnosis of ADHD to implement. The guidelines also discourage the use of medication in children under four except for extreme cases. The sixth statement addresses the importance of adjusting medication dosage for optimal control of behavior. The seventh statement reiterates the importance of addressing comorbid disorders, which may require specialized intervention.

Medication treatment

It has been recognized since 1937 that stimulant medication is effective in treating hyperactivity. The initial observations were incidental because amphetamine was used to treat headaches in children with disruptive behavior who underwent invasive medical procedures. It seemed to have the "paradoxical" effect of slowing them down. We now know that the effects are not paradoxical (Rapoport et al., 1978) and, as we discuss below, not specific to ADHD behavior. Stimulants have an energizing effect on the nervous system and increase inhibitory control, which has a secondary effect on hyperactivity. Children who take stimulants for ADHD are more alert, less distractible, better able to persist and exert sustained mental effort, and are less impulsive. There is not a direct effect on aggression except to the extent that impulsive responding is reduced.

There are two main stimulants as well as nonstimulant medications used with children identified with ADHD (Wolraich et al., 2019).

The main stimulants are methylphenidate, historically representing Ritalin, and Dextroamphetamine, with Adderall a common trade name.

The AAP guidelines note that one or both of these stimulants are effective with about 80% of children with ADHD. Thus, if one stimulant does not seem effective, the other should be tried. With both, as Key Action Statement 6 states, the dosage should be adjusted until there is evidence of adequate response and no major adverse side effects. The side effects can include loss of appetite and insomnia, which often disappear after a short time. Stimulants can exercise adverse effects on mood and make children appear lethargic and unhappy, prompting a medication change.

A positive response to stimulants is not a diagnostic marker for ADHD. Stimulants enhance alertness and learning in people without ADHD, which is one reason they are potentially drugs of abuse, especially in high doses. In a classic study, Rapoport et al. (1978) administered amphetamine to typically developing children who volunteered for the study and were children of healthcare professionals. Compared to a placebo, these children showed improvement in tasks involving attentional persistence, reaction time, verbal learning, and had decreased motor reactivity. The difference is that stimulant medication reduces the adaptive impairment in children and adults with ADHD.

Many parents worry about medication interventions for children with ADHD. However, evidence suggests that they are often very effective when they are actively managed (Connor, 2015). When the secondary consequences of ADHD for overall adaptation are considered, early use of medication may help prevent subsequent behavioral and academic problems. However, the AAP guidelines recommend parent-based behavior management and classroom interventions for children under six and discourage use of medications except in extreme cases. In children 6–12 years of age, methylphenidate and amphetamine preparations are recommended, along with parent-based behavior management training and classroom interventions, if available. In adolescents 12–18 years of age, the guidelines recommend use of medications. Classroom-based interventions and supports are recommended.

Psychosocial interventions

Psychosocial interventions for ADHD include parent-based training, interventions focused on the adolescent (e.g., goal-directed counseling), social skills training, and school-based interventions. Here we focus on parent-based and school-based interventions.

The most important psychosocial intervention for children with ADHD is training in behavior management and parenting (Barkley, 2013; Kazdin, 2005). There are well-defined approaches to behavior management that involve structuring the household by introducing routines and schedules to make the child's day more predictable. Specific approaches to discipline are taught, with the focus on the use of immediate incentives and consequences for misbehavior that are reliably administered. Goals are set and monitored by identifying target behaviors and tracking their frequency. Parents often need help in identifying target behaviors, working together as a unit, and not undermining one another by disagreements over expectations. Consistent with normative development and the transition to independence, these types of interventions may be less effective for adolescents and it may be better to focus on individual forms of intervention. Even then, treatment should be practical, didactic, and goal-directed.

School-based interventions also focus on increasing the amount of structure and routine at school (Pfiffner & DuPaul, 2015). Although parent–school partnerships are essential, ADHD-related behavior has to be addressed in the context in which it occurs. Part of addressing ADHD in the school is educating teachers and administrators about the nature of ADHD as a biologically based disorder of self-control and moving them away from explanations focused on motivation or inability to learn or behave. In addition to education, a functional behavior assessment should be completed to identify antecedents and consequences of the child's behavior and to set targets for behavior change. Teachers may learn a set of consequences for specific target behaviors and participate in token reward programs where appropriate behavior is rewarded and charted with tokens (and supplemented at home). Perhaps most importantly, children with ADHD need help with organization at school. Even through adolescence, they have trouble keeping up with their assignments and remembering to turn in completed work. Punishment in the way of bad grades or negative interactions with teachers and parents discourages the child and perpetuates the behavior, so explicit assistance with these kinds of organizational skills is essential.

Combined interventions

Common sense would suggest that combined interventions would be best, but resources for combined interventions are often not available. The National Children's Health Survey reported that 77% of children with ADHD were receiving treatment: 30% received only medication, 15% received only behavior management, and 32% received a combined intervention. The largest and most ambitious treatment study of ADHD, the National Institute of Mental Health Multimodal Treatment of ADHD Study (MTA; Jensen, 1999), found that medication-only and medication with behavior modification conditions were not different, but outcomes were better than the behavior modification-only and the community controls. It is striking that in these analyses, there was no obvious additive effect of the behavioral treatments. However, alternative analyses showed that the combined interventions might have been more effective, especially if composite outcomes were used and in relation to comorbid externalizing disorders (Swanson et al., 2008). Further, in many respects, children with ADHD need combined interventions (Smith & Shapiro, 2015): medication does not last 24 hours a day, long-term medication use may be contraindicated, and medications may not affect comorbid symptoms.

Chapter Summary

ADHD is the most prevalent childhood behavior disorder. Characterized by impairments on two primary dimensions, inattention and hyperactivity/impulsivity, ADHD is a disorder of the ability to regulate behavior, emotion, and cognition. It is widely considered a brain-based disorder with important environmental contributions. ADHD is highly heritable, and children identified with ADHD often have parents with ADHD and other disorders. Molecular genetic studies are advancing rapidly, but ADHD is a complex, polygenetic disorder that involves many combinations of genes. At the level of the brain, ADHD is associated with quantitative reductions in gray matter and cortical thickness, especially in the prefrontal regions and the striatum. These impairments are closely related to the problems with executive function, attention, working memory, and motivational responding demonstrated by children with ADHD. It is a chronic disorder that persists into adulthood, which means that long-term intervention may be needed. The most effective interventions involve careful medication management and psychosocial interventions.

Further Reading

Barkley, R.A. (Ed.) (2015). *Attention-deficit hyperactivity disorder (4th ed.). A handbook for diagnosis and treatment*. New York, NY: Guilford Press.

Hinshaw, S.P., & Scheffler, R.M. (2014). *The ADHD explosion*. New York, NY: Oxford University Press.

Wolraich, M. L., Hagan, J.F., Allan, C, et al. (2019). AAP subcommittee on children and adolescents with Attention-Deficit/Hyperactive Disorder. Clinical practice guideline for the diagnosis, evaluation, and treatment of Attention-Deficit/Hyperactivity Disorder in children and adolescents. *Pediatrics*, *144*(4), e20192528.

Discussion/Essay Questions

1. What is the relation of the two primary dimensions of ADHD? Can they be accounted for by a single factor?
2. If the traits associated with ADHD are highly heritable, what are some of the reasons why specific genes have not been reliably linked to ADHD or show small effects?
3. What are the most important components of intervention for children and adolescents with ADHD? How do these components change if there is evidence for (a) SLD; (b) oppositional defiant disorder; and (c) depression?
4. The NIMH Multimodal Treatment of ADHD Study has been controversial because of the finding that medication-only and medication + behavior modification treatments were statistically equivalent. How would you interpret these results and help resolve the controversy? Why should children with ADHD not just receive medication treatment?
5. Why do prevalence rates for ADHD vary?

Glossary

Basal ganglia is a subcortical region involved in motor control, motivation, and goal-directed behavior.

Bifactor models are statistical models that posit that data is organized into a common factor with several specific factors.

Clinical samples are drawn from outpatient or inpatient mental health clinics for research.

Concordance refers to the rate of agreement, for instance the rate of agreement between two parents who are rating the ADHD symptoms of their child.

Diffusion tensor imaging measures the integrity of the white matter pathways that link different regions of the brain.

Disinhibition refers to lack of control over one's actions.

Disruptive behavior disorders are those that involve, for example, rule breaking, aggression, and temper tantrums, like Oppositional Defiant Disorder.

Dizygotic refers to fraternal, non-identical, twins.

Executive control refers to manipulating and organizing material, usually in working memory.

Executive functions, often referred to as *cognitive control* in neuroscience research, is a broad term for skills involved in the regulation of cognitive and affective behavior.

Generative informant refers to the person who is completing an interview or rating scale and is therefore the one providing information about the child being assessed.

Inhibitory control or *response inhibition* refer to abilities including restraint and cancellation of responses to the environment.

Magnetic resonance imaging is a form of neuroimaging that uses magnetic fields to generate images of internal organs like the brain.

Metacognition is an overarching awareness of the self in action.

Moderators are variables that affect the statistical relation between the independent and dependent variables.

Monozygotic refers to identical twins that share identical genetic material.

Pervasiveness indicates that symptoms occur in more than one setting.

Polygenetic disorder means that multiple genes, rather than just one, are involved in causing a disorder.

Procedural learning refers to the effects of repeated efforts to learn a task, where there is incidental learning that occurs in the process of acquiring a skill and is different from the knowledge of skill that is acquired.

Response control refers to attention processes that are voluntary, such as selection and disinhibition.

Self-regulated learning involves strategies for managing behavior in relation to goals.

Shifting is the ability to move attention from one task or strategy to another.

Stimulus control includes attention components that are involuntary, involving alerting and arousal.

Working memory is the ability to manipulate and maintain information in a short-term store.

References

Achenbach, T. M., & Rescorla, L. (2001). *Manual for the ASEBA school-age forms & profiles: An integrated system of multi-informant assessment.* Burlington, VT: Aseba.

Barkley, R. A. (2013). *Defiant children: A clinician's manual for assessment and parent training* (3rd ed.). New York, NY: Guilford Press.

Barkley, R. A. (2015a). Emotional regulation is a core component of ADHD. In R. A. Barkley (Ed.), *Attention-Deficit Hyperactivity Disorder. A handbook for diagnosis and treatment* (4th ed., pp. 81–115). New York, NY: Guilford Press.

Barkley, R.A. (2015b). Etiologies of ADHD. In R. A. Barkley (Ed.), *Attention-Deficit Hyperactivity Disorder. A handbook for diagnosis and treatment* (4th ed., pp. 356–390). New York, NY: Guilford Press.

Centers for Disease Control and Prevention (2020). Data and statistics about ADHD. Available at: https://www.cdc.gov/ncbddd/adhd/data.html.

Cirino, P. T., Ahmed, Y., Miciak, J., Taylor, W. P., Gerst, E. H., & Barnes, M. A. (2018). A framework for executive function in the late elementary years. *Neuropsychology, 32*, 176–189.

Connor, D. F. (2015). Pharmacological management of pediatric patients with comorbid attention-deficit hyperactivity disorder oppositional defiant disorder. *Pediatric Drugs, 17*(5), 361–371.

Danielson, M. L., Bitsko, R. H., Ghandour, R. M., Holbrook, J. R., Kogan, M. D., & Blumberg, S. J. (2018). Prevalence of parent-reported ADHD diagnosis and associated treatment among US children and adolescents, 2016. *Journal of Clinical Child & Adolescent Psychology, 47*(2), 199–212.

Dennis, M., Sinopoli, K. J., Fletcher, J. M., & Schachar, R. (2008). Puppets, robots, critics, and actors within a taxonomy of attention for developmental disorders. *Journal of the International Neuropsychological Society, 14*, 1–18.

Duda, T. A., Casey, J. E., O'Brien, A. M., Frost, N., & Phillips, A. M. (2019). Reduced graphomotor procedural learning in children and adolescents with ADHD. *Human Movement Science, 65*, 60–70.

Faraone, S. V., & Larsson, H. (2019). Genetics of attention deficit hyperactivity disorder. *Molecular Psychiatry, 24*(4), 562–575.

Fernández-Jaén, A., López-Martín, S., Albert, J., Fernández-Mayoralas, D. M., Fernández Perrone, A. L., de La Peña, M. J., & Muñoz-Jareño, N. (2015). Cortical thickness differences in the prefrontal cortex in children and adolescents with ADHD in relation to dopamine transporter (DAT1) genotype. *Psychiatry Research: Neuroimaging, 233*(3), 409–417.

First, M.B., Williams, J.B.W., Karg, R.S., & Spitzer, R.L. (2016). *User's guide for the structured clinical interview for DSM-5 disorders, clinician version (SCID-5-CV).* Arlington, VA: American Psychiatric Association.

Franke, B., & Buitelaar, J. K. (2018). Gene-environment interactions. In T. Banaschewski, D. Coghill, & A. Zuddas (Eds.), *Oxford handbook of Attention Deficit Hyperactivity Disorder* (pp. 35–51). New York, NY: Oxford.

Gallo, E. F., & Posner, J. (2016). Moving towards causality in attention-deficit hyperactivity disorder: Overview of neural and genetic mechanisms. *The Lancet Psychiatry, 3*(6), 555–567.

Haslam, N., Williams, B., Prior, M., Haslam, R., Graetz, B., & Sawyer, M. (2006). The latent structure of attention-deficit/hyperactivity disorder: A taxometric analysis. *Australian & New Zealand Journal of Psychiatry, 40*(8), 639–647.

Hinshaw, S. P., Owens, E. B., Zalecki, C., Huggins, S. P., Montenegro-Nevado, A. J.,

Schrodek, E., & Swanson, E. N. (2012). Prospective follow-up of girls with attention-deficit/hyperactivity disorder into early adulthood: Continuing impairment includes elevated risk for suicide attempts and self-injury. *Journal of Consulting and Clinical Psychology*, *80*(6), 1041.

Hinshaw, S. P., & Scheffler, R. M. (2014). *The ADHD explosion*. New York, NY: Oxford University Press.

Hoogman, M., Muetzel, R., Guimaraes, J. P., Shumskaya, E., Mennes, M., Zwiers, M. P., & Soliva Vila, J. C. (2019). Brain imaging of the cortex in ADHD: A coordinated analysis of large-scale clinical and population-based samples. *American Journal of Psychiatry*, *176*(7), 531–542.

Janssen, T. W., Heslenfeld, D. J., van Mourik, R., Logan, G. D., & Oosterlaan, J. (2015). Neural correlates of response inhibition in children with attention-deficit/hyperactivity disorder: A controlled version of the stop-signal task. *Psychiatry Research: Neuroimaging*, *233*(2), 278–284.

Jensen, P. S. (1999). A 14-month randomized clinical trial of treatment strategies for attention deficit/hyperactivity disorder. *Archives of General Psychiatry*, *56*(12), 1073–1086.

Johnston, C., & Chronis-Tuscano, A. (2015). Families and ADHD. In R. A. Barkley (Ed.), *Attention-Deficit Hyperactivity Disorder. A handbook for diagnosis and treatment* (4th ed., pp. 191–209). New York, NY: Guilford Press.

Kang, S., & Harvey, E.A. (2020). Racial differences between black parents' and white teachers' perceptions of Attention-Deficit/Hyperactivity Disorder behavior. *Journal of Abnormal Child Psychology*, *48*(5), 661-672.

Kazdin, A. (2005). *Parent management training: Treatment for oppositional, aggressive, and antisocial behavior in children and adolescents*. New York, NY: Oxford.

Kessler, R. C., Adler, L., Barkley, R., Biederman, J., Conners, C. K., Demler, O., & Spencer, T. (2006). The prevalence and correlates of adult ADHD in the United States: Results from the National Comorbidity Survey Replication. *American Journal of Psychiatry*, *163*(4), 716–723.

Marcus, D. K., Norris, A. L., & Coccaro, E. F. (2012). The latent structure of attention deficit/hyperactivity disorder in an adult sample. *Journal of Psychiatric Research*, *46*(6), 782–789.

Meehl, P. E. (1962). Schizotaxia, schizotypy, schizophrenia. *American Psychologist*, *17*(12), 827–838.

Miller, T. W., Nigg, J. T., & Miller, R. L. (2009). Attention deficit hyperactivity disorder in African American children: What can be concluded from the past ten years? *Clinical Psychology Review*, *29*(1), 77–86.

Nigg, J. T., & Barkley, R. A. (2014). Attention-Deficit/Hyperactivity Disorder. In E. J. Mash and R. A. Barkley (Eds.), *Child psychopathology* (3rd ed., pp. 75–144). New York, NY: Guilford.

Nigg, J. T., Goldsmith, H. H., & Sachek, J. (2004). Temperament and attention deficit hyperactivity disorder: The development of a multiple pathway model. *Journal of Clinical Child and Adolescent Psychology*, *33*(1), 42–53.

Owens, E. B., Cardoos, S. L., & Hinshaw, S. P. (2015). Developmental progression and gender differences among individuals with ADHD. In R. A. Barkley (Ed.), *Attention-Deficit Hyperactivity Disorder. A handbook for diagnosis and treatment* (4th ed., pp. 223–255). New York, NY: Guilford Press.

Pfiffner, L. J., & DuPaul, G. P. (2015). Treatment of ADHD in school settings. In R. A. Barkley (Ed.). *Attention-Deficit Hyperactivity Disorder. A handbook for diagnosis and treatment* (4th ed., pp. 596–629). New York, NY: Guilford Press.

Rapoport, J. L., Buchsbaum, M. S., Zahn, T. P., Weingartner, H., Ludlow, C., & Mikkelsen, E. J. (1978). Dextroamphetamine: Cognitive and behavioral effects in normal prepubertal boys. *Science*, *199*(4328), 560–563.

Rowland, A. S., Skipper, B. J., Rabiner, D. L., Qeadan, F., Campbell, R. A., Naftel, A. J., & Umbach, D. M. (2018). Attention-Deficit/

Hyperactivity Disorder (ADHD): Interaction between socioeconomic status and parental history of ADHD determines prevalence. *Journal of Child Psychology and Psychiatry, 59*(3), 213–222.

Russell, A. E., Ford, T., & Russell, G. (2015). Socioeconomic associations with ADHD: Findings from a mediation analysis. *PloS One, 10*(6), e0128248. Available at: https://doi.org/10.1371/journal.pone.0128248.

Satterfield, J. H., Faller, K. J., Crinella, F. M., Schell, A. M., Swanson, J. M., & Homer, L. D. (2007). A 30-year prospective follow-up study of hyperactive boys with conduct problems: Adult criminality. *Journal of the American Academy of Child & Adolescent Psychiatry, 46*(5), 601–610.

Smith, B.H., & Shapiro, C.J. (2015). Combined treatments for ADHD. In R. A. Barkley (Ed.). *Attention-Deficit Hyperactivity Disorder. A handbook for diagnosis and treatment* (4th ed., pp. 686–704). New York, NY: Guilford Press.

Still, G.F. (1902). Some abnormal psychological conditions in children. *Lancet, 1*, 1077–1082.

Swanson, J., Arnold, L. E., Kraemer, H., Hechtman, L., Molina, B., Hinshaw, S., & Greenhill, L. (2008). Evidence, interpretation, and qualification from multiple reports of long-term outcomes in the Multimodal Treatment Study of Children with ADHD (MTA) Part I: Executive Summary. *Journal of Attention Disorders, 12*(1), 4–14.

Thomas, R., Sanders, S., Doust, J., Beller, E., & Glasziou, P. (2015). Prevalence of attention deficit/hyperactivity disorder: A systematic review and meta-analysis. *Pediatrics, 135*(4), e994–e1001.

Weiss, G., & Hechtmann, L.T. (1993). *Hyperactive children grown up: ADHD in children, adolescents, and adults*. New York, NY: Guilford Press.

Wender, P. H. (1987). *The hyperactive child, adolescent, and adult: Attention deficit disorder through the lifespan*. New York, NY: Oxford University Press.

Weyandt, L.L., & Gudmundsdottir, B.G. (2015) Developmental and psychological deficits in children with ADHD. In R. A. Barkley (Ed.), *Attention-Deficit Hyperactivity Disorder. A handbook for diagnosis and treatment* (4th ed., pp. 116–139). New York, NY: Guilford Press.

Willcutt, E. G. (2012). The prevalence of DSM-IV attention-deficit/hyperactivity disorder: A meta-analytic review. *Neurotherapeutics, 9*(3), 490–499.

Wolraich, M. L., Hagan, J. F., Allan, C., et al. (2019). AAP Subcommittee on Children and Adolescents with Attention-Deficient/ Hyperactive Disorder. Clinical practice guideline for the diagnosis, evaluation, and treatment of Attention-Deficit/Hyperactivity Disorder in children and adolescents. *Pediatrics, 144*(4), e20192528.

World Health Organization (2020). International statistical classification of diseases and related health problems (11th ed.). https://icd.who.int/.

Xu, G., Strathearn, L., Liu, B., Yang, B., & Bao, W. (2018). Twenty-year trends in diagnosed attention-deficit/hyperactivity disorder among US children and adolescents, 1997–2016. *JAMA Network Open, 1*(4), e181471–e181471.

Zelazo, P. D., & Carlson, S. M. (2012). Hot and cool executive function in childhood and adolescence: Development and plasticity. *Child Development Perspectives, 6*(4), 354–360.

Chapter 6

Autism Spectrum Disorder

RACHEL H. FEIN, AMANDA VENTA, ALLISON C. MEINERT, SARAH S. MIRE, AND KATHERINE BERGEZ

Chapter Overview

In this chapter, we will discuss *Autism Spectrum Disorder (ASD)*, a classification in the DSM-5 that replaced the DSM-IV-TR categories of Autistic Disorder, Asperger's Disorder, Childhood Disintegrative Disorder, Rett's Disorder, and Pervasive Developmental Disorder Not Otherwise Specified. Research shows that 91% of children diagnosed using the DSM-IV can now be categorized with ASD (Huerta et al., 2012). This disorder is characterized by impairments in social communication and interaction as well as restricted, repetitive patterns of interest or behavior that are noted early in development.

Features of ASD have been documented in children for several decades. Leo Kanner (1943) first identified a group of children in the United States who experienced difficulties with regard to social interaction, communication, and repetitive interests. In addition to noting that these children seem to have difficulty relating to others, he noticed several anomalies in their spoken language, including a delay in language acquisition, *echolalia*, and pronoun reversal. He also wrote that these children engaged in repetitive interests and stereotyped play. He eventually coined the term "infantile autism" to describe these behaviors. Within the same time period, an Austrian psychiatrist, Hans Asperger (1944) made similar findings; however, his research included a wider range of individuals and abilities, including those with typical speech and language development but with a tendency to be pedantic and use repetitive or scripted speech. The current understanding of ASD is that it is a

Developmental Psychopathology, First Edition. Edited by Amanda Venta, Carla Sharp, Jack M. Fletcher, and Peter Fonagy.

spectrum disorder, with a unique set of strengths and challenges for each individual diagnosed with ASD. Below, we provide an example of a case from our clinical work.

Case study in ASD

Simon is a five-year-old Caucasian male who lives with both of his parents in a middle-income suburban neighborhood. Simon's parents say that they have always thought that Simon was different from other children. From a young age, he appeared more independent than his siblings; he was able to entertain himself quietly for long periods of time and rarely sought his parents' attention. However, over the last two years, Simon's parents have become concerned about his behavior. They describe him having "tantrums" during which he cries, screams, and bangs his head on the floor when the family experiences a change in routine or asks him to stop playing on his tablet—his favorite toy. They also say that he is defiant with his teacher and parents—refusing to eat the food served in the school cafeteria due to textural aversions to some foods and refusing to wear the clothes that his mother picks for him each morning because the clothing tags bother him so much. Simon is bright, but his teacher worries that he does not pay attention in class because he often seems distracted by items around the room and talks excessively about games he plays on his tablet. Simon's teacher and parents are worried about how to manage his "tantrums" and keep him from falling behind in school.

As the clinician seeing this family, discuss possible diagnoses you would give Simon and supporting evidence for each differential diagnosis, as well as other factors to consider. What other information would you gather during an assessment to guide diagnosis and treatment of Simon's behaviors?

Definition, Diagnosis, and Clinical Features

ASD is characterized by two core deficits: (a) persistent impairments in social communication and interaction and (b) restricted, repetitive patterns of interest and behavior. A clinical diagnosis is warranted when a child demonstrates symptoms in each of these domains and when these symptoms produce clinically significant impairment. Symptoms must be present in early development, though they may not fully manifest until an individual is older and social demands increase. Further, an individual can meet criteria for ASD by history, especially if deficits have improved significantly with intervention.

Impairments in social communication and interaction can take many forms, and the heterogeneity of behaviors observed can make assessing for ASD difficult. The DSM-5 provides three areas in which these impairments might be noted, and deficits across all three areas must be met in order to meet criteria for ASD. First, children may show deficits in social–emotional reciprocity, which includes the ability to engage in back-and-forth conversation, share interests and emotions with others, and initiate or respond to social interactions. For example, when a three-year-old child is playing with toys while their parent is sitting next to them, one would expect the child to occasionally check-in with the parent by glancing at them, bringing toys to them, or asking them to play. However, a child with ASD of the same age may not engage in these behaviors as they may struggle with initiating social interactions. Second, children may show deficits in non-verbal communication abilities, including eye contact, body language, gestures, and facial expressions. Third, difficulties may be noted with regard to maintaining and understanding relationships, for instance, struggling to appropriately change behavior to match a social context (e.g., being quiet in the library), struggling to make or play with friends, or understanding relationships (e.g., the meaning of friendship or the reason why people get married).

Restricted, repetitive patterns of interest or behavior also vary widely across individuals with ASD. The DSM-5 criteria emphasize behavior in four areas; however, an individual only needs to exhibit deficits in two out of the four areas in order to meet criteria for ASD. First, behavior may be stereotyped or repetitive, such that children may be observed to engage in repetitive speech (e.g., repeating the same phrase with the same intonation), repetitive use of objects (e.g., lining up toy animals rather than using them for creative, spontaneous play), and/or repetitive motor mannerisms (e.g., hand flapping or body rocking). Second, children may show an insistence on sameness or focus on routines and rituals that is accompanied by distress when routines or expectations are changed, and needing to do certain things (e.g., getting dressed) the same way. Third, restricted interests that are abnormally strong or narrow are common in individuals with ASD. For example, children may demonstrate a strong interest in one toy, like dinosaurs, such that they acquire unusual knowledge about that subject, which dominates their interest, play, and conversation. Finally, many children with ASD demonstrate unusual interest in or aversions to sensory aspects of the environment. Common examples include visually inspecting or looking closely at the wheels of a toy car while spinning them repeatedly, intolerance for certain food textures, distress at loud noises, or indifference to pain.

You may be thinking that you have observed many of the behaviors associated with ASD diagnoses in your young siblings, and you are right—many of these behaviors are common in early, typical development. For instance, newborn babies are not expected to make eye contact or use facial expressions, and these behaviors are not considered symptoms of ASD, but rather typical stages of early development. Likewise, repeating the same phrase is a common stage of learning language, but becomes worrisome if children do not grow out of this phase and acquire more complex language. In order to detect symptoms of ASD, then, clinicians must have a sound understanding of typical development. By paying attention to these developmental milestones, and whether or not they are met, parents can help professionals identify developmental delays like ASD.

You will remember from the chapter overview that, until recently, ASD included several separate disorders: Autistic Disorder, Asperger's Disorder, Rett's Disorder, Childhood Disintegrative Disorder, and Pervasive Developmental Disorder Not Otherwise Specified (PDD-NOS). In the DSM-5, though, these categories were eliminated, leaving only one category—ASD. The rationale for this change was outlined by a workgroup dedicated to the creation of the DSM-5, who said that the separate diagnoses were not consistently applied across settings and, instead, supported an overarching diagnosis (American Psychiatric Association, 2013). This chapter will describe ASD as currently defined in the DSM-5, although some research referred to will focus on one of the DSM-IV subgroups specifically.

Another key difference between the DSM-IV and the DSM-5 is that Asperger's Disorder has been subsumed by the broad heading of ASD. In the DSM-IV, the main difference between Asperger's Disorder and Autistic Disorder was that language development delay and cognitive deficits are not associated with Asperger's Disorder whereas "qualitative impairments in communication" was a component of Autistic Disorder. However, in reality, these diagnostic categories were not really so distinct. Indeed, studies found that up to 80% of individuals with Asperger's met the DSM-IV criteria for Autistic Disorder (Gilchrist et al., 2001) and *discriminant validity* studies demonstrate insufficient evidence to consider these two subtypes as separate conditions. Based upon cluster analytic studies (e.g., Prior et al., 1998), researchers have long considered Asperger's Disorder and Autistic Disorder as levels of severity on the same diagnostic spectrum (Frith, 2003) and this is just the approach that was selected in creating the DSM-5.

Prevalence

The Center for Disease Control (CDC) currently estimates that 1 in 54 children in the United States (US) meets criteria for ASD. This rate is higher than many other childhood conditions, including childhood cancer and Type 1 diabetes. Prevalence rates identified in other nations vary widely, as noted in Elsabbagh et al. (2012), a systematic review of previous *epidemiological* surveys of ASD.

The prevalence of ASD has been a topic of controversy and recent media attention due to concerns that rates are rapidly rising. Some data supports this concern. In 2000, the Center for Disease Control (CDC) estimated the prevalence at 1 in 150 children. By 2004, this estimate had increased to 1 in 125 children and it continued to increase to 1 in 88 children in 2008 and 1 in 68 children in 2010. This pattern of generally increasing prevalence has been noted for several decades, contributing to concerns that there is an epidemic in the US. However, this concern was refuted in a recent study that systematically reviewed epidemiological data gathered between 1990 and 2010 and reported no clear evidence of increasing prevalence (Baxter et al., 2015). Possible explanations for these conflicting findings include better mental health and diagnostic resources. In other words, more resources have contributed to an increase in the *diagnosis* of ASD, but not their true prevalence per se. Tsai (2014) adds that methodological factors, like changes in diagnostic criteria and increased awareness of ASD among parents, healthcare providers, and the public, are likely to account for the upward trend in prevalence.

PREVALENCE BY GENDER AND AGE

Data from a large-scale study (CDC, Baio, 2014) of children aged eight years across 11 Autism and Developmental Disabilities Monitoring (ADDM) Network sites in the US provides recent evidence that the prevalence of ASD in males (estimated at 1 in 42) is significantly higher than the prevalence in females (estimated at 1 in 189). Researchers are mixed in explaining these gender differences, suggesting that there are differences in the clinical presentation of symptoms of ASD (Kirkovski et al., 2013), that girls are better able to "camouflage" their symptoms (Kirkovski et al., 2013), and that the typical profile of ASD presented in the current literature is the stereotypically male profile, potentially leading to under and/or misdiagnosis among females (Kirkovski et al., 2013). Regarding true genetic relations between sex and ASD, studies (see Section 6.5.1) have begun to show that there are no sex-specific genetic influences in ASD, suggesting that the decreased prevalence observed in females may be attributable to environmental factors (Constantino & Todd, 2003).

It is widely believed that ASD is biologically based and present at birth. However, documenting the presence of the disorder is not possible until symptoms begin to emerge. Just because a child has not received a diagnosis until, for example, five years of age, does not mean that the disorder was not present at birth. Indeed, researchers have noted key differences between the home videos (at one year of age) of children later diagnosed with ASD and children without an ASD diagnosis. Specifically, children who would ultimately receive the diagnosis looked at others less consistently and oriented to their names less often than the typically developing children (Osterling & Dawson, 1994).

Current research indicates that children as young as six months old can be identified in research laboratory settings (Maestro et al., 2002), although characteristic symptoms become more apparent after 12 months. Indeed, Shumway and colleagues (2011) found that 62% of their participants with ASD were reported to have symptoms present in the first year of life. Notably, ASD can be reliably diagnosed as early as two years of age; however, most children are not diagnosed with ASD until after four years of age (CDC, Baio, 2014). To address this issue, The National Institute of Child Health and Human Development has published five indicators that a child should receive further evaluation: (a) does not babble or coo by 12 months; (b) does not gesture by 12 months, (c) does not say single words by 16 months; (d) does not say two-word phrases by 23 months, and (e) has any loss of language or social skill at any age.

ASD is a life-long disorder and the prevalence is not known to vary with age. Indeed, the vast majority of youth diagnosed with ASD experience limited attainment of adaptive skills (e.g., employment, education, social relationships) as adults (Eaves & Ho, 2008), and without treatment the symptoms of ASD are highly likely to persist (McLeod, Wood, & Klebanoff, 2015). In a large-scale study of the developmental course of ASD, Kobayashi and colleagues (1992) assessed nearly 200 adults with a prior diagnosis of ASD. The majority of the adults they followed required close supervision, although 27% lived independently and nearly half had adequate communication skills. Interestingly, research conducted by Helt and colleagues (2008) found that between 3% and 25% of individuals with ASD eventually "lost" their diagnosis, though it is unclear if the social and communicative behaviors of these individuals would have been described as "typical." These same researchers also found that predictors of better outcomes for individuals with ASD included higher cognitive abilities, receptive language, imitation and motor skills, earlier diagnosis and treatment, and less impairing symptoms of ASD. Fein and colleagues (2013) explored characteristics of the "optimal outcome" (OO) population, which includes individuals who previously met the criteria for ASD, but no longer met criteria following intervention. Adaptive behavior did not differ between the OO group and the neurotypical group, and language scores were in the average range. These studies are important in highlighting the range of outcomes for individuals with ASD, but simultaneously point to the general persistence of ASD.

PREVALENCE BY RACE, ETHNICITY, AND SOCIOECONOMIC STATUS (SES)

Although the incidence of ASD is reported in all racial, ethnic, linguistic, and socioeconomic (SES) groups (Baio et al., 2018; Durkin et al., 2017) and across the world (May, Sciberras, Brignell, & Williams, 2017), diagnostic prevalence varies among diverse groups. Data collected from the 11 U.S. sites of the ADDM Network provide recent evidence that the prevalence of ASD varies by race and ethnicity (Baio et al., 2018). Based on data from this collaborative network, which tracks children diagnosed with ASD across the US, non-Hispanic white children consistently are diagnosed with ASD at higher rates than their black and Hispanic peers.

Baio and colleagues (2018) did note, however, that racial and ethnic differences appear to be decreasing compared to ADDM data from previous years. When examining the most recent data from all ADDM sites together, prevalence of ASD diagnosis for white children was 7% higher than for their black peers, which they noted was significantly lower than the previous estimates of 20–30% higher prevalence among white children. Similarly, previous ADDM findings (e.g., Baio, 2014) indicated that ASD diagnoses for white children were approximately 50% higher than for their Hispanic peers, but in the ADDM report published in 2018 the difference was 22%. This suggests better identification practices for children of all backgrounds, yet the authors noted that ASD estimates do continue to vary by race and ethnicity.

Socioeconomic status (SES) has also been associated with U.S. ASD diagnostic prevalence. Parents' education, household income, insurance status, and residential location are interrelated factors that contribute to prevalence. For example, using data from the National Center for Health Statistics (NCHS), Zablotsky and colleagues (2019) found that children who had only private insurance (i.e., did not have public insurance) were more likely to have an ASD diagnosis than were uninsured children. Additionally, children from low-income families were more likely to have *all* of diagnoses queried in this study (e.g., ADHD, learning disability, intellectual disability) *except for* ASD.

Greater ASD prevalence among higher SES groups has been a consistent finding of studies of U.S. children (Durkin et al., 2017), and ASD diagnoses are often made significantly later for lower income families and/or families with lower parental education (Mazurek et al., 2014). Moreover, SES has been found to be a stronger predictor of the age at first diagnosis than actual severity of ASD symptoms (Fountain et al., 2011). Though beyond the scope of the current chapter, recent work related to disparities in ASD offers detailed information about contributing factors to disparities and considerations for researchers and practitioners in addressing these issues (e.g., Karpur, Lello, Frazier, Dixon, & Shih, 2019).

Comorbidity

Emotional and behavioral comorbidities are exceptionally common among individuals with ASD throughout the lifespan. Among young children (4.5–9.8 years of age), 90.5% of individuals have been shown to meet criteria for at least one co-occurring psychiatric disorder (Salazar et al., 2015). Estimates among youths 10–14 years of age indicate similarly high rates of one (70%) or two or more (41%) comorbid conditions (Simonoff et al., 2008).

A large proportion of individuals with ASD meet criteria for any anxiety disorder, with prevalence estimates ranging from 78.9% among younger children to 41.9% among older children (Salazar et al., 2015). However, individuals with ASD also commonly appear anxious in response to sensory stimuli to which they are hyper-reactive, making it difficult to disentangle sensory sensitivity from a comorbid anxiety disorder (Green & Ben-Sasson, 2010). Rates of depressive disorders may be impacted by age and methodology, as rates for young children (14.6%), older children (1.4%), and adults (48% lifetime; 19% current) vary greatly across studies (Salazar et al., 2015).

Many individuals with ASD also meet diagnostic criteria for attention deficit/hyperactivity disorder (ADHD), with prevalence estimates ranging from 59.1% to 28.2% among younger and older children, respectively (Salazar et al., 2015; Simonoff et al., 2008). While the DSM-IV did not allow for the diagnosis of both ASD and ADHD, the DSM-5 now permits the provision of both diagnoses (APA, 2013). Oppositional Defiant Disorder is also prevalent in this population, with estimates nearly identical across younger (28.7%) and older (28.1%) children. Many individuals with ASD are also impacted by co-occurring medical conditions, including seizure and gastrointestinal disorders (Doshi-Velez, Ge, & Kohane, 2014).

Although many individuals with ASD have average and above average intellectual abilities (44%), data collected from the ADDM Network reveals that 31% of children with an ASD were classified as having an intellectual disability and 25% were classified as having intellectual functioning in the borderline range (Baio et al., 2018). Given that the diagnostic criteria for ASD included a requirement for language impairment until the recent revision in the DSM-5, it is common for children with an ASD to have noted language difficulties (Kjelgaard & Tager-Flusberg, 2001).

Developmental Continuities and Discontinuities (Course)

There is widespread evidence of *homotypic continuity* for ASD and the disorder is considered chronic. Indeed, the two key impairments characteristic of ASD (impairments in social communication and interaction and restricted, repetitive patterns of interest and behavior) can be observed in very young children—providing strong evidence of homotypic continuity in the developmental course of ASD.

As early as six months of age, an infant who will go on to receive a diagnosis of ASD evidences reduced vocalizations, attempts to seek physical contact, orientations towards faces, and social smiles (Maestro et al., 2002). Further, non-response to name has been observed by 8–10 months, as have anomalies in visual attending (Werner et al., 2000). Non-response to name is often cited as a behavior that best distinguishes between ASD and other developmental delays (Dawson & Faja, 2008), correctly classifying children less than one year of age in 85% of cases (Osterling et al., 2002). These symptoms continue to be characteristic of infants with ASD as they age—in fact, symptoms become more pronounced by 12 months (e.g., Zwaigenbaum et al., 2005). Additionally, reduced showing and pointing, social smiling, and imitation are noted in children with ASD at 12 months (Maestro et al., 2002).

As children age, impairments in social communication become more pronounced with regard to language. By 12 months, children with ASD can be distinguished from their at-risk siblings based upon *receptive and expressive language* abilities as well as non-verbal communication like gestures (Zwaigenbaum et al., 2005). Although expressive language development is often more readily observed and focused on by clinicians and parents, numerous studies have shown that both are developmentally delayed in ASD (Hudry et al., 2013; Landa & Garret-Mayer, 2006). Communication difficulties continue across developmental stages such that by two years of age, children with ASD differ from typically developing children in their ability to understand verbal instructions, make complex vocalizations themselves, imitate verbal prompts, and use words and phrases (Werner & Dawson, 2005).

The second key feature of ASD, repetitive patterns of interest and behavior, has also been documented in very young children. For instance, Zwaigenbaum and colleagues (2005) noted that 12-month-old children who would later receive a diagnosis of ASD displayed greater fixation on a single object, demonstrated less visual exploration, and, by 24 months old, demonstrated observable impairments in shifting attention.

Although the convergence of evidence certainly suggests that homotypic continuity is most characteristic of the developmental course of ASD, an example of heterogeneity in the developmental course of ASD is *autistic regression.* Autistic regression is estimated to occur in a third of children with ASD and is characterized by largely typical early development, followed by a loss of skills and emergence of symptoms between 15 and 30 months of age (Barger, Campbell, & McDonough, 2013). Following this developmental regression, children follow the typical development of ASD (Duffy et al., 2014).

A Developmental Psychopathology Model of the Etiology of ASD

Figure 6.1 depicts a developmental psychopathology model of ASD, thereby laying out the etiology of the disorder. This framework organizes etiological factors for which empirical support exists by *level of explanation* (see Chapter 2) and shows how risk and protective factors interact in the development of ASD.

GENETIC FACTORS (DISTAL RISK FACTORS)

Family and twin studies

It is widely agreed upon that genetics play a role in the development of ASD. Findings from twin and family studies indicate high heritability for ASD and are largely the basis for this current consensus. Estimated *concordance rates* vary widely across twin studies (Tick, Bolton, Happé, & Risdijk, 2016) with rates among *monozygotic twins* ranging between 64% and 91% and rates among *dizygotic twins* estimated as high as 31%. In the families of an individual with ASD, nearly 20% of siblings will meet diagnostic criteria for ASD (Sandin et al., 2014) and many siblings will show some symptoms (Rubenstein & Chawla, 2018).

Because concordance rates are much higher among monozygotic twins than among dizygotic twins or siblings, it is hypothesized that ASD is caused by multiple genes interacting (Ronemus, Iossifov, Levy, & Wigler, 2014). That is, ASD likely has an underlying *genetic heterogeneity*. In other words, the fact that concordance rates drop rapidly as the two individuals in question become more genetically dissimilar (i.e., monozygotic twins → dizygotic twins → non-twin siblings) suggests to researchers that ASD susceptibility is caused by several genes rather than just one.

Molecular genetic studies

ASD cannot be traced to a single genetic mutation or chromosomal abnormality (De Rubeis et al., 2014). Though more than 100 specific genes have been examined in relation to ASD (Iossifov et al., 2014), researchers have derived limited conclusions in this area. Still, a genetic cause for ASD can be identified in approximately 20–30% of children (Ronemus et al., 2014) and genetic research in ASD has converged on three core chromosomal regions: chromosome 2q (Li, Zou, & Brown, 2012), 7q (Klein-Tasman & Mervis, 2018), and 17q (Reilly, Gallagher, Chen, Leader, & Shen, 2017). Regarding chromosome 7, several studies have tied specific genes associated with cerebellar development to ASD.

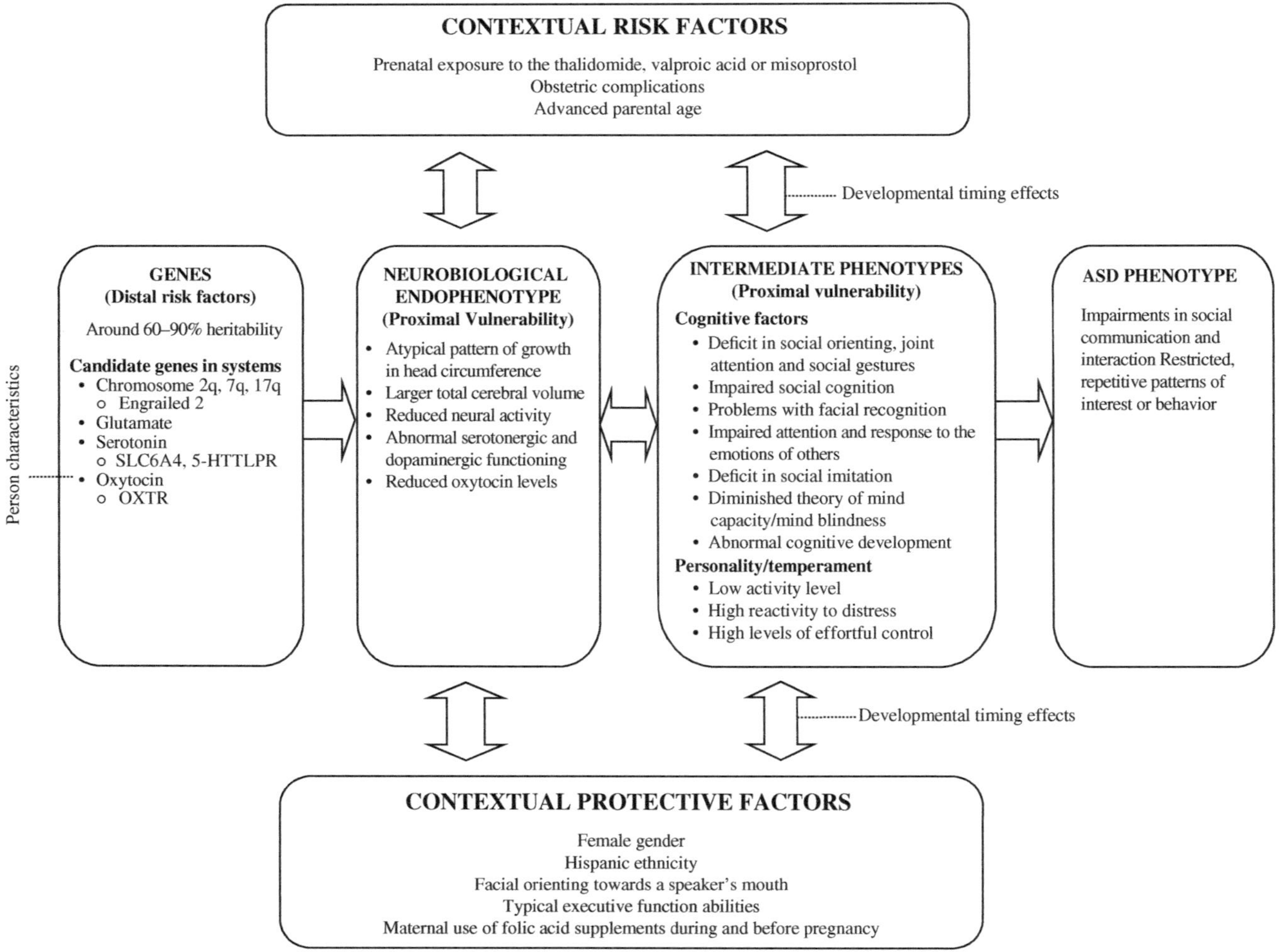

FIGURE 6.1 A Developmental Psychopathology Model of ASD

Specifically, a gene called Engrailed 2 has been linked with ASD and, in mice, is key to cerebellar development (Soltani et al., 2017), a known area of abnormality among many individuals with ASD (James et al., 2013).

Additionally, genes associated with various neurotransmitters, including glutamate and serotonin, have been linked to ASD. Specifically, the deletion of a gene called Neurexin 1, which is involved in the neurotransmitter *glutamate*, has been linked to ASD (Schaaf et al., 2012). Further, the *serotonin* transporter gene, SLC6A4 (located in chromosomal region 17q), has been implicated in several studies examining the genetic basis of ASD (Jaiswal et al., 2015), and research is beginning to link this gene and symptom severity in ASD. In a large study of more than 1,500 individuals, a short allele (5-HTTLPR) associated with this gene of the serotonin system was noted in individuals with an ASD (Devlin et al., 2005). This same short allele has been linked with increased cerebral size, a commonly noted neurological feature associated with ASD (Brandenburg & Blatt, 2019).

A number of studies have also identified links between ASD and genes related to *oxytocin*, a neuropeptide hormone implicated in a range of social interactions. Variants of the oxytocin receptor gene, OXTR, for instance, have been associated with ASD (LoParo & Waldman, 2015) and, together, suggest that this is a promising area of continued research.

Family history studies

Although continued research on the genetic bases of ASD is needed, a number of studies suggest that autistic traits are significantly heritable—with heritability estimates ranging from 60 to 90% (Meek et al., 2013). For instance, research has shown that first-degree relatives of individuals with ASD demonstrated autistic traits that were above normative values in the general population (Berthoz, Lalanne, Crane, & Hill, 2013; Rubenstein & Chawla, 2018). The collection of sub-diagnostic autistic traits seen in relatives is commonly referred to as the broader autism phenotype (Gerdts & Bernier, 2011) and has become a burgeoning area of research (Rubenstein & Chawla, 2018).

NEUROBIOLOGICAL FACTORS (PROXIMAL VULNERABILITY FACTORS)

Head circumference

An atypical pattern of growth in head circumference has been identified in individuals with ASD (Sacco, Gabriele, & Persico, 2015). Specifically, small or average circumference at birth is followed by rapid growth beginning at approximately 4 months (Sacco et al., 2015). This growth then slows after 12 months such that circumference returns to normal limits (McKeague et al., 2015). The rapid head growth that occurs between 4 and 12 months precedes and overlaps with the first behavioral symptoms of ASD whereas the deceleration of circumference growth appears to coincide with deceleration in the acquisition (or loss) of skills (McKeague et al., 2015).

Structural and functional brain imaging findings

Structural brain imaging studies conducted in children with ASD indicate atypical brain development. Anomalies with regard to the brain size, amygdala, and brain lateralization appear to be most consistent. Specifically, individuals with ASD have larger total cerebral volume—or brain weight— than children with comparable IQ between the ages of two and four when examined via *magnetic resonance imaging*. The increase in volume has been attributed to enlargement of white matter in the cerebrum and cerebellum as well as enlargement of gray matter in the cerebrum (Fernández, Mollinedo-Gajate, & Peñagarikano, 2018). The brains of children with ASD grow more rapidly than in typically developing children shortly after birth, thought to lead to an anomalous developmental trajectory. The amygdala, specifically, is enlarged among children with ASD, which has been linked to more severe symptom expression (Fernández et al., 2018). Anatomical differences have also been noted in other structures including the hippocampus and precuneus, as well as white matter structures (Lai, Lombard, & Baron-Cohen, 2014). In addition to these areas of structural anomaly, several researchers have identified reduced neural activity in a network of brain regions—including the medial prefrontal cortex and amygdala, among other regions (Lai et al., 2014)—during tasks that require the individual to think and make accurate judgments about social stimuli (Fernández et al., 2018).

Neurotransmitters

Current research has noted anomalies in several neurotransmitters, the chemical messengers of the brain, in individuals with ASD. In particular, studies have identified abnormal functioning of neurotransmitter systems related to serotonin and dopamine. Elevated levels of serotonin, a neurotransmitter that innervates brain regions associated with emotional expression and social behavior (Ettinger, 2017), have been documented in individuals with ASD (Gabriele, Sacco, & Persico, 2014). Chevallier and colleagues (2012) have also proposed the Social Motivation Theory of Autism, which implicates the dopaminergic system—a key reward processing center of the brain. Early in development, infants attend to others and their social cues, because social contact activates the dopamine reward circuit, thereby producing a sense of pleasure. Researchers hypothesize that this experience of pleasure contributes to continued attention towards social cues (e.g., faces) throughout development and related growth in social abilities (Greene, Walsh, Mosner, & Dichter, 2019).

Hormones

Blood oxytocin levels are reduced in children with ASD (Yang et al., 2015) and ASD has been linked to anomalies in the oxytocin receptor gene (see Section 6.5.1, Genetic Factors). While findings are mixed (Wang, Wang, Rong, He, & Yang, 2019), there is some support for the oxytocin suppression hypothesis in ASD from studies that demonstrated reduced repetitive behaviors (Hollander et al., 2003) and improved social functioning (Anagnostou et al., 2012) after oxytocin administration. Indeed, even small doses of synthetic oxytocin delivered via a nasal spray have produced changes in the social behavior of individuals with ASD, including increased eye contact (Andari et al., 2010) and emotion recognition (Guastella et al., 2010). Building on previous research, Dadds and colleagues (2014) published the first randomized control trial evaluating intranasally administered oxytocin as an intervention for children with ASD. However, during the 5-day intervention, intranasal oxytocin *did not* significantly improve any of the symptoms or social interaction variables measured.

TEMPERAMENT

Researchers have documented unique *temperament* profiles among infants and young children who go on to receive a diagnosis of ASD (del Rosario et al., 2014). Zwaigenbaum and colleagues (2005) conducted a large-scale *longitudinal* study of infant siblings of children with ASD in order to assess a high-risk group, as well as infants without any family risk of ASD. Children who went on to develop ASD were rated as less active by their parents at 6 months and demonstrated less visual exploration at 12 months. Further, the same children demonstrated more frequent and intense reactivity to distress by 12 months of age and continued to demonstrate diminished inhibitory control at 24 months. Bolton and colleagues (2012) found that increased activity levels and reduced distractibility at 24 months differentiated toddlers with ASD from neurotypical controls. Additionally, they reported that elevated traits of ASD at 6 months of age were associated with less activity and intensity while elevated traits of ASD at 24 months of age were associated with more activity and intensity. Unique temperament profiles are also apparent among older children with ASD (del Rosario et al., 2014). Children with ASD between 3 and 8 years of age exhibit reduced adaptability, persistence, and sensory responsiveness (Hepburn & Stone, 2006) and decreased attention focusing, inhibitory control, and soothability (Konstantareas & Stewart 2006) relative to neurotypical controls. De Pauw and colleagues (2011) reported that children with ASD between 8 and 12 years of age were rated higher in negative affect and lower on effortful control and surgency than typical controls.

COGNITIVE FACTORS

The cognitive factors described below are among those that play a key role in ASD. Although it should be noted that individuals with ASD have differing degrees of impairment in each of these domains, and, therefore, these factors influence individual developmental trajectories differently, research has identified important links between these factors and ASD.

Social cognitive

Social cognitive factors, the mental processes that facilitate understanding people and interactions, underlie social communication and social behaviors (Happé et al., 2017). Such factors are present in infancy and provide the foundations for increasingly complex social behaviors (Davis & Carter, 2014). Faja and Dawson (2017) described five domains of social functioning affected in ASD—social orienting, face processing, attention to emotional cues, joint attention, and motor imitation. The term "*social orienting*" describes the spontaneous tendency to orient towards social stimuli (Dawson, Meltzoff, Osterling, Rinaldi, & Brown, 1998). Children with ASD often have difficulty recognizing and attending to others' social cues (e.g., facial expressions) (Jellema et al., 2009). Further, infants who fail to spontaneously orient towards social stimuli miss the opportunity to engage in appropriate social interactions, thereby altering their developmental pathways (Mundy & Neal, 2001). Notably, Dawson and colleagues (2004) found that children with ASD demonstrated more impairments in both social and non-social orienting than did children with intellectual disability or typically developing children, and impairments were substantially more profound for social stimuli, specifically.

Perhaps also hinged upon social orienting, *facial recognition and processing* is impaired in individuals with ASD. Children with ASD attend less to faces, overall, and less to key facial features than individuals without ASD (Trepagnier, Sebrechts, & Peterson, 2002). Further, while typical facial processing includes focus on the eyes of others, individuals with ASD do not give preference to this region and, instead, look at the eyes of others as often as their chins (Pelphrey et al., 2002). Diminished visual attention toward faces in ASD has been found in toddlers (Dawson et al., 1998), adolescents (Klin, Jones, Schultz, Volkmar, & Cohen, 2002), and adults (Volkmar & Mayes, 1990) and seem to be unique to ASD. These impairments tend to co-occur with impaired attention to emotional cues of others. Difficulties attending to, or recognizing, social cues such as others' facial expressions, body language, and emotional states are often observed in ASD (Chawarska, Volkmar, & Klin, 2010; Pelphrey et al., 2002).

Joint attention, which is the ability to coordinate attention with another person such that awareness of an object is shared (Mundy et al., 1986), provides a foundation for social communication and theory of mind (Murza, Schwartz, Hahs-Vaughn, & Nye, 2016). A child smiling and pointing at something that captures their interest, then looking back and forth between the object and another person in the room exemplifies *initiating* joint attention; a child following an adults' gaze and/or point toward an interesting out-of-reach object represents an example of *responding* to joint attention. Reduced initiation of and response to joint attention has been found among toddlers who later receive a diagnosis of ASD (Cornew, Dobkins, Akshoomoff, McCleery & Carver, 2012), and noted in children with ASD as early as one year of age (Osterling & Dawson, 1994).

Finally, *imitation* of motor movements (Hertzig, Snow, & Sherman, 1989), facial expressions (Loveland et al., 1994), imaginary actions (Rogers et al., 1996), and vocalizations (Dawson & Adams, 1984) is impaired in many children with ASD and considered an early core deficit (Dawson & Lewy, 1989). In fact, infants later diagnosed with ASD displayed atypical imitation within the first 12 months of life (Zwaigenbaum et al., 2005). Difficulties with imitation differentiate young children who have ASD from those who have other developmental delays and/or communication disorders (Stone, Ousley, & Littleford, 1997).

Theory of mind

Theory of mind, the ability to represent mental states of oneself and others, is thought to contribute to social problems in ASD (Happé et al., 2017). In a landmark study conducted by Baron-Cohen, Leslie, and Frith (1985), 11-year-old children with ASD were compared with age-matched children who had Down's Syndrome and with four-year-old typically developing children on a "false belief" task. This activity was designed to detect their ability to form theories about others' thinking, and it described a doll character (Sally) placing an object in a basket (see Figure 6.2). Then, another character (Anne) hid the object in a different location while Sally was out of the room. Participants were asked where Sally would look for the object on return. The majority of children with ASD said that Sally would look for the object in its actual location, whereas the typically developing preschoolers and children with Down's syndrome believed Sally would look for the object where she left it. That is, most children with ASD did not demonstrate an understanding that their own knowledge and the knowledge they could attribute to others

FIGURE 6.2 Sally Anne Task. *Source:* Frith, U. (1989). Reproduced with permissions of John Wiley & Sons.

(i.e., Sally) could be different. Based upon this study, it was suggested that some children with ASD might be unable to consider others' thoughts or beliefs—a deficit famously coined "mindblindness" (Baron-Cohen et al., 1995).

While theory of mind deficits are widely considered central to ASD (Baron-Cohen, 2000), theory of mind capabilities are increasingly viewed as being on a continuum, wherein individuals with ASD show differing levels of difficulty with, but not a complete lack of, a theory of mind (Sharp & Venta, 2012). For instance, children with ASD display difficulties in understanding complex mental states (Baron-Cohen, 1991), have reduced insight into deception (Yirmiya & Shulman, 1996), and tend to conflate memories of their own actions with memories of the actions of other people (Russell & Jarrold, 1999). Although many individuals with ASD will pass a false belief task later in development, they continue to struggle with more complex tasks, such as understanding others' behavior in broad social contexts and making inferences about others' thoughts or understanding non-literal speech (Happé, 1994). Taken together, a solid body of literature supports reduced theory of mind capacity in individuals with ASD, although the belief that theory of mind is completely absent in ASD has been abandoned.

Intellectual development

Cognitive abilities related to the measurement of intelligence vary widely among individuals with ASD, with scores on measures of intelligence (i.e., "IQ") ranging from the severely impaired to gifted range. The co-occurrence of intellectual disability (ID) with ASD is common, with current large-scale data gathered by the ADDM Network indicating that 31% of children in the sample had measured intelligence in the ID range, while 44% had scores in the average or above average range (Baio et al., 2018). Zablotsky and colleagues (2019) also noted that ID comorbid with ASD has been decreasing, a finding they attributed to broadened ASD diagnostic criteria.

Understanding the intellectual functioning level of a person with ASD can help with discussing prognosis and also with developing plans of treatment and care (Matson & Shoemaker, 2009). Predictors of impaired intellectual ability can be detected quite early—by 14 months, and many children with ASD demonstrate difficulties in motor skills, language, and intelligence compared to language-delayed children without ASD (Landa & Garrett-Mayer, 2006). One domain of early cognitive functioning, sensorimotor as early as 6 months, was found to predict ASD diagnosis at 24 months (Estes et al., 2015). This led the researchers to hypothesize that "[e]arly motor deficits could play a role in later motor impairments, atypical control of eye movements, and/or delays in development of gestures such as pointing, associated with the emergence of joint attention" (p. 7). Further, impaired language has been linked to early social orienting impairments in individuals with ASD (Sullivan et al., 2007), suggesting that language impairment may underlie (or share a common etiology) other difficulties noted in ASD.

Intelligence appears to predict, to some degree, the course of ASD. Bryson and colleagues (2007), for instance, identified two groups of children with ASD: one group that demonstrated cognitive decline between one and two years of life and a second group that did not. The subgroup that experienced cognitive decline was characterized by more severe and earlier emerging symptoms. However, researchers have found that children with ASD often demonstrate individual cognitive profile variability (Nowell et al., 2015), though research in this area has yielded mixed findings with regard to the nature and meaning of intra-individual profile variability (Nowell, Goin-Kochel, McQuillin, & Mire, 2017).

Even individuals who have ASD *without* intellectual disabilities often have atypical intellectual development. For instance, while typically developing children demonstrate improved problem-solving abilities when mathematical calculations, for example, are placed in the context of daily life, individuals with ASD do not benefit from this additional context. Numerous studies examining problem-solving behavior among individuals with ASD suggest that detailed, focused thinking is characteristic of ASD, whereas global, broad-strokes thinking is de-emphasized (Frith, 2003).

Contextual Risk Factors

Although variation in twin concordance rates indicates that environmental factors are key in the emergence of ASD, this research has proven largely inconsistent. One of the first contextual risk factors investigated is prenatal exposure to thalidomide. In one study of 100 adults exposed to thalidomide prenatally, one-third developed ASD (Miller & Strömland, 1993). However, no additional studies have investigated the relationship between thalidomide and ASD (Ornoy, Weinstein-Fudim, & Ergaz, 2015). In utero exposures to other substances, including insecticides, pesticides, misoprostol, and SSRIs, as well as folic acid deficiency, have also been recognized as possible contributors of ASD (Ornoy et al., 2015). Additionally, maternal fever, diabetes, and Rubella infection during pregnancy (Ornoy et al., 2015) as well as prenatal exposure to valproate (a drug used to control seizures) (Bromley, Mawer, Clayton-Smith, & Baker, 2008) have been linked to increased risk of ASD in children.

Additionally, a large study of perinatal risk factors among children with ASD (Glasson et al., 2004) showed that individuals with ASD experienced higher rates of reported obstetric complications. Specifically, mothers reported experiencing more frequent threatened abortion, epidural caudal anesthesia use, and labor induction, and noted that infants were more likely to have experienced distress or been delivered via cesarean section (though not specified whether these were planned or emergent) (Glasson et al. 2004). Other studies have identified advanced parental reproductive age as conferring risk for ASD, although the mechanism of transmission is not yet well understood (Lai et al., 2014).

It should be noted, however, that these risk factors are not directly causally linked with ASD, as there are a large number of children who experience these obstetric complications and do not go on to receive a diagnosis of ASD.

Recent controversy has surrounded the possible risk for ASD conferred by the measles–mumps–rubella (MMR) vaccine. Support for a link between this vaccine and ASD was first published by Andrew Wakefield and colleagues in 1999, resulting in an increased fear of the MMR vaccine and a subsequent decline in vaccination rates. However, a number of studies have failed to confirm the findings that Wakefield reported (e.g., Jacobson, 2004; Wilson et al., 2003) and, in 2010, the study was officially retracted due to questionable participant sampling and manipulated evidence. In the same year, Andrew Wakefield was found guilty of professional misconduct and lost the right to practice medicine in the United Kingdom. The Wakefield study is currently widely regarded as fraudulent and consensus of evidence indicates no connection between the MMR vaccine and ASD.

An older controversy regarding the causes of ASD includes the belief that it is caused by a cold, rejecting parent—termed a "refrigerator mother." Indeed, numerous scholars described the parents of children with ASD as detached, uninterested, vague, and cold (e.g., Bettelheim, 1967). This belief is considered a substantial misstep in developing theories of the etiology of ASD and supporting families with a child with this condition. Indeed, this belief, propagated by many clinicians, compounded difficulties for parents—in addition to navigating the developmental disability of their child, they also carried guilt and blame for being the cause. Although interactions between parents and children with ASD may appear atypical to outside observers, it is now well established that these interactions are characteristic of the biologically based predispositions of the child, rather than the result of insufficient or inadequate caregiving. Indeed, research has suggested that the parents of children with ASD are really quite similar to those of children with other disabilities (Doussard-Roosevelt et al., 2003).

Contextual Protective Factors

Few studies have focused on contextual factors that protect against the development of ASD, and instead research has aimed to identify factors that improve treatment outcomes. Based upon a few, tentative explorations of protective factors in ASD, those that show possible promise are: female gender (although findings are mixed and research suggests that females may be critically under-diagnosed, see Section 6.2.2) (Werling & Geschwind, 2013), Hispanic ethnicity (though this is likely to be more related to access barriers to healthcare) (Palmer, Walker,

Mandell, Bayles, & Miller, 2010), and facial movement towards a speaker's mouth. Additionally, it has been hypothesized that typical executive function abilities (e.g., regulatory function) should be thought of as a protective factor in the development of ASD, rather than thinking of deficits in executive functioning as a specific risk factor (Bedford et al., 2019). Regarding maternal behaviors, use of folic acid supplements during and before pregnancy as well as breastfeeding (Tseng et al., 2019) have received early support as potential protective factors. Additionally, typical levels of maternal and fetal melatonin during pregnancy have recently been hypothesized to play a protective role (Jin et al., 2018).

GENE–ENVIRONMENT INTERPLAY

As genetic studies of ASD suggest, most researchers agree that multifactorial origins and heterogeneous etiologies are common in ASD. Genetic and environmental interactions may be one reason why this heterogeneity is so common.

Gene–environment correlations

These correlations suggest that genetic origins predict the types of environments that people are likely to experience. Research on gene–environment correlations in children with ASD is lacking (Mandy & Lai, 2016); however, Meek and colleagues (2013) conducted a review of related research, allowing them to draw some preliminary conclusions. For instance, they reviewed evidence showing that children with ASD tend to engage in more solitary and less cooperative play—behaviors that are known to have genetic roots. They posited a conceptual "multiplier" model in which genes produce certain behaviors in individuals with ASD, which, in turn, predict the environments to which they are exposed and subsequent behaviors. In their model, genetic influences set a trajectory for the individual, creating a self-reinforcing cycle, wherein, for example, a child is born with some genetically influenced capacity for joint engagement that is reinforced by parenting behaviors (e.g., following the child's lead) and thereby improves and predicts future joint engagement. In the case of a child with a tendency to avoid joint engagement, the parent may match non-engagement over time and reinforce the child's own non-engagement, multiplying the child's preference for non-engagement (Meek et al., 2013)

Gene–environment interactions

Two epidemiological studies of ASD and perinatal events point to important gene–environment interactions. As discussed previously, Glasson and colleagues (2004) examined a group of 465 children with ASD, their siblings, and a control group. They noted that perinatal complications (including advanced parental age, epidural caudal anesthesia use, labor induction, and fetal distress) were most common in the ASD group, but also more common in the unaffected siblings than in the control group. Chien and colleagues (2019) replicated these findings in a study of 323 children with ASD, their siblings, and a control group of children of typical development. These results suggest that ASD might result from a biologically based sensitivity to the same environmental stimuli experienced by unaffected siblings. Despite enthusiasm about these emerging gene–environment interaction studies among individuals with ASD, Chaste and Leboyer (2012) note that the number of studies conducted in humans is very limited and difficult to conduct due to both a low statistical power to detect these interactions and a lack of replication across studies. Moreover, researchers consistently remark about the vast amount of heterogeneity in the genetic basis of ASD, making the study of gene–environment interactions highly complex (Mandy & Lai, 2016).

Developmental Timing Effects: The Interplay of Normal and Abnormal Development

The developmental psychopathology model of ASD points to the emergence of symptoms very early in life and their continuity across the lifespan. Dawson and colleagues (2005) have put forth the *social motivation hypothesis* to explain developmental timing effects in ASD, suggesting that many social impairments in ASD are secondary to a primary impairment in social motivation occurring very early in life. Moreover, Dawson and colleagues (2005) cite evidence suggesting that there is a genetic basis to social motivation that manifests in early social impairments in infants with ASD. Importantly, in this hypothesis, reduced social motivation is thought to limit the amount of time that children spend focused on social stimuli like faces, voices, and gestures. This hypothesis points to important timing effects—that is, *early* impairments in social motivation place a child on a trajectory that ultimately can result in the profound social impairments noted in ASD. Notably, their hypothesis is critically focused on the sequential order of emerging deficits, and it could be speculated that social a-motivation later in life (as might be observed in depression) would not be associated with increasing social impairments to the same degree.

Based on what we know about early, typical development, we can imagine how being born with reduced social motivation might affect all aspects of development later on. For instance, if an infant is not motivated to look towards his or her caregivers, he will miss exposure to smiles and frowns. Decreased exposure to facial expressions in others, then, might contribute to a later difficulty in making his or her own facial expressions as a form of communication. By the same token, the same child may then grow up and continue struggling to understand and succeed in relationships because he or she is not able to extract social and emotional information from facial expressions. Of course, development is complex and the social motivation hypothesis does not paint such a simple or linear picture of developing social impairments in ASD. However, the basic premise is that children with ASD are predisposed, by reduced social motivation, to miss out on typical learning experiences (which take place in a social context), thereby leading to more profound social impairments later on.

Interventions

Evidence is accumulating in support of early interventions focused on social functioning and language among children with ASD. Chorpita and colleagues (2011) reported the strongest support for intensive behavioral interventions, including Applied Behavior Analysis (ABA), which are currently considered the gold standard for early intervention in children with ASD.

INTENSIVE BEHAVIORAL INTERVENTIONS

Behavioral treatments were studied among individuals with ASD as early as 1987 (Lovaas, 1987) with promising results. Intensive behavioral treatment includes aspects of ABA and discrete trial training; a traditional intensive early behavioral intervention program recommends on average 40 hours per week of direct intervention conducted by the child's therapists and parents in different settings. ABA is a more general term that refers to the use of principles to teach new skills and shape behavior. In general, learning is based upon giving an instruction (called an antecedent), waiting for the child's behavior, and providing an immediate consequence. The repeated pairing of these three components produces learning. Several *meta-analytic studies* have documented the effectiveness of intensive behavioral treatments for improving core impairments, as well as IQ, language, and *adaptive behavior* in individuals with ASD (Kuppens et al., 2011). In discrete trial training, skills (including self-help, communication, and social skills; Sturmey & Fitzer, 2007) are task analyzed (reduced into simple components) and taught to the individual one-on-one using properties from *operant conditioning* including reinforcement, chaining, shaping, prompts, and extinction (Peters-Scheffer, Didden, Korzilius, & Sturmey, 2011). In this treatment, once a skill is task analyzed, trained therapists teach the small components to a child one by one and with frequent repetition.

Positive reinforcement (e.g., provision of a positive, motivating stimulus, such as candy or praise) is used each time that a child produces the desired behavior. To teach a skill, such as putting on shoes, a therapist might first start by modeling how to open the closet door where the shoes are located, for instance, and then prompt the child to do the same thing. She would then reward the child for compliance and rehearse the task several more times until mastery before moving on to the next step. Once each step of the behavior is learned, the behaviors can then be strung together to form the desired behavior. A similar process would be used to teach communication, play, social, and other adaptive skills. An example of discrete trial training can be seen online at https://www.youtube.com/watch?v=cp_gzUTCm8g. Due to its repetitive and highly structured nature, discrete trial training can take many hours per week to make progress.

EARLY SCHOOL-BASED INTERVENTIONS

Early intervention is critical for children with ASD; therefore, professionals have focused on providing early, intense intervention with children—often times through the public education system. Dawson and Faja (2008) summarize common factors present in early interventions, including a curriculum focused on imitation, language, play, and social functioning; developmental consideration, supportive teaching, behavioral intervention for reducing interfering behaviors, parental involvement, and transition to naturalistic environments; delivery by highly trained staff and supervision and review mechanisms; intensive delivery lasting at least 25 hours per week for 2 years or more; and initiation of the intervention by ages 2–4. Interventions containing these elements show a positive impact on cognitive and language abilities, as well as educational placement (Faja & Dawson, 2006) for up to 50% of children with ASD (Dawson & Faja, 2008). Additionally, children with ASD often receive other school-based services including therapeutic interventions (speech, occupational, and physical therapy) as well as academic modifications and accommodations.

OTHER PSYCHOSOCIAL TREATMENTS

Other treatments, including Parent-Mediated Interventions (e.g., *Early Start Denver Model* and *Parent Training for Disruptive Behavior-The RUBI Autism Network*), Cognitive Behavioral Therapy, and Social Skills training often occur in clinical settings and have been identified as "established" interventions for children with ASD based on careful review from the National Standards Project. The National Standards Project, developed with the aim of addressing the need for evidence-based standards in the treatment of ASD, places several treatments into the "established level of evidence" category (2015). Further information on the National Standards Project can be found at their website, http://www.nationalautismcenter.org/national-standards-project/. It should be noted that the heterogeneity of ASD presentations (noted throughout this chapter) makes traditional *randomized controlled trials* (RCTs) somewhat difficult to execute and interpret. Though some RCTs have been conducted, much of the research used to identify evidence-based treatments for ASD is based upon single-subject case designs.

PSYCHOPHARMACOLOGICAL TREATMENTS

There are no medications that are approved by the Food and Drug Administration (FDA) to treat the *core* symptoms of ASD (Volkmar et al., 2014), but almost half (48.5%) of insured children in the US with an ASD diagnosis are prescribed at least one medication (Madden et al., 2017). Medications are most often prescribed for children with ASD to target comorbidities (Madden et al., 2017). Evidence supporting psychopharmacological treatments for symptoms typically associated with ASD (e.g., hyperactivity, irritability, anxiety) is limited, although medications have been shown to reduce some symptoms that commonly cause problems for individuals with ASD. Currently, there are two FDA-approved medications meant to address *secondary* symptoms within the pediatric population with ASD: Abilify (aripiprazole) and Risperdal (risperidone) (Food and Drug Administration, 2005, 2014). Abilify, a second-generation antipsychotic medication, has been shown to reduce irritability in children with ASD. Risperdal, also a second-generation antipsychotic medication, has been shown to reduce tantrums, aggression, social withdrawal, and self-injurious behavior in children with ASD (FDA, 2005, 2014). Additionally, the use of serotonin reuptake inhibitors has shown some promise in reducing repetitive behaviors (Lai, Lombardo, & Baron-Cohen, 2014). Finally, the use of stimulant medications has been recommended for individuals with ASD who also experience symptoms of ADHD (Volkmar et al., 2014).

Chapter Summary

This chapter discusses ASD, a diagnosis characterized by persistent impairments in social functioning and restricted, repetitive interests and behaviors. It is a highly prevalent childhood condition, affecting more children than medical diagnoses like cancer and Type 1 diabetes. Although ASDs are chronic, their etiology and prognosis are multifactorial. We described the contextual, genetic, and neurobiological factors associated with ASD and briefly introduced currently well-supported interventions tailored to this diagnosis.

Further Reading

Dapretto, M., Davies, M. S., Pfeifer, J. H., Scott, A. A., Sigman, M., Bookheimer, S. Y., & Lacoboni, M. (2006). Understanding emotions in others: Mirror neuron dysfunction in children with ASD. *Nature Neuroscience*, 9(1), 28–30. doi: 10.1038/nn1611.

Faja, S., & Dawson, G. (2006). Early intervention for autism. In J. L. Luby (Ed.), *Handbook of preschool mental health: Development, disorders, and treatment* (pp. 388–416). New York, NY, USA: Guilford Press.

Wilson, K., Mills, E., Ross, C., McGowan, J., & Jadad, A. (2003). Association of autistic spectrum disorder and the measles, mumps, and rubella vaccine: A systematic review of current epidemiological evidence. *Archives of Pediatrics & Adolescent Medicine*, 157(7), 628–634.

Discussion/Essay Questions

1. Discuss how impaired social orienting might underlie a trajectory of increasing social dysfunction among individuals with ASD.
2. How might the prognosis of an individual with ASD be affected by their race/ethnicity and gender? Discuss at least three ways in which these factors would be expected to affect prognosis.
3. There is little current research on protective factors in ASD research. Propose one protective factor that you would like to see studied and use evidence from the chapter to support your choice.
4. Controversy surrounds the relation between the MMR vaccine and ASD that was reported by Andrew Wakefield in 1999. Hypothesize and discuss how this fraudulent study has affected research and treatment of ASD, as well as public health more generally.

Glossary

Adaptive behavior allows an individual to complete tasks of daily living independently.

Applied Behavior Analysis (ABA) is application of evidence-based strategies to change socially significant behaviors in a systematic manner.

Autism Spectrum Disorder (ASD) is a neurodevelopmental disorder characterized by deficits in social communication and interaction as well as restricted interests and repetitive patterns of behavior.

Autistic regression is when a child appears to follow a typical developmental trajectory but then either loses or stops gaining speech and social skills and is subsequently diagnosed with ASD.

Concordance rates is the likelihood that two persons (e.g., siblings) with shared genes will develop the same certain characteristic, such as an organic disease.

Discriminant validity is used to determine whether specific concepts that are not supposed to related are in reality unrelated.

Dizygotic twins are siblings born in the same pregnancy that developed separate eggs which were fertilized by separate sperm cells. Often referred to as fraternal twins.

Echolalia is non-functional repetition of another person's speech.

Epidemiological studies explore how often diseases or disorders occur in different groups of individuals and why.

Expressive language is the use of words, sentences, gestures, and writing to convey meaning and messages to others.

Facial recognition and processing is the ability of individuals to follow another person's gaze, identify a familiar person by their face and/or recognize emotions in others based on their facial expressions.

Genetic heterogeneity is the occurrence of the same phenotypes (e.g., observable characteristics) despite differing genotypes between individuals.

Glutamate is an excitatory neurotransmitter that is involved in cognitive processes such as learning and memory.

Homotypic continuity is a term used when disorder predicts itself at a later point in time.

Imitation is the ability to copy another person's speech or behavior.

Joint attention is the ability to coordinate attention with another person such that awareness of an object is shared (Mundy et al., 1986).

Longitudinal research involves gathering information about an individual or group of individuals over a long time period.

Magnetic resonance imaging (MRI) is a procedure in which magnets and radio waves are used to create an image of organs and soft tissue inside the body.

Meta-analytic studies- are research studies that involve a statistical analysis combining the results of multiple scientific studies that address the same or very similar questions.

Monozygotic twins are siblings born from the same pregnancy that developed from one egg and one sperm cell, which then split into two separate embryos after fertilization. Often referred to as identical twins.

Operant conditioning is a type of learning that occurs through systematically reinforcing specific behaviors to increase or strengthen behavior over time and punishing specific behaviors in order to decrease or weaken a behavior over time.

Oxytocin **is** a hormone and neurotransmitter that is created by the pituitary gland and influences social interactions, such as attachment and pair bonding.

Receptive language is the ability to understand spoken language.

Serotonin is a neurotransmitter that influences social behavior, mood, emotions, impulsivity, aggression, memory, sleep, and appetite.

Social Motivation Hypothesis is the idea that individuals with ASD display deficits in processing social rewards.

Social orienting is the spontaneous tendency to orient towards social stimuli, and deficits are notable among children with ASD (Dawson et al., 1998).

Temperament covers relatively stable individual differences in behavioral tendencies that exert bidirectional influences upon the social environment (Thomas and Chess, 1977)

Theory of Mind is the ability to represent mental states of oneself and others, or mentalizing, and is sometimes considered a social cognitive factor and is thought to contribute to social problems in ASD (Happé et al., 2017)

References

Anagnostou, E., Soorya, L., Chaplin, W., Bartz, J., Halpern, D., Wasserman, S., & Hollander, E. (2012). Intranasal oxytocin versus placebo in the treatment of adults with ASD: A randomized controlled trial. *Molecular Autism*, 3(1), 16. https://doi-org.ezproxy.lib.uh.edu/10.1186/2040-2392-3-16.

Andari, E., Duhamel, J., Zalla, T., Herbrecht, E., Leboyer, M., & Sirigua, A. (2010). Promoting social behavior with oxytocin in high-functioning ASD. *PNAS Proceedings of The National Academy of Sciences of The United States of America*, 107(9), 4389–4394. doi: 10.1073/pnas.0910249107.

American Psychiatric Association (2013). *Diagnostic and statistical manual of mental disorders* (5th ed.). Arlington, VA.

Asperger, H. (1944). Die "Autistischen Psychopathen" im Kindesalter. *European Archives of Psychiatry and Clinical Neuroscience*, 117(1), 76–136.

Baio, J. (2014). Developmental Disabilities Monitoring Network Surveillance Year 2010 Principal Investigators; Centers for Disease Control and Prevention (CDC). Prevalence of ASD among children aged 8 years—Autism and developmental disabilities monitoring network, 11 sites, United States, 2010. *MMWR Surveillance Summaries*, 63, 1–21.

Baio, J., Wiggins, L., Christensen, D. L., Maenner, M. J., Daniels, J., Warren, Z., & Dowling, N. F. (2018). Prevalence of autism spectrum disorder among children aged 8 years—Autism and Developmental Disabilities Monitoring Network, 11 sites, United States, 2014. *MMWR Surveillance Summaries* 67(6), 1–23. doi: 10.15585/mmwr.ss6706a1.

Barger, B. D., Campbell, J. M., & McDonough, J. D. (2013). Prevalence and onset of regression within ASD: A meta-analytic review. *Journal of Autism and Developmental Disorders*, 43(4), 817–828. doi: 10.1007/s10803-012-1621-x.

Baron-Cohen, S. (1991). The theory of mind deficit in autism: How specific is it? *British Journal of Developmental Psychology*, 9(2), 301–314. doi: 10.1111/j.2044-835X.1991.tb00879.x.

Baron-Cohen, S. (2000). Theory of mind and autism: A fifteen year review. In S. Baron-Cohen, H. H. Tager-Flusberg, & D. J. Cohen (Eds.), *Understanding other minds: Perspectives from developmental cognitive neuroscience* (pp. 3–20). Oxford, UK: Oxford University Press.

Baron-Cohen, S., Campbell, R., Karmiloff-Smith, A., Grant, J., & Walker, J. (1995). Are children with autism blind to the mentalistic significance of the eyes? *British Journal of Developmental Psychology*, 13(4), 379–398. doi: 10.1111/j.2044-835X.1995.tb00687.x.

Baron-Cohen, S., Leslie, A. M., & Frith, U. (1985). Does the autistic child have a "theory of mind?" *Cognition*, 21, 37–46.

Baxter, A. J., Brugha, T. S., Erskine, H. E., Scheurer, R. W., Vos, T., & Scott, J. G. (2015). The epidemiology and global burden of ASD. *Psychological Medicine*, 45(3), 601–613.

Bedford, R., Gliga, T., Hendry, A., Jones, E. J. H., Pasco, G., Charman, T., & Pickles, A. (2019). Infant regulatory function acts as a protective factor for later traits of autism spectrum disorder and attention deficit/hyperactivity disorder but not callous unemotional traits. *Journal of Neurodevelopmental Disorders*, 11, 14. https://doi-org.ezproxy.lib.uh.edu/10.1186/s11689-019-9274-0.

Berthoz, S., Lalanne, C., Crane, L., & Hill, E. L. (2013). Investigating emotional impairments in adults with ASD and the broader autism phenotype. *Psychiatry Research*, 208(3), 257–264. doi: 10.1016/j.psychres.2013.05.014.

Bettelheim, B. (1967). *The empty fortress: Infantile autism and the birth of the self.* Oxford, UK: Free Press of Glencoe.

Bolton, P., Golding, J., Emond, A., & Steer, C. (2012). Autism spectrum disorder and autistic traits in the Avon longitudinal study of parents and children: Precursors and early signs. *Journal of the American Academy of Child and Adolescent Psychiatry*, 51(3), 249–260.

Brandenburg, C., & Blatt, G. J. (2019). Differential serotonin transporter (5-HTT) and 5-HT2 receptor density in limbic and neocortical areas of adults and children with ASD: Implications for selective serotonin reuptake inhibitor efficacy. *Journal of Neurochemistry*, 151(5), 642–655. doi: 10.1111/jnc.14832.

Bromley, R. L., Mawer, G., Clayton-Smith, J., & Baker, G. A. (2008). ASD following in utero exposure to antiepileptic drugs. *Neurology*, 71(23), 1923–1924. doi: 10.1212/01.wnl.0000339399.64213.1a.

Bryson, S. E., Zwaigenbaum, L., Brian, J., Roberts, W., Szatmari, P., Rombough, V., & McDermott, C. (2007). A prospective case series of high-risk infants who developed autism. *Journal of Autism and Developmental Disorders*, 37(1), 12–24. doi: 10.1007/s10803-006-0328-2.

Chaste, P., & Leboyer, M. (2012). Autism risk factors: Genes, environment, and gene–environment interactions. *Dialogues in Clinical Neuroscience*, 14(3), 281.

Chawarska, K., Volkmar, F., & Klin, A. (2010). Limited attentional bias for faces in toddlers with autism spectrum disorders. *Archives of General Psychiatry*, 67(2), 178–185.

Chevallier, C., Kohls, G., Troiani, V., Brodkin, E. S., & Schultz, R. T. (2012). The social motivation theory of autism. *Trends in Cognitive Sciences*, 16(4), 231–239. https://doi-org.ezproxy.lib.uh.edu/10.1016/j.tics.2012.02.007.

Chien, Y.-L., Chou, M.-C., Chou, W.-J., Wu, Y.-Y., Tsai, W.-C., Chiu, Y.-N., & Gau, S. S.-F. (2019). Prenatal and perinatal risk factors and the clinical implications on autism spectrum disorder. *Autism: The International Journal of Research and Practice*, 23(3), 783–791. doi: 10.1177/1362361318772813.

Chorpita, B. F., Rotheram-Borus, M. J., Daleiden, E. L., Bernstein, A., Cromley, T., Swendeman, D., & Regan, J. (2011). The old solutions are the new problem: How do we better use what we already know about reducing the burden of mental illness? *Perspectives on Psychological Science*, 6(5), 493–497. doi: 10.1177/1745691611418240.

Constantino, J. N., & Todd, R. D. (2003). Autistic traits in the general population: A twin study. *Archives of General Psychiatry*, 60(5), 524–530. doi: 10.1001/archpsyc.60.5.524.

Cornew, L., Dobkins, K. R., Akshoomoff, N., McCleery, J. P., & Carver, L. J. (2012). Atypical social referencing in infant siblings of children with autism spectrum disorders. *Journal of Autism and Developmental Disorders*, 42(12), 2611–2621. doi: org.ezproxy.lib.uh.edu/10.1007/s10803-012-1518-8.

Dadds, M. R., MacDonald, E., Cauchi, A., Williams, K., Levy, F., & Brennan, J. (2014). Nasal oxytocin for social deficits in childhood autism: A randomized controlled trial. *Journal of Autism and Developmental Disorders*, 44(3), 521–531. doi: 10.1007/s10803-013-1899-3.

Davis, N. O., & Carter, A. S. (2014). Social development in autism. In F. R. Volkmar, S. J. Rogers, R. Paul, & K. A. Pelphrey (Eds.), *Handbook of autism and developmental disorders* (4th ed., pp. 212–229). Hoboken, NJ: John Wiley & Sons, Inc.

Dawson, G., & Adams, A. (1984). Imitation and social responsiveness in autistic children. *Journal of Abnormal Child Psychology*, 12(2), 209–225. doi: 10.1007/BF00910664.

Dawson, G., & Faja, S. (2008). ASD: A developmental perspective. In T. P. Beauchaine, S. P. Hinshaw, T. P. Beauchaine, & S. P. Hinshaw (Eds.), *Child and adolescent psychopathology* (pp. 575–613). Hoboken, NJ: John Wiley & Sons, Inc.

Dawson, G., & Lewy, A. (1989). Reciprocal subcortical-cortical influences in autism: The role of attentional mechanisms. In G. Dawson & G. Dawson (Eds.), *Autism: Nature, diagnosis, and treatment* (pp. 144–173). New York, NY: Guilford Press.

Dawson, G., Meltzoff, A. N., Osterling, J., Rinaldi, J., & Brown, E. (1998). Children with autism fail to orient to naturally occurring social stimuli. *Journal of Autism and Developmental Disorders*, 28(6), 479–485. doi: 10.1023/A:1026043926488.

Dawson, G., Toth, K., Abbott, R., Osterling, J., Munson, J., Estes, A., & Liaw, J. (2004). Early social attention impairments in autism: Social orienting, joint attention, and attention to distress. *Developmental Psychology*, 40(2), 271–283. doi: 10.1037/0012-1649.40.2.271.

Dawson, G., Webb, S. J., Wijsman, E., Schellenberg, G., Estes, A., Munson, J., & Faja, S. (2005). Neurocognitive and electrophysiological evidence of altered face processing in parents of children with autism: Implications for a model of abnormal development of social brain circuitry in autism. *Development and Psychopathology*, 17(3), 679–697. doi: 10.1017/S0954579405050327.

del Rosario, M., Gillespie-Lynch, K., Johnson, S., Sigman, M., & Hutman, T. (2014). Parent-reported temperament trajectories among infant siblings of children with autism. *Journal of autism and developmental disorders*, 44(2), 381–393. doi: 10.1007/s10803-013-1876-x.

Devlin, B., Cook, E. H., Coon, H., Dawson, G., Grigorenko, E. L., McMahon, W., & Rodier, P. M. (2005). Autism and the serotonin transporter: The long and short of it. *Molecular Psychiatry*, 10(12), 1110–1116.

De Pauw, S. S. W., Mervielde, I., Van Leeuwen, K. G., & De Clercq, B. J. (2011). How temperament and personality contribute to the maladjustment of children with autism. *Journal of Autism and Developmental Disorders*, 41, 196–212.

De Rubeis, S., He, X., Goldberg, A. P., Poultney, C. S., Samocha, K., Cicek, A. E., & Buxbaum, J. D. (2014). Synaptic, transcriptional and chromatin genes disrupted in autism. *Nature*, 515(7526), 410–413. Retrieved from: http://search.ebscohost.com.ezproxy.lib.uh.edu/login.aspx?direct=true&db=psyh&AN=2014-49517-003&site=ehost-live.

Doshi-Velez, F., Ge, Y., & Kohane, I. (2014). Comorbidity clusters in autism spectrum disorders: An electronic health record time-series analysis. *Pediatrics*, 133(1), e54–e63.

Doussard-Roosevelt, J., Joe, C., Bazhenova, O., & Porges, S. (2003). Mother–child interaction in autistic and nonautistic children: Characteristics of maternal approach behaviors and child social responses. *Development and Psychopathology*, 15(2), 277–295. doi: 10.1017/S0954579403000154.

Duffy, F. H., Shankardass, A., McAnulty, G. B., Eksioglu, Y. Z., Coulter, D., Rotenberg, A., & Als, H. (2014). Corticosteroid therapy in regressive autism: A retrospective study of effects on the Frequency Modulated Auditory Evoked Response (FMAER), language, *and behavior. BMC Neurology*, 14, 70.

Durkin, M. S., Maenner, M. J., Baio, J., Christensen, D., Daniels, J., Fitzgerald, R., & Yeargin-Allsopp, M. (2017). Autism spectrum disorder among U.S. children (2002–2010): Socioeconomic, racial, and ethnic disparities. *American Journal of Public Health*, 107, 1818–1826. doi: 10.2105/AJPH.2017.304032.

Eaves, L. C., & Ho, H. H. (2008). Young adult outcome of ASD. *Journal of Autism and Developmental Disorders*, 38(4), 739–747. doi: 10.1007/s10803-007-0441-x.

Elsabbagh, M., Divan, G., Koh, Y., Kim, Y. S., Kauchali, S., Marcín, C., & Fombonne, E. (2012). Global prevalence of autism and other pervasive developmental disorders. *Autism Research*, 5(3), 160–179. doi: 10.1002/aur.239.

Estes, A., Zwaigenbaum, L., Gu, H., St. John, T., Paterson, S., Elison, J. T., & IBIS network (2015). Behavioral, cognitive, and adaptive development in infants with autism spectrum disorder in the first two years of life. *Journal of Neurodevelopmental Disorders*, 7, 24. doi: 10.1186/s11689-015-9117-6.

Ettinger, R.H. (2017). *Psychopharmacology* (2nd ed.). New York, NY: Routledge.

Faja, S., & Dawson, G. (2006). Early intervention for Autism. In J. L. Luby & J. L. Luby (Eds.), *Handbook of preschool mental health: Development, disorders, and treatment* (pp. 388–416). New York, NY: Guilford Press.

Faja, S., & Dawson, G. (2017). Autism spectrum disorder. In T. P. Beauchaine & S. P. Hinshaw (Eds.), *Child and adolescent psychopathology* (3rd ed., pp. 762–799). Hoboken, NJ: John Wiley & Sons, Inc.

Fein, D., Barton, M., Eigsti, I., Kelley, E., Naigles, L., Schultz, R., Stevens, M., Helt, M., Orinstein, A., Rosenthal, M., Troyb, E., & Tyson, K. (2013). Optimal outcome in individuals with a history of autism. *Journal of Child Psychology and Psychiatry*, 54(2), 195–205. doi: 10.1111/jcpp.12037.

Fernández, M., Mollinedo-Gajate, I., & Peñagarikano, O. (2018). Neural circuits for social cognition: Implications for Autism. *Neuroscience*, 370, 148–162. doi: 10.1016/j.neuroscience.2017.07.013.

Food and Drug Administration (2014). Abilify. Retrieved from: https://www.accessdata.fda.gov/drugsatfda_docs/label/2014/021436s038,021713s030,021729s022,021866s023lbl.pdf.

Food and Drug Administration (2005). Risperdal. Retrieved from: https://www.accessdata.fda.gov/drugsatfda_docs/label/2005/020272s042,020588s030,021444s016,021346s010lbl.pdf.

Fountain, C., King, M. D., & Bearman, P. S. (2011). Age of diagnosis for autism: Individual and
community factors across 10 birth cohorts. *Journal of Epidemiology & Community Health*, 65, 503–510.

Frith, U. (1989). *Autism: Explaining the enigma* (1st ed.). Oxford, UK: Blackwell.

Frith, U. (2003). *Autism: Explaining the enigma* (2nd ed.). Malden, MA: Wiley-Blackwell Publishing.

Gabriele, S., Sacco, R., & Persico, A. M. (2014). Blood serotonin levels in autism spectrum disorder: A systematic review and meta-analysis. *European Neuropsychopharmacology*, 24(6), 919–929. doi: 10.1016/j.euroneuro.2014.02.004.

Gerdts, J. & Bernier, R. (2011). The broader autism phenotype and its implications on the etiology and treatment of ASD. *Autism Research and Treatment*, vol. 2011, Article ID 545901. Available at: https://doi.org/10.1155/2011/545901.

Gilchrist, A., Green, J., Cox, A., Burton, D., Rutter, M., & Le Couteur, A. (2001). Development and current functioning in adolescents with Asperger syndrome: A comparative study. *Journal of Child Psychology and Psychiatry*, 42(2), 227–240. doi: 10.1111/1469-7610.00714.

Glasson, E. J., Bower, C., Petterson, B., de Klerk, N., Chaney, G., & Hallmayer, J. F. (2004). Perinatal factors and the development of autism: A population study. *Archives of General Psychiatry*, 61(6), 618–627. doi: 10.1001/archpsyc.61.6.618.

Green, S. A., & Ben-Sasson, A. (2010). Anxiety disorders and sensory over-responsivity in children with autism spectrum disorders: Is there a causal relationship? *Journal of Autism and Developmental Disorders*, 40(12), 1495–1504.

Greene, R. K., Walsh, E., Mosner, M. G., & Dichter, G. S. (2019). A potential mechanistic role for neuroinflammation in reward processing impairments in autism spectrum disorder. *Biological Psychology*, 142, 1–12. doi: 10.1016/j.biopsycho.2018.12.008.

Guastella, A. J., Einfeld, S. L., Gray, K. M., Rinehart, N. J., Tonge, B. J., Lambert, T. J., & Hickie, I. B. (2010). Intranasal oxytocin improves emotion recognition for youth with ASD. *Biological Psychiatry*, 67(7), 692–694. doi: 10.1016/j.biopsych.2009.09.020.

Happé, F. G. (1994). An advanced test of theory of mind: Understanding of story characters' thoughts and feelings by able autistic, mentally handicapped, and normal children and adults. *Journal of Autism and Developmental Disorders*, 24(2), 129–154.

Happé, F., Cook, J. L., & Bird, G. (2017). The structure of social cognition: In(ter)dependence of sociocognitive processes. *Annual Review of Psychology*, 68, 243–267.

Helt, M., Kelley, E., Kinsbourne, M., Pandey, J., Boorstein, H., Herbert, M., & Fein, D. (2008). Can children with autism recover? If so, how? *Neuropsychology Review*, 18(4), 339–366.

Hepburn, S. L., & Stone, W. L. (2006). Using Carey temperament scales to assess behavioral style in children with autism spectrum disorders. *Journal of Autism and Developmental Disorders*, 36, 637–642.

Hertzig, M. E., Snow, M. E., & Sherman, M. (1989). Affect and cognition in autism. *Journal of The American Academy of Child & Adolescent Psychiatry*, 28(2), 195–199. doi: 10.1097/00004583-198903000-00008.

Hollander, E., Phillips, A. T., & Yeh, C. (2003). Targeted treatments for symptom domains in child and adolescent autism. *The Lancet*, 362(9385), 732–734. doi: 10.1016/S0140-6736(03)14236-5.

Hudry, K., Aldred, C., Wigham, S., Green, J., Leadbitter, K., Temple, K., & McConachie, H. (2013). Predictors of parent–child interaction style in dyads with autism. *Research in Developmental Disabilities*, 34(10), 3400–3410. doi: 10.1016/j.ridd.2013.07.015.

Huerta, M., Bishop, S. L., Duncan, A., Hus, V., & Lord, C. (2012). Application of DSM-5 criteria for ASD to three samples of children with DSM-IV diagnoses of pervasive developmental disorders. *The American Journal of Psychiatry*, 169(10), 1056–1064. doi: 10.1176/appi.ajp.2012.12020276.

Iossifov, I., O'Roak, B.J., Sanders, S.J., Ronemus, M., Krumm, N., Levy, D., & Wigler, M. (2014). The contribution of de novo coding mutations to autism spectrum disorder. *Nature*, 515(7562), 216–221. doi: 10.1038/nature13908.

Jacobson, R. M. (2004). Association of autistic spectrum disorder and the measles, mumps, and rubella vaccine–A systematic review of current epidemiological evidence. *Child: Care, Health and Development*, 30(1), 91–92.

Jaiswal, P., Guhathakurta, S., Singh, A. S., Verma, D., Pandey, M., Varghese, M., & Rajamma, U. (2015). SLC6A4 markers modulate platelet 5-HT level and specific behaviors of autism: A study from an Indian population. *Progress in Neuro-Psychopharmacology & Biological Psychiatry*, 56, 196–206. https://doi: 10.1016/j.pnpbp.2014.09.004.

James, S. J., Shpyleva, S., Melnyk, S., Pavliv, O., & Pogribny, I. P. (2013). Complex epigenetic regulation of engrailed-2 (EN-2) homeobox gene in the autism cerebellum. *Translational Psychiatry*, 3, e232. https://doi-org.ezproxy.lib.uh.edu/10.1038/tp.2013.8.

Jellema, T., Lorteije, J., Van Rijn, S., Wout, M., de Haan, E., van Engeland, H., & Kemner, C. (2009). Involuntary interpretation of social cues is compromised in autism spectrum disorders. *Autism Research*, 2, 192–204.

Jin, Y., Choi, J., Won, J., & Hong, Y. (2018). The relationship between Autism Spectrum Disorder and melatonin during fetal development. *Molecules*, 23(1), 198. https://doi-org.ezproxy.lib.uh.edu/10.3390/molecules23010198.

Kanner, L. (1943). Autistic disturbances of affective contact. *Nervous Child*, 2(3), 217–250).

Karpur, A., Lello, A., Frazier, T., Dixon, P., & Shih, A. (2019). Health disparities among children with autism spectrum disorders: Analysis of the National Survey of Children's Health 2016. *Journal of Autism and Developmental Disorders*, 49(4), 1652–1664. doi.org/10.1007/s10803-018-3862-9.

Kirkovski, M., Enticott, P. G., & Fitzgerald, P. B. (2013). A review of the role of female gender in autism spectrum disorders. *Journal of Autism and Developmental*

Disorders, 43(11), 2584–2603. doi: 10.1007/s10803-013-1811-1.

Kjelgaard, M. M., & Tager-Flusberg, H. (2001). An investigation of language impairment in autism: Implications for genetic subgroups. *Language and Cognitive Processes*, 16(2–3), 287–308. doi: 10.1080/01690960042000058.

Klein-Tasman, B. P. & Mervis, C. B. (2018). Autism spectrum symptomatology among children with duplication 7q11.23 syndrome. *Journal of Autism and Developmental Disorders*, 48(6), 1982–1994. doi: 10.1007/s10803-017-3439-z.

Klin, A., Jones, W., Schultz, R., Volkmar, F. R., & Cohen, D. J. (2002). Visual fixation patterns during viewing of naturalistic social situations as predictors of social competence in individuals with autism. *Archives of General Psychiatry*, 59(9), 809–816.

Kobayashi, R., Murata, T., & Yoshinaga, K. (1992). A follow-up study of 201 children with autism in Kyushu and Yamaguchi areas, *Japan. Journal of Autism and Developmental Disorders*, 22(3), 395–411. doi: 10.1007/BF01048242.

Konstantareas, M. M., & Stewart, K. (2006). Affect regulation and temperament in children with autism spectrum disorder. *Journal of Autism and Developmental Disorders*, 36(2), 143–154.

Kuppens, S., Heyvaert, M., Van den Noortgate, W., & Onghena, P. (2011). Sequential meta-analysis of single-case experimental data. *Behavior Research Methods*, 43(3), 720–729. doi: 10.3758/s13428-011-0080-1.

Lai, M., Lombardo, M. V., & Baron-Cohen, S. (2014). Autism. *The Lancet*, 383 (9920), 896–910. doi: 10.1016/S0140-6736(13)61539-1.

Landa, R., & Garrett-Mayer, E. (2006). Development in infants with ASD: A prospective study. *Journal of Child Psychology and Psychiatry*, 47(6), 629–638. doi: 10.1111/j.1469-7610.2006.01531.x.

Li, X., Zou, H., & Brown, W. T. (2012). Genes associated with autism spectrum disorder. *Brain Research Bulletin*, 88(6), 543–552. https://doi-org.ezproxy.lib.uh.edu/10.1016/j.brainresbull.2012.05.017.

LoParo, D., & Waldman, I. D. (2015). The oxytocin receptor gene (OXTR) is associated with autism spectrum disorder: a meta-analysis. *Molecular Psychiatry*, 20(5), 640–646. https://doi-org.ezproxy.lib.uh.edu/10.1038/mp.2014.77

Lovaas, O. I. (1987). Behavioral treatment and normal educational and intellectual functioning in young autistic children. *Journal of Consulting and Clinical Psychology*, 55(1), 3–9. doi: 10.1037/0022-006X.55.1.3.

Loveland, K. A., Tunali-Kotoski, B., Pearson, D. A., Brelsford, K. A., Ortegon, J., & Chen, R. (1994). Imitation and expression of facial affect in autism. *Development and Psychopathology*, 6(3), 433–444. doi: 10.1017/S0954579400006039.

Madden, J. M., Lakoma, M. D., Lynch, F. L., Rusniak, D., Owen-Smith, A. A., Coleman, K. J., Quinn, V. P., Yau, V. M., Qian, Y. X., & Croen, L. A. (2017). Psychotropic medication use among insured children with autism spectrum disorder. *Journal of Autism and Developmental Disorders*, 47(1), 144–154. https://doi-org.ezproxy.lib.uh.edu/10.1007/s10803-016-2946-7.

Maestro, S., Muratori, F., Cavallaro, M. C., Pei, F., Stern, D., Golse, B., & Palacio-Espasa, F. (2002). Attentional skills during the first 6 months of age in autism spectrum disorder. *Journal of the American Academy of Child & Adolescent Psychiatry*, 41(10), 1239–1245. doi: 10.1097/00004583-200210000-00014.

Mandy, W., & Lai, M.-C. (2016). Annual Research Review: The role of the environment in the developmental psychopathology of autism spectrum condition. *Journal of Child Psychology and Psychiatry, and Allied Disciplines*, 57(3), 271–292. https://doi-org.ezproxy.lib.uh.edu/10.1111/jcpp.12501.

Matson, J. L., & Shoemaker, M. (2009). Intellectual disability and its relationship to autism spectrum disorders. *Research in*

Developmental Disabilities, 30, 1107–1114. https://doi.org/10.1016/j.ridd.2009.06.003.

May, T., Sciberras, E., Brignell, A., & Williams, K. (2017). Autism spectrum disorder: updated prevalence and comparison of two birth cohorts in a nationally representative Australian sample. *BMJ Open*, 7(5), e015549. https://doi.org/10.1136/bmjopen-2016-015549.

Mazurek, M. O., Handen, B. L., Wodka, E. L., Nowinski, L., Butter, E., & Engelhardt, C. R. (2014). Age at first autism spectrum disorder diagnosis: The role of birth cohort, demographic factors, and clinical features. *Journal of Developmental & Behavioral Pediatrics*, 35(9), 561–569.

McKeague, I. W., Brown, A. S., Bao, Y., Hinkka-Yli-Salomäki, S., Huttunen, J., & Sourander, A. (2015). Autism with intellectual disability related to dynamics of head circumference growth during early infancy. *Biological Psychiatry*, 77(9), 833–840. https://doi-org.ezproxy.lib.uh.edu/10.1016/j.biopsych.2014.08.008.

McLeod, B. D., Wood, J. J., & Klebanoff, S. (2015). Advances in evidence-based intervention and assessment practices for youth with an autism spectrum disorder. *Behavior Therapy*, 46(1), 1–6. doi: 10.1016/j.beth.2014.07.004.

Meek, S. E., Lemery-Chalfant, K., Jahromi, L. B., & Valiente, C. (2013). A review of gene–environment correlations and their implications for autism: A conceptual model. *Psychological Review*, 120(3), 497–521. doi: 10.1037/a0033139.

Miller, M. T., & Strömland, K. (1993). Thalidomide embryopathy: An insight into autism. *Teratology*, 47, 387–388.

Mundy, P., & Neal, A. R. (2001). Neural plasticity, joint attention, and a transactional social-orienting model of autism. In L. M. Glidden (Ed.), *International review of research in mental retardation: Autism* (vol. 23, pp. 139–168). San Diego, CA: Academic Press.

Mundy, P., Sigman, M. D., Ungerer, J., & Sherman, T. (1986). Defining the social deficits of autism: The contribution of non-verbal communication measures. *Child Psychology & Psychiatry & Allied Disciplines*, 27(5), 657–669. doi: 10.1111/j.1469-7610.1986.tb00190.x.

Murza, K. A., Schwartz, J. B., Hahs-Vaughn, D. L., & Nye, C. (2016). Joint attention interventions for children with autism spectrum disorder: A systematic review and meta-analysis. *International Journal of Language & Communication Disorders*, 51(3), 236–251.

Nowell, K. P., Goin-Kochel, R. P., McQuillin, S. D., & Mire, S. S. (2017). Intellectual functioning and ASD: Can profiles inform identification of subpopulations? *Review Journal of Autism and Developmental Disorders*, 4(4), 339–349. doi: 10.1007/s40489-017-0118-0.

Nowell, K. P., Schanding, G. T. S., Kanne, S. M., & Goin-Kochel, R. P. (2015). Cognitive profiles in youth with autism spectrum disorder: An investigation of base rate discrepancies using the Differential Ability Scales, Second Edition. *Journal of Autism and Developmental Disorders*, 45, 1978–1988. doi.org/10.1007/s10803-014-2356-7.

Ornoy, A., Weinstein-Fudim, L., & Ergaz, Z. (2015). Prenatal factors associated with autism spectrum disorder (ASD). *Reproductive Toxicology*, 56, 155–169.

Osterling, J., & Dawson, G. (1994). Early recognition of children with autism: A study of first birthday home videotapes. *Journal of Autism and Developmental Disorders*, 24(3), 247–257. doi: 10.1007/BF02172225.

Osterling, J. A., Dawson, G., & Munson, J. A. (2002). Early recognition of 1-year-old infants with ASD versus mental retardation. *Development and Psychopathology*, 14(2), 239–251. doi: 10.1017/S0954579402002031.

Palmer, R. F., Walker, T., Mandell, D., Bayles, B., & Miller, C. S. (2010). Explaining low rates of autism among Hispanic school children in Texas. *American Journal of Public Health*, 100(2), 270–272. doi: 10.2105/AJPH.2008.150565.

Pelphrey, K. A., Sasson, N. J., Reznick, J. S., Paul, G., Goldman, B. D., & Piven, J. (2002). Visual scanning of faces in autism. *Journal of Autism and Developmental Disorders*, 32(4), 249–261. doi: 10.1023/A:1016374617369.

Peters-Scheffer, N., Didden, R., Korzilius, H., & Sturmey, P. (2011). A meta-analytic study on the effectiveness of comprehensive ABA-based early intervention programs for children with ASD. *Research in ASD*, 5(1), 60–69. doi: 10.1016/j.rasd.2010.03.011.

Prior, M., Eisenmajer, R., Leekam, S., Wing, L., Gould, J., Ong, B., & Dowe, D. (1998). Are there subgroups within the autistic spectrum? A cluster analysis of a group of children with autistic spectrum disorders. *Journal of Child Psychology and Psychiatry*, 39(6), 893–902. doi: 10.1111/1469-7610.00389.

Reilly, J., Gallagher, L., Chen, J. L., Leader, G., & Shen, S. (2017). Bio-collections in autism research. *Molecular Autism*, 8(1), 34. doi: 10.1186/s13229-017-0154-8.

Rogers, S. J., Bennetto, L., McEvoy, R., & Pennington, B. F. (1996). Imitation and pantomime in high-functioning adolescents with ASD. *Child Development*, 67(5), 2060–2073. doi: 10.2307/1131609.

Ronemus, M., Iossifov, I., Levy, D., & Wigler, M. (2014). The role of de novo mutations in the genetics of ASD. *Nature Reviews Genetics*, 15, 144–141. doi: https://doi.org/10.1038/nrg3585.

Rubenstein, E., & Chawla, D. (2018). Broader autism phenotype in parents of children with autism: A systematic review of percentage estimates. *Journal of Child and Family Studies*, 27(6), 1705–1720. https://doi-org.ezproxy.lib.uh.edu/10.1007/s10826-018-1026-3.

Russell, J., & Jarrold, C. (1999). Memory for actions in children with autism: Self versus other. *Cognitive Neuropsychiatry*, 4(4), 303–331.

Sacco, R., Gabriele, S., & Persico, A. M. (2015). Head circumference and brain size in autism spectrum disorder: A systematic review and meta-analysis. *Psychiatry Research: Neuroimaging*, 234(2), 239–251. https://doi-org.ezproxy.lib.uh.edu/10.1016/j.pscychresns.2015.08.016.

Salazar, F., Baird, G., Chandler, S., Tseng, E., O'Sullivan, T., Howlin, P., & Simonoff, E. (2015). Co-occurring psychiatric disorders in preschool and elementary school-aged children with autism spectrum disorder. *Journal of Autism and Developmental Disorders*, 45(8), 2283–2294.

Sandin, S., Lichtenstein, P., Kuja-Halkola, R., Larsson, H., Hultman, C. M., & Reichenberg, A. (2014). The familial risk of autism. *JAMA: Journal of the American Medical Association*, 311(17), 1770–1777. https://doi- org.ezproxy.lib.uh.edu/10.1001/jama.2014.4144.

Schaaf, C. P., Boone, P. M., Sampath, S., Williams, C., Bader, P. I., Mueller, J. M., & Cheung, S.W. (2012). Phenotypic spectrum and genotype–phenotype correlations of NRXN1 exon deletions. *European Journal of Human Genetics*, 20, 1240–1247. doi: 10.1038/ejhg.2012.95.

Sharp, C., & Venta, A. (2012). Mentalizing problems in children and adolescents. In N. Midgley, I. Vrouva, N. Midgley, & I. Vrouva (Eds.), *Minding the child: Mentalization-based interventions with children, young people and their families* (pp. 35–53). New York, NY: Routledge/Taylor & Francis Group.

Shumway, S., Thurm, A., Swedo, S. E., Deprey, L., Barnett, L. A., Amaral, D. G., & Ozonoff, S. (2011). Brief report: Symptom onset patterns and functional outcomes in young children with ASD. *Journal of Autism and Developmental Disorders*, 41(12), 1727–1732. doi: 10.1007/s10803-011-1203-3.

Simonoff, E., Pickles, A., Charman, T., Chandler, S., Loucas, T., & Baird, G. (2008). Psychiatric disorders in children with autism spectrum disorders: Prevalence, comorbidity, and associated factors in a population-derived sample. *Journal of the American Academy of Child & Adolescent Psychiatry*, 47(8), 921–929.

Soltani, A., Lebrun, S., Carpentier, G., Zunino, G., Chantepie, S., Maïza, A., & Stettler, O. (2017). Increased signaling by the autism-related Engrailed-2 protein enhances dendritic branching and spine density, alters synaptic structural matching, and exaggerates protein synthesis. *Plos One*, 12(8), e0181350. https://doi-org.ezproxy.lib.uh.edu/10.1371/journal.pone.0181350.

Stone, W. L., Ousley, O. Y., & Littleford, C. D. (1997). Motor imitation in young children with autism: What's the object? *Journal of Abnormal Child Psychology*, 25, 475–485.

Sturmey, P., & Fitzer, A. (Eds.) (2007). *ASD: Applied behavior analysis, evidence, and practice*. Austin, TX: Pro-ed.

Sullivan, M., Finelli, J., Marvin, A., Garrett-Mayer, E., Bauman, M., & Landa, R. (2007). Response to joint attention in toddlers at risk for autism spectrum disorder: A prospective study. *Journal of Autism and Developmental Disorders*, 37(1), 37–48. doi:.10.1007/s10803-006-0335-3.

Thomas, A., & Chess, S. (1977). *Temperament and development*. Oxford, UK: Brunner/Mazel.

Tick, B., Bolton, P., Happé, F., Rutter, M., & Rijsdijk, F. (2016). Heritability of ASD: A meta-analysis of twin studies. *Journal of Child Psychology and Psychiatry*, 57(5), 585–595. https://doi-org.ezproxy.lib.uh.edu/10.1111/jcpp.12499.

Trepagnier, C., Sebrechts, M. M., & Peterson, R. (2002). Atypical face glaze in autism. *Cyberpsychology & Behavior*, 5(3), 213–217. doi: 10.1089/109493102760147204.

Tsai, L. Y. (2014). Impact of DSM-5 on epidemiology of autism spectrum disorder. *Research in ASD*, 8(11), 1454–1470. doi: 10.1016/j.rasd.2014.07.016.

Tseng, P. T., Chen, Y. W., Stubbs, B., Carvalho, A. F., Whiteley, P., Tang, C. H., & Yang, W. C. (2019). Maternal breastfeeding and autism spectrum disorder in children: A systematic review and meta-analysis. *Nutritional Neuroscience*, 22(5), 354–362.

Volkmar, F. R., & Mayes, L. C. (1990). Gaze behavior in autism. *Developmental and Psychopathology*, 2(1), 61–69.

Volkmar, F., Siegel, M., Woodbury-Smith, M., King, B., McCracken, J., & State, M. (2014). Practice parameter for the assessment and treatment of children and adolescents with autism spectrum disorder. *Journal of the American Academy of Child & Adolescent Psychiatry*, 53(2), 237–257. doi: 10.1016/j.jaac.2013.10.013.

Wakefield, A. J. (1999). MMR vaccination and autism. *The Lancet*, 354(9182), 949–950.

Wang, Y., Wang, M.-J., Rong, Y., He, H.-Z., & Yang, C.-J. (2019). Oxytocin therapy for core symptoms in autism spectrum disorder: An updated meta-analysis of randomized controlled trials. *Research in ASD*, 64, 63–75. doi: 10.1016/j.rasd.2019.03.007.

Werling, D. M., & Geschwind, D. H. (2013). Sex differences in autism spectrum disorders. *Current Opinion in Neurology*, 26(2), 146.

Werner, E., & Dawson, G. (2005). Validation of the phenomenon of autistic regression using home videotapes. *Archives of General Psychiatry*, 62(8), 889–895. doi: 10.1001/archpsyc.62.8.889.

Werner, E., Dawson, G., Osterling, J., & Dinno, N. (2000). Brief report: Recognition of ASD before one year of age: A retrospective study based on home videotapes. *Journal of Autism and Developmental Disorders*, 30(2), 157–162.

Wilson, K., Mills, E., Ross, C., McGowan, J., & Jadad, A. (2003). Association of autistic spectrum disorder and the measles, mumps, and rubella vaccine: A systematic review of current epidemiological evidence. *Archives of Pediatrics & Adolescent Medicine*, 157(7), 628–634.

Yang, C.-J., Tan, H.-P., Yang, F.-Y., Wang, H.-P., Liu, C.-L., He, H.-Z., & Du, Y.-J. (2015). The cortisol, serotonin and oxytocin are associated with repetitive behavior in autism spectrum disorder. *Research in ASD*, 18, 12–20. https://doi-org.ezproxy.lib.uh.edu/10.1016/j.rasd.2015.07.002.

Yirmiya, N., & Shulman, C. (1996). Seriation, conservation, and theory of mind abilities in individuals with autism, individuals with mental retardation, and normally developing children. *Child Development*, 67(5), 2045–2059. doi: 10.2307/1131608.

Zablotsky, B., Black, L. I., Maenner, M. J., Schieve, L. A., Danielson, M. L., Bitsko, R. H., & Boyle, C. A. (2019). Prevalence and trends of developmental disabilities among children in the United States: 2009-2017. *Pediatrics*, 144(4), e20190811. doi: https://doi.org/10.1542/peds.2019-0811.

Zwaigenbaum, L., Bryson, S., Rogers, T., Roberts, W., Brian, J., & Szatmari, P. (2005). Behavioral manifestations of autism in the first year of life. *International Journal of Developmental Neuroscience*, 23(2–3), 143–152. doi: 10.1016/j.ijdevneu.2004.05.001.

Chapter 7

Emergence of Antisocial Behavior in Middle Childhood

Peter Fonagy

Chapter Overview

Although intuitively we may feel able to identify "antisocial behavior," the various disorders associated with conduct problems (CPs), coupled with the wide range of disruptive, externalizing, or "acting out" behaviors that CPs encompass, make it difficult to develop a universally applicable scientific definition. What we do know is that problem behaviors should not be viewed in isolation, but rather as elements of a complex spectrum that can develop into Antisocial Personality Disorder (ASPD), Oppositional Defiant Disorder (ODD), or Conduct Disorder (CD).

In this chapter we will consider how breakdowns in emotional and behavioral regulation contribute to the onset of these disorders, taking our lead from DSM-5 (American Psychiatric Association, 2013). For example, CD emerges with behaviors that violate either societal norms or the rights of others, or both. In contrast, in ODD, poorly controlled emotion, manifested as, for example, outbursts of anger, is more prominent and generates interpersonal problems. Although the criteria for ODD include behaviors (e.g., argumentativeness or defiance), these may also be associated with the angry emotional outbursts and acute irritation. A case from our clinical work is given below.

Developmental Psychopathology, First Edition. Edited by Amanda Venta, Carla Sharp, Jack M. Fletcher, and Peter Fonagy.

Case vignette

Theo is now 14 but he has been "trouble," according to his mother, since he was six or seven. Theo's parents have more or less given up as Theo seems "out of control." Theo is described as an adventurous little boy who fearlessly explored things. However, Theo's parents went through a rough patch in their own lives and Theo became an increasingly problematic child. His early independence turned into uncontrollable behavior around second grade, and he refused to do his schoolwork or go to bed when asked, and started to speak disrespectfully to his teachers and swear and shout at his mother. On such occasions his father's authority would be invoked but his harsh (sometimes physical) discipline made things worse rather than better. Theo had friends, but he often got into fights with them. On one occasion his best friend's parents complained that Theo hit his friend in the face hard enough to cause a nosebleed. As he turned 11, Theo started staying out late with older children. At school he was disrespectful and was suspended twice in the 6th grade. As Theo got older his behaviour became even worse and he started staying out late at night with his parents not knowing where he was. At school he was significantly behind educationally and shunned by other students, who reported being frightened of him. There was suspicion that he might have joined a local gang and was involved in destruction of property and theft. Ultimately Theo's school insisted that mental health support be sought.

As the clinician seeing this family, discuss possible diagnoses you would give Theo and consider the course his problems have taken and what that might mean in terms of his likely outcome. What other information would you gather during an assessment to guide diagnosis and treatment of Theo's behaviors?

Definition, Diagnosis, and Clinical Features

The definitions of CD and ODD have been refined in DSM-5. It is worth bearing in mind, however, that many of the treatment studies considered in this chapter have not used formal diagnostic criteria.

OPPOSITIONAL DEFIANT DISORDER

Table 7.1 shows the DSM-5 diagnostic criteria for ODD. ODD includes a repetitive pattern of symptoms such as angry/irritable mood, argumentativeness/defiance, or vindictiveness, of at least six months' duration. This grouping is new to DSM-5 and reflects the fact that ODD involves emotional symptoms alongside behaviors. Given that many ODD behaviors are also shown by normally developing children, the criteria have been developmentally calibrated: for children younger than five years, they are expected to occur on most days, while older children should show the behaviors once per week. The persistence and frequency of the symptoms should exceed what is normative for an individual's age, gender, and culture.

CONDUCT DISORDER

Table 7.1 contains the diagnostic criteria for CD. Although the definitions of ODD and CD overlap, unlike ODD, CD entails violation of others' basic rights or of age-appropriate societal norms or rules. DSM-5 distinguishes two subtypes of CD on the basis of age at onset. In the *childhood-onset type*, at least one of the 15 behaviors must appear before the age of 10, whereas in the *adolescent-onset type*, none appear before the age of 10. Evidence suggests that these two subtypes predict different courses and prognoses for patients, with findings of differential risk for child-onset versus adolescent-onset CD (Johnson, Kemp, Heard, Lennings, & Hickie, 2015) and relatively poorer outcomes for the child-onset group (Bevilacqua, Hale, Barker, & Viner, 2018).

Recent longitudinal research has led to the suggestion that a third subtype, *childhood-limited* CD, should be distinguished. Children in this group, identified in follow-up studies, do not become antisocial adults. They do, however, tend to become adults who suffer from depression (Sentse, Kretschmer, de Haan, & Prinzie, 2017) and are socially isolated and financially dependent on others (Wiesner, Kim, & Capaldi, 2005).

Callous and unemotional traits

It is important to note that even when individuals do meet the criteria for CD, there is considerable heterogeneity in presentation. Perhaps one of the most crucial elements worth observing is whether the behavior of the child is marked by a callous and unemotional (CU) interpersonal style. CU traits are widely observed among 12–46% of all those with CD (Fanti, 2018). A CU interpersonal style is denoted when individuals have displayed at least two of the following characteristics: (1) lack of remorse and guilt, (2) callous lack of empathy, (3) lack of concern about performance, and (4) shallow or deficient affect. These children and adolescents typically see dominance and aggression in social scenarios as appropriate, tend to underestimate the likelihood that they will be punished, and are often insensitive to punishment cues.

The presence of high or low CU traits will impact how CPs manifest. Although there is some overlap, a distinction must be drawn between aggressive and rule-breaking CD. Lower CU traits are more commonly

TABLE 7.1 Externalizing Disorders as Defined by the DSM-5, ICD-11, and the Dimensional ASEBA Scales

DSM-5	*ICD-11*	*ASEBA Syndrome scales*	*ASEBA DSM scales*
Oppositional Defiant Disorder A. A pattern of angry/irritable mood, argumentative/defiant behavior, or vindictiveness lasting at least 6 months as evidenced by at least four symptoms from any of the following categories, and exhibited during interaction with at least one individual who is not a sibling. • Angry/Irritable Mood 1. Often loses temper. 2. Is often touchy or easily annoyed. 3. Is often angry and resentful. • Argumentative/Defiant Behavior. 4. Often argues with authority figures or, for children and adolescents, with adults. 5. Often actively defies or refuses to comply with requests from authority figures or with rules. 6. Often deliberately annoys others. 7. Often blames others for his or her mistakes or misbehavior. • Vindictiveness 8. Has been spiteful or vindictive at least twice within the past 6 months. B. The disturbance in behavior is associated with distress in the individual or others in his or her immediate social context (e.g., family, peer group, work colleagues), or it impacts negatively on social, educational, occupational, or other important areas of functioning. C. The behaviors do not occur exclusively during the course of a psychotic, substance use, depressive, or bipolar disorder. Also, the criteria are not met for disruptive mood dysregulation disorder.	**Oppositional Defiant Disorder** Oppositional defiant disorder is a persistent pattern (e.g., 6 months or more) of markedly defiant, disobedient, provocative, or spiteful behavior that occurs more frequently than is typically observed in individuals of comparable age and developmental level and that is not restricted to interaction with siblings. Oppositional defiant disorder may be manifest in prevailing, persistent, angry, or irritable mood, often accompanied by severe temper outbursts or in headstrong, argumentative, and defiant behaviour. The behaviour pattern is of sufficient severity to result in significant impairment in personal, family, social, educational, occupational, or other important areas of functioning.	**1.5–5 year olds** ***Aggressive Problems*** Can't wait Defiant Demanding Destroys things Disobedient Doesn't feel guilty Easily frustrated Fights Hits Hurt by accident Angry moods Physically attacks Punishment doesn't change behavior Screams Selfish Stubborn Temper tantrums Uncooperative Wants a lot of attention **6–18 year olds** ***Rule Breaking Behavior*** Drinks alcohol Lacks guilt	**1.5–5 year olds** ***Oppositional Defiant*** Defiant Disobedient Angry moods Stubborn Temper tantrums Uncooperative **6–18 year olds** ***Oppositional Defiant Problems*** Argues a lot Disobeys at home Disobeys at school Stubborn Temper tantrums ***Conduct Problems*** Cruel to animals Mean Destroys others' things Lacks guilt Breaks rules Fights

DSM-5	*ICD-11*	*ASEBA Syndrome scales*	*ASEBA DSM scales*
Conduct Disorder A. A repetitive and persistent pattern of behavior in which the basic rights of others or major age-appropriate societal norms or rules are violated, as manifested by the presence of at least three of the following 15 criteria in the past 12 months from any of the categories below, with at least one criterion present in the past 6 months: • Aggression to People and Animals 1. Often bullies, threatens, or intimidates others. 2. Often initiates physical fights. 3. Has used a weapon that can cause serious physical harm to others (e.g., a bat, brick, broken bottle, knife, gun). 4. Has been physically cruel to people. 5. Has been physically cruel to animals. 6. Has stolen while confronting a victim (e.g., mugging, purse snatching, extortion, armed robbery). 7. Has forced someone into sexual activity. • Destruction of Property 8. Has deliberately engaged in fire setting with the intention of causing serious damage. 9. Has deliberately destroyed others' property (other than by fire setting).	**Conduct-Dissocial Disorder** Conduct-dissocial disorder is characterized by a repetitive and persistent pattern of behavior in which the basic rights of others or major age-appropriate societal norms, rules, or laws are violated, such as aggression towards people or animals; destruction of property; deceitfulness or theft; and serious violations of rules. The behavior pattern is of sufficient severity to result in significant impairment in personal, family, social, educational, occupational, or other important areas of functioning. To be diagnosed, the behavior pattern must be enduring over a significant period of time (e.g., 12 months or more). Isolated dissocial or criminal acts are thus not in themselves grounds for the diagnosis.	Breaks rules at home Deviant friends Lies or cheats Prefers older kids Runs away Sets fires Sexual problems Steals at home Steals at other locations Swears Thinks about sex too much Uses tobacco Skips school Uses drugs Vandalism ***Aggressive Behavior*** Argues a lot Mean Demands attention Destroys own things Destroys others' things Disobeys at home Disobeys at school Fights Physically attacks Screams a lot Stubborn	Deviant friends Lies or cheats Physically attacks Runs away Sets fires Steals at home Steals at other locations Swears Threatens others Skips school Vandalism

(Continued)

TABLE 7.1 (Continued)

DSM-5	*ICD-11*	*ASEBA Syndrome scales*	*ASEBA DSM scales*
• Deceitfulness or Theft 10. Has broken into someone else's house, building, or car. 11. Often lies to obtain goods or favors or to avoid obligations (i.e., "cons" others). 12. Has stolen items of non-trivial value without confronting a victim (e.g., shoplifting, but without breaking and entering; forgery). • Serious Violations of Rules 13. Often stays out at night despite parental prohibitions, beginning before age 13 years. 14. Has run away from home overnight at least twice while living in the parental or parental surrogate home, or once without returning for a lengthy period. 15. Is often truant from school, beginning before age 13 years. B. The disturbance in behavior causes clinically significant impairment in social, academic, or occupational functioning. C. If the individual is age 18 years or older, criteria are not met for antisocial personality disorder.		Sudden mood changes Sulks Suspicious Teases a lot Temper tantrums Threatens Loud	

observed in the "aggressive" strand of CD, a variant of the disorder that is also characterized by neuroticism and affective regulation dysfunction. By contrast, the "rule-breaking" manifestation is typically accompanied by slightly higher CU traits and greater impulsivity. Notably, rule-breaking CD increases from childhood to early adolescence, while CD with aggression tends to decrease after childhood.

Prevalence

Disorders of conduct are the most common mental health disorders in children and adolescents in the USA (Ghandour et al., 2019). A cross-sectional and longitudinal review (Boylan, Vaillancourt, Boyle, & Szatmari, 2007) found that the reported prevalence of ODD ranged between 2.6 and 15.6% in community samples, rising to 28–65% in clinical samples. Furthermore, there is evidence suggesting that the prevalence of adolescent CPs has been increasing over the past 30 years (Collishaw, Maughan, Goodman, & Pickles, 2004), although there are indications of a sight reversal of this trend in recent years (Comeau et al., 2019).

Prevalence By Age

Typically, antisocial behavior emerges in childhood or adolescence, and it is very rare for either ODD or CD to first develop in adulthood. The first symptoms of ODD tend to appear during the preschool years and early childhood in particular (Vasileva, Graf, Reinelt, Petermann, & Petermann, 2020). However, prevalence rates for CD continue to rise during childhood (Steinhausen & Jakobsen, 2019), such that the highest prevalence rates are recorded in adolescence.

Prevalence By Gender

During childhood more males than females appear to suffer from ODD (Demmer, Hooley, Sheen, McGillivray, & Lum, 2017). Conduct disorder follows a similar pattern, with males primarily affected by childhood-onset CD. This gender disparity may, however, be lower in the adolescent-onset type (Moore, Silberg, Roberson-Nay, & Mezuk, 2017) and there is some evidence to suggest that the gender disparity might be narrowing (Tracy, Kempf-Leonard, & Abramoske-James, 2009).

In addition to gendered patterns in the prevalence of antisocial disorders, the behavioral manifestations of CD also appear to bifurcate according to gender. Males with CD frequently exhibit fighting, stealing, vandalism, and school discipline problems. Females with CD are more likely to exhibit lying, truancy, running away, substance use, and prostitution. Whereas males tend to exhibit both physical aggression and relational aggression, females tend to exhibit relatively more relational aggression (Ackermann et al., 2019).

PREVALENCE BY RACE AND ETHNICITY

Prevalence of ODD and CD is relatively consistent across countries that differ in race and ethnicity, although there is mixed evidence on a racial difference in the prevalence of adolescent-onset conduct disorder.

PREVALENCE BY SOCIOECONOMIC STATUS

Children and adolescents who are from a lower socioeconomic background are three to four times as likely to have ODD (Piotrowska et al., 2015) or CD as those in the highest socioeconomic status (SES) bracket.

Comorbidity

Analysis of individuals suffering from behavioral disorders reveals a strong correlation between ODD and Attention Deficit and Hyperactivity Disorder (ADHD), as well as between CD and ADHD (Fonagy et al., 2014). It is estimated that about one-third of boys with an ADHD diagnosis proceed to develop CD. Children with both disorders have a higher probability of worse academic, social, and emotional problems.

Similarly, studies show that rates of ODD are much higher in samples of children and adolescents with ADHD (Mitchison & Njardvik, 2019), and while the precise association between the two illnesses is not known, increased vulnerability may result from shared temperamental risk factors. After ADHD, the most common co-occurring disorder with ODD is CD, suggesting significant overlap in antisocial behavioral disorders.

From the point of view of treatment, the association between ADHD and disturbance of conduct is perhaps the most significant. Twin studies suggest that ADHD and CD may have common genetic components (Moffitt, 2005). ADHD and ODD are both common in individuals with CD, and comorbid presentations predict worse outcomes (Galán, Wang, Shaw, & Forbes, 2020); therefore, early identification and intervention is paramount.

Besides ADHD, disorders of conduct can coincide with a number of other disorders, including, but not limited to, specific learning disorders, anxiety disorders, depressive or bipolar disorders, and substance-related disorders. In fact, data from the National Survey of Children's Health reveals that although ADHD is most commonly associated with CD (27% of cases), 18% of children with ADHD have comorbid depression, with 14% recording comorbid anxiety (Larson, Russ, Kahn, & Halfon, 2011).

Different manifestations of CPs will also carry differential risks for comorbidity. The extent to which internalizing disorders co-occur with CPs is in part affected by what form of CD the child has, i.e., whether it is CD with CU traits or without. Consistent with the observation that youth with CU traits tend to underestimate the likelihood of punishment and/or are less concerned by disciplinary actions, they also typically show very low levels of anxiety. By contrast, youth with CD without CU traits have much higher rates of comorbid anxiety and display hyperreactivity to threatening social cues. Disturbance of conduct is also a risk factor for substance misuse, and for children who suffer from both CD and depression, the risk of substance misuse increases (Egerton et al., 2020).

Developmental Continuities and Discontinuities

For most adolescents and adults who have persistent patterns of CPs, disruptive behavior begins early and becomes increasingly stable through middle childhood and adolescence. The Dunedin longitudinal study reported that 60% of adults with ASPD had a prior diagnosis of CD (Kim-Cohen et al., 2003).

Looking first to ODD, it is worth reiterating that although this disorder can often precede the development of CD, especially for those with childhood-onset CD, the majority of children who suffer from ODD do not go on to develop CD (Husby & Wichstrøm, 2017). However, even when ODD does not develop into CD, the risk of developing anxiety disorders and major depressive disorder is still significant. CD tends to be more stable than ODD, with persistence over several years following diagnosis estimated at around 50–60% (Rowe et al., 2010).

Homotypic Continuity

Research using data drawn from the Development Trends Study highlighted that homotypic continuity was found in ODD, ADHD, and CD, such that "the number of symptoms of one phase significantly predicted the number of symptoms in the same disorder the following year" (Burke et al., 2005, p. 1206).

Heterotypic Continuity

There is a closely documented relationship between CPs and substance use, with the former being a risk factor for the latter (Nock et al., 2006).

The association between the disorders appears to follow a unidirectional path, such that CD is more likely to precede substance use disorders than vice versa.

As with the association between CD and substance use, there is an additional link between antisocial behavior and depression. In a population-based study (Rice, Lifford, Thomas, & Thapar, 2007), diagnosis of depression in early adolescence approximately doubled the risk of antisocial behavior four years later.

A Developmental Psychopathology Model of the Etiology of Antisocial Behavior

A developmental psychopathology model summarizing the findings we will review in this section appears in Figure 7.1. Risk factors for antisocial behavior include impulsiveness, low IQ, and low school achievement (Murray, Irving, Farrington, Colman, & Bloxsom, 2010). Children brought up with poor parental supervision, punitive or erratic parental discipline, cold parental attitudes, physical abuse, parental conflict, and/or antisocial parents are more at risk of CPs (Fleming, McMahon, & King, 2017). This can be compounded by family disruption, large family size, low family income, and high-crime neighbourhoods, as well as antisocial peer networks and schools with high delinquency rates (Murray et al., 2010).

GENETIC FACTORS

CD with CU traits appears to have a stronger genetic basis. There is evidence to suggest that there is increased heritability of CD with CU traits, highlighting the potential for its intergenerational transmission (Fonagy & Luyten, 2018).

Molecular genetic studies

In a meta-analysis of twin and adoption studies, Mason and Frick (1994) discovered that 50% of the variance found in measures of antisocial behavior could be ascribed to genetic effects. Of particular significance is the MAOA gene, which encodes an enzyme that metabolizes neurotransmitters such as noradrenaline, serotonin, and dopamine, rendering them inactive. Notably, a functional polymorphism in the MAOA gene has been found to moderate the effect of maltreatment. Caspi et al. (2002) genotyped this polymorphism in a birth cohort study, finding that maltreated children with a genotype conferring high levels of MAOA expression were less likely to develop antisocial problems. However, subsequent attempts to replicate these findings have had only mixed success (Ouellet-Morin et al., 2016).

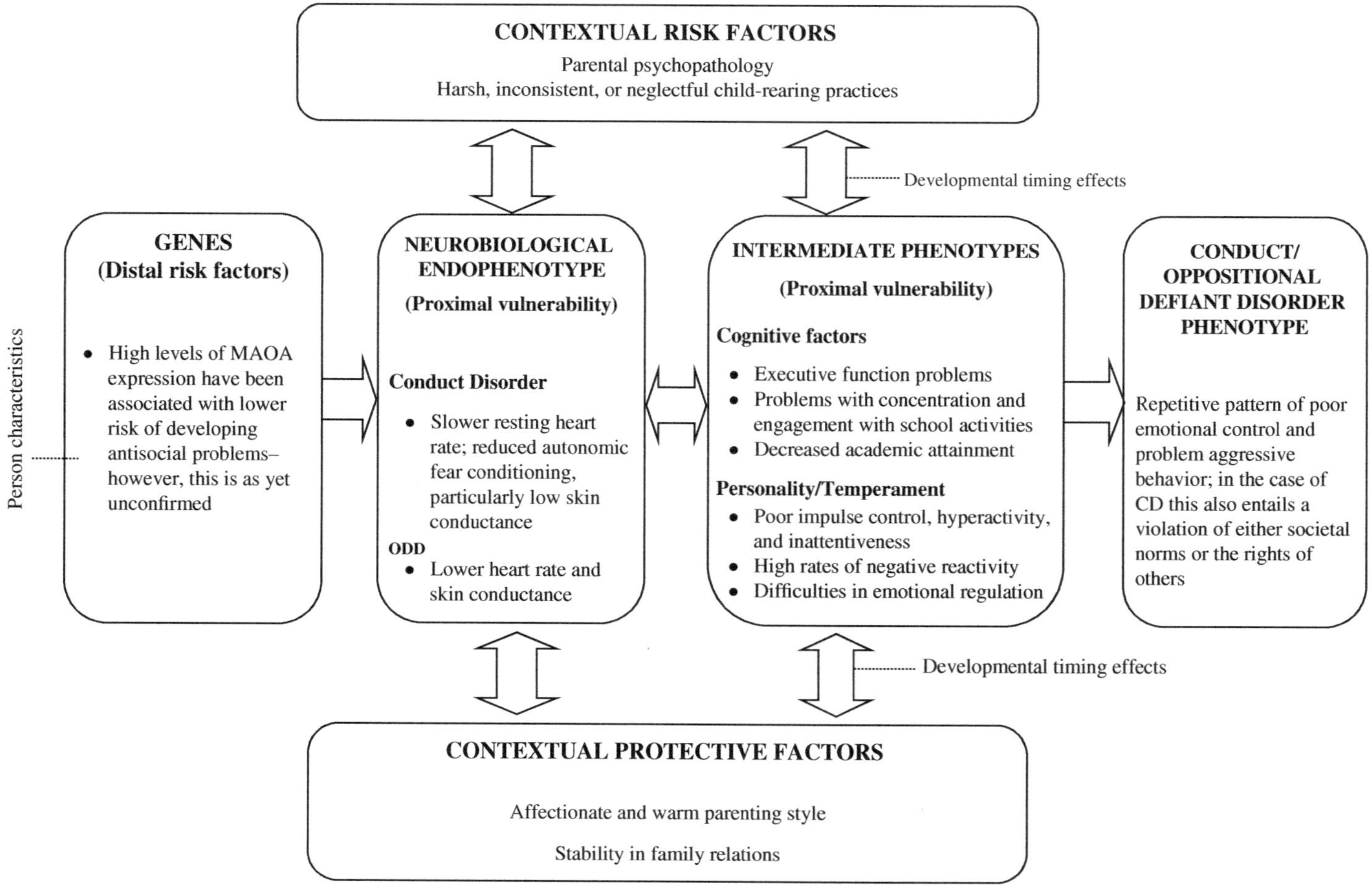

FIGURE 7.1 A Developmental Psychopathology Model of Conduct or Oppositional Defiant Disorder

NEUROBIOLOGICAL FACTORS

Consistent with existing findings from animal models and studies of adult ASPD, several studies examining neurotransmitters have found low central serotonin levels in physically aggressive children in comparison to age-matched non-aggressive children (Holmes, Slaughter, & Kashani, 2001).

Structural and functional differences in brain areas associated with affect regulation and affect processing, particularly frontotemporal-limbic connections involving the brain's ventral prefrontal cortex and amygdala, have been consistently noted in individuals with CD (Blair & Zhang, 2020). Reduced autonomic fear conditioning, particularly low skin conductance, is also well documented in patients with CD, while both high and low resting heart rate have been associated with antisocial behaviour (Fanti, 2018). Although it is relatively easy to identify unique traits of CD, it is much harder to do so for ODD. The vast majority of studies have not separated children with ODD from those with CD, making it difficult to isolate specific neurobiological differences between the disorders.

It is important to note that additional structural and functional differences have been identified for those with CU traits. Recent research has found that boys with CPs coupled with CU traits had increased grey matter concentration and decreased white matter concentration (De Brito et al., 2011).

TEMPERAMENT

The association between CPs and poor self-control is robust across gender and age groups (Frick & Morris, 2004). Poor impulse control, hyperactivity, and inattentiveness are the most highly related predisposing factors for the presentation of antisocial behavior (Holmes et al., 2001). In fact, childhood-onset CPs are often considered to be more strongly linked to temperamental vulnerabilities than adolescent-onset CPs. How parents and guardians react to poor behavioral outbursts can affect the consequent developmental trajectory, with negative reactivity associated with and predictive of CPs (Fleming et al., 2017).

EMOTIONAL REGULATION

Difficulties with emotional regulation are consistently associated with CPs, in particular high levels of negative emotional reactivity. A failure to develop an adequate emotional regulatory system may be a critical contributory factor in the development of CPs.

Cognitive Factors

An additional correlative factor for CPs appears to be IQ. Research has found that lower IQ and language skills during the preschool years are significant predictors of antisocial behavior in later life (Holmes et al., 2001). However, the direction of the causal chain may also work in reverse. CD can affect the student's ability to concentrate and engage with school activities, while behaviors such as disruptiveness and truancy may contribute to decreased academic attainment.

Contextual Risk Factors

Although individual-level factors such as emotional regulation, temperament, and IQ affect the probability of the child developing CPs, social and environmental influences are also important factors. We know that the environment in which the child is raised does have a bearing on disorder development, in particular the family environment and peer associations.

Environmental context

Historically, it was believed that environmental influences account for *differences* between siblings, otherwise known as non-shared or child-specific outcomes, with genetics believed to account for sibling similarities. However, recently this conjecture has been debunked. A meta-analysis of 490 twin and adoption studies of internalizing and externalizing psychopathology prior to adulthood (Burt, 2009b) revealed that shared environmental influences account for 10–15% of the variance within externalizing disorders. While situational factors at both familial and community level do contain risk for the development of conduct disorders, their effect appears to have a greater magnitude for the childhood-onset subtype of CD, although their impact is persistent over time up until adulthood.

Family context

The nature of the relationship between parent and child has particular relevance when attempting to predict the probability of behavioral disorder onset (Pinquart, 2017). Harsh, inconsistent, or neglectful child-rearing practices are more common in families of children and adolescents with ODD. Aligned to this, a strong link has been established between abuse in childhood and antisocial behavior in adolescence (Braga, Cunha, & Maia, 2018).

Stability in family relations is also of importance, with ODD being more prevalent in families where childcare is disrupted by a succession of different caregivers (Murray et al., 2010; Navarro-Soria, Servera, & Burns, 2020). An associated risk factor is parental demeanor, with research revealing that parental hostility can contribute towards ODD progressing to CD (Kolko, Dorn, Bukstein, & Burke, 2008), while the presence of an alcoholic father, parental conflict or violence, single parenthood, and maternal depression are correlated with the development of CD in the first instance (Holmes et al., 2001).

Social context

Aside from familial circumstances, social environment and, in particular, peer-group relations can be an important predictor of behavioral problems. Conduct disorder may emerge as a result of association with delinquent peer groups or as a consequence of peer rejection. Social withdrawal, childhood aggression, and a lack of social skills can contribute to deteriorating social relations and peer group rejection as early as the preschool years (Holmes et al., 2001).

CONTEXTUAL PROTECTIVE FACTORS

As we have seen, familial and peer-group factors can affect the probability of a child presenting with CD, but certain contextual elements can act as a buffer against risk. A stable and supportive home life can have a protective effect on children's general mental health (Ogden & Hagen, 2019) and an affectionate and warm parenting style is effective in protecting against progression to psychopathy.

GENE–ENVIRONMENT INTERPLAY

Genetics also play a role in determining susceptibility to CD (Azeredo, Moreira, & Barbosa, 2018). While the onset of CD is influenced by environmental factors, the risk of developing CD is increased in children with a parent or sibling with CD. CD also appears to be genetically linked with both alcohol and substance use disorder (Salvatore & Dick, 2018). The relevance of family medical history is amplified for those individuals who have childhood-onset CD. Genetic and social factors can intertwine with significant outcomes for children's behavioral patterns, with numerous research projects finding evidence of gene–environment interactions (Holz et al., 2018).

DEVELOPMENTAL TIMING EFFECTS: THE INTERPLAY OF NORMAL AND ABNORMAL DEVELOPMENT

Antisocial behavior tends to first emerge in childhood or adolescence (Steinhausen & Jakobsen, 2019). The critical period for the onset of CD is middle childhood through to middle adolescence. In cases where the

CD emerges prior to puberty, it is usually severe and more likely to be connected to neuropsychological deficits than adolescent-onset antisocial behavior (Johnson et al., 2015), which may be partially caused by peer influence. Furthermore, it is important to remember that the symptoms of CD can vary with age. While symptoms may become more severe with time, a meta-analysis highlights the necessity of distinguishing between aggressive and non-aggressive rule-breaking forms of antisocial behavior at the offset (Burt, 2009a). This distinction is important because the etiological roots of the two types of behavior are different, with the evidence pointing towards the high heritability associated with the aggressive form—genetic factors account for 65% of the variance, with a shared or common environment, particularly after childhood, only having a minor influence. This is notably different to the rule-breaking form, for which environmental factors appear to be instrumental, such that genetic influences only account for 48% of the variance.

Interventions

Evidence indicates poor long-term outcomes of disturbance of conduct (Wertz et al., 2018), even in children who do not meet diagnostic criteria (Fergusson et al., 2010). Therefore, we mainly discuss the treatment of disturbance of conduct rather than the treatment of ODD or CD. We use the terms ODD and CD when the studies report that the individuals sampled met formal diagnostic criteria. We simply refer to "CPs" or "disturbance of conduct" where the criteria were not specified.

While oppositional behavior in young children is often a developmental precursor of antisocial behavior in adolescence, early disruptive behavior does tend to improve without assistance over the first 10 years of life, indicating that not all childhood aggression necessarily progresses to CPs in later life. What we do know, however, is that where CD presents with a CU interpersonal style, the child is at increased risk of persistent and treatment-resistant antisocial and offending behavior (Bansal et al., 2019). This risk is somewhat reduced by adaptive parenting practices that emphasize warm parent–child relationships (Waller, Hyde, Klump, & Burt, 2018), and concentrated parental support may also buffer the child against some biological risk factors for psychopathy (e.g., fearlessness).

PARENT-TRAINING PROGRAMS

Family-level interventions have been found to be particularly constructive, with a large number of studies finding parental training as effective for addressing child behavioral issues. In fact, of the children under the age of 11 with CPs whose parents participate in parent training, on average, about two-thirds improve (Fonagy et al., 2014). However, there is also evidence from RCT data that substantial subgroups of families with children with CPs are likely neither to be suitable for, nor to persist with, this form of treatment (Chacko et al., 2016). While families at greatest risk often respond to treatment, the magnitude of these effects is attenuated by risk factors (Fonagy et al., 2014). It appears that the most positive gains from parenting programs are found when children have a higher level of CPs and when there are higher baseline levels of critical parenting (Sanders, Kirby, Tellegen, & Day, 2014). It is also conditional on the parents accepting the need for intervention and overcoming barriers such as stressors related to treatment, perceived treatment demands, and barriers concerning the therapist (Kazdin, 2018).

The parenting programs that are considered the most effective are the Incredible Years (IY) program and the Triple-P (Positive Parenting Program), which in many respects is comparable to the IY program but involves a number of levels of increasing intensity (Menting, Orobio de Castro, & Matthys, 2013; Sanders et al., 2014). There is also strong evidence for the effectiveness of the Oregon Social Leaning Centre (OSLC) program, which has been applied in a wide range of contexts, with different modifications, and is effective for a somewhat wider age range (Forgatch & Kjøbli, 2016).

The key to successful parenting interventions lies in shifting to a positive parenting model. Reducing harsh or negative parenting alone appears insufficient (Pasalich et al, 2016). Emerging evidence also suggests that positive parenting is more effective with high-CU rather than low-CU youth. Given the greater genetic basis of CD with high CU traits than CD without CU traits, it may be expected that high CU traits would negate the impact of positive parenting. Yet, in a study of over 800 children with high and low CU traits, positive parenting was actually associated with lower CD in children with high CU traits (Crum, Waschbusch, Bagner, & Coxe, 2015).

There is only limited evidence that training in adjunctive treatments—such as social problem-solving skills for single parents, partner support training for families with marital discord, and community-based treatment for high-risk families (Fonagy et al., 2014)—are effective. Similarly, the precise impact of self-directed parent training is still ambiguous. While there is some evidence to recommend this intervention strategy (Tarver, Daley, Lockwood, & Sayal, 2014), as well as the obvious economic arguments in its favor, it should be endorsed with caution given that the evidence is primarily drawn from universal or indicated prevention implementations of parent training, rather than clinic referrals.

Some possible difficulties have been associated with parenting interventions. First, there is evidence that perceived barriers to treatment reported by parents, such as demands and stressors associated with participation and perceived relevance of treatment, is a robust moderator (Kazdin, 2018). The programs can involve activities such as the review of educational material, systematic observation of the child, implementation of reinforcement procedures, maintenance of telephone contact with the therapist, and attendance at clinic sessions. For some families this level of engagement may be overwhelming, and the dropout from parent training can be as high as 26% in high-risk population samples (Chacko et al., 2016). Second, there is some concern regarding the long-term maintenance of treatment gains. We also know from meta-analytic findings (Lundahl, Risser, & Lovejoy, 2006) that the benefit of social support gained from group-based interventions does not outweigh the cost of individually delivered training, at least for disadvantaged families.

Psychodynamic Treatments

There is little evidence that psychodynamic approaches are effective for children with CPs (Midgley, O'Keeffe, French, & Kennedy, 2017). Rates of clinically significant improvement appear to be lower in psychodynamic therapy than in other treatments, while treatment length and number of sessions are greater.

Cognitive Behavioral Therapy

Compared to family-level interventions such as the parent training programs discussed above, there is mixed evidence on the relative effectiveness of CBT for children (Hendriks, Bartels, Colins, & Finkenauer, 2018). However, we do know that when CBT focuses on increasing self-control—through anger management, cognitive social skills training, and verbal self-instruction—this has a moderate effect and can result in reductions in CPs (Powell, Lochman, Boxmeyer, Barry, & Pardini, 2017). This evidence, however, is based on RCTs of just a single intensive intervention package (the Coping Power Program). When this program has been found to be successful, counsellors have received intensive training (Lochman et al., 2009), and a parenting component can also enhance long-term effects (Lochman & Wells, 2004). Some researchers have tested the effectiveness of a combined cognitive behavioral intervention such as Problem-Solving Skills Training (PSST) with a family-based therapy, Parent Management Training (PMT), with very positive results (Kazdin, 2017). Not only is PSST-PMT effective across multiple outcome domains for the child, but it also improves family relations, reducing stress and parental dysfunction. Furthermore, these gains are maintained at one-year follow-up. However, there are population groups for whom this treatment may be less effective, with negative moderators including child IQ, parent psychopathology, parent stress, and greater severity of impairment (Kazdin, 2017).

SCHOOL-LEVEL INTERVENTIONS

Interventions limited to a school setting are unlikely to have a lasting impact on the behavioral problems of children and adolescents. There is some evidence that training to modify teachers' behavior can result in improvements in children's externalizing behavior (Plueck et al., 2015) and classroom contingency management methods also seem to be effective in addressing challenging and aggressive behavior in clinical, at-risk, and community samples (Veenman, Luman, & Oosterlaan, 2018). For school-based strategies to have greater effectiveness, parent-administered reinforcements may be necessary in order to enhance classroom-based preventative programs. While school-based interventions may not be effective for long-term reductions in CPs, there is evidence from meta-analytic studies that interventions aimed at reducing the prevalence of bullying, specifically, can be effective (Zych, Ortega-Ruiz, & Del Rey, 2015). There is some evidence that school-wide, systemic interventions show promise in terms of maintaining behavioral improvements after formal termination of the program (Bradshaw, Waasdorp, & Leaf, 2012).

MULTISYSTEMIC THERAPY

Multisystemic therapy (MST) is a manualized treatment for young people exhibiting antisocial behaviour and their families. The programme uses a social-ecological approach with the aim of simultaneously affecting the multiple systems around the young person, including home life, school, peer relationships, and the wider community. MST is an intensive family-focused programme (Henggeler, 1999) drawing on CBT behavioral therapy, strategic family therapy, and structural family therapy. MST has been identified as a promising intervention for improving the prognosis of antisocial and offending behavior in adolescence, mitigating effects on public health, and improving individual and family morbidity (van der Stouwe, Asscher, Stams, Dekovic, & van der Laan, 2014). In the USA, there has been some evidence that MST can reduce criminal activity (Henggeler, Clingempeel, Brondino, & Pickrel, 2002) and recidivism (Schaeffer & Borduin, 2005), and improve antisocial behavior and family cohesion, compared with management as usual. However, a recent large randomized trial in the UK did not find strong evidence supporting MST (Fonagy et al., 2018) and reported a slightly greater number of convictions in those who were offered MST compared to management as usual (Fonagy et al., 2020).

Chapter Summary

In this chapter, we examined the prevalence, etiology, and treatment of behavioral disorders. Behavioral disorders are the most commonly occurring mental health conditions in children and adolescents, with estimates suggesting that up to 16% of children in the community will suffer from either Conduct Disorder (CD) or Oppositional Defiant Disorder (ODD). Multiple factors have been identified as contributing to the onset and development of both disorders, from emotional regulation and temperamental problems to environmental factors such as disruptive, abusive, and unstable family relations, parental psychopathology, and delinquent peer networks. There are a number of evidence-based treatment paths for conduct problems. Overall, parent-training programs provided the greatest evidence for effectiveness and should be considered as the first-step intervention for behavioral disorders.

Further Reading

Bakker, M. J., Greven, C. U., Buitelaar, J. K., & Glennon, J. C. (2017). Practitioner Review: Psychological treatments for children and adolescents with conduct disorder problems—A systematic review and meta-analysis. Journal of Child Psychology and Psychiatry, *58*(1), 4–18. doi: 10.1111/jcpp.12590.

Fonagy, P., & Luyten, P. (2018). CPs in youth and the RDoC approach: A developmental, evolutionary-based view. Clinical Psychology Review, *64*, 57–76. doi: 10.1016/j.cpr.2017.08.010.

Frick, P. J., & Marsee, M. A. (2018). Psychopathy and developmental pathways to antisocial behavior in youth. In C. J. Patrick (Ed.), *Handbook of Psychopathy* (pp. 456–475). New York, NY: Guilford Press.

Vitaro, F., Brendgen, M., & Tremblay, R. E. (2017). Interplay between genetic and environmental influences on the development of aggressive–antisocial behavior during childhood and adolescence. In P. Sturmey (Ed.), *The Wiley Handbook of Violence and Aggression (Chapter 22)*. Hoboken, NJ: Wiley-Blackwell.

Discussion/Essay Questions

1. How do you understand the differences (or similarities) between oppositional defiant disorder and conduct disorder?
2. How does the concept of callous-unemotional traits help us to understand antisocial behavior in children and young people?
3. Discuss the most important potential causal factors involved in the development of antisocial behavior.
4. What are the relative merits of the main interventions available for antisocial behavior in children and young people?

Glossary

Additive genetic influences refer to genetic influences where the total effect on a trait is equal to the net sum of the combined effects of the individual alleles that influence that trait. For example, two copies of a risk allele will confer twice as much risk as having only one copy. The contributions of these alleles to the trait are independent of other alleles or the environment.

CPs refer to a range of oppositional or antisocial forms of behavior in childhood and adolescence.

Non-additive genetic influences refer to genetic influences that have a nonlinear effect. These include dominance (where the presence of a dominant allele masks the expression of its recessive equivalent), epistasis (where alleles act differently depending on what other alleles are present), or gene–environment effects (where the contribution of an allele changes depending on the environment).

Non-shared environmental influences are environmental influences that result in differences between siblings.

Relational aggression is aggressive behavior that harms social relationships of others.

Shared environmental influences are environmental influences that result in similarities between siblings.

References

Ackermann, K., Kirchner, M., Bernhard, A., Martinelli, A., Anomitri, C., Baker, R., & Freitag, C. M. (2019). Relational aggression in adolescents with conduct disorder: Sex differences and behavioral correlates. Journal of Abnormal Child Psychology, *47*(10), 1625–1637. doi: 10.1007/s10802-019-00541-6.

American Psychiatric Association. (2013). *Diagnostic and Statistical Manual of Mental Disorders, (DSM-5)* (5th ed.) Washington, DC.

Azeredo, A., Moreira, D., & Barbosa, F. (2018). ADHD, CD, and ODD: Systematic review of genetic and environmental risk factors. Research into Development Disability, *82*, 10–19. doi:https://doi.org/10.1016/j.ridd.2017.12.010.

Bansal, P. S., Waschbusch, D. A., Haas, S. M., Babinski, D. E., King, S., Andrade, B. F., & Willoughby, M. T. (2019). Effects of intensive behavioral treatment for children with varying levels of CPs and callous-unemotional traits. Behavior Therapies, *50*(1), 1–14. doi:https://doi.org/10.1016/j.beth.2018.03.003.

Bevilacqua, L., Hale, D., Barker, E. D., & Viner, R. (2018). CPs trajectories and psychosocial outcomes: A systematic review and meta-analysis. European Child Adolescent Psychiatry, *27*(10), 1239–1260. doi: 10.1007/s00787-017-1053-4.

Blair, R. J. R., & Zhang, R. (2020). Recent neuro-imaging findings with respect to conduct disorder, callous-unemotional traits and psychopathy. Current Opinion Psychiatry, *33*(1), 45–50. doi: 10.1097/yco.0000000000000559.

Boylan, K., Vaillancourt, T., Boyle, M., & Szatmari, P. (2007). Comorbidity of internalizing disorders in children with oppositional defiant disorder. European Child Adolescent Psychiatry, *16*(8), 484–494. doi: 10.1007/s00787-007-0624-1.

Bradshaw, C. P., Waasdorp, T. E., & Leaf, P. J. (2012). Effects of school-wide positive behavioral interventions and supports on child behavior problems. Pediatrics, *130*(5), e1136–e1145. doi: 10.1542/peds.2012-0243.

Braga, T., Cunha, O., & Maia, A. (2018). The enduring effect of maltreatment on antisocial behavior: A meta-analysis of longitudinal studies. Aggression and Violent Behavior, *40*, 91–100. doi: 10.1016/j.avb.2018.04.003.

Burke, J. D., Loeber, R., Lahey, B. B., & Rathouz, P. J. (2005). Developmental transitions among affective and behavioral disorders in adolescent boys. Journal of Child Psychological Psychiatry, *46*(11), 1200–1210. doi: 10.1111/j.1469-7610.2005.00422.x.

Burt, S. A. (2009a). Are there meaningful etiological differences within antisocial behavior? Results of a meta-analysis. Clincal Psychology Review, *29*(2), 163–178. doi: 10.1016/j.cpr.2008.12.004.

Burt, S. A. (2009b). Rethinking environmental contributions to child and adolescent psychopathology: A meta-analysis of shared environmental influences. Psychological Bulletin, *135*(4), 608–637. doi: 10.1037/a0015702.

Caspi, A., McClay, J., Moffitt, T. E., Mill, J., Martin, J., Craig, I. W., & Poulton, R. (2002). Role of genotype in the cycle of violence in maltreated children. Science, *297*(5582), 851–854. doi: 10.1126/science.1072290.

Chacko, A., Jensen, S. A., Lowry, L. S., Cornwell, M., Chimklis, A., Chan, E., & Pulgarin, B. (2016). Engagement in behavioral parent training: Review of the literature and implications for practice. Clinical Child and Family Psychological Review, *19*(3), 204–215. doi: 10.1007/s10567-016-0205-2.

Collishaw, S., Maughan, B., Goodman, R., & Pickles, A. (2004). Time trends in adolescent mental health. Journal of Child Psychology and Psychiatry, *45*(8), 1350–1362. doi: 10.1111/j.1469-7610.2004.00335.x.

Comeau, J., Georgiades, K., Duncan, L., Wang, L., Boyle, M. H., & Team, O. C. H.

S. (2019). Changes in the prevalence of child and youth mental disorders and perceived need for professional help between 1983 and 2014: Evidence from the Ontario child health study. The Canadian Journal of Psychiatry, *64*(4), 256–264.

Crum, K. I., Waschbusch, D. A., Bagner, D. M., & Coxe, S. (2015). Effects of callous-unemotional traits on the association between parenting and child CPs. Child Psychiatry and Human Development, *46*(6), 967–980. doi: 10.1007/s10578-015-0535-1.

De Brito, S. A., McCrory, E. J., Mechelli, A., Wilke, M., Jones, A. P., Hodgins, S., & Viding, E. (2011). Small, but not perfectly formed: Decreased white matter concentration in boys with psychopathic tendencies. Molecular Psychiatry, *16*(5), 476–477. doi: mp201074 [pii] 10.1038/mp.2010.74.

Demmer, D. H., Hooley, M., Sheen, J., McGillivray, J. A., & Lum, J. A. G. (2017). Sex differences in the prevalence of oppositional defiant disorder during middle childhood: A meta-analysis. Journal of Abnormal Child Psychology, *45*(2), 313-325. doi: 10.1007/s10802-016-0170-8.

Egerton, G. A., Jenzer, T., Blayney, J. A., Kimber, J., Colder, C. R., & Read, J. P. (2020). Distress-related internalizing symptoms interact with externalizing symptoms to predict alcohol problems in an inpatient adolescent sample. The American Journal on Addictions, *29*(1), 57-64. doi:10.1111/ajad.12980

Fanti, K. A. (2018). Understanding heterogeneity in conduct disorder: A review of psychophysiological studies. Neuroscience & Biobehavioral Reviews, *91*, 4–20. doi:https://doi.org/10.1016/j.neubiorev.2016.09.022.

Fleming, A. P., McMahon, R. J., & King, K. M. (2017). Structured parent–child observations predict development of CPs: The importance of parental negative attention in child-directed play. Prevention Science, *18*(3), 257–267. doi: 10.1007/s11121-016-0672-1.

Fonagy, P., Butler, S., Cottrell, D., Scott, S., Pilling, S., Eisler, I., & Goodyer, I. M. (2018). Multisystemic therapy versus management as usual in the treatment of adolescent antisocial behaviour (START): A pragmatic, randomised controlled, superiority trial. Lancet Psychiatry, *5*(2), 119–133. doi: 10.1016/S2215-0366(18)30001-4.

Fonagy, P., Butler, S., Cottrell, D., Scott, S., Pilling, S., Eisler, I., & Goodyer, I. M. (2020). Multisystemic therapy versus management as usual in the treatment of adolescent antisocial behaviour (START): 5-year follow-up of a pragmatic, randomised, controlled, superiority trial. The Lancet Psychiatry, *7*(5), 420–430.

Fonagy, P., Cottrell, D., Phillips, J., Bevington, D., Glaser, D., & Allison, E. (2014). *What works for whom?: A critical review of treatments for children and adolescents*. New York, NY: Guilford Publications.

Fonagy, P., & Luyten, P. (2018). CPs in youth and the RDoC approach: A developmental, evolutionary-based view. Clinical Psychology Review, *64*, 57–76. doi:https://doi.org/10.1016/j.cpr.2017.08.010.

Forgatch, M. S., & Kjøbli, J. (2016). Parent management training—Oregon model: Adapting intervention with rigorous research. Family Process, *55*(3), 500–513. doi: 10.1111/famp.12224.

Frick, P. J., & Morris, A. S. (2004). Temperament and developmental pathways to CPs. Journal of Clinical Child & Adolescent Psychology, *33*(1), 54–68. doi: 10.1207/S15374424JCCP3301_6.

Galán, C. A., Wang, F. L., Shaw, D. S., & Forbes, E. E. (2020). Early childhood trajectories of CPs and hyperactivity/attention problems: Predicting adolescent and adult antisocial behavior and internalizing problems. Journal of Clinical Child & Adolescent Psychology, *49*(2), 200–214. doi: 10.1080/15374416.2018.1534206.

Ghandour, R. M., Sherman, L. J., Vladutiu, C. J., Ali, M. M., Lynch, S. E., Bitsko, R. H., & Blumberg, S. J. (2019). Prevalence and treatment of depression, anxiety, and CPs in US children. Journal of Pediatrics, *206*, 256–267, e253. doi:https://doi.org/10.1016/j.jpeds.2018.09.021.

Hendriks, A. M., Bartels, M., Colins, O. F., & Finkenauer, C. (2018). Childhood aggression: A synthesis of reviews and meta-analyses to reveal patterns and opportunities for prevention and intervention strategies. Neuroscience & Biobehavioral Reviews, *91*, 278–291. doi:https://doi.org/10.1016/j.neubiorev.2018.03.021.

Henggeler, S. W. (1999). Multisystemic therapy: An overview of clinical procedures, outcomes, and policy implications. Child Psychology and Psychiatry Review, *4*, 2–10. doi:https://doi.org/10.1017/S1360641798001786.

Henggeler, S. W., Clingempeel, W. G., Brondino, M. J., & Pickrel, S. G. (2002). Four-year follow-up of multisystemic therapy with substance-abusing and substance-dependent juvenile offenders. Journal of the American Academy of Child and Adolescent Psychiatry, *41*(7), 868–874. doi: 10.1097/00004583-200207000-00021.

Holmes, S. E., Slaughter, J. R., & Kashani, J. (2001). Risk factors in childhood that lead to the development of conduct disorder and antisocial personality disorder. Child Psychiatry & Human Development, *31*(3), 183–193. doi: 10.1023/A:1026425304480.

Holz, N. E., Zohsel, K., Laucht, M., Banaschewski, T., Hohmann, S., & Brandeis, D. (2018). Gene × environment interactions in conduct disorder: Implications for future treatments. Neuroscience & Biobehavioral Reviews, *91*, 239–258. doi:https://doi.org/10.1016/j.neubiorev.2016.08.017.

Husby, S. M., & Wichstrøm, L. (2017). Interrelationships and continuities in symptoms of oppositional defiant and conduct disorders from age 4 to 10 in the community. Journal of Abnormal Child Psychology, *45*(5), 947–958. doi: 10.1007/s10802-016-0210-4.

Johnson, V. A., Kemp, A. H., Heard, R., Lennings, C. J., & Hickie, I. B. (2015). Childhood versus adolescent-onset antisocial youth with conduct disorder: Psychiatric illness, neuropsychological and psychosocial function. PLoS One, *10*(4), e0121627–e0121627. doi: 10.1371/journal.pone.0121627.

Kazdin, A. E. (2017). Parent management training and problem-solving skills training for child and adolescent CPs. Evidence-Based Psychotherapies for Children and Adolescents, 142–158.

Kazdin, A. E. (2018). Implementation and evaluation of treatments for children and adolescents with CPs: Findings, challenges, and future directions. Psychotherapy Research, *28*(1), 3–17. doi: 10.1080/10503307.2016.1208374.

Kim-Cohen, J., Caspi, A., Moffitt, T. E., Harrington, H., Milne, B. J., & Poulton, R. (2003). Prior juvenile diagnoses in adults with mental disorder: Developmental follow-back of a prospective longitudinal cohort. Archives of General Psychiatry, *60*(7), 709–717. doi: 10.1001/archpsyc.60.7.709.

Kolko, D. J., Dorn, L. D., Bukstein, O., & Burke, J. D. (2008). Clinically referred ODD children with or without CD and healthy controls: Comparisons across contextual domains. Journal of Child and Family Studies, *17*(5), 714–734.

Larson, K., Russ, S. A., Kahn, R. S., & Halfon, N. (2011). Patterns of comorbidity, functioning, and service use for US children with ADHD, 2007. Pediatrics, *127*(3), 462–470. doi: 10.1542/peds.2010-0165.

Lochman, J. E., Boxmeyer, C., Powell, N., Qu, L., Wells, K., & Windle, M. (2009). Dissemination of the Coping Power Program: Importance of intensity of counselor training. Journal of Consulting Clinical Psychology, *77*(3), 397–409. doi: 10.1037/a0014514.

Lochman, J. E., & Wells, K. C. (2004). The Coping Power Program for Preadolescent Aggressive Boys and Their Parents: Outcome effects at the 1-year follow-up. Journal of Consulting Clinical Psychology, *72*(4), 571–578. doi: 10.1037/0022-006X.72.4.571.

Lundahl, B., Risser, H. J., & Lovejoy, M. C. (2006). A meta-analysis of parent training: Moderators and follow-up effects. Clinical Psychology Review, *26*(1), 86–104.

Mason, D. A., & Frick, P. J. (1994). The heritability of antisocial behavior: A meta-analysis of twin and adoption studies. Journal of Psychopathology and Behavioral Assessment, *16*(4), 301–323. doi: 10.1007/BF02239409.

Menting, A. T. A., Orobio de Castro, B., & Matthys, W. (2013). Effectiveness of the Incredible Years parent training to modify disruptive and prosocial child behavior:

A meta-analytic review. Clinical Psychology Review, *33*(8), 901–913. doi:https://doi.org/10.1016/j.cpr.2013.07.006.

Midgley, N., O'Keeffe, S., French, L., & Kennedy, E. (2017). Psychodynamic psychotherapy for children and adolescents: An updated narrative review of the evidence base. Journal of Child Psychotherapy, *43*(3), 307–329. doi: 10.1080/0075417X.2017.1323945.

Mitchison, G. M., & Njardvik, U. (2019). Prevalence and gender differences of ODD, anxiety, and depression in a sample of children with ADHD. Journal of Attention Disorders, *23*(11), 13391345. doi: 10.1177/1087054715608442.

Moffitt, T. E. (2005). Genetic and environmental influences on antisocial behaviors: Evidence from behavioral–genetic research. Advances in Genetics, *55*, 41–104. doi: 10.1016/S0065-2660(05)55003-X [pii].

Moore, A. A., Silberg, J. L., Roberson-Nay, R., & Mezuk, B. (2017). Life course persistent and adolescence limited conduct disorder in a nationally representative US sample: Prevalence, predictors, and outcomes. Social Psychiatry and Psychiatric Epidemiology, *52*(4), 435–443. doi: 10.1007/s00127-017-1337-5.

Murray, J., Irving, B., Farrington, D. P., Colman, I., & Bloxsom, C. A. (2010). Very early predictors of CPs and crime: Results from a national cohort study. Journal of Child Psychology and Psychiatry, *51*(11), 1198–1207.doi:10.1111/j.1469-7610.2010.02287.x.

Navarro-Soria, I., Servera, M., & Burns, G. L. (2020). Association of Foster Care and its duration with clinical symptoms and impairment: Foster care versus non-foster care comparisons with Spanish children. Journal of Child and Family Studies, *29*(2), 526–533. doi: 10.1007/s10826-019-01596-1.

Nock, M. K., Kazdin, A. E., Hiripi, E., & Kessler, R. C. (2006). Prevalence, subtypes, and correlates of DSM-IV conduct disorder in the National Comorbidity Survey Replication. Psychological Medicine, *36*(5), 699–710.doi:10.1017/S0033291706007082.

Ogden, T., & Hagen, K. (2019). *Adolescent Mental Health: Prevention and intervention* (2nd ed.). London, UK: Routledge.

Ouellet-Morin, I., Côté, S. M., Vitaro, F., Hébert, M., Carbonneau, R., Lacourse, É., & Tremblay, R. E. (2016). Effects of the MAOA gene and levels of exposure to violence on antisocial outcomes. British Journal of Psychiatry, *208*(1), 42–48. doi: 10.1192/bjp.bp.114.162081.

Pasalich, D. S., Witkiewitz, K., McMahon, R. J., Pinderhughes, E. E., & The CPs Prevention Research (2016). Indirect effects of the fast track intervention on conduct disorder symptoms and callous-unemotional traits: Distinct pathways involving discipline and warmth. Journal of Abnormal Child Psychology, *44*(3), 587–597. doi: 10.1007/s10802-015-0059-y.

Pinquart, M. (2017). Associations of parenting dimensions and styles with externalizing problems of children and adolescents: An updated meta-analysis. Devevelopmental Psychology, *53*(5), 873–932. doi: 10.1037/dev0000295.

Piotrowska, P. J., Stride, C. B., Maughan, B., Goodman, R., McCaw, L., & Rowe, R. (2015). Income gradients within child and adolescent antisocial behaviours. British Journal of Psychiatry, *207*(5), 385–391. doi: 10.1192/bjp.bp.113.143636.

Plueck, J., Eichelberger, I., Hautmann, C., Hanisch, C., Jaenen, N., & Doepfner, M. (2015). Effectiveness of a teacher-based indicated prevention program for preschool children with externalizing problem behavior. Prevention Science, *16*(2), 233–241. doi: 10.1007/s11121-014-0487-x.

Powell, N. P., Lochman, J. E., Boxmeyer, C. L., Barry, T. D., & Pardini, D. A. (2017). The Coping power program for aggressive behavior in children. *Evidence-based psychotherapies for children and adolescents* (pp. 159–176). New York, NY: Guilford.

Rice, F., Lifford, K. J., Thomas, H. V., & Thapar, A. (2007). Mental health and functional outcomes of maternal and adolescent reports of adolescent depressive symptoms. Journal of the American Academy of Child and Adolescent Psychiatry, *46*(9), 1162–1170. doi: 10.1097/chi.0b013e3180cc255f.

Rowe, R., Costello, E. J., Angold, A., Copeland, W. E., & Maughan, B. (2010).

Developmental pathways in oppositional defiant disorder and conduct disorder. Journal of Abnormal Psychology, *119*(4), 726–738. doi: 10.1037/a0020798.

Salvatore, J. E., & Dick, D. M. (2018). Genetic influences on conduct disorder. Neuroscience & Biobehavioral Reviews, *91*, 91–101. doi: https://doi.org/10.1016/j.neubiorev.2016.06.034.

Sanders, M. R., Kirby, J. N., Tellegen, C. L., & Day, J. J. (2014). The Triple P-Positive Parenting Program: A systematic review and meta-analysis of a multi-level system of parenting support. Clin Psychol Rev, *34*(4), 337-357. doi:https://doi.org/10.1016/j.cpr.2014.04.003

Schaeffer, C. M., & Borduin, C. M. (2005). Long-term follow-up to a randomized clinical trial of multisystemic therapy with serious and violent juvenile offenders. Journal of Consulting and Clinical Psychology, *73*(3), 445–453. doi: 10.1037/0022-006X.73.3.445.

Sentse, M., Kretschmer, T., de Haan, A., & Prinzie, P. (2017). CP trajectories between age 4 and 17 and their association with behavioral adjustment in emerging adulthood. Journal of Youth Adolescence, *46*(8), 1633–1642. doi: 10.1007/s10964-016-0476-4.

Steinhausen, H.-C., & Jakobsen, H. (2019). Incidence rates of treated mental disorders in childhood and adolescence in a complete nationwide nirth cohort. Journal of Clinical Psychiatry, *80*(3). doi: 10.4088/jcp.17m12012 (Accession No. 31050232).

Tarver, J., Daley, D., Lockwood, J., & Sayal, K. (2014). Are self-directed parenting interventions sufficient for externalising behaviour problems in childhood? A systematic review and meta-analysis. European Child Adolescence Psychiatry, *23*(12), 1123–1137. doi: 10.1007/s00787-014-0556-5.

Tracy, P. E., Kempf-Leonard, K., & Abramoske-James, S. (2009). Gender differences in delinquency and juvenile justice processing: Evidence from national data. Crime & Delinquency, *55*(2), 171–215. doi: 10.1177/0011128708330628.

van der Stouwe, T., Asscher, J. J., Stams, G. J., Dekovic, M., & van der Laan, P. H. (2014). The effectiveness of Multisystemic Therapy (MST): A meta-analysis. Clinical Psychology Review, *34*(6), 468–481. doi: 10.1016/j.cpr.2014.06.006.

Vasileva, M., Graf, R. K., Reinelt, T., Petermann, U., & Petermann, F. (2020). Research review: A meta-analysis of the international prevalence and comorbidity of mental disorders in children between 1 and 7 years. *Journal of Child Psychology and Psychiatry* (not yet available). https://acamh.onlinelibrary.wiley.com/doi/epdf/10.1111/jcpp.13261.

Veenman, B., Luman, M., & Oosterlaan, J. (2018). Efficacy of behavioral classroom programs in primary school. A meta-analysis focusing on randomized controlled trials. PLoS One, *13*(10), e0201779–e0201779. doi: 10.1371/journal.pone.0201779.

Waller, R., Hyde, L. W., Klump, K. L., & Burt, S. A. (2018). Parenting is an environmental predictor of callous-unemotional traits and aggression: A monozygotic twin differences study. Journal of the American Academy of Child & Adolescent Psychiatry, *57*(12), 955–963. doi:https://doi.org/10.1016/j.jaac.2018.07.882.

Wertz, J., Agnew-Blais, J., Caspi, A., Danese, A., Fisher, H., Goldman-Mellor, S., & Arseneault, L. (2018). From childhood CPs to poor functioning at age 18 years: Examining explanations in a longitudinal cohort study. Journal of American Academy Child Adolescent Psychiatry, *57*(1), 54–60. doi: 10.1016/j.jaac.2017.09.437.

Wiesner, M., Kim, H. K., & Capaldi, D. M. (2005). Developmental trajectories of offending: Validation and prediction to young adult alcohol use, drug use, and depressive symptoms. Development and Psychopathology, *17*(1), 251–270. doi: 10.1017/S0954579405050133.

Zych, I., Ortega-Ruiz, R., & Del Rey, R. (2015). Systematic review of theoretical studies on bullying and cyberbullying: Facts, knowledge, prevention, and intervention. Aggression and Violent Behavior, *23*, 1–21. doi:https://doi.org/10.1016/j.avb.2015.10.001.

Chapter 8

Fear and Anxiety

Andres G. Viana, Erika S. Trent, Haley E. Conroy, and Elizabeth M. Raines

Chapter Overview

Fear, a universal human experience with deep evolutionary roots, is defined as a set of behavioral, physical, and emotional reactions to defend the body from an identifiable threat (Öhman, 2008). An angry dog, a burglar trying to break into our home, a loud bang in the middle of the night, or a terrorist attack can trigger our *fight-or-flight response*, a physiological reaction that prepares the body by concentrating resources to either confront the threat or escape it. As children mature, they experience a number of common fears that are considered normative. Infants and toddlers fear strangers and separation from their caregivers; young children often report fears of the dark, storms, and imaginary creatures; for adolescents and young adults, fear of social and evaluative situations help them navigate intimacy and romantic relationships. In most cases, children master these common fears by developing coping skills through exposure—gradually confronting the feared situations—in order to correct erroneous beliefs and learn to tolerate their fearful responses (Ale, McCarthy, Rothschild, & Whiteside, 2015).

Although fear and anxiety are closely related emotional phenomena, there are important distinctions between the two constructs. How is anxiety different from fear? While fear is typically our body's response to an immediate threat, *anxiety is considered a future-oriented emotion characterized by an unpleasant feeling of foreboding, nervousness, tension, or apprehension, and a belief that there is little control over it* (Öhman, 2008). Consistent with this definition, the DSM-5 (American Psychiatric Association, 2013), defines anxiety as the "anticipation of

Developmental Psychopathology, First Edition. Edited by Amanda Venta, Carla Sharp, Jack M. Fletcher, and Peter Fonagy.

future threat . . . often associated with muscle tension and vigilance in preparation for future danger and cautious or avoidant behaviors" (p. 189). Thus, when a child experiences anxiety, there is typically no identifiable fear stimulus; rather, it is the *perception of threat*. As Öhman (2008) eloquently described, "in fear, therefore, it is an obvious (albeit not necessarily clearly perceived) danger located in space and time that must be dealt with; in anxiety, on the other hand, the nature and location of the threat remain more obscure and thus are difficult to cope with by active defensive maneuvers" (p. 710). Below is an example of a child with an *anxiety disorder*.

Case vignette

Mary is an eight-year-old girl who lives with her biological parents and two younger brothers. Mary was a "nervous child" growing up, often requesting to sleep in her parents' bedroom because of a fear of the dark that had since subsided. During the day, Mary was often seen biting her nails and, despite living in a very safe neighborhood, she worried about a burglar breaking into their house at night. Two months ago, while grocery shopping with her mom for their family Thanksgiving holiday, Mary became distracted by the cereal boxes and did not notice she had separated from her mother. Mary began to scream and search frantically for her mother, but given the crowds of holiday shoppers, it took almost 10 minutes to find each other. Upon their reunion, Mary was crying inconsolably and breathing heavily. Mary refuses to go anywhere without her mother since then. She phones her mother repeatedly at work to make sure she is safe and begs her parents not to go out on date nights. Although Mary used to enjoy sleepovers at her best friend's house, she has declined the last five invitations. Mary was also recently invited to a birthday party and, upon learning that her mother would have to drop her off instead of staying with her at the party, she began to cry uncontrollably, refusing to go.

Which diagnoses would you consider for Mary and why? What other information would you gather during an assessment to guide the diagnosis and treatment of Mary's behaviors?

Definition, Diagnosis, and Clinical Features

Although both fear and anxiety are considered ubiquitous emotional experiences, it is important to distinguish between clinical (e.g., anxiety disorders and phobias) and normal manifestations of fear and anxiety. Such distinctions are made on the basis of their frequency (how often), severity (how intense), and duration (for how long), as well as the degree to which the child's *psychosocial functioning* is impaired. Children with anxiety disorders experience a persistent sense of dread that is disproportionate to the identified fear stimulus and may express this in many ways, including excessive crying, tantrums, avoidance of feared situations, clinginess, and freezing responses. This chapter does not address specific anxiety disorders exhaustively, but will rather examine anxiety disorders as a cluster from a developmental psychopathology lens. Anxiety disorders, as a cluster, share several characteristics, such as physiological arousal, catastrophic thoughts, and avoidance; yet, there are specific features of each anxiety disorder that distinguish one from another another (see Table 8.1). For example, in generalized anxiety disorder, chronic and uncontrollable worry is a core feature, whereas a significant fear of negative evaluation is a central aspect of social anxiety disorder.

Prevalence

Anxiety disorders are the most common form of psychopathology in children and adolescents (Merikangas et al., 2010b). The DSM-5 (APA, 2013) identifies 11 types of anxiety disorders that can be diagnosed in youth and adults. *Epidemiological studies* suggest that, in any given year, approximately 13% of children are diagnosed with an anxiety disorder (Costello, Egger, Copeland, Erkanli, & Angold, 2011).

Gender Differences

Large-scale, nationally representative studies of adolescents have found that girls are significantly more likely to meet criteria for an anxiety disorder than boys (Merikangas et al., 2010b). Girls are also more likely to exhibit *comorbidity*, such as depression (Nolen-Hoeksema, 2000). *Longitudinal research* looking at this association suggests that anxiety disorders tend to precede the developmental onset of a mood disorder.

Age differences

As many as 30% of youth will develop an anxiety disorder by the time they are 18 years old (Merikangas et al., 2010b). Most childhood anxiety disorders emerge sometime in middle childhood (Merikangas et al., 2010a), but as many as 7-11% of children under the age of five years exhibit clinically significant anxiety symptoms (Costello, Egger, & Angold, 2005). In some cases, published estimates regarding the onset of anxiety disorders are influenced by contextual factors that can make certain problems noticeable across development. For example, a child's separation anxiety may only become problematic when they start school, even though the child may have been struggling with anxiety before then.

TABLE 8.1 Anxiety Disorders in the DSM-5, ICD-11, and ASEBA Scales

	DSM-5		*ICD-11*	
Anxiety Disorder	*Core Feature*	*Example*	*Description*	*ASEBA DSM Scales*
Separation Anxiety Disorder	Excessive fear or anxiety concerning separation from those to whom the individual is attached.	Matt experiences intense fear every morning when his mom drops him off at school.	Separation anxiety disorder is characterized by marked and excessive fear or anxiety about separation from specific attachment figures. In children, separation anxiety typically focuses on caregivers, parents, or other family members; in adults, it is typically a romantic partner or children. Manifestations of separation anxiety may include thoughts of harm or untoward events befalling the attachment figure, reluctance to go to school or work, recurrent excessive distress upon separation, reluctance or refusal to sleep away from the attachment figure, and recurrent nightmares about separation. The symptoms persist for at least several months and are sufficiently severe to result in significant distress or significant impairment in personal, family, social, educational, occupational, or other important areas of functioning.	**Anxiety Problems 1.5–5 years old** Dependent Not sleep alone Out of home Fears Upset by separation Nervous Nightmares Shows panic Fearful Worries
Selective Mutism	Consistent failure to speak in specific social situations in which there is an expectation for speaking (e.g., at school) despite speaking in other situations.	Sally speaks fluently when she is home with her parents, but does not speak when she goes to school.	Selective mutism is characterized by consistent selectivity in speaking, such that a child demonstrates adequate language competence in specific social situations, typically at home, but consistently fails to speak in others, typically at school. The disturbance lasts for at least one month, is not limited to the first month of school, and is of sufficient severity to interfere with educational or occupational achievement or with social communication. Failure to speak is not due to a lack of knowledge of, or comfort with, the spoken language required in the social situation (e.g., a different language spoken at school than at home).	

(Continued)

TABLE 8.1 (Continued)

	DSM-5		*ICD-11*	
Anxiety Disorder	*Core Feature*	*Example*	*Description*	*ASEBA DSM Scales*
Specific Phobia	Marked fear or anxiety about a specific object or situation (e.g., animals, needles, thunderstorms).	Sam is afraid of snakes so he avoids going anywhere where there might be a snake.	Specific phobia is characterized by a marked and excessive fear or anxiety that consistently occurs when exposed to one or more specific objects or situations (e.g., proximity to certain animals, flying, heights, closed spaces, the sight of blood, or injury) and that is out of proportion to the actual danger. The phobic objects or situations are avoided or else endured with intense fear or anxiety. Symptoms persist for at least several months and are sufficiently severe to result in significant distress or significant impairment in personal, family, social, educational, occupational, or other important areas of functioning.	**Anxiety Problems** **6–18 years old** Dependent fears Fears school Fears do bad Nervous Nightmares Fearful Self- conscious Worries
Social Anxiety Disorder (Social Phobia)	Marked fear or anxiety about one or more social situations in which the individual is exposed to possible scrutiny by others.	Quinn is scared of getting on the bus because he knows it will be full of other people.	Social anxiety disorder is characterized by marked and excessive fear or anxiety that consistently occurs in one or more social situations such as social interactions (e.g., having a conversation), being observed (e.g., eating or drinking), or performing in front of others (e.g., giving a speech). The individual is concerned that he or she will act in a way, or show anxiety symptoms, that will be negatively evaluated by others. The social situations are consistently avoided or else endured with intense fear or anxiety. The symptoms persist for at least several months and are sufficiently severe to result in significant distress or significant impairment in personal, family, social, educational, occupational, or other important areas of functioning.	

Agoraphobia	Marked fear or anxiety triggered by the real or anticipated exposure to a wide range of situations.	Pam is afraid to leave her apartment because she is scared of being in open spaces.	Agoraphobia is characterized by marked and excessive fear or anxiety that occurs in response to multiple situations where escape might be difficult or help might not be available, such as using public transportation, being in crowds, being outside the home alone (e.g., in shops, theatres, standing in line). The individual is consistently anxious about these situations due to a fear of specific negative outcomes (e.g., panic attacks, other incapacitating or embarrassing physical symptoms). The situations are actively avoided, entered only under specific circumstances such as in the presence of a trusted companion, or endured with intense fear or anxiety. The symptoms persist for least several months, and are sufficiently severe to result in significant distress or significant impairment in personal, family, social, educational, occupational, or other important areas of functioning.
Generalized Anxiety Disorder	Excessive anxiety and worry about a number of events or activities.	Riley is worried about many things, including his grades and performance in sports. His worry makes it hard for him to focus, relax, or sleep.	Generalized anxiety disorder is characterized by marked symptoms of anxiety that persist for at least several months, for more days than not, manifested by either general apprehension (i.e., 'free-floating anxiety') or excessive worry focused on multiple everyday events, most often concerning family, health, finances, and school or work, together with additional symptoms such as muscular tension or motor restlessness, sympathetic autonomic over-activity, subjective experience of nervousness, difficulty maintaining concentration, irritability, or sleep disturbance. The symptoms result in significant distress or significant impairment in personal, family, social, educational, occupational, or other important areas of functioning. The symptoms are not a manifestation of another health condition and are not due to the effects of a substance or medication on the central nervous system.

(*Continued*)

TABLE 8.1 (Continued)

	DSM-5		*ICD-11*	
Anxiety Disorder	*Core Feature*	*Example*	*Description*	*ASEBA DSM Scales*
Substance/ Medication-Induced Anxiety Disorder	Excessive nervousness, anxiety and worry caused by using, or stopping the use of, a substance (e.g., alcohol, illicit drugs) or medication.	John has begun to experience severe anxiety, panic attacks, and tingling sensations after stopping his illicit use of benzodiazepines.	Not included	
Anxiety Disorder Due to Another Medical Condition	Excessive nervousness, anxiety and worry directly caused by a physical health condition.	Carlos has been experiencing severe panic and anxiety symptoms since having been diagnosed with cancer.	Not included	

Note. Not included are Other Specified Anxiety Disorder and Unspecified Anxiety Disorder, two diagnostic labels that are used among youth who experience significant and interfering anxiety but do not have enough symptoms to warrant one of the more specific anxiety disorder diagnoses.

PREVALENCE BY RACE AND ETHNICITY

Findings regarding racial and ethnic differences in the prevalence of anxiety disorders have been mixed, with some studies demonstrating higher rates of anxiety disorders among ethnic minorities while other studies fail to find such differences. For example, Beidel and colleagues found higher rates of test anxiety and social anxiety disorder among African American youth compared to European Americans (Beidel, Turner, & Trager, 1994). In studies of *clinic-referred youth*, higher rates of self-reported fears have been found among African American youth compared to European Americans (Last & Perrin, 1993). Several researchers have also found higher rates of separation anxiety disorder and greater worry among Latinx youth relative to European Americans (Pina & Silverman, 2004). Likewise, studies have shown that Asian American children reported higher levels of test anxiety than European American children (Pang, 1991).

In contrast, several studies of children *seeking treatment* for anxiety disorders have failed to find racial and/or ethnic differences. One study comparing African American and European American youth did not find differences in the duration of their anxiety disorder or their lifetime history of anxiety disorders (Last & Perrin, 1993). Ferrell and colleagues (2004) also failed to find differences in the severity of social phobia between African American and European American youth (Ferrell et al., 2004). Overall, the research suggests that racial and ethnic minority children *endorse* higher levels of anxiety symptoms than European American children, but data regarding racial and ethnic differences in the actual prevalence of anxiety disorders among treatment-seeking youth are more mixed (Anderson & Mayes, 2010).

Interestingly, there is also evidence that Latinx and Asian children may be more likely to endorse somatic symptoms of anxiety (e.g., breathing difficulties, perspiration) than European Americans (Varela, Weems, Berman, Hensley, & de Bernal, 2007). Although the reasons are not fully understood, researchers hypothesize that the stigma associated with psychological problems in some cultures may be partially responsible for the higher endorsement of somatic symptoms (Varela et al., 2007).

Comorbidity

Childhood anxiety disorders increase the risk for mood, substance use, and externalizing disorders as well as suicidal behaviors (Verduin & Kendall, 2003; Woodward & Fergusson, 2001). For instance, one study of adolescents and young adults found that *social anxiety disorder* preceded 85.2% of comorbid substance abuse disorders, 81.6% of mood disorders, and 64.6% of non-phobic anxiety disorders (Wittchen, Stein, & Kessler, 1999), suggesting that childhood anxiety may serve as a warning of what may lie ahead if left untreated.

Childhood anxiety disorders are also associated with significant functional impairments, such as poor academic performance, peer difficulties, and family relationship problems (Towe-Goodman, Franz, Copeland, Angold, & Egger, 2014). Somatic complaints, such as stomachaches, headaches, and *autonomic reactivity* are also common among anxious children (Albano, Chorpita, & Barlow, 2003). Children with anxiety report feeling lonelier and having fewer friends than their non-anxious peers (Albano et al., 2003). Avoidance behaviors may also impede the achievement of key developmental milestones, including dating, holding jobs, completing school and college, becoming socially independent and assertive, developing social supports, and learning about the world (Albano et al., 2003).

Developmental Course

Historically, childhood anxiety problems were seen as transient issues that a child would "grow out of." However, a sizable body of research has found that, for many, anxiety problems begin early in life, follow a chronic course, and increase the risk for the development of other psychopathologies (Albano et al., 2003; Beesdo, Knappe, & Pine, 2009). Research has found evidence of both *homotypic* and *heterotypic continuity* of childhood anxiety disorders. For instance, a study by Costello and colleagues (2003) found that *separation anxiety disorder (SAD)* in childhood predicted SAD in adolescence (homotypic continuity), and that overanxious disorder in childhood (a diagnosis in the DSM-III that was later substituted with *generalized anxiety disorder*) was predictive of depression in adolescence (heterotypic continuity). Likewise, Ferdinand and colleagues (Ferdinand, Dieleman, Ormel, & Verhulst, 2007) examined symptoms (vs. diagnoses) of anxiety and found that separation, social, and generalized anxiety symptoms assessed at the ages of 10–12 years significantly predicted those same classes of symptoms two years later. However, symptoms of separation anxiety also predicted anxiety symptoms unrelated to separation (e.g., social anxiety) two years later.

A Developmental Psychopathology Model of Anxiety Disorders

As you have learned throughout this book, consideration of risk and protective factors is a central tenet of developmental psychopathology investigations that aim to understand how pathological processes are set in motion. In the following sections, research on risks and protective factors for anxiety is described (Figure 8.1).

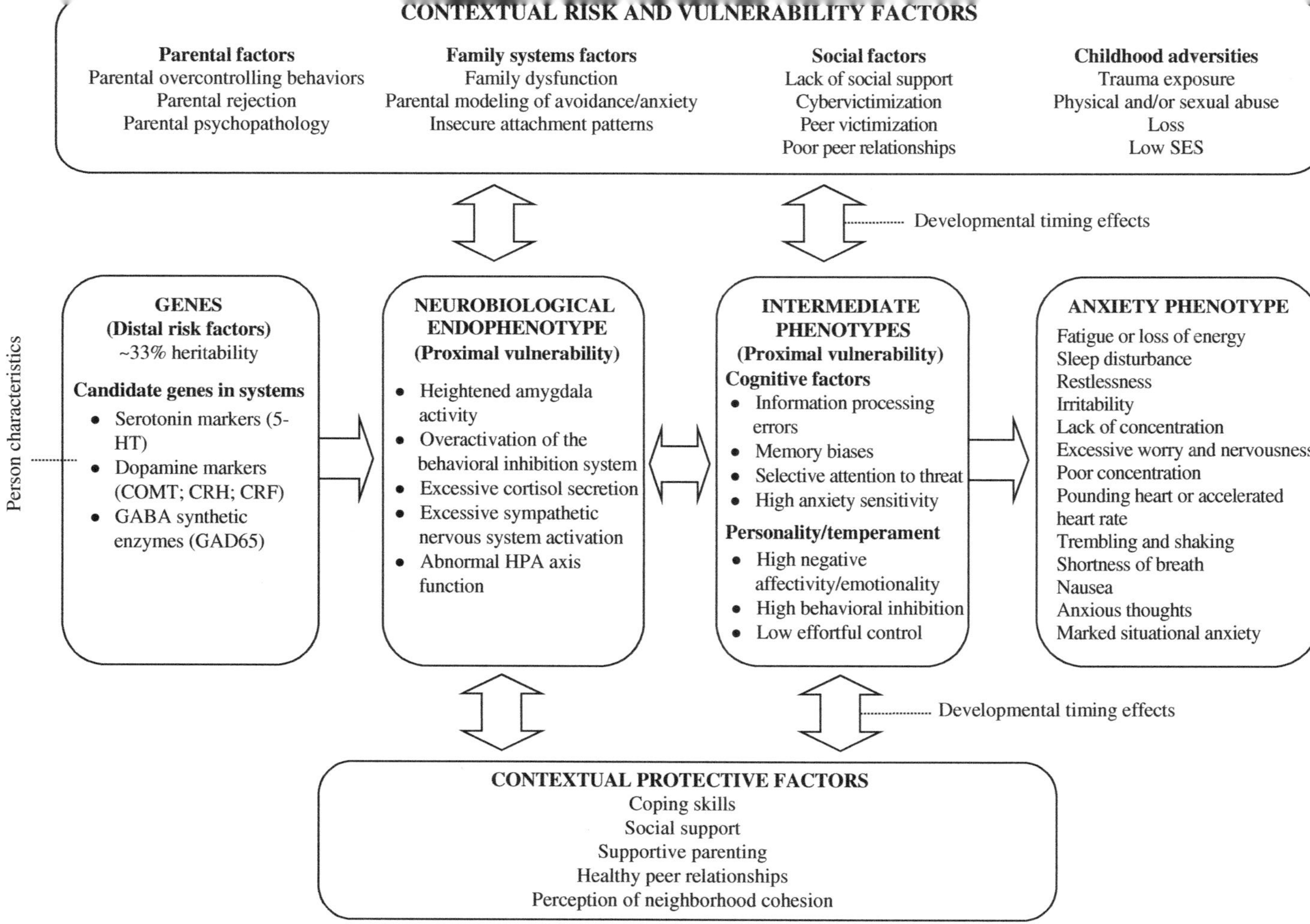

FIGURE 8.1 A Developmental Psychopathology Model of Childhood Anxiety

GENETIC FACTORS

Family and twin studies

Findings from *family and twin studies* provide substantial support for the genetic transmission of anxiety. Twin studies suggest that 33% of the variance in child anxiety is attributable to genetic heritability (Gregory & Eley, 2007). Children of clinically anxious parents are seven times as likely to be diagnosed with an anxiety disorder than children of parents without mental health problems, and twice as likely to meet criteria for an anxiety disorder diagnosis than children of parents with dysthymic disorder (a chronic yet less severe form of depression; Turner, Beidel, & Costello, 1987). Heritability may explain children's anxious disposition in early childhood, including behavioral withdrawal and avoidance, physiological reactivity, and response styles. However, recent work suggests that the strength of genetic influences on anxiety symptoms increases as children transition into adolescence and young adulthood (Bergen, Gardner, & Kendler, 2007). In addition to age, the effects of genetic factors may also be influenced by the child's sex (Gregory & Eley, 2007), such that anxiety symptoms may be more heritable among female than male children (Feigon, Waldman, Levy, & Hay, 2001).

Molecular genetic association studies

Though anxiety is a complex disorder that likely involves multiple genes (Gregory & Eley, 2007), researchers have relied on molecular genetic association studies to identify specific gene variants that may be related to anxiety. In these studies, scientists compare allele frequencies between anxious and healthy individuals. Most molecular genetic association studies have focused on markers of serotonin, a neurotransmitter implicated in emotional states including anxiety and depression (Gregory & Eley, 2007). Additionally, three genes related to dopamine (a neurotransmitter involved in reward-motivated behavior) have been examined as candidate genes for anxiety. However, despite the heritable nature of anxiety, association studies are yet to report robust associations between specific genes and anxiety disorders (Gregory & Eley, 2007; Trzaskowski et al., 2013).

Recent work suggests strong links between specific genes and *anxiety-related traits*. For example, the gene encoding of the gamma-aminobutyric acid (GABA)-synthetic enzyme GAD65 has been linked to behavioral inhibition, withdrawal, and avoidance among anxious children, but no GABA receptors have been directly linked to youth anxiety disorders (Gordon & Hen, 2004). Findings also suggest that polymorphisms in the promoter region (involved in the activation or suppression of a gene) of the serotonin transporter (5-HTT) may be related to behavioral inhibition and withdrawal, but not to specific anxiety disorders (Fox et al., 2005). Finally, although the field has taken large strides towards identifying associations between specific genes and anxiety disorders, recent *genome-wide association studies (GWAS)* have found that it is more likely that many genetic variants exert small influences on childhood anxiety (Trzaskowski et al., 2013).

NEUROBIOLOGICAL FACTORS

Structural and functional imaging findings

Rapid progress in *neuroscience* has allowed researchers to identify several neurobiological factors that contribute to anxiety. One of the most notable brain structures linked to the experience of anxiety is the *amygdala*, the hub of a "fear circuit" in the brain (LeDoux & Pine, 2016). One of the amygdala's primary functions is to evaluate the emotional content of incoming stimuli and project this to other systems in the brain, such as the *frontal cortex*, *hippocampus*, and *striatum*, which process this information and determine how to respond (LeDoux & Pine, 2016). Youth with anxiety disorders tend to show greater activation in the amygdala, compared with healthy controls. For example, when shown masked angry faces, anxiety-disordered youth showed greater right-side amygdala activation than healthy controls; the level of amygdala activation also positively correlated with their anxiety disorder severity (Monk et al., 2008). Moreover, anxiety-disordered youth showed a weaker coordination between the right amygdala and right ventrolateral prefrontal cortex than their non-anxious peers, with the ventrolateral prefrontal cortex not effectively modulating the amygdala's overactivation (Monk et al., 2008).

Functional brain studies have also found differential hemispheric activation between individuals with and without anxiety disorders. *Electroencephalogram (EEG)* research shows anxious children generally showed greater right than left frontal activation at baseline, whereas healthy controls showed no such asymmetry (Baving, Laucht, & Schmidt, 2002). *Functional magnetic resonance imaging (fMRI)* techniques have also expanded our understanding of how various brain regions are activated during anxiety-provoking experiences. Table 8.2 summarizes brain regions, their functions, and their role in anxiety.

Neurotransmitters

Anxiety research has focused on the neurotransmitters *serotonin (5-HT)* and *GABA*, as well as neurotransmitter systems such as the GABAergic, serotonergic, and noradrenergic systems (i.e., systems pertaining to the neurotransmitter noradrenaline; Gordon & Hen, 2004). Specifically, *anxiolytic medications* that treat anxiety symptoms, such as *benzodiazepines* and *selective serotonin reuptake inhibitors (SSRIs)* target GABAergic and serotonergic neurotransmitter systems. Benzodiazepines

TABLE 8.2 Summary of Brain Regions Associated with Child and Adolescent Anxiety

Brain Region	*Function*	*Significance in Anxiety*
Frontal lobes Right prefrontal lobe Left prefrontal cortex Ventrolateral prefrontal cortex (VLPC)	Goal-directed behaviors, affect-guided planning, suppression of startle response, interpretation of threat	Cognitive impairments, social-cognitive impairments, poor decision making
Midline and medial temporal structures Amygdala Hippocampus Hypothalamus Brain stem	Stress response, autonomic response, startle response, corticosteroid response, threat detection, emotional memory, decision making, contextual memory	Poor decision making, avoidance, behavioral inhibition, fearfulness, physiological hyperarousal, negative emotionality

increase GABA activity; since GABA is an inhibitory neurotransmitter, increased GABA activity leads to decreased feelings of anxiety. SSRIs prevent the reuptake of leftover serotonin in the synaptic gap, which increases overall levels of serotonin in the brain and can result in improved mood. These findings have led researchers to examine in more detail the role of these neurotransmitter systems in the etiology of anxiety symptoms and disorders.

Central nervous system

The *nervous system* is divided into two parts: the *central nervous system (CNS)*, which includes the brain and spinal cord, and the *peripheral nervous system (PNS)*, which includes all the nerves that branch from the brain and spinal cord to communicate with other parts of the body. One subsystem within the CNS that deserves particular attention is the *behavioral inhibition system*, which consists of several parts: the amygdala, noradrenergic projections of the locus coeruleus, and serotonergic projections of the median raphe (Gray & McNaughton, 2000). Overactivation of the behavioral inhibition system is associated with anxiety, excessive fear, hyperarousal, and negative emotionality. Another important subsystem within the CNS is the *hypothalamic–pituitary–adrenal (HPA) axis*, the "stress response" system. When you experience psychological or physical stress, the hypothalamus releases *corticotropin-releasing hormone (CRH)*, which causes the pituitary gland to release *adrenocorticotropic hormone (ACTH)*. ACTH, in turn, causes the adrenal cortex to release cortisol, which activates the body's cells and the brain to help you cope with the stressor in the moment. Cortisol also signals to the hypothalamus and pituitary gland to stop releasing CRH and ACTH, completing a feedback loop. Although cortisol can help you handle stressors in the short term, there are harmful consequences of prolonged cortisol secretion, including anxiety (Gunnar, Morison, Chisholm, & Schuder, 2001).

Peripheral nervous system

The peripheral nervous system is comprised of the enteric system and the *autonomic nervous system (ANS)*, which is further divided into the sympathetic nervous system and the parasympathetic nervous system. The *sympathetic nervous system* is active in response to perceived stress or threat, while the *parasympathetic nervous system* is active when energy is being conserved (e.g., restful states). Although these two branches of the ANS have seemingly opposing functions, at any given time, both branches are working. Excessive sympathetic nervous system activation has been consistently associated with child anxiety psychopathology (El-Sheikh, Arsiwalla, Hinnant, & Erath, 2011). Such overactivation is manifested in increased heart rate, blood pressure, and electrodermal responding. For instance, youth with anxiety disorders showed increased skin conductance and increased heart rate when they were exposed to a fear-eliciting stimulus (Weems, Zakem, Costa, Cannon, & Watts, 2005). Parasympathetic nervous system withdrawal has also been linked to child anxiety psychopathology, although findings are more mixed (Graziano & Derefinko, 2013).

TEMPERAMENT

Several *temperamental* traits are robustly associated with childhood anxiety disorders. One such trait is *behavioral inhibition*, defined as a general tendency to react cautiously and with restraint to novel stimuli or situations (Kagan, 2008). In contrast, behaviorally uninhibited children are said to have "an affectively spontaneous approach" to the unfamiliar (Kagan, 2008, p. 163). Children high in behavioral inhibition share some of the same behavioral, affective, and physiological characteristics seen among children with anxiety disorders, such as greater avoidance of novel situations, fear and clinginess to caregivers, and heightened levels of physiological arousal (Kagan, 2008; Weems & Silverman, 2008). Accordingly, behaviorally inhibited children are significantly more likely than behaviorally uninhibited children to receive an anxiety disorder diagnosis three years later (Biederman et al., 1993). Other studies have shown that behavioral inhibition in preschool-aged children significantly increased the risk of being diagnosed with social anxiety disorder in middle childhood (Hirshfeld-Becker et al., 2007). Relative to children with no behavioral inhibition, behaviorally inhibited children are also more likely to come from a family in which one or both parents have or have had an anxiety disorder (Rosenbaum et al., 1991). Twin studies have demonstrated high heritability of behavioral inhibition (DiLalla, Kagan, & Reznick, 1994), and its behavioral, affective, and physiological signs have been found to be moderately stable across childhood (Kagan, 2008) and related to later anxious symptoms (Kagan & Snidman, 2004). Despite its robust role as a risk factor for anxiety psychopathology, it is worth noting that only a small proportion of behaviorally inhibited children go on to develop a full-blown anxiety disorder. For example, Biederman and colleagues (2001) found that only 17% of behaviorally inhibited children met criteria for social anxiety disorder, relative to 5% of children without behavioral inhibition. Consistent with the developmental psychopathology perspective, these findings suggest that although behavioral inhibition is an important risk factor for the development of anxiety disorders, other factors are clearly at play as well.

Indeed, children who are prone to experience negative emotions, such as sadness, anger, and fear—a temperamental trait known as *negative affectivity/emotionality* (Rothbart, 2007)—are also at increased risk for anxiety psychopathology. Longitudinal and prospective studies have shown that children high in negative emotionality exhibited higher anxiety symptoms later in life (Caspi & Silva, 1995). Negative emotionality may compound the risk for anxiety symptoms in children exposed to traumatic events, such as natural disasters (Kopala-Sibley et al., 2016).

In contrast, a growing body of research has found that greater *effortful control*, a temperamental trait involving voluntary control of behaviors and attentional processes in order to modulate emotional expressions (Rothbart, 2007), may *protect* youth from anxiety pathology. For example, greater effortful control buffered against later anxiety pathology even among children who were rated high on behavioral inhibition as toddlers (Niditch & Varela, 2018). Several other investigators have replicated associations between low effortful control and increased child anxiety symptoms (Niditch & Varela, 2018; Scheper et al., 2017). Accumulating evidence also suggests that the combination of high negative emotionality with low effortful control may be a particularly risky temperamental profile for child anxiety psychopathology (Lonigan, Vasey, Phillips, & Hazen, 2004).

ATTACHMENT AND EMOTION REGULATION

As a review of what you learned in Chapter 4, *attachment theory* (Bowlby, 1980) posits that from the moment of birth, humans strive to establish long-lasting, meaningful connections to others. During the early years, primary caretakers—and their behavior towards the child—assume a prominent role in the development of secure attachments (Cassidy, 1994). Parental displays of sensitive and responsive behavior to the child's needs allow the child to learn that the caregiver is a reliable figure who will provide comfort in times of distress. This provides the ideal environment for the expression of emotions and the eventual development of *emotion regulation*, a correlate of the temperamental variables we have just discussed. The quality of these early attachments is also influential in terms of how the child will perceive others in interpersonal interactions later in life.

In contrast, insecure attachment has been linked to anxiety problems (Kobak, Cassidy, Lyons-Ruth, & Ziv, 2006; Warren, Huston, Egeland, & Sroufe, 1997). Warren and colleagues (1997) found that adolescents who had been classified as insecurely attached at the age of 12 months using the *Strange Situation procedure* had significantly higher rates of anxiety disorders than those who had been classified as securely attached. In addition, insecure attachment (i.e., anxious/resistant type) significantly predicted child and adolescent anxiety disorders even after controlling for maternal anxiety and child temperament (Warren et al., 1997). Insecure attachment has also been found to predict a higher number of anxiety disorders, as well as higher symptoms of separation anxiety, social anxiety, and school phobia (Borelli, David, Crowley, & Mayes, 2010). Notably, some researchers have suggested that, compared to temperament, attachment insecurity may contribute to anxiety problems to a relatively lesser degree (Groh, Roisman, van Ijzendoorn, Bakermans-Kranenburg, & Fearon, 2012).

COGNITIVE AND INFORMATION PROCESSING FACTORS

Theories of cognitive processing emphasize cognitive vulnerabilities shared by both adults and children with anxiety disorders (Vasey & Dadds, 2001). These vulnerabilities include cognitive processing errors (i.e., interpreting events in a threatening manner), memory biases (i.e., tendency to recall threatening information), selective attention to threatening stimuli (in the context of other, non-threatening stimuli), and a hypersensitivity to anxiety-related sensations. These various cognitive factors are thought to work independently as well as additively in the etiology and maintenance of anxiety.

Interpretation biases

Ambiguity is often the status quo in life. An explosive noise may be the sound of fireworks or that of a gunshot. A door may slam shut because someone angrily slammed it or because a drafty window let the wind in. The steps of someone walking behind us may be those of a friend or an approaching robber. Research has found that the manner in which children interpret situations plays a significant role in the development and maintenance of anxiety symptoms. Children with (vs. without) clinical anxiety are more likely to interpret neutral or ambiguous situations in a threatening manner (Taghavi, Neshat-Doost, Moradi, Yule, & Dalgleish,

1999), and prospective studies have found that interpretation biases in childhood are associated with the maintenance of anxiety symptoms over time (Dodd, Hudson, Morris, & Wise, 2012). Experimental studies have also found that providing threatening information about animals to children aged 6–13 years induced threat interpretations as well as behavioral avoidance of the animal, which persisted up to six months later (Field, Lawson, & Banerjee, 2008).

Memory biases

Memory biases refer to a heightened tendency to recall threatening information (Vasey & MacLeod, 2001). Several studies have linked memory biases to childhood anxiety problems (Dalgleish et al., 2003; Watts & Weems, 2006). Clinically anxious youth also more easily recall threat-related (e.g., "horror") and depression-related words (e.g., "hopeless") than clinically depressed, clinically traumatized, and healthy control counterparts (Dalgleish et al., 2003). Notably, the association between memory biases and anxiety is not restricted to youth at the extreme end of anxiety psychopathology, as these relationships have also been replicated in community samples (Watts & Weems, 2006). Interestingly, research has shown that anxious individuals not only tend to display greater recall for threatening information, but they also exhibit worse recall of positive or neutral information (Mitte, 2008).

Attention biases

You receive written feedback on a midterm paper into which you poured time and effort. Of your instructor's many comments, which ones do you likely pay more attention to? Youth who struggle with anxiety would probably pay more attention to the critical comments than the positive ones. This is an example of an attention bias. Research shows that anxious individuals preferentially attend to threatening or negative information, as opposed to positive or neutral information (Weems & Watts, 2005). The relationship between attention biases and anxiety has been tested in two experimental paradigms: the emotional Stroop task and the visual probe task. In the emotional Stroop task, a participant sees words of varying colors appear on a screen, one by one. Some words are threatening (e.g., "failure") and others are non-threatening (e.g., "holiday"). The participant is asked to name the color of the word (while ignoring the actual word) as quickly as they can, and the researcher records the response time during each trial. Studies using this task have found that anxious (vs. non-anxious) children take longer to name the color of threatening words, suggesting that the meaning of the threatening word may capture some of their attentional capacity (Taghavi, Dalgleish, Moradi, Neshat-Doost, & Yule, 2003). While the emotional Stroop task is commonly used, it has been criticized because it involves other processes such as color-naming. The visual probe task is a more direct measure of attention bias, and is more widely used to capture attentional processes. In the visual probe task, one threatening stimulus and one non-threatening stimulus are presented briefly, side-by-side, on a computer screen (e.g., an angry face and a neutral face). Then, the stimuli disappear and one is replaced by a dot probe. The participant indicates, as quickly as they can, the side on which the dot appears by pressing a button. Overall, anxious youth tend to respond more quickly when the dot probe appears where the threatening stimulus used to be, whereas non-anxious youth do not show this attentional preference (Roy et al., 2008). However, following a recent three-year-long longitudinal study that found that adolescents' performance on the visual probe task was not very stable across time, researchers caution against making prospective inferences from this task (Booth, Songco, Parsons, Heathcote, & Fox, 2019).

Anxiety sensitivity

Expectancy theory (Reiss, 1991) states that avoidant behavior and fears are generally determined by the intensity of danger expectancies, anxiety expectancies, and anxiety sensitivity. Danger expectancies refer to the ability of a feared stimulus to signal danger in the environment (e.g., the sight of a dog eliciting a fear of being bitten). An anxiety expectancy is the ability of a particular stimulus to elicit anxiety; for example, a child may fear going near a dog because she anticipates becoming uncontrollably anxious. Therefore, danger and anxiety expectancies are situationally bound and depend on the type of stimulus presented. In contrast, anxiety sensitivity is defined as a cognitive-affective predisposition to interpret the sensations of anxiety (e.g., rapid heart rate, perspiration, blushing) as dangerous. A child with high anxiety sensitivity may interpret a racing heart as an impending heart attack or may interpret difficulties concentrating as a sign of "losing one's mind." Anxiety sensitivity serves as a risk factor for the development of anxiety disorders by increasing preexisting levels of anxiety (Hayward, Killen, Kraemer, & Taylor, 2000). Specifically, a child with high anxiety sensitivity may detect and subsequently interpret their anxiety symptoms as potentially catastrophic, which, in turn, generates more anxiety. This positive feedback mechanism results in an escalating response that may culminate in a full-blown anxiety attack.

Learning experiences

Studies have found that exposure to certain experiences, such as traumatic events (e.g., child abuse, natural disasters), places individuals at risk for anxiety disorders (La Greca, Silverman, Vernberg, & Prinstein, 1996). Additionally, individuals may acquire fears and anxieties by observing others' reactions to stimuli (Ollendick & King, 1991). For example, a child who sees their father react with extreme fear to a rollercoaster may begin to model the same fear. Finally, children may develop anxiety through conversations about fearful objects or events (e.g., birthday parties) with parents, caregivers, or acquaintances. A study by Field, Argyris, and Knowles (2001) found that children (aged 7–9 years) who received negative information about an unknown monster doll reported higher fear ratings than those who received positive information.

CONTEXTUAL RISK FACTORS

Parental overcontrolling behaviors

Parental maladaptive behaviors, such as overprotection (limiting the child's exposure to new people or situations) and intrusive behaviors (taking over the child's activity as soon as the child shows signs of struggling; e.g., while building a puzzle), increase children's risk for anxiety (Chorpita & Barlow, 1998). Rapee (1997) argued that overcontrolling, overinvolved, and intrusive parental behaviors may prevent children from approaching fear-provoking situations, thereby hindering their capacity to cope with fear and practice emotion regulation independently. In addition, these parental behaviors may reinforce the child's fears by inadvertently conveying the message that certain stimuli are threatening (Rapee, 1997). A large body of research has found that parental overcontrol is associated with child anxiety symptoms and associated traits such as social withdrawal (e.g., Kalomiris, Phelps, & Kiel, 2019). Though it may indeed be that overprotection disrupts the development of adequate emotion regulation in the child, which in turn leads to anxiety problems (Kiel & Kalomiris, 2019), parent–child relationships are transactional in nature, and it is likely that an anxious child displays behaviors that elicit parental overcontrol.

Parental rejection

Another dimension of parenting behaviors that may contribute to childhood anxiety is *parental rejection*. Parental rejection consists of low levels of parental warmth, approval, and responsiveness. A rejecting parent may appear cold, disapproving, and unresponsive towards their child. Imagine a child who turns to their parent in distress, only to be dismissed, ignored, or criticized in return. Repeated experiences of rejection are theorized to thwart children's ability to regulate negative emotions, which increases their sensitivity to anxiety and contributes to problematic anxiety (Wood, McLeod, Sigman, Hwang, & Chu, 2003). Although a number of influential theories have highlighted the role of parenting in children's anxiety outcomes (Wood et al., 2003) and some associations between parental rejection and child anxiety are reported in the literature (Rapee, 1997), the findings have been mixed. In a *meta-analysis* of 47 studies testing associations between parenting and child anxiety, McLeod and colleagues (McLeod, Wood, & Weisz, 2007) found that parental rejection was associated with child anxiety, but only to a small degree. In fact, parental rejection accounted only for approximately 4% of the variance in childhood anxiety, while parental overcontrolling behaviors accounted for approximately 6% of the variance in childhood anxiety (McLeod et al., 2007). Taken together, parenting factors may exert a modest role in childhood anxiety while other factors, such as genetics and *non-shared environmental influences* (e.g., peer relationships, traumatic events), may explain a larger proportion of the variance in child anxiety outcomes (Eley et al., 2003).

Childhood adversities

There are robust associations between childhood anxiety and various *adverse childhood experiences (ACEs)*, such as trauma and physical/sexual abuse, family dysfunction (e.g., parent separation, death of a parent, parental psychopathology), and socioeconomic risk (Hudson, 2005; Xue, Leventhal, Brooks-Gunn, & Earls, 2005). On average, anxious youth experience more childhood adversities in the year preceding the onset of anxiety symptoms compared to non-anxious peers (Goodyer, Wright, & Altham, 1990). Moreover, the effects of ACEs on childhood anxiety remain many years later; one study found that experiencing an ACE before the age of five predicted increases in anxiety during adolescence, even after controlling for current negative experiences (Phillips, Hammen, Brennan, Najman, & Bor, 2005). However, the processes through which ACEs increase risk for anxiety psychopathology are undoubtedly complex. Early adversity may interfere with developing stress systems (e.g., the HPA axis; Phillips et al., 2005) and parenting practices (Creswell & Cartwright-Hatton, 2007), as well as contribute to the development of threat-related cognitions associated with anxiety problems (Chorpita & Barlow, 1998). Such findings underscore the inherent difficulty in parsing apart the multiple systems that are impacted by childhood adversity.

Trauma exposure

One specific form of adversity that has received considerable attention in terms of anxiety psychopathology is exposure to traumatic situations involving perceived or actual threat of death or serious injury. Multiple forms of traumatic experiences of this nature, such as sexual abuse, exposure to natural disasters, and transportation accidents, have been linked to childhood anxiety problems (La Greca, 2002). The effects may be more pronounced among younger children, among whom concerns regarding safety, security, and separation from loved ones and caretakers following traumatic disaster experiences may be especially relevant (La Greca, 2002).

Parental psychopathology

Parental psychopathology is a long-standing risk factor for the development and maintenance of anxiety problems among children and adolescents (Connell & Goodman, 2002). Research has found that children of anxious parents are more likely to develop an anxiety disorder than children of non-anxious parents (Hirshfeld-Becker, Micco, Simoes, & Henin, 2008). Notably, there are several pathways through which parental psychopathology may influence childhood anxiety outcomes (Connell & Goodman, 2002). First, parental psychopathology is thought to increase risk via genetic transmission of risk for anxiety (Gregory & Eley, 2007). Second, parental psychopathology, such as anxiety, depression, and substance and alcohol abuse are thought to contribute to the development of dysfunctional neuroregulatory mechanisms, thus putting the child in a position of increased risk. Indeed, parental psychopathology and substance use during pregnancy are linked with a number of pre- and postnatal complications, including pre-term delivery, low birth weight, intrauterine growth restriction, neuroregulation problems (e.g., HPA-axis dysfunction), and emotional difficulties such as anxiety (Connell & Goodman, 2002). Third, parental anxiety may increase the extent to which parents model avoidant, controlling, and anxious behaviors for their children (Ginsburg & Schlossberg, 2002). Generally, the magnitude of the effects of parental psychopathology on children's functioning declines as children age and gain exposure to other social environments and sources of influence (Connell & Goodman, 2002). Therefore, younger children may be more vulnerable to parental psychopathology than older children. Finally, contextual stressors (e.g., family problems, marital problems, unemployment, economic strain) associated with parental psychopathology may further exacerbate youth anxiety symptoms.

Peer victimization

Peer difficulties, such as low peer acceptance and peer victimization, are associated with childhood anxiety problems (Bierman, 2004). Peer victimization can take many forms, including aggression, bullying, cybervictimization, and social exclusion (Bierman, 2004). Victimized children demonstrate significantly higher levels of depression, anxiety, and loneliness than their peers (Hawker & Boulton, 2000), as well as associated difficulties such as decreased self-confidence, self-esteem problems, negative self-evaluations, and avoidance of social situations (Baumeister & Leary, 1995). Notably, while peer victimization can lead to anxiety, anxiety problems can also precede peer victimization (Storch & Ledley, 2005). Specifically, the fearfulness, submissiveness, and social withdrawal often displayed by anxious youth may lead to peer relationship difficulties, unpopularity, and bullying. Electronic forms of victimization—*cybervictimization*, defined as aggression communicated online with the intent to hurt a peer (Fisher, Gardella, & Teurbe-Tolon, 2016)—are also robustly associated with increased risk for childhood anxiety psychopathology (Kowalski, Giumetti, Schroeder, & Lattanner, 2014). Bidirectional relationships between cybervictimization and anxiety symptoms have also been reported (Fisher et al., 2016).

Contextual Protective Factors

As is the case with most childhood psychopathologies, research examining *protective factors* for childhood anxiety disorders has not kept pace with investigations documenting the risks related to this cluster of disorders. Nevertheless, several protective factors have been identified, such as children's coping skills, social support (Donovan & Spence, 2000), supportive parenting (Hurrell, Hudson, & Schniering, 2015), and healthy attachments to their peer group (Oliva, Parra, & Reina, 2014). Likewise, children's perception of neighborhood cohesion (trusting relationships and shared values of residents in a neighborhood) may also serve as a protective factor by decreasing exposure to traumatic and/or negative life events, as well as providing additional coping resources outside their home, such as supportive adults (Butler, Kowalkowski, Jones, & Raphael, 2012). For instance, among children exposed to violence, greater neighborhood cohesion is associated with lower internalizing symptoms, including anxiety (Kliewer et al., 2004). Notably, protective factors for childhood anxiety may be influenced by cultural factors. In a study of African American children, stronger parental endorsement of cultural pride predicted lower childhood anxiety symptoms (Bannon Jr, McKay, Chacko, Rodriguez, & Cavaleri Jr, 2009). Protective factors related to culture, race, and ethnicity remains an area of research that requires further attention.

Gene–Environment Interplay

Gene–environment correlations

Genetic and environmental influences on anxiety are thought to unfold across development (Gregory & Eley, 2007) and may be correlated in three ways (Jaffee & Price, 2008). *Passive gene–environment correlation (rGE)* refers to the genotype a child inherits and the environment in which the child grows up (Jaffee & Price, 2008). Thus, anxious parents may confer genetic risk to their children yet also shape the rearing environment in a way that increases the likelihood that the child will exhibit anxiety problems (e.g., modeling of anxious behavior).

Evocative or reactive rGE refers to the association between a child's genetically influenced characteristics and the environment's reaction to such characteristics. A child's genetic risk may therefore interact with the environment in a way that might make it more (positive reactive rGE) or less likely (negative reactive rGE) that they will manifest problematic anxiety. For example, negative emotionality or behavioral inhibition (temperamental traits considered moderately heritable; Kagan, 2008) can elicit negative parenting practices (e.g., rejecting and overcontrolling parenting) that promote childhood anxiety symptoms (van der Bruggen, Stams, Bögels, & Paulussen-Hoogeboom, 2010).

Finally, *active rGE* describes the association between a child's heritable characteristics and their propensity to seek environments that magnify a particular trait or disorder. For example, behaviorally inhibited children who are prone to avoid novel situations may select experiences that do not challenge their assumptions (e.g., "birthday parties are scary so I will decline this invitation"), which may subsequently reinforce the child's anxiety.

Gene–environment interactions

As with most psychiatric disorders, there is ample evidence of an interactive relationship between genes and the environment in terms of childhood anxiety and its disorders. For example, the interaction between the serotonin transporter (5-HTT) genotype and adverse childhood experiences has been shown to predict childhood anxiety symptoms (Schiele et al., 2016). Likewise, research has shown that genetic effects on childhood anxiety/depression symptoms are significantly greater among youth who have experienced negative life events (Silberg, Rutter, & Eaves, 2001). It is also noteworthy that a particular genotype may have protective or deleterious effects on the development of anxiety psychopathology depending on the environmental context (Belsky & Beaver, 2011). Consistent with the developmental psychopathology framework, childhood anxiety disorders are undoubtedly a complex cluster of disorders emerging from a multitude of factors (e.g., genetic, neurobiological, cognitive, behavioral, social) with reciprocal relationships over time.

Interventions

Cognitive-Behavioral Therapy (CBT)

The cognitive-behavioral theory of childhood anxiety disorders suggests that pathological anxiety emerges from a dysfunctional pattern of thoughts, behaviors, and emotions (Rapee, Schniering, & Hudson, 2009). Specifically, childhood anxiety disorders are conceptualized from a cognitive-behavioral perspective as the result of erroneous evaluations of stimuli as threats (cognition), which trigger unpleasant emotional reactions, resulting in efforts to escape the anxiety-provoking stimulus (avoidant behavior). The goal of CBT for anxiety is to correct this maladaptive response pattern by using psychoeducation, problem solving, cognitive restructuring, and, most importantly, graded exposures (Ale et al., 2015). Psychoeducation aims to increase treatment compliance and empower patients to become experts in their own course of treatment by providing information about anxiety and the patient's treatment plan. Problem-solving involves the identification of distorted thoughts, evaluation of choices, and selection of a helpful plan of action. Patients are encouraged to challenge and modify anxious thoughts by generating alternative explanations, monitoring the functions behind anxious thoughts, and recalling positive experiences to disprove maladaptive thoughts. This therapeutic process of challenging irrational and anxious thoughts, and replacing them with more realistic thoughts, is termed *cognitive restructuring*. Finally, patients participate in *exposures*, wherein they gradually confront the situations that make them anxious in order to learn to tolerate (and eventually extinguish) the fear and correct preexisting fear beliefs (Ale et al., 2015).

CBT and exposure-based therapies are well-established treatments for youths with anxiety disorders (Higa-McMillan, Francis, Rith-Najarian, & Chorpita, 2016). The most comprehensive meta-analysis to date of youth anxiety treatment (which included data from 6,978 youth) found support for CBT as an efficacious treatment for childhood anxiety disorders (Wang et al., 2017). Research has also shown that CBT is effective across various ages, genders, sexual orientations, races/ethnicities, and socioeconomic groups (Hofmann, Asnaani, Vonk, Sawyer, & Fang, 2012). Nevertheless, youth with severe baseline psychopathology and youth whose parents experience high levels of psychopathology and stress are less likely to benefit from CBT (Compton et al., 2014). Conversely, successful implementation of adaptive coping strategies (i.e., problem solving, cognitive restructuring) predicts increased benefit from CBT among youth with anxiety disorders (Hogendoorn et al., 2014).

EXPOSURE THERAPY

Exposure is a key feature of CBT (Ale et al., 2015), but it is also implemented as a standalone treatment. Exposure therapy can take the form of in vivo exposure, interoceptive exposure, or imaginal exposure. *In vivo exposure* involves real-life confrontation of feared experiences, wherein the individual, with the help of a therapist, works to gradually and systematically confront the feared situations (e.g., snakes). *Interoceptive exposure* involves the intentional exposure to uncomfortable physiological symptoms that are characteristic of anxiety in order to learn that these sensations, while uncomfortable, are not dangerous. Thus, a patient may be asked to breathe rapidly through a straw for 1–2 minutes to mimic shortness of breath, or to shake their head from side to side for 2 minutes to recreate feelings of dizziness. Lastly, *imaginal exposure* requires the patient to imagine themselves being in a feared situation (e.g., giving an oral presentation in front of the class) and to imagine as vividly as possible all the details associated with the situation. Exposure therapy works by providing opportunities for corrective learning and facilitating extinction of fear by habituating the patient to the experience of anxiety (Ale et al., 2015). Cognitive-behavioral and exposure-based therapies also utilize homework to ensure that patients practice these skills between sessions.

Parental Involvement

Parental involvement in CBT treatment has been found to predict increased treatment gains (Manassis et al., 2014). Parents aid in homework reinforcement, facilitate homework exposure, discourage anxiety-driven avoidance of triggers and fear-inducing situations, and model non-anxious behaviors. Cognitive-behavioral and exposure-based therapies are effective with and without parental involvement, but may be most effective when parents learn to employ *contingency management* strategies at home (Manassis et al., 2014), such as rewarding brave behavior when the child complets exposure assignments. This form of parental support and involvement is thought to bolster long-term treatment outcomes.

Chapter Summary

Anxiety disorders, as a cluster, are the most prevalent form of psychopathology among youth. In this chapter, we have described the multifactorial nature of childhood anxiety disorders (see Figure 8.1) and many of the risk and protective factors associated with the development and maintenance of these debilitating problems, including genes, temperament, attachment relationships, parenting processes, and cognitive variables. Finally, we provided an overview of evidence-based practices for childhood anxiety and its disorders.

Further Reading

Cohen, J. R., Andrews, A. R., Davis, M. M., & Rudolph, K. D. (2018). Anxiety and depression during childhood and adolescence: Testing theoretical models of continuity and discontinuity. *Journal of Abnormal Child Psychology*, *46*(6), 1295–1308.

Gray, J. A. & McNaughton, N. (2003) *The neuropsychology of anxiety: An enquiry into the functions of the septo-hippocampal system.* New York, NY: Oxford University Press, Inc.

Gregory, A. M., & Eley, T. C. (2007). Genetic influences on anxiety in children: What we've learned and where we're heading. *Clinical Child and Family Psychology Review, 10*(3), 199–212.

Kiel, E. J., & Kalomiris, A. E. (2019). Emotional development and anxiety. In V. LoBue & K. Perez-Edgar (Eds.), *Handbook of emotional development* (pp. 665–693). Cham, Switzerland: Springer.

McKay, D. & Storch, E. A. (Eds.) (2011). *Handbook of child and adolescent anxiety disorders*. New York, NY: Springer.

McLeod, B. D., Wood, J. J., & Weisz, J. R. (2007). Examining the association between parenting and childhood anxiety: A meta-analysis. *Clinical Psychology Review, 27*(2), 155–172.

Discussion/Essay Questions

1. How can one distinguish between fears that are developmentally normative (i.e., appropriate) versus clinically significant?
2. Which temperamental characteristics contribute to problematic anxiety in childhood?
3. Discuss the role of parenting behaviors in childhood anxiety.
4. What considerations does a clinician need to make when choosing a treatment option for a child with an anxiety disorder?
5. To what extent are childhood anxiety disorders based in biology versus caused by one's environment? Provide evidence for both sides of your argument.
6. Which treatments are considered to have a solid scientific base for use with children with anxiety disorders?

Glossary

Fear is defined as a set of behavioral, physical, and emotional reactions to defend the body from an identifiable threat.

Fight-or-flight response is a physiological reaction that prepares the body by concentrating resources to either confront the threat or escape it in the interest of self-preservation.

Exposure is a technique used in therapy, in which a patient gradually confronts situations that make them afraid.

Anxiety is a future-oriented emotion characterized by an unpleasant feeling of foreboding, nervousness, tension, or apprehension, and a belief that there is little control over it. Whereas fear is a response to an immediate and identifiable threat, anxiety is the future-oriented *perception of threat* that is often not attributable to an identifiable fear stimulus.

Psychosocial functioning refers to one's ability to function within domains such as work, interpersonal relationships, life satisfaction, and recreation.

Anxiety disorders are a cluster of psychological disorders that share several core characteristics, such as physiological arousal, catastrophic thinking, and avoidance of anxiety-triggering situations.

Epidemiological studies examine the distribution, patterns, and determinants of disorders among the population.

Comorbidity refers to the presence of more than one mental disorder within an individual.

Longitudinal research is a type of research design in which the same group of people are studied multiple times over a period of time.

Clinic-referred youth refers to children who are referred to clinical treatment for psychological problems.

Social anxiety disorder is a type of anxiety disorder in which a child is fearful of social situations and situations in which public shame or embarrassment are possible.

Autonomic reactivity refers to the extent to which one responds physiologically to a stressor. See *autonomic nervous system* for more information.

Homotypic continuity is observed when a behavioral or emotional problem manifests itself in similar ways throughout development. For example, a young child who struggles with social anxiety may continue to struggle with those same feelings in adolescence and into adulthood.

Heterotypic continuity is observed when a behavioral or emotional problem at one point in time predicts a different type of problem later in life. For example, a child who struggles with an anxiety disorder in childhood may later develop a depressive disorder in adolescence.

Separation anxiety disorder is a type of anxiety disorder.

Generalized anxiety disorder is a type of anxiety disorder.

Molecular genetic association studies are used to compare allele frequencies between groups of people to determine a genetic cause.

Allele is a is one of two (or more) versions of a gene. A person inherits two alleles for each gene, one from each biological parent.

Genotype is the collection of an individual's genes. It can only be observed through specialized biological equipment.

Phenotype is an observable trait that is determined by the individual's genotype and environment. Phenotypes can be physical, psychological, or behavioral.

Serotonin is a neurotransmitter involved in various physiological functions, including sleep, appetite, and reproduction, and is implicated in emotional states including anxiety and depression.

Dopamine is a neurotransmitter involved in reward-motivated behavior.

Gamma-aminobutyric acid (GABA) is an inhibitory neurotransmitter that reduces feelings of fear and anxiety.

Genome-wide association study (GWAS) is a type of research study that helps scientists identify genetic risk factors for diseases. It involves examining a comprehensive set of genetic variances in many individuals to identify if any particular variant is associated with a certain trait or disease.

Neuroscience is the scientific study of the nervous system.

Amygdala is an almond-shaped part of the brain that comprises the limbic system. It is involved in emotions and memories related to survival, such as fear and aggression.

Frontal cortex is the largest of the four lobes of the brain. It is involved in problem-solving, decision-making, and planning.

Hippocampus is another part of the limbic system, which plays an important role in memory, learning, and spatial navigation.

Striatum is a part of the basal ganglia. It is associated with the reward system, such as motivation and reinforcement learning.

Electroencephalogram (EEG) is a test that records electrical activity in the brain.

Functional magnetic resonance imaging (fMRI) is a technique used to measure brain activity by detecting changes associated with blood flow.

Neurotransmitters are chemicals that cary and alter signals between neurons and other cells in the body. Examples of neurotransmitters involved in anxiety disorders include serotonin, gamma-aminobutyric acid, dopamine, epinephrine, and acetylcholine.

Anxiolytic medications are medications used to treat symptoms of anxiety disorders.

Benzodiazepines are medications that are primarily used for treating anxiety by affecting neurotransmitters in the brain. They are often used for other conditions such as insomnia, epilepsy, and alcohol dependence.

Selective-serotonin reuptake inhibitors (SSRIs) are a class of antidepressant medications that are used to treat symptoms of depression and often anxiety.

Nervous system is a collection of nerves and neurons that transmit signals throughout the body in response to bodily and environmental changes.

Central nervous system (CNS) is the part of the nervous system that includes the brain and spinal cord.

Behavioral inhibition system consists of the amygdala, noradrenergic projections of the locus coeruleus, and serotonergic projections of the median raphe.

Hypothalamic-pituitary-adrenal (HPA) axis, often called the "stress response," is a feedback loop linking the hypothalamus, pituitary gland, and adrenal glands.

Corticotropin-releasing hormone (CRH) is a hormone involved in the HPA axis. It is released by the hypothalamus and causes the anterior pituitary gland to stimulate the secretion of adrenocorticotropic hormone (corticotropin).

Adrenocorticotropic hormone (ACTH) is a hormone involved in the HPA axis. It is released by the anterior pituitary gland and causes the adrenal glands to make cortisol.

Autonomic nervous system (ANS) is a part of the peripheral nervous system; it is divided into the sympathetic nervous system and parasympathetic nervous system.

Sympathetic nervous system is active in response to perceived stress or threat.

Parasympathetic nervous system is active when energy is being conserved (e.g., restful states).

Temperament refers to individual differences in emotional, motor, and attentional reactivity to stimulation and patterns of behavioral and attentional self-regulation.

Behavioral inhibition is defined as a general tendency to react cautiously and with restraint to novel stimuli or situations.

Negative affectivity/emotionality is a personality variable that involves the frequency and intensity of the experience of negative emotions, such as anger, sadness, fear, and nervousness.

Effortful control, a dimension of temperament, is the ability to inhibit, activate, or adapt behaviors as needed.

Attachment theory describes how children develop relational styles (attachment styles) with others based on their relationship with their early caregivers, and how these attachment styles influence their relationships with other people later in life.

Emotion regulation is the ability to recognize and modulate one's emotions in order to meet environmental demands.

Strange Situation procedure was developed by Mary Ainsworth in the 1970s, and it is used to examine a child's attachment style by presenting children with a series of unusual, but not overly distressing, separations from and reunions with their caregiver.

Interpretation biases refer to the tendency to perceive ambiguous or neutral situations in a threatening or negative manner.

Memory biases refer to a heightened tendency to recall threatening information.

Attention bias refers to the tendency to pay more attention to certain stimuli than to others. Specifically, anxious individuals tend to preferentially attend to threatening or negative information, as opposed to positive or neutral information.

Emotional Stroop task is a paradigm used to measure attention bias, in which participants are shown a mix of threatening and nonthreatening words in a variety of colors. Participants must state what color the word is written in and researchers record the response time.

Visual probe task is another paradigm used to measure attention bias, in which participants are shown a threatening and a neutral stimulus side by side on a computer screen. The stimuli disappear and a dot probe appears on one side of the screen. Participants indicate the side on which the dot appears by pressing a button.

Anxiety sensitivity is defined as a cognitive-affective predisposition to interpret the physical sensations of anxiety as catastrophic or dangerous.

Parental overcontrolling behaviors refer to specific parenting behaviors that diminish a child's autonomy and independence.

Parental rejection refers to patterns of low levels of parental warmth, approval, and responsiveness, which may contribute to childhood anxiety.

Meta-analysis is a research technique that combines the results of previous studies to determine the overall results found in that area of research.

Non-shared environmental influence refers to any influence that occurs outside of the body and is not shared with other subjects.

Adverse childhood experiences (ACEs) are defined as potentially traumatic events that occur in childhood. There are three broad categories of ACEs: abuse (physical, emotional, sexual), neglect (physical, emotional), and household dysfunction (e.g., parental mental illness, witness to domestic abuse, parental divorce or separation, parental incarceration, or parental substance abuse).

Cybervictimization is defined as aggression communicated online with the intent to hurt a peer.

Protective factors are conditions or attributes (e.g., resources, strengths) that help mitigate an individual's risk of developing a disorder.

Resiliency is an example of a protective factor. It refers to the ability to adapt well in the face of adversity.

Passive gene–environment correlation (rGE) refers to the association between the genotype inherited by one's parents and the environment in which one is raised.

Evocative or reactive rGE occurs when a child's heritable behavior evokes a particular response from the environment.

Active rGE occurs when a child has a heritable inclination to select a particular environment.

Family and twin studies are research studies that focus on differences and similarities within families and between twins.

Cognitive-behavioral therapy (CBT) is a type of psychotherapy that involves the use of psychoeducation, problem solving, cognitive restructuring, behavioral experiments, and graded exposure to help patients overcome their problems.

Cognitive restructuring is a technique widely used in CBT, which involves disputing irrational, maladaptive, and anxious thoughts by generating alternate explanations, explaining anxious thought processes, monitoring the functions behind anxious thoughts, and recalling positive experiences.

In vivo exposure involves real-life confrontation of feared experiences. Individuals create a hierarchy of anxiety-provoking situations and, with the help of a therapist, work gradually and systematically to confront the feared situations.

Interoceptive exposure involves the intentional exposure to uncomfortable physiological symptoms characteristic of anxiety, to learn that these sensations are not dangerous.

Imaginal exposure is a therapeutic procedure in which the patient is asked to imagine being in a feared situation as vividly as possible.

Contingency management is a technique that involves controlling the stimulus and rewarding desired behavior while punishing undesired behaviors.

References

Albano, A. M., Chorpita, B. F., & Barlow, D. H. (2003). Childhood anxiety disorders. In E. J. Mash & R. A. Barkley (Eds.), *Child psychopathology*. (2nd ed., pp. 279–329). New York, NY, USA: Guilford Press.

Ale, C. M., McCarthy, D. M., Rothschild, L. M., & Whiteside, S. P. H. (2015). Components of cognitive Behavioral Therapy Related to outcome in childhood anxiety disorders. *Clinical Child and Family Psychology Review*, *18*(3), 240–251. doi: 10.1007/s10567-015-0184-8.

American Psychiatric Association (2013). *Diagnostic and statistical manual of mental disorders: DSM-5*. Washington, DC: Author.

Anderson, E. R., & Mayes, L. C. (2010). Race/ethnicity and internalizing disorders in youth: A review. *Clinical Psychology Review*, *30*(3), 338–348. doi: 10.1016/j.cpr.2009.12.008.

Bannon Jr, W. M., McKay, M. M., Chacko, A., Rodriguez, J. A., & Cavaleri Jr, M. (2009). Cultural pride reinforcement as a dimension of racial socialization protective of urban African American child anxiety. *Families in Society*, *90*(1), 79–86.

Baumeister, R. F., & Leary, M. R. (1995). The need to belong—Desire for interpersonal attachments as a fundamental human-motivation. *Psychological Bulletin*, *117*(3), 497–529.doi:10.1037/0033-2909.117.3.497.

Baving, L., Laucht, M., & Schmidt, M. H. (2002). Frontal brain activation in anxious school children. *Journal of Child Psychology and Psychiatry*, *43*(2), 265–274. doi: 10.1111/1469-7610.00019.

Beesdo, K., Knappe, S., & Pine, D. S. (2009). Anxiety and anxiety disorders in children and adolescents: Developmental issues and implications for DSM-V. *Psychiatric Clinics*, *32*(3), 483–524.

Beidel, D. C., Turner, M. W., & Trager, K. N. (1994). Test anxiety and childhood anxiety disorders in African American and White school children. *Journal of Anxiety Disorders*, *8*(2), 169–179.doi:10.1016/0887-6185(94)90014-0.

Belsky, J., & Beaver, K. M. (2011). Cumulative-genetic plasticity, parenting and adolescent self-regulation. *Journal of Child Psychology and Psychiatry*, *52*(5), 619–626.

Bergen, S. E., Gardner, C. O., & Kendler, K. S. (2007). Age-related changes in heritability of behavioral phenotypes over adolescence and young adulthood: A meta-analysis. *Twin Research and Human Genetics*, *10*(3), 423–433. doi:10.1375/twin.10.3.423

Biederman, J., Hirshfeld-Becker, D. R., Rosenbaum, J. F., Herot, C., Friedman, D., Snidman, N., & Faraone, S. V. (2001). Further evidence of association between behavioral inhibition and social anxiety in children. *American Journal of Psychiatry*, *158*(10), 1673–1679.

Biederman, J., Rosenbaum, J. F., Bolduc-Murphy, E. A., Faraone, S. V., Chaloff, J., Hirshfeld, D. R., & Kagan, J. (1993). A 3-year follow-up of children with and without behavioral inhibition. *Journal of the American Academy of Child & Adolescent Psychiatry*, *32*(4), 814–821. doi: 10.1097/00004583-199307000-00016.

Bierman, K. L. (2004). *Peer rejection: Developmental processes and intervention strategies*. New York, NY: Guilford Press.

Booth, C., Songco, A., Parsons, S., Heathcote, L. C., & Fox, E. (2019). The CogBIAS longitudinal study of adolescence: Cohort profile and stability and change in measures across three waves. *BMC Psychology*, *7*(1), 73. doi: 10.1186/s40359-019-0342-8.

Borelli, J. L., David, D. H., Crowley, M. J., & Mayes, L. C. (2010). Links between disorganized attachment classification and clinical symptoms in school-aged children. *Journal of Child and Family Studies*, *19*(3), 243–256. doi: 10.1007/s10826-009-9292-8.

Bowlby, J. (1980). *Attachment and loss*. New York, NY: Basic Books.

Butler, A. M., Kowalkowski, M., Jones, H. A., & Raphael, J. L. (2012). The relationship of reported neighborhood conditions with child mental health. *Academic Pediatrics*, *12*(6), 523–531. doi: 10.1016/j.acap.2012.06.005.

Caspi, A., & Silva, P. A. (1995). Temperamental qualities at age three predict personality traits in young adulthood: Longitudinal evidence from a birth cohort. *Child Development*, *66*(2), 486–498.

Cassidy, J. (1994). Emotion regulation: Influences of attachment relationships. *Monographs of the Society for Research in Child Development*, *59*(2–3), 228–283. doi: 10.2307/1166148.

Chorpita, B. F., & Barlow, D. H. (1998). The development of anxiety: The role of control in the early environment. *Psychological Bulletin*, *124*(1), 3.

Compton, S. N., Peris, T. S., Almirall, D., Birmaher, B., Sherrill, J., Kendall, P. C., & Albano, A. M. (2014). Predictors and moderators of treatment response in childhood anxiety disorders: Results from the CAMS trial. *Journal of Consulting and Clinical Psychology*, *82*(2), 212–224. doi: 10.1037/a0035458.

Connell, A. M., & Goodman, S. H. (2002). The association between psychopathology in fathers versus mothers and children's internalizing and externalizing behavior problems: A meta-analysis. *Psychological Bulletin*, *128*(5), 746–773. doi: 10.1037//0033-2909.128.5.746.

Costello, E. J., Egger, H. L., & Angold, A. (2005). The developmental epidemiology of anxiety disorders: Phenomenology, prevalence, and comorbidity. *Child and Adolescent Psychiatric Clinics of North America*, *14*(4), 631–648. doi: http://dx.doi.org/10.1016/j.chc.2005.06.003.

Costello, E. J., Egger, H. L., Copeland, W., Erkanli, A., & Angold, A. (2011). The developmental epidemiology of anxiety disorders: Phenomenology, prevalence, and comorbidity. In A. P. Field & W. K. Silverman (Eds.), *Anxiety disorders in children and adolescents* (2 ed., pp. 56–75). Cambridge, UK: Cambridge University Press.

Costello, E. J., Mustillo, S., Erkanli, A., Keeler, G., & Angold, A. (2003). Prevalence and development of psychiatric disorders in childhood and adolescence. *Archives of General Psychiatry*, *60*(8), 837–844. doi: 10.1001/archpsyc.60.8.837.

Creswell, C., & Cartwright-Hatton, S. (2007). Family treatment of child anxiety: Outcomes, limitations and future directions. *Clinical Child and Family Psychology Review*, *10*(3), 232–252. doi: 10.1007/s10567-007-0019-3.

Dalgleish, T., Taghavi, R., Neshat-Doost, H., Moradi, A., Canterbury, R., & Yule, W. (2003). Patterns of processing bias for emotional information across clinical disorders: A comparison of attention, memory, and prospective cognition in children and adolescents with depression, generalized anxiety, and posttraumatic stress disorder. *Journal of Clinical Child and Adolescent Psychology*, *32*(1), 10–21. doi: 10.1207/15374420360533022.

DiLalla, L. F., Kagan, J., & Reznick, J. S. (1994). Genetic etiology of behavioral inhibition among 2-year-old children. *Infant Behavior & Development*, *17*(4), 405–412. doi: 10.1016/0163-6383(94)90032-9.

Dodd, H. F., Hudson, J. L., Morris, T. M., & Wise, C. K. (2012). Interpretation bias in preschool children at risk for anxiety: A prospective study. *Journal of Abnormal Psychology*, *121*(1), 28–38. doi: 10.1037/a0024589.

Donovan, C. L., & Spence, S. H. (2000). Prevention of childhood anxiety disorders. *Clinical Psychology Review*, *20*(4), 509–531.

Eley, T. C., Bolton, D., O'Connor, T. G., Perrin, S., Smith, P., & Plomin, R. (2003). A twin study of anxiety-related behaviours in pre-school children. *Journal of Child Psychology and Psychiatry and Allied Disciplines*, *44*(7), 945–960. doi: 10.1111/1469-7610.00179.

El-Sheikh, M., Arsiwalla, D. D., Hinnant, J. B., & Erath, S. A. (2011). Children's internalizing symptoms: The role of interactions between cortisol and respiratory sinus arrhythmia. *Physiological Behavior*, *103*(2), 225–232. doi: 10.1016/j.physbeh.2011.02.004.

Feigon, S. A., Waldman, I. D., Levy, F., & Hay, D. A. (2001). Genetic and environmental influences on separation anxiety disorder symptoms and their moderation by age and sex. *Behavior Genetics*, *31*(5), 403–411. doi: 10.1023/A:1012738304233.

Ferdinand, R. F., Dieleman, G., Ormel, J., & Verhulst, F. C. (2007). Homotypic versus heterotypic continuity of anxiety symptoms in young adolescents: Evidence for distinctions between DSM-IV subtypes. *Journal of Abnormal Child Psychology*, *35*(3), 325–333. doi: 10.1007/s10802-006-9093-0.

Ferrell, C. B., Beidel, D. C., & Turner, S. M. (2004). Assessment and treatment of socially phobic children: A cross cultural comparison. *Journal of Clinical Child and Adolescent Psychology*, *33*(2), 260–268. doi: 10.1207/s15374424jccp3302_6.

Field, A. P., Argyris, N. G., & Knowles, K. A. (2001). Who's afraid of the big bad wolf?: A prospective paradigm to test Rachman's indirect pathways in children. *Behaviour Research and Therapy*, *39*(11), 1259–1276. doi: 10.1016/S0005-7967(00)00080-2.

Field, A. P., Lawson, J., & Banerjee, R. (2008). The verbal threat information pathway to fear in children: The longitudinal effects on fear cognitions and the immediate effects on avoidance behavior. *Journal of Abnormal Psychology*, *117*(1), 214–224. doi: 10.1037/0021-843x.117.1.214.

Fisher, B. W., Gardella, J. H., & Teurbe-Tolon, A. R. (2016). Peer cybervictimization among adolescents and the associated internalizing and externalizing problems: A meta-analysis. *Journal of Youth and Adolescence*, *45*(9), 1727–1743. doi: 10.1007/s10964-016-0541-z.

Fox, N. A., Nichols, K. E., Henderson, H. A., Rubin, K., Schmidt, L., Hamer, D., & Pine, D. S. (2005). Evidence for a gene–environment interaction in predicting behavioral inhibition in middle childhood. *Psychological Science*, *16*(12), 921–926. doi: 10.1111/j.1467-9280.2005.01637.x.

Ginsburg, G. S., & Schlossberg, M. C. (2002). Family-based treatment of childhood anxiety disorders. *International Review of Psychiatry*, *14*(2), 143–154.

Goodyer, I., Wright, C., & Altham, P. (1990). Recent achievements and adversities in anxious and depressed school-age-children. *Journal of Child Psychology and Psychiatry and Allied Disciplines*, *31*(7), 1063–1077. doi: 10.1111/j.1469-7610.1990.tb00846.x.

Gordon, J. A., & Hen, R. (2004). Genetic approaches to the study of anxiety. *Annual Review of Neuroscience*, *27*(1), 193–222. doi: 10.1146/annurev.neuro.27.070203.144212.

Gray, J. A., & McNaughton, N. (2000). *The neuropsychology of anxiety: An enquiry into the functions of the septo-hippocampal system*. Oxford, UK: Oxford University Press.

Graziano, P., & Derefinko, K. (2013). Cardiac vagal control and children's adaptive functioning: A meta-analysis. *Biological Psychology*, *94*(1), 22–37. doi: 10.1016/j.biopsycho.2013.04.011.

Gregory, A. M., & Eley, T. C. (2007). Genetic influences on anxiety in children: What we've learned and where we're heading. *Clinical Child and Family Psychology Review*, *10*(3), 199–212. doi: 10.1007/s10567-007-0022-8.

Groh, A. M., Roisman, G. I., van Ijzendoorn, M. H., Bakermans-Kranenburg, M. J., & Fearon, R. P. (2012). The significance of insecure and disorganized attachment for children's internalizing symptoms: A meta-analytic study. *Child Development*, *83*(2), 591–610.

Gunnar, M. R., Morison, S. J., Chisholm, K., & Schuder, M. (2001). Salivary cortisol levels in children adopted from Romanian orphanages. *Development and Psychopathology*, *13*, 17.

Hawker, D. S. J., & Boulton, M. J. (2000). Twenty years' research on peer victimization and psychosocial maladjustment: A meta-analytic review of cross-sectional studies. *Journal of Child Psychology and Psychiatry*, *41*(4), 441–455. doi: 10.1017/S0021963099005545.

Hayward, C., Killen, J. D., Kraemer, H. C., & Taylor, C. B. (2000). Predictors of panic attacks in adolescents. *Journal of the American Academy of Child and Adolescent Psychiatry*, *39*(2), 207–214. doi: 10.1097/00004583-200002000-00021.

Higa-McMillan, C. K., Francis, S. E., Rith-Najarian, L., & Chorpita, B. F. (2016).

Evidence base update: 50 years of research on treatment for child and adolescent anxiety. *Journal of Clinical Child and Adolescent Psychology*, *45*(2), 91–113. doi: 10.1080/15374416.2015.1046177.

Hirshfeld-Becker, D. R., Biederman, J., Henin, A., Faraone, S. V., Davis, S., Harrington, K., & Rosenbaum, J. F. (2007). Behavioral inhibition in preschool children at risk is a specific predictor of middle childhood social anxiety: A five-year follow-up. *Journal of Developmental Behavior Pediatrics*, *28*(3), 225–233. doi: 10.1097/01.DBP.0000268559.34463.d0.

Hirshfeld-Becker, D. R., Micco, J. A., Simoes, N. A., & Henin, A. (2008). High risk studies and developmental antecedents of anxiety disorders. *American Journal of Medical Genetics Part C—Seminars in Medical Genetics*, *148c*(2), 99–117. doi: 10.1002/ajmg.c.30170.

Hofmann, S. G., Asnaani, A., Vonk, I. J. J., Sawyer, A. T., & Fang, A. (2012). The efficacy of cognitive behavioral therapy: A review of meta-analyses. *Cognitive Therapy and Research*, *36*(5), 427–440. doi: 10.1007/s10608-012-9476-1.

Hogendoorn, S. M., Prins, P. J. M., Boer, F., Vervoort, L., Wolters, L. H., Moorlag, H., & de Haan, E. (2014). Mediators of cognitive behavioral therapy for anxiety-disordered children and adolescents: Cognition, perceived control, and coping. *Journal of Clinical Child and Adolescent Psychology*, *43*(3), 486–500. doi: 10.1080/15374416.2013.807736.

Hudson, J. L. (2005). Interparental conflict, violence and psychopathology. In J. L. Hudson & R. Rapee (Eds.), *Psychopathology and the Family*. (1st ed., pp. 53-69). Oxford, UK: Elsevier Ltd.

Hurrell, K. E., Hudson, J. L., & Schniering, C. A. (2015). Parental reactions to children's negative emotions: Relationships with emotion regulation in children with an anxiety disorder. *Journal of Anxiety Disorders*, *29*, 72–82. doi: 10.1016/j.janxdis.2014.10.008.

Jaffee, S. R., & Price, T. S. (2008). Genotype–environment correlations: Implications for determining the relationship between environmental exposures and psychiatric illness. *Psychiatry*, *7*(12), 496–499.

Kagan, J. (2008). Behavioral inhibition as a risk factor for psychopathology. In T. P. Beauchaine, S. P. Hinshaw, T. P. Beauchaine, & S. P. Hinshaw (Eds.), *Child and adolescent psychopathology* (pp. 157–179). Hoboken, NJ, USA: John Wiley & Sons, Inc.

Kagan, J., & Snidman, N. (2004). *The long shadow of temperament*. Cambridge, MA, USA: Belknap Press/Harvard University Press.

Kalomiris, A. E., Phelps, R. A., & Kiel, E. J. (2019). The relation between specific parenting behaviors and toddlers' early anxious behaviors is moderated by toddler cortisol reactivity. *Journal of Abnormal Child Psychology*, *47*(8), 1367–1377. doi: 10.1007/s10802-019-00522-9.

Kiel, E. J., & Kalomiris, A. E. (2019). Emotional development and anxiety. In V. LoBue & K. Perez-Edgar (Eds.), *Handbook of emotional development* (pp. 665–693). Cham, Switzerland: Springer.

Kliewer, W., Cunningham, J. N., Diehl, R., Parrish, K. A., Walker, J. M., Atiyeh, C., & Mejia, R. (2004). Violence exposure and adjustment in inner-city youth: Child and caregiver emotion regulation skill, caregiver–child relationship quality, and neighborhood cohesion as protective factor. *Journal of Clinical Child and Adolescent Psychology*, *33*(3), 477–487.

Kobak, R., Cassidy, J., Lyons-Ruth, K., & Ziv, Y. (2006). Attachment, stress, and psychopathology: A developmental pathways model. In D. Cicchetti & D. J. Cohen (Eds.), *Developmental psychopathology: Theory and method* (vol. *1*, 2nd ed., pp. 333–369). Hoboken, NJ: John Wiley & Sons, Inc.

Kopala-Sibley, D. C., Danzig, A. P., Kotov, R., Bromet, E. J., Carlson, G. A., Olino, T. M., & Klein, D. N. (2016). Negative emotionality and its facets moderate the effects of exposure to Hurricane Sandy on children's postdisaster depression and anxiety symptoms. *Journal of Abnormal Psychology*, *125*(4), 471.

Kowalski, R. M., Giumetti, G. W., Schroeder, A. N., & Lattanner, M. R. (2014). Bullying in the digital age: A critical review and meta-analysis of cyberbullying research among youth. *Psychological Bulletin, 140*(4), 1073–1137. doi: 10.1037/a0035618.

La Greca, A. M. (2002). *Helping children cope with disasters and terrorism*. Washington, DC: American Psychological Association.

La Greca, A. M., Silverman, W. K., Vernberg, E. M., & Prinstein, M. J. (1996). Symptoms of posttraumatic stress in children after Hurricane Andrew: A prospective study. *Journal of Consulting and Clinical Psychology, 64*(4), 712.

Last, C. G., & Perrin, S. (1993). Anxiety disorders in African-American and White children. *Journal of Abnormal Child Psychology, 21*(2), 153–164. doi: 10.1007/BF00911313.

LeDoux, J. E., & Pine, D. S. (2016). Using neuroscience to help understand fear and anxiety: A two-system framework. *American Journal of Psychiatry, 173*(11), 1083–1093. doi: 10.1176/appi.ajp.2016.16030353.

Lonigan, C. J., Vasey, M. W., Phillips, B. M., & Hazen, R. A. (2004). Temperament, anxiety, and the processing of threat-relevant stimuli. *Journal of Clinical Child and Adolescent Psychology, 33*(1), 8–20.

Manassis, K., Lee, T. C., Bennett, K., Zhao, X. Y., Mendlowitz, S., Duda, S., & Wood, J. J. (2014). Types of parental involvement in CBT with anxious youth: A preliminary meta-analysis. *Journal of Consulting and Clinical Psychology, 82*(6), 1163–1172. doi: 10.1037/a0036969.

McLeod, B. D., Wood, J. J., & Weisz, J. R. (2007). Examining the association between parenting and childhood anxiety: A meta-analysis. *Clinical Psychology Review, 27*(2), 155–172. doi: 10.1016/j.cpr.2006.09.002.

Merikangas, K. R., He, J.-P., Brody, D., Fisher, P. W., Bourdon, K., & Koretz, D. S. (2010). Prevalence and treatment of mental disorders among US children in the 2001–2004 NHANES. *Pediatrics, 125*(1), 75-81. doi:10.1542/peds.2008-2598

Merikangas, K. R., He, J.-p., Burstein, M., Swanson, S. A., Avenevoli, S., Cui, L., & Swendsen, J. (2010). Lifetime prevalence of mental disorders in US adolescents: Results from the National Comorbidity Survey Replication–Adolescent Supplement (NCS-A). *Journal of the American Academy of Child and Adolescent Psychiatry, 49*(10), 980–989.

Mitte, K. (2008). Memory bias for threatening information in anxiety and anxiety disorders: A meta-analytic review. *Psychological Bulletin, 134*(6), 886–911. doi: 10.1037/a0013343.

Monk, C. S., Nelson, E. E., McClure, E. B., Mogg, K., Bradley, B. P., Leibenluft, E., & Pine, D. S. (2008). Ventrolateral prefrontal cortex activation and attentional bias in response to angry faces in adolescents with generalized anxiety disorder. *American Journal of Psychiatry, 163*(6), 1091–1097. doi: 10.1176/ajp.2006.163.6.1091.

Niditch, L. A., & Varela, R. E. (2018). A longitudinal study of inhibited temperament, effortful control, gender, and anxiety in early childhood. *Child and Youth Care Forum, 47*(4), 463–479. doi: 10.1007/s10566-018-9447-0.

Nolen-Hoeksema, S. (2000). The role of rumination in depressive disorders and mixed anxiety/depressive symptoms. *Journal of Abnormal Psychology, 109*(3), 504–511. doi: 10.1037/0021-843x.109.3.504.

Öhman, A. (2008). Fear and anxiety: Overlaps and dissociations. In M. Lewis, J. M. Haviland-Jones, & L. F. Barrett (Eds.), *Handbook of emotions* (3rd ed., pp. 709–728). New York, NY: The Guilford Press.

Oliva, A., Parra, Á., & Reina, M. C. (2014). Personal and contextual factors related to internalizing problems during adolescence. *Child and Youth Care Forum, 43*(4), 505–520.

Ollendick, T. H., & King, N. J. (1991). Origins of childhood fears: An evaluation of Rachman's theory of fear acquisition. *Behaviour Research and Therapy, 29*(2), 117–123. doi: 10.1016/0005-7967(91)90039-6.

Pang, V. O. (1991). The relationship of test anxiety and math achievement to parental values in Asian-American and European-American middle school students. *Journal of Research & Development in Education*, *24*(4), 1–10.

Phillips, N. K., Hammen, C. L., Brennan, P. A., Najman, J. M., & Bor, W. (2005). Early adversity and the prospective prediction of depressive and anxiety disorders in adolescents. *Journal of Abnormal Child Psychology*, *33*(1), 13–24. doi: 10.1007/s10802-005-0930-3.

Pina, A. A., & Silverman, W. K. (2004). Clinical phenomenology, somatic symptoms, and distress in Hispanic/Latino and European American youths with anxiety disorders. *Journal of Clinical Child and Adolescent Psychology*, *33*(2), 227–236.

Rapee, R. M. (1997). Potential role of childrearing practices in the development of anxiety and depression. *Clinical Psychology Review*, *17*(1), 47–67.

Rapee, R. M., Schniering, C. A., & Hudson, J. L. (2009). Anxiety disorders during childhood and adolescence: Origins and treatment. *Annual Review of Clinical Psychology*, *5*, 311–341. doi: 10.1146/annurev.clinpsy.032408.153628.

Reiss, S. (1991). Expectancy model of fear, anxiety, and panic. *Clinical Psychology Review*, *11*(2), 141–153.

Rosenbaum, J. F., Biederman, J., Hirshfeld, D. R., Bolduc, E. A., Faraone, S. V., Kagan, J., & Reznick, J. S. (1991). Further evidence of an association between behavioral inhibition and anxiety disorders: Results from a family study of children from a non-clinical sample. *Journal of Psychiatric Research*, *25*(1–2), 49–65. doi: 10.1016/0022-3956(91)90015-3.

Rothbart, M. K. (2007). Temperament, development, and personality. *Current Directions in Psychological Science*, *16*(4), 207–212.

Roy, A. K., Vasa, R. A., Bruck, M., Mogg, K., Bradley, B. P., Sweeney, M., & Team, C. (2008). Attention bias toward threat in pediatric anxiety disorders. *Journal of the American Academy of Child & Adolescent Psychiatry*, *47*(10), 1189–1196. doi: 10.1038/jid.2014.371.

Scheper, F. Y., Majdandžić, M., van de Ven, P. M., Jansen, L. M. C., Doreleijers, T. A. H., Schuengel, C., & de Vries, A. L. C. (2017). Temperament traits and psychopathology in young clinically referred children compared to a general population sample. *Child Psychiatry and Human Development*, *48*(6), 841–850. doi: 10.1007/s10578-016-0708-6.

Schiele, M. A., Ziegler, C., Holitschke, K., Schartner, C., Schmidt, B., Weber, H., & Zwanzger, P. (2016). Influence of 5-HTT variation, childhood trauma and self-efficacy on anxiety traits: A gene-environment-coping interaction study. *Journal of Neural Transmission*, *123*(8), 895–904.

Silberg, J. L., Rutter, M., & Eaves, L. (2001). Genetic and environmental influences on the temporal association between earlier anxiety and later depression in girls. *Biological Psychiatry*, *49*(12), 1040–1049. doi: 10.1016/S0006-3223(01)01161-1.

Storch, E. A., & Ledley, D. R. (2005). Peer victimization and psychosocial adjustment in children: Current knowledge and future directions. *Clinical Pediatrics*, *44*(1), 29–38. doi: 10.1177/000992280504400103.

Taghavi, M. R., Dalgleish, T., Moradi, A. R., Neshat-Doost, H. T., & Yule, W. (2003). Selective processing of negative emotional information in children and adolescents with Generalized Anxiety Disorder. *British Journal of Clinical Psychology*, *42*(3), 221–230. doi: 10.1348/014466503360703348.

Taghavi, M. R., Neshat-Doost, H. T., Moradi, A. R., Yule, W., & Dalgleish, T. (1999). Biases in visual attention in children and adolescents with clinical anxiety and mixed anxiety-depression. *Journal of Abnormal Child Psychology*, *27*(3), 215–223. doi: 10.1023/A:1021952407074.

Towe-Goodman, N. R., Franz, L., Copeland, W., Angold, A., & Egger, H. (2014). Perceived family impact of preschool anxiety disorders. *Journal of the American Academy of Child & Adolescent Psychiatry*, *53*(4), 437–446. doi: 10.1016/j.jaac.2013.12.017.

Trzaskowski, M., Eley, T. C., Davis, O. S. P., Doherty, S. J., Hanscombe, K. B., Meaburn, E. L., & Plomin, R. (2013). First Genome-Wide Association Study on Anxiety-Related

Behaviours in Childhood. *PloS One*, *8*(4), e58676. doi: 10.1371/journal.pone.0058676

Turner, S. M., Beidel, D. C., & Costello, A. (1987). Psychopathology in the offspring of anxiety disorders patients. *Journal of Consulting and Clinical Psychology*, *55*(2), 229–235. doi: 10.1037/0022-006X.55.2.229.

van der Bruggen, C. O., Stams, G. J. J. M., Bögels, S. M., & Paulussen-Hoogeboom, M. C. (2010). Parenting behaviour as a mediator between young children's negative emotionality and their anxiety/depression. *Infant and Child Development*, *19*(4), 354–365.

Varela, R. E., Weems, C. F., Berman, S. L., Hensley, L., & de Bernal, M. C. R. (2007). Internalizing symptoms in Latinos: The role of anxiety sensitivity. *Journal of Youth and Adolescence*, *36*(4), 429–440. doi: 10.1007/s10964-007-9168-4.

Vasey, M. W., & Dadds, M. R. (2001). *The developmental psychopathology of anxiety*. New York, NY: Oxford University Press.

Vasey, M. W., & MacLeod, C. (2001). Information-processing factors in childhood anxiety: A review and developmental perspective. In M. W. Vasey & M. R. Dadds (Eds.), *The developmental psychopathology of anxiety* (pp. 253–277). New York, NY: Oxford University Press.

Verduin, T. L., & Kendall, P. C. (2003). Differential occurrence of comorbidity within childhood anxiety disorders. *Journal of Clinical Child and Adolescent Psychology*, *32*(2), 290–295. doi: 10.1207/S15374424JCCP3202_15.

Wang, Z., Whiteside, S. P. H., Sim, L., Farah, W., Morrow, A. S., Alsawas, M., & Murad, M. H. (2017). Comparative effectiveness and safety of cognitive behavioral therapy and pharmacotherapy for childhood anxiety disorders: A systematic review and meta-analysis. *JAMA Pediatrics*, *171*(11), 1049–1056. doi: 10.1001/jamapediatrics.2017.3036.

Warren, S. L., Huston, L., Egeland, B., & Sroufe, L. A. (1997). Child and adolescent anxiety disorders and early attachment. *Journal of the American Academy of Child & Adolescent Psychiatry*, *36*(5), 637–644. doi: 10.1097/00004583-199705000-00014.

Watts, S. E., & Weems, C. F. (2006). Associations among selective attention, memory bias, cognitive errors and symptoms of anxiety in youth. *Journal of Abnormal Child Psychology*, *34*(6), 841–852. doi: 10.1007/s10802-006-9066-3.

Weems, C., & Silverman, W. (2008). Anxiety disorders. In T. P. Beauchaine, S. P. Hinshaw, T. P. Beauchaine, & S. P. Hinshaw (Eds.), *Child and adolescent psychopathology* (pp. 447–476). Hoboken, NJ: John Wiley & Sons, Inc.

Weems, C. F., & Watts, S. E. (2005). Cognitive models of childhood anxiety. In C. M. Velotis (Ed.), *Anxiety Disorder Research* (pp. 205–232). Hauppauge, NY: Nova Science Publishers, Inc.

Weems, C. F., Zakem, A. H., Costa, N. M., Cannon, M. F., & Watts, S. E. (2005). Physiological response and childhood anxiety: Association with symptoms of anxiety disorders and cognitive bias. *Journal of Clinical Child and Adolescent Psychology*, *34*(4), 712–723. doi: 10.1207/s15374424jccp3404_13.

Wittchen, H.-U., Stein, M. B., & Kessler, R. C. (1999). Social fears and social phobia in a community sample of adolescents and young adults: Prevalence, risk factors and co-morbidity. *Psychological Medicine*, *29*(2), 309–323. doi: 10.1017/S0033291798008174.

Wood, J. J., McLeod, B. D., Sigman, M., Hwang, W. C., & Chu, B. C. (2003). Parenting and childhood anxiety: Theory, empirical findings, and future directions. *Journal of Child Psychology and Psychiatry and Allied Disciplines*, *44*(1), 134–151. doi: 10.1111/1469-7610.00106.

Woodward, L. J., & Fergusson, D. M. (2001). Life course outcomes of young people with anxiety disorders in adolescence. *Journal of the American Academy of Child and Adolescent Psychiatry*, *40*(9), 1086–1093. doi: 10.1097/00004583-200109000-00018.

Xue, Y. G., Leventhal, T., Brooks-Gunn, J., & Earls, F. J. (2005). Neighborhood residence and mental health problems of 5- to 11-year-olds. *Archives of General Psychiatry*, *62*(5), 554–563. doi: 10.1001/archpsyc.62.5.554.

Part III

Problems of Adolescence and Early Adulthood

In Chapter 3 we talked about adolescence as a developmental period between puberty and legal adulthood. It is also a period during which rates of psychopathology arise. In the largest epidemiological study to cover both childhood and early adolescence (the British Child and Adolescent Mental Health Survey; BCAMHS) with over 10,000 children aged 5–15 years, rates of DSM-IV psychiatric disorders increased from 8.6% at 8–10 years old to 9.6% at 11–12 years old and 12.2% at 13–15 years old. Adolescence is therefore an important transition period for thinking about how and why psychopathology develops.

In this part of your textbook, we will talk about the typical emotional and behavioral problems that emerge in adolescence. As we will discuss, research has shown that many of these problems co-occur. For example, an adolescent struggling with depression will also be likely to struggle with a substance use disorder or perhaps even an eating disorder. Keep this in mind as you work through each of the different emotional and behavioral problems in this section. Towards the end of Part III, we hope that you will have formed a comprehensive picture of adolescence as a unique period in the study of developmental psychopathology. We will cover the following topics:

Chapter 9

Depression

FRANCESCA PENNER AND CARLA SHARP

Chapter Overview

It is appropriate for us to begin Part III with *depressive disorders* because this group of disorders is very typical of adolescence. Depressive disorders refer to a spectrum of disorders that relate to problems in *mood* (or *affect* or *emotion*) (American Psychiatric Association, 2013). The DSM-5 separates depressive disorders and bipolar and related disorders into two classes. We will focus on the depressive disorders here (see Figure 9.1) and, in particular, on Major Depressive Disorder (MDD) as the most prominent of the depressive disorders.

Prior to the mid-1970s, there was a general belief that children could not experience some of the complex emotions characteristic of depression, like hopelessness, shame, or guilt (Rie, 1966). However, by the 1980s, thanks to the research of several leaders in the field of child and adolescent depression, it became accepted that children and adolescents could meet criteria for MDD (Klein, Kujawa, Black, & Pennock, 2013), though it is more commonly seen among adolescents and adults relative to children. Below, we provide an example of an adolescent case.

Definition, Diagnosis, and Clinical Features

Depression is complex because the term can encompass a variety of conditions. *Depression as a transient mood or affective state* refers to the feeling of being "down" or "having the blues." Most of us have experienced depression in this way and it is quite normative to have days of

Developmental Psychopathology, First Edition. Edited by Amanda Venta, Carla Sharp, Jack M. Fletcher, and Peter Fonagy.

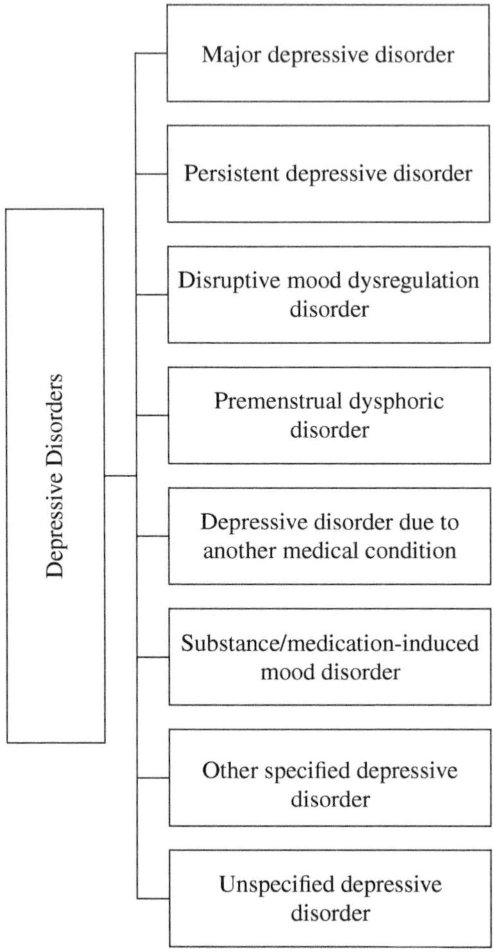

FIGURE 9.1 DSM-5 Classification of Depressive Disorders

Case vignette

Silvia is a 13-year-old Hispanic girl who lives with her mother, Monica, in an apartment complex. Her parents divorced a few years ago and there is ongoing discord regarding multiple issues, including custody of Silvia. Since she was very young, Silvia has been a shy child who sleeps very little and is hard to soothe. She has begun to display episodes of irritability and moodiness and, when feeling down or angry, tends to withdraw socially from her friends and her mom. In the past couple years, she has been displaying more defiant behaviors with her parents.

Discuss possible diagnoses you would give Silvia, as well as other factors to consider. What other information would you gather to guide diagnosis and treatment for Silvia?

low mood. In contrast, *depression as a clinical syndrome* refers to a constellation of symptoms that occur together, as described in Table 9.1 for the DSM-5.

Depression is a leading cause of disability worldwide and tends to onset during adolescence. Therefore, it is a particularly important mental health disorder to study during adolescence. Adolescent depression can be a significant risk for impairment later in life, such as poor physical health, other mental health problems, or difficulties at work and in relationships. It is also a major risk factor for suicide for teens and adults (Nock et al., 2013).

Think back to Chapter 1 when we considered the DSM-5's categorical approach to psychological disorders. Using this approach, disorders are categorized as discrete entities that occur independently of other disorders (though they can co-occur, known as *comorbidity*). Depression as a categorical construct is how it is conceptualized in the DSM, when an individual meets criteria of at least five of nine symptoms of MDD in the DSM, or does not meet criteria.

On the other hand, *depression as a dimensional construct* refers to the principle that mild and severe depression are at different ends of the same continuum. Whether depression should be considered as a discrete category or on a continuum (dimension) of severity is a controversial issue and is the subject of much debate. While the categorical approach is necessary for clinicians to communicate and make clinical decisions, there are also advantages to taking a dimensional approach, because it allows for the examination of the full spectrum of severity. In Table 9.1, alongside the categorical approaches of the DSM and the International Classification of Diseases (ICD), we also list depressive symptoms from a dimensional approach, the ASEBA assessment system. Research in this area is now turning a focus toward understanding depression using a latent dimensional model, which considers a dimension of depression with some symptoms unique to depression and some that are held in common with broader factors (e.g., distress, internalizing, and general psychopathology; Kotov et al., 2017).

Depression as a subclinical syndrome assumes a dimensional approach in which individuals below threshold for clinical depression are identified. This approach may be especially relevant in developmental psychopathology where we are interested in early identification and intervention, as well as early markers of disorder. Indeed, both subclinical depression and MDD are associated with a higher risk of MDD during young adulthood (Rohde et al., 2013), as well as with impairment and later mental health problems (Angold et al., 1999).

There are some features of depression that are similar across different age groups, and some that are different (see the summary in Table 9.2). Most notably, the DSM-5 requires that for children and adolescents, one of the five symptoms must be depressed *or* irritable mood (irritability is considered a manifestation of depressed mood in youth), or *anhedonia*, which

TABLE 9.1 Depression as Defined by the DSM 5, ICD-11, and the Dimensional ASEBA Scales

DSM 5	*ICD-11*	*ASEBA DSM scales (anxious-depressed)*	*ASEBA DSM scales (withdrawn-depressed)*
A. Five (or more) of the following symptoms have been present during the same 2-week period and represent a change from previous functioning; at least one of the symptoms is either (1) depressed mood or (2) loss of interest or pleasure. (Note: do not include symptoms that are clearly attributable to another medical condition.) 1. Depressed mood most of the day, nearly every day, as indicated by either subjective report (e.g., feels sad, empty, hopeless) or observation made by others (e.g., appears tearful). (Note: in children and adolescents, can be irritable mood.) 2. Markedly diminished interest or pleasure in all, or almost all, activities most of the day, nearly every day (as indicated by either subjective account or observation). 3. Significant weight loss when not dieting or weight gain (e.g., a change of more than 5% of body weight in a month), or decrease or increase in appetite nearly every day. 4. Insomnia or hypersomnia nearly every day. 5. Psychomotor agitation or retardation nearly every day (observable by others, not merely subjective feelings of restlessness or being slowed down).	A depressive episode is characterized by a period of almost daily depressed mood or diminished interest in activities lasting at least two weeks accompanied by other symptoms such as difficulty concentrating, feelings of worthlessness or excessive or inappropriate guilt, hopelessness, recurrent thoughts of death or suicide, changes in appetite or sleep, psychomotor agitation or retardation, and reduced energy or fatigue. There have never been any prior manic, hypomanic, or mixed episodes, which would indicate the presence of a bipolar disorder.	**1.5–5-year-olds** *Depression* Sad Looks unhappy *Anxiety* Fearful Nervous Self-conscious Upset by separation Clings **6-18-year-olds** *Depression* Talks or thinks of suicide Feels worthless Feels unloved Feels too guilty Must be perfect Anxious to please Afraid to make mistakes Feels hurt when criticized *Anxiety* Fearful and anxious Nervous Self-conscious	**1.5–5-year-olds** *Depression* Shows little interest Shows little affection Unresponsive to affection *Social withdrawal* Withdrawn Avoids eye contact Doesn't answer when spoken to Refuses to play active games Daydreams Acts too young Apathetic **6–18-year-olds** *Depression* Sad Enjoys little Lacks energy *Social withdrawal* Withdrawn Shy Secretive Would rather be alone Refuses to talk

6. Fatigue or loss of energy nearly every day. 7. Feelings of worthlessness or excessive or inappropriate guilt (which may be delusional) nearly every day (not merely self-reproach or guilt about being sick). 8. Diminished ability to think or concentrate, or indecisiveness, nearly every day (either by subjective account or as observed by others). 9. Recurrent thoughts of death (not just fear of dying), recurrent suicidal ideation without a specific plan, or a suicide attempt or a specific plan for committing suicide. B. The symptoms cause clinically significant distress or impairment in social, occupational, or other important areas of functioning. C. The episode is not attributable to the physiological effects of a substance or to another medical condition. **Note:** Criteria A–C represent a major depressive episode. **Note:** Responses to a significant loss (e.g., bereavement, financial ruin, losses from a natural disaster, a serious medical illness or disability) may include the feelings of intense sadness, rumination about the loss, insomnia, poor appetite, and weight loss noted in Criterion A, which may resemble a depressive episode. Although such symptoms may be understandable or considered appropriate to the loss, the presence of a major depressive episode in addition to the normal response to a significant loss should also be carefully considered. This decision inevitably requires the exercise of clinical judgment based on the individual's history and the cultural norms for the expression of distress in the context of loss.	Has many fears Fears school Fears doing bad things Worries Cries a lot

(Continued)

TABLE 9.1 (Continued)

DSM 5	*ICD-11*	*ASEBA DSM scales (anxious-depressed)*	*ASEBA DSM scales (withdrawn-depressed)*
D. The occurrence of the major depressive episode is not better explained by schizoaffective disorder, schizophrenia, schizophreniform disorder, delusional disorder, or other specified and unspecified schizophrenia spectrum and other psychotic disorders. E. There has never been a manic episode or a hypomanic episode. (Note: This exclusion does not apply if all of the manic-like or hypomanic-like episodes are substance-induced or are attributable to the physiological effects of another medical condition.)			

Note: The DSM-5 (APA, 2013), ICD-11 (WHO, 2018), ASEBA (Achenbach & Rescorla, 2000, 2001).

TABLE 9.2 Developmental Differences in the Symptoms and Syndrome of Depression

1. Somatic complaints are common expressions of depression in prepubertal children but decrease with age.
2. Hypersomnia and reduced appetite (for girls) increase during adolescence, but are uncommon in preadolescent children.
3. While suicide is relatively uncommon in prepubertal children, it peaks during middle (girls) or late (boys) adolescence.
4. Irritability is a core feature of depression in children and adolescents but not in adults.
5. The prevalence of depression in preadolescents is significantly lower than adolescence.
6. The prevalence of depression increases significantly for girls relative to boys beginning in adolescence.
7. Adolescents may demonstrate more vegetative symptoms (e.g., low energy, sleep problems, and appetite/weight problems), suicidality, and hopelessness relative to adults.
8. Depressed adolescent females may more often report weight/appetite disturbance and worthlessness/guilt, relative to boys.

Sources: APA, 2013; Garber & Rao, 2014; Klein et al., 2013; Lewinsohn, Rohde, & Seeley, 1998; Rice et al., 2019.

is decreased pleasure or interest in everyday activities (APA, 2013). In general, prevalence rates for MDD are significantly higher in adolescence and adulthood relative to childhood, and there is an increase in prevalence for girls relative to boys beginning in adolescence. However, recurrence rates, rates of comorbidity, and episode duration have been shown to be similar between adolescents and adults with MDD (Rohde et al., 2013).

Prevalence

Nationally representative estimates of MDD among youth ages 13–18 years in the United States, from the National Comorbidity Survey—Adolescent Supplement (NCS-A; Merikangas et al., 2009), show a *12-month prevalence* of 7.5% and a *lifetime prevalence* of 11.0% (Avenvoli et al., 2015). Comparatively, estimates show a 12-month prevalence of 2.7% for 8–15-year-olds (Merikangas et al., 2010). More recent data from the 2017 Substance Abuse and Mental Health Services Administration (SAMHSA) National Survey on Drug Use and Health suggest a 12-month prevalence of 13.3% among adolescents aged 12–17 (SAMHSA, 2017).

Prevalence By Gender and Age

Data from the NCS-A and from the 2017 SAMHSA National Survey are presented in Table 9.3 and Figure 9.2. These data clearly demonstrate two important features of the prevalence of depression. First, there are significant

TABLE 9.3 Lifetime Prevalence of DSM-IV-TR/CIDI Mood Disorders by Age and Gender in the National Comorbidity Survey Replication (NCS-R) and Adolescent Supplement (NCS-A)

	Ages 13–17						*Ages 18–64*					
	Female		*Male*		*Total*		*Female*		*Male*		*Total*	
	Percent	*(SE)*	*Percent*	*(SE)*	*Percent*	*(SE)*	*Percent*	*(SE)*	*Percent*	*(SE)*	*Percent*	*(SE)*
Major depressive episode												
Single	3.7	(0.6)	2.5	(0.5)	3.1	(0.4)	6.4*	(0.4)	4.7	(0.3)	5.6	(0.3)
Recurrent episodes	13.1*	(1.1)	6.0	(0.8)	9.5	(0.8)	18.8*	(0.7)	10.8	(0.7)	15.4	(0.6)
Total	16.8*	(1.3)	8.5	(0.9)	12.6	(0.9)	25.2*	(0.7)	16.5	(0.8)	20.9	(0.6)
Major depressive disorder												
Single	3.4	(0.5)	2.4	(0.5)	2.9	(0.4)	6.0*	(0.4)	4.2	(0.4)	5.2	(0.3)
Recurrent episodes	10.8*	(1.1)	4.8	(0.7)	7.7	(0.8)	16.1*	(0.7)	10.1	(0.7)	13.2	(0.6)
Total	14.2*	(1.2)	7.2	(0.8)	10.6	(0.8)	22.1*	(0.7)	14.4	(0.7)	18.3	(0.6)
Bipolar disorder												
BPD I	0.3	(0.2)	0.1	(0.0)	0.2	(0.1)	1.3	(0.2)	0.9	(0.2)	1.1	(0.2)
BPD II	2.8	(0.5)	2.8	(0.5)	2.8	(0.4)	1.6	(0.2)	1.2	(0.2)	1.4	(0.1)
BPD I or II	3.1	(0.5)	2.8	(0.5)	3.0	(0.4)	2.9	(0.3)	2.1	(0.2)	2.5	(0.2)
Any mood disorder	18.2	(1.3)	10.8	(1.2)	14.4	(1.0)	25.7	(0.7)	16.9	(0.8)	21.4	(0.5)
(n)	(3,219)		(3,024)		(6,243)		(2,978)		(2,245)		(5,223)	

The NCS-A (ages 13–17) and NCS-R (ages 18+) samples were combined without weighting to adjust for the higher probability of selection of adolescents than adults in the two surveys.
[*] Significant gender difference within the subsample.
Source: Kessler et al., (2012). Reproduced with permissions of John Wiley & Sons.

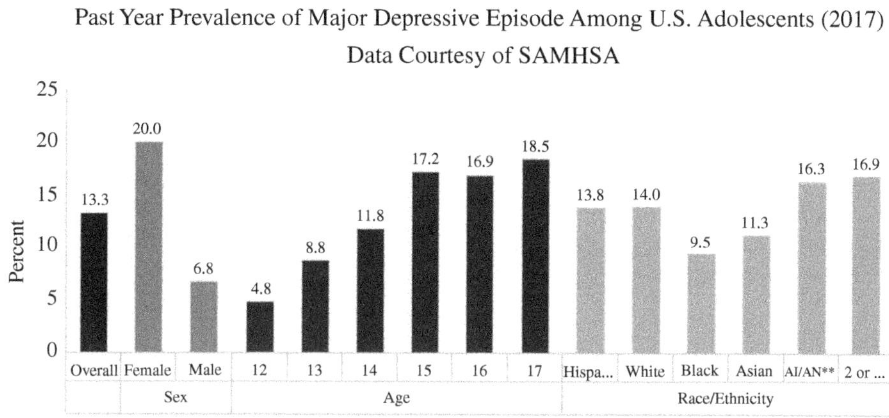

FIGURE 9.2 12-Month Depression Prevalence in Adolescents. Source: National Institutes of Mental Health (NIMH). (2019). Major depression. Retrieved from https://www.nimh.nih.gov/health/statistics/major-depression.shtml. Accessed on 4 February 2020. Public Domain.

gender differences in adolescent depression, with nearly twice the rates among girls compared to boys. Research has shown that this gender difference only becomes apparent in adolescence, around age 13 (Hankin et al., 2015). Second, these data indicate that there is a striking increase in prevalence rates across the adolescent years from 13 to 18, typically starting after puberty, for both genders (Avenevoli et al., 2015). Data from the NCS-A also showed that 25% of adults with MDD or *persistent depressive disorder* (previously called dysthymia) reported onset prior to young adulthood. *Prospective follow-up studies* also show a dramatic increase in the prevalence of MDD after age 11 and again after age 15, with flattening rates in young adulthood (Kim-Cohen et al., 2003).

Prevalence By Socioeconomic Status (Ses), Race, and Ethnicity

There are mixed findings for the link between SES and depression. A large meta-analysis conducted in 2002 (Twenge & Nolen-Hoeksema, 2002) suggested no relation between depression and SES in youth. The NCS-A data also found no difference across SES categories as indexed by the poverty index ratio (Avenevoli et al., 2015). In adults, the picture looks different, with a higher likelihood of incurring and persisting depression with low SES (Lorant et al., 2003). Lower SES may increase risk for depression because SES is associated with increased life stress or early adversity, which, in turn, can lead to depression (Dohrenwend, 2000).

In terms of prevalence in different racial and ethnic groups, NCS-A data suggest that Hispanic youth had a past-year MDD prevalence of 8.9%, compared to 8.0% in non-Hispanic Black youth, 7.1% in non-Hispanic White youth, and 8.3% for youth of other racial/ethnic backgrounds; these differences were not significant (Avenevoli et al., 2015). In the 2017 SAMHSA National Survey on Drug Use and Health, results indicated that past-year prevalence of depression was highest among adolescents who reported belonging to two or more racial/ethnic groups (16.9% prevalence in this group), and also high among American Indian/Alaska Native teens (16.3%). See Figure 9.2 for the 2017 data reprinted from SAMHSA.

Comorbidity

MDD in children and adolescents is a highly comorbid disorder (Avenevoli, Knight, Kessler, & Merikangas, 2008). Adolescents with MDD who experience comorbid problems are likely to have greater impairment and worse outcomes, including longer depressive episodes and higher rates of recurrence, as well as more suicide attempts (Garber & Rao, 2014). In the NCS-A, among 13–18-year-old adolescents reporting an MDD in the last 12 months, 63.7% of adolescents had a comorbid disorder, including anxiety, ADHD, behavior disorders, and substance use, with anxiety and behavior disorders most commonly represented (Avenevoli et al., 2015).

Developmental Continuities and Discontinuities (Course)

Think back to Chapter 2 when we talked about the meaning of homotypic and heterotypic continuity. *Homotypic continuity* is defined as stability in the same or similar behavioral responses over time; that is, the *same* disorder predicts itself over time (e.g., earlier depression predicting later depression). *Heterotypic continuity* is defined as stability of an underlying construct that is manifested differently across time as a result of developmental changes, that is, *different* disorders predict one another over time (e.g., anxiety predicting later depression).

There is widespread evidence of *homotypic continuity* for depression. For instance, the cumulative probability of recurrence of depression is 40% by two years after a depressive episode and 70% by five years (Birmaher et al., 1996). Evidence for *heterotypic continuity* comes from studies that demonstrate that somatic problems (Ryan et al., 1987), anxiety (Finsaas et al., 2018), and conduct problems (McDonough-Caplan, Klein, & Beauchaine, 2018) predict later depression. In all, it appears that both homotypic and heterotypic processes of continuity are relevant and may reflect the *heterogeneity* (subgroups, or many possible ways that the disorder may present) of youth depression, as well as its high comorbidity and overlap with other disorders.

helpful discussion of the most promising neurobiological *endophenotypes* for depression. These include impaired reward function, stress reactivity (dysfunctional cortisol responses associated with abnormal HPA axis function), and tryptophan depletion (an index of serotonergic function).

Structural and functional imaging findings

Table 9.4, adapted from reviews of the neurobiology of depression in youth (Nantel-Vivier & Pihl, 2008; Weir, Zakama, & Rao, 2012), presents a list of the major brain regions associated with depression in children and adolescents identified through structural and functional neuroimaging studies. Abnormalities in the HPA axis, prefrontal cortex, and the limbic system including the amygdala, subgenual anterior cingulate cortex, and hippocampus have been related to risk for depression in adolescence, as have abnormalities in the connections between the prefrontal cortex and the limbic system (i.e., corticolimbic circuit). These abnormalities make emotion regulation and impulse control more difficult. There is also evidence for problems in the connections between the striatum and the prefrontal cortex, which underlie reward circuitry, and problems in the connections between the inferior and dorsolateral prefrontal cortex, anterior cingulate gyrus, and striatal regions, which underlie cognitive control and attention (see Blom et al., 2016).

TABLE 9.4 Summary of Brain Regions Associated with Child and Adolescent Depression

Brain Region	*Function*	*Significance in Depression*
Frontal lobes Dorsolateral prefrontal cortex (DLPC) Dorsomedial prefrontal cortex (DMPC) Ventrolateral prefrontal cortex (VLPC) Orbital prefrontal cortex Subgenual prefrontal cortex Insula	Goal-directed behaviors Affect-guided planning Reward responses	Cognitive impairments (executive functioning) Social-cognitive impairments Depressogenic cognitions Altered reward and punishment responses Suicidality Poor decision making
Midline and medial temporal structures Cingulate Amygdala Hippocampus Caudate nucleus Putamen Thalamus	Emotion responses Stress responses Emotional memory Reward responses Decision-making Contextual memory	Anhedonia Vegetative symptoms Poor decision-making Anxiety

Neurotransmitters

The identification of neurotransmitters in the brain that influence depression is important, because they help researchers design psychiatric medications. Of all the neurotransmitters, serotonin has received the most attention. Research has shown that psychiatric medications that increase the flow of serotonin in the brain (selective serotonin reuptake inhibitors, or SSRIs) are effective in reducing depression symptoms, even for adolescents. Other neurotransmitters that have been implicated in adult depression include norepinephrine, dopamine, brain-derived neurotrophic factor, neurotransmitters involved in the neuroendocrine system, glutamate, and gamma-aminobutyric acid (GABA) (aan het Rot, Mathew, and Charney, 2009), with many of these having evidence for a role in adolescent depression as well.

Hormones

The hypothalamic–pituitary–adrenal (HPA) system plays an important role in the regulation of stress hormones, including cortisol. While results in children and adolescents have been mixed, there is a general belief that the HPA system is important in the etiology of depression (Goodyer, Herbert, Tamplin, & Altham, 2000). In addition to cortisol, other neuroendocrine risks for depression in youth suggested by previous research include problems in growth hormone levels or in prolactin (Garber, 2006). The effect of hormones is also one important explanatory factor for the difference in depression prevalence rates between the sexes. As we explained in Chapter 3, the neuroendocrine system plays a crucial role in the changes associated with pubertal development. Animal studies have shown that the effect of sex steroids on the maturing HPA axis makes girls more sensitive to the effects of stress, whereas androgens appear to play a protective role in boys (Naninck, Lucassen, & Bakker, 2011). While biological theories are important for explaining sex differences in depression, it is also important to consider psychosocial explanations. Differences in stress coping, mother–child relationships, and gender-specific expectations have been cited as important factors (Nolen-Hoeksema, 2001). Further, there is evidence that teenage girls experience more life stressors that increase risk for depression, such as sexual assault and chronic stressors (e.g., poverty, childcare burden, and sexual harassment) (Nolen-Hoeksema, 2001). Girls may experience low self-esteem due to pubertal changes or early pubertal timing (Hyde, Mezulis, & Abramson, 2008), and may demonstrate greater rejection sensitivity, negative cognitive style, or rumination (Lenroot & Giedd, 2010).

Temperament

In Chapter 2 we talked about temperament in the context of normative development. In the context of depression research, Compas, Connor-Smith, and Jaser (2004) highlighted three major dimensions of temperament: *negative emotionality (NE)* or neuroticism, *positive emotionality (PE)* or extroversion, and *attentional control (AC)*. NE refers to the inclination toward experiencing intense discomfort, such as fear and anger, and reacting more easily to stress. PE refers to the tendency to seek pleasure and reward from the environment and AC refers to the ability to control emotions and behaviors and the ability to retain focus. Typically, the combination of high NE and low PE has been found to relate to depression in children and adolescents in longitudinal, observational, and laboratory studies (Klein, Kotov, & Bufferd, 2011), and may impact the ability to regulate emotion, specifically AC (or effortful control). Indeed, studies have shown that depressed adolescents show increased levels of effortful control over positive emotions, thereby not allowing themselves to experience pleasure and reward (Forbes & Dahl, 2012). Several studies of adults and adolescents with depression (e.g., Forbes et al., 2006) have demonstrated reduced brain activation in response to either rewards or anticipation of reward, and difficulty distinguishing between rewards of high versus low value (Forbes, Shaw, & Dahl, 2007). Reduction in reward function has also been demonstrated in non-depressed biological children of mothers with depression (Sharp et al., 2014), suggesting that reduced reward dysfunction may precede the onset of depression in high-risk samples. In our study (Sharp et al., 2014), we found that reduced reward activation can be observed in the non-depressed daughters of depressed mothers, similar to the depressed daughters of depressed mothers (see Figure 9.4). This means that the brains of children of depressed mothers may look similar in terms of reward function to the brains of already depressed adolescents. This is important because it suggests that a teenager may be genetically predisposed to a reduced reward function if he or she has a depressed mother.

COGNITIVE FACTORS

Broadly speaking, these different theories are based on the fundamental principle that individuals with depression (and those at risk) show impairments or biases in attention, interpretation, and memory processes for emotionally salient stimuli (Hankin et al., 2009).

Beck's cognitive theory of depression

Beck's cognitive diathesis-stress theory (Beck, 1967) has been incredibly influential and forms the basis of *cognitive-behavior therapy*. Beck's theory suggests that schemas (defined as mental representations of the self and others) come about through early childhood experience and are relatively stable. These schemas are activated in environmental conditions that resemble the early childhood experience.

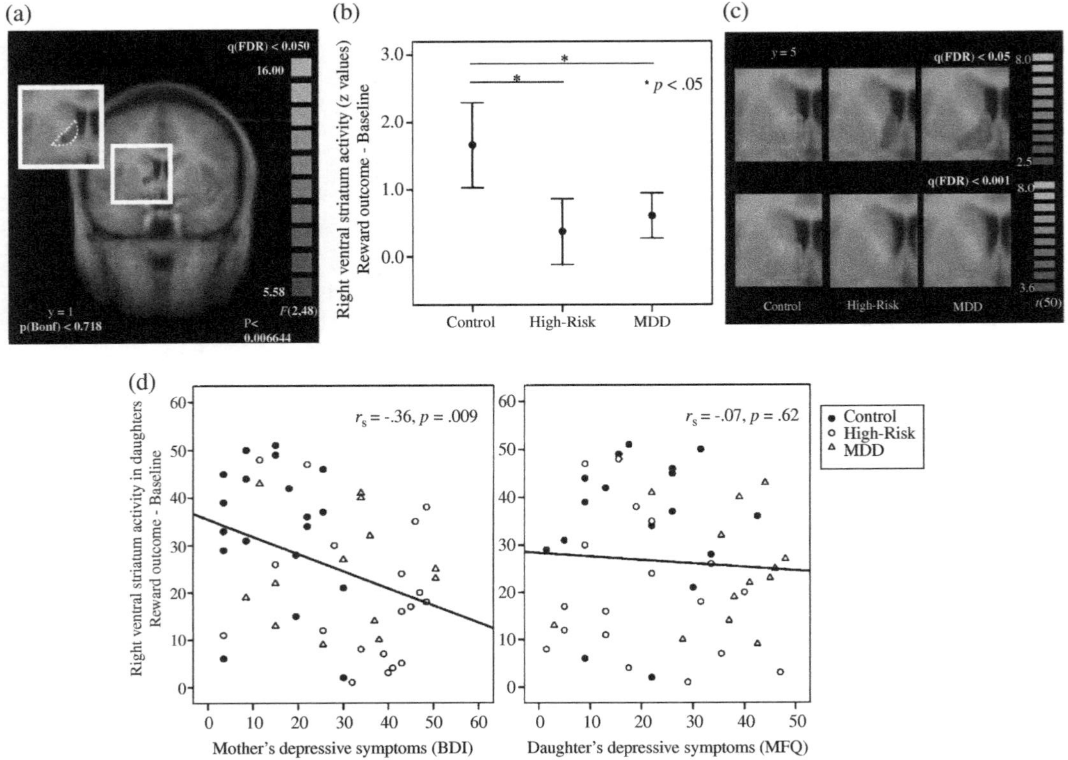

FIGURE 9.4 (a) Reward outcome x group interaction observed at a subregion (369 mm^3) of the right ventral striatum (x =10, y = 1, z = 10, p < .007, FDR corrected, q < .05). Inset of magnified right ventral striatum superimposed on the anatomical mask used to define ventral striatum region of interest. (b) Both MDD and high-risk groups show attenuated right ventral striatum activation in response to reward outcome

A depressive schema is likely to be associated with negative self-referential thoughts, negative thoughts about the world, and negative thoughts about one's future (the "cognitive triad"), and when the schema is activated, it can lead to altered information processing. For instance, an individual with depression may carry a depressogenic schema ("I am unlovable"), which stems from early rejection by a parental figure. When this individual, as a teenager, is dumped by her boyfriend, the schema is activated without her conscious awareness. Activation of the schema results in negative attitudes and negative thinking errors such as "Nobody loves me," or "I will never be loved," which in turn leads to symptoms of depression.

Hopelessness theory

Abramson, Alloy, and Metalsky (1989) developed hopelessness theory, another cognitive *diathesis-stress* theory that focuses on a negative cognitive style related to the attributions for causes of negative events. This theory suggests that when confronted with a negative event (e.g., being rejected by a boyfriend), individuals with a negative cognitive style attribute the causes of such an event to internal ("It is because I'm ugly"), stable ("I will always be rejected"), and global ("Everything about me is stupid") factors. This attributional style is thought to increase vulnerability to hopelessness and depression.

Response styles theory

Nolen-Hoeksema's (1991) theory of depression suggests that rumination (i.e., reviewing a problem over and over, dwelling on meaning, causes, and consequences) can maintain depressive mood or behavioral inactivation, or make individuals less likely to cope effectively. Research suggests that women are more likely to ruminate in response to stress or to negative life events, which is one hypothesis for why there are higher rates of depression among women, beginning in adolescence (Nolen-Hoeksema, 2001).

(both $p < .05$). Error bars depict 95% confidence interval. (c) Activation for the reward outcome versus baseline contrast within the ventral striatum region of interest, presented at FDR corrected $q < .05$ (top row) and $q < .001$ (bottom row). (d) Adolescent daughter's right ventral striatum BOLD response to reward outcome correlates negatively with her mother's depressive symptoms (BDI), but not with her own (MFQ). BOLD signal values were extracted from the anatomically defined right ventral striatum mask for each subject. For graphical representations of spearman's rank-order correlations, x and y axes were converted to ranks and are not presented in the original units of measurement. Source: Sharp, C., et al. (2014). Reproduced with permissions of John Wiley & Sons.

Social-cognitive vulnerabilities

Youth depression occurs within an interpersonal context and depressed youth have been shown to have problems in relationships with peers and parents (Rudolph, Flynn, & Abaied, 2008). These difficulties may be related to deficits in social-cognitive functioning, such as distorted mental representations, biased attention, memory, and information processing in social situations, impaired social decision-making, and ineffective social coping (Kyte & Goodyer, 2008).

The interaction among different cognitive vulnerability factors

In Chapter 2, we introduced the term "*cognitive vulnerabilities*" to refer to cognitive processes that may put an individual at risk for psychopathology (e.g., depressogenic schemas). Recent work in the field of cognitive vulnerability has focused on integrating different cognitive vulnerability factors into one design, given that it is unlikely that each cognitive vulnerability theory is presenting a distinct etiological pathway leading to the development of depression (Abela & Hankin, 2008).

CONTEXTUAL RISK FACTORS

Life stress

The link between life stress and depression is a very robust finding in the depression literature (Hammen, 2018). Stress, including negative life events as well as chronic stressors such as neglect, abuse, separation from a parent, parental psychopathology, and poverty, is linked strongly to depression (Risch et al., 2009). However, not all children who are exposed to negative life events become depressed. This suggests there is likely to be an interaction between life events and other vulnerability factors (Hammen, 2018).

While *independent life events* (beyond the control of an individual, e.g., a parent dying of a heart attack) are related to depression, depressed adolescents may also create stress for themselves (i.e., *dependent life events*). This process is called *stress generation*, which tends to occur more in depressed individuals, including adolescents, and can lead to further depression (Liu & Alloy, 2010). The work of Hammen and colleagues (see Hammen, 2018) has also shown that interpersonal life events (e.g. the death of a parent, a break-up) are a risk for depression.

Parental psychopathology

A very important form of potential life stress and a potent contextual risk factor for depression in children relates to parenting factors. Children of depressed parents are four times more likely to have an episode of MDD compared to normal controls (National Research Council and Institute of Medicine, 2009). Parents with depression can transfer risk to their children in multiple ways. Symptoms of depression may directly interfere with the ability to parent: depressed mothers have been shown to display more negative/hostile and disengaged behavior and less positive social behavior compared to non-depressed mothers (Lovejoy, Graczyk, O'Hare, & Neuman, 2000). In addition, depressed parents may model a depressogenic cognitive style, negative cognitions and affect, or poor coping strategies (Goodman & Gotlib, 1999). Finally, parent depression may lead to other stressors in the home such as parental conflict and parent stress, which, in turn, have negative effects on children and can expose children to chronic stress (Hammen, Brennan, & Shih, 2004).

Interpersonal theories

Attachment theory suggests that humans have an innate need for social bonds, including secure bonds to attachment figures, and that disruptions in social bonds can lead to distress (Bowlby, 1973). Sullivan's interpersonal theory of depression posits that positive interpersonal relationships and social support are important factors for adaptive mental health (Sullivan, 1953). Together, these theories underline the developmental risk for depression that may arise from interpersonal contexts. Importantly, social relationships and identity building are particularly important milestones during adolescence, making the interpersonal context even more salient for adolescent depression. These theories form the foundation for *interpersonal psychotherapy for adolescent depression* (IPT-A; Mufson, Dorta, Moreau, & Weissman, 2004).

Maladaptive parenting and abuse

Low levels of parental warmth and care, lower levels of communication, higher levels of emotional expression (hostility and criticism), and higher levels of intrusiveness and emotional overinvolvement have been associated with increased levels of depressive symptoms (Restifo & Bogels, 2009). In addition, experiences of maltreatment, such as physical, sexual, or emotional abuse, have also been associated with increased rates of depression (Kim & Cicchetti, 2006).

Low peer acceptance and bullying

Studies have shown that difficulties in peer relationships predict increases in depressive symptoms. For example, Allen and colleagues (2006) showed that withdrawn, angry, or dependent patterns of behavior with a best friend predicted depressive symptoms one year later. Studies have also demonstrated that children who are bullied are more likely to experience depression (e.g., Copeland, Wolke, Anfold, & Costello, 2013).

CONTEXTUAL PROTECTIVE FACTORS

Comparatively less research has been conducted on the protective factors for the development of depression. One of the most important protective factors identified thus far is social support (Rueger et al., 2016). In addition, Costello and colleagues (2008) showed that a two-parent family structure, and feeling connected to parents, peers, or school, were protective factors for adolescent depression.

GENE–ENVIRONMENT INTERPLAY

Consistent with a developmental psychopathology framework, no factor causes depression on its own. Two factors often examined together are genetic factors and other variables in one's environment, such as where one lives or stressors one has experienced.

Gene–environment correlations

Having certain genes may contribute to increased environmental risks for depression, while also increasing depression risk on their own (Lau & Eley, 2008b). This phenomenon is called gene–environment correlation, or *rGE*. Research on rGE in depression has found evidence that genes influence several environmental factors that are known to be risks for depression, such as negative life events, parental discipline, parent–child bonding and mutuality, sibling relationships, and divorce; these genes also contribute to depressive symptoms on their own (see Wilkinson, Trzaskowski, Haworth, & Eley, 2013, for a review).

Gene–environment interactions

Interactions refer to the idea that one variable may affect another variable differently depending on levels of a third variable. Gene–environment interactions arise when environmental risk affects change as a function of genetic risks, or when genetic risks are expressed only in the presence of a certain environmental stressor. Caspi et al. (2003) carried out a famous study demonstrating gene–environment interaction for depression. They showed an interaction where the combination of a certain *polymorphism* in the serotonin (5-HT) transporter promoter region and the experience of stressful life events was associated with higher depression symptoms in adults (see Figure 9.5). This finding was replicated in adolescents (Petersen et al. 2012).

DEVELOPMENTAL TIMING EFFECTS: THE INTERPLAY OF NORMAL AND ABNORMAL DEVELOPMENT

Research is still determining when certain vulnerability factors for depression emerge, and whether and how they change over time. In terms of

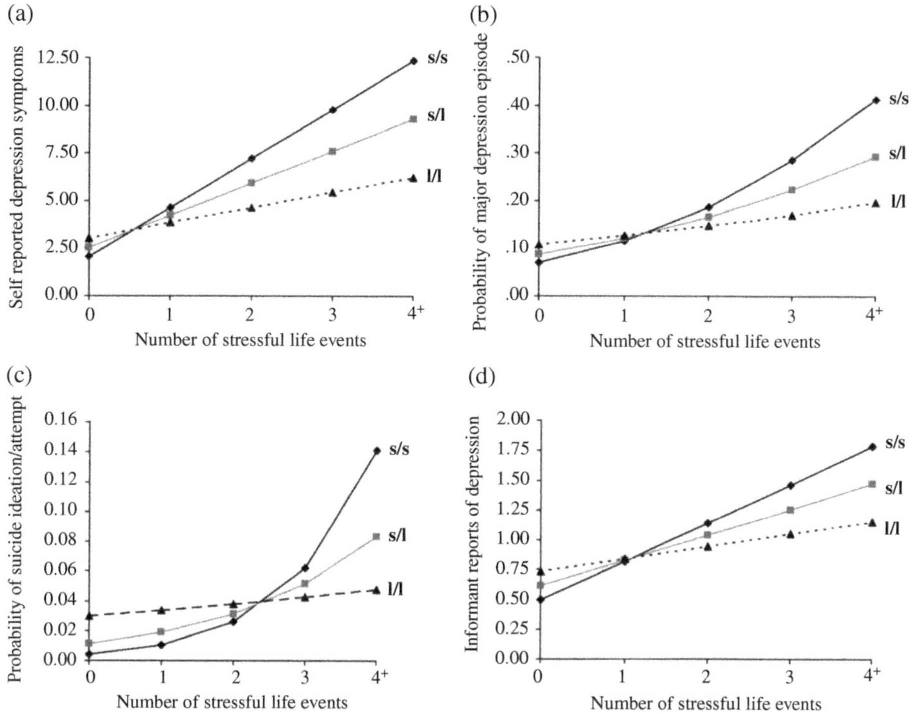

FIGURE 9.5 Results of Multiple Regression Analyses Estimating the Association Between Number of Stressful Life Events (between ages 21 and 26 years) and Depression Outcomes at age 26 as a Function of 5-HT T Genotype (Caspi et al., 2003) Results of multiple regression analyses estimating the association between number of stressful life events (between ages 21 and 26 years) and depression outcomes at age 26 as a function of 5-HT T genotype. Among the 146 s/s homozygotes, 43 (29%), 37(25%), 28 (19%), 15 (10%), and 23 (16%) study members experienced zero, one, two, three, and four or more stressful events, respectively. Among the 435 s/l heterozygotes, 141 (32%), 101 (23%), 76 (17%), 49 (11%), and 68 (16%) experienced zero, one, two, three, and four or more stressful events. Among the 264 l/l homozygotes, 79 (29%), 73 (28%), 57 (21%), 26 (10%), and 29 (11%) experienced zero, one, two, three, and four or more stressful events. (A) Self-reports of depression symptoms. The main effect of 5-HT TLPR (i.e., an effect not conditional on other variables) was marginally significant ($b = -0.96$, SE = 0.52, $t = 1.86$, $P = 0.06$), the main effect of stressful life events was significant ($b = 1.75$, SE = 0.23, $t = 7.45$, $P < 0.001$), and the interaction between 5-HT TLPR and life events was in the predicted direction ($b = -0.89$, SE = 0.37, $t = 2.39$, $P = 0.02$). The interaction showed that the effect of life events on self-reports of depression symptoms was stronger among individuals carrying an s allele ($b = 2.52$, SE = 0.66, $t = 3.82$, $P < 0.001$ among s/s homozygotes, and $b = 1.71$, SE = 0.34, $t = 5.02$, $P < 0.001$ among s/l heterozygotes) than among l/l homozygotes ($b = 0.77$, SE = 0.43, $t = 1.79$, $P = 0.08$). (B) Probability of major depressive episode. The main effect of 5-HT TLPR was not significant ($b = -0.15$, SE = 0.14, $z = 1.07$, $P = 0.29$), the main effect of life events was significant ($b = 0.37$, SE = 0.06, $z = 5.99$, $P < 0.001$), and the G × E was in the predicted direction ($b = -0.19$, SE = 0.10, $z = 1.91$, $P = 0.056$). Life events predicted a diagnosis of major depression among s carriers ($b = 0.52$, SE = 0.16, $z = 3.28$, $P = 0.001$ among s/s homozygotes, and $b = 0.39$, SE = 0.09, $z = 4.24$, $P < 0.001$ among s/l heterozygotes) but not among l/l homozygotes ($b = 0.16$,

vulnerability factors that may emerge in adolescence, Forbes and Dahl (2012) argue that adolescence may be a developmental period in which the reward function in depression is most strikingly disrupted. Another feature of adolescent brain development that may affect depression risk is that the emotion regions of the brain (subcortical affective regions) develop more quickly than the areas that support behavioral and emotional control (prefrontal cortex), making it more difficult for adolescents to control their emotions and behavior. Pubertal development is another factor that may influence the rise of depression. In particular, early pubertal timing, when one matures earlier than one's peers, has been associated with increased risk for adolescent depression (Ullsperger & Nikolas, 2017).

Evidence-Based Interventions

The most established evidence-based mental health interventions for adolescent depression are *Cognitive Behavioral Therapy* (CBT) and *Interpersonal Psychotherapy for Adolescents* (IPT-A), and there is growing evidence for *Attachment-Based Family Therapy* (ABFT). Pharmacotherapy is also a form of treatment for adolescent depression. Research most strongly supports the combination of therapy and psychiatric medications for youth depression.

Psychotherapy

Cognitive Behavioral Therapy (CBT) is considered an empirically supported, evidence-based approach for treating adolescent depression. CBT aims to address maladaptive thoughts, behaviors, and emotions through cognitive restructuring, behavioral activation, problem solving,

SE = 0.13, $z = 1.18$, $P = 0.24$). (C) Probability of suicide ideation or attempt. The main effect of 5-HT TLPR was not significant ($b = -0.01$, SE = 0.28, $z = 0.01$, $P = 0.99$), the main effect of life events was significant ($b = 0.51$, SE = 0.13, $z = 3.96$, $P < 0.001$), and the G × E interaction was in the predicted direction ($b = -0.39$, SE = 0.20, $t = 1.95$, $P = 0.051$). Life events predicted suicide ideation or attempt among s carriers ($b = 0.48$, SE = 0.29, $z = 1.67$, $P = 0.09$ among s/s homozygotes, and $b = 0.91$, SE = 0.25, $z = 3.58$, $P < 0.001$ among s/l heterozygotes) but not among l/l homozygotes ($b = 0.13$, SE = 0.26, $z = 0.49$, $P = 0.62$). (D) Informant reports of depression. The main effect of 5-HT TLPR was not significant (b = –0.06, SE = 0.06, t = 0.98, $P = 0.33$), the main effect of life events was significant ($b = 0.23$, SE = 0.03, $t = 8.47$, $P < 0.001$), and the G × E was in the predicted direction ($b = -0.11$, SE = 0.04, $t = 2.54$, $P < 0.01$). The effect of life events on depression was stronger among s carriers ($b = 0.39$, SE = 0.07, $t = 5.23$, $P < 0.001$ among s/s homozygotes, and $b = 0.17$, SE = 0.04, $t = 4.51$, $P < 0.001$ among s/l heterozygotes) than among l/l homozygotes ($b = 0.14$, SE = 0.05, $t = 2.69$, $P < 0.01$). Source: Caspi, A., et al. (2003). reproduced with permissions of John Wiley & Sons.

communication skills, relaxation training, and social skills (Jeffreys & Weersing, 2014). Another psychotherapy intervention that has strong empirical support and is considered evidence-based for the treatment of adolescent depression is Interpersonal Psychotherapy for Adolescents (IPT-A) (Mufson et al., 2004). IPT-A is a manualized treatment designed for 12–18-year-olds, which focuses on 1–2 interpersonal problem areas based on the adolescent's specific interpersonal difficulties precipitating depression. Attachment-Based Family Therapy (ABFT) also has growing support as a treatment for adolescent depression. ABFT is a manualized form of family therapy that focuses on improving attachment security as the primary mechanism of change. It uses five tasks to build trust and repair attachment ruptures (Diamond, Russon, & Levy, 2016).

PSYCHOPHARMACOLOGY (PSYCHIATRIC MEDICATIONS)

The psychiatric medication that has been shown to be most helpful in treating adolescent depression is SSRIs (Selective Serotonin Reuptake Inhibitors), which increase the flow of serotonin in the brain (Fonagy et al., 2014). While some previous research showed that suicidal thinking increased for some adolescents when they were taking SSRIs, leading the FDA to add a "black box warning," these risks have been shown to be small, and later review papers showed benefits of using SSRIs to reduce adolescent depressive symptoms (Hetrick et al., 2012).

COMBINED TREATMENT

The combination of psychiatric medication and therapy have been shown to be more effective than therapy by itself or medication by itself (Fonagy et al., 2014). It is thought that medication may help prompt an immediate decline in symptoms, whereas therapy may help with long-term effects. Combined treatment may be particularly beneficial for youth who have comorbid mental health conditions (Fonagy et al., 2014).

Chapter Summary

This chapter was the first of Part III that deals with problems of adolescence and early adulthood. Depression is one of the most prevalent disorders of this developmental period; depression rates increase significantly during adolescence, particularly among girls. Depression has many effects on other aspects of functioning and is often comorbid with other mental health disorders. As we showed in Figure 9.3, depression in adolescence is multifactorial in its etiology. We described the contextual risk and protective factors that contribute to the causes and maintenance of depression. We also described the genetic, neurobiological, cognitive, and temperamental factors that help to maintain and cause depression. Finally, we gave you a glimpse into the evidence-based interventions for depression in adolescence.

Further Reading

Caspi, A., Sugden, K., Moffitt, T. E., Taylor, A., Craig, I. W., Harrington, H., & Poulton, R. (2003). Influence of life stress on depression: Moderation by a polymorphism in the 5-HTT gene. *Science*, *301*(5631), 386–389.

Disner, S. G., Beevers, C. G., Haigh, E. A. P., & Beck, A. T. (2011). Neural mechanisms of the cognitive model of depression. *Nature Reviews Neuroscience*, *12*(8), 467–477.

Forbes, E. E. & Dahl, R. E. (2012). Research review: Altered reward function in adolescent depression: What, when and how? *Journal of Child Psychology and Psychiatry*, *53*(1), 3–15.

Hankin, B. L. (2012). Future directions in vulnerability to depression among youth: Integrating risk factors and processes across multiple levels of analysis. *Journal of Clinical Child and Adolescent Psychology*, *41*, 695–718.

Discussion/Essay Questions

1. What are two important changes in terms of depression prevalence during adolescence?
2. Discuss how the developmental psychopathology principles of homotypic and heterotypic continuity can be applied to depression from childhood to adulthood.
3. Discuss at least three cognitive theories of depression.
4. What is the role of life stress in depression during adolescence?
5. Name three ways that parents can increase a teenager's risk for depression.
6. What are evidence-based treatments for adolescent depression?
7. Is depression a biologically-based illness? Provide evidence for your answer.

Glossary

Affect refers to an individual's outward expression of emotional states or mood.

Alleles refer to different versions of stretches of DNA that vary across individuals. As each individual possesses two alleles at a given locus (part of the gene), the particular combination of a person's alleles defines his or her genotype.

Anhedonia is characterized by decreased interest and pleasure in everyday activities.

Attachment-Based Family Therapy (ABFT) is an evidence-based treatment for depression that aims to improve attachment security as a means of reducing depression symptoms.

Beck's cognitive theory focuses on negative schema and dysfunctional attitudes, which are rigid cognitive structures that negatively filter and bias social and affective information.

Cognitive-Behavioral Therapy (CBT) is an evidence-based therapy for adolescent depression. CBT aims to address teenagers' maladaptive thoughts, behaviors, and emotions.

Cognitive vulnerabilities refer to cognitive (i.e., thought) processes that may put an individual at risk for psychopathology.

Comorbidity occurs when an individual is experiencing two or more disorders at one time.

Dependent life events refer to stressors that occur because of the actions of an individual, such as parking illegally and getting a ticket.

Depression as a clinical syndrome refers to a constellation of symptoms that occur together as described in the DSM-5.

Depression as a dimensional construct refers to the principle that mild and severe depression are different ends of the same continuum.

Depression as a subclinical syndrome (or minor depression) assumes a dimensional approach in which individuals below the threshold for clinical depression are identified.

Depression as a transient mood or affective state refers to the feeling of being "down" or "having the blues."

Depressive disorders refer to a spectrum of disorders that relate to problems in mood (or affect or emotion).

Diathesis-stress models refer to the idea that one may have a certain vulnerability (diathesis) to depression based on certain individual or biological factors, but this vulnerability may not exert an effect until a stressful event (or multiple stressors) occur.

Endophenotypes are risk markers or vulnerability traits that are proximal to, and thus more directly influenced by, genes than are the signs and symptoms.

Emotion refers to an internal, automatic response (i.e., fear, anger, sadness, disgust, joy), usually to an event or stimulus.

Heterogeneity of disorder refers to the idea that, among individuals meeting criteria for depression, there may be subgroups who have similar clusters of symptoms.

Heterotypic continuity is the idea that different disorders predict one another over time due to developmental changes (e.g., anxiety predicting depression).

Homotypic continuity is defined as stability in the same or similar behavioral responses over time; that is, a disorder predicting itself over time.

Hopelessness theory focuses on a negative cognitive style, which comprises negative inferences that are global, stable, and internal about the causes of events and their consequences.

Independent life events refer to stressors that are beyond the control of an individual, such as experiencing the death of a parent due to a heart attack.

Interpersonal Psychotherapy for Adolescents (IPT-A) is an evidence-based treatment for depression in adolescents.

Lifetime prevalence refers to the rates of depression experienced among a particular group over the span of their entire lifetimes.

Major Depressive Disorder, or MDD, is diagnosed when an individual is experiencing at least five of nine symptoms for more than half the time for at least two weeks. For youth, one of the symptoms must be a depressed mood, loss of interest, or irritable mood.

Mood refers to an individual's emotional state.

Persistent Depressive Disorder, previously called dysthymia, is diagnosed in adolescents when they have been experiencing depressed or irritable mood more than half the time for at least a year, in addition to at least two other symptoms.

Polymorphisms are different variations of the same allele. Individuals have two alleles at a given locus (part of the gene), and therefore may have two copies of the same allele (homozygous), or two different alleles (heterozygous).

Probands refers to individuals seeking treatment for a disorder who become the starting point for studying genetics associated with the disorder.

Prospective follow-up studies are a type of longitudinal research design that chooses a cohort of individuals based on certain criteria and then follows-up with those people over time.

Psychopharmacotherapy refers to psychiatric medications that may be prescribed to treat mental health symptoms, such as SSRIs for depression.

Response styles theory emphasizes rumination as a process of repeatedly focusing on or dwelling on symptoms of depression and the meaning, causes, and consequences of the symptoms.

rGE refers to gene-environment correlations, and can take three forms: Passive rGE, Evocative rGE, or Active rGE.

Serotonin is a neurotransmitter, or a chemical produced by cells in the nervous system that helps to send signals. It helps in the regulation of many processes, including mood and sleep.

The stress generation hypothesis refers to the idea that individuals who are depressed are more likely to act in a manner that may cause or generate further stress in their lives.

Temperament refers to individual differences in children's basic emotional reactivity, as well as children's emotional and behavioral tendencies across different contexts.

Twelve-month prevalence refers to the rates of a depression experienced among a particular group over the span of one year.

References

aanhet Rot, M., Mathew, S. J., & Charney, D. S. (2009). Neurobiological mechanisms in major depressive disorder. *CMAJ: Canadian Medical Association Journal, 180*(3), 305–313.

Abela, J. R. Z., & Hankin, B. L. (2008). Cognitive vulnearbility to depression in children and adolescents: A developmental psychopathology perspective. In J. R. Z. Abela & B. L. Hankin (Eds.), *Handbook of depression in children and adolescents* (pp. 35–78). New York, NY: The Guilford Press.

Achenbach, T. M., & Rescorla, L. A. (2000). *Manual for the ASEBA Preschool Forms & Profiles*. Burlington, VT: University of Vermont, Research Center for Children, Youth, & Families.

Achenbach, T. M., & Rescorla, L. A. (2001). *Manual for the ASEBA School-Age Forms & Profiles*. Burlington, VT: University of Vermont, Research Center for Children, Youth, & Families.

Abramson, L. Y., Alloy, L. B., & Metalsky, G. I. (1989). Hopelessness depression—A theory-based subtype of depression. *Psychological Review, 96*(2), 358–372.

Allen, J. P., Insabella, G., Porter, M. R., Smith, F. D., Land, D., & Phillips, N. (2006). A social-interactional model of the development of depressive symptoms in adolescence. *Journal of Consulting and Clinical Psychology, 74*(1), 55–65.

American Psychiatric Association (2013). *Diagnostic and Statistical Manual of Mental Disorders* (5th ed.). Washington, DC.

Angold, A., Costello, E. J., Farmer, E. M. Z., Burns, B. J., & Erkanli, A. (1999). Impaired but undiagnosed. *Journal of the American Academy of Child and Adolescent Psychiatry, 38*(2), 129–137.

Avenevoli, S., Knight, E., Kessler, R. C., & Merikangas, K. R. (2008). Epidemiology of depression in children and adolescents. In J. R. Z. Abela & B. L. Hankin (Eds.), *Handbook of depression in children and adolescents*. New York, NY: The Guilford Press.

Avenevoli, S., Swendsen, J., He, J.-P., Burstein, M., & Merikangas, K. R. (2015). Major depression in the National Comorbidity Survey–Adolescent Supplement: Prevalence, correlates, and treatment. *Journal of the American Academy of Child & Adolescent Psychiatry, 54*(1), 37–44.

Beck, A. T. (1967). *Depression: Clinical, experimental, and theoretical aspects*. New York, NY, USA: Harper.

Birmaher, B., Ryan, N. D., Williamson, D. E., Brent, D. A., Kaufman, J., Dahl, R. E., & Nelson, B. (1996). Childhood and adolescent depression: A review of the past 10 years. *Part I. Journal of the American Academy of Child Adolescent Psychiatry, 35*(11), 1427–1439.

Bowlby, J. (1973). *Attachment and loss: Separation*. New York, NY: Basic Books.

Caspi, A., Sugden, K., Moffitt, T. E., Taylor, A., Craig, I. W., Harrington, H., & Poulton, R. (2003). Influence of life stress on depression: Moderation by a polymorphism in the 5-HTT gene. *Science, 301*(5631), 386–389.

Compas, B. E., Connor-Smith, J., & Jaser, S. S. (2004). Temperament, stress reactivity, and coping: Implications for depression in childhood and adolescence. *Journal of Clinical Child and Adolescent Psychology, 33*(1), 21–31.

Copeland, W.E., Wolke, D., Angold, A., & Costello, E.J. (2013). Adult psychiatric outcomes of bullying and being bullied by peers in childhood and adolescence. *JAMA Psychiatry, 70*(4), 419–426.

Costello, D. M., Swendsen, J., Rose, J. S., & Dierker, L. C. (2008). Risk and protective factors associated with trajectories of depressed mood from adolescence to early adulthood. *Journal of Consulting and Clinical Psychology, 76*(2), 173–183.

Diamond, G., Russon, J., & Levy, S. (2016). Attachment-based family therapy: A review of the empirical support. *Fam Process. 55*(3), 595–610. doi:10.1111/famp.12241

Dohrenwend, B. P. (2000). The role of adversity and stress in psychopathology: Some evidence and its implications for theory and research. *Journal of Health and Social Behavior*, *41*(1), 1–19.

Finsaas, M. C., Bufferd, S. J., Dougherty, L. R., Carlson, G. A., & Klein, D. N. (2018). Preschool psychiatric disorders: Homotypic and heterotypic continuity through middle childhood and early adolescence. *Psychological Medicine*, *48*(13), 2159–2168.

Fonagy, P., Cottrell, D., Phillips, J., Bevington, D., Glaser, D., & Allison, E. (2014). *What works for whom? A critical review of treatments for children and adolescents* (2nd ed.). New York, NY: Guilford Press.

Forbes, E. E., Christopher May, J., Siegle, G. J., Ladouceur, C. D., Ryan, N. D., Carter, C. S., & Dahl, R. E. (2006). Reward-related decision-making in pediatric major depressive disorder: An fMRI study. *Journal of Child Psychology and Psychiatry*, *47*(10), 1031–1040.

Forbes, E. E., & Dahl, R. E. (2012). Research Review: Altered reward function in adolescent depression: What, when and how? *Journal of Child Psychology and Psychiatry*, *53*(1), 3–15.

Forbes, E. E., Shaw, D. S., & Dahl, R. E. (2007). Alterations in reward-related decision making in boys with recent and future depression. *Biology and Psychiatry*, *61*(5), 633–639.

Garber, J. (2006). Depression in children and adolescents: Linking risk research and prevention. American Journal of Prevention Medicine, 31(6 Suppl. 1), S104–S125.

Garber, J. & Rao, U. (2014). Depression in children and adolescents. In M. Lewis and K. D. Rudolph (Eds.), *Handbook of developmental psychopathology* (3rd ed., pp. 489–520). New York, NY: Springer Science + Business Media.

Goodman, S. H., & Gotlib, I. H. (1999). Risk for psychopathology in the children of depressed mothers: A developmental model for understanding mechanisms of transmission. *Psychological Review*, *106*(3), 458–490.

Goodyer, I. M., Herbert, J., Tamplin, A., & Altham, P. M. E. (2000). Recent life events, cortisol, dehydroepiandrosterone and the onset of major depression in high-risk adolescents. *British Journal of Psychiatry*, *177*, 499–504.

Hammen, C. (2018). Risk factors for depression: An autobiographical review. *Annual Review of Clinical Psychology*, *14*, 1–28. doi: 10.1146/annurev-clinpsy-050817-084811.

Hammen, C., Brennan, P. A., & Shih, J. H. (2004). Family discord and stress predictors of depression and other disorders in adolescent children of depressed and nondepressed women. *Journal of the American Academy of Child & Adolescent Psychiatry*, *43*(8), 994–1002.

Hankin, B. L., Oppenheimer, C., Jenness, J., Barrocas, A., Shapero, B. G., & Goldband, J. (2009). Developmental origins of cognitive vulnerabilities to depression: Review of processes contributing to stability and change across time. *Journal of Clinical Psychology*, *65*(12), 1327–1338.

Hankin, B. L., Young, J. F., Abela, J. R. Z., Smolen, A., Jenness, J. L., Gulley, L. D., Technow, J. R., Gottlieb, A. B., Cohen, J. R., & Oppenheimer, C. W. (2015). Depression from childhood into late adolescence: Influence of gender, development, genetic susceptibility, and peer stress. *Journal of Abnormal Psychology*, *124*(4), 803–816.

Hasler, G., Drevets, W. C., Manji, H. K., & Charney, D. S. (2004). Discovering endophenotypes for major depression. *Neuropsychopharmacology*, *29*(10), 1765–1781.

Henje Blom, E., Ho, T. C., Connolly, C. G., LeWinn, K. Z., Sacchet, M. D., Tymofiyeva, O., Weng, H. Y., & Yang, T. T. (2016). The neuroscience and context of adolescent depression. *Acta Paediatrica*, *105*(4), 358–365. https://doi.org/10.1111/apa.13299.

Hetrick, S.E., McKenzie, J.E., Cox, G.R., Simmons, M.B., & Merry, S.N. (2012). Newer generation antidepressants for depressive disorders in children and adolescents. *Cochrane Database of Systematic Reviews, 10.*

Hyde, J. S., Mezulis, A. H., & Abramson, L. Y. (2008). The ABCs of depression: Integrating affective, biological, and cognitive models to explain the emergence of the gender difference in depression. *Psychological Review, 115*(2), 291–313.

Jeffreys, M. & Weersing, V.R. (2014). Depressive disorders in adolescents. In C.A. Alfano & D.C. Beidel (Eds.), *Comprehensive evidence-based interventions for children and adolescents* (pp. 147–162). Hoboken, NJ: John Wiley & Sons, Inc.

Kessler, R. C., Petukhova, M., Sampson, N. A., Zaslavsky, A. M., & Wittchen, H. U. (2012). Twelve-month and lifetime prevalence and lifetime morbid risk of anxiety and mood disorders in the United States. *International Journal of Methods in Psychiatric Research* doi: 10.1002/mpr.1359.

Kim-Cohen, J., Caspi, A., Moffitt, T. E., Harrington, H., Milne, B. J., & Poulton, R. (2003). Prior juvenile diagnoses in adults with mental disorder: Developmental follow-back of a prospective-longitudinal cohort. *Archives of General Psychiatry, 60*(7), 709–717.

Kim, J., & Cicchetti, D. (2006). Longitudinal trajectories of self-system processes and depressive symptoms among maltreated and nonmaltreated children. *Child Development, 77*(3), 624–639.

Klein, D. N., Kotov, R., & Bufferd, S. J. (2011). Personality and depression: Explanatory models and review of the evidence. *Annual Review of Clinical Psychology, 7*, 269–295.

Klein, D. N., Kujawa, A. J., Black, S R., & Pennock, A. T. (2013). Depressive disorders. In T. D. Beauchaine & S. P. Hinshaw (Eds.), *Child and Adolescent Psychopathology* (2nd ed., pp. 543–575). Hoboken, NJ: John Wiley & Sons, Inc.

Kotov, R., Krueger, R. F., Watson, D., Achenbach, T. M., Althoff, R. R., Bagby, R. M., Brown, T. A., Carpenter, W. T., Caspi, A., Clark, L. A., Eaton, N. R., Forbes, M. K., Forbush, K. T., Goldberg, D., Hasin, D., Hyman, S. E., Ivanova, M. Y., Lynam, D. R., Markon, K., & Zimmerman, M. (2017). The hierarchical taxonomy of psychopathology (HiTOP): A dimensional alternative to traditional nosologies. *Journal of Abnormal Psychology, 126*(4), 454–477. https://doi.org/10.1037/abn0000258.

Kyte, Z., & Goodyer, I. (2008). Social cognition in depressed children and adolescents. In C. Sharp, P. Fonagy & I. Goodyer (Eds.), *Social cognition and developmental psychopathology* (pp. 201–237). Oxford, UK: Oxford University Press.

Lau, C., & Eley, T. C. (2008a). New behavioral genetic approaches to depression in childhood and adolescence. In J. R. Abela & B. L. Hankin (Eds.), *Handbook of depression in children and adolescence* (pp. 124–148). New York, NY: The Guilford Press.

Lau, J. Y. F., & Eley, T. C. (2008b). Disentangling gene–environment correlations and interactions on adolescent depressive symptoms. *Journal of Child Psychology and Psychiatry, 49*(2), 142–150.

Lenroot, R. K., & Giedd, J. N. (2010). Sex differences in the adolescent brain. *Brain and Cognition, 72*(1), 46–55.

Lewinsohn, P. M., Rohde, P., & Seeley, J. R. (1998). Major depressive disorder in older adolescents: Prevalence, risk factors, and clinical implications. *Clinical Psychology Review, 18*(7), 765–794.

Liu, R.T., & Alloy, L.B. (2010). Stress generation in depression: A systematic review of the empirical literature and recommendations for future study. *Clinical Psychology Review, 30*(5), 582–593.

Lorant, V., Deliege, D., Eaton, W., Robert, A., Philippot, P., & Ansseau, M. (2003). Socioeconomic inequalities in depression: A meta-analysis. *American Journal of Epidemiology, 157*(2), 98–112.

Lovejoy, M. C., Graczyk, P. A., O'Hare, E., & Neuman, G. (2000). Maternal depression and parenting behavior: A meta-analytic review. *Clinical Psychology Review, 20*(5), 561–592.

McDonough-Caplan, H., Klein, D. N., & Beauchaine, T. P. (2018). Comorbidity and continuity of depression and conduct problems from elementary school to adolescence. *Journal of Abnormal Psychology, 127*(3), 326–337.

Merikangas, K., Avenevoli, S., Costello, J., Koretz, D., & Kessler, R. C. (2009). National comorbidity survey replication adolescent supplement (NCS-A): I. Background and measures. *Journal of American Academy of Child Adolescent Psychiatry, 48*(4), 367–369.

Merikangas K. R., He J. P., Brody D., Fisher P.W., Bourdon K., & Koretz D.S. (2010). Prevalence and treatment of mental disorders among US Children in the 2001–2004 NHANES. *Pediatrics, 125*(1), 75– 81.

Mufson, L., Dorta, K., Moreau, D., & Weissman, M. (2004) *Interpersonal psychotherapy for depressed adolescents* (2nd ed.). New York, NY: The Guilford Press.

Naninck, E. F., Lucassen, P. J., & Bakker, J. (2011). Sex differences in adolescent depression: Do sex hormones determine vulnerability? [Research Support, Non-U.S. Government Review]. *Journal of Neuroendocrinol, 23*(5), 383–392.

Nantel-Vivier, A., & Pihl, R. O. (2008). Biological vulnerability to depression. In J. R. Abela & B. L. Hankin (Eds.), *Handbook of depression in children and adolescents* (pp. 103–123). New York, NY: The Guilford Press.

National Research Council and Institute of Medicine (2009). Depression in parents, parenting, and children: Opportunities to improve identification, treatment, and prevention. In M. J. England & L. J. Sim (Eds.), *Committee on depression, parenting practices, and the healthy development of children*. Washington, DC: The National Academies Press.

Nock M. K., Green J. G., Hwang I., McLaughlin, K. A., Sampson, N. A., Zaslavsky, A. M., & Kessler, R. C. (2013). Prevalence, correlates, and treatment of lifetime suicidal behavior among adolescents: Results from the National Comorbidity Survey Replication Adolescent Supplement. *JAMA Psychiatry, 70*(3), 300–310. doi: 10.1001/2013.jamapsychiatry.55.

Nolen-Hoeksema, S. (1991). Responses to depression and their effects on the duration of depressive episodes. *Journal of Abnormal Psychology, 100*(4), 569–582.

Nolen-Hoeksema, S. (2001). Gender differences in depression. *Current Directions in Psychological Science, 10*(5), 173–176.

Petersen, I. T., Bates, J. E., Goodnight, J. A., Dodge, K. A., Lansford, J. E., Pettit, G. S., & Dick, D. M. (2012). Interaction between serotonin transporter polymorphism (5-HTTLPR) and stressful life events in adolescents' trajectories of anxious/depressed symptoms. *Developmental Psychology, 48*(5), 1463–1475.

Restifo, K., & Bogels, S. (2009). Family processes in the development of youth depression: Translating the evidence to treatment. *Clinical Psychology Review, 29*(4), 294–316.

Rice, F., Riglin, L., Thapar, A. K., Heron, J., Anney, R., O'Donovan, M. C., & Thapar, A. (2019). Characterizing developmental trajectories and the role of neuropsychiatric genetic risk variants in early-onset depression. *JAMA Psychiatry, 76*(3), 306–313.

Rie, H. E. (1966). Depression in childhood. A survey of some pertinent contributions. *Journal of the American Academy of Child Psychiatry, 5*(4), 653–685.

Risch, N., Herrell, R., Lehner, T., Liang, K.-Y., Eaves, L., Hoh, J., & Merikangas, K. R. (2009). Interaction between the serotonin transporter gene (5-HTTLPR), stressful life events, and risk of depression: A meta-analysis. *JAMA, 301*(23), 2462–2471.

Rohde, P., Lewinsohn, P. M., Klein, D. N., Seeley, J. R., & Gau, J. M. (2013). Key characteristics of major depressive disorder occurring in childhood, adolescence, emerging adulthood, adulthood. *Clinical Psychological Science, 1*(1), 41–53.

Rudolph, K., Flynn, M., & Abaied, J. L. (2008). A developmental perspective on interpersonal theories of youth depression.

In J. R. Z. Abela & B. L. Hankin (Eds.), *Handbook of depression*. New York, NY: Guilford Press.

Rueger, S. Y., Malecki, C. K., Pyun, Y., Aycock, C., & Coyle, S. (2016). A meta-analytic review of the association between perceived social support and depression in childhood and adolescence. *Psychological Bulletin*, *142*(10), 1017–1067.

Ryan, N.D., Puig-Antich, J., Ambrosini, P., Rabinovich, H., Robinson, D., Nelson, B., & Twomey, J. (1987). The clinical picture of major depression in children and adolescents. *Archives of General Psychiatry*, *44*, 854–861.

Substance Abuse and Mental Health Services Administration (SAMHSA) (2017). Results from the 2017 National Survey on Drug Use and Health: Detailed tables Retrieved from: https://www.samhsa.gov/data/sites/default/files/cbhsq-reports/NSDUHDetailedTabs2017/NSDUHDetailedTabs2017.htm#tab8-56A. Accessed on 4 February 2020.

Sharp, C., Kim, S., Herman, L., Pane, H., Reuter, T., & Strathearn, L. (2014). Major depression in mothers predicts reduced reward-related brain processing in adolescent daughters, with or without depression. *Journal of Abnormal Psychology*, *123*(2), 298–309.

Smoller, J. W. (2016). The genetics of stress-related disorders: PTSD, depression, and anxietydisorders. *Neuropsychopharmacology*, *41*(1), 297–319.

Sullivan, H. S. (1953). *The interpersonal theory of psychiatry*. New York, NY: Norton.

Sullivan, P. F., Neale, M. C., & Kendler, K. S. (2000). Genetic epidemiology of major depression: Review and meta-analysis. *The American Journal of Psychiatry*, *157*(10), 1552–1562.

Twenge, J. M., & Nolen-Hoeksema, S. (2002). Age, gender, race, socioeconomic status, and birth cohort differences on the children's depression inventory: A meta-analysis. *Journal of Abnormal Psychology*, *111*(4), 578–588.

Ullsperger, J. M., & Nikolas, M. A. (2017). A meta-analytic review of the association between pubertal timing and psychopathology in adolescence: Are there sex differences in risk? *Psychological Bulletin*, *143*(9), 903–938.

Weir, J. M., Zakama, A., & Rao, U. (2012). Developmental risk I: Depression and the developing brain. *Child and Adolescent Psychiatric Clinics of North America*, *21*(2), 237–259.

Wilkinson, P. O., Trzaskowski, M., Haworth, C. M., & Eley, T. C. (2013). The role of gene–environment correlations and interactions in middle childhood depressive symptoms. *Development and Psychopathology*, *25*(1), 93–104.

World Health Organization (2018). International classification of diseases for mortality and morbidity statistics (11th revision). Retrieved from: https://icd.who.int/browse11/l-m/en.

Chapter 10

Eating Disorders

Deborah Michel and Amanda Venta

Chapter Overview

If you reflect on your transition from childhood to teenage years, you may remember that the physical, emotional, and social changes that accompany puberty often result in feelings of insecurity around physical appearance and peer acceptance. While these feelings are a normal part of adolescence, *eating disorders* can also emerge during this time. They are described in the DSM-5 as "persistent disturbance of eating or eating-related behavior that results in the altered consumption or absorption of food that significantly impairs physical health or psychosocial functioning" (American Psychiatric Association, 2013). In this chapter, we will discuss the eating disorders that have been most widely researched in adolescence, anorexia nervosa and bulimia nervosa, with mention of binge-eating disorder as well. Below, we provide a case example.

Case study in anorexia nervosa

Mia is a 14-year-old Asian Indian female who lives with her parents in a suburban neighborhood. Mia's family is very health conscious. Her parents are vegetarians and avid runners. Mia has always followed their example by maintaining a vegetarian diet. However, as Mia entered puberty, her parents noticed a focus on weight control, with recent weight loss rendering her significantly underweight. They added that she has been withdrawn lately, spending less time with friends and family. When you meet with Mia privately, you discover

Developmental Psychopathology, First Edition. Edited by Amanda Venta, Carla Sharp, Jack M. Fletcher, and Peter Fonagy.

that her dietary intake is limited to a few small meals per day and that, despite her low weight, she sees nothing wrong with her a "healthy" lifestyle.

Did anything about Mia's case surprise you? Which information leads you to believe that she has an eating disorder? Are there aspects of her behavior that are normative? Is there additional information you would like to obtain?

Definition, Diagnosis, and Clinical Features

Let us first consider the DSM-5 definitions for the eating disorders that we will discuss. Table 10.1 includes a summary of the diagnostic criteria for each of these disorders as it is presented in the DSM-5, as well as how they are conceptualized using other diagnostic systems.

Anorexia nervosa (AN) consists of three main features. First, there are behaviors such as food restriction to the degree that the person is below the minimum expected weight for age, stature, previous weight trajectory, and sex. This may occur through weight loss or failure to achieve the weight gain that would be expected as a child or adolescent matures (American Psychiatric Association, 2013). The second criterion is that the individual displays an intense fear of weight gain (APA, 2013) or a pattern of behavior that interferes with the person's ability to gain or maintain weight. A binge-eating/purging subtype is assigned when the person shows a pattern of eating an unusually large quantity of food (*binge eating*) or *purging behavior*, which may include self-induced vomiting, laxative and/or diuretic abuse, enema abuse, or misuse of other medications to compensate for calories consumed during a binge. Non-purging means of compensating for calories ingested include fasting and excessive exercise. Notice that we said binge eating *or* purging, as some individuals will purge after eating small or normal amounts of food. Finally, diagnosis requires a disturbance in the way in which a person perceives personal weight, shape, and/or parts of their body (APA, 2013), which is commonly referred to as *body image distortion*. Oftentimes, individuals see themselves as overweight and/or perceive certain body parts as larger than what others observe. They may engage in "body checking" behaviors such as weighing, measuring body parts, or scrutinizing themselves in a mirror. Further, weight and/or body shape plays an overly important role in the person's self-esteem and self-worth, such that internal qualities are minimized. Alternatively, this criterion can manifest in a failure to recognize the seriousness of one's low body weight and/or other medical complications of the disorder, which is often referred to as *denial* or *minimization* of the disorder.

TABLE 10.1 Eating Disorders as Defined by the DSM-5 and ICD-11

Disorder	*DSM-5*	*ICD-11*
Anorexia nervosa	A. Restriction of energy intake relative to requirements, leading to a significantly low body weight in the context of age, sex, developmental trajectory, and physical health. Significantly low weight is defined as a weight that is less than minimally normal or, for children and adolescents, less than that minimally expected. B. Intense fear of gaining weight or of becoming fat, or persistent behavior that interferes with weight gain, even though at a significantly low weight. C. Disturbance in the way in which one's body weight or shape is experienced, undue influence of body weight or shape on self-evaluation, or persistent lack of recognition of the seriousness of the current low body weight.	Anorexia nervosa is characterized by significantly low body weight for the individual's height, age, and developmental stage (body mass index (BMI) less than 18.5 kg/m^2 in adults and BMI-for-age under fifth percentile in children and adolescents) that is not due to another health condition or to the unavailability of food. Low body weight is accompanied by a persistent pattern of behaviors to prevent restoration of normal weight, which may include behaviors aimed at reducing energy intake (restricted eating), purging behaviors (e.g., self-induced vomiting, misuse of laxatives), and behaviors aimed at increasing energy expenditure (e.g., excessive exercise), typically associated with a fear of weight gain. Low body weight or shape is central to the person's self-evaluation or is inaccurately perceived to be normal or even excessive.
Bulimia nervosa	A. Recurrent episodes of binge eating. An episode of binge eating is characterized by both of the following: 1. Eating, in a discrete period of time (e.g., within any 2-hour period), an amount of food that is definitely larger than what most individuals would eat in a similar period of time under similar circumstances. 2. A sense of lack of control over eating during the episode (e.g., a feeling that one cannot stop eating or control what or how much one is eating).	Bulimia nervosa is characterized by frequent, recurrent episodes of binge eating (e.g., once a week or more over a period of at least one month). A binge eating episode is a distinct period of time during which the individual experiences a subjective loss of control over eating, eating notably more or differently than usual, and feels unable to stop eating or limit the type or amount of food eaten. Binge eating is accompanied by repeated inappropriate

	B. Recurrent inappropriate compensatory behaviors in order to prevent weight gain, such as self-induced vomiting; misuse of laxatives, diuretics, or other medications; fasting; or excessive exercise. C. The binge eating and inappropriate compensatory behaviors both occur, on average, at least once a week for 3 months. D. Self-evaluation is unduly influenced by body shape and weight. E. The disturbance does not occur exclusively during episodes of anorexia nervosa.	compensatory behaviors aimed at preventing weight gain (e.g., self-induced vomiting, misuse of laxatives or enemas, strenuous exercise). The individual is preoccupied with body shape or weight, which strongly influences self-evaluation. The individual is not significantly underweight and therefore does not meet the diagnostic requirements of anorexia nervosa.
Binge eating disorder	A. Recurrent episodes of binge eating. An episode of binge eating is characterized by both of the following: 1. Eating, in a discrete period of time (e.g., within any 2-hour period), an amount of food that is definitely larger than what most people would eat in a similar period of time under similar circumstances. 2. A sense of lack of control over eating during the episode (e.g., a feeling that one cannot stop eating or control what or how much one is eating). B. The binge-eating episodes are associated with three (or more) of the following: 1. Eating much more rapidly than normal. 2. Eating until feeling uncomfortably full.	Binge eating disorder is characterized by frequent, recurrent episodes of binge eating (e.g., once a week or more over a period of several months). A binge eating episode is a distinct period of time during which the individual experiences a subjective loss of control over eating, eating notably more or differently than usual, and feels unable to stop eating or limit the type or amount of food eaten. Binge eating is experienced as very distressing, and is often accompanied by negative emotions such as guilt or disgust. However, unlike in bulimia nervosa, binge eating episodes are not regularly followed by inappropriate compensatory behaviors aimed at preventing weight gain (e.g., self-induced vomiting, misuse of laxatives or enemas, strenuous exercise).

(Continued)

TABLE 10.1 (Continued)

Disorder	*DSM-5*	*ICD-11*
	3. Eating large amounts of food when not feeling physically hungry. 4. Eating alone because of feeling embarrassed by how much one is eating. 5. Feeling disgusted with oneself, depressed, or very guilty afterward. C. Marked distress regarding binge eating is present. D. The binge eating occurs, on average, at least once a week for 3 months. E. The binge eating is not associated with the recurrent use of inappropriate compensatory behavior as in bulimia nervosa and does not occur exclusively during the course of bulimia nervosa or anorexia nervosa.	

Bulimia nervosa (BN) is characterized by the binging and purging behaviors we mentioned earlier. Binge eating is defined as eating an amount of food that is "definitely larger than what most individuals would eat in a similar period of time under similar circumstances" (APA, 2013). A binge must occur during a discrete period of time, such as within two hours, does not describe routine food consumption, and there is a sense of loss of control over eating. Binging is often done in secret and eating may be very rapid. Family members may notice food disappearing or find empty food wrappers or containers. Following a binge, a person with BN will engage in behavior, like purging, to compensate for the calories consumed in an effort to avoid weight gain. Outside of these episodes, most individuals with BN restrict their diets to some degree. Finally, the criteria specify that the individual displays an overconcern with body shape or weight as a means of self-worth, such as that seen in AN. Overall, the majority of those with BN are within an average weight range or overweight range.

Binge eating disorder (BED) was included in the DSM-5 as a distinct eating disorder in 2013. A BED diagnosis may be warranted for an individual who repeatedly binge eats, feels a lack of control over the binging, and does not regularly engage in any compensatory behaviors (APA, 2013). Additionally, diagnosis requires that the episodes are associated with three or more of the following: rapid eating, eating until uncomfortably full, solitary eating due to embarrassment, eating when not physically hungry, and/or feelings of disgust, depression, shame, or guilt afterwards. Further, there must be significant distress over the binge eating and the episodes must occur at least once per week for three months.

With respect to medical complications, food restriction, binge eating, and purging can affect every organ system of the body (Peebles & Sieke, 2019). In fact, eating disorders have one of the highest mortality rates of any psychiatric disorders, second only to opioid addiction (Chesney, Goodwin, & Fazel, 2014). For example, food restriction may result in a semi-starvation state. Severe complications can arise in each of the organ systems, with approximately 80% of those with AN presenting with cardiac complications such as low heart rate, low blood pressure, and abnormal heart rhythms (Peebles & Sieke, 2019). Food restriction can also lead to amenorrhea (loss of three consecutive menstrual cycles) in females, and loss of bone density, osteoporosis, and increased bone fracture risk in males and females (Nagata, Golden, Leonard, Copelovitch, & Denburg, 2017). Stunted growth, changes in resting metabolic rate, and delayed gastric emptying leading to early fullness, bloating, and/or constipation are observed as well (Peebles & Sieke, 2019). Outward signs of food restriction skin include dry skin, an orange tint to the skin (carotenemia) in response to excessive consumption of certain vegetables containing carotene (e.g., carrots), and *lanugo*—fine, downy hair that grows on the body to provide warmth following excessive weight loss.

Purging behaviors can also have dangerous consequences for bodily systems (Peebles & Sieke, 2019). Resulting electrolyte imbalances can lead to complications such as cardiac arrhythmias (irregular heartbeat), which can be life threatening. Gastrointestinal complications from repeated laxative use include diarrhea, constipation, and cathartic colon syndrome, a condition in which nerve cells in the colon are permanently damaged, resulting in refractory constipation (Mehler, 2017). In females, irregular menstrual cycles may result and can pose reproductive system challenges (Peebles & Sieke, 2019). Dental caries, tooth enamel erosion, and gingivitis may result from chronic self-induced vomiting (Brown & Mehler, 2017). Additionally, scars or calluses may form on the knuckles or fingers that are used to induce vomiting. This scarring is called *Russell's sign* (see Figure 10.1; Peebles & Sieke, 2019), named after the British psychiatrist who first described the condition.

Binge eating has been linked to serious gastrointestinal complications including sudden enlargement of the gastric system in response to a binge, which may result in perforation of body tissue, infection, and potentially death (Young, Henderson, & Thompson, 2011). Binging has also been correlated to obesity, which has been linked to a wide array of medical consequences (Anderson, 2017).

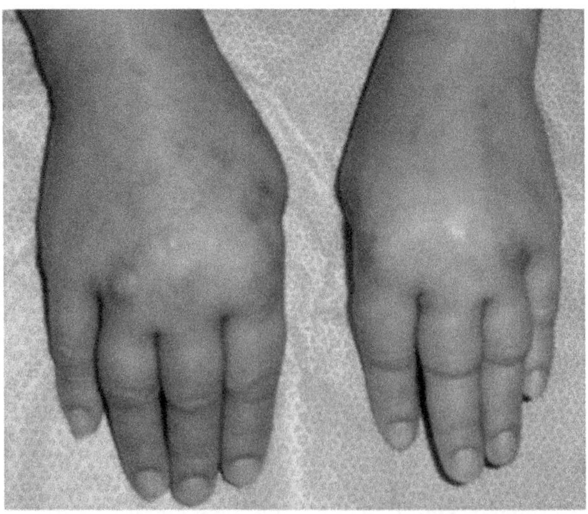

FIGURE 10.1 Russell's Sign on the Hands of a 32-Year-Old Woman. Reprinted with permission of Springer from Young, Henderson, & Thompson (2011).

Prevalence

A large study examining prevalence as defined by DSM-5 in adolescents reported a lifetime prevalence of 1.7% for AN, 0.8% for BN, and 2.3% for BED (Smink, van Hoeken, Oldehinkel, and Hoek, 2014). The authors note that the rates were similar to those found using the broader DSM-IV diagnostic criteria. Smink et al. (2014) also compared prevalence rates using both DSM-IV and DSM-5 criteria and noted an increase of 28.9% in lifetime prevalence of any eating disorder from DSM-IV to DSM-5, with an increase of 50% for AN and 40% for BN. Current thought supports the contention that a greater number of individuals are developing eating disorders over time (Galmiche, Dechelotte, Lambert, & Tavolacci, 2019).

PREVALENCE BY GENDER AND AGE

Prevalence values are consistently higher for females compared to males. Estimates provided by Smink and colleagues (2014) are presented in Table 10.2 and clearly demonstrate significant gender differences across the diagnoses. Data currently suggests a 1:3–4 ratio of males to females

TABLE 10.2 DSM-5 Eating Disorder Prevalence in a Community Cohort of Adolescents

		Lifetime Prevalence % (95% CI)[b]		*Point Prevalence % (95% CI)*	
DSM-5 Eating Disorder[b]	*Number of Cases (% Female)*	*Women*	*Men*	*Women*	*Men*
AN[a]	16 (93.8)	1.7 (1.0–2.9)	0.1 (0.0–0.8)	1.2 (0.6–2.1)	0.1 (0.0–0.8)
BN	8 (87.5)	0.8 (0.3–1.7)	0.1 (0.0–0.8)	0.6 (0.2–1.3)	0.1 (0.0–0.8)
BED	25 (80.0)	2.3 (1.4–3.6)	0.7 (0.2–1.6)	1.6 (0.9–2.7)	0.3 (0.0–1.0)
OSFED	7 (71.4)	0.6 (0.2–1.3)	0.3 (0.0–1.0)	0.3 (0.1–1.0)	0
Unspecified FED	2 (100.0)	0.2 (0.0–0.8)	0	0	0
Any ED	58 (84.5)	5.7 (4.2–7.5)	1.2 (0.6–2.3)	3.7 (2.6–5.2)	0.5 (0.1–1.4)

[a]Total n = 1,597 (53.9% female) with completed CIDI and/or measured BMI at the fourth assessment wave of the TRAILS study (mean age 19.1 years); mean age at diagnostic interview by eating disorder experts 20.6 years.
[b]AN: anorexia nervosa; BN: bulimia nervosa; BED: binge eating disorder; OSFED: other specified feeding and eating disorder; FED: feeding and eating disorder: ED: eating disorder; 95% CI: 95% confidence interval.
Source: Smink et al. (2014). Reproduced with permissions of John Wiley & Sons.

(Anderson, 2017) with gender distribution more equivalent among younger children (Rojo-Moreno et al., 2015).

Longitudinal studies show an increase in the prevalence of eating disorders from childhood to adolescence (Attia & Walsh, 2007). Smink et al. (2014) reported average ages of onset of 15.1 for AN, 16.0 for BN, and 13.29 for BED (using DSM-5). Notably, the usual age of onset for BN is often somewhat later than that of AN, with some investigators pointing to an age of onset in late adolescence and early adulthood (Lewinsohn, Striegel-Moore, & Seeley, 2000).

Prevalence By Socioeconomic Status (SES), Race, and Ethnicity

Eating disorders affect people across a variety of SES groups, races, and ethnicities though differences in type of eating disorder among groups have been observed. For example, in the largest national study to date (Udo & Grilo, 2018), lifetime prevalence of AN was lower in Blacks compared to Whites, BN was not significantly different among racial/ethnic groups, and lifetime BED prevalence was greater for Whites than for Blacks. Lower lifetime prevalence rates of AN in Hispanics have also been reported with comparable rates of rates of BED and BN compared to Whites (Perez, Ohrt, & Hoek, 2016). As research continues to include more diverse samples, we will advance our understanding of how race, ethnicity, and culture relate to eating disorder development.

Comorbidity

Eating disorders are highly comorbid with other psychological disorders, and overall estimates show that individuals diagnosed with AN are more likely than not to meet criteria for a second disorder (Hughes, 2012). The two most common comorbid diagnoses in youth with eating disorders are depression and anxiety. These conditions can predate, coincide with, or follow eating disorder development, though approximately two-thirds of those with eating disorders report anxiety symptoms prior to eating disorder development (Tagay, Schlottbohm, Reyes-Rodriguez, Repic, & Senf, 2014). Lifetime prevalence of *mood disorders* is 42% for AN, 71% for BN, and 46% for BED (Uniake & Broft, 2016). Suicide is regularly identified as the second most common cause of death in those with eating disorders (Uniake & Broft, 2016), with approximately one in five deaths resulting from suicide (Papadopoulos, Ekbom, Brandt, & Ekselius, 2008).

Developmental Continuities and Discontinuities (Course)

There is substantial support for *homotypic continuity* in eating disorders with early, disordered eating associated with greater risk for developing AN, BN, or continued disordered eating of greater severity into adulthood (APA, 2013). Still, strides in treatment practices have resulted in improved recovery rates for both AN and BN, recent data indicating that two-thirds of those with AN or BN are fully recovered at long-term follow-up (Eddy et al., 2016). Recovery from BN was found to occur more rapidly during the first decade, whereas a subset of those with AN required another decade to achieve recovery (Eddy et al., 2016). Binge-eating disorder is described as a persistent disorder (APA, 2013), but less is presently known about its full course and treatment outcomes.

When eating disorders are examined as distinct diagnostic entities, significant evidence of *heterotypic continuity*, or crossover, emerges. For example, approximately 20–40% of individuals who are diagnosed with AN will crossover into some symptoms of BN and may eventually meet full criteria for the disorder (Castellini et al., 2011; Monteleone, De Geno, Monteleone, De Filippo, & Maj, 2011). Similarly, 20–30% of individuals with BN will eventually migrate into AN (Eddy et al., 2008), and it is not unusual for those with binge eating to crossover into BN (Allen, Bryne, Oddy, & Crosby, 2013).

Additional evidence of heterotypic continuity emerges when considering relations between eating disorders, depression, and anxiety. Research suggests that depression typically onsets after AN, whereas anxiety disorders typically predate the diagnosis of AN (Hughes, 2012). There is often improvement in depressive symptoms as weight is restored and eating disorder symptoms are decreased (Hughes, 2012). Similarly, anxiety and related obsessions can be exacerbated by starvation and lessen with a return to healthy body weight (Pollice, Kaye, Greeno, & Weltzin, 1997).

A Developmental Psychopathology Model of the Etiology of Eating Disorders

Figure 10.2 depicts a developmental psychopathology model of eating disorder development based on what is presently known about these conditions.

Genetic Factors (Distal Risk Factors)

Genetic risk for eating disorders has been established with consensus that multiple genes are likely to be involved (Bulik, Blake, & Austin, 2019). There is also research implicating genes related to neurotransmitter and hormonal function in the emergence of eating disorders. As you read, you

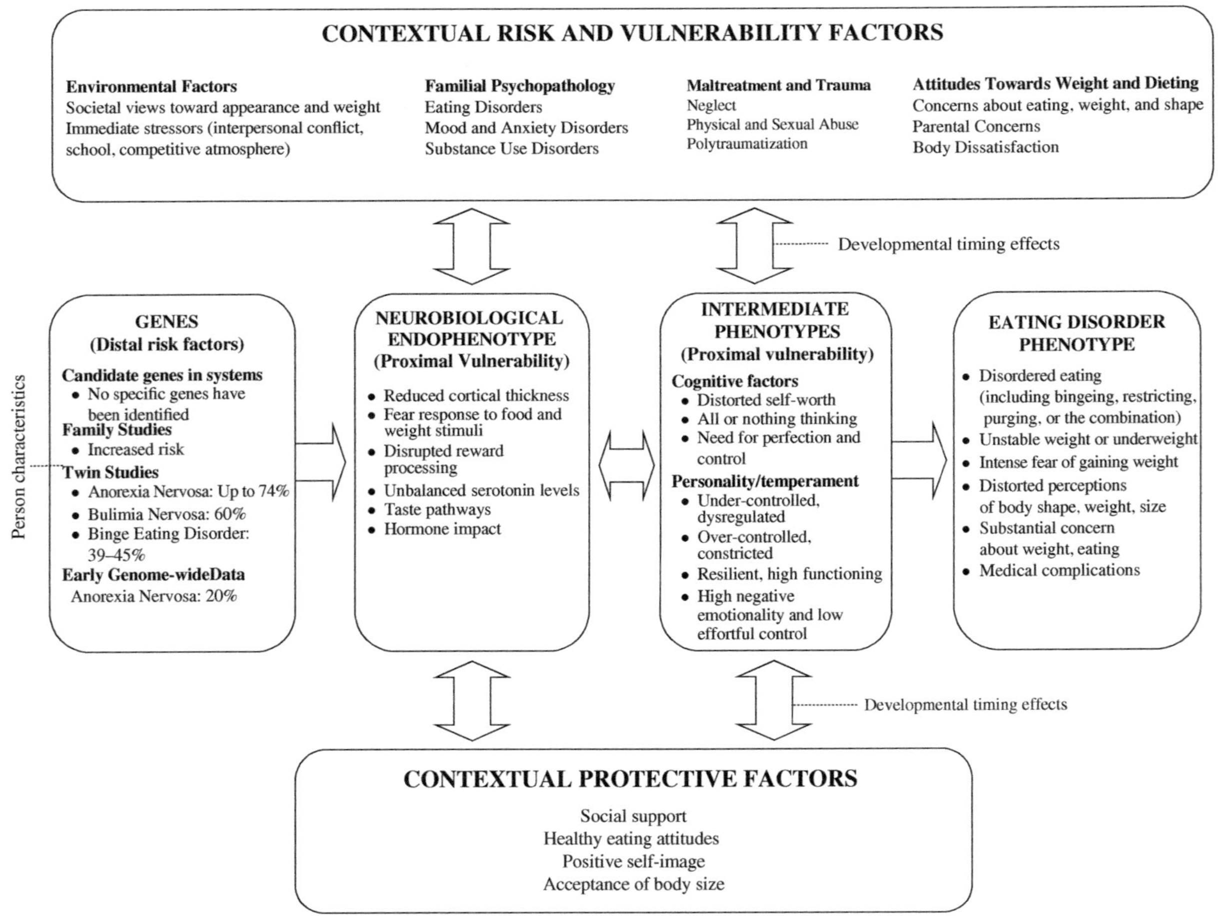

FIGURE 10.2 Developmental Psychopathology Model of Eating Disorders

will learn that heritability estimates for eating disorders derived from family and twin studies are on a par with some of the most biologically based disorders, such as bipolar disorder and schizophrenia (Kaye, Frank, Bailer, & Henry, 2005).

Family studies

Bulik and colleagues (2019) explain that family studies clearly demonstrate familial risk for eating disorders, with a substantially increased risk for first degree relatives of those with AN or BN as well as increased but less robust risk for BED. Further, the researchers noted an increased risk for disordered eating in the relatives of someone with a diagnosed eating disorder, suggesting that familial risk is related to a spectrum of disordered eating and that some familial risk may be shared among AN, BN, and BED.

Twin studies

Across eating disorders, *concordance rates* among monozygotic (i.e., identical) twins are greater than among dizygotic (i.e., fraternal) twin pairs, indicating substantial genetic heritability with heritability estimates of 0.28 to 0.74 (Bulik et al., 2019). Heritability estimates for BN tend to hover around 60%, while estimates for BED are lower, ranging from 39 to 45% (Bulik et al., 2019).

Genome-wide data

Bulik and colleagues (2019) note that scientists are currently utilizing *genome-wide data* to directly estimate heritability of eating disorders, as opposed to calculating indirect estimates from family and twin studies. Early data revealed a heritability estimate of 0.20 for AN with efforts underway to collect data for BN and BED. As research continues, we expect to learn more about genetic risk and generate additional treatments.

NEUROBIOLOGICAL FACTORS (PROXIMAL VULNERABILITY FACTORS)

Structural and functional imaging findings

Research related to neurobiological factors has revealed some anomalies in cortical volume related to eating disorders. One study (Marsh et al., 2015) examining young women with BN, for instance, found reduced cortical thickness in frontal regions of the brain associated with impulse control, while another study (Berner et al., 2018) found similar results in a slightly different area of the brain that implicated difficulties with attention and regulatory control. Among adolescents with AN, reduced cortical thickness is also observed, as is reduced volume in other brain areas, but, after recovery from AN, the brain returns to a normal structure when healthy weight is established (King et al., 2015). Additional research is needed to understand the neurobiological mechanisms related to these findings as well as to ascertain whether observed structural differences between those with eating disorders and healthy individuals are a result of eating disorder behavior or neurological vulnerability for the disorder.

Functional imaging findings including fear responses to food- and weight-related stimuli, reward processing difficulties, and serotonergic system dysregulation are also implicated in the development of eating disorders (Schmidt & Campbell, 2013). Much of this research has centered on disrupted reward processing among individuals with AN. Two brain circuits seem to be particularly important in this regard: a ventral, limbic system related to deficits in emotion regulation, and a dorsal, cognitive system, which might lead to overreliance on cognitive rules to manage limbic deficits (Connan, Campbell, Katzman, Lightman, & Treasure, 2003; Kaye, Fudge, & Paulus, 2009). Although more research is needed, existing evidence suggests that cortical development during puberty may cause vulnerabilities for eating disorders and interact with neurotransmitter dysfunction, hormonal changes, and environmental factors to produce eating disordered behavior (Kaye et al., 2009).

Neurotransmitters

Most research on the role of neurotransmitters in eating disorders has focused on serotonin—a neurotransmitter that plays a significant role in feelings of fullness and satiety that most people experience after eating. Serotonin is also implicated in obsessive thinking, depression, and anxiety, constructs we previously explained as correlated to eating disorder development. Among individuals with AN, Kaye and colleagues (2005) posit that unbalanced serotonin levels lead to low mood, and restricted food intake is used to enhance mood and reduce overactivity of serotonin in the brain, thereby making the restricting behavior more likely to occur in the future. Duvvuri, Bailer, and Kaye (2010) suggest that serotonin imbalance and related anxiety may predate the onset of AN and that the disorder represents a "vicious cycle" in which food restriction functions to reduce serotonin, temporarily enhancing mood. Ensuing malnutrition further alters neurotransmitter function, leading to an even lower mood, and thus more efforts at mood enhancement through restriction continue. Studies have also revealed that individuals with BN have reduced serotonin activity in the brain (Pichika et al., 2012). It is important to mention that nutrition impacts neurotransmitter levels, making it difficult to determine to what degree neurotransmitter imbalances are a cause or a consequence of altered nutrition in eating disorders (Kaye et al., 2005; Pichika et al., 2012).

Hormones

The effects of hormones during puberty, particularly estrogen, have been of interest due to activating and organizational effects on the brain (Klump, 2014). Genetic research has also documented a link between estrogen receptor genes, AN (Versini et al., 2010), and BN (Nilsson et al., 2004), suggesting a complex etiology that is likely to involve interactions between hormonal, genetic, and developmental variables. Many have hypothesized that puberty-related changes in sex hormones may relate to the typical age of onset for eating disorders and that puberty may play a differential role in triggering genetic risk for eating disorders in girls when compared to boys (Klump, 2014; Fairweather-Schmidt & Wade, 2015).

TEMPERAMENT

As you have probably noticed, there is substantial heterogeneity across eating disorders. There is also heterogeneity *within* eating disorder groups, partly due to individual differences in temperament. Turner et al. (2014) identified three groups based on the temperamental factors of behavioral inhibition, behavioral activation, and effortful control. *Behavioral inhibition* is the tendency to avoid situations/things that might be dangerous or aversive; *behavioral activation* is the motivation to approach situations/things that might be pleasant; and *effortful control* is the ability to control one's own emotions and behaviors. First, they described an under-controlled, dysregulated group characterized as impulsive, extraverted, and affectively unstable. This group showed high scores for behavioral activation with low scores for effortful control and largely represented individuals with BN. Second, there was an overcontrolled, emotionally constricted group that showed high behavioral inhibition and effortful control, low behavioral activation, and largely represented patients with AN. Finally, there was a relatively more resilient, high functioning group characterized by fewer comorbid disorders and better functioning. The resilient group demonstrated low behavioral inhibition, high effortful control, and had the least severe psychopathology. Though the identified temperamental clusters do not perfectly map on to eating disorder classifications, temperament may be important in predicting the disorder course.

COGNITIVE FACTORS

Next, we will discuss how an individual's thinking style might contribute to eating disorder development. Try to notice, as you read this next section, which cognitive factors seem more specific to AN or BN and which seem to present a general vulnerability for disordered eating.

Cognitive distortions

Many *cognitive distortions* that are commonly observed in individuals with eating disorders center around the body. Among individuals with BN and AN, there is a distorted system of self-worth that links shape, size and weight, or *body image*, directly to personal value (APA, 2013). Notably, body image dissatisfaction is both a contributing and maintaining factor for eating disorders as well as a major risk factor for relapse (McLean & Paxton, 2019).

Individuals with eating disorders also tend to display all-or-none thinking, or *dichotomous thinking*, characterized by thinking in polar extremes of good or bad (Fairburn, Cooper, & Cooper, 1986). When applied to rigid dietary rules, once a rule has been broken, the cognitive distortion takes center stage with extreme thoughts and fuels eating disorder behavior (e.g., "I already blew my diet, so I might as well binge").

Perfectionism and need for control

While perfectionism can be present in any of the eating disorders, it is especially correlated with AN and restricting behaviors. Clinical perfectionism, or adherence to high personal standards and concern about making mistakes, has been indirectly associated with dietary restraint through the overevaluation of weight and shape (Dakanalis et al., 2015). Perfectionism has also been linked to BN by contributing to dichotomous thinking (Shafran, Cooper, & Fairburn, 2002).

It has long been speculated that restricted eating comes from a desire to exert control over elements in one's life and it has been demonstrated that eating disorder symptoms are particularly associated with an individual's perceived need to control their own thoughts (Olstad, Solem, Hjemdal, and Hagen, 2015). Indeed, those with AN report an elevated need for control, though paradoxicallythey perceive their thoughts as uncontrollable (Woolrich, Cooper, & Turner, 2008).

Ego-syntonicity and -dystonicity

Many disorders in this book are categorized as *ego-dystonic*, meaning that they are perceived by the individual as being inconsistent with their sense of self and are not intrinsically rewarding. On the other hand, some psychological disorders are *ego-syntonic*, meaning that they are considered by the individual to be consistent with their broader sense of self. Ego-syntonic symptoms are more difficult to change because they are internally rewarding (Vandereycken, 2006). AN is typically ego-syntonic as symptoms often create a sense of safety, power, control, and value (Marzola, Panepinto, Delsedime, Fassino, & Abbate-Daga, 2016). On the other hand, bingeing and purging behaviors are typically considered ego-dystonic (APA, 2013).

Contextual Risk Factors

Societal

Over time, there have been changing views about beauty ideal, thinness, fitness, and muscularity in society, as well as the sexualization of adolescents in media outlets. These factors have been linked to depression, low self-esteem, body dissatisfaction, and eating disorders in adolescents (Dakanalis, 2017; Ng, 2016). Widespread use of social media in a manner that equates one's "likes" with approval and acceptance as well as bullying (Lie, Ro, & Bang, 2019) create an environment ripe for misguided messages to establish emotional stability through weight during this developmental stage (Anderson et al., 2018). For gender questioning adolescents as well as sexual and gender minority youth, there is an even wider array of complex issues rendering them at much greater risk of a multitude of psychiatric issues, including body dissatisfaction and eating disorders (Goldhammer, Maston, & Keuroghlian, 2019).

Family interactions

Dysfunctional interaction patterns in families of individuals with eating disorders have been described for several decades. Empirical research has identified enmeshment in the families of adolescents with both AN (Rowa, Kerig, & Geller, 2001) and BN (Leon, Fulkerson, Perry, & Dube, 1994) as well as high family conflict and hostility (Dancyger, Fornari, Scionti, Wisotsky, & Sunday, 2005). It is important to point out that an overwhelming majority of these investigations have been *concurrent* studies that do not allow interpretations of *causality*. We therefore cannot ascertain if the family interaction patterns contributed to eating disorder development, or are the result of the eating disorder's impact on family interactions.

Parental psychopathology

As previously mentioned, an eating disorder in a first-degree relative is a substantial risk factor for eating disorder development. Other forms of parental psychopathology have also been identified as risk factors. Individuals with AN are more likely than a control group to have parents with affective disorders, fathers with substance use disorders and mothers with anxiety and personality disorders (Steinhausen et al., 2014). These findings as well as others point to parental depression and substance abuse as risk factors for eating disorders (Fairburn et al., 1997), suggesting that the risk for eating disorders is partially conferred by other forms of parental psychopathology.

Maltreatment and trauma

Across many disorders in this book, you learned that exposure to trauma places children at risk of developing psychopathology. Multiple studies describe a link among eating disorders and physical abuse, sexual abuse, and other traumatic stressors (Brewerton, 2007). Trauma is considered a non-specific risk factor for eating disorders, but polytraumatization, or experiencing repeated traumatic events, especially sexual abuse and interpersonal stressors, appears to be particularly common in those with eating disorders (Hazzard, Bauer, Mukherjee, Miller, & Sonneville, 2019). It is hypothesized that the degree of emotional dysregulation following traumatic events may be the factor most closely associated with development of these illnesses (Trottier & MacDonald, 2017).

Attitudes towards weight and dieting

Although there are few *prospective studies* of risk factors for bingeing and purging, Allen and colleagues (2014) published a longitudinal study showing that 14-year-olds who reported concerns about their eating, weight, and shape were at risk of later developing an eating disorder. Additionally, parental concern about their child's weight early in life can increase weight and shape concerns in adolescence as well as later body dissatisfaction, thereby contributing to the risk of emerging eating disordered behavior (Allen, Byrne, Forbes, & Oddy, 2009).

Contextual Protective Factors

The bulk of research on contextual protective factors has focused on social support, showing that increased social support is associated with less disordered eating (Ferreiro, Seoane, & Senra, 2012). Further, social support seems to buffer the risk for eating disorders conferred by the risk factors we just outlined. Skomorovsky and colleagues (2006) posit that perhaps enlistment of social support persons serves as a coping strategy that protects individuals from resorting to maladaptive coping behaviors, which can include disordered eating. Similarly, Wonderlich-Tierney and Vander Wal (2010) found that the link between social anxieties and symptoms of eating disorders were lessened in a group of college women who reported high levels of social support, adding to the notion that the latter protects against eating disorder behavior. Other protective factors represent the converse of several risk factors already discussed, including healthy eating attitudes, positive self-image, and acceptance of body size (Gustafsson, Edlund, Kjellin, & Norring, 2009).

Gene–Environment Interplay

Gene–environment interactions

A literature review by Culbert, Racine, and Klump (2015) examined behavioral genetic models of disordered eating. Age (early versus late adolescence), pubertal status, and dietary restraint emerged as prominent environmental moderators of genetic risk. The authors suggested that a broader environmental moderator is likely to be development itself, which can be represented by both age and pubertal status. Additionally, parenting (Karwautz et al., 2011), abuse, and adverse experiences (Akkerman et al., 2012; Steiger et al., 2011) have also emerged as moderators of genetic risk.

Gene–environment interactions across time

Interactions between genetic vulnerability and development have been shown to change the heritability and risk factors of eating disorders in interesting ways. A study of adolescent twins conducted by Fairweather-Schmidt and Wade (2015) revealed that gene and environment interactions increased as subjects aged, with significant new sources of genetic and environmental risk emerging as the adolescents got older. Weight-related teasing by peers was particularly related to the emergence of disordered eating in late adolescence. In sum, the authors suggested an especially sensitive period of gene–environment interaction during late adolescence.

DEVELOPMENTAL TIMING EFFECTS: THE INTERPLAY OF NORMAL AND ABNORMAL DEVELOPMENT

Treasure, Stein, and Maguire (2015) described a "staging heuristic" model of eating disorder development. They post that risk factors and *prodromal factors*, or markers of pathology that exist before the full disorder, emerge first during childhood and adolescence. Sub-threshold disorders develop shortly thereafter and eventually transition to the full disorder. According to the model, as the disorder progresses, it becomes more severe, more resistant to treatment, and is often accompanied by comorbid conditions. Their review suggests that this pattern holds true for AN, with more evidence needed regarding BN and BED. For AN, perfectionism and obsessive-compulsive behavior often seem to exist before the eating disorder behavior is observed (Wade et al., 2008), probably emerging in childhood and existing outside of weight-related distress. Similarly, impulse control difficulties appear to emerge early in development for individuals who will progress to BN (Lilenfeld, Wonderlich, Riso, Crosby, & Mitchell, 2006).

Adolescence represents a particularly vulnerable period in the emergence of eating disorders, representing a complicated interplay among genetic, biological, temperamental, and environmental factors that result in eating disorder behavior. The behaviors then exert effects on the vulnerable adolescent brain, which may propel the youngster on an eating disorder trajectory and eventually lead to a diagnosable disorder (Treasure et al., 2015).

Interventions

PSYCHOTHERAPEUTIC TREATMENTS

In a review of existing interventions for eating disorders in youth, Lock and LeGrange (2015) arranged treatments according to their level of empirical support. As you can see from Table 10.3, treatments are categorized from "well-established treatments" to "treatments of questionable efficacy." You may have noticed that, in Table 10.3, there is no treatment that is either "well-established" or "probably efficacious" for BN or BED (Lock & LeGrange, 2015). The best evidence-based treatments for those disorders are cognitive behavioral therapies, which employ challenging *cognitive distortions*, monitoring eating disorder

TABLE 10.3 Evidence-Based Therapies for Eating Disorders in Adolescents

	Anorexia Nervosa	*Bulimia Nervosa*	*Binge Eating Disorder*
Level 1: Well-Established Treatments	Family Therapy-Behavioral	None	None
Level 2: Probably Efficacious Treatments	Family Therapy-Systemic; Insight Oriented Psychotherapy (Individual)	None	None
Level 3: Possibly Efficacious Treatments	None	Family Therapy–Behavioral; Cognitive Behavioral Therapy (Guided Self-Help) (Individual)	Internet Facilitated Cognitive BehaviorTherapy–Self-Help
Level 4: Experimental Treatments	Cognitive–Behavioral Therapy–Broad (Individual); Cognitive Training (Individual)	Cognitive Behavior Therapy (Individual); Supportive Psychotherapy (Individual)	Interpersonal Psychotherapy (Individual) Dialectical Behavior Therapy (Individual and Family)
Level 5: Treatments of Questionable Efficacy	None	None	None

Source: Lock (2015). Reproduced with permissions of John Wiley & Sons.

behavior, and using *behavior modification* techniques to extinguish eating disorder behavior and increase healthy behaviors.

Newer therapies that have shown promise in the treatment of eating disorders include acceptance and commitment therapy (ACT) and dialectical behavior therapy (DBT; Starzomska, Wilkos, & Kucharska, 2018). ACT (Hayes, Luoma, Bond, Masuda, & Lillis, 2006) focuses on changing one's relationship to thoughts as opposed to attempting to change and/or replace the thoughts themselves. It emphasizes acceptance of uncomfortable thoughts, feelings, and sensations followed by intentional commitment to engage in behaviors that are consistent with one's personal values. For those with eating disorders, avoidance of emotional and situational discomfort is typical, and it is precisely this avoidance that is specifically addressed by ACT. DBT (Linehan et al., 1999) emphasizes client mindfulness of the present moment as well as validation of a client's emotional pain while simultaneously teaching tolerance of emotional discomfort and avoidance of impulsive, maladaptive behaviors. As with ACT, data is encouraging for the utility of DBT in eating disorder treatment, particularly BN and BED (Davis & Attia, 2019).

Family-based treatment (FBT) is the one well-established treatment for AN, and evidence for its utility among adolescents with BN is also accumulating (Rieneke, 2017). FBT is described in a treatment manual written by Drs. Lock and Le Grange (2015) using a family approach with a behavioral focus. The family is "exonerated" from blame and the clinician takes a curious, non-judgmental stance towards the eating disorder behavior and family interactions. Adolescents are considered unable to resolve eating disorder behaviors due to the eating disorder-related thoughts. Parents actively participate in feeding their child and learn to re-conceptualize eating disorder behavior as symptoms of disease. Family interactions are carefully observed to understand how the illness affects familial strengths and weaknesses. Treatment then progresses through three phases: weight restoration, transitioning control of eating back to the adolescent, and resolving remaining adolescent issues and discussing termination.The excerpt below (quoted from Doyle & Le Grange, 2015) describes how these principles are incorporated into a treatment session. The dialogue took place after Charlotte, the client, was repeatedly prompted by her parents to eat one small piece of chicken. After resisting for 25 minutes, Charlotte finally ate the chicken while crying. As you read the dialogue, pay attention to how the therapist is attempting to change the perspectives of each family member:

CHARLOTTE: (*weeping quietly*) Why did you make me do that? I hate you . . . I hate you . . .

MOTHER: I know you are upset, honey. (*Reaches out to stroke Charlotte's arm, who initially pulls back, but then relents and lets her mother touch her.*)

FATHER: (*in a warm and intense tone*) We love you, honey. We know that was hard.

THERAPIST: (*in a quiet, serious tone*) Charlotte, that was extremely difficult, I know. The eating disorder has really made it hard to eat foods that used to be so easy to eat. (*speaking to parents*) It is clear how strong the anorexia is, seeing how hard it was for Charlotte to have just one bite of chicken. I imagine you thought that the anorexia would never give in, especially knowing how hard these past meals have been.

FATHER: Yeah, normally, one of us would have gotten upset and left the table by this point.

MOTHER: I can't believe it took all of this time to eat one bite, though.

THERAPIST: It may seem like a small step, but you have just demonstrated that when the two of you are working together and not leaving any room for the anorexia to get out of eating, the anorexia will eventually give up. If you are able to do this meal after meal, the anorexia will really get the message that it can no longer torment Charlotte with its drive to restrict.

Did you notice how the therapist attempted to separate Charlotte from the symptoms and behavior of AN as well as involve her parents in supporting behavior change? The therapist also emphasized the positive aspects of the process to convey hope for future change in a difficult moment. Lastly, reflect on how the session integrated both a concern for Charlotte's inner world—her thoughts and feelings—as well as maintaining the focus on her behavioral success (i.e., eating). While FBT is recommended as a first-line intervention due to its evidence base, the approach does not work for everyone (Rieneke, 2017). It is an intensive outpatient therapy to which all families are not able to commit.

MEDICAL NUTRITION THERAPY

Medical nutrition therapy has long been recognized as the standard of care in comprehensive eating disorder treatment (Ozier & Henry, 2011). It is crucial that the dietitian be trained and experienced in the treatment of eating disorders as specific eating disorder knowledge for various levels of care is required. (Woodside, Halpert, & Dimitropoulos, 2015).

PHARMACOLOGICAL TREATMENTS

While medications alone are not recommended for the treatment of eating disorders, Crow (2019) described how they can be useful to address certain symptoms. With respect to AN, atypical antipsychotics may assist with weight gain and reduction of eating-related preoccupations. For BN, only one antidepressant to date, fluoxetine, has been approved for use to decrease binge eating with a few antidepressants, anticonvulsants, and one stimulant shown to decrease binge eating associated with BED. For those with comorbid conditions, such as depression and/or anxiety, antidepressants may be utilized to diminish those symptoms, thereby benefitting overall treatment (Lutter, 2017).

Chapter Summary

Eating disorders are a serious medical and psychological threat to the healthy development of children and adolescents with potentially lethal consequences. We have reviewed research showing that disordered eating and eating disorders are widespread, may be persistent, and may grow more severe over time. It is therefore critical that early identification and comprehensive intervention are immediately initiated as these factors have been shown to increase the probability of recovery (Lock, 2002). While treatment research in youth is limited, new treatments are demonstrating better outcomes. The biological and environmental risk factors as well as protective factors we covered, in addition to new strides in research, will undoubtedly set the stage for improving the identification of children and adolescents at risk for eating disorders, allowing for the advancement of treatment and prevention.

Further Reading

American Psychiatric Association (2006). *Practice guideline for the treatment of patients with eating disorders* (3rd ed.), Washington, DC.

Lock, J. (2015). An update on evidence-based psychosocial treatments for eating disorders in children and adolescents. *Journal of Clinical Child and Adolescent Psychology*, *44*(5), 707–721. doi: 10.1080/15374416.2014.971458.

Mehler, P. S., & Anderson, A. (Eds.) (2017). *Eating disorders: A guide to medical care and complications* (3rd ed.). Balimore, MD, Johns Hopkins University Press.

Discussion/Essay Questions

1. The relationship among anxiety, depression, and eating disorders is complex. Why do you think there is a high proportion of people who experience difficulties with anxiety prior to developing eating disorder?
2. Given that eating disorders commonly begin in youth, why do you hypothesize that there are few evidence-based treatments for eating disorders for children and adolescents?
3. If this chapter were written 10 years from now, when BED has been in the DSM for many years, do you expect research to show that individuals with BED are more similar in course to individuals with AN, BN, or show an entirely different course?

References

Akkermann, K., Kaasik, K., Kiive, E., Nordquist, N., Oreland, L., & Harro, J. (2012). The impact of adverse life events and the serotonin transporter gene promoter polymorphism on the development of eating disorder symptoms. *Journal of Psychiatric Research*, *46*(1), 38–43.

Allen, K. L., Byrne, S. M., Oddy, W. H., & Crosby, R. D. (2013). DSM–IV–TR and DSM-5 eating disorders in adolescents: Prevalence, stability, and psychosocial correlates in a population-based sample of male and female adolescents. *Journal of Abnormal Psychology*, *122*(3), 720.

Allen, K. L., Byrne, S. M., Forbes, D., & Oddy, W. H. (2009). Risk factors for full- and partial-syndrome early adolescent eating disorders: A population-based pregnancy cohort study. *Journal of the American Academy of Child & Adolescent Psychiatry*, *48*(8), 800–809.

Allen, K. L., Byrne, S. M., Oddy, W. H., Schmidt, U., & Crosby, R. D. (2014). Risk factors for binge eating and purging eating disorders: Differences based on age of onset. *International Journal of Eating Disorders*, *47*(7), 802–812. doi: 10.1002/eat.22299.

American Psychiatric Association (2013). *Diagnostic and Statistical Manual of Mental Disorders* (5th ed.). Arlington, VA.

Anderson, A.E. (2017). Diagnosis and treatment of the eating disorders spectrum in primary care medicine In P.S. Mehler and A.E. Anderson (Eds.), *Eating disorders: A guide to medical care and complications* (3rd ed., pp. 1–5). Baltimore, MD: Johns Hopkins University Press.

Anderson, L. K., Claudat, K., Cusack, A., Brown, T. A., Trim, J., Rockwell, R., Nakamura, T., Gomez, L., & Kaye, W. H. (2018). Differences in emotion regulation difficulties among adults and adolescents across eating disorder diagnoses. Journal of Clinical Psychology, 1–7, doi: 10.1002/jclp.22638.

Attia, E., & Walsh, B. T. (2007). Anorexia nervosa. *The American Journal of Psychiatry*, *164*(12), 1805–1810. doi: 10.1176/appi.ajp.2007.07071151.

Berner, L.A., Stefan, M., Lee, S., Wang, Z., Terranova, K., Attia, E., & Marsh, R. (2018). Altered cortical thickness and attentional deficits in adolescent girls and women with bulimia nervosa. *Journal of Psychiatry and Neuroscience*, *43*(2), 1–10.

Brewerton, T. (2007). Eating disorders, trauma, and comorbidity: Focus on PTSD. *European Eating Disorders Review*, *15*(4), 285–304, doi: 10.1080/10640260701454311.

Brown, C., & Mehler, P. (2017). Oral, dental, ear, and eye complications. In P.S. Mehler and A.E. Anderson (Eds.), *Eating disorders: A guide to medical care and complications* (3rd ed., pp. 207–218). Baltimore, MD: Johns Hopkins University Press.

Bulik, C.M., Blake, L., & Austin, C.M. (2019). Genetics of eating disorders: What clinicians need to know. *Psychiatric Clinics of North America*, *42*, 59–73.

Castellini, G., Sauro, C. L., Mannucci, E., Ravaldi, C., Rotella, C. M., Faravelli, C., & Ricca, V. (2011). Diagnostic crossover and outcome predictors in eating disorders according to DSM-IV and DSM-V proposed criteria: A 6-year follow-up study. *Psychosomatic Medicine*, *73*(3), 270–279.

Chesney, E., Goodwin, G.M., & Fazel, S. (2014). Risks of all-cause and suicide mortality in patients with anorexia nervosa and other eating disorders. *Archives of General Psychiatry*, *68*(7), 724–731.

Connan, F., Campbell, I. C., Katzman, M., Lightman, S. L., & Treasure, J. (2003). A neurodevelopmental model for anorexia nervosa. *Physiology and Behavior*, *79*(1), 13–24.

Crow, S. (2019). Pharmacologic treatment of eating disorders. *Psychiatric Clinics of North America*, *42*(2), 253–262. doi: 10/1016/j.psc.2019.01.007.

Culbert, K. M., Racine, S. E., & Klump, K. L. (2015). Research review: What we have learned about the causes of eating disorders—A synthesis of sociocultural, psychological, and biological research. *Journal of Child Psychology and Psychiatry*, *56*(11), 1141–1164.

Dakanalis, A. (2017). Social standards of beauty, body image, and eating disorders. The SAGE Encyclopedia of Abnormal and Clinical Psychology, 3246–3248. doi: 10.4135/9781483365817.n1289.

Dakanalis, A., Carrà, G., Calogero, R., Zanetti, M. A., Gaudio, S., Caccialanza, R., & Clerici, M. (2015). Testing the cognitive-behavioural maintenance models across DSM-5 bulimic-type eating disorder diagnostic groups: A multi-centre study. *European Archives of Psychiatry and Clinical Neuroscience*, *265*(8), 663–676. doi: 10.1007/s00406-014-0560-2.

Dancyger, I., Fornari, V., Scionti, L., Wisotsky, W., & Sunday, S. (2005). Do daughters with eating disorders agree with their parents' perception of family functioning? *Comprehensive Psychiatry*, *46*(2), 135–139.

Davis, L.E., & Attia, E. (2019). Recent advances in therapies for eating disorders. *F1000 Research*, *8*(F1000 Faculty Rev): 1693. doi: 10.12688/f1000research.19847.1.

Duvvuri, V., Bailer, U. F., & Kaye, W. H. (2010). Altered serotonin function in anorexia and bulimia nervosa. In C. P. Müller, B. L. Jacobs, C. P. Müller, B. L. Jacobs (Eds.), *Handbook of the behavioral neurobiology of serotonin* (pp. 715–729). San Diego, CA: Elsevier Academic Press.

Eddy, K. T., Dorer, D. J., Franko, D. L., Tahilani, K., Thompson-Brenner, H., & Herzog, D. B. (2008). Diagnostic crossover in anorexia nervosa and bulimia nervosa: Implications for DSM-V. *American Journal of Psychiatry*, *165*(2), 245–250.

Eddy, K. T., Tabri, N., Thomas, J. J., Murray, H. B., Keshavia, A., Hastings, E., Edkins, K., Krishna, M., Herzog, D. B., Keel, P. K., & Franko, D. L. (2016). Recovery from anorexia and bulimia nervosa at 22-year follow-up. *Journal of Clinical Psychiatry*, *78*(2), 184–189. doi: 10.4088/JCP.15m10393.

Fairburn, C. G., Cooper, Z., & Cooper, P. J. (1986). The clinical features and maintenance of bulimia nervosa. *Handbook of eating disorders: Physiology, psychology and treatment of obesity, anorexia and bulimia* (pp. 389–404). New York, NY: Basic Books, Inc.

Fairburn, C. G., Welch, S. L., Doll, H. A., Davies, B. A., & O'Connor, M. E. (1997). Risk factors for bulimia nervosa: A community-based case-control study. *Archives of General Psychiatry*, *54*(6), 509–517. doi: 10.1001/archpsyc.1997.01830180015003.

Fairweather-Schmidt, A. K., & Wade, T. D. (2015). Piloting a perfectionism intervention for pre-adolescent children. *Behaviour Research and Therapy*, *73*, 67–73.

Ferreiro, F., Seoane, G., & Senra, C. (2012). Gender-related risk and protective factors for depressive symptoms and disordered eating in adolescence: A 4-year longitudinal study. *Journal ofYouth and Adolescence*, *41*(5), 607–622.

Galmiche, M., Dechelotte, P., Lambert, G., & Pierre Tavolacci, M. (2019). Prevalence of eating disorders over the 2000–2018 period: A systematic literature review. *American Journal of Clinical Nutrition*, *109*, 1402–1413.

Goldhammer, S. M., Maston, E. D., & Keuroghlian, A. S. (2019). Addressing eating disorders and body dissatisfaction in sexual and gender minority youth. *American Journal of Preventive Medicine*, *56*(2), 318–322. doi: 10.1016/j.amepre.2018.09.011.

Gustafsson, S. A., Edlund, B., Kjellin, L., & Norring, C. (2009). Risk and protective factors for disturbed eating in adolescent girls—Aspects of perfectionism and attitudes to eating and weight. *European Eating Disorders Review*, *17*(5), 380–389.

Hayes, S. C., Luoma, J. B., Bond, F. W., Masuda, A., & Lillas, J. (2006). Acceptance and commitment therapy: Model, *processes and outcomes. Behavior Research and Therapy*, *44*(1), 1–25. doi: 10.1016/j.brat.2005.06.006.

Hazzard, V. M., Bauer, K. W., Mukherjee, B., Miller, A. L., & Sonneville, K. R. (2019). Associations between childhood maltreatment latent classes and eating disorder symptoms in a nationally representative sample of young adults in the United States. *Child Abuse and Neglect*, *98*, 1–9. doi: 10.1016/j.chiabu.2019.104171.

Hughes, E. K. (2012). Comorbid depression and anxiety in childhood and adolescent anorexia nervosa: Prevalence and implications for outcome. *Clinical Psychologist*, *16*(1), 15–24.

Karwautz, A. K., Wagner, G., Waldherr, K., Nader, I. W., Fernandez-Aranda, F., Estivill, X., & Treasure, J. L. (2011). Gene–environment interaction in anorexia nervosa: Relevance of non-shared environment and the serotonin transporter gene. *Molecular Psychiatry*, *16*(6), 590–592. doi: 10.1038/mp.2010.125.

Kaye, W. H., Frank, G. K., Bailer, U. F., & Henry, S. E. (2005). Neurobiology of anorexia nervosa: Clinical implications of alterations of the function of serotonin and other neuronal systems. *International Journal of Eating Disorders*, *37*(S1), S15–S19.

Kaye, W. H., Fudge, J. L., & Paulus, M. (2009). New insights into symptoms and neurocircuit function of anorexia nervosa. *Nature Reviews Neuroscience*, *10*(8), 573–584.

King, J. A., Geisler, D., Ritschel, F., Boehm, I., Seidel, M., Roschinski, B., & Roessner, V. (2015). Global cortical thinning in acute anorexia nervosa normalizes following long-term weight restoration. *Biological Psychiatry*, *77*(7), 624–632.

Klump, K. L. (2014). Puberty as a critical risk period for eating disorders: A review of human and animal studies. *Hormones and Behavior*, *64*(2), 399–410.

Leon, G. R., Fulkerson, J. A., Perry, C. L., & Dube, A. (1994). Family influences, school behaviors, and risk for the later development of an eating disorder. *Journal of Youth and Adolescence*, *23*(5), 499–515.

Lewinsohn, P. M., Striegel-Moore, R. H., & Seeley, J. R. (2000). Epidemiology and natural course of eating disorders in young women from adolescence to young adulthood. *Journal of the American Academy of Child & Adolescent Psychiatry*, *39*(10), 1284–1292.

Lie, S.O., Ro, O, & Bang, L. (2019). Is bullying and teasing associated with eating disorders? A systematic review and meta-analysis. *International Journal of Eating Disorders*, *52*(5), 497–514.

Lilenfeld, L. R., Wonderlich, S., Riso, L. P., Crosby, R., & Mitchell, J. (2006). Eating disorders and personality: A methodological and empirical review. *Clinical Psychology Review*, *26*(3), 299–320.

Linehan, M. M., Schmidt, H., Dimeff, L. A., Craft, J. C., Kanter, J., & Comtois, K. A. (1999). Dialectical behavior therapy for patients with borderline personality disorder and drug-dependence. *American Journal of Addiction*, *8*(4), 279–292.

Lock, J. (2002). Treating adolescents with eating disorders in the family context: empirical and theoretical considerations. *Child and Adolescent Psychiatric Clinics of North America*, *11*(2), 331–342.

Lock, J., & Le Grange, D. (2015). *Treatment manual for anorexia nervosa: A family-based approach*. New York, NY: Guilford Publications.

Lutter, M. (2017). Emerging treatment in eating disorders. *Neurotherapeutics*, *14*, 614–622.

Marsh, R., Stefan, M., Bansal, R., Hao, X., Walsh, B. T., & Peterson, B. S. (2015). Anatomical characteristics of the cerebral surface in bulimia nervosa. *Biological Psychiatry*, *77*, 616–623.

Marzola, E., Panepinto, C., Delsedime, N., Federico, A, Fassino, S., & Abbate-Daga, G. (2016). A factor analysis of the meanings of anorexia nervosa: Intrapsychic, relational, and avoidant dimensions and their clinical correlates. *BMC Psychiatry*, *16*, 1–9. doi: 10.1186/s12888-016-0894-6.

McLean, S. A., & Paxton, S. J. (2019). Body image in the context of eating disorders, *Psychiatric Clinics of North America*, *42*(1), 145–156. doi: 10.1016/j.psc.2018.10.006.

Mehler, P. S. (2017). Gastrointestinal complications. In P. S. Mehler and A. E.

Anderson (Eds.), *Eating disorders: A guide to medical care and complications* (3rd ed., pp. 126–142). Baltimore, MD: Johns Hopkins University Press.

Monteleone, P., Di Genio, M., Monteleone, A. M., Di Filippo, C., & Maj, M. (2011). Investigation of factors associated to crossover from anorexia nervosa restricting type (ANR) and anorexia nervosa binge-purging type (ANBP) to bulimia nervosa and comparison of bulimia nervosa patients with or without previous ANR or ANBP. *Comprehensive Psychiatry*, *52*(1), 56–62. doi: 10.1016/j.comppsych.2010.05.002.

Nagata, J. M., Golden, N. H., Leonard, M. B., Copelovitch, L., & Denburg, M. R. (2017). Assessment of sex differences in fracture risk among patients with anorexia nervosa: A population-based cohort study using The Health Improvement Network. *Journal of Bone Mineral Research*, *32*(5), 1082–1089.

Ng, S. (2016). Social media and the sexualization of adolescent girls. *The American Journal of Psychiatry Residents' Journal*, *11*(12), 14. doi: 10.1176/appi.ajp-rj.2016.111206.

Nilsson, M., Naessen, S., Dahlman, I., Hirschberg, A. L., Gustafsson, J. Å., & Dahlman Wright, K. (2004). Association of estrogen receptor β gene polymorphisms with bulimic disease in women. *Molecular Psychiatry*, *9*(1), 28–34.

Olstad, S., Solem, S., Hjemdal, O., & Hagen, R. (2015). Metacognition in eating disorders: Comparison of women with eating disorders, self-reported history of eating disorders or psychiatric problems, and healthy controls. *Eating Behaviors*, *16*, 17–22.

Ozier, A. D., & Henry, B. W. (2011). Position of the American Dietetic Association: Nutrition intervention in the treatment of eating disorders. *Journal of the American Dietetic Association*, *111*(8), 1236–1241. doi: 10.1016/j.jada.2011.06.016.

Papadopoulos, F. C., Ekbom, A., Brandt, L., & Ekselius, L. (2008). Excess mortality, causes of death and prognostic factors in anorexia nervosa. *The British Journal of Psychiatry*, *194*(1), 10–17.

Peebles, R., & Sieke, E. H. (2019). Medical complications of eating disorders in youth. *Child and Adolescent Psychiatric Clinics of North America*, *28*, 593–615.

Perez, M., Ohrt, T. K., & Hoek, H. W. (2016). Prevalence and treatment of eating disorders among Hispanics/Latino Americans in the United States. *Current Opinion of Psychiatry*, *29*(6), 378–382.

Pichika, R., Buchsbaum, M. S., Bailer, U., Hoh, C., DeCastro, A., Buchsbaum, B. R., & Kaye, W. (2012). Serotonin transporter binding after recovery from bulimia nervosa. *International Journal of Eating Disorders*, *45*(3), 345–352.

Pollice, C., Kaye, W. H., Greeno, C. G., & Weltzin, T. E. (1997). Relationship of depression, anxiety, and obsessionality to state of illness in anorexia nervosa. *International Journal of Eating Disorders*, *21*(4), 367–376.

Rieneke, R. (2017). Family-based treatment of eating disorders in adolescents: Current insights. *Adolescent Health, Medicine, and Therapeutics*, *8*, 69–79.

Rojo-Moreno L., Arribas P., Plumed, J., Gimeneo, N., Garcia-Blanco, A., Vaz-Leal, F., Vila, M. L., & Livianos, L. (2015). Prevalence and comorbidity of eating disorders among a community sample of adolescents: 2-year follow-up. *Psychiatry Research* [serial online]. May 30, 2015; *227*(1), 52–57.

Rowa, K., Kerig, P. K., & Geller, J. (2001). The family and anorexia nervosa: Examining parent–child boundary problems. *European Eating Disorders Review*, *9*(2), 97–114.

Schmidt, U., & Campbell, I. C. (2013). Treatment of eating disorders cannot remain "brainless": The case for brain-directed treatments. *European Eating Disorders Review*, *21*(6), 425–427. doi: 10.1002/erv.2257.

Shafran, R., Cooper, Z., & Fairburn, C. G. (2002). Clinical perfectionism: A cognitive-behavioural analysis. *Behavior Research and Therapy*, *40*, 773–791. https://doi.org/10.1016/S0005-7967(01)00059-6.

Skomorovsky, A., Matheson, K., & Anisman, H. (2006). The buffering role of social support perceptions in relation to eating disturbances among women in abusive dating relationships. *Sex Roles*, *54*(9–10), 627–638.

Smink, F. R., Hoeken, D., Oldehinkel, A. J., & Hoek, H. W. (2014). Prevalence and severity of DSM-5 eating disorders in a community cohort of adolescents. *International Journal of Eating Disorders*, *47*(6), 610–619.

Starzomska, M., & Wilkos, E., & Kucharska, K. (2018). Modern approaches to the treatment of anorexia nervosa: "The third wave" of cognitive behavioral therapy. *Psychiatria. Polska*, *52*(4), 651–662.

Steiger, H., Bruce, K., Gauvin, L., Groleau, P., Joober, R., Israel, M., & Kin, F. Y. (2011). Contributions of the glucocorticoid receptor polymorphism (Bcl1) and childhood abuse to risk of bulimia nervosa. *Psychiatry Research*, *187*(1–2), 193–197. doi: 10.1016/j.psychres.2010.10.021.

Steinhausen, H-C. E., Jakobsen, H., Helenius, D., Bisgaard, C., Munk-Jørgensen, P., & Strober, M. (2014). Family aggregation and risk factors in major mental disorders over three generations in a nation-wide study. *Poster session presented at NordCAP*, Middelfart, Denmark.

Tagay, S., Schlottbohm, E., Reyes-Rodriguez, M. L., Repic, N., & Senf, W. (2014). Eating disorders, trauma, PTSD, and psychosocial resources. *Eating Disorders*, *22*(1), 33–49.

Treasure, J., Stein, D., & Maguire, S. (2015). Has the time come for a staging model to map the course of eating disorders from high risk to severe enduring illness? An examination of the evidence. *Early Intervention in Psychiatry*, *9*(3), 173–184.

Trottier, K., & MacDonald, D. E. (2017). Update on psychological trauma, other severe adverse experiences and eating disorders: State of the research and future research directions. *Current Psychiatry Reports*, *19*(45), 1–9, doi: 10.1007/s11920-017-0806-6.

Turner, B. J., Claes, L., Wilderjans, T. F., Pauwels, E., Dierckx, E., Chapman, A. L., & Schoevaerts, K. (2014). Personality profiles in eating disorders: Further evidence of the clinical utility of examining subtypes based on temperament. *Psychiatry Research*, *219*(1), 157–165.

Udo, T., & Grilo, C. M. (2018). Prevalence and correlates of DSM-5 eating disorders in nationally representative sample of United States adults. *Biological Psychiatry*, *84*(5), 345–354. doi: 10.1016/j.biopsych.2018.03.014.

Uniacke, B., & Broft, A. (2016). The interplay of mood disorders and eating disorders. *Psychiatric Times*, *33*(5), 1–4.

Vandereycken, W. (2006). Denial of illness in anorexia nervosa—A conceptual review: Part 1: Diagnostic significance and assessment. *European Eating Disorders Review*, *14*(5), 341–351. doi: 10.1002/erv.721.

Versini, A., Ramoz, N., Le Strat, Y., Scherag, S., Ehrlich, S., Boni, C., Hinney, A., Hebebrand, J., Romo, L., Guelfi, J., & Gorwood, P. (2010). Estrogen receptor 1 gene (ESR1) is associated with restrictive anorexia nervosa. *Neuropsychopharmacology*, *35*(8), 1818–1825.

Wade, T. D., Tiggemann, M., Bulik, C. M., Fairburn, C. G., Wray, N. R., & Martin, N. G. (2008). Shared temperament risk factors for anorexia nervosa: A twin study. *Psychosomatic Medicine*, *70*(2), 239–244.

Wonderlich-Tierney, A. L., & Vander Wal, J. S. (2010). The effects of social support and coping on the relationship between social anxiety and eating disorders. *Eating Behaviors*, *11*(2), 85–91.

Woodside, B., Halpert, B., & Dimitropoulos, G. (2015). *Implementing behavioral family therapy in complex settings. Family therapy for adolescent eating and weight disorders: New applications* (pp. 361–371). New York, NY: Routledge.

Woolrich, R. A., Cooper, M. J., & Turner, H. M. (2008). Metacognition in patients with anorexia nervosa, dieting and non-dieting women: A preliminary study. *European Eating Disorders Review*, *16*(1), 11–20.

Young, J., Henderson, M. C., & Thompson III, G. R. (2011). Anorexia nervosa: Russell's sign with concurrent tetany. *Journal of General Internal Medicine*, *26*(6), 668–668.

Chapter 11

Substance Use Disorders

Maxwell R. Christensen, Emma Anderson-White, Lauren J. Ryan, Mia M. Ricardo, Beata A. Krembuszewski, Cody Sze, and Craig E. Henderson

Chapter Overview

This chapter examines the development, maintenance, and amelioration of substance use disorders (SUDs) over time. Although epidemiological data suggests experimental substance use may be a common feature of adolescent development (e.g., Substance Abuse and Mental Health Services Administration, 2019), problematic use is associated with harmful consequences that often persist into adulthood (including sexually transmitted infections, unintended pregnancy, criminal involvement, school truancy, psychiatric disorders, and physical health problems) and are even leading causes of death among youth (Keyes, Brady, & Li, 2015; National Center on Addiction and Substance Abuse, 2011; Wong, Zhou, Goebert, & Hishinuma, 2013). These disorders therefore demand adequate attention from psychologists and other professionals who seek to improve quality of life for teens and their families. Below, we provide an example of an adolescent case from our clinical work.

Case vignette

John is a 17-year-old European-American male currently detained in a juvenile correctional facility following arrest for possession of cocaine. John started using tobacco and alcohol when he was 13 alongside his older brother and a number of his brother's friends. John gradually became more involved in illicit drug use himself, including becoming very close with one member of the social group who used marijuana and cocaine. After his arrest, John admitted that he

Developmental Psychopathology, First Edition. Edited by Amanda Venta, Carla Sharp, Jack M. Fletcher, and Peter Fonagy.

had used either cocaine, marijuana, or alcohol every day over the last 2 years and, of late, had used substances on his own, without his friends or brother.

As the clinician seeing this young man, discuss possible diagnoses you would give John and supporting evidence for each differential diagnosis, as well as other factors to consider. What other information would you gather during an assessment to guide diagnosis and treatment of John's substance use?

Definition, Diagnosis, and Clinical Features

When thinking about substances, whether alcohol, tobacco, marijuana, or other illicit drugs, how do you define when use becomes a disorder? Is it engaging in use that violates the law? Or do you define it differently depending on the drug? How does addiction differ from an SUD, or does it? Such questions pose a challenge for psychologists. When we turn to DSM-5, we see a basic, core framework:

> "The essential feature of a substance use disorder is a cluster of cognitive, behavioral, and physiological symptoms indicating that the individual continues using the substance despite significant substance-related problems"
>
> (American Psychiatric Association, 2013, p. 483).

Accordingly, DSM-5 diagnoses of SUD exist for 10 different substance classes (e.g., alcohol, cannabis), and generally consist of a problematic use pattern that results in clinically significant impairment or distress manifested over a long period of time (i.e., 12 months) and evidenced by at least 2 of 11 symptoms listed in Table 11.1 below. Table 11.1 provides an overview of the specific symptoms that are considered as manifestations of these disorders and how those symptoms differ across the diagnostic systems introduced in Chapter 1. However, across systems, symptoms can generally be classified into the following domains: (1) *impaired control* (e.g., taking a substance in larger amounts or for a longer period of time than was intended), (2) *social impairment* (e.g., failure to fulfill major role obligations at work, school, or home), (3) *risky use of the substance* (e.g., recurrent substance use in situations where it is physically hazardous), and (4) *pharmacological criteria* (e.g., *tolerance* and *withdrawal*). Furthermore, the DSM-5 introduced a severity classification, with ratings of mild, moderate, and severe, representing a change from previous iterations (i.e., DSM-IV-TR; APA, 2000), in which SUDs were instead labeled as *substance abuse* and/or *substance dependence* based on the presence of specific criteria.

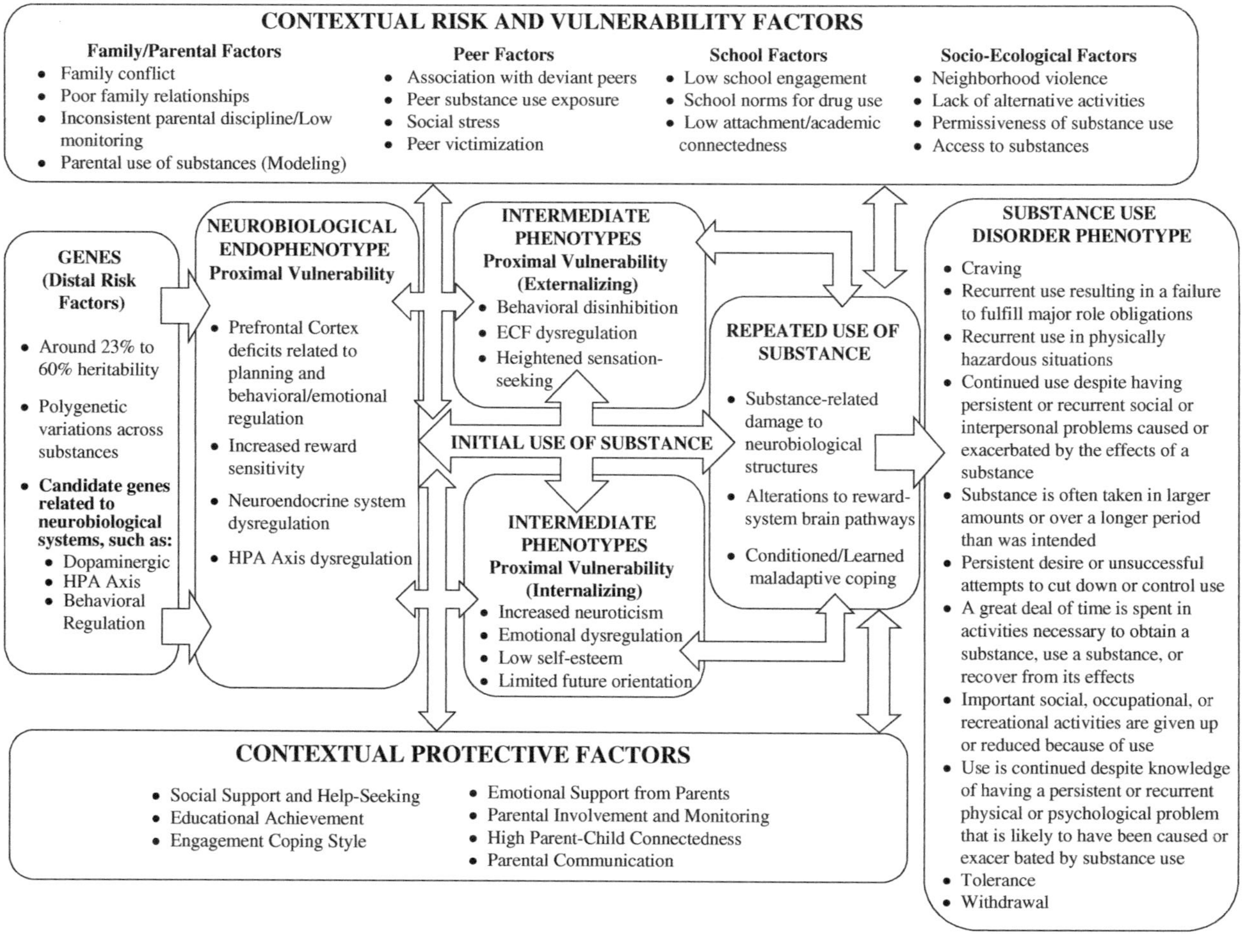

FIGURE 11.1 A Developmental Psychopathology Model of Substance Use Disorder

factors that increase and decrease the risk of problematic substance use patterns being developed and maintained. Across all of the models, you will spot the categories you are used to thinking about: biological factors, temperamental variables, cognitive factors, and contextual factors. Etiology must be examined using a holistic approach that considers contributions from each of these pathways. Although we present these trajectories as distinct, remember that factors commonly overlap and collectively contribute to an individual's overall risk for disorder. Think of these trajectories as a collection of risk factors that are related to a particular, underlying mechanism, which in turn place youth on a course for alcohol and drug use to become problematic.

EXTERNALIZING PATHWAY

The externalizing pathway frames SUDs as stemming from behavioral difficulties that result in problematic engagement with our environment. Although many of these environmental components will be discussed later as part of the contextual pathway, we will first characterize the externalizing pathway by discussing specific, underlying mechanisms, primarily those related to executive cognitive functioning and behavioral control.

Executive cognitive functioning (ECF), or the planning, initiation, and regulation of goal-oriented behavior, consists of highly related characteristics, such as reasoning, foresight, attention, judgment, self-monitoring, and motor control (Giancola, Martin, Tarter, Pelham, & Moss, 1995). Low ECF has consistently been related to increased substance use in adolescents (Giancola & Mezzich, 2003; Tarter et al., 2004; Giancola & Tarter, 1999). Dysregulation of ECF is believed to be caused by functional deficits in the prefrontal cortex of the brain (Giancola & Tarter, 1999; Tarter et al., 2004) and is related to antisocial behavior as well as diagnoses of conduct disorder in adolescent females ages 14–18 (Giancola, Mezzich, & Tarter, 1998). Additionally, aggressive behavior (Giancola, et al., 1995) and difficult temperaments are linked to low ECF (Giancola & Tarter, 1999). *Neurobehavioral disinhibition*, which includes a lack of behavior control, dysregulated emotions, and low ECF, explains the association between parental substance use and substance use in adolescent males and predicts continued substance use in young adulthood (Tarter et al., 2004). Those with temperaments that include heightened sensation/novelty-seeking and impulsivity are more likely to have problems with behaviors such as substance use (Gerra et al., 2005). As such, these combined affective, cognitive, and behavioral functions create vulnerability for substance use in adolescents (Giancola & Tarter, 1999).

Many disorders, such as attention-deficit/hyperactivity disorder (ADHD), which we covered in Chapter 5, and substance use, share underlying genetic vulnerability. For instance, ADHD and SUD are both linked to the ADGRL3 gene and related to impulsivity (Arcos-Burgos et al., 2019). Underlying difficulty inhibiting behavior that can increase the likelihood of acquiring an SUD (Iacono, Malone, & McGue, 2003), just as it can increase other symptoms of behavioral disinhibition—like conduct disorder and ADHD—which are intercorrelated in adolescence, point to an underlying biological component (Young et al., 2009).

Genes that are specifically related to the reward system of the brain, which runs on the neurotransmitter dopamine, have also been studied. Whenever we receive any rewarding or pleasurable stimuli (e.g., drugs, chocolate, sex, etc.), this *mesolimbic pathway* becomes highly active (Volkow et al., 2012). Some people may be predisposed to be more sensitive to dopamine activity in the reward pathway because of dysfunction in certain brain receptors, meaning that pleasurable and rewarding stimuli (like substances) are more reinforcing (Blum et al., 1996). A longitudinal study showed that adolescents with higher sensitivity to reward were more likely to abuse substances (Colder et al., 2013).

Externalizing problems, such as aggression and delinquency, can interact with family conflict to contribute to substance use (Skeer, McCormick, Normand, Buka, & Gilman, 2009). Additionally, externalizing symptoms together predict diagnoses of SUDs (Kirisci et al., 2015), and individuals with comorbid externalizing and internalizing disorders at age 18 have also been found to endorse significantly higher rates of substance use at age 22 compared to young adults with no diagnoses, comorbid internalizing disorders, or only behavioral disorders (Lansford et al., 2008). Other longitudinal studies have also shown that externalizing behaviors contribute to adolescent substance use over time. For example, higher rates of aggressive behavior, delinquency, and social problems at ages 4, 6, 9, 10, and 11 have been found to be predictors of adolescent substance use (Min et al., 2018). Research also suggests youth meeting diagnostic criteria for externalizing disorders demonstrate increasing substance use throughout adolescence and significantly higher rates of use at age 18 (Lansford et al., 2008). Although these studies do not suggest that substance use is a specific consequence of behavioral disorders (e.g., as suggested by independence of diagnoses, deficits in behavioral control appear to be cross-cutting mechanisms underlying these conditions (Merikangas et al, 2010).

INTERNALIZING PATHWAY

Although you may think of substance use as an "externalizing" disorder because of its behavioral nature, research suggests that some people may also use substances to escape from negative emotions. The link between internalizing disorders, such as depression, and adolescent substance use seems to be weaker and less clear than externalizing disorders and adolescent substance use, but it remains influential for some (King, Iacono, & McGue, 2004).

Though research is mixed (Scalco et al., 2014), most studies support an internalizing pathway toward the development of SUDs. Genetics may predispose individuals toward a temperament characterized by *neuroticism*—the tendency to experience negative mood states—which are common features of internalizing disorders (Barlow, Ellard, Sauer-Zavala, Bullis, & Carl, 2014). This may predispose individuals towards *emotional dysregulation* and use of substances to cope (Poon et al., 2016; Schwinn, Schinke, Hopkins, & Thom, 2016). Longitudinal research has shown that emotional dysregulation beginning in childhood and continuing through adolescence is associated with the development of SUDs (Kirisci et al., 2015). Internalizing symptoms have also been associated with substance use among adolescents, particularly for youth low in externalizing pathology or experiencing depressive symptoms (Khoddam, Jackson, & Leventhal, 2016). There is a stronger influence of internalizing symptoms—specifically depressive symptoms—on the development of SUDs among females (Schwinn et al., 2016), and adolescent girls characterized as having difficult temperaments are also more likely to engage in substance use than girls with easier temperaments (Giancola & Mezzich, 2003).

Historically, research on the influence of internalizing symptoms has given rise to the *self-medication hypothesis*, which states that engaging in substance use relieves emotional distress (Khantzian, 1997). Accordingly, research has found that *negative urgency*, acting impulsively when experiencing negative emotions, mediates the effect of child abuse and neglect on alcohol and marijuana use in adolescents (Oshri et al., 2018). As another example, anxiety symptoms explain the relation between certain personality traits (e.g., impulsive-irresponsible psychopathic traits) and use of alcohol or marijuana as a coping mechanism for negative emotions among adolescent males (Gillen, Barry, & Bater, 2016). Additional psychological factors, such as low self-esteem, negative body image, a lack of future planning, and a tendency to blame oneself following negative events, may also give rise to SUDs as part of the internalizing pathway (Schwinn et al., 2016; Stumper, Olino, Abramson, & Alloy, 2019), with drug and alcohol use mainly serving to manage distress.

REPEATED USE PATHWAY

By this point, we have reviewed risk factors pertaining to individual characteristics that predispose people to SUDs. Before we proceed to a discussion of contextual influences and their interactions with these factors, it is important to investigate an additional avenue of disorder progression—how drugs and alcohol change brain functioning. We therefore will now explore how neurological changes may function to increase risk for pathology and drug addiction (Volkow et al., 2012), specifically under the framework of a *repeated use pathway.*

Previously, we discussed the impact of dopamine on the brain's reward system and noted a person may use drugs to experience the resulting pleasurable effects. When the drug is removed after neurons have become accustomed to frequent exposure, the brain is then deprived of the neurotransmitters and the likelihood of continued use increases (Volkow et al., 2012). Similarly, additional neurotransmitter systems undergo changes with drug use during adolescence (e.g., cannabis use and the endocannabinoid system), contributing to downstream vulnerability to addiction and psychological disorders (Hurd, Michaelides, Miller, & Jutras-Aswad, 2014). These neurological changes can also occur during the early lifespan. For example, use of substances during pregnancy may disrupt the development of the fetus's neuroendocrine system, which influences the regulation of the brain pathway that deals with stress (i.e., *Hypothalamus-Pituitary-Adrenal (HPA) axis*; Tarter, 2002).

Repeated use is not only reinforcing at the neuronal level, but also at the brain's structural level. The prefrontal cortex (which controls executive functioning) is not fully developed during adolescence (Lubman, Yücel, & Hall, 2007), meaning the brain is more susceptible to damage from substances (Monti et al., 2005). Repeated drug use alters the structure of the mesolimbic pathway of the brain that is responsible for rewards and motivation and decreases the prefrontal cortex's control over executive functioning, thus leading to decreased impulse inhibition and attention for non-drug related activities (Volkow et al., 2012). In other words, the more a person uses substances (especially as an adolescent with a still-developing brain), the less ability they will have to direct their attention toward decreasing substance use. This contributes to a physiological basis for the development and progression of SUDs, something best encapsulated by the term *addiction.*

Beginning in the early to mid-1900s, perspectives on addiction began shifting from being perceived as an affliction to a choice that is based on characterological problems and moral failings (White & Miller, 2007). Often deemed the "Moral Weakness Model," this concept encompasses beliefs that an individual is solely responsible for their substance use, as they willfully make the decision to initiate and continue such use (Morse, 2004). In the 1990s, the National Institute on Drug Abuse (NIDA) published a seminal article detailing support for what was deemed the "*brain disease model of addiction*" (BDMA; Leshner, 1997). This model cites a body of research identifying structural and functional changes in the brain that occurs when recreational use develops into physical dependence (Volkow, Koob, & McLellan, 2016). Scientific support for the BDMA indicates that such neurobiological changes in the brain influence one's ability to feel pleasure and contribute to difficulty controlling impulses, increased depression and negative affect, poor distress tolerance, and difficulty with rational decision making (Koob & Volkow, 2010; Volkow et al., 2016). Further, these changes inhibit one's ability to remain abstinent once sobriety is achieved (Leshner, 1997; NIDA, 2016; Volkow et al., 2016). Given this body of literature, the NIDA and the American Society of Addiction Medicine (ASAM) both define addiction as a "chronic, relapsing disease of the brain" (ASAM, 2011; NIDA, 2016); however, *exactly how much* a person's drug-seeking behavior patterns might be out of their control remains controversial.

CONTEXTUAL PATHWAY

Along with the externalizing, internalizing, and repeated use pathways, research supports a fourth pathway to the development of SUDs, which we term the *contextual pathway*. The contextual pathway operates in conjunction with other pathways, enhancing both risk and protection depending on the particular circumstances in place. For instance, youth who begin engaging in oppositional and delinquent behaviors at young ages tend to associate with delinquent peers, who in turn shape further delinquency and eventually substance use. In addition, children who are the victims of parental abuse and neglect are likely to develop depressive symptoms, which might move them towards the internalizing pathway. However, the contextual pathway operates at more molar, relational levels than the genetic and psychological factors that tend to be major explanatory factors in the other pathways we described.

Drawing from *Bronfenbrenner's ecological systems theory* (1977, 1979), the contextual pathway views substance use as emerging from an interaction between individuals and their environment at multiple levels or systems. This theory posits that there are many different levels of environmental influence that affect a child's development, starting from people and institutions immediately surrounding the individual to nationwide cultural forces; later versions of this theory also took into account change over time, such as cultural change. The contextual factors that seem most pertinent to the development of SUDs include family, peer groups, school bonding, neighborhood effects, and socioeconomic status.

Family relationships

Family conflict, or other disruptions to the *family system*, can adversely affect adolescent development. Parent–child conflict and adolescents' negative perceptions of their relationship with their parents have both been positively correlated with substance use (Wills & Yaeger, 2003).

Poor parent–child relationships feature frequent arguments, lack of enjoyment and satisfaction regarding quality time, and feelings of being unheard by the other (Rusby, Light, Crowley, Westling, 2018). Other life events, such as parental conflict, family illnesses, or unemployment, may damage relationships as extenuating circumstances override emotional needs (Wills & Yaeger, 2003).

Poor family management and lower parental monitoring have been associated with higher alcohol and marijuana use (Rusby et al., 2018). Adolescents in households without explicit and consistently enforced rules find more freedom to engage with deviant peers who may be using substances themselves. In addition, family discipline practices influence the development of SUDs, with lower levels of parental reinforcement, control through guilt, and lack of control or strictness associated with higher likelihood of use (Muchiri & dos Santos, 2018). Finally, parents' own use of substances can model maladaptive coping and promotion of mental health symptoms in adolescents (Brook et al., 2010), as well as possibly increase access to substances (Rusby et al., 2018).

Peer relationships

Associating with deviant peers has been repeatedly shown to put one at risk for substance use (Obando, Trujillo, & Trujillo, 2014; Pereyra & Bean, 2017). Sibling and peer substance use is also predictive of adolescent drinking frequency and volume (Yurasek et al., 2019), and research has found positive associations between perceptions of peers engaging in opioid abuse and endorsement of both personal use and use by others (Egan, Gregory, Osborne, & Cottler, 2019). Factors such as low parental monitoring, emotional maltreatment, and low maternal involvement can exacerbate the influence deviant peers have on substance use (e.g., Cheng & Lo, 2017). Lastly, social stress and peer victimization (e.g., bullying) have also been linked to substance use (e.g., Barbieri et al., 2019). Intersecting with the internalizing pathway, interpersonal stress can indirectly influence use through the emergence of depressive symptoms, particularly for female adolescents (Zapolski, Rowe, Fisher, Hensel, & Barnes-Najor, 2018).

Broader socioecological factors

Researchers have also found that less proximal factors such as school, neighborhood, and socioeconomic status also exert an influence on SUD. In terms of school-related factors, substance use is generally higher in educational settings where students report lower attachment to school and higher peer acceptability of use (Ennett, Flewelling, Lindrooth, & Norton, 1997). Interestingly, examining the relation between substance use and school achievement alone has yielded counterintuitive findings. For instance, the most prevalent group of substance users have high grades, social reasons for attending school, and affiliate with peers who also do well in school (Bryant-Ludden & Eccles, 2007). Low achievement is often only a risk factor for substance use when combined with other variables, such as experiencing little fun at school (Bryant-Ludden & Eccles, 2007) or affiliating with peers that use substances (Haller, Handley, Chassin & Bountress, 2010). Of note, these results may suggest the importance of examining school achievement in a more holistic manner that also accounts for school bonding.

Literature on the impact of neighborhood factors on adolescent substance use is limited; however, existing research suggests that the neighborhoods in which adolescents live can influence the development of SUDs. Specifically, exposure to neighborhood violence appears to be the most consistent predictor (Löfving-Gupta et al., 2018; Mason & Mennis, 2010), even after controlling for adolescents' own level of violent behavior and emotional problems (Löfving-Gupta et al., 2018). Evidence suggests that neighborhood permissiveness of substance use can also increase the likelihood of problematic use (Lee et al, 2017). Some research further indicates that neighborhood disorder (e.g., broken windows, vacant lots) is associated with increased probability of marijuana use in adolescents and young adults (Furr-Holden et al., 2015); however, other studies have not replicated these findings (Fagan, Wright & Pinchevsky, 2015). Longitudinal studies have shown that lower parental education is associated with greater likelihood of later marijuana and alcohol use, although this association is explained by lack of alternative non-drug related social activities, indicating that lower parental education alone does not entirely account for this association (e.g., Lee et al., 2018).

Regarding neighborhood advantage, youth raised in middle-class, White, urban neighborhoods appear to have higher odds of substance use compared to peers from most other neighborhood types (Warner, 2016). Neighborhood advantage also moderates the relation between sensation-seeking and substance use such that adolescents residing in the most advantaged neighborhoods exhibit the strongest link between sensation seeking and substance use initiation (Jensen, Chassin & Gonzalez, 2017). Similarly, among adolescents who have experienced maltreatment, neighborhood disadvantage has been found to result in more marijuana dependence symptoms as compared to non-maltreated adolescents, especially for those who experienced multiple types of maltreatment (Handley, Rogosch, Guild & Cicchetti, 2015). These differential effects within broad social systems (i.e., neighborhoods, families, etc.) showcase how context can provide a precarious environment for youth who may already be at risk for developing pathology.

FACTORS PROTECTING AGAINST SUBSTANCE USE

Protective factors themselves are not just the *absence* of a risk factor, but rather (somewhat) independent buffers that reduce the risk of developing a disorder. These are important pieces of the developmental picture regarding substancc use, as they counterbalance the risk factors established in the literature.

Genetic factors

There is at least one protective genetic factor associated with substance-related psychopathology, specifically for alcohol dependence. When alcohol is consumed, it is broken down by enzymes in the liver. The presence of certain polymorphisms of genes (most notably, the ALDH2 gene) makes these enzymes metabolize alcohol differently, which leads to a decreased risk for alcohol dependence (Li, Zhao, & Gelernter, 2012). This is likely because people with these polymorphisms have more negative side effects from drinking (e.g., vomiting, flushing), deterring them from consuming alcohol (Wall, Luczak, & Hiller-Sturmhöfel, 2016). Research has shown that a few alleles produce this protective factor, with their frequencies differing among ethnic groups. People of Asian descent, for example, are more likely to possess one of these protective allele forms and are less likely to develop alcohol dependence (Wall et al., 2016).

Coping style

Coping style has been found to protect against adolescent substance use and intentions to use substances among adolescents (McConnell, Memetovic, & Richardson, 2014). Specifically, engagement coping, or interacting with others to reduce distressing emotions, is associated with less substance use when adolescents encounter stressful life events (Wills, Sandy, Yaeger, Cleary, & Shinar, 2001). Further, a longitudinal study found that religion-based coping significantly reduced frequency of drugs used, drug-related problems, and a number of drugs used for adolescent boys (Brechting & Giancola, 2007). These psychological processes therefore remain important focal points for prevention and treatment.

Family relationships and communication

Emotional support and high parent–child connectedness have both been associated with reduced substance use, particularly during the transition into high school and through later adolescence (Van Ryzin, Fosco, & Dishion, 2012). High parent–child relationship quality often operates in tandem with increased parental involvement and emotional support, which are respectively associated with delayed initiation and reduced levels of substance use (Ryan, Jorm, & Lubman, 2010). Furthermore, good communication has been associated with delayed alcohol initiation and lower levels of use (Carver, Elliot, Kennedy, & Hanley, 2017).

Likewise, open parent–child communication has been found to protect against substance use (Muchiri & dos Santos, 2018), and communication about substances may also be protective depending on content. For example, research indicates expressions of disapproval and messages about specific health risks are related to reduced use (Carver et al., 2017).

As reduced parental monitoring is associated with increased substance use, more monitoring can serve a protective function if done in a supportive family relationship. Youth may abstain due to adherence to rules and fear of associated penalties for rule violations, suggesting consistent and reasonable discipline within the home can protect young people from developing problems with substance use (Wills & Yaeger, 2003). Higher monitoring may also include specifically limiting availability of alcohol and implementing discipline, both of which have been associated with reduced alcohol use. Monitoring also includes parental knowledge of their children's activities, which is likewise associated with less frequent alcohol use and decreased illicit substance use (Muchiri & dos Santos, 2018; Ryan et al., 2010).

Finally, other factors that may serve to buffer against the influence of interpersonal stressors on substance use outcomes include social support and help seeking, higher levels of drug resistance self-efficacy, higher GPA and educational achievement, and greater future orientation (Dastgerdi & Eslami, 2018; Heerde and Hemphill, 2018; Whaley, Hayes, & Smith, 2016). Further, stronger parental attachment serves a protective function for both genders, and, while stronger attachment to peers may be protective for females, among males it has conversely been associated with higher rates of substance use (Lee and Kim, 2017).

SUMMARY

Above, we provided a glimpse of the developmental trajectories established in the scientific literature on SUDs (for further examination of these etiological pathways, see Chassin, Colder, Hussong, & Sher, 2016). Consistent with the developmental psychopathology concepts of *multifinality* and *equifinality*, there is no global risk profile or developmental course that accounts for SUDs, especially when considering the expansive range of drugs and alcohol that exists today. Instead, problematic substance use is promoted by a variety of interrelated factors across the lifespan, with contributions from biological, physiological, and sociological components.

Gene–Environment Interactions

While we have already touched on some genetic factors in the previous section, in order to fully examine the etiology of SUDs, we first must acknowledge how genetics and environmental factors may independently and interdependently contribute to psychopathology. Similar to many psychological constructs, interrelationships between "nature" and "nurture" are important when it comes to SUDs. When discussing "nature," we typically consider genetic contributions. Twin studies can be extremely helpful in identifying genetic contributions to psychological disorders, and SUDs more specifically. For example, many twin studies have shown that genetics are a key factor in the development of SUDs, with estimates of the specific contributions of genes ranging from 23% (Han, McGue, & Iacono, 1999) up to 60% (McGue, Elkins, & Iacono, 2000) depending on the study and the substance examined. There is not just one gene that predicts overall substance use, or even one gene per substance (Kreek, Nielsen, Butelman, & LaForge, 2005). For example, one recent review found 566 genetic variants that are implicated in tobacco use, depending on the stage of use (e.g., initiation, cessation; Liu et al., 2019). Tobacco/nicotine use has frequently been shown to have a higher genetic component than other substances, indicating that genes influence use unequally across substances (Maes et al., 1999; McGue et al. 2000). There are also specific genetic factors that predict substance use in adolescence but not adults (Stone, Becker, Huber, & Catalano, 2012). However, it is important to consider that despite the influence that genes exert, environmental contributions are also always present (Hopfer, Crowley, & Hewitt, 2003). As we explore the various risk factors related to adolescent substance use, keep in mind that from a developmental psychopathology framework, it is the *combination* of such genetic predispositions and environmental factors that produce an increased risk for SUDs. This process is likely to be best encapsulated by the effects of time and age on the development of pathology.

For example, a proposed explanation for inconsistent results in research linking a gene called DAT1 (which works in the reward pathway of the brain) to drug use in adolescence is that the gene exerts more influence in a period of development when the brain is maturing quickly. Therefore, the time of life in which an individual begins using substances can influence whether they will eventually encounter problems with substance use (Schmid et al., 2009). In their study, Schmid and colleagues (2009) found that the DAT1 gene interacts more potently with earlier drug use to predict substance use in the future. Basically, the DAT1 gene is more influential the earlier the person begins using substances. This reflects the broader scientific literature on adolescent substance use, suggesting that early age of onset is a key predictor of later dysfunction (Chassin, et al., 2016), and highlights the complicated relationship between genes, development, and environmental influences.

Developmental Timing Effects

Broadly speaking, the developmental period of adolescence is its own risk factor for substance use. Just as there are critical periods of development for vision and language, it has been proposed that adolescence may be a sensitive period for substance use (Fuhrmann, Knoll, & Blakemore, 2015). Adolescence is a time of change within the body, with hormones increasing during puberty and increased risk-taking behavior overall (Tarter, 2002). Hormonal changes lead to increased risk-taking in all adolescents, but they impact some groups more than others. Early-maturing girls and early- and late-maturing boys, for example, appear to have an especially greater risk for substance use (Stumper et al, 2019). Similarly, increased reward sensitivity during childhood, as identified through neuroimaging techniques, has been found to predict initiation of substance use during adolescence (Cope, Martz, Hardee, Zucker, & Heitzig, 2019). These examples suggest that developmental timing of substance use is critical to consider when conceptualizing disordered use of drugs and alcohol. Although prevalence rates indicating substance use, particularly of alcohol and marijuana, may be considered normative among older adolescents (Johnston et al., 2019), research also suggests that disordered use may appear at an earlier time, with the median age of onset for SUDs among adolescents at approximately 15 years of age (Merikangas et al., 2010).

Assessment of Substance Use Disorders

As the prevalence of SUDs appears to significantly increase among older adolescents (Johnston et al., 2019), early assessment and intervention is critical. Considering these developments, the American Academy of Pediatrics has provided guidance for medical professionals regarding appropriate screening procedures for youth (Levy & Williams, 2016), with the intent of utilizing healthcare interactions as opportunities to efficiently identify problematic use among adolescents. This triage-based public health approach, specifically known as Screening, Brief Intervention, and Referral to Treatment (SBIRT), has also been endorsed by the Substance Abuse and Mental Health Services Administration (SAMHSA), and incorporates a three-stage process of: (1) identifying a youth's risk level, (2) increasing insight and motivation for treatment, and (3) referring to specialty care in line with youth needs (Levy & Williams, 2016; Pilowsky & Wu, 2013; SAMHSA, 2017).

It is important to note that a variety of assessment tools and measures exist, including short instruments and longer interviews, as well as biological drug testing (e.g., urinalysis; Pilowsky & Wu, 2013; Winters & Kaminer, 2008). Within the SBIRT framework, screening instruments particularly allow for a broad canvassing of potential problems that may otherwise avoid detection. For example, the CRAFFT (Knight et al., 1999) is a six-item screening tool for adolescent substance difficulties that allows for versatile application in healthcare settings and efficient re-evaluations over time, with more in-depth measures serving as appropriate follow-ups (Winters & Kaminer, 2008). In conjunction with screening instruments, comprehensive tools can help to fill out the details regarding a youth's clinical presentation and use patterns. Considering the comorbidity of SUDs and other psychiatric problems (Merikangas et al., 2010), along with the interrelated risk factors that we have summarized above, these assessments can also help to identify the range of difficulties that adolescents may experience (Winters & Kaminer, 2008).

Intervention with Substance Use Disorders

Outpatient treatment is the most common treatment modality for youth in the United States, hosting over 80% of teenagers receiving substance use services (SAMHSA, 2014). Readers interested in research on the effectiveness of prevention services are encouraged to see the Cochrane review published by Faggiano, Minozzi, Versino, and Buscemi (2014), and those interested in research on the effectiveness of alcohol use interventions are invited to see the systematic review published by Tripodi, Bender, Litschge, and Vaughn (2010). Finally, consistent with research on adults, medication-assisted treatment (MAT), defined as opioid agonist or antagonist medication combined with appropriate behavioral interventions, is the only evidence-based treatment for youth opiate use disorder (Committee on Substance Use, 2016).

The *Journal of Clinical Child and Adolescent Psychology* (JCCAP) has published three evidence-based reviews summarizing the results of treatment effectiveness studies for an array of problems faced by children and adolescents, including adolescent substance use. The editors of JCCAP defined five levels of empirical support, three of which pertain to the treatments summarized below: (a) Well-Established, in which a treatment demonstrated efficacy in at least two independent research settings by two different investigatory teams showing the experimental treatment to be either statistically significantly superior to a *placebo* or another active treatment or equivalent to an already well-established treatment; (b) Probably Efficacious, which included the previous specifications with the exception being the independent replication criterion; and (3) Possibly Efficacious, which required only one randomized trial.

The first of these reviews conducted by Waldron and Turner (2008) documented that protocol-based treatments for adolescent substance use were more effective than no treatment or usual care and classified discrete treatment models and broad treatment approaches into two categories of empirical support: Well-Established, which contained Multidimensional Family Therapy (MDFT), Functional Family Therapy (FFT), and Group *Cognitive-Behavioral Therapy* (CBT-G); and Probably Efficacious, which contained Brief Strategic Family Therapy (BSFT), *Behavioral Family-Based Treatment* (FBT-B), and Multisystemic

Therapy (MST). Hogue, Henderson, Ozechowski, and Robbins (2014) updated Waldron and Turner via a cumulative review of studies published between 2007 and 2013, focusing on broad treatment approaches and refining the empirical support classifications. The revised Well-Established category included *Ecological Family-Based Treatment* (FBT-E), CBT-G, Individual CBT (CBT-I), and two multicomponent treatments (i.e., treatment packages containing more than one evidence-based approach for ASU): *Motivational Enhancement Therapy* + CBT (MET/CBT), and MET/CBT + FBT-B. The revised Probably Efficacious category included FBT-B, standalone Motivational Interviewing/MET (MI/MET), and two multicomponent treatments: FBT-E + *Contingency Management* (CM), and MET/CBT + FBT-B + CM. Finally, the category Possibly Efficacious was added to accommodate the drug counseling/*12 step (DC/12) approach*. Finally, Hogue, Henderson, Becker, and Knight (2018) concluded that the current evidence base is highly consistent with the previous review. Specifically, there are now five treatment approaches deemed Well-Established: FBT-E, CBT-G, CBT-I, MET/CBT, and MET/CBT + FBT-B. Another five approaches are deemed Probably Efficacious: FBT-B, MI/MET, FBT-E + CM, MET/CBT + CM, and MET/CBT + FBT-B + CM. One approach remains Possibly Efficacious: DC/12.

It is also notable to mention a common treatment modality that has often been highlighted as possibly *iatrogenic* (literally, "illness caused by the intended medicine"): group-based treatment for adolescent substance use (GBT). GBT has been cautioned against in previous writings due to putative peer deviancy training, a process by which deviant or rule-breaking conversation or behavior is reinforced by peers (Dishion, Spracklen, Andrews, & Patterson, 1996; Dodge, Dishion, & Lansford, 2006). However, as highlighted from the results of studies showing that CBT-G is a well-established treatment, it is apparent that treatments that share a broad characteristic such as "modality" (e.g., individual, family, group) may nonetheless differ substantially with regard to the treatment approach each represents (e.g., CBT, motivational, twelve-step) as well as the specific therapeutic techniques that constitute them. In other words, modality does not equal model, and GBT can be effective depending on the context in which it is used and the types of interventions that are employed.

The scope of available treatments for adolescent SUDs provides empirically supported methods of addressing these conditions. Additionally, the primary use of family- and systems-based interventions reflects the interdependent nature of risk factors, with treatment provided in a manner that is consistent with a developmental conceptualization of drug and alcohol psychopathology. In light of the outsized role parents and families play in the trajectories of youth substance use, caregivers can be an important bridge to treatment for their children, and family relationships exert powerful curative effects. Yet, it is easy to conceive how having helpful conversations around difficult topics like substance use would be quite challenging. The following provides an example of how such a conversation could go, depicting work with a mother (M) and son (R) in which the therapist (T) attempts to understand the emotion under a parent's statements that had taken an accusatory turn. These examples come from the Multidimensional Family Therapy Treatment Manual (Liddle, 2000).

M: Well, I can't follow R out in the street and keep him away from the boys who are into stealing and staying out till all hours.

T: I agree with you, Mrs. Williams. There are a lot of things you can't control. But that doesn't mean there aren't ways you can influence him. I can help him listen to you.

M: Well, I sure hope so. I must have been up most of the night on Thursday. R went out right after dinner and wasn't back when I went to bed. I don't think he got in until 3 in the morning or so.

T: And I'll bet you were worried sick. What were you thinking about when you lay there awake?

M: I was thinking, "The police'll be by any minute to tell me R has been shot." That's what I was thinking. I don't think I could bear losing R.

T: Does R know what you went through that night?

M: Well, he sure knows I was angry, 'cause when he did come in I went downstairs and I guess I really went off. I was just screaming and carrying on and he kind of stood there until I finished and then we both went to bed. We haven't talked much since then.

T: So, R doesn't know really what you go through when he stays out? I really think it's important for him to know. I think it would be good for him to hear that today when he comes back in. You and he have a relationship. Don't assume that it doesn't matter to him what you go through.

The following shows how the adolescent can then be brought into the conversation:

T: R, what's going on in there? You and I agreed that it was important for you to tell your mom how angry you were when she told you off in front of your friends. Don't bail out on me here. I can help her hear you, but you need to do your part, too.

R: I know I said that, but she's not gonna listen to me. She never does.

T: It sounds as if you're feeling really hopeless about what we can do together to make things change. What do you think will happen if we bring this stuff up today?

R: Well, she'll say all the right things when we're here, and then we'll go home and everything will be the same.

T: R, if that's so, I also want us to say that to her—that you don't really trust her yet to follow through. I want to help you with this, R, but I can't do it without you. Can we agree to go back in there and at least try?

The fundamental point of the treatment is to arrange meaningful conversations between parents and adolescents to help them discuss their emotions and understand each other around difficult subjects like substance use.

Chapter Summary

Adolescent substance use remains a focal point of concern for mental health and public policy professionals due to its potential influence on a variety of developmental domains. In this chapter, we reviewed the landscape of substance use and substance use disorders among adolescents and young adults within the United States. We also presented developmental frameworks for SUDs and discussed the interrelated effects of biological, psychological, and sociological factors on the onset and maintenance of alcohol- and drug-related pathology. Further, we highlighted empirically supported treatments established for this clinical population.

Further Reading

Hawkins, J. D., Catalano, R. F., & Miller, J. Y. (1992). Risk and protective factors for alcohol and other drug problems in adolescence and early adulthood: Implications for substance abuse prevention. *Psychological Bulletin*, *112*, 64–105. doi: 10.1037/0033-2909.112.1.64.

Hogue, A., Henderson, C. E., Becker, S. J., & Knight, D. K. (2018). Evidence based on outpatient behavioral treatments for adolescent substance use, 2014–2017: Outcomes, treatment delivery, and promising horizons. *Journal of Clinical Child and Adolescent Psychology*, *47*, 499–526. doi: 10.1080/15374416.2018.1466307.

Khoddam, R., Jackson, N. J., & Leventhal, A. M. (2016). Internalizing symptoms and conduct problems: Redundant, incremental, or interactive risk factors for adolescent substance use during the first year of high school? *Drug and Alcohol Dependence*, *169*, 48–55. doi: 10.1016/j.drugalcdep.2016.10.007.

Discussion/Essay Questions

1. What are some ways in which parents may attempt to foster resilience in their children to combat social and interpersonal risk factors related to the development of substance use?
2. How does the Brain Disease Model of Addiction account for the development of substance use disorders? Is it effective as an explanation that might increase support for rehabilitation and treatment? Why or why not?

3. Based on the biological and genetic risk factors discussed in this chapter, describe who would be the most at risk for an adolescent substance use disorder. What environmental factors would decrease this person's risk?
4. Thinking back to the clinical case vignette at the start of this chapter, explain which developmental psychopathology model might best explain why this adolescent has developed a substance use disorder.

Glossary of Terms

30-Day prevalence is the proportion of a given population that has exhibited a disorder (or behavior; e.g., substance use) over a specified period of 30 days.

Addiction is a severe form of substance use characterized by a chronic, physiological dependency involving processes of reward seeking and relief.

Behavioral family-based treatment is an intervention approach that focuses on decreasing substance use by using behavioral principles such as reinforcement and punishment while concurrently working with a youth and their caregivers/family members.

Brain disease model of addiction is the perspective that addiction develops as a chronic, relapsing disease of the brain and is maintained by neurobiological changes at the structural, functional, molecular, and cellular levels, which in turn interfere with one's ability to obtain and maintain sobriety.

Bronfrenbrenner's ecological systems theory is a theoretical framework proposed by Urie Bronfrenbrenner that conceptualizes an individual's functioning within the context of multiple, interacting, environmental systems.

Cognitive-behavioral therapy is a psychological treatment approach that targets maladaptive thought and behavior patterns contributing to the maintenance of substance use.

Contingency management is an approach to decreasing substance use that incorporates motivational incentives (e.g., monetary prizes) rewarding desired behaviors such as treatment attendance and clean drug tests.

Ecological family-based treatment is a systems-focused treatment approach that implements services with families in order to address problematic family dynamics and address external systems such as school in a coordinated fashion to decrease adolescent substance use.

Emotional dysregulation is a pattern of difficulty in the ability to control or manage the experience of emotions.

Equifinality is the principle that different combinations of risk and protective factors can result in the same outcome (e.g., pathology) and that there is not a singular, unique, developmental course for a given disorder.

Executive cognitive functioning is the planning, initiation, and regulation of goal-oriented behavior.

Family system is conceptualization of the family as a singular unit, whose influences act in a bidirectional manner on one another, rather than in isolation.

Hypothalamus-pituitary-adrenal (HPA) axis is the pathway of the brain that connects the hypothalamus, pituitary gland, and adrenal glands and is important for reactions to stress and other bodily processes.

Iatrogenic is illness caused by treatment or diagnostic evaluation.

Lifetime prevalence is the proportion of a given population that has exhibited a disorder (or behavior; e.g., substance use) at some point in their lifetime.

Mesolimbic pathway is also known as the reward system, the connection between the ventral tegmental area to the ventral striatum that requires dopamine.

Motivational enhancement therapy is an intervention approach that reinforces internal motivations for behavior change in order to assist individuals with overcoming feelings of ambivalence about discontinuing substance use.

Multifinality is the principle that identical sets of risk and protective factors can lead to different outcomes over development, with no predetermined end point or course associated with specific factors.

Negative urgency is the impulsivity that occurs in response to the experience of negative emotions.

Neurobehavioral disinhibition is a pattern of psychological functioning that consists of a lack of behavioral control, dysregulation of emotions, and low executive cognitive functioning.

Neuroticism is a personality trait characterized by a tendency to experience negative mood states.

Placebo is a treatment that has no therapeutic effect and is used as a control for extraneous factors in treatment evaluation research.

Self-medication hypothesis is a theory that individuals may engage in substance use as a means to relieve emotional distress.

Substance abuse is a former diagnostic category of problematic substance use recognized by the American Psychological Association that represented a mild form of disordered use.

Substance dependence is a former diagnostic category of problematic substance use recognized by the American Psychological Association that represented a moderate to severe form of disordered use.

Temperament is an individual's nature, or psychological disposition.

Tolerance is a symptom of substance use disorders characterized by either (a) the need for a markedly increased dose of the substance to achieve the desired effect or (b) a markedly reduced effect when the usual dose is consumed.

Twin studies are those conducted on identical or fraternal twins with the purpose of examining the role of genes and environment on disorders or traits.

Withdrawal is a syndrome that consists of substance-specific problematic behavioral change, with physiological and cognitive features, that is due to the cessation of, or reduction in, heavy and prolonged substance use.

References

American Psychiatric Association (2000). *Diagnostic and statistical manual of mental disorders* (4th ed., text rev.). Arlington, VA: American Psychiatric Publishing.

American Psychiatric Association (2013). *Diagnostic and statistical manual of mental disorders* (5th ed.). Arlington, VA: American Psychiatric Publishing.

American Society of Addiction Medicine (2011). Public policy statement: Definition of addiction. Retrieved from: http://www.asam.org/docs/default-source/publicpolicy-statements/1definition_of_addiction_short_4-11.pdf?sfvrsn=0.

Arcos-Burgos, M., Vélez, J. I., Martinez, A. F., Ribasés, M., Ramos-Quiroga, J. A., Sánchez-Mora, C., & Muenke, M. (2019). ADGRL3 (LPHN3) variants predict substance use disorder. *Translational Psychiatry*, *9*(1), 42. doi: 10.1038/s41398-019-0396-7.

Barbieri, N., Clipper, S. J., Narvey, C., Rude, A., Craig, J. M., & Piquero, N. L. (2019). Assessing general strain theory and measures of victimization, 2002–2018. *Aggression and Violent Behavior*, *49*, 1–12. doi: 10.1016/j.avb.2019.06.005.

Barlow, D. H., Ellard, K. K., Sauer-Zavala, S., Bullis, J. R., & Carl, J. R. (2014). The origins of neuroticism. *Perspectives on Psychological Science*, *9*(5), 481–496. doi: 10.1177/1745691614544528.

Blum, K., Sheridan, P. J., Wood, R. C., Braverman, E. R., Chen, T. J., Cull, J. G., & Comings, D. E. (1996). The D2 dopamine receptor gene as a determinant of reward deficiency syndrome. *Journal of the Royal Society of Medicine*, *89*(7), 396–400. doi: 10.1177/014107689608900711.

Brechting, E. H., & Giancola, P. R. (2007). A longitudinal study of coping strategies and substance use in adolescent boys. *Journal of Child & Adolescent Substance Abuse*, *16*(2), 51–67. doi: 10.1300/J029v16n02_03.

Bronfenbrenner, U. (1977). Toward an experimental ecology of human development. *American Psychologist*, *32*(7), 513–531. doi: 10.1037/0003-066X.32.7.513.

Bronfenbrenner, U. (1979). *The ecology of human development*. Cambridge, MA: Harvard University Press.

Brook, J. S., Balka, E. B., Crossman, A. M., Dermatis, H., Galanter, M. & Brook, D. W. (2010). The relationship between parental alcohol use, early and late adolescent alcohol use, and young adult psychological symptoms: A longitudinal study. *American Journal on Addictions*, *19*(6), 534–542. doi: 10.1111/j.1521-0391.2010.00083.x.

Bryant-Ludden, A., & Eccles, J. S. (2007). Psychosocial, motivational, and contextual profiles of youth reporting different patterns of substance use during adolescence. *Journal of Research on Adolescence*, *17*(1), 51–88. doi: 10.1111/j.1532-7795.2007.00512.x.

Carver, H., Elliott, L., Kennedy, C., & Hanley, J. (2017). Parent–child connectedness and communication in relation to alcohol, tobacco and drug use in adolescence: An integrative review of the literature. *Drugs: Education, Prevention & Policy*, *24*(2), 119–133. doi: 10.1080/09687637.2016.1221060.

Centers for Disease Control and Prevention (2018). Youth risk behavior survey—United States, 2017. *Data Summary & Trends Report, 2007–2017*, pp, 1–91.

Chassin, L., Colder, C. R., Hussong, A., & Sher, K. J. (2016). Substance use and substance use disorders. In D. Cicchetti (Ed.), *Developmental psychopathology* (pp. 833–897). New York, NY: John Wiley & Sons, Inc.

Cheng, T. C., & Lo, C. C. (2017). Social risk and protective factors in adolescents' reduction and cessation of alcohol use. *Substance Use & Misuse*, *52*(7), 916–928. doi: 10.1080/10826084.2016.1267220.

Colder, C. R., Hawk Jr., L. W., Lengua, L. J., Wiezcorek, W., Eiden, R. D., & Read, J. P. (2013). Trajectories of reinforcement sensitivity during adolescence and risk for substance use. *Journal of Research on*

Adolescence, *23*(2), 345–356. doi: 10.1111/jora.12001.

Collins, F. S., Koroshetz, W. J., & Volkow, N. D. (2018). Helping to end addiction over the long-term: The research plan for the NIH HEAL Initiative. *JAMA*, *320*(2), 129–130. doi: 10.1001/jama.2018.8826.

Committee on Substance Use (2016). Medication-assisted treatment of adolescents with opioid use disorders. *Pediatrics*, *138*(3). 1–4. doi: 10.1542/peds.2016-1893.

Conway, K. P., Swendsen, J., Husky, M. M., He, J., & Merikangas, K. R. (2016). Association of lifetime mental disorders and subsequent alcohol and illicit drug use: Results from the National Comorbidity Survey–Adolescent Supplement. *Journal of the American Academy of Child and Adolescent Psychiatry*, *55*(4), 280–288. doi: 10.1016/j.jaac.2016.01.006.

Cope, L. M., Martz, M. E., Hardee, J. E., Zucker, R. A., & Heitzeg, M. M. (2019). Reward activation in childhood predicts adolescent substance use initiation in a high-risk sample. *Drug and Alcohol Dependence*, *194*, 318–325. doi: 10.1016/j.drugalcdep.2018.11.003.

Dastgerdi, Z. F., & Eslami, A. A. (2018). The relationship between social influences and adolescents' substance use-related cognitions. *Journal of Substance Use*, *23*(3), 268–273. https://doi-org.ezproxy.shsu.edu/10.1080/14659891.2017.1394377.

Dishion, T. J., Spracklen, K. M., Andrews, D. W., & Patterson, G. R. (1996). Deviancy training in male adolescent friendships. *Behavior Therapy*, *27*, 373–390. doi: 10.1016/S0005-7894(96)80023-2.

Dodge, K. A., Dishion, T. J., & Lansford, J. E. (2006). Deviant peer influences in intervention and public policy for youth. *Social Policy Report*, *20*(1), 1–20. doi: 10.1002/j.2379-3988.2006.tb00046.x.

Egan, K. L., Gregory, E., Osborne, V. L., & Cottler, L. B. (2019). Power of the peer and parent: Gender differences, norms, and nonmedical prescription opioid use among adolescents in south central Kentucky. *Prevention Science*, *20*(5), 665–673.

Ennett, S. T., Flewelling, R. L., Lindrooth, R. C., & Norton, E. C. (1997). School and neighborhood characteristics associated with school rates of alcohol, cigarette, and marijuana use. *Journal of Health and Social Behavior*, *38*(1), 55–71. Retrieved from: www.jstor.org/stable/2955361.

Fagan, A. A., Wright, E. M., & Pinchevsky, G. M. (2015). A multi-level analysis of the impact of neighborhood structural and social factors on adolescent substance use. *Drug and Alcohol Dependence*, *153*, 180–186. doi: 10.1016/j.drugalcdep.2015.05.022.

Faggiano, F., Minozzi, S., Versino, E., & Buscemi, D. (2014). Universal school-based prevention for illicit drug use. *Cochrane Database of Systematic Reviews, 12*, Art. No.: CD003020. doi: 10.1002/14651858.CD003020.pub3.

Fuhrmann, D., Knoll, L. J., & Blakemore, S. J. (2015). Adolescence as a sensitive period of brain development. *Trends in Cognitive Sciences*, *19*(10), 558–566. doi: 10.1016/j.tics.2015.07.008.

Furr-Holden, C. D. M., Lee, M. H., Johnson, R., Milam, A. J., Duncan, A., Reboussin, B. A., & Ialongo, N. S. (2015). Neighborhood environment and marijuana use in urban young adults. *Prevention Science*, *16*(2), 268–278. doi: 10.1007/s11121-014-0497-8.

Gaither, J. R., Shabanova, V., & Leventhal, J. M. (2018). US national trends in pediatric deaths from prescription and illicit opioids, 1999-2016. *JAMA Network Open*, *1*(8), e186558-e186558.

Gerra, G., Garofano, L., Castaldini, L., Rovetto, F., Zaimovic, A., Moi, G., & Donnini, C. (2005). Serotonin transporter promoter polymorphism genotype is associated with temperament, personality traits and illegal drugs use among adolescents. *Journal of Neural Transmission*, *112*(10), 1397–1410. doi: 10.1007/s00702-004-0268-y.

Giancola, P. R., Martin, C., Tarter, R. E., Pelham, W. E., & Moss, H. B. (1995). Executive cognitive functioning and aggressive behavior in preadolescent boys at high risk for substance abuse/dependence. *Journal of Studies on Alcohol*, *57*(4), 352–359. doi: 10.15288/jsa.1996.57.352

Giancola, P. R., & Mezzich, A. C. (2003). Executive functioning, temperament, and drug use involvement in adolescent females with a substance use disorder. *Journal of Child Psychology & Psychiatry & Allied Disciplines*, *44*(6), 857–866. doi: 10.1111/1469-7610.00170.

Giancola, P. R., Mezzich, A. C., & Tarter, R. E. (1998). Executive cognitive functioning, temperament, and antisocial behavior in conduct-disordered adolescent females. *Journal of Abnormal Psychology*, *107*(4), 629.

Giancola, P. R., & Tarter, R. E. (1999). Executive cognitive functioning and risk for substance use. *Psychological Science*, *10*(3), 203–205. doi: 10.1111/1467-9280.00135.

Gillen, C. T. A., Barry, C. T., & Bater, L. R. (2016). Anxiety symptoms and coping motives: Examining a potential path to substance use-related problems in adolescents with psychopathic traits. *Substance Use & Misuse*, *51*(14), 1920–1929. doi: 10.1080/10826084.2016.1201510.

Haller, M., Handley, E., Chassin, L., & Bountress, K. (2010). Developmental cascades: Linking adolescent substance use, affiliation with substance use promoting peers, and academic achievement to adult substance use disorders. *Development and Psychopathology*, *22*(4), 899–916. doi: 10.1017/S0954579410000532.

Han, C., McGue, M. K., & Iacono, W. G. (1999). Lifetime tobacco, alcohol and other substance use in adolescent Minnesota twins: Univariate and multivariate behavioral genetic analyses. *Addiction*, *94*(7), 981–993. doi: 10.1046/j.1360-0443.1999.9479814.x.

Handley, E. D., Rogosch, F. A., Guild, D. J., & Cicchetti, D. (2015). Neighborhood disadvantage and adolescent substance use disorder: The moderating role of maltreatment. *Child Maltreatment*, *20*(3), 193–202. doi: 10.1177/1077559515584159.

Heerde, J. A., & Hemphill, S. A. (2018). Examination of associations between informal help-seeking behavior, social support, and adolescent psychosocial outcomes: A meta-analysis. *Developmental Review*, *47*, 44–62. doi: 10.1016/j.dr.2017.10.001.

Hogue, A., Henderson, C. E., Ozechowski, T. J., & Robbins, M. S. (2014). Evidence base on outpatient behavioral treatments for adolescent substance use: Updates and recommendations 2007–2013. *Journal of Clinical Child and Adolescent Psychology*, *43*, 697–720. doi: 10.1080/15374416.2014.915550.

Hogue, A., Henderson, C. E., Becker, S. J., & Knight, D. K. (2018). Evidence base on outpatient behavioral treatments for adolescent substance use, 2014–2017: Outcomes, treatment delivery, and promising horizons. *Journal of Clinical Child and Adolescent Psychology*, *47*, 499–526. doi: 10.1080/15374416.2018.1466307.

Hogue, A., Henderson, C. E., Ozechowski, T., J., Becker, S. J., & Coatsworth, J. D. (2019). Can the group harm the individual? Examining potential iatrogenic effects of group treatment for adolescent substance use. *Clinical Psychology: Science and Practice*. doi: 10.1111/cpsp.12307.

Hopfer, C. J., Crowley, T. J., & Hewitt, J. K. (2003). Review of twin and adoption studies of adolescent substance use. *Journal of the American Academy of Child & Adolescent Psychiatry*, *42*(6), 710–719. doi: 10.1097/01.CHI.0000046848.56865.54.

Hurd, Y. L., Michaelides, M., Miller, M. L., & Jutras-Aswad, D. (2014). Trajectory of adolescent cannabis use on addiction vulnerability. *Neuropharmacology*, *76*, 416–424. doi:10.1016/j.neuropharm.2013.07.028.

Iacono, W. G., Malone, S. M., & McGue, M. (2003). Substance use disorders, externalizing psychopathology, and P300 event-related potential amplitude. *International Journal of Psychophysiology*, *48*(2), 147–178. doi: 10.1016/S0167-8760(03)00052-7.

Jensen, M., Chassin, L., & Gonzales, N. A. (2017). Neighborhood moderation of sensation seeking effects on adolescent substance use initiation. *Journal of Youth and Adolescence*, *46*(9), 1953–1967. doi: 10.1007/s10964-017-0647-y.

Johnston, L. D., Miech, R. A., O'Malley, P. M., Bachman, J. G., Schulenberg, J. E., & Patrick, M. E. (2019). *Monitoring the future national survey results on drug use, 1975–2018: Overview, key findings on adolescent drug use*. Ann Arbor, MI: Institute for Social Research, University of Michigan.

Keyes, K. M., Brady, J. E., & Li, G. (2015). Effects of minimum legal drinking age on alcohol and marijuana use: Evidence from toxicological testing data for fatally injured drivers aged 16 to 25 years. *Injury Epidemiology*, *2*(1), 1–10. doi: 10.1186/s40621-014-0032-1.

Khantzian, E. J. (1997). The self-medication hypothesis of substance use disorders: A reconsideration and recent applications. *Harvard Review of Psychiatry*, *4*, 231–244. doi: 10.3109/10673229709030550.

King, S. M., Iacono, W. G., & McGue, M. (2004). Childhood externalizing and internalizing psychopathology in the prediction of early substance use. *Addiction*, *99*(12), 1548–1559.doi:10.1111/j.1360-0443.2004.00893.x.

Kirisci, L., Tarter, R., Ridenour, T., Reynolds, M., Horner, M., & Vanyukov, M. (2015). Externalizing behavior and emotion dysregulation are indicators of transmissible risk for substance use disorder. *Addictive Behaviors*, *42*, 57–62. doi: 10.1016/j.addbeh.2014.10.028.

Khoddam, R., Jackson, N. J., & Leventhal, A. M. (2016). Internalizing symptoms and conduct problems: Redundant, incremental, or interactive risk factors for adolescent substance use during the first year of high school? *Drug and Alcohol Dependence*, *169*, 48–55. doi: 10.1016/j.drugalcdep.2016.10.007.

Knight, J. R., Shrier, L. A., Bravender, T. D., Farrell, M., Vander Bilt, J., & Shaffer, H. J. (1999). A new brief screen for adolescent substance abuse. *Archives of Pediatrics & Adolescent Medicine*, *153*, 591–596.

Koob, G. F., & Volkow, N. D. (2010). Neurocircuitry of addiction. *Neuropsychopharmacology*, *35*, 217–238. doi: 10.1038/npp.2009.110.

Kreek, M. J., Nielsen, D. A., Butelman, E. R., & LaForge, K. S. (2005). Genetic influences on impulsivity, risk taking, stress responsivity and vulnerability to drug abuse and addiction. *Nature Neuroscience*, *8*(11), 1450. doi: 10.1038/nn1583.

Lansford, J. E., Erath, S., Yu, T., Pettit, G. S., Dodge, K. A., & Bates, J. E. (2008). The developmental course of illicit substance use from age 12 to 22: Links with depressive, anxiety, and behavior disorders at age 18. *Journal of Child Psychology and Psychiatry*, *49*(8), 877–885. doi: 10.1111/j.1469-7610.2008.01915.x.

Lee, J. O., Cho, J., Yoon, Y., Bello, M. S., Khoddam, R., & Leventhal, A. M. (2018). Developmental pathways from parental socioeconomic status to adolescent substance use: Alternative and complementary reinforcement. *Journal of Youth and Adolescence*, *47*(2), 334–348. doi: 10.1007/s10964-017-0790-5.

Lee, J. O., Jones, T. M., Kosterman, R., Rhew, I. C., Lovasi, G. S., Hill, K. G., & Hawkins, J. D. (2017). The association of unemployment from age 21 to 33 with substance use disorder symptoms at age 39: The role of childhood neighborhood characteristics. *Drug and Alcohol Dependence*, *174*, 1–8. doi: 10.1016/j.drugalcdep.2017.01.005.

Lee, Y., & Kim, J. (2017). Developmental patterns of substance use by gender and their relation to individual, parental, and peer factors. *Criminal Justice and Behavior*, *44*(11), 1413–1443. doi: 10.1177/0093854817717291.

Leshner, A. I. (1997). Addiction is a brain disease, and it matters. *Science*, *278*(5335), 45–47.

Levy, S. J. L., & Williams, J. F. (2016). Substance use screening, brief intervention, and referral to treatment. *Pediatrics*, *138*(1), e20161211. doi: 10.1542/peds.2016-1211.

Li, D., Zhao, H., & Gelernter, J. (2012). Strong protective effect of the aldehyde dehydrogenase gene (ALDH2) 504lys (* 2) allele against alcoholism and alcohol-induced medical diseases in Asians. *Human Genetics*, *131*(5), 725–737. doi: 10.1007/s00439-011-1116-4.

Liddle, H. A. (2000). Multidimensional Family Therapy for adolescent cannabis users. *Cannabis Youth Treatment (CYT) series: Vol. 5*. Rockville, MD: Center for Substance Use Treatment, Substance

Abuse and Mental Health Services Administration.

Liu, M., Jiang, Y., Wedow, R., Li, Y., Brazel, D. M., Chen, F., & Vrieze, S. (2019). Association studies of up to 1.2 million individuals yield new insights into thc genetic etiology of tobacco and alcohol use. *Nature Genetics*, *51*(2), 237–244.

Löfving-Gupta, S., Willebrand, M., Koposov, R., Blatný, M., Hrdlička, M., Schwab-Stone, M., & Ruchkin, V. (2018). Community violence exposure and substance use: Cross-cultural and gender perspectives. *European Child & Adolescent Psychiatry*, *27*(4), 493–500. doi: 10.1007/s00787-017-1097-5.

Lubman, D. I., Yücel, M., & Hall, W. D. (2007). Substance use and the adolescent brain: A toxic combination? *Journal of Psychopharmacology*, *21*(8), 792–794.

Maes, H. H., Woodard, C. E., Murrelle, L., Meyer, J. M., Silberg, J. L., Hewitt, J. K., & Neale, M. C. (1999). Tobacco, alcohol and drug use in eight- to sixteen-year-old twins: The Virginia twin study of adolescent behavioral development. *Journal of Studies on Alcohol*, *60*(3), 293–305. doi: 10.15288/jsa.1999.60.293.

Mason, M. J., & Mennis, J. (2010). An exploratory study of the effects of neighborhood characteristics on adolescent substance use. *Addiction Research & Theory*, *18*(1), 33–50.

McConnell, M. M., Memetovic, J., & Richardson, C. G. (2014). Coping style and substance use intention and behavior patterns in a cohort of BC adolescents. *Addictive Behaviors*, *39*(10), 1394–1397. doi: 10.1016/j.addbeh.2014.05.018.

McGue, M., Elkins, I., & Iacono, W. G. (2000). Genetic and environmental influences on adolescent substance use and abuse. *American Journal of Medical Genetics*, *96*(5), 671–677. doi: 10.1002/1096-8628(20001009)96:5<671::AID-AJMG14>3.0.CO;2-W.

Merikangas, K. R., He., J., Burstein, M., Swanson, S. A., Avenevoli, S., Cui, L., Benjet, C., Georgiades, K., & Swendsen, J. (2010). Lifetime prevalence of mental disorders in U.S. adolescents: Results from the National Comorbidity Survey Replication—Adolescent Supplement (NCS-A). *Journal of the American Academy of Child & Adolescent Psychiatry*, *49*(10), 980–989.

Min, M. O., Minnes, S., Park, H., Ridenour, T., Kim, J.-Y., Yoon, M., & Singer, L. T. (2018). Developmental trajectories of externalizing behavior from ages 4 to 12: Prenatal cocaine exposure and adolescent correlates. *Drug and Alcohol Dependence*, *192*, 223–232.

Minozzi, S., Amato, L., Bellisario, C., & Davoli, M. (2014). Maintenance treatments for opiate-dependent adolescents. *Cochrane Database of Systematic Reviews*. doi: 10.1002/14651858.CD007210.pub3.

Monti, P. M., Miranda Jr, R., Nixon, K., Sher, K. J., Swartzwelder, H. S., Tapert, S. F., & Crews, F. T. (2005). Adolescence: Booze, brains, and behavior. *Alcoholism: Clinical and Experimental Research*, *29*(2), 207–220. doi: 10.1097/01.ALC.0000153551.11000.F3.

Morse, S. J. (2004). Medicine and morals, craving and compulsion. *Substance Use & Misuse*, *39*(3), 437–460. doi: 10.1081/JA-120029985.

Muchiri, B. M., & dos Santos, M. (2018). Family management risk and protective factors for adolescent substance use in South Africa. *Substance Abuse Treatment, Prevention, and Policy*, *13*(24), 1–10. doi: 10.1186/s13011-018-0163-4.

National Center on Addiction and Substance Abuse (2011). *Adolescent substance use: America's #1 public health problem*. New York, NY: The National Center on Addiction and Substance Abuse. Retrieved from: http://www.centeronaddiction.org/addiction-research/reports/adolescent-substance-use.

National Institute on Drug Abuse (2016). *Drug facts: Understanding drug use and addiction*. Retrieved from: https://www.drugabuse.gov/publications/drugfacts/understanding-drug-use-addiction.

Obando, D., Trujillo, A., & Trujillo, C. A. (2014). Substance use and antisocial behavior in adolescents: The role of family and peer-individual risk and protective factors. *Substance Use & Misuse*, *49*(14), 1934–1944. doi: 10.3109/10826084.2014.956365.

Oshri, A., Kogan, S. M., Kwon, J. A., Wickrama, K. A. S., Vanderbroek, L., Palmer, A. A., & MacKillop, J. (2018). Impulsivity as a mechanism linking child abuse and neglect with substance use in adolescence and adulthood. *Development and Psychopathology*, *30*(2), 417–435. doi: 10.1017/S0954579417000943.

Pereyra, S. B., & Bean, R. A. (2017). Latino adolescent substance use: A mediating model of inter-parental conflict, deviant peer associations, and parenting. *Children and Youth Services Review*, *76*, 154–162. doi: 10.1016/j.childyouth.2017.03.001.

Pilowsky, D. J., & Wu, L-T. (2013). Screening instruments for substance use and brief interventions targeting adolescents in primary care: A literature review. *Addictive Behaviors*, *38*, 2146–2153. doi: 10.1016/j.addbeh.2013.01.015.

Poon, J. A., Turpyn, C. C., Hansen, A., Jacangelo, J., & Chaplin, T. M. (2016). Adolescent substance use & psychopathology: Interactive effects of cortisol reactivity and emotion regulation. *Cognitive Therapy and Research*, *40*(3), 368–380.

Rusby, J. C., Light, J. M., Crowley, R., & Westling, E. (2018). Influence of parent–youth relationship, parental monitoring, and parent substance use on adolescent substance use onset. *Journal of Family Psychology*, *32*(3), 310–320. doi: 10.1037/fam0000350.

Ryan, S. M., Jorm, A. F., & Lubman, D. I. (2010). Parenting factors associated with reduced adolescent alcohol use: A systematic review of longitudinal studies. *Australian & New Zealand Journal of Psychiatry*, *44*(9), 774–783. doi: 10.1080/00048674.2010.501759.

Scalco, M. D., Colder, C. R., Hawk, L. W., Jr., Read, J. P., Wieczorek, W. F., & Lengua, L. J. (2014). Internalizing and externalizing problem behavior and early adolescent substance use: A test of a latent variable interaction and conditional indirect effects. *Psychology of Addictive Behaviors*, *28*(3), 828–840. doi: 10.1037/a0035805.

Schmid, B., Blomeyer, D., Becker, K., Treutlein, J., Zimmermann, U. S., Buchmann, A. F., & Laucht, M. (2009). Genetic study: The interaction between the dopamine transporter gene and age at onset in relation to tobacco and alcohol use among 19-year-olds. *Addiction Biology*, *14*(4), 489–499. doi: 10.1111/j.1369-1600.2009.00171.x.

Schwinn, T. M., Schinke, S. P., Hopkins, J., & Thom, B. (2016). Risk and protective factors associated with adolescent girls' substance use: Data from a nationwide Facebook sample. *Substance Abuse*, *37*(4), 564–570. doi: 10.1080/08897077.2016.1154495.

Skeer, M., McCormick, M. C., Normand, S-L. T., Buka, S. L., Gilman, S. E. (2009). A prospective study of familial conflict, psychological stress, and the development of substance use disorders in adolescence. *Drug and Alcohol Dependence*, *104*, 65–72.

Stone, A. L., Becker, L. G., Huber, A. M., & Catalano, R. F. (2012). Review of risk and protective factors of substance use and problem use in emerging adulthood. *Addictive Behaviors*, *37*(7), 747–775. doi: 10.1016/j.addbeh.2012.02.014.

Stumper, A., Olino, T. M., Abramson, L. Y., & Alloy, L. B. (2019). Pubertal timing and substance use in adolescence: An investigation of two cognitive moderators. *Journal of Abnormal Child Psychology*, *47*(9), 1509–1520. doi: 10.1007/s10802-019-00524-7.

Subramaniam, G. A., Fishman, M. J., & Woody, G. (2009). Treatment of opioid-dependent adolescents and young adults with buprenorphine. *Current Psychiatry Reports*, *11*(5), 360–363.

Substance Abuse and Mental Health Services Administration (2014). *Discharges from substance abuse treatment services*. Treatment Episode Data Set (TEDS): 2011. BHSIS Series S-70, HHS Publication No. (SMA) 14-4846. Rockville, MD: SAMHSA.

Substance Abuse and Mental Health Services Administration (2017). *About screening, brief intervention, and referral to treatment*

(SBIRT). Retrieved from: https://www.samhsa.gov/sbirt.

Substance Abuse and Mental Health Services Administration. (2019). *Key substance use and mental health indicators in the United States: Results from the 2018 National Survey on Drug Use and Health.* HHS Publication No. PEP19-5068, NSDUH Series H-54. Center for Behavioral Health Statistics and Quality, Substance Abuse and Mental Health Services Administration, Rockville, MD. Retrieved from: https://www.samhsa.gov/data/.

Tarter, R. E. (2002). Etiology of adolescent substance abuse: A developmental perspective. *American Journal on Addictions*, *11*(3), 171–191. doi: 10.1080/105504902900879.

Tarter, R. E., Kirisci, L., Habeych, M., Reynolds, M., & Vanyukov, M. (2004). Neurobehavior disinhibition in childhood predisposes boys to substance use disorder by young adulthood: Direct and mediated etiologic pathways. *Drug and Alcohol Dependence*, *73*, 121–132. doi: 10.1016/j.drugalcdep.2003.07.004.

Tripodi, S. J., Bender, K., Litschge, C., & Vaughn, M. G. (2010). Interventions for reducing adolescent alcohol abuse: A meta-analytic review. *Archives of Pediatrics & Adolescent Medicine*, *164*, 85–91. doi: 10.1001/archpediatrics.2009.235.

Van Ryzin, M. J., Fosco, G. M., & Dishion, T. J. (2012). Family and peer predictors of substance use from early adolescence to early adulthood: An 11-year prospective analysis. *Addictive Behaviors*, *37*(12), 1314–1324. doi: 10.1016/j.addbeh.2012.06.020.

Volkow, N. D., Frieden, T. R., Hyde, P. S., & Cha, S. S. (2014). Medication-assisted therapies—Tackling the opioid-overdose epidemic. *New England Journal of Medicine*, *370*(22), 2063–2066. doi: 10.1056/NEJMp1402780.

Volkow, N. D., Koob, G. F., & McLellan, A. T. (2016). Neurobiologic advances from the brain disease model of addiction. *The New England Journal of Medicine*, *374*(4), 363–371. doi: 10.1056/NEJMra1511480.

Volkow, N. D., Wang, G. J., Fowler, J. S., & Tomasi, D. (2012). Addiction circuitry in the human brain. *Annual Review of Pharmacology and Toxicology*, *52*, 321–336. doi: 10.1146/annurev-pharmtox-010611-134625.

Waldron, H. B., & Turner, C. W. (2008). Evidence-based psychosocial treatments for adolescent substance abuse. *Journal of Clinical Child and Adolescent Psychology*, *37*(1), 238–261.

Wall, T. L., Luczak, S. E., & Hiller-Sturmhöfel, S. (2016). Biology, genetics, and environment: Underlying factors influencing alcohol metabolism. *Alcohol Research: Current Reviews*, *38*(1), 59–68.

Warner, T. D. (2016). Up in smoke: Neighborhood contexts of marijuana use from adolescence through young adulthood. *Journal of Youth and Adolescence*, *45*(1), 35–53.

Wenner, A., & Gigli, K. H. (2016). Opioid addiction in adolescents: A background and policy brief. *Journal of Pediatric Health Care*, *30*(6), 606–609. doi: 10.1016/j.pedhc.2016.08.001.

Whaley, R. B., Hayes, R., & Smith, J. M. (2016). Differential reactions to school bonds, peers, and victimization in the case of adolescent substance use: The moderating effect of sex. *Crime & Delinquency*, *62*(10), 1263–1285. doi: 10.1177/0011128714541195.

White, W., & Miller, W. (2007). The use of confrontation in addiction treatment: History, science and time for change. *Counselor*, *8*(4), 12–30.

Wills, T. A., Sandy, J. M., Yaeger, A. M., Cleary, S. D., & Shinar, O. (2001). Coping dimensions, life stress, and adolescent substance use: A latent growth analysis. *Journal of Abnormal Psychology*, *110*(2), 309–323. doi: 10.1037/0021-843X.110.2.309.

Wills, T. A., & Yaeger, A. M. (2003). Family factors and adolescent substance use: Models and mechanisms. *Current Directions in Psychological Science*, *12*(6), 222–226.

Winters, K. C., & Kaminer, Y. (2008). Screening and assessing adolescent substance use disorders in clinical populations. *Journal of the American Academy of*

Child and Adolescent Psychiatry, *47*(7), 740–744. doi: 10.1097/CHI.0b013e31817395cf.

Wong, S. S., Zhou, B., Goebert, D., & Hishinuma, E. S. (2013). The risk of adolescent suicide across patterns of drug use: A nationally representative study of high school students in the United States from 1999 to 2009. *Social Psychiatry and Psychiatric Epidemiology*, *48*(10), 1611–1620. doi: 10.1007/s00127-013-0721-z.

Young, S. E., Friedman, N. P., Miyake, A., Willcutt, E. G., Corley, R. P., Haberstick, B. C., & Hewitt, J. K. (2009). Behavioral disinhibition: Liability for externalizing spectrum disorders and its genetic and environmental relation to response inhibition across adolescence. *Journal of Abnormal Psychology*, *118*(1), 117–130. doi: 10.1037/a0014657.

Yurasek, A. M., Brick, L., Nestor, B., Hernandez, L., Graves, H., & Spirito, A. (2019). The effects of parent, sibling and peer substance use on adolescent drinking behaviors. *Journal of Child and Family Studies*, *28*(1), 73–83. doi: 10.1007/s10826-018-1251-9.

Zapolski, T. C. B., Rowe, A. T., Fisher, S., Hensel, D. J., & Barnes-Najor, J. (2018). Peer victimization and substance use: Understanding the indirect effect of depressive symptomatology across gender. *Addictive Behaviors*, *84*, 160–166. doi: 10.1016/j.addbeh.2018.04.010.

Chapter 12

Schizophrenia

Amanda Venta and Jessica R. Hart

Chapter Overview

In this chapter, we focus on the etiology, correlates, and treatment of schizophrenia. Though we will review research on individuals who meet full diagnostic criteria for schizophrenia, the disorder is conceptualized as forming part of a *schizophrenia spectrum*, which contains disorders that have in common either hallucinations, delusions, or disorganized thinking, speech, or behavior.

Schizophrenia is typically a disorder associated with adults, but many of the symptoms first emerge in childhood, and risk and protective factors related to the emergence and course of schizophrenia are well studied in youth. Consider this case example, which describes the emergence of psychotic symptoms in late adolescence, a common presentation for developing schizophrenia.

Case study in schizophrenia

Brian is an 18-year-old who is living on campus during his freshman year of college. Brian earned high grades in early high school and, despite a decline during his senior year, he was admitted to a competitive college. During his first semester, Brian's grades were low and his parents noticed increasingly odd behavior during visits. They noticed he did not acknowledge making any friends at college. During the spring semester, Brian's roommate contacted Brian's parents to let them know he had stopped speaking, rarely left the apartment, ate little, and seemed really "worried." Brian's parents encouraged

Developmental Psychopathology, First Edition. Edited by Amanda Venta, Carla Sharp, Jack M. Fletcher, and Peter Fonagy.

him to see the campus psychiatrist, who discovered Brian was preoccupied with what he described as the "certain decline of the US to foreign spies living among us." Brian shared his beliefs that he was being targeted by these spies with poisoned foods and video surveillance, and that they were removing thoughts from his mind, leading to the behaviors his roommate reported.

As the clinician seeing this family, discuss possible diagnoses you would give Brian and supporting evidence for each differential diagnosis. What other information would you gather during an assessment to guide diagnosis and treatment of Brian's behaviors?

Definition, Diagnosis, and Clinical Features

Schizophrenia is a severe, persistent mental disorder characterized by *positive symptoms*, *negative symptoms*, and/or disorganized speech or behavior. Delusions and hallucinations are positive symptoms—experiences individuals with schizophrenia have that others do not have. The diagnosis also requires significant impairment and a persistent course that isn't better explained by drugs or another disorder. Table 12.1 describes the specific diagnostic criteria for schizophrenia in the DSM-5 and other diagnostic systems.

The DSM-5 defines *delusions* as "fixed beliefs that are not amenable to change in light of conflicting evidence (American Psychiatric Association, 2013). An individual with a delusion may hang on to a belief with conviction, despite contrary evidence. Common delusions in schizophrenia are persecutory (concern about impending harm), referential (perceptions that gestures or messages are being directed to the individual), grandiose (exceptional abilities), and erotomanic (erroneous belief that someone is in love with the individual). Somatic delusions, in which the individual is preoccupied with their health, are also sometimes present.

Hallucinations are perceptive experiences, rather than thoughts. Patients with schizophrenia describe seeing (visual hallucinations), hearing (auditory), feeling (tactile), smelling (olfactory), and/or tasting (gustatory) things that are not present. Hallucinations require occurrence without an external stimulus and when the individual is in a lucid state, so experiences that only occur while falling asleep, waking up, using drugs, or running a high fever may not qualify (APA, 2013). Hallucinations are often religious or spiritual, such as hearing God's voice or seeing angels. It can be difficult to discern whether these are psychotic hallucinations or culturally/religiously normative experiences.

Negative symptoms are things that are present for most people but absent in an individual with schizophrenia, such as reduced facial expressions, eye contact, speech intonation, and motivation (avolition).

TABLE 12.1 Schizophrenia as Defined by the DSM-5, ICD-11, and the Dimensional ASEBA Scales

DSM 5	*ICD-11*	*ASEBA*
A. Two (or more) of the following, each present for a significant portion of time during a 1-month period (or less if successfully treated). At least one of these must be (1), (2), or (3): 1. Delusions. 2. Hallucinations. 3. Disorganized speech (e.g., frequent derailment or incoherence). 4. Grossly disorganized or catatonic behavior. 5. Negative symptoms (i.e., diminished emotional expression or avolition). B. For a significant portion of the time since the onset of the disturbance, the level of functioning in one or more major areas, such as work, interpersonal relations, or self-care, is markedly below the level achieved prior to the onset (or when the onset is in childhood or adolescence, there is failure to achieve the expected level of interpersonal, academic, or occupational functioning). C. Continuous signs of the disturbance persist for at least 6 months. This 6-month period must include at least 1 month of symptoms (or less if successfully treated) that meet Criterion A (i.e., active-phase symptoms) and may include periods of prodromal or residual symptoms. During these prodromal or residual periods, the signs of the disturbance may be manifested by only negative symptoms or by two or more symptoms listed in Criterion A present in an attenuated form (e.g., odd beliefs, unusual perceptual experiences).	Schizophrenia is characterized by disturbances in multiple mental modalities, including thinking (e.g., delusions, disorganization in the form of thought), perception (e.g., hallucinations), self-experience (e.g., the experience that one's feelings, impulses, thoughts, or behavior are under the control of an external force), cognition (e.g., impaired attention, verbal memory, and social cognition), volition (e.g., loss of motivation), affect (e.g., blunted emotional expression), and behavior (e.g., behavior that appears bizarre or purposeless, unpredictable or inappropriate emotional responses that interfere with the organization of behavior). Psychomotor disturbances, including catatonia, may be present. Persistent delusions, persistent hallucinations, thought disorder, and experiences of influence, passivity, or control are considered core symptoms. Symptoms must have persisted for at least one month in order for a diagnosis of schizophrenia to be assigned. The symptoms are not a manifestation of another health condition (e.g., a brain tumor) and are not due to the effect of a substance or medication on the central nervous system (e.g., corticosteroids), including withdrawal (e.g., alcohol withdrawal).	**Ages 1.5–5 Years** • Not included **Ages 6–18 Years** **Thought Problems** • Can't get mind off certain thoughts • Harms self • Hears things • Twitches • Picks skin • Plays with own sex parts in public • Plays with own sex parts too much • Repeats acts • Sees things • Sleeps less • Stores up too many things he/she doesn't need • Strange behavior • Strange ideas • Sleep walk • Sleep problems

(Continued)

TABLE 12.1 (Continued)

DSM 5	*ICD-11*	*ASEBA*
D. Schizoaffective disorder and depressive or bipolar disorder with psychotic features have been ruled out because either (1) no major depressive or manic episodes have occurred concurrently with the active-phase symptoms or (2) if mood episodes have occurred during active-phase symptoms, they have been present for a minority of the total duration of the active and residual periods of the illness. E. The disturbance is not attributable to the physiological effects of a substance (e.g., a drug of abuse, a medication) or another medical condition. F. If there is a history of autism spectrum disorder or a communication disorder of childhood onset, the additional diagnosis of schizophrenia is made only if prominent delusions or hallucinations, in addition to the other required symptoms of schizophrenia, are also present for at least 1 month (or less if successfully treated).		

It is also common for individuals with schizophrenia to experience loss of pleasure in things they once enjoyed (anhedonia) or lack of interest in social interactions (asociality). Negative symptoms often persist even after the positive symptoms have been successfully treated (APA, 2013).

Finally, individuals with schizophrenia are likely to experience disorganized speech and behavior. A patient with *disorganized speech* may move from one topic to another in a manner that is hard to follow. It can be difficult for them to communicate their thoughts and experiences, and the quality of the voice can be somewhat unusual (e.g., monotone). An example of disorganized speech is as follows:

THERAPIST: How are you today?
CLIENT: Good, feeling like a million bucks. Yep, sitting around a campfire with lots of friends. Like a fish in a stream. What a headache! (Example of loose associations)
THERAPIST: You have a headache?
CLIENT: My head, my head. More like bed with red and a shed. (Example of *clang*)
THERAPIST: I'm sorry to hear that your head hurts. When did it start?
CLIENT: The thing about my head is . . . that I used to collect all kinds of things—like pencils—I just loved collecting pencils. (Example of derailment)

The most common form of disorganized behavior is *catatonia*—a decrease in movement in which one position can be held for a long period of time, with absent verbal and motor responses. *Catatonic excitement* is characterized by repeated, non-functional movements, echoed speech or movements, and staring—behaviors you may associate with autism spectrum disorders (APA, 2013). With our current diagnostic system, an individual with autism should only receive an additional diagnosis of schizophrenia if delusions or hallucinations are significant (APA, 2013).

Prevalence

Schizophrenia is uncommon, with a *lifetime prevalence* ranging from 0.3 to 0.7% (van Os & Kapur, 2009). In a recent literature review, the lifetime prevalence was estimated at 0.48% and the *point prevalence* at 0.32% (Simeone et al., 2015).

PREVALENCE BY GENDER AND AGE

Schizophrenia occurs more often in men than in women, with a risk ratio estimate of 1.4 males to 1 female (Saha et al., 2005). The diagnosis typically emerges in late adolescence or early adulthood, though there are rare cases of childhood-onset (in which psychosis emerges before age 12 or 13). Men typically experience their first psychotic episode in the early-to-mid-20s, whereas the first episode typically occurs in the late-20s for women (McGrath, Saha, Chant, & Williams, 2008). Men diagnosed with schizophrenia typically experience a poorer prognosis, including more prominent symptoms and poorer outcome.

Prevalence By Socioeconomic Status (SES), Race, and Ethnicity

Several studies have documented racial/ethnic differences in the prevalence of schizophrenia. In the United Kingdom, rates of schizophrenia are higher among African-Caribbean and Black African individuals and lower among South Asian groups, as compared with white individuals (Qassem et al., 2015). Increased prevalence among Black individuals has also been noted in the United States (Bresnahan et al., 2007).

However, studies examining racial/ethnic differences in prevalence rates are controversial. Numerous researchers have suggested that these studies confound life experiences and SES with race/ethnicity and lead to mischaracterization of the link between race and prevalence. Economic disadvantage is associated with increased prevalence and, critically, when studies statistically control for SES, the relation between Black race and schizophrenia is significantly reduced (Bresnahan et al., 2007). Moreover, there is evidence that cultural isolation and discrimination are risk factors for schizophrenia, and significant concerns have been raised about overdiagnosis among Black Americans.

Comorbidity

In adults with schizophrenia, comorbid diagnoses most frequently include substance-related disorders, as well as anxiety and depressive disorders (Buckley, Miller, Kohrer, & Castle, 2009). Comorbidity is the majority experience—affecting 56% of individuals with schizophrenia. A comorbid substance use disorder, known as *dual diagnosis*, is related to lower functioning and poorer prognosis.

Given the low base rate of childhood onset schizophrenia, studies of comorbidity in youth have focused on samples considered to be at high risk of developing psychosis. In those studies, high rates of mood, anxiety, and substance use disorders have been reported, with ADHD, externalizing, developmental, tic, and learning disorders also co-occurring (Algon, Calkins, Kohler, & Borgmann-Winter, 2012). Early developmental delays, particularly in speech and language, are strongly associated with later childhood-onset schizophrenia.

Developmental Continuities and Discontinuities (Course)

Schizophrenia is considered a persistent disease from which the likelihood of full remission is low. The course is generally *homotypic*, with approximately 80% of children diagnosed continuing to meet diagnostic criteria into adulthood, and similar remission rates are reported for adult-onset schizophrenia (APA, 2013). The majority will experience severe impairment from the disorder, including difficulty completing school, securing a job, and maintaining employment; social isolation and relational instability; and impaired abilities of daily living.

The *premorbid phase*, in which early symptoms start to emerge, comes first and occurs before the true disorder begins. The *acute phase* is the time during which full diagnostic criteria for the disorder are met. Once this phase occurs, the individual is unlikely to experience full remission, but periods of waxing and waning are common. Schizophrenia is discussed in terms of *episodes*, during which individuals experience more positive symptoms. Although positive symptoms may decrease across the lifespan (and in between acute episodes), negative symptoms are more persistent; these periods are known as *residual phases*.

A number of premorbid developmental anomalies have been identified in people who later develop schizophrenia. The bulk of research on premorbid development in schizophrenia has pointed to delays in early language production and motor control/development that emerge during infancy and continue into middle childhood (Gooding & Iacono, 1995). Social difficulties are also noted early in life (Schenkel & Silverstein, 2004), with parents reporting many autism-like traits in their children as early as infancy. Walker and Lewine (1990) examined childhood home videos of individuals who would go on to develop schizophrenia and their unaffected siblings. The footage revealed that the group with schizophrenia was more socially withdrawn and displayed reduced eye contact, social responsiveness, and emotional expressiveness. Similarly, teacher ratings of social functioning were significantly predictive of later diagnosis (Tsuji et al., 2013). It is widely speculated that these social deficits, usually considered premorbid characteristics, may actually constitute the earliest expression of negative symptoms.

Cognitive impairments are widely reported among individuals with schizophrenia and research has identified these impairments during the premorbid phase as well. In a meta-analytic review, Woodberry, Giuliani, and Seidman (2008) noted a robust impairment in premorbid IQ that was about one half of a standard deviation below that of control subjects. These deficits are noted as early as the first grade and the decline continues across school ages, with school performance and achievement test scores also affected. Intellectual functioning is further impaired after onset of schizophrenia (Trotta, Murray, & MacCabe, 2015).

Many of these premorbid features continue throughout the prodromal and acute phases, with generally increasing severity, though motor difficulties tend to remit in adolescence. Social deficits in early childhood may grow into social isolation by adolescence, which may be exacerbated by an odd presentation or unusual interpretation of social interactions. Although it might be tempting to think that these premorbid characteristics continuously increase in severity until they warrant a diagnosis in the acute phase, that would be an oversimplification of what we currently know about the course of schizophrenia, in which heterogeneity is the norm.

A Developmental Psychopathology Model of the Etiology of Schizophrenia

Figure 12.1 depicts a developmental psychopathology model of schizophrenia.

GENETIC FACTORS (DISTAL RISK FACTORS)

Family and twin studies

In the Maudsley Twin Psychosis studies, 106 monozygotic and 118 dizygotic twins with a diagnosis of psychosis were assessed alongside a same-sex co-twin (Cardno et al., 1999). They found that when one twin was diagnosed with schizophrenia, 40.8% of monozygotic twins also had the disorder and only 5.3% of dizygotic twins also had the disorder. A number of similar studies have produced similar or higher estimates, and a review of 12 existing twin studies pointed to an 81% heritability estimate for schizophrenia based on research with twins, with approximately 11% attributable to shared environmental influences (Sullivan, Kendler, & Neale, 2003).

A number of large-scale studies have examined familial (but non-twin) risk for schizophrenia. A Consortium on the Genetics of Schizophrenia Study investigated 296 families that included an individual with schizophrenia, both parents, and an unaffected sibling (Light et al., 2014). The authors reported the heritability of schizophrenia was 31% among nuclear families and 44% for extended families. This heritability estimate is quite lower than the 81% based on twin studies, pointing to the importance of research design in contextualizing heritability estimates.

Molecular genetic studies

A review of thousands of individuals conducted by Farrell and colleagues (2015) presented evidence for each of 25 candidate genes for schizophrenia. The authors concluded that no single candidate gene for schizophrenia has repeatedly panned out; however, they also surveyed prominent scientists

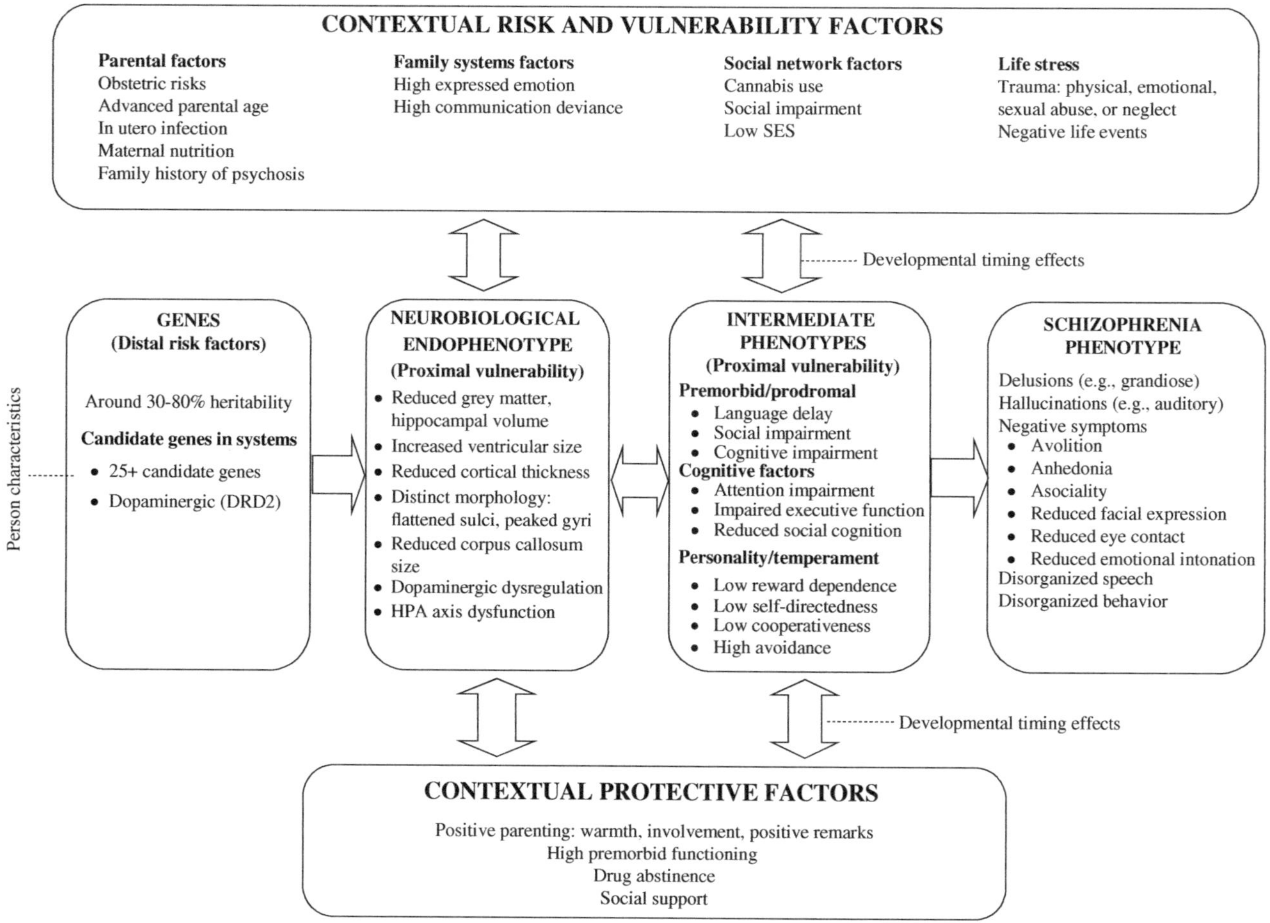

FIGURE 12.1 A Developmental Psychopathology Model of Schizophrenia

regarding their opinions on the potential of various genes. The findings repeatedly pointed to DRD2, a dopamine receptor gene and the target of antipsychotic drugs that typically improve the positive symptoms of schizophrenia. Although studies on this gene are mixed, current research suggests that polymorphisms of DRD2 may confer risk for schizophrenia (Glatt, Faraone, & Tsuang, 2003).

NEUROBIOLOGICAL FACTORS (PROXIMAL VULNERABILITY FACTORS)

Structural anomalies

Schizophrenia has been consistently linked to reduced grey matter and hippocampal volume and increased ventricular volume. A recent study of childhood-onset schizophrenia provided evidence that less decrease in hippocampal volume (across three or more brain scans) was associated with fewer negative symptoms and improved general functioning (Anvari et al., 2015). Decreases in grey matter, hippocampal, and amygdala volume have also been noted in youth at risk for schizophrenia prior to the prodromal phase. These studies show that brain volume decreases are not just a consequence of schizophrenia, but rather are present prior to the disease onset.

Studies of brain structure with schizophrenia have also shown anomalies in the structure of the corpus callosum, which connects the left and right hemispheres (Woodruff, McManus, & David, 1995). Similar reductions have been found in children with symptoms of schizophrenia. Still, this area of research is relatively small and mixed, and the largest longitudinal study found no significant differences in corpus callosum volume (Johnson et al., 2013).

Neurotransmitters

Two prominent neurotransmitter hypotheses currently center on the importance of dopamine in schizophrenia. The *dopamine hypothesis* suggests that overactive mesolimbic dopaminergic neurons produce positive symptoms, while underactive mesocortical dopaminergic neurons produce negative, cognitive, and mood symptoms (Steiner, Schiltz, Bernstein, & Bogerts, 2015). The *glutamate hypothesis* posits that reduced function of glutamate receptors is responsible for impaired control of dopaminergic neurons, which, in turn, leads to the aforementioned dysregulation of the dopaminergic system (Steiner et al., 2015). The dopamine hypothesis was updated by Howes and Kapur (2009) to include many of the other risk factors discussed in this chapter (see Figure 12.2).

This model suggests that drugs, stress, and genetic and neurological factors contribute to dopaminergic dysregulation, which increases the risk for psychosis. They also suggest that dopamine dysregulation may affect how individuals make sense of their world. The "aberrant salience"

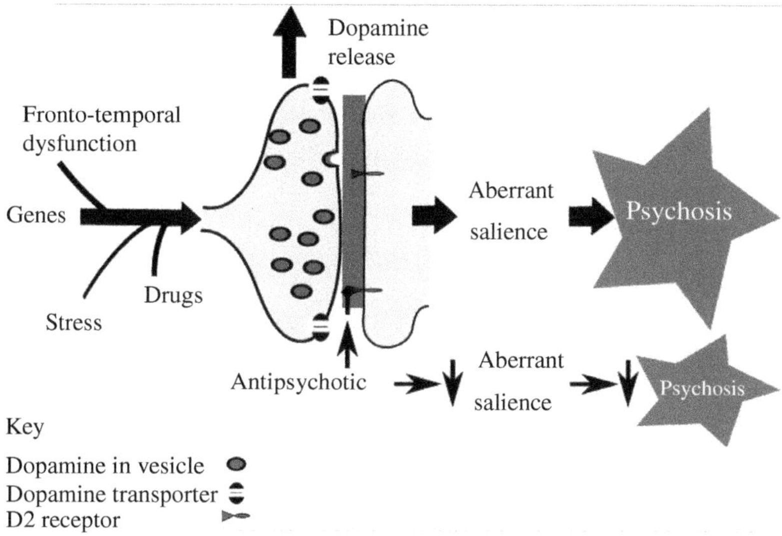

FIGURE 12.2 The Dopamine Hypothesis of Schizophrenia by Howes and Kapur, 2009
Source: Howes and Kapur, 2009. Reproduced with permissions of Oxford University Press.

construct suggests that, in psychosis, an individual's attention is drawn to life experiences that would not capture others' attention, and, over time, they make sense of the altered state of consciousness through delusions (Kapur, 2003). Similarly, abnormal salience to internal experiences may produce hallucinations.

Hormones

A number of studies show that individuals with schizophrenia experience dysfunction of the hypothalamic–pituitary–adrenal (HPA) axis, which controls the body's stress reaction. Bradley and Dinan (2010) reviewed existing research on schizophrenia, the HPA axis, and cortisol, finding significant evidence of both hypo- and hyper-reactivity in these systems. Individuals with schizophrenia commonly have elevated cortisol levels during their first episode (and sometimes chronically), while they also commonly experience low cortisol levels and a blunted HPA response to stress. Though heterogeneous, the evidence points to significant differences in aspects of HPA response and subsequent cortisol levels.

TEMPERAMENT

Jetha, Goldber, and Schmidt (2013) reviewed many prior studies, showing that individuals with schizophrenia tend to be high in avoidance and low in extroversion, novelty seeking, and sociability. Several other studies have identified low reward dependence (which includes warmth, sensitivity, and social attachment), low self-directedness, and low cooperativeness among individuals with schizophrenia. In a study of temperament in individuals with schizophrenia, harm avoidance and self-directedness (among other variables) were predictive of quality of life (Margetić, Jacovliević, Ivanec, & Margetić, 2011).

COGNITIVE FACTORS

Attention

Attention impairments have been consistently noted in patients with schizophrenia, as well as those in remission and first-degree relatives. In perhaps the largest study (Neuchterlein et al., 2015), attention and vigilance across 2,251 participants were examined using the Continuous Performance Test (CPT). In this task, letters or numbers appear on a computer screen and the participant is instructed to press the space bar only in response to some letters or numbers. The authors confirmed the link between schizophrenia and impaired attention, and also linked CPT performance to educational achievement and overall functioning. Similar studies have found youth at high risk for developing psychosis demonstrate impairment comparable to youth experiencing a first psychotic episode.

Executive functions

Executive functioning, which includes planning, working memory, and problem-solving abilities, is impaired among individuals with a diagnosis of schizophrenia, though it is difficult to establish whether these difficulties are a cause, correlate, or consequence of schizophrenia. In a longitudinal study, Woodberry and colleagues (2013) followed youth for one year and found that the group at high risk for psychosis experienced significant progressive impairment across time, particularly on tests of executive function. This study shows the progression of neuropsychological impairment and suggests that differences observed in adults are not simply indicative of premorbid differences.

Social cognition

Social cognitive abilities are those that allow us to interact with others—to detect what they might be thinking and feeling, and to understand how their mental states underlie their actions and intentions. Individuals with schizophrenia have demonstrated deficits in their social cognitive abilities in addition to premorbid social impairments and acute negative symptoms. For example, they tend to perform poorly on tasks requiring them to identify faces or recognize emotions (Kohler et al., 2009). A meta-analysis conducted by Bora, Yucel, and Pantelis (2010) showed that social cognitive deficits remained for individuals in whom schizophrenia was characterized as "remitted," suggesting *theory of mind* impairments are not simply a symptom of the disorder.

CONTEXTUAL RISK FACTORS

A number of risk and protective factors have been identified and, in this section and the next, we will follow the literature review conducted by Schlosser, Pearson, Perez, and Loewy (2012), which summarizes environmental factors important in the development of psychosis.

Obstetric risks

Complications during the prenatal and perinatal periods have been identified as risk factors for schizophrenia. Fetal hypoxia (lack of oxygen to a fetus) has been linked to schizophrenia, but only in families with a history of psychosis (Cannon et al., 2000), suggesting an interaction between this risk factor and a biological vulnerability. Maternal infection, an activated immune response, and advanced paternal age, have also been linked to schizophrenia (Gilmore & Jarskog, 1997). Maternal malnutrition, particularly vitamin deficiencies, has been linked to the risk of schizophrenia in offspring. Interestingly, deficiency in vitamin D (typically absorbed through sunlight exposure) might explain why schizophrenia has been associated with winter and spring births as well as birth in the northern latitudes.

Trauma

Higher rates of childhood trauma have been reported in both retrospective and longitudinal studies. Studies have begun to show that increased trauma exposure is associated with increased positive symptoms severity, with particularly high risk for a psychotic disorder associated with sexual abuse (Bechdolf et al., 2010). Together, these studies suggest that traumatic experiences may exacerbate or expose biological vulnerabilities for schizophrenia during development, and researchers have begun to examine the mechanism for this risk by studying cortisol and the stress response system.

Family factors

Much of the research examining the families of individuals with schizophrenia has focused on a construct called *expressed emotion*, which is characterized by hostility, emotional overinvolvement, and critical comments. This type of family environment has been repeatedly associated with increased risk for schizophrenia and with greater likelihood of symptom relapse (Butzlaff & Hooley, 1998). Table 12.2 presents examples of how researchers conceptualize some aspects of the family environment using the Camberwell Family Interview.

Positive parenting variables have been associated with an improved course of emerging psychosis in longitudinal studies. For example, parental involvement, warmth, and positive remarks were associated with symptom improvement in a group of adolescents from baseline to three-month follow-up (O'Brien et al., 2006).

TABLE 12.2 Examples of Family Factors Related to Risk for Schizophrenia from the Camberwell Family Interview

1. CRITICAL COMMENT: An unambiguous statement expressing dislike, disapproval, or resentment of a behavior/characteristic of the other. Example: "He just doesn't put forth effort for anything. . . . I do get angry, and it's like 'when the hell are you gonna wake up and do this stuff?'"
2. POSITIVE REMARK: An unambiguous statement expressing praise, approval or appreciation of another's behavior or personality. Example: "I think he is very bright and I really admire that."
3. WARMTH: Rated on a scale ranging from 0 (no warmth) to 5 (high warmth). Higher ratings (up to a rating of 3) are assigned to those who express understanding, sympathy and concern for their son or daughter, and who speak in a caring tone. The highest ratings (4–5 range) are reserved for those who not only express care and concern, but also express enthusiasm, interest in and enjoyment of the person. This rating is based on evidence compiled throughout the interview.

Rating of 1:
This father's voice tone is neutral. He does not spend much time with his son. However, he does notice that his son seems distracted, and he identifies with his son's tendencies to be rebellious. He demonstrates a bit of compassion for his son's illness and isolation. This father seems to know very little about his son's daily life and about who his son is as a person.

Rating of 5:
This mother's enthusiasm and warm tone of voice throughout the interview communicate that she cares for her daughter and is very interested in who she is as a person. She communicates concern for her daughter's happiness and sensitivity to her need for peer interaction given her frequent bouts of depression and tendency to become socially isolated. For example, she states "Even though her grades are bad, I let her go to the library for a while after school to hang out with her friends." She is able to separate her daughter's personality from the symptoms her daughter is currently exhibiting, and to continue to value who her daughter is as a person. For example, she states "I'm not critical of who she is at all. I'm very proud of who she is. I know she is a kind person, but her behavior is just a mess." She frequently empathizes with the patient's difficult situation and encourages her. This mother provides many details regarding her daughter's activities and friendships. Throughout the interview it is obvious that this mother is very connected to her daughter, has a lot of insights about her, and truly enjoys and values the time she spends with her. For example, she states "I like to see her smile. . .we have a great relationship. . .we are very affectionate."

4. EMOTIONAL INVOLVEMENT: Rated on a scale ranging from 0 (no involvement) to 5 (high involvement). This is a global rating that is made after listening to the whole interview, listing evidence "for" and "against" involvement, and then deciding upon a summary score. This category is comprised of three main dimensions: dramatization/emotionality, self sacrifice/devoted behavior, and protective behavior.

Rating of 0:
This father does not convey much emotion as he talks about his son. He is essentially uninvolved in his son's life and continues with all aspects of his own independent life. He enjoys working full time and meets daily with friends, largely buffered from family stress by his wife who deals with the children.

Table 12.2 (Continued)

Rating of 3:

No dramatization was noted. This working mother spends a lot of time supporting her son. She brings him to doctors and hospitals, participates in his Individual Education Plan meetings at school, and spends time talking to him and comforting him. All of these efforts have made it difficult for this mother to maintain her job. For example, this mother reports that "son had a bad episode that lasted several hours and he called me at work again and asked for me to come home so I did." "I spend so much time in therapy and with psychiatrists and making sure I am there for him that I can't be as productive as I used to be." This mom has made serious financial sacrifices for her child. For example, before the school district agreed to pay for a specialized school placement, this mother agreed to pay for it out of her own personal savings ($2500/month) because she was convinced her son could only participate in school with these additional supports. At the same time, this mother does try to set some limits in terms of requiring her son to do some work around the house. "He empties the garbage, keeps his room clean, and keeps his bathroom clean. I make him pick up his things, and he helps with food preparation." Mother continues her involvement with the church choir, and tries to meet occasionally with friends for lunch.

Rating of 5:

This mother cried throughout the interview and made many dramatic statements. This mother has been unable to work because of the demands of caring for her daughter, which has greatly impacted the family finances. "I can't work now because I can't leave her alone. I pretty much take her with me wherever I go." This mother hasn't gone on vacation for many years due to her inability to leave her daughter. She has taken her to many doctors in an effort to get her help. All of the symptoms that her daughter has been experiencing have taken a toll on the mother's health. "This has been really stressful to me. I've gone through my own depression and I'm typically a really upbeat person." She has changed her routine entirely, no longer going to the gym or participating in activities with her own friends or pursuing romantic relationships of her own in order to care for her daughter.

Source: O'Brien et al., (2006). Reproduced with permissions of Elsevier.

Cannabis use

Cannabis use has been established as a risk factor for the development of schizophrenia; however, controversy exists as to whether it plays a causal role. A prospective study conducted by McGrath and colleagues (2010) attempted to address the potential role of cannabis in developing schizophrenia more fully during a 21-year study. They found cannabis use was associated with risk for psychosis and that heavy use exacerbated this risk. Other studies have noted that cannabis use seems to elevate risk even in individuals without a predisposition for psychosis.

Contextual Protective Factors

Less is known about protective factors compared to risk factors in the etiology of schizophrenia, though higher premorbid functioning, early intervention, decreased severity of symptoms, and later age of onset are commonly cited as protective factors. Many studies describe the absence of risk factors as protective factors, such as lack of cannabis consumption. More broadly, social support is associated with improved functioning and fewer positive symptoms (Norman et al., 2005). Positive, warm family environments also serve as significant protective factors. In the next section, we will discuss how positive family factors even seem to mitigate a strong genetic risk for schizophrenia.

GENE–ENVIRONMENT INTERPLAY

Gene–environment correlations

Many of the risk factors discussed have been conceptualized as reflecting a gene–environment correlation. For instance, van Os and colleagues (2008) suggest gene–environment correlations may account for identified links between obstetric complications and later psychosis due to some underlying genetic vulnerability contributing to both events. Similar hypotheses have been put forth regarding links between cannabis use and schizophrenia. Power and colleagues (2014) examined the cannabis use and genetic profile of 2,082 healthy adults. They found the polygenetic risk for schizophrenia was significantly predictive of the individual's cannabis use—suggesting the relation between cannabis use and psychotic symptoms may be complicated by a shared genetic basis for both variables.

Gene–environment interactions

One of the strongest examples of a gene-environment interaction in schizophrenia comes from the Finnish Adoptive Family Study of Schizophrenia (Tienari et al., 2004). This study followed adopted individuals and compared those whose biological mother had schizophrenia with those whose biological mother did not. The researchers (blind to the biological mother's diagnostic status) rated the adoptive family's functioning and found a significant interaction. For adoptees whose biological mother had schizophrenia, 36% of those in unhealthy adoptive families (e.g., critical, conflictual) developed a psychotic disorder, versus only 6% in the healthy families—suggesting family functioning can exacerbate and attenuate genetic risk for psychosis.

DEVELOPMENTAL TIMING EFFECTS: THE INTERPLAY OF NORMAL AND ABNORMAL DEVELOPMENT

Whether childhood-onset schizophrenia is continuous with the more common, adult-onset course of the disorder is a key question in understanding developmental timing effects. Accumulating research suggests that, though the incidence of schizophrenia rises sharply in early adolescence, early and late onset cases share basic clinical and biological features and can be diagnosed under the same criteria (Kumra et al., 2001). However, differences in the premorbid functioning and prognosis suggest developmental timing effects are present. Before developing psychosis, individuals who will develop childhood-onset schizophrenia demonstrate more language impairments and autistic traits than individuals with adult-onset presentations and may have a stronger family history of psychosis (Kumra et al., 2001). Likewise, the prognosis for childhood-onset schizophrenia is poor compared to adult-onset schizophrenia.

Together, this research suggests that the timing of schizophrenia onset may play an important role in determining the prognosis of the disease. Imagine, for instance, that language impairment was present since birth instead of emerging as a symptom of schizophrenia (e.g., disorganized speech). How might this affect an individual's ability to make use of group housing, engage in psychotherapy, or communicate medication side effects? Given the normal developmental progression of language, social, and cognitive abilities, it makes sense that the earlier difficulties set in, the more difficult the course and prognosis of the illness will be.

Intervention

Schizophrenia is often first diagnosed when family, friends, health care professionals, or law officers became concerned about the individual's safety, leading to psychiatric hospitalization. In most hospitals in the US, stabilization is accomplished using antipsychotic medication—the core component of treatment for schizophrenia since the 1950s (National Institute for Health and Care Excellence, 2014). While their side effects are serious and varied, medication is typically effective in reducing the positive symptoms of schizophrenia. During the last 10 years, psychotherapy has gained attention as a treatment component to enhance the effectiveness of medication; indeed, this combination is cited as recommended treatment. The research is mixed, though, with studies showing that CBT is no better than supportive therapy in individuals with schizophrenia and does not significantly reduce relapse (Newton-Howes & Wood, 2013).

The rarity of childhood-onset schizophrenia has led to limited research on treatments for youth. Though existing research on the safety and effectiveness of antipsychotic medications in youth suggests promise, the research base is slim and serious side effects have been documented. Similarly, although individual psychotherapy and family therapy have been recommended, little research supports the effectiveness of specific psychosocial treatments. Recently, Armando, Pontillo, and Vicari (2015) completed a review of psychosocial interventions in youth, reporting preliminary evidence for cognitive remediation, a behaviorally based training that attempts to remediate cognitive deficits such as difficulties in attention, memory, executive functions, and social cognition. It has shown promise in adult samples across multiple studies (Revell et al., 2015). Cognitive remediation is goal-based, such that an individual's problems are translated to a positive goal with specific strategies that can be practiced and enhanced through repetition. Examples of common goals that could be addressed with Cognitive Enhancement Therapy (a specific cognitive remediation program) are presented in Table 12.3.

TABLE 12.3 Examples of Goals and Strategies That Can Be Included in Cognitive Remediation Therapies for Schizophrenia

Example A
Goal: To improve my attention during conversations
Problem: Difficulty maintaining attention/easily distracted
Strategies:

1. Cue myself to pay attention
2. Take notes in the CET group to avoid distraction
3. Actively listen and ask questions in conversations
4. Focus on the gist when talking with others
5. Paraphrase back to the other person in conversations
6. Use computer training to boost attention

Example B
Goal: To better understand other people
Problem: Difficulty with understanding others' thoughts and feelings
Strategies:

1. Use active listening (observe verbal and non-verbal cues, take the person's emotional temperature; ask open-ended questions).
2. Evaluate whether this is a good time for the person to talk.
3. Ask questions to better understand the other person's point of view and check whether my understanding is correct.
4. Practice active listening and perspective-taking during CET computer and group sessions. Make supportive statements ("I like what you said/did").
5. After giving my feedback following a CET group exercise, see if my observations of the participants' thoughts and feelings are correct.

Example C
Goal: To increase my network of friends
Problem: Having a small social network
Strategies:

1. Assess situations to decide who I want to get to know further. Work on initiating and maintaining conversations.
2. Use CET strategies: active listening, perspective taking, foresightfulness, social context appraisal.
3. Make an effort to know new people while keeping up with current friends.
4. Use humor in conversations. Try to be less serious and more relaxed. Coach myself using positive self-talk.
5. Express myself more to others – use elaborated speech.

Source: Eack, 2012. Reproduced with permissions of Oxford University Press.

Chapter Summary

In this chapter, we discussed the different presentations and courses of schizophrenia with a particular emphasis on the role that developmental timing plays in the emergence and prognosis of the disorder. Though schizophrenia is uncommon in children, many of the risk factors we reviewed are present in youth, and the premorbid phases of the disorder are increasingly well-researched and understood. As a disorder with a strong biological basis, studies of schizophrenia make for a particularly rich literature on the interaction between environmental and genetic variables.

Further Reading

Eack, S. M. (2012). Cognitive remediation: A new generation of psychosocial interventions for people with schizophrenia. *Social Work, 57*(3), 235–246.

Keefe, R. E. (2014). The longitudinal course of cognitive impairment in schizophrenia: An examination of data from premorbid through posttreatment phases of illness. *Journal of Clinical Psychiatry, 75*(Suppl 2), 8–12. doi: 10.4088/JCP.13065su1.02.

Schlosser, D. A., Pearson, R., Perez, V. B., & Loewy, R. L. (2012). Environmental risk and protective factors and their influence on the emergence of psychosis. *Adolescent Psychiatry, 2*(2), 163–171.

Discussion/Essay Questions

1. What are the similarities and differences between the diagnostic criteria for autism spectrum disorder and schizophrenia? At what point in the course of schizophrenia might the disorder be easiest to mislabel as an autism spectrum disorder?
2. Describe variables that complicate the following statement: Schizophrenia is more common in Black individuals.
3. Is schizophrenia a biological disorder? Explain your answer.
4. Given the relation between cannabis use and psychotic disorders, how might you expect the prevalence of schizophrenia to change in states that have legalized recreational use of cannabis?

Glossary

Bizarre delusions are those that are odd and implausible.

Catatonia is a decrease in movement in which one position can be held for a long period of time, with absent verbal and motor responses.

Catatonic excitement is characterized by repeated, non-functional movements, echoed speech or movements, and staring.

Clanging is speech in which words are associated by sound rather than meaning.

Delusions are fixed beliefs that are not amenable to change in the light of conflicting evidence.

Disorganized speech includes moving from one topic to another in a manner that is hard to follow or connecting topics that are not apparently related.

Dopamine hypothesis suggests that overactive mesolimbic dopaminergic neurons produce positive symptoms of schizophrenia and that underactive mesocortical dopaminergic neurons produce the other symptoms of schizophrenia.

Dual diagnosis refers to being diagnosed both with a non-substance related mental disorder and a substance use disorder at the same time.

Expressed emotion includes hostility, emotional overinvolvement, and critical comments, and this type of family environment has been repeatedly associated with risk for schizophrenia.

Glutamate hypothesis posits that reduced function of glutamate receptors is responsible for impaired control of dopaminergic neurons, which, in turn, leads to dysregulation of the dopaminergic system.

Hallucinations are sensory perceptive experiences of something not present.

Homotypic continuity is when the same condition is expressed in the same manner across development.

Lifetime prevalence refers to the percentage of individuals diagnosed with a condition across their lifetime.

Negative symptoms are things that are absent in an individual with schizophrenia, such as reduced facial expressions communicating emotion, eye contact, emotional intonation in speaking, and decreased motivation.

Point prevalence refers to the percentage of individuals diagnosed with a condition at a given point in time.

Positive symptoms are things that are present in an individual with schizophrenia but absent in healthy individuals, such as hallucinations and delusions.

Premorbid refers to the time period before the onset of illness.

Schizophrenia spectrum is the continuum of disorders including schizophrenia as well as other psychotic disorders and schizotypal personality disorder.

Theory of mind is a general term for detecting the mental states of others.

References

Algon, S., Yi, J., Calkins, M. E., Kohler, C., & Borgmann-Winter, K. E. (2012). Evaluation and treatment of children and adolescents with psychotic symptoms. *Current Psychiatry Reports*, *14*(2), 101–110.

American Psychiatric Association (APA) (2013). *Diagnostic and statistical manual of mental disorders* (5th ed.). American Psychiatric Publication.

Anvari, A. A., Friedman, L. A., Greenstein, D., Gochman, P., Gogtay, N., & Rapoport, J. L. (2015). Hippocampal volume change relates to clinical outcome in childhood-onset schizophrenia. *Psychological Medicine*, *45*, 1–8.

Armando, M., Pontillo, M., & Vicari, S. (2015). Psychosocial interventions for very early and early-onset schizophrenia: A review of treatment efficacy. *Current Opinion Psychiatry*, *28*, 312–323.

Bechdolf, A., Thompson, A., Nelson, B., Cotton, S., Simmons, M. B., Amminger, G. P., & Sidis, A. (2010). Experience of trauma and conversion to psychosis in an ultra-high-risk (prodromal) group. *Acta Psychiatrica Scandinavica*, *121*(5), 377–384.

Bora, E., Yücel, M., & Pantelis, C. (2010). Neurocognitive markers of psychosis in bipolar disorder: A meta-analytic study. *Journal of Affective Disorders*, *127*(1), 1–9.

Bradley, A. J., & Dinan, T. G. (2010). Review: A systematic review of hypothalamic–pituitary–adrenal axis function in schizophrenia: Implications for mortality. *Journal of Psychopharmacology*, *24*(4 Suppl.), 91–118.

Bresnahan, M., Begg, M. D., Brown, A., Schaefer, C., Sohler, N., Insel, B., & Susser, E. (2007). Race and risk of schizophrenia in a US birth cohort: Another example of health disparity? *International Journal of Epidemiology*, *36*(4), 751–758.

Buckley, P. F., Miller, B. J., Lehrer, D. S., & Castle, D. J. (2009). Psychiatric comorbidities and schizophrenia. *Schizophrenia Bulletin*, *35*(2), 383–402.

Butzlaff, R. L., & Hooley, J. M. (1998). Expressed emotion and psychiatric relapse: A meta-analysis. *Archives of General Psychiatry*, *55*(6), 547–552.

Cannon, T. D., Huttunen, M. O., Lonnqvist, J., Tuulio-Henriksson, A., Pirkola, T., Glahn, D., & Koskenvuo, M. (2000). The inheritance of neuropsychological dysfunction in twins discordant for schizophrenia. *The American Journal of Human Genetics*, *67*(2), 369–382.

Cardno, A. G., Marshall, E. J., Coid, B., Macdonald, A. M., Ribchester, T. R., Davies, N. J., & Gottesman, I. I. (1999). Heritability estimates for psychotic disorders: The Maudsley twin psychosis series. *Archives of General Psychiatry*, *56*(2), 162–168.

Eack, S. M. (2012). Cognitive remediation: A new generation of psychosocial interventions for people with schizophrenia. *Social Work*, *57*(3), 235–246.

Farrell, M. S., Werge, T., Sklar, P., Owen, M. J., Ophoff, R. A., O'Donovan, M. C., & Sullivan, P. F. (2015). Evaluating historical candidate genes for schizophrenia. *Molecular Psychiatry*, *20*(5), 555–562.

Gilmore, J. H., & Jarskog, L. F. (1997). Exposure to infection and brain development: Cytokines in the pathogenesis of schizophrenia. *Schizophrenia Research*, *24*(3), 365–367.

Glatt, S. J., Faraone, S. V., & Tsuang, M. T. (2003). Meta-analysis identifies an association between the dopamine D2 receptor gene and schizophrenia. *Molecular Psychiatry*, *8*(11), 911–915.

Gooding, D. C., & Iacono, W. G. (1995). Schizophrenia through the lens of a developmental psychopathology perspective. In D. Cicchetti & D. J. Cohen (Eds.), *Wiley series on personality processes, vol 2, Risk, disorder, and adaptation* (pp. 535–580). Hoboken, NJ: John Wiley & Sons, Inc.

Howes, O. D., & Kapur, S. (2009). The dopamine hypothesis of schizophrenia: Version III—The final common pathway. *Schizophrenia Bulletin*, *35*(3), 549–562.

Jetha, M. K., Goldberg, J. O., & Schmidt, L. A. (2013). Temperament and its relation to social functioning in schizophrenia. *International Journal of Social Psychiatry*, *59*(3), 254–263.

Johnson, S. L., Greenstein, D., Clasen, L., Miller, R., Lalonde, F., Rapoport, J., & Gogtay, N. (2013). Absence of anatomic corpus callosal abnormalities in childhood-onset schizophrenia patients and healthy siblings. *Psychiatry Research: Neuroimaging*, *211*(1), 11–16.

Kapur, S. (2003). Psychosis as a state of aberrant salience: A framework linking biology, phenomenology, and pharmacology in schizophrenia. *American Journal of Psychiatry*, *160*(1), 13–23.

Keefe, R. E. (2014). The longitudinal course of cognitive impairment in schizophrenia: An examination of data from premorbid through posttreatment phases of illness. *Journal of Clinical Psychiatry*, *75*(Suppl. 2), 8–13. doi: 10.4088/JCP.13065su1.02.

Kohler, C. G., Walker, J. B., Martin, E. A., Healey, K. M., & Moberg, P. J. (2009). Facial emotion perception in schizophrenia: A meta-analytic review. *Schizophrenia Bulletin*, *36*(5), 1009–1019.

Kumra, S., Shaw, M., Merka, P., Nakayama, E., & Augustin, R. (2001). Childhood-onset schizophrenia: research update. *Canadian Journal of Psychiatry (Revue Canadienne de Psychiatrie)*, *46*(10), 923.

Light, G., Greenwood, T. A., Swerdlow, N. R., Calkins, M. E., Freedman, R., Green, M. F., & Olincy, A. (2014). Comparison of the heritability of schizophrenia and endophenotypes in the COGS-1 Family Study. *Schizophrenia Bulletin*, *40*(6), 1404–1411.

Margetić, B. A., Jakovljević, M., Ivanec, D., & Margetić, B. (2011). Temperament, character, and quality of life in patients with schizophrenia and their first-degree relatives. *Comprehensive Psychiatry*, *52*(4), 425–430.

McGrath, J., Saha, S., Chant, D., & Welham, J. (2008). Schizophrenia: A concise overview of incidence, prevalence, and mortality. *Epidemiologic Reviews*, *30*(1), 67–76.

McGrath, J., Welham, J., Scott, J., Varghese, D., Degenhardt, L., Hayatbakhsh, M. R., & Najman, J. M. (2010). Association between cannabis use and psychosis-related outcomes using sibling pair analysis in a cohort of young adults. *Archives of General Psychiatry*, *67*(5), 440–447.

National Institute for Health and Care Excellence (2014). Psychosis and schizophrenia in adults: Prevention and management. *NICE Clinical Guidelines*. Available at: https://www.nice.org.uk/guidance/cg178.

Newton-Howes, G., & Wood, R. (2013). Cognitive behavioural therapy and the psychopathology of schizophrenia: Systematic review and meta-analysis. *Psychology and Psychotherapy: Theory, Research and Practice*, *86*(2), 127–138.

Norman, R. M., Malla, A. K., Manchanda, R., Harricharan, R., Takhar, J., & Northcott, S. (2005). Social support and three-year symptom and admission outcomes for first episode psychosis. *Schizophrenia Research*, *80*(2), 227–234.

Nuechterlein, K. H., Green, M. F., Calkins, M. E., Greenwood, T. A., Gur, R. E., Gur, R. C., & Braff, D. L. (2015). Attention/vigilance in schizophrenia: Performance results from a large multi-site study of the Consortium on the Genetics of Schizophrenia (COGS). *Schizophrenia Research*, *163*(1–3), 38–46. doi: 10.1016/j.schres.2015.01.017.

O'Brien, M. P., Gordon, J. L., Bearden, C. E., Lopez, S. R., Kopelowicz, A., & Cannon, T. D. (2006). Positive family environment predicts improvement in symptoms and social functioning among adolescents at imminent risk for onset of psychosis. *Schizophrenia Research*, *81*(2–3), 269–275.

Power, R. A., Verweij, K. J., Zuhair, M., Montgomery, G. W., Henders, A. K., Heath, A. C., & Martin, N. G. (2014). Genetic predisposition to schizophrenia associated with increased use of cannabis. *Molecular Psychiatry*, *19*(11), 1201–1204.

Qassem, T., Bebbington, P., Spiers, N., McManus, S., Jenkins, R., & Dein, S. (2015). Prevalence of psychosis in Black ethnic minorities in Britain: Analysis based on three national surveys. *Social Psychiatry and Psychiatric Epidemiology*, *50*(7), 1057–1064. doi: 10.1007/s00127-014-0960-7.

Revell, E. R., Neill, J. C., Harte, M., Khan, Z., & Drake, R. J. (2015). A systematic review and meta-analysis of cognitive remediation in early schizophrenia. *Schizophrenia Research*, *168*(1), 213–222.

Saha, S., Chant, D., Welham, J., & McGrath, J. (2005). A systematic review of the prevalence of schizophrenia. *PLoS Medicine*, *2*(5), 413.

Schenkel, L. S., & Silverstein, S. M. (2004). Dimensions of premorbid functioning in schizophrenia: A review of neuromotor, cognitive, social, *and behavioral domains. Genetic, Social, and General Psychology Monographs*, *130*(3), 241–272.

Schlosser, D. A., Pearson, R., Perez, V. B., & Loewy, R. L. (2012). Environmental risk and protective factors and their influence on the emergence of psychosis. *Adolescent Psychiatry*, *2*(2), 163–171.

Schlosser, D. A., Zinberg, J. L., Loewy, R. L., Casey-Cannon, S., O'Brien, M. P., Bearden, C. E., & Cannon, T. D. (2010). Predicting the longitudinal effects of the family environment on prodromal symptoms and functioning in patients at-risk for psychosis. *Schizophrenia Research*, *118*(1), 69–75.

Simeone, J. C., Ward, A. J., Rotella, P., Collins, J., & Windisch, R. (2015). An evaluation of variation in published estimates of schizophrenia prevalence from 1990–2013: A systematic literature review. *BMC Psychiatry*, *15*, 1–14.

Steiner, J., Schiltz, K., Bernstein, H. G., & Bogerts, B. (2015). Antineuronal antibodies against neurotransmitter receptors and synaptic proteins in schizophrenia: Current knowledge and clinical implications. *CNS Drugs*, *29*(3), 197–206.

Sullivan, P. F., Kendler, K. S., & Neale, M. C. (2003). Schizophrenia as a complex trait: Evidence from a meta-analysis of twin studies. *Archives of General Psychiatry*, *60*(12), 1187–1192.

Tienari, P., Wynne, L. C., Sorri, A., Lahti, I., Läksy, K., Moring, J., & Wahlberg, K. E. (2004). Genotype–environment interaction in schizophrenia-spectrum disorder: Long-term follow-up study of Finnish adoptees. *The British Journal of Psychiatry*, *184*(3), 216–222.

Trotta, A., Murray, R. M., & MacCabe, J. H. (2015). Do premorbid and post-onset cognitive functioning differ between schizophrenia and bipolar disorder? A systematic review and meta-analysis. *Psychological Medicine*, *45*(02), 381–394.

Tsuji, T., Kline, E., Sorensen, H. J., Mortensen, E. L., Michelsen, N. M., Ekstrom, M., & Schiffman, J. (2013). Premorbid teacher-rated social functioning predicts adult schizophrenia-spectrum disorder: A high-risk prospective investigation. *Schizophrenia Research*, *151*(1), 270–273.

Van Os, J., & Kapur, S. (2009). Psychosis: From diagnosis to syndrome. *Nederlands Tijdschrift voor Geneeskunde*, *154*, A1874–A1874.

Van Os, J., Rutten, B. P., & Poulton, R. (2008). Gene–environment interactions in schizophrenia: Review of epidemiological findings and future directions. *Schizophrenia Bulletin*, *34*(6), 1066.

Walker, E., & Lewine, J. (1990). Prediction of adult-onset schizophrenia. *American Journal of Psychiatry*, *1*, 47.

Woodberry, K. A., Giuliano, A. J., & Seidman, L. J. (2008). Premorbid IQ in schizophrenia: A meta-analytic review. *The American*

Journal of Psychiatry, *165*(5), 579–587. doi: 10.1176/appi.ajp.2008.07081242.

Woodberry, K. A., McFarlane, W. R., Giuliano, A. J., Verdi, M. B., Cook, W. L., Faraone, S. V., & Seidman, L. J. (2013). Change in neuropsychological functioning over one year in youth at clinical high risk for psychosis. *Schizophrenia Research*, *146*(1), 87–94.

Woodruff, P. W., McManus, I. C., & David, A. S. (1995). Meta-analysis of corpus callosum size in schizophrenia. *Journal of Neurology, Neurosurgery & Psychiatry*, *58*(4), 457–461.

Chapter 13

Emerging Personality Disorders

SOPHIE KERR, PETER FONAGY, AND CARLA SHARP

Chapter Overview

Personality disorders are defined by pervasive and inflexible patterns of feeling and behavior that onset in adolescence or early adulthood and lead to significant distress or impairment (American Psychiatric Association, 2013). The term "pervasive" indicates that, unlike disorders such as anxiety or depression, personality disorders are part of someone's personality functioning. However, personality disorders are not as persistent and unremitting as historically assumed and there are now multiple evidence-based treatments available. We focus the current chapter on *borderline personality disorder* (BPD), which is characterized by patterns of instability in interpersonal relationships, self-image, and emotion, as well as impulsive behavior. We focus on BPD for two reasons. First, personality disorders have overlapping features and often co-occur with each other, and evidence suggests that BPD represents the "core" of all personality disorders (Sharp et al., 2015). Therefore, much of what we discuss regarding BPD may be common to personality disorders in general. Second, there is a large body of research on BPD in young people, and we know more about the development and treatment of BPD in adolescents than of any other personality disorders.

Despite widespread evidence that BPD usually onsets in adolescence, many practitioners are reluctant to diagnose BPD prior to age 18. However, the diagnosis of BPD has been shown to be as valid and reliable in adolescence as it is in adulthood (Sharp & Fonagy, 2015). Additionally, while it is true that significant stigma surrounds the diagnosis, research has demonstrated that disorder-specific treatment is

Developmental Psychopathology, First Edition. Edited by Amanda Venta, Carla Sharp, Jack M. Fletcher, and Peter Fonagy.

effective. Therefore, identifying people with BPD early in life is crucial for prevention and intervention. Below, we present an example of an adolescent who shows features of BPD.

Case Vignette

Lisa is a 16-year-old girl who lives with her mother and stepfather. According to her mother, she has been "extremely moody" since she was a young child and has always shown stronger emotional reactions than her peers ("she gets triggered so easily, and usually it seems like for no reason," said her mother). Throughout her life, Lisa has had periods of sadness and has been in trouble at school for acting out. However, her mental health problems have become much worse over the past few years. She was recently hospitalized after she told her boyfriend that she was going to overdose on her anti-depressant medication while arguing with him on the phone. This is consistent with past extreme efforts to keep others from leaving her (e.g., lying to friends, calling her boyfriend sobbing when he spends time with other people). Her boyfriend was very concerned, especially considering she had seriously attempted suicide one year ago, and called Lisa's mother to tell her about the suicidal statement. Lisa's mother went to Lisa's room where Lisa was acting "calm and zoned out" and said that she felt like she was floating above her body. Lisa has often described these kinds of experiences when distressed. After she appeared "somewhat back to normal" half an hour later, her parents explained the plan to bring her to the hospital. She became extremely angry and hit the wall of her bedroom, injuring her hand. She frequently has anger outbursts and also engages in non-suicidal self-injurious behaviors including cutting her arms and thighs using a razor and scratching her arms to draw blood. During the assessment at the hospital, she reported that she cuts herself when she feels overwhelmed or "just to feel something" because she feels empty or numb. In addition to the self-harm and suicidal statements, her parents expressed concern for her safety because she has been binge-drinking and using drugs over the past year and was recently arrested for reckless driving while under the influence. When asked about her social life, her parents report that she is extraverted and always seems to have a few friends, but that she tends to quickly shift from acting "obsessed" with friends or boyfriends to believing that they are out to get her, and therefore she has difficulty maintaining long-term relationships. They also noted that she seems to frequently change the groups she hangs out with and the way she presents herself, like she is "taking on a new identity." When the therapist at the hospital asked Lisa to describe herself as a person, Lisa reported that she had "no idea what to say."

As the clinician treating Lisa and her family, what diagnoses would you consider? Describe supporting information for each possible diagnosis. Provide any other information you would want to gather during an assessment with Lisa to guide diagnosis and treatment.

Definition, Diagnosis, and Clinical Features

There are two parallel systems for diagnosing personality disorders in the DSM-5: the traditional, categorical approach and the *Alternative Model of Personality Disoder* (AMPD) (APA, 2013). The categorical approach in Section II of the DSM-5 (see Table 13.1) presents ten personality disorders as distinct syndromes each requiring a certain number of behavioral criteria: paranoid, schizoid, schizotypal, antisocial, borderline, histrionic, narcissistic, avoidant, dependent, and obsessive-compulsive personality disorders. As discussed in Chapter 1, this system has been heavily criticized as invalid. Therefore, a group of researchers and clinicians proposed a new system that integrates categorical and dimensional approaches: the AMPD. Although the board of the American Psychiatric Association rejected the proposal because they did not believe enough work had been done to translate the workgroup's proposal into clinical practice, this classification system is presented in Section III (Emerging Models and Measures) of the DSM-5 (see Table 13.1). It is recommended that both the categorical and alternative models are used to inform clinical practice and research.

Using the AMPD, a personality disorder can be diagnosed when an individual shows moderate or greater impairment in *personality (self/ interpersonal) functioning* (Criterion A) and at least one *pathological personality trait* (Criterion B) (APA, 2013). Criteron A describes core dysfunction shared among all personality disorders and Criterion B describes behavioral expressions of personality pathology. Criterion A function includes two domains (self and interpersonal) and four elements (self: identity and self-direction, interpersonal: empathy and intimacy), and each element contains three facets (see Table 13.2). For Criterion B, pathological personality traits are described across five domains (negative affectivity, detachment, antagonism, disinhibition, and psychoticism) and includes 25 specific trait facets (see Table 13.3). Based on the trait facets met, one of six categorical diagnoses can be assigned: antisocial, avoidant, borderline, narcissistic, obsessive-compulsive, and

TABLE 13.1 DSM-5 Diagnostic Criteria for Borderline Personality Disorder (adapted from APA, 2013)

DSM-5 Section II	*DSM-5 Section III*
BPD criteria (APA, 2013, p. 663) requires "a pervasive pattern of instability of interpersonal relationships, self-image, and affects, and marked impulsivity" indicated by at least 5 of the 9 following personality traits: 1. Frantic efforts to avoid abandonment 2. Unstable and intense interpersonal relationships, alternating between idealization and devaluation 3. Identity disturbance, with unstable self-image or sense of self 4. Impulsivity in at least two areas (e.g., spending, substance abuse, reckless driving, binge eating) 5. Recurrent suicidal or self-mutilating behavior 6. Affective instability 7. Chronic feelings of emptiness 8. Inappropriate, intense anger, or difficulty controlling anger 9. Transient, stress-related paranoid ideation or severe dissociative symptoms	Proposed BPD criteria (APA, 2013, pp. 766–767) requires: A. Moderate or greater impairment in personality functioning, indicated by at least two of the following four areas of difficulty: 1. **Identity:** poorly developed or unstable self-image, excessive self-criticism, chronic emptiness, or dissociative states under stress 2. **Self-direction:** instability in goals, aspirations, values, or career plans 3. **Empathy:** difficulty recognizing the feelings and needs of others, interpersonal hypersensitivity 4. **Intimacy:** intense, unstable, and conflicted close relationships, preoccupation with abandonment; alternating between idealization and devaluation B. At least 4 of the following 7 pathological personality trait facets (at least one must be impulsivity, risk taking, or hostility): 1. ***Emotional lability*** (an aspect of Negative Affectivity) 2. ***Anxiousness*** (an aspect of Negative Affectivity) 3. ***Separation insecurity*** (an aspect of Negative Affectivity) 4. ***Depressivity*** (an aspect of Negative Affectivity) 5. ***Impulsivity*** (an aspect of Disinhibition) 6. ***Risk taking*** (an aspect of Disinhibition) 7. ***Hostility*** (an aspect of Antagonism)
General PD criteria that must also be met (APA, 2013): 1. Symptoms must relatively inflexible and pervasive across multiple contexts (i.e., the symptoms do not occur only at home or during certain times) 2. Symptoms must result in significant distress or impairment in functioning 3. Symptoms or patterns of behavior are stable across time and their onset can be traced back to adolescence or early adulthood 4. Symptoms are not better explained by another mental disorder 5. Symptoms are not attributable to physiological effects of a substance or another medical condition	General PD criteria that must also be met (APA, 2013): 1. Personality dysfunction and trait expression must be relatively inflexible and pervasive across multiple contexts (i.e., the symptoms do not occur only at home or during certain times) 2. Personality dysfunction is stable across time and onset can be traced back to adolescence or early adulthood 3. Not better explained by another mental disorder 4. Not attributable to physiological effects of a substance or another medical condition 5. Impairments are not better understood as normal for an individual's developmental stage or sociocultural environment
Onset and duration (APA, 2013): • Onset in adolescence or early adulthood • Personality disorders may be applied to children or adolescents in "relatively unusual instances in which the individual's particular maladaptive personality traits appear to be pervasive, persistent, and unlikely to be limited to a particular developmental stage or another mental disorder" (APA, 2014, p. 647) • Individuals under 18: features must be present for at least one year • Adults: features must be present for at least two years	Onset and duration (APA, 2013): • Onset in adolescence or early adulthood • Duration is the same for youth and adults, with no specific requirement except that dysfunction is "relatively stable across time" (APA, 2013, p. 761)

TABLE 13.2 Elements of Personality Functioning (Criterion A of AMPD)

Core domains	*Elements*	*Facets*
Self-functioning	Identity	Experience of oneself as unique, with clear boundaries between self and others
		Stability of self-esteem and accuracy of self-appraisal
		Capacity for, and ability to regulate, a range of emotional experiences
	Self-direction	Pursuit of coherent and meaningful short-term and life goals
		Utilization of constructive and prosocial internal standards of behavior
		Ability to self-reflect productively
Interpersonal functioning	Empathy	Comprehension and appreciation of others' experiences and motivations
		Tolerance of differing perspectives
		Understanding the effects of one's own behavior on others
	Intimacy	Depth and duration of connection with others
		Desire and capacity for closeness
		Mutuality of regard reflected in interpersonal behavior

TABLE 13.3 Pathological Personality Trait Domains and Facets (Criterion B of AMPD)

Trait domains	*Facets*
Negative affectivity	Emotional Lability; Anxiousness; Separation Insecurity; Submissiveness; Hostility; Perseveration; Depressivity; Suspiciousness; Restricted Affectivity
Detachment	Withdrawal; Intimacy Avoidance; Anhedonia; Depressivity; Restricted Affectivity; Suspiciousness
Antagonism	Manipulativenss; Deceitfulness; Grandiosity; Attention Seeking; Callousness; Hostility
Disinhibition	Irresponsibility; Impulsivity; Distractibility; Risk Taking; Rigid Perfectionism
Psychoticism	Unusual Beliefs and Experiences; Eccentricity; Cognitive and Perceptual Dysregulation

schizotypal personal disorder. When an individual shows moderate or greater self/interpersonal impairment and at least one pathological personality trait, but the traits do not align with criteria for a specific disorder, PD-Trait Specified (PD-TS) is diagnosed.

The categorical criteria for BPD require five of nine behavioral traits (see Table 13.1 for criteria). The criteria are the same across adolescents and adults, but adolescents must show these features for at least one year compared to two years in adults (APA, 2013). To diagnose BPD using the AMPD, moderate or greater difficulty in at least two of the four elements of self/other functioning (identity, self-direction, empathy, intimacy), and at least four of seven pathological personality traits need to be identified (see Table 13.1). The necessary duration is the same for adolescents and adults, with no specific timeframe but instead a requirement that symptoms are "relatively stable across time" (APA 2013, p. 761). Because the AMPD was published only in 2013, most research on BPD in adolescents has been based on Section II-defined BPD, although research on Section III is rapidly growing.

BPD can be difficult to diagnose because it shares features with both internalizing and externalizing disorders, and individuals with BPD usually present with a number of other disorders. Additionally, some features of BPD resemble normal aspects of adolescence. Adolescence is a time of rapid development and change, and many adolescents struggle with mood swings, forming an identity, maintaining positive relationships, or impulse control. While adolescents generally show an increase in these problems but then improve as they enter adulthood, a subgroup of adolescents present with severe symptoms (e.g., very risky behavior, persistent suicidality and self-harm, or dissociation) that persist into adulthood, and these are the adolescents who would meet BPD criteria (Cohen, Crawford, Johnson, & Kasen, 2005).

BPD is associated with extremely high risk and severe impairment. In adolescents, persistent self-harm and suicidal behaviors are one of the most distinguishing features of BPD (Yen et al., 2013). Additionally, difficulties with impulsivity and regulating negative emotions can lead to high-risk behaviors such as unsafe sexual activity or substance abuse. Adolescents with BPD also have significant social and academic difficulties and low quality of life, even compared to adolescents with other psychopathology (Chanen, Jovev, & Jackson, 2007). Adolescents with BPD show high rates of psychiatric treatment utilization and frequent hospitalization, with some evidence that costs associated with adolescent BPD are even higher than in adults (Hutsebaut, Feenstra, & Luyten, 2013). It is also important to note that the presence of BPD features, even when individuals do not meet the diagnostic threshold, is still associated with significant risk and impairment.

Prevalence

Studies suggest that BPD occurs in 1–3% of the general adult population and, though there is less data, it is estimated that the prevalence is also about 1–3% in the general adolescent population (Sharp &

Fonagy, 2015). However, BPD is much more common in clinical settings, with prevalence estimates of 15–22% in adolescent outpatient settings and 33–49% in adolescent inpatient settings. Longitudinal studies suggest that BPD features typically emerge in adolescence, peak in late adolescence and early adulthood, then decline over the following decades, making the diagnosis less common in older adults (Cohen et al., 2005).

Gender differences in the prevalence of BPD have been a particular topic of interest among researchers. It is consistently reported that BPD is more common in women in samples of adults seeking psychiatric treatment, with the DSM-5 reporting a 3:1 female to male gender ratio in diagnoses (APA, 2013). However, some studies using samples from the general population report no significant gender difference (Grant et al., 2008). Few studies have examined gender differences in adolescents, but existing data also suggests generally higher prevalence among females in clinical samples, but no significant gender differences in a large population-based study (Zanarini et al., 2011). It is unclear whether the unequal gender distribution in treatment-seeking samples reflects bias in diagnosis or sample selection versus true gender differences.

Surprisingly few studies have meaningfully compared prevalence estimates based on sociodemographic variables. Population-based studies report significantly higher rates of BPD in lower-income, Native American, and Black adults and significantly lower rates in Asian adults (Grant et al., 2008). While further research is needed, such disparities may reflect greater mental distress and exposure to traumatic stress among low-SES and racial minority populations.

Comorbidity

Individuals with BPD almost always suffer from additional psychological disorders. The rate of *comorbidity* in adolescents with BPD is significantly higher than in adolescents with other types of psychopathology and may be even higher than in adults with BPD (Chanen et al., 2007). Common comorbidities include mood, anxiety, externalizing, eating, posttraumatic stress, and substance use disorders, as well as other personality disorders. However, BPD cannot be fully explained by internalizing or externalizing psychopathology (Eaton et al., 2011). Instead, personality pathology appears to be a confluence of internalizing and externalizing symptoms and at the same time a qualitatively distinct construct characterized by underlying problems in self/interpersonal functioning (Sharp & Wall, 2017).

Developmental Continuities and Discontinuities (Course)

During adolescence, individuals face new challenges that make them particularly vulnerable for the development of BPD symptoms (Sharp & Wall, 2017). This includes new interpersonal demands (e.g., creating a social network, developing romantic relationships) and the development of identity and sense of self. When these processes go awry, the self/interpersonal dysfunction described by Criterion A in DSM-5 Section III may emerge. Therefore, although younger children may show temperamental and behavioral indicators of risk for BPD, it is not until the *sensitive period* of adolescence, during which developmental changes in self and interpersonal processes take place, that personality disorder onsets.

There is evidence that Section II-defined BPD demonstrates *homotypic continuity* (the same disorder predicts itself over time). In both adolescents and adults, BPD shows moderate to strong *rank-order stability*, meaning that individuals maintain a fairly consistent placement relative to the rest of the population on their level of BPD traits (Bornovalova, Hicks, Iacono, & McGue, 2009). However, *categorical stability*, defined as the continuity of a categorical diagnosis (i.e., meeting at least five of the nine DSM-5 Section II features), is not as stable as traditionally assumed. Even adults show high rates of change and remission from a categorical diagnosis (Zanarini, Frankenburg, Reich, & Fitzmaurice 2012). This does not imply that individuals in remission are completely healthy. These individuals often continue to showimpairment in social and occupational domains and other areas of functioning.

BPD also shows *heterotypic continuity*. Individuals who go on to develop BPD often show traits and symptoms early in childhood that may reflect an underlying vulnerability for personality pathology that manifests differently across developmental stages. These early indicators include emotionality, impulsivity, noncomformity, and aggression (Stepp & Lazarus, 2017). Studies also suggest that BPD manifests as more acute, externalizing behaviors (outbursts, self-harm, extreme risk-taking) in adolescents compared to adults (Stepp, Burke, Hipwell, & Loeber, 2012). Internalizing symptoms (chronic emptiness, negative emotionality) and comorbid internalizing disorders become more prominent with age, while externalizing symptoms decrease into adulthood and then are retained (Eaton et al., 2011). These age-related differences in externalizing symptoms coincide with the developmental trajectory of impulsivity, which tends to decrease from adolescence to young adulthood and then remains relatively stable. In summary, homotypic continuity is demonstrated by moderate stability of the disorder in adolescence and adulthood while heterotypic continuity is reflected by persistent distress and impairment (likely arising from problems in self- and interpersonal function) despite changes in the manifestation and number of symptoms across age.

A Developmental Psychopathology Model of Borderline Personality Disorder

Contemporary etiological theories of BPD emphasize dynamic interactions between genetic, temperamental, cognitive, and environmental factors that together increase the risk of developing BPD. In the *biosocial model*, BPD is characterized as a disorder of *emotion dysregulation* (Linehan, 1993). This emotion dysregulation develops when underlying biological and temperamental features of emotionality and impulsivity interact with failures in the social environment, particularly an *invalidating environment*. The *mentalization-based theory* posits that a core feature of BPD is a reduced or unstable capacity for *mentalizing*, which is the ability to reflect on one's own and others' mental states and to understand the relationships between mental states and behaviors (Fonagy & Bateman, 2008). In this model, early disruption in the attachment (caregiver–child) relationship and later traumatic experiences in the attachment context interact with neurobiological development to disrupt social-cognitive development, thereby leading to BPD. Though they differ in their focus on specific processes and factors, each etiological theory of BPD describes complex interactions between internal (child) and external (environmental) factors that together increase the risk of BPD, with particular attention to factors related to *interpersonal relatedness* and functioning, such as emotional sensitivity, attachment, experiences of parenting, and social cognition. Our developmental psychopathology model of BPD (see Figure 13.1) includes aspects of these theoretical approaches and organizes empirical evidence on risk and protective factors for BPD by their level of explanation to depict the complex etiology of BPD.

GENETIC FACTORS

Family and twin studies

Research suggests that BPD is moderately heritable in adults, with heritability estimates ranging from 42–69% (Sharp & Fonagy, 2015). There have been fewer studies with youth, but existing evidence supports the idea that genetic vulnerabilities interact with environmental factors to result in BPD. For example, Belsky and colleagues (2012) measured BPD features in a large sample of twins at age 12 and found that traits were both heritable and associated with harsh parental treatment. It is more likely that individuals inherit predispositions and vulnerabilities for traits that underlie the symptoms of BPD, rather than inheriting the actual disorder. The heritable predispositions may lead to a variety of outcomes or psychological symptoms, depending on other genetic factors and the environment.

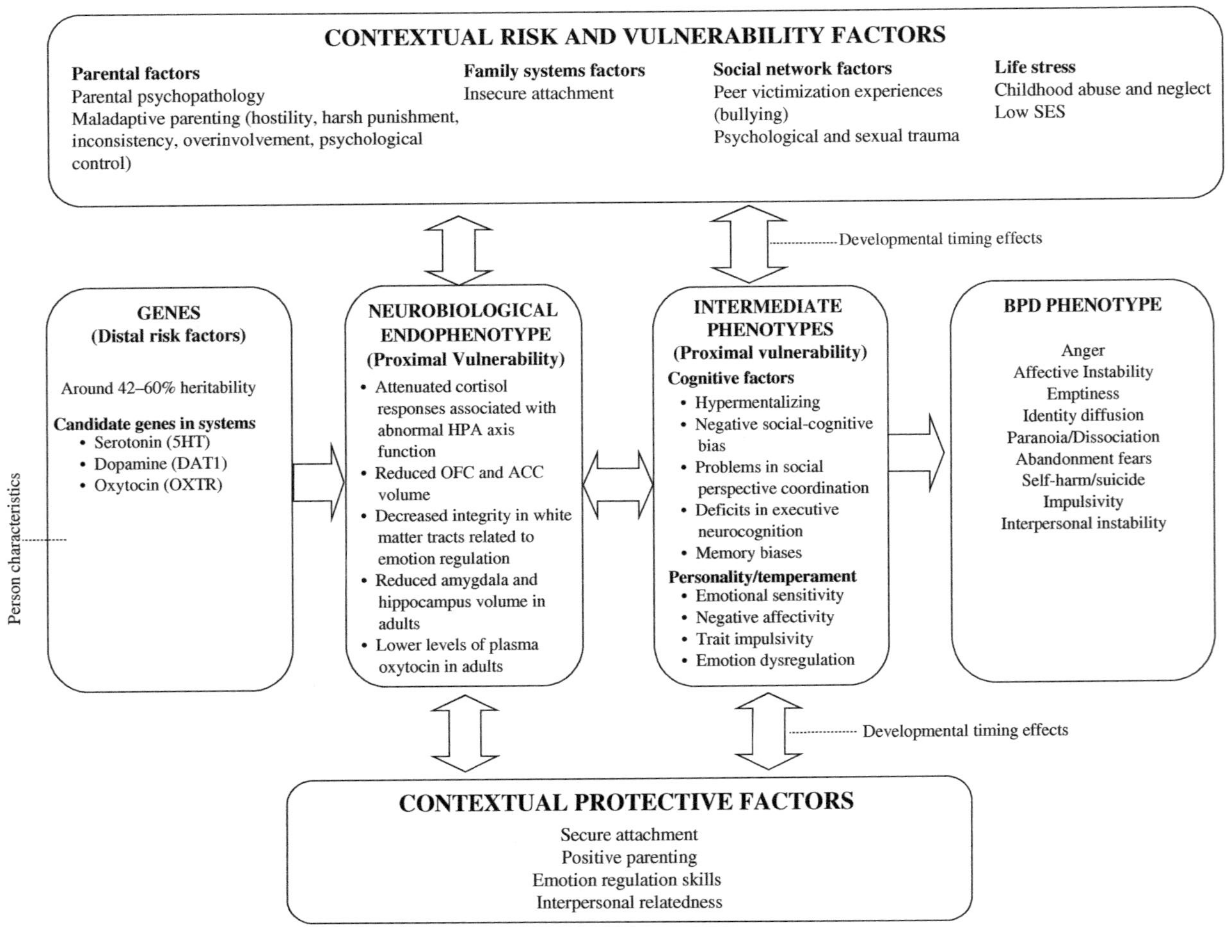

FIGURE 13.1 A Developmental Psychopathology Model of Borderline Personality

Molecular genetic studies

Studies have found preliminary evidence that genes implicated in *serotonin, dopamine, hypothalamic–pituitary–adrenal (HPA) axis*, and *oxytocin* systems play a role in the development of BPD. For example, in community samples of youth age 9–15, carriers of the short allele of the serotonin transporter promoter gene 5-HTTLPR exhibited the highest levels of BPD traits, consistent with findings in adults (Hankin et al., 2011). It would make sense that the serotonin system is involved in BPD given its role in suicide, impulsivity, and emotional instability. Researchers hypothesize that high novelty seeking (tendencies to be excitable, anger-prone, and impulsive) in BPD may be related to altered dopaminergic function. The role of the HPA-axis and oxytocin will be discussed further in the *hormonal systems* and *neuropeptides* sections, respectively.

With these preliminary findings in mind, researchers have not identified reliable, well-established *candidate genes* related specifically to BPD. There have only been two genome-wide association studies on BPD, and both were conducted in adults. The lack of consistent, specific genetic findings likely reflects the complex and multifactorial nature of BPD and of psychopathology more generally. Studies may benefit from a focus on the genetic transmission of underlying vulnerabilities or endophenotypes of BPD such as impulsivity, problems in social cognition, altered neural structure and circuitry, or other neurobiological pathways.

NEUROBIOLOGICAL FACTORS

Neurotransmitters

Underlying dysregulation in *neurotransmitters*, including serotonin, dopamine, and norepinephrine, may also play a role in the development of BPD. Research suggests that traumatic stress in childhood, which is very common in individuals with BPD, may be responsible for altering aspects of the serotonin system, particularly serotonin receptors (Rinne, Westernberg, den Boer, & van den Brink, 2000). However, most research on the relation between BPD and the serotonergic and dopaminergic systems has focused on the genes we reviewed above, rather than the neurotransmitters directly. Lastly, norepinephrine may be implicated in the aggressive behaviors and dissociative symptoms found in BPD (Simeon et al., 2007).

Hormonal systems

Behaviors associated with BPD such as mood swings, anger, dissociation, and self-harm are highly reactive to stress, particularly interpersonal stress. This has led to research on the neurobiology of stress responses associated with BPD by examining hypothalamic–pituitary–adrenal (HPA) axis function. Stressful experiences activate the HPA axis, which triggers the production of the hormone cortisol. Over time, prolonged stress can lead to dysregulation of this cortisol stress response. Preliminary research suggests that early childhood trauma impacts HPA axis function, which may lead to the maladaptive stress responses (suppressed or delayed cortisol response) found in individuals with BPD (Kaess et al., 2012).

Neuropeptides

Oxytocin is a neuropeptide that plays a major role in parent–child attachment, interpersonal relationships, and social cognitive processes. Given that BPD is characterized by problems in these areas, oxytocin has been hypothesized to play a role in the development and maintenance of BPD. For example, one study found that the oxytocin receptor gene predicted BPD at age 20 through interaction with early family variables (Hammen, Bower, & Cole, 2015). Researchers have also begun to investigate the exciting question of whether intranasally administered oxytocin could improve social functioning in individuals with BPD. Thus far, findings have been mixed in adolescents and adults and additional investigation is needed to determine its treatment potential.

Structural and functional imaging findings

Research on structural brain differences related to BPD suggest abnormalities in *frontolimbic networks*, which are thought to be involved in emotion processing and regulation as well as social cognition. Adults show reduced volume of the hippocampus, amygdala, and regions of the prefrontal cortex (PFC), including the dorsolateral prefrontal cortex (DLPFC), orbitofrontal cortex (OFC), and anterior cingulate cortex (ACC). Researchers have shown that OFC and ACC alterations found in adult samples are already present in adolescents (Brunner et al., 2010; Goodman et al., 2011), but most adolescent studies have failed to replicate adult hippocampal and amydala differences. Evidence also suggests that adolescents with BPD have decreased structural integrity in the white matter tract connecting the amygdala to the ACC and PFC (Maier-Hein et al., 2014). These white matter changes have been linked to emotion dysregulation and are thought to result from myelin loss, which often follows stressful life events. Therefore, these findings might reflect how environmental factors can impact brain structure and lead to problems associated with BPD.

Similar to structural findings, functional neuroimaging research on the correlates of BPD in adults suggests that dysfunction in frontolimbic circuitry may underlie problems in emotion regulation and social cognition. More specifically, studies have identified patterns of altered function in cortical regions including the prefrontal cortex (PFC) and temporal cortex, as well as limbic regions, including the amygdala and insula (Schulze, Schmahl, & Niedtfeld, 2016). These findings extend to recent, preliminary research in adolescents, but further research is needed in youth samples (Safar et al., 2019).

It is important to note that these neurobiological factors are implicated in a broad range of psychopathology and it is difficult to determine relations that are specific to BPD. Rather, these structural and functional alterations are likely to be transdiagnostic, which makes sense given the high comorbidity between BPD and other disorders.

TEMPERAMENT

The biosocial model provides a helpful framework for understanding the role of temperament in the development of BPD. In this model, BPD is characterized as a disorder of emotion dysregulation, which arises when temperamental vulnerabilities interact with an unsupportive and invalidating environment (Linehan, 1993). The model originally defined the temperamental vulnerability as heightened *emotional sensitivity and reactivity*, reflected by a low threshold for having an emotional reaction, a tendency for very strong emotional reactions, and needing an extended period of time to return to a calm state after experiencing an emotion. More recently, the biosocial theory has been expanded to include *negative affectivity* and *trait impulsivity* (Crowell, Beauchaine, & Linehan, 2009). Negative affectivity is defined by intense and frequent negative emotions (e.g., sadness, fear, anger, and frustration) and difficulty regulating these emotions. Trait impulsivity refers to the propensity for rapid and unplanned behaviors and acting on urges without regard for consequences. Individuals with BPD often engage in impulsive behaviors as attempts to manage or distract from negative emotions. Research shows that emotionality, negative affectivity, and impulsivity in childhood is associated with later BPD (Stepp, Lazarus, & Byrd, 2016).

COGNITIVE FACTORS

Social cognition and mentalization

Given the highly interpersonal nature of the disorder, it makes sense that *social cognition* is the most researched cognitive factor in BPD. The mentalization-based theory hypothesizes that core features of BPD reflect difficulties in *mentalizing*, the social-cognitive capacity to think about own's own and others' thoughts and feelings and understand how mental states (i.e., intentions, thoughts, beliefs) relate to behavior (Fonagy & Luyten, 2009). Early parent–child relationships and attachment to caregivers play a crucial role in the development of social cognition and mentalizing, as we discussed in Chapter 4. In a secure attachment relationship, caregivers display interest in the child's thoughts and feelings and treat the child as their own psychological agent, fostering a coherent sense of self in the child and a curiosity to explore their own and others' minds, as well as epistemic trust (the belief that they can learn from others). Conversely, disruptions in early attachment experiences can derail social cognitive development. More specifically, if caregivers fail to adequately represent and mirror their child's mental states, the child may develop failures in understanding their own and other's mental states and tendencies to misinterpret thoughts and behaviors and mistrust others. This disrupted mentalizing is thought to underly the behaviors and symptoms associated with BPD. Research has shown mentalizing failures in BPD, particularly *hypermentalizing*, the tendency to overattribute mental states to others beyond observable data (Sharp &Vanwoerden, 2015). Further, individuals with BPD tend to overattribute malevolent, rejecting, or hostile mental states to others, reflecting a *negative social-cognitive bias*. For example, if a friend says they need to cancel plans because they are sick, an individual with BPD may misinterpret this as the friend rejecting them because they did not want to spend time together despite no objective evidence to suggest this. Adolescents with BPD also show problems in *social perspective coordination*, which is the capacity to differentiate and integrate the perspective of the self with the perspectives of others (Jennings, Hulbert, Jackson, & Chanen, 2012).

Executive neurocognition and memory

Although BPD is not a neurocognitive disorder, some aspects of executive neurocognition, such as the ability to plan ahead and inhibit responses, are implicated in the development and maintenance of BPD symptoms. Youth with BPD show a preference for immediate gratification and a tendency to discount longer-term rewards, which appears to be connected to trait impulsivity (Lawrence, Allen, & Chanen, 2010). Studies also report that adults with BPD perform worse on assessments of verbal and non-verbal memory, which is also associated with impulsivity (Seres et al., 2009). Across neurocognitive and memory domains, tasks using emotionally charged stimuli led to worsened performance for individuals with BPD, emphasizing the interplay between affective and cognitive vulnerabilities.

CONTEXTUAL RISK FACTORS

Adolescents and adults with BPD usually report histories of trauma, difficulties in the parent–child relationship, and other adverse childhood experiences. These environmental factors have been widely researched and play a pivotal role in etiological models of BPD. For example, the biosocial model emphasizes the role of an invalidating environment in which caregivers or other people in the child's life chronically punish, dismiss, or trivialize their emotions and experiences (Linehan, 1993).

Childhood abuse and neglect

Research supports that childhood abuse (physical, sexual, and emotional) and neglect (e.g. prolonged separation from parents, inadequate supervision, or poor parental care) increase the risk for developing BPD (Stepp, Lazarus, & Byrd, 2016). Maltreatment appears to have a cumulative effect over time, such that greater severity and chronicity confers an even higher risk of BPD. Children who experience maltreatment may adapt to prolonged experiences of threat by becoming more sensitive or reactive to threat, which could generate the lack of trust and interpersonal sensitivity found in individuals with BPD. While it has been historically believed that BPD is largely a consequence of sexual abuse, empirical evidence suggests it is actually a rather weak and nonspecific risk factor (Fossati, Mededdu, & Maffei, 1999). Therefore, it is important to consider broader definitions of maltreatment, including emotional abuse.

Parental psychopathology

As we discussed in our section on genetic factors, studies support intergenerational transmission of BPD and BPD features. Additionally, parental internalizing and externalizing disorders also increase the risk of BPD (Stepp, Lazarus, & Byrd, 2016). This may result from inherited vulnerabilities for general psychopathology or from parental psychopathology affecting parenting behaviors and thereby affecting offspring development.

Attachment

Given the highly interpersonal nature of the disorder, it makes sense that *attachment* has long been theorized as an important factor in the development of BPD. Attachment plays an important role in the prominent theories of BPD: emotion regulation and mentalizing capacities are both thought to develop in the context of secure attachment. In a secure attachment relationship, caregivers communicate to the child that others can be regarded as reliable, responsible, and trustworthy. In contrast, disruptions in the attachment relationship may lead to an internal working model characterized by expectations that others will be unreliable, unresponsive, or lacking in care. This might help explain why individuals with BPD display hypersensitivity to interpersonal threats and intense fears of abandonment. The vast majority of adults with BPD are classified as insecurely attached (Levy, 2005). The adult attachment styles most characteristic of BPD are unresolved, fearful, and preoccupied, which each reflect a simultaneous desire for intimacy and concerns of dependency or rejection. Moreover, longitudinal studies report that attachment insecurity in infancy, childhood, and adolescence predict later BPD features (Stepp et al., 2016).

Maladaptive parenting

In addition to attachment, studies suggest that parenting practices including low warmth, high hostility, and harsh disciplinary practices increase the risk of BPD. Studies that used observational assessments to measure parenting found that disrupted maternal communication at 18 months predicted BPD symptoms at age 18, maternal hostility at 42 months predicted BPD symptoms at age 28, and maternal expressed negative emotion in middle childhood predicted BPD features at age 12 (Stepp, Lazarus, & Byrd, 2016). It is important to note that parent–child dynamics are transactional and reciprocal, not one-way causal pathways. For example, Stepp and colleagues (2014) found that parental low warmth and harsh punishment predicted subsequent increases in adolescent BPD symptoms while adolescent BPD symptoms predicted subsequent increases in parental levels of low warmth and harsh punishment.

Peer victimization

As children age, they spend increasingly more time with peers and less time with parents. Although most research on contextual risk factors has focused on family variables, emerging research suggests that bullying and psychological or sexual violence by peers contribute to the development of BPD (Sansone, Lam, & Wiederman, 2010; Vanwoerden et al., 2019; Wolke, Schreier, Zanarini, & Winsper, 2012).

Contextual Protective Factors

Relatively little evidence exists on potential protective factors that may buffer against the risk factors that we have reviewed thus far. Retrospective reports of validating parenting experiences appeared to be a protective factor against BPD features in a community sample of adults (Gill & Warburton, 2014). In adolescents, attachment security appears to buffer against BPD symptoms through adaptive regulation of positive emotions (Kim, Sharp, & Carbone, 2014). Additionally, we can assume that factors that are opposite of prominent risk factors, such as positive parenting and the development of interpersonal relatedness, would also act as protective factors.

Gene–Environment Interplay

We have reviewed many factors from a variety of levels (e.g. genetic, neurobiological, contextual) that are each associated with the development of BPD. However, these should not be regarded as independent causal factors; instead, they interact and influence each other over time, together leading to the development of BPD. We now discuss the emerging evidence that illustrates this interplay between factors at different levels, though further research on the interactions between risk and protective factors is sorely needed.

Gene–environment correlations and interactions

Consistent with the stress-diathesis approach, several studies support the interactive effects of genetic and environmental factors. For example, Distel and colleagues (2011) investigated the contributions of heritability and life events to BPD features and found gene–environment correlations. Genetic risk factors for BPD increased the likelihood that individuals would also experience environmental risk factors for BPD (divorce, sexual assault, and job loss). They also found gene–environment interactions where genetic factors exerted less influence on BPD features in individuals who experienced sexual assault, suggesting that the risk associated with sexual assault is large enough to predict BPD features even in individuals with low levels of genetic vulnerability. Other evidence of gene–environment interaction includes the finding that variations in the tryptophan hydroxylase 1 gene increase the risk of BPD when combined with a history of childhood abuse (Wilson et al., 2012). Studies have also investigated *epigenetic* mechanisms in which experiences of maltreatment may affect DNA methylation, thereby affecting gene function and expression. Evidence suggests that methylation of genes involved in the HPA-axis stress response system relates to both childhood maltreatment and BPD severity in adults, which may indicate gene–environment interaction (Martín-Blanco et al., 2014). Beyond maltreatment, other family variables appear to contribute greater risk for BPD when combined with genetic vulnerability. For example, effects of family functioning on BPD features were only observed in individuals with a polymorphism of the oxytocin receptor gene (Hammen et al., 2015).

Environment–temperament interactions

We would never argue that the onset of BPD in adolescence is predicted from the behaviors and tendencies displayed in infancy or early childhood alone. Temperamental predispositions or vulnerabilities interact with environmental risk factors including abuse, parenting, and family adversity. For example, one study found that the relationship between childhood abuse and BPD symptoms depended on temperament; specifically, abuse was only associated with BPD in children with low levels of affiliation (a desire for and pleasure in warmth and closeness with others; Jovev et al., 2013). Evidence also suggests that poor self-control (which relates to trait impulsivity) predicts BPD symptoms through reciprocal effects with parental harsh discipline (Hallquist, Hipwell, & Stepp, 2015). Lastly, another study reported an interaction between negative affectivity and family adversity, with high levels of both predicting the highest levels of BPD symptoms (Stepp et al., 2016).

DEVELOPMENTAL TIMING EFFECTS

Very little research has considered timing effects for the development of BPD. One example of such findings is that children with early experiences of childhood maltreatment and children with chronic experiences of maltreatment (spanning more developmental periods) were at higher risk for BPD than children who began to experience maltreatment later in childhood (Hecht, Cicchetti, Rogosch, & Crick, 2014). With the goal to prevent the disorder before it emerges in mind, it is unfortunate that few studies have examined predictors of the onset of BPD, rather than symptom severity. Therefore, researchers recommend that future studies assess BPD during developmentally sensitive windows, use samples that will have a high likelihood of onset during these windows, and use retrospective data to identify precursors or prodromes to onset (Stepp, Lazarus, & Byrd., 2016). One key window may be adolescence. As discussed in Section 13.2, studies consistently support that BPD onsets during adolescence and it is during this time that crucial interpersonal and identity formation processes may go awry, leading to the development of personality pathology (Sharp & Wall, 2017). Moving forward, research on risk and protective factors during the *sensitive period* of adolescence may be particularly informative.

THE GENERAL FACTOR FOR PSYCHOPATHOLOGY

A rapidly growing area of research in mental health has been around the concept of a general risk factor for psychopathology, labelled the "p" (for psychopathology) factor, echoing the widely used concept of a general factor for intelligence known as the g factor (Caspi et al., 2014). The idea of a p factor is appealing in that it would explain why current definitions of mental health disorders do not always align with reality in two respects. First, manifestations of mental health symptoms and disorders do not often fit within discrete diagnostic categories—i.e., many people experience comorbidity, or they might suffer from a particular disorder at one stage and a quite different disorder later on in life. A typical example is an individual receiving a diagnosis of conduct disorder in adolescence and a diagnosis of severe depression in adulthood. These are two categorically distinct disorders but there may be a continuity in the pathology that underpins them. Second, research at statistical, microbiological, and genetic levels has been surprisingly unsuccessful at identifying disease entities. Indeed, the p factor concept originates in statistical research using a particular approach known as bifactor analysis. This form of analysis looks for what different diagnoses may have in common. For example, irritability and impulsive behavior are common symptoms for a range of disorders. Bifactor analyses of the symptoms of large groups of adults, adolescents, and children have shown that after accounting for the symptoms that different diagnoses share, what is left might be best undersood as a general vulnerability for psychopathology (i.e., the p factor). This general psychopathology risk "measures a person's liability to mental disorder, comorbidity among disorders, persistence of disorders over time, and severity" (Lahey et al., 2018, p. 1).

The p factor has recently been applied to understanding BPD. In a large sample of inpatients, such analysis revealed that once the common symptoms across different PD diagnoses were accounted, BPD was best understood as itself the general factor that underpins an individual's level vulnerability to PD symptoms of all kinds, rather than as a separate psychiatric diagnosis (Sharp et al., 2015). In other words, BPD might represent the core features of most, if not all, PD symptomatology. It has been further suggested that BPD could be an expression of an individual's position on the p factor spectrum, associated with greater risk, higher levels of comorbidity, and symptom severity (Fonagy et al., 2017).

Evidence-Based Interventions

BPD is not as persistent and untreatable as traditionally assumed and multiple evidence-based treatments have been established for BPD and related problems in adults. Less research exists on treatment for adolescents, but there is a growing focus on tailoring evidence-based treatments for youth with BPD and developing prevention programs for individuals who display emerging symptoms. Though many adults with BPD take psychiatric medications, there are no evidence-based pharmacological interventions for BPD. Therefore, we only review psychotherapeutic interventions and prevention programs in this chapter.

Psychotherapy Interventions

Dialectical behavior therapy (DBT) is the most widely investigated treatment for BPD and its efficacy is supported by numerous randomized-controlled trials in adults (RCTs). DBT is based on the biosocial model of BPD that we have described throughout this chapter and targets emotion dysregulation as the core problem in BPD. The treatment evolved from cognitive-behavioral therapy and represents a blend of three theoretical orientations: behavioral science, dialectical philosophy, and Zen practice. Through balancing principles of change and acceptance, the treatment targets emotion regulation, mindfulness, distress tolerance, and interpersonal effectiveness. Treatment includes weekly group classes focused on teaching behavioral skills, weekly individual therapy, and phone coaching between sessions in which clients can call their therapist for guidance on in-the-moment skill use. DBT for adolescents (DBT-A) follows the same structure but includes family members in skills groups and provides an optional family therapy component. Two RCTs support the efficacy of DBT-A for BPD.

Mentalization-based treatment (MBT) is another empirically supported treatment for BPD in adults that has been adapted for adolescents. MBT aligns with the mentalization-based theory of BPD and aims to improve and stabilize emotional expression, sense of self, and interpersonal relationships by enhancing mentalizing capacities (Bateman & Fonagy, 2010). MBT can be delivered in individual and group therapy formats. MBT for adolescents (MBT-A) adds a family therapy component and more explicitly focuses on impulsivity and affect regulation, given that these problems are more pronounced in adolescence. Individual and group MBT-A have each been examined by an RCT and were found to be effective.

These studies provide preliminary support that the evidence-based treatments for BPD in adults extend to younger populations. Transference-focused psychotherapy, a psychodynamic treatment that has received support for treatment of BPD in adults, has also been adapted for use in adolescents, but has yet to be evaluated in an RCT.

PREVENTION PROGRAMS AND CLINICAL STAGING MODELS

Other psychotherapy programs aim for prevention by targeting adolescents with emerging BPD features or risk factors rather than those with a diagnosis. The Helping Young People Early program is a comprehensive prevention and early intervention program that incorporates *cognitive analytic therapy* (CAT), a treatment that shares features with MBT and integrates psychoanalytic object relations theory with cognitive psychology. In an RCT, CAT was effective for adolescents with at least one childhood risk factor and at least three BPD criteria (Chanen et al., 2009). The Dutch Emotion Regulation Training (ERT) treatment program is a relatively brief group training for adolescents suffering from two or more BPD criteria. ERT was adapted from Systems Training for Emotional Predictability and Problem Solving (STEPPS), and shares features with DBT. An RCT found that symptoms decreased and were maintained at 6-month follow-up, but that ERT did not demonstrate additional benefits compared to treatment as usual (Marieke Schuppert et al., 2012).

Recently, researchers have proposed *clinical staging models* that suggest treatments in proportion to the progression of personality dysfunction (Chanen, Berk, & Thompson, 2016; Hutsebaut, Videler, Verheul, & Van Alphen, 2019; Sharp, Kerr, & Chanen, 2021). As used in other fields of psychology and medicine, these models describe the progression of a disorder through five stages based on severity and duration, beginning with individuals who are at risk but do not show symptoms and ending with a persistent and unremitting form of the disorder. For example, an adolescent in an early stage of BPD may benefit from brief psychoeducation and parenting skills training for the family, whereas an adolescent in a late stage of the disorder may require inpatient hospitalization for stabilization as well as long-term intensive outpatient psychotherapy. Future work should focus on elaborating these models, as this approach offers exciting potential for developmentally appropriate, cost-effective, and evidence-based prevention and early intervention.

Chapter Summary

Borderline personality disorder onsets during adolescence and is associated with severe risk, impairment, and burden. In this chapter, we began by discussing contemporary diagnostic conceptualizations of personality disorders and the typical clinical features associated with BPD. As shown in Figure 13.1, the etiology of BPD is complex and multifactorial. Using the developmental psychopathology model, we presented evidence on the dynamic interplay between genetic, neurobiological, temperamental, cognitive, and environmental factors that contribute to the development and maintenance of BPD. Lastly, we provided an overview of evidence-based treatments with an emphasis on the need for prevention and early intervention of this severe and life-threatening psychological disorder.

Further Reading

Belsky, D. W., Caspi, A., Arseneault, L., Bleidorn, W., Fonagy, P., Goodman, M., Houts, R., & Moffitt, T. E. (2012). Etiological features of borderline personality related characteristics in a birth cohort of 12-year-old children. *Development and Psychopathology*, 24(1), 251–265. https://doi.org/10.1017/S0954579411000812.

Chanen, A. M. (2015). Borderline personality disorder in young people: Are we there yet? *Journal of Clinical Psychology*, 71(8), 778–791.

Sharp, C., & Fonagy, P. (2015). Practitioner review: Borderline personality disorder in adolescence—Recent conceptualization, intervention, and implications for clinical practice. *Journal of Child Psychology and Psychiatry*, 56(12), 1266–1288. https://doi.org/10.1111/jcpp.12449.

Sharp, C., & Wall, K. (2017). Personality pathology grows up: Adolescence as a sensitive period. *Current Opinions in Psychology*, 21, 111–116. https://doi.org/10.1016/j.copsyc.2017.11.010.

Stepp, S. D., Lazarus, S. A., & Byrd, A. L. (2016). A systematic review of risk factors prospectively associated with borderline personality disorder: Taking stock and moving forward. *Personality Disorders: Theory, Research, and Treatment*, 7(4), 316–323. https://doi.org/10.1037/per0000186.

Discussion/Essay Questions

1. Describe differences between the categorical (DSM-5, Section II) diagnostic system for personality disorders and the alternative model for PD (AMPD) presented in DSM-5, Section III. How is borderline personality disorder diagnosed using each model?
2. Explain similarities and differences between the biosocial and mentalization-based models of BPD. What risk factors are emphasized by each theory?
3. Why is adolescence considered a sensitive period for the development of BPD?
4. Describe two examples of how biological and environmental risk factors for BPD may interact and transact with each other.
5. Discuss how certain aspects of the parent–child relationship might increase the risk for developing BPD.
6. Describe two evidence-based treatments for BPD.

Glossary

Affective instability is a feature of BPD that describes marked mood reactivity, with intense feelings of sadness, irritability, or anxiousness that usually last a few hours.

Alternative DSM-5 Model for Personality Disorders (AMPD) is an alternate model for PD diagnosis presented in the Emerging Measures and Models section of the DSM-5. The AMPD is a hybrid categorical/dimensional model that characterizes personality disorders by impairments in personality (self/interpersonal) functioning and by pathological personality traits.

Biosocial model characterizes BPD as primarily a disorder of emotion dysregulation and proposes that this emotion dysregulation results from transactions between biologically based emotional vulnerabilities and an invalidating environment.

Borderline personality disorder (BPD) is a psychiatric disorder defined by pervasive patterns of instability in interpersonal relationships, self-image, and emotion, as well as impulsivity.

Candidate genes are thought to cause a particular disease or disorder.

Categorical stability is the continuity of meeting a categorical diagnosis over time.

Clinical staging models describe stages of disorder based on duration and severity and suggest treatment strategies that are in proportion to the stage of disorder.

Cognitive analytic therapy (CAT) is a psychotherapeutic treatment that integrates psychoanalytic object relations theory and cognitive psychology.

Dialectical Behavior Therapy (DBT) is an evidence-based treatment for BPD focused on emotion regulation, mindfulness, distress tolerance, and interpersonal effectiveness.

Dissociative symptoms refer to experiences of depersonalization (feeling of separation between oneself and one's body), derealization (feeling detached from the outside world or like things are strange or not real), or both. Individuals with BPD often experience transient (lasting minutes or hours) dissociative symptoms when under severe stress.

Dopamine is a chemical that functions as both a neurotransmitter and hormone and is involved in a variety of processes related to psychopathology including motivation and reward pathways.

Emotional sensitivity/reactivity is described by the biosocial model of BPD as a low threshold for having an emotional reaction, a tendency for very strong emotional reactions, and needing an extended period of time to return to a calm state after experiencing an emotion.

Emotion dysregulation is a core feature of BPD. Broadly, emotion regulation refers to the processes of monitoring, evaluating, and modifying emotional reactions.

Epigenetic processes are when external (e.g., environmental) factors affect gene activity or expression.

Epistemic trust refers to the willingness to consider communication from others as authentic, generalizable, and relevant to the self.

Frontolimbic network is a set of neural structures including the amygdala, anterior cingulate cortex (ACC), hypothalamus, the orbitofrontal cortex (OFC), and the nucleus accumbens and is involved in emotional processing.

Heterotypic continuity refers to the stability of an underlying construct that is manifested or expressed differently across development.

Homotypic continuity is when a psychological problem presents or manifests similarly throughout development or when a particular disorder predicts itself over time.

Hypermentalizing is the tendency to overattribute mental states (intentions, thoughts, beliefs) to others beyond observable data.

Identity disturbance is a feature of BPD characterized by marked and persistently unstable self-image and sense of self.

Interpersonal hypersensitivity describes intense fears of abandonment, sensitivity to rejection, and intolerance of being alone that are associated with BPD.

Interpersonal relatedness refers to the ability to relate to others.

Invalidating environment is a context that responds erratically or inappropriately to the child's emotions and behaviors such that their experiences are punished, dismissed, and trivialized.

Mentalization-based theory posits that disruption in the attachment relationship interacts with neurobiological development to disrupt social-cognitive development (mentalizing), thereby leading to BPD.

Mentalization-based treatment (MBT) is an empirically supported treatment for BPD that aims to improve and stabilize emotional expression, sense of self, and interpersonal relationships through enhancing mentalizing capacities.

Mentalizing refers the ability to reflect on one's own and others' mental states and to understand the relationships between mental states and behaviors.

Negative affectivity is defined by intense and frequent negative emotions (e.g., sadness, fear, anger, and frustration) and difficulty regulating these emotions.

Negative social-cognitive bias is the tendency to attribute negative mental states or intentions to others beyond objective data.

Neurotransmitters are chemicals produced by cells in the nervous system that transmit signals between neurons.

Oxytocin is a chemical that functions as both a hormone and neuropeptide that plays a major role in social bonding and parent–child attachment.

Pathological personality traits are the behavioral expressions or traits of personality pathology described by the AMPD. The model includes five broad trait domains (negative affectivity, detachment, antagonism, disinhibition, and psychoticism) and 25 specific trait facets.

Personality disorders are a group of psychiatric disorders defined by pervasive and inflexible patterns of feelings and behaviors that onset in adolescence or early adulthood and lead to significant distress or impairment.

Personality (self/interpersonal) functioning is the defining feature (Criterion A) of personality disorders in the AMPD. Self-functioning involves elements of identity and self-direction and interpersonal functioning includes elements of empathy and intimacy.

Rank-order stability refers to individuals maintaining a fairly consistent placement relative to the population.

Sensitive period refers to a developmental stage or window of time in which certain factors or experiences have a particularly strong effect.

Serotonin is a neurotransmitter involved in regulation of many processes including mood, sleep, learning, memory, and cognition.

Social cognition involves the processes of perceiving, attending to, remembering, and reflecting on others and interactions with others, as well as the ability to understand the self and others as individuals with their own beliefs, feelings, and personalities.

Social perspective coordination is the capacity to differentiate and integrate the perspective of the self with the perspectives of others.

Trait impulsivity has been defined as tendencies for rapid and unplanned behaviors and to act on urges without regard for consequences.

References

American Psychiatric Association (2013). *Diagnostic and statistical manual of mental disorders* (5th ed.). Washington, DC.

Bateman, A., & Fonagy, P. (2010). Mentalization based treatment for borderline personality disorder. *World Psychiatry: Official Journal of the World Psychiatric Association (WPA)*, 9(1), 11–15.

Belsky, D. W., Caspi, A., Arseneault, L., Bleidorn, W., Fonagy, P., Goodman, M., Houts, R., & Moffitt, T. E. (2012). Etiological features of borderline personality related characteristics in a birth cohort of 12-year-old children. *Development and Psychopathology*, 24(1), 251–265. https://doi.org/10.1017/S0954579411000812.

Bornovalova, M. A., Hicks, B. M., Iacono, W. G., & McGue, M. (2009). Stability, change, and heritability of borderline personality disorder traits from adolescence to adulthood: A longitudinal twin study. *Development and Psychopathology*, 21(4), 1335–1353. https://doi.org/10.1017/S0954579409990186.

Brunner, R., Henze, R., Parzer, P., Kramer, J., Feigl, N., Lutz, K., Essig, M., Resch, F., & Stieltjes, B. (2010). Reduced prefrontal and orbitofrontal gray matter in female adolescents with borderline personality disorder: Is it disorder specific? *NeuroImage*, 49(1), 114–120. https://doi.org/10.1016/j.neuroimage.2009.07.070.

Caspi, A., Houts, R. M., Belsky, D. W., Goldman-Mellor, S. J., Harrington, H., Israel, S., Meier, M. H., Ramrakha, S., Shalev, I., Poulton, R., & Moffitt, T. E. (2014). The p factor: One general psychopathology factor in the structure of psychiatric disorders? *Clinical Psychological Science*, 2(2), 119–137. https://doi.org/10.1177/2167702613497473.

Chanen, A. M., Berk, M., & Thompson, K. (2016). Integrating early intervention for borderline personality disorder and mood disorders. *Harvard Review of Psychiatry*, 24(5), 330–341. https://doi.org/10.1097/HRP.0000000000000105.

Chanen, Andrew M., Jovev, M., & Jackson, H. J. (2007). Adaptive functioning and psychiatric symptoms in adolescents with borderline personality disorder. *The Journal of Clinical Psychiatry*, 68(02), 297–306. https://doi.org/10.4088/JCP.v68n0217.

Chanen, Andrew M., Mccutcheon, L. K., Germano, D., Nistico, H., Jackson, H. J., & Mcgorry, P. D. (2009). The HYPE Clinic: An early intervention service for borderline personality disorder. *Journal of Psychiatric Practice*, 15(3), 163–172. https://doi.org/10.1097/01.pra.0000351876.51098.f0.

Cohen, P., Crawford, T. N., Johnson, J. G., & Kasen, S. (2005). The Children in the Community Study of Developmental Course of Personality Disorder. *Journal of Personality Disorders*, 19(5), 466–486. https://doi.org/10.1521/pedi.2005.19.5.466.

Crowell, S. E., Beauchaine, T. P., & Linehan, M. M. (2009). A biosocial developmental model of borderline personality: Elaborating and extending Linehan's theory. *Psychological Bulletin*, 135(3), 495–510. https://doi.org/10.1037/a0015616.

Distel, M. A., Middeldorp, C. M., Trull, T. J., Derom, C. A., Willemsen, G., & Boomsma, D. I. (2011). Life events and borderline personality features: The influence of gene–environment interaction and gene–environment correlation. *Psychological Medicine*, 41(4), 849–860. https://doi.org/10.1017/S0033291710001297.

Eaton, N. R., Krueger, R. F., Keyes, K. M., Skodol, A. E., Markon, K. E., Grant, B. F., & Hasin, D. S. (2011). Borderline personality disorder co-morbidity: Relationship to the internalizing–externalizing structure of common mental disorders. *Psychological Medicine*, 41(5), 1041–1050. https://doi.org/10.1017/S0033291710001662.

Fonagy, P., & Bateman, A. (2008). The development of borderline personality disorder—A mentalizing model. *Journal of Personality Disorders*, 22(1), 4–21. https://doi.org/10.1521/pedi.2008.22.1.4.

Fonagy, P., & Luyten, P. (2009). A developmental, mentalization-based approach to the understanding and treatment of borderline personality disorder. *Development and Psychopathology*, 21(4), 1355–1381. https://doi.org/10.1017/S0954579409990198.

Fossati, A., Madeddu, F., & Maffei, C. (1999). Borderline personality disorder and childhood sexual abuse: A meta-analytic study. *Journal of Personality Disorders*, 13(3), 268–280. https://doi.org/10.1521/pedi.1999.13.3.268.

Gill, D., & Warburton, W. (2014). An investigation of the biosocial model of borderline personality disorder: Investigating the biosocial model of BPD. *Journal of Clinical Psychology*, 70(9), 866–873. https://doi.org/10.1002/jclp.22074.

Goodman, M., Hazlett, E. A., Avedon, J. B., Siever, D. R., Chu, K.-W., & New, A. S. (2011). Anterior cingulate volume reduction in adolescents with borderline personality disorder and co-morbid major depression. *Journal of Psychiatric Research*, 45(6), 803–807. https://doi.org/10.1016/j.jpsychires.2010.11.011.

Grant, B. F., Chou, S. P., Goldstein, R. B., Huang, B., Stinson, F. S., Saha, T. D., Smith, S. M., Dawson, D. S., Pulay, A. J., Pickering, R. P., & Ruan, W. J. (2008). Prevalence, correlates, disability, and comorbidity of DSM-IV borderline personality disorder: Results from the Wave 2 National Epidemiologic Survey on Alcohol and Related Conditions. *The Journal of Clinical Psychiatry*, 69(4), 533–545. https://doi.org/10.4088/JCP.v69n0404.

Hallquist, M. N., Hipwell, A. E., & Stepp, S. D. (2015). Poor self-control and harsh punishment in childhood prospectively predict borderline personality symptoms in adolescent girls. *Journal of Abnormal Psychology*, 124(3), 549–564. https://doi.org/10.1037/abn0000058.

Hammen, C., Bower, J. E., & Cole, S. W. (2015). Oxytocin receptor gene variation and differential susceptibility to family environment in predicting youth borderline symptoms. *Journal of Personality Disorders*, 29(2), 177–192. https://doi.org/10.1521/pedi_2014_28_152.

Hankin, B. L., Barrocas, A. L., Jenness, J., Oppenheimer, C. W., Badanes, L. S., Abela, J. R. Z., Young, J., & Smolen, A. (2011). Association between 5-HTTLPR and borderline personality disorder traits among youth. *Frontiers in Psychiatry*, 2. https://doi.org/10.3389/fpsyt.2011.00006.

Hecht, K. F., Cicchetti, D., Rogosch, F. A., & Crick, N. R. (2014). Borderline personality features in childhood: The role of subtype, developmental timing, and chronicity of child maltreatment. *Development and Psychopathology*, 26(3), 805–815. https://doi.org/10.1017/S0954579414000406.

Hutsebaut, J., Feenstra, D. J., & Luyten, P. (2013). Personality disorders in adolescence: Label or opportunity? *Clinical Psychology: Science and Practice*, 20(4), 445–451. https://doi.org/10.1111/cpsp.12052.

Hutsebaut, J., Videler, A. C., Verheul, R., & Van Alphen, S. P. J. (2019). Managing borderline personality disorder from a life course perspective: Clinical staging and health management. *Personality Disorders–Theory Research and Treatment*, 10(4), 309–316. https://doi.org/10.1037/per0000341.

Jennings, T. C., Hulbert, C. A., Jackson, H. J., & Chanen, A. M. (2012). Social perspective coordination in youth with borderline personality pathology. *Journal of Personality Disorders*, 26(1), 126–140. https://doi.org/10.1521/pedi.2012.26.1.126.

Jovev, M., McKenzie, T., Whittle, S., Simmons, J. G., Allen, N. B., & Chanen, A. M. (2013). Temperament and maltreatment in the emergence of borderline and antisocial personality pathology during early adolescence. *Journal of the Canadian Academy of Child and Adolescent Psychiatry (Journal de l'Academie Canadienne de Psychiatrie de L'Enfant et de L'Adolescent)*, 22(3), 220–229.

Kaess, M., Hille, M., Parzer, P., Maser-Gluth, C., Resch, F., & Brunner, R. (2012). Alterations in the neuroendocrinological stress response to acute psychosocial stress in adolescents engaging in nonsuicidal self-injury. *Psychoneuroendocrinology*, 37(1), 157–161. https://doi.org/10.1016/j.psyneuen.2011.05.009.

Kim, S., Sharp, C., & Carbone, C. (2014). The protective role of attachment security for adolescent borderline personality disorder features via enhanced positive emotion regulation strategies. *Personality Disorders: Theory, Research, and Treatment*, 5(2), 125–136. https://doi.org/10.1037/per0000038.

Lahey, B. B., Zald, D. H., Perkins, S. F., Villalta-Gil, V., Werts, K. B., Van Hulle, C. A., Rathouz, P. J., Applegate, B., Class, Q. A., Poore, H. E., Watts, A. L., & Waldman, I. D. (2018). Measuring the hierarchical general factor model of psychopathology in young adults. *International Journal of Methods in Psychiatric Research*, 27(1), e1593. https://doi.org/10.1002/mpr.1593.

Lawrence, K. A., Allen, J. S., & Chanen, A. M. (2010). Impulsivity in borderline personality disorder: Reward-based decision-making and its relationship to emotional distress. *Journal of Personality Disorders*, 24(6), 786–799. https://doi.org/10.1521/pedi.2010.24.6.785.

Levy, K. N. (2005). The implications of attachment theory and research for understanding borderline personality disorder. *Development and Psychopathology*, 17(04). https://doi.org/10.1017/S0954579405050455.

Linehan, M. M. (1993). *Cognitive-behavioral treatment of borderline personality disorder* (pp. 56–58), New York, NY: Guilford Press.

Maier-Hein, K. H., Brunner, R., Lutz, K., Henze, R., Parzer, P., Feigl, N., Kramer, J., Meinzer, H.-P., Resch, F., & Stieltjes, B. (2014). Disorder-specific white matter alterations in adolescent borderline personality disorder. *Biological Psychiatry*, 75(1), 81–88. https://doi.org/10.1016/j.biopsych.2013.03.031.

Marieke Schuppert, H., Timmerman, M. E., Bloo, J., van Gemert, T. G., Wiersema, H. M., Minderaa, R. B., Emmelkamp, P. M. G., & Nauta, M. H. (2012). Emotion regulation training for adolescents with borderline personality disorder traits: A randomized controlled trial. *Journal of the American Academy of Child & Adolescent Psychiatry*, 51(12), 1314–1323.e2. https://doi.org/10.1016/j.jaac.2012.09.002.

Martín-Blanco, A., Ferrer, M., Soler, J., Salazar, J., Vega, D., Andión, O., Sanchez-Mora, C., Arranz, M. J., Ribases, M., Feliu-Soler, A., Pérez, V., & Pascual, J. C. (2014). Association between methylation of the glucocorticoid receptor gene, childhood maltreatment, and clinical severity in borderline personality disorder. *Journal of Psychiatric Research*, 57, 34–40. https://doi.org/10.1016/j.jpsychires.2014.06.011.

Rinne, T., Westenberg, H. G. M., den Boer, J. A., & van den Brink, W. (2000). Serotonergic blunting to meta-chlorophenylpiperazine (m-CPP) highly correlates with sustained childhood abuse in impulsive and autoaggressive female borderline patients. *Biological Psychiatry*, 47(6), 548–556. https://doi.org/10.1016/S0006-3223(99)00181-X.

Safar, K., Sato, J., Ruocco, A. C., Korenblum, M. S., O'Halpin, H., & Dunkley, B. T. (2019). Disrupted emotional neural circuitry in adolescents with borderline personality traits. *Neuroscience Letters*, 701, 112–118. https://doi.org/10.1016/j.neulet.2019.02.021.

Sansone, R. A., Lam, C., & Wiederman, M. W. (2010). Being bullied in childhood: Correlations with borderline personality in adulthood. *Comprehensive Psychiatry*, 51(5), 458–461. https://doi.org/10.1016/j.comppsych.2010.02.002.

Schulze, L., Schmahl, C., & Niedtfeld, I. (2016). Neural correlates of disturbed emotion processing in borderline personality disorder: A multimodal meta-analysis. *Biological Psychiatry*, 79(2), 97–106. https://doi.org/10.1016/j.biopsych.2015.03.027.

Seres, I., Unoka, Z., Bódi, N., Áspán, N., & Kéri, S. (2009). The neuropsychology of borderline personality disorder: Relationship with clinical dimensions and comparison with other personality disorders. *Journal of Personality Disorders*, 23(6), 555–562. https://doi.org/10.1521/pedi.2009.23.6.555.

Sharp, C., & Wall, K. (2017). Personality pathology grows up: Adolescence as a sensitive period. *Current Opinion in Psychology*, 21, 111–116. https://doi.org/10.1016/j.copsyc.2017.11.010.

Sharp, C. & Fonagy, P. (2015). Practitioner Review: Borderline personality disorder in adolescence—Recent conceptualization, intervention, and implications for clinical practice. *Journal of Child Psychology and Psychiatry*, 56(12), 1266–1288. https://doi.org/10.1111/jcpp.12449.

Sharp, C., Kerr, S., & Chanen, A. (2021). Early identification and prevention of personality pathology: An AMPD informed model of clinical staging. In A. Skodol and J. Oldham (Eds). *The American Psychiatric Association Textbook of Personality Disorders* (pp. 285-337). Washington, DC: American Psychiatric Association.

Sharp, C., & Vanwoerden, S. (2015). Hypermentalizing in borderline personality disorder: A model and data. *Journal of Infant, Child, and Adolescent Psychotherapy*, 14(1), 33–45. https://doi.org/10.1080/15289168.2015.1004890.

Sharp, C., Wright, A. G. C., Fowler, J. C., Frueh, B. C., Allen, J. G., Oldham, J., & Clark, L. A. (2015). The structure of personality pathology: Both general ('g') and specific ('s') factors? *Journal of Abnormal Psychology*, 124(2), 387–398. https://doi.org/10.1037/abn0000033.

Simeon, D., Knutelska, M., Smith, L., Baker, B. R., & Hollander, E. (2007). A preliminary study of cortisol and norepinephrine reactivity to psychosocial stress in borderline personality disorder with high and low dissociation. *Psychiatry Research*, 149(1–3), 177–184. https://doi.org/10.1016/j.psychres.2005.11.014.

Stepp, S. D., Burke, J. D., Hipwell, A. E., & Loeber, R. (2012). Trajectories of attention deficit hyperactivity disorder and oppositional defiant disorder symptoms as precursors of borderline personality disorder symptoms in adolescent girls. *Journal of Abnormal Child Psychology*, 40(1), 7–20. https://doi.org/10.1007/s10802-011-9530-6.

Stepp, S. D., & Lazarus, S. A. (2017). Identifying a borderline personality disorder prodrome: Implications for community screening: BPD prodrome for community screening. *Personality and Mental Health*, 11(3), 195–205. https://doi.org/10.1002/pmh.1389.

Stepp, S. D., Lazarus, S. A., & Byrd, A. L. (2016a). A systematic review of risk factors prospectively associated with borderline personality disorder: Taking stock and moving forward. *Personality Disorders: Theory, Research, and Treatment*, 7(4), 316–323. https://doi.org/10.1037/per0000186.

Stepp, S. D., Scott, L. N., Jones, N. P., Whalen, D. J., & Hipwell, A. E. (2016b). Negative emotional reactivity as a marker of vulnerability in the development of borderline personality disorder symptoms. *Development and Psychopathology*, 28(1), 213–224. https://doi.org/10.1017/S0954579415000395.

Stepp, S. D., Whalen, D. J., Scott, L. N., Zalewski, M., Loeber, R., & Hipwell, A. E. (2014). Reciprocal effects of parenting and borderline personality disorder symptoms in adolescent girls. *Development and Psychopathology*, 26(2), 361–378. https://doi.org/10.1017/S0954579413001041.

Vanwoerden, S., Leavitt, J., Gallagher, M. W., Temple, J. R., & Sharp, C. (2019). Dating violence victimization and borderline personality pathology: Temporal associations from late adolescence to early adulthood. *Personality Disorders: Theory, Research, and Treatment*, 10(2), 132–142. https://doi.org/10.1037/per0000324.

Wilson, S. T., Stanley, B., Brent, D. A., Oquendo, M. A., Huang, Y., Haghighi, F., Hodgkinson, C. A., & Mann, J. J. (2012). Interaction between tryptophan hydroxylase I polymorphisms and childhood abuse is associated with increased risk for borderline personality disorder in adulthood. *Psychiatric Genetics*, 22(1), 15–24.

Wolke, D., Schreier, A., Zanarini, M. C., & Winsper, C. (2012). Bullied by peers in childhood and borderline personality symptoms at 11 years of age: A prospective study: Peer victimisation and borderline personality disorder symptoms. *Journal of*

Child Psychology and Psychiatry, 53(8), 846–855. https://doi.org/10.1111/j.1469-7610.2012.02542.x.

Yen, S., Weinstock, L. M., Andover, M. S., Sheets, E. S., Selby, E. A., & Spirito, A. (2013). Prospective predictors of adolescent suicidality: 6-month post-hospitalization follow-up. *Psychological Medicine*, 43(5), 983–993. https://doi.org/10.1017/S0033291712001912.

Zanarini, M. C., Frankenburg, F. R., Reich, D. B., & Fitzmaurice, G. (2012). Attainment and stability of sustained symptomatic remission and recovery among patients with borderline personality disorder and axis II comparison subjects: A 16-year prospective follow-up study. *American Journal of Psychiatry*, 169(5), 476–483.

Zanarini, M. C., Horwood, J., Wolke, D., Waylen, A., Fitzmaurice, G., & Grant, B. F. (2011). Prevalence of DSM-IV borderline personality disorder in two community samples: 6,330 English 11-year-olds and 34,653 American adults. *Journal of Personality Disorders*, 25(5), 607–619. https://doi.org/10.1521/pedi.2011.25.5.607.

Part IV

Special Topics and Conclusions

Having reviewed specific classes of psychopathology that tend to emerge in early and middle childhood (Part II) and in adolescence and young adulthood (Part III) we now move away from psychopathology to other important topics in developmental psychopathology. Indeed, this section begins with a chapter on maltreatment (Chapter 14), a common experience for youth that is known to confer **cross-cutting** risk for mental health disorders, meaning that it increases the risk for disorders across the categories we discussed in Parts II and III. Likewise, Chapter 15 describes what is known about the impact of parental divorce, separation, and loss on individuals across development.

You may also have noticed that this is the last part of your textbook and, thus, we close with a chapter aiming to answer "quo vadis?" or "where are you going?" At this point, we hope that you have a sound understanding of the developmental psychopathology approach and feel comfortable with its application. That means that you are ready to imagine how developmental psychopathology will shape the future (Chapter 16). We will cover the following topics:

Chapter 14

Child Maltreatment

Brian Allen, Michelle P. Desir, and Chad E. Shenk

Preparation of this chapter was supported in part by the National Institutes of Health, Eunice Kennedy Shriver National Institute of Child Health and Human Development, under Award Number P50HD089922 supporting Brian Allen and Chad E. Shenk. The content is solely the responsibility of the authors and does not necessarily represent the official views of the National Institutes of Health.

Chapter Overview

Child maltreatment is a pervasive concept within the field of developmental psychopathology, both for its detrimental effect on myriad developmental processes and as a prime etiological factor for various forms of psychopathology. Unfortunately, defining child maltreatment can be difficult and, as a result, adequately estimating its prevalence is challenging. Even gauging the impact of maltreatment on a developing child can depend on the definition one uses of the term. Nonetheless, research over the past 50 years clearly demonstrates the harmful effect of child maltreatment, and various efforts to prevent its occurrence and intervene when it has occurred provide useful directions for clinical practice.

Varying Definitions of a Multifaceted Construct

To begin this discussion of the challenges in defining child maltreatment, consider the vignette below, which is likely to resemble any number of clinical cases one might encounter.

Developmental Psychopathology, First Edition. Edited by Amanda Venta, Carla Sharp, Jack M. Fletcher, and Peter Fonagy.

Case vignette

Amy is a 10-year-old girl residing with both of her biological parents. Although she is fairly well-behaved, when discipline occurs Amy is typically sent to her room and loses certain privileges. On rare occasions, her father will use a belt and spank Amy across the buttocks. Most days in the home are peaceful; however, at least once per month Amy's parents have heated verbal disagreements, often resulting in one of them storming out of the home and threatening to leave the family. When it is the mother who leaves, Amy's father drinks heavily for the remainder of the evening and occasionally watches pornography in the living room of the home, where Amy can readily see the images. When it is the father who leaves, Amy's mother typically continues using profanity, storms around the house, and screams about how terrible a person the father is for another 30 minutes.

In thinking about the case of Amy, would you characterize the spanking with a belt that she endures as physical abuse? Do you consider Amy's exposure to pornography as sexual abuse? Although neither parent becomes physically aggressive toward the other, do these repeated heated arguments constitute domestic/inter-partner violence? As for her father's drinking, might these experiences qualify Amy as substance exposed? Are there any other events within the vignette that suggest Amy is subjected to psychological abuse? This vignette demonstrates how difficult it is to clearly define child maltreatment. Certainly, the events described may have a negative impact on Amy's development, but whether she is viewed as having been the victim of any type of maltreatment is debatable. However, many times the resources available to Amy's family, the clinical direction taken, and other outcomes are a direct result of the determination made regarding her maltreatment status.

In the United States, federal legislation provides a broad definition of maltreatment that creates a form of minimal standard for individual states that each develop their own definitions. The Child Abuse Prevention and Treatment Act (CAPTA) defines *child maltreatment* as "Any recent act or failure to act on the part of a parent or caregiver, which results in death, serious physical or emotional harm, sexual abuse or exploitation, or an act or failure to act which presents an imminent risk of serious harm" (Child Welfare Information Gateway, 2019). The Centers for Disease Control and Prevention (CDC, n.d.) defines child maltreatment as "any act, intentional or not, that results in harm, the potential for harm, or the threat of harm to a child." Other similar definitions are present, but each typically includes three core elements. First, child maltreatment as a broad term includes *acts of commission*, where an individual performs a specific behavior toward a child (i.e., abuse), and *acts of omission*, where an individual fails to provide the necessary attention or care to prevent adverse outcomes to a child (i.e., neglect). Second, the abusive or neglectful act(s) must cause or create the potential for harm to the child. These definitions recognize that harm may occur in various forms, including physical, sexual, and psychological. Third, there is commonly a threshold of harm that must be met for the act to be defined as maltreatment. The CAPTA definition uses the term "serious" to indicate the level of actual or potential harm that must occur, while individual states use more specific threshold specifiers as diverse as "substantial harm" for physical abuse and "material impairment" for psychological abuse (Texas) to specific types of injuries, such as "soft tissue swelling, skin bruising, and any other such nontrivial injury" for physical abuse and "substantial reduction in the child's ability to function" for psychological abuse (Massachusetts).

Returning to the example of Amy, it is certainly the case that her father spanking her qualifies as an act of commission, and any time one is being hit there is a potential for harm (indeed, the rationale of spanking as a discipline technique is to inflict pain). Therefore, spanking meets the first two criteria, but whether it meets the threshold set by a given state determines whether the spanking technically qualifies as *physical abuse*. In the examples provided above, it is unlikely that common uses of spanking would qualify as "substantial harm" in Texas; however, if the spanking leaves any form of marks on the child, it may very well be considered physical abuse in Massachusetts. The same can be said for the issue of *psychological abuse*. It may be difficult to show that Amy's parents arguing and the general chaos of those moments creates the "material impairment" required in Texas, but if Amy displays difficulty functioning in school because she is preoccupied with her parents' argument from the night before, then she may be judged to show an observable reduction in her ability to function and psychological abuse may be indicated in Massachusetts.

The definition of *sexual abuse* is often more uniform across countries and jurisdiction, as the commission of a sexual act does not require the subjective opinion of whether the intensity of the act reached an abstract threshold. However, variability does exist regarding what constitutes a "sexual act." Commonly regarded acts of sexual abuse across jurisdictions include touching of genital areas and exposing oneself to a child for sexual gratification, but non-contact and non-confrontational acts become more difficult to define. For instance, in most states, the child passively being exposed to pornography as a result of a parent watching it for their own purposes, such as what occurred with Amy, is not considered sexual abuse. On the other hand, if the perpetrator specifically directed the child to view pornography, concerns about the potential grooming of the child for sexual abuse emerge and may qualify as sexual abuse under some statutes. In addition, new definitional challenges have developed with the advent of the Internet and smart phones. Given that most states and countries legally define some form of sexual exploitation of a child to include the production and distribution of child pornography, jurisdictions are currently grappling with how to respond when pornographic images of children are taken and distributed by the children themselves (i.e., "sexting"), and whether to consider a child protective service and/or law enforcement approach.

Depending on the jurisdiction, various other forms of maltreatment may be defined. The most obvious example is in the definition of *neglect*. It is common for neglect to be broken into several distinct subgroups: failure to provide adequate food, clothing, and shelter (i.e., physical neglect), failure to provide the necessary comfort and support for healthy development (i.e., emotional neglect), failure to ensure the child attends school (i.e., educational neglect), and the failure to seek appropriate care when the child is sick or injured (i.e., medical neglect). In some jurisdictions, repeatedly exposing the child to forms of domestic violence may be included in the statute defining psychological abuse, while in others there is very limited consideration of domestic violence in child protection laws. The use of illicit drugs or excessive amounts of alcohol in the home are considered maltreating by some jurisdictions within their definitions of neglect, while others have a separate statute to define such exposure, and others do not explicitly address the topic.

CONTROVERSIAL ISSUE: PHYSICAL DISCIPLINE OR PHYSICAL ABUSE?

Spanking or otherwise physically inflicting pain on a child is a traditional parenting technique in use for millennia as a way of punishing children for misdeeds. Such physical discipline is viewed by many parents as a foundational approach to raising their children, as it is meant to instill respect and provide necessary correction. In the past 30 years, however, a substantial amount of research has called into question the wisdom of this approach. A number of meta-analyses have demonstrated that physical discipline is actually associated with an increased risk of the child displaying aggression, antisocial behavior, and delinquency, as well as a host of other negative outcomes (Gershoff & Grogan-Kaylor, 2016). These studies also find no evidence that spanking is an effective technique for enhancing any of the outcomes examined. From a theoretical perspective, physical discipline teaches children that physical force is an acceptable tool for achieving a desired result and does not offer sufficient instruction and development of important developmental capacities, such as emotion regulation and social skills. Such repeated and consistent results have led professional organizations, such as the American Academy of Pediatrics and the American

Psychological Association, to definitively state that spanking is harmful to children and should not be used. However, advocates of spanking counter with various arguments. One often invokes a religious perspective, arguing that the Bible sanctions physical discipline of children. Specifically, scripture in Proverbs 13:24 states that "He that spareth the rod hateth his son," in the King James version. Newer versions of the text, such as the New Living Translation, interpret the phrase differently: "If you refuse to discipline your children, it proves you don't love them." Given that discipline does not necessarily mean spanking or striking a child, and the translation of the phrase is debatable, arguments are ongoing within theological circles as to whether spanking is actually directed by scripture. Another argument for maintaining spanking similarly utilizes a cultural perspective and highlights that the prevalence of physical discipline is higher among African-American parents than parents of other ethnicities, which is likely due to multiple historical factors, such as cultural heritage, and social factors, such as socioeconomic and educational disparities. Spanking is also generally more acceptable among less educated individuals and those at the lower end of the socioeconomic continuum (Smith, Davern, Freese, & Morgan, 2018). As such, attempts to ban or restrict the use of spanking would disproportionately impact African-American, poor, and/or less educated parents. Nonetheless, attitudes regarding spanking have seen a drastic shift in the American consciousness, with 83.5% agreeing with spanking in 1986 and only 66.9% agreeing with spanking in 2018 (Smith et al., 2018). Globally, over 50 countries have banned spanking and seen drastic results, with significant reductions in varied outcomes, such as physical fighting among adolescents and suicide, when compared to other countries that have not banned spanking (e.g., Elgar et al., 2018). What do you think; should spanking be prohibited?

Prevalence, Incidence, and Economic Impact

The varying definitions of child maltreatment within the United States make it difficult to provide accurate estimates domestically. For instance, all states report to the federal government statistics related to *child maltreatment investigations*. Such an investigation is conducted by a state-operated *child protection agency* to determine whether maltreatment has occurred and may include interviewing the child directly, interviewing the alleged perpetrator, and/or collection of any physical evidence by a medical professional. Following an investigation, the child protection agency makes a decision as to whether to *substantiate* the allegation and potentially implement any number of possible actions. In 2017, the rate of children referred for investigation of alleged maltreatment in the United States was 55.7 per 1,000 children (U.S. Department of Health and Human Services, 2019). However, this rate varied widely from a low of 14.5 per 1,000 children in Hawaii to a high of 169.1 per 1,000 children in Vermont. The types of maltreatment investigated showed similar variability based on the state. Whereas nationally the most commonly substantiated form of maltreatment was neglect, accounting for 74.9% of all substantiated maltreatment cases, neglect was only 2.4% and 8.0% of substantiated cases in Vermont and Pennsylvania, respectively. In Vermont, physical abuse was the most commonly substantiated (57.9%) while sexual abuse was the most commonly substantiated in Pennsylvania (45.8%). Clearly, state-based differences exist for the rate at which allegations of maltreatment are investigated and which forms of maltreatment are most likely to be substantiated upon investigation.

Given these concerns related to governmentally reported statistics, epidemiology studies are likely to provide a more helpful estimate of prevalence and incidence of child maltreatment. The National Incidence Study (NIS) is a Congressionally mandated attempt to discern the incidence of child maltreatment in the United States that aims to recruit and assess a nationally representative sample and use standardized definitions of both abuse and neglect.

The most recent study, NIS-4, found that approximately 2.9 million children experienced some form of maltreatment in the study year of 2005–2006, where 29% experienced some form of abuse and 77% experienced neglect (Sedlak et al., 2010). The NIS reports data based on two standards, Harm and Endangerment. The Harm Standard requires the act of omission or commission results in harm to the child to be considered as maltreatment. The Endangerment Standard is less stringent as it includes cases where a maltreating act occurred that may have caused harm to the child. The statistics provided here are those reported for the Endangerment standard. For those children experiencing abuse, the majority were physically abused (57%) and/or psychologically abused (57%), with the fewest number having been sexually abused (22%). These incidence rates were similar to data collected 10 years earlier during NIS-3.

To gain an understanding of the true prevalence of child maltreatment, one must examine the multitude of epidemiological studies available. In the third National Survey of Children's Exposure to Violence (NatSCEV), 38.1% of older adolescents reported having experienced at least one type of maltreatment in childhood, with psychological abuse being the most prevalent form (23.9%) followed closely by neglect (18.4%) and physical abuse (18.1%) (Finkelhor, Turner, Shattuck, & Hamby, 2015). Other epidemiological studies with adolescents document lower physical abuse rates ranging from 4% to 9%, primarily because of differences in definition (Kilpatrick & Saunders, 1997; McLaughlin et al., 2012). Rates of contact sexual abuse range from 8% to 12% across studies; however, when sexual abuse is expanded to include non-contact acts, such as sexual harassment and adults intentionally exposing their genitals, the rate of sexual victimization climbs to approximately 28%, with females commonly reporting higher rates of victimization than males. In addition, approximately 9% to 32% of adolescents report witnessing family violence, depending on the definition used in the study (Finkelhor et al., 2015). Of growing interest to researchers is the frequency of *poly-victimization*, which is one's exposure to multiple forms of interpersonal trauma, including maltreatment. Depending on the number of traumatic events assessed in the study, estimates can vary widely. In the original NatSCEV, youth between the ages of 10 and 17 were surveyed about their exposure to 51 separate forms of victimization. Nearly 50% of all respondents reported experiencing two or more victimization types, while the median number of exposure types was three (Finkelhor, Turner, Hamby, & Ormrod, 2011). It should be remembered that these numbers refer only to the number of discrete forms of exposure and does not include the frequency with which each type of exposure was experienced.

Similarly, varying definitions across countries makes it difficult to provide global estimates of abuse and neglect, including examining differences across cultures. For instance, consider that a population-based study in Sweden found that 14.2% of children in grades 2, 7, and 9 reported being physically abused (Annerbäck, Wingren, Svedin, & Gustafsson, 2010); however, the definition used in the study included any form of physical violence, including spanking, as corporal punishment toward children was banned in Sweden in 1979. Another population-based study from the United Kingdom, sampling 18 to 24-year-olds, also used a broad definition of physical abuse and found 25% of the sample reported such experiences (May-Chahal & Cawson, 2005). Using these two studies as an example, it is tempting to assert that physical abuse is significantly less common in Sweden, potentially validating the ban on corporal punishment; however, the U.K. study included "endangerment" types of parental behaviors that did not actually cause harm to the child under the broad definition of physical abuse. When the types of experiences qualifying as physical abuse in the U.K. study were restricted to only those that caused some form of injury, and thus eliminated potentially legal corporal punishment cases, the percentage endorsing physical abuse dropped to 6%. Further, the data reported in the U.K. study suggested a similar prevalence of physical abuse to that found in the NatSCEV study from the United States, even though the U.S. population typically has more permissive attitudes toward the use of physical discipline with children (Scotland banned corporal punishment in 2019 and similar legislation is pending in Wales).

Prevalence estimates of child sexual abuse globally show both variability and consistency. A meta-analysis of 331 separate studies examining the prevalence of sexual abuse internationally found an aggregate global prevalence of 12.7% when using self-report methods, regardless of the study definition of sexual abuse (Stoltenborgh, van IJzendoorn, Euser, & Bakermans-Kranenburg, 2011). However, analyses yielded higher prevalence rates when using a broader definition of sexual abuse (21.2% of females; 10.7% of males) than when using a stricter definition requiring physical contact (14.1% of females; 6.9% of males). Interestingly, regional differences emerged. For both men and women, the lowest rates of sexual abuse were reported in studies from Asia (11.3% for females; 4.1% for males) while the highest rates were derived from studies in Africa (20.2% for females; 19.3% for males). In only one global region did males report a higher rate of sexual abuse (South America), but only two studies reported on rates among males from this region. In summary, across studies of sexual abuse prevalence, higher rates are typically found among females and when using more liberal definitions. It is also apparent that regional differences exist, although it is not clear the extent to which these rates are influenced by cultural, political, economic, and/or social differences.

Given these rates of child maltreatment, an important public health and policy discussion involves the economic impact on society. Fang and colleagues (2012) published a comprehensive examination of the financial burden of various forms of maltreatment in the United States. Their analyses suggested that the lifetime cost of non-fatal child maltreatment per victim is $210,012 with the single greatest contributor of this estimate being lost productivity, followed by childhood medical expenses. Other costs considered in the analysis included medical costs in adulthood, child welfare services, criminal justice costs, and special education services. All totaled, they estimated that each year in the United States, $121.6 billion of new lifetime costs are incurred as a result of child maltreatment. A more recent analysis focused specifically on sexual abuse in the United States found comparable per victim costs of $282,734 (Letourneau, Brown, Fang, Hassan, & Mercy, 2018). This analysis suggested that the United States accrues a lifetime cost of over $9 billion each year from sexual abuse incidents alone. Another analysis examining the economic burden of child maltreatment in the East Asia and Pacific region also revealed staggering results with the total annual burden being $194 billion (Fang et al., 2015). This equates to roughly 2% of gross domestic product in the East Asia and Pacific region.

Child Maltreatment Within a Developmental Psychopathology Framework

It is clear that childhood maltreatment is a pervasive and concerning problem in society, but why does it occur? Figure 14.1 depicts a developmental psychopathology model of childhood maltreatment and includes

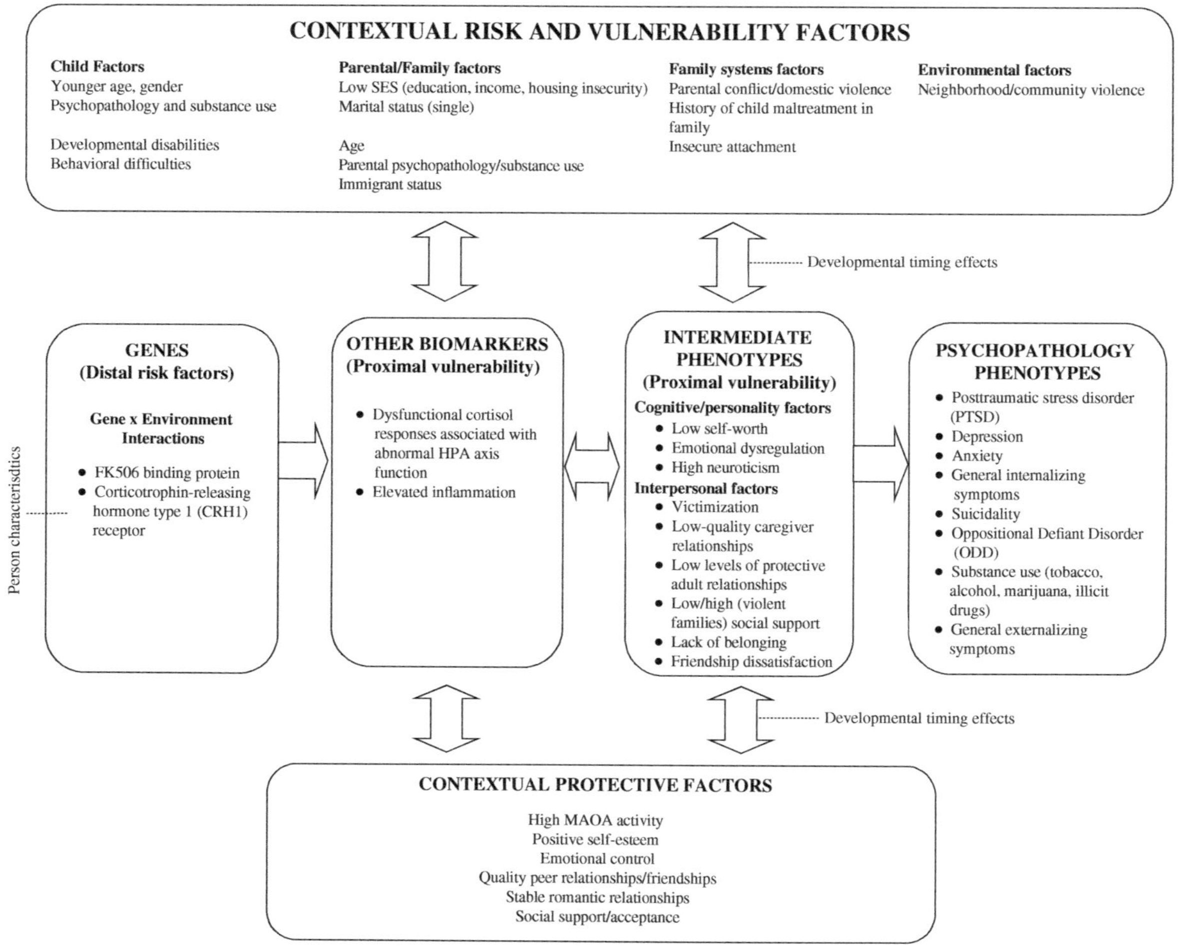

FIGURE 14.1 A Developmental Psychopathology Model of Child Maltreatment

some risk and vulnerability factors to aid our discussion regarding the etiology of child maltreatment. Because maltreatment is considered a risk factor for various forms of psychopathology, a discussion of its etiology will differ from how we would think about a mental health disorder such as depression, as occurred in Parts II and III of this book. However, there are some key risk factors for maltreatment that are important to discuss. The framework provided in Figure 14.1 also includes the multitude of systems on which maltreatment exerts a negative impact, which are related to risk of psychopathology. Contextual protective factors for preventing the development of psychopathology among individuals who have experienced maltreatment are listed as well.

Risk Factors For Maltreatment

Child factors

There are some characteristics of children that increase their risk of becoming the victim of childhood maltreatment. For instance, youth who have problems related to drug and alcohol use, including infants who were exposed to alcohol and drugs in utero, are at heightened risk of experiencing child maltreatment (U.S. Department of Health and Human Services, 2019). Children with a multitude of medical and psychological problems, including those with mental health disorders, behavioral difficulties, and developmental disabilities, are at increased risk as well. Beyond these factors, there are certain demographic variables that increase risk. For example, as discussed earlier, females are more likely to be the victims of child sexual abuse than males. In addition, throughout the age range that encompasses childhood and adolescence, children under the age of five years are at the most heightened risk of being a victim of child maltreatment as they are the least likely to resist, the most susceptible to injury, and are commonly incapable of coherently describing their experiences.

Parental and family factors

In addition to child factors, there are several parental and family factors that have been identified in the literature that increase risk for maltreatment, which are similar to those for many mental health disorders. The National Longitudinal Study of Adolescent Health was a prospective longitudinal study of over 15,000 adolescents followed up into adulthood, which found several sociodemographic factors that increased the risk of maltreatment, including lower level of parental education, lower family income, and immigrant status (Hussey, Chang, & Kotch, 2006). Other sources have identified parental age as a factor as well. Specifically, younger parents are more likely to be perpetrators of child maltreatment (Lau et al., 2005). Additionally, single parents, parents with psychopathology and/or substance abuse problems, and parents who are experiencing difficulties with housing security are more likely to be perpetrators of maltreatment occurrence and recurrence (Cicchetti, 2013; Hindley, Ramchandani, & Jones 2006). Consider for a moment why these factors might be related to child maltreatment rates. Hopefully, the answers you develop center on the concept of stress. Each of the factors just mentioned are related to increasing levels of personal stress, which in turn increases the risk for child maltreatment, as well as any number of other unfortunate outcomes.

Family systems and environmental factors

Additional risk factors for maltreatment occurrence and recurrence include characteristics of the family and wider environment. Environments that are characterized by high levels of conflict and violence, including parental conflict, domestic violence, and neighborhood and community violence increase the likelihood of maltreatment (Hindley et al., 2006; Valentino, Nuttall, Comas, Borkowski, & Akai, 2012). Similarly, previous experiences with maltreatment also increase the likelihood that maltreatment will occur. Maltreatment is more common if a family has a history of childhood maltreatment with any children in the home or if a caregiver experienced maltreatment during their own childhood (Cicchetti, 2013; Valentino et al., 2012). However, even if there has not been any maltreatment or violence present in the family history or in the neighborhood, a poor-quality relationship between a parent and child can be a risk factor.

MALTREATMENT AS AN ETIOLOGICAL FACTOR FOR PSYCHOPATHOLOGY

One of the reasons why childhood maltreatment is such an extensively studied topic in developmental psychopathology research is because of the wide array of research evidence that it is associated with an increased risk of the various forms of psychopathology covered in this textbook. *Posttraumatic stress disorder* (PTSD) in particular is one of the most commonly studied forms of psychopathology post-maltreatment. Table 14.1 shows how PTSD is measured in the classification systems we have been using throughout this book. Overall, PTSD is a disorder that can occur following exposure to actual or threatened death, serious injury, or sexual violence. Once considered primarily as a reaction exhibited by veterans returning from combat, it is now long established that PTSD can emerge following various types of traumatic events, including childhood maltreatment. PTSD includes multiple categories of symptoms including distressing memories or thoughts of the trauma coming to mind when the person does not want them to (e.g., nightmares, flashbacks), avoidance of things that would remind the person of the

TABLE 14.1 PTSD According to DSM-5, ICD-11, and the ASEBA System

DSM-5	*ICD-II*	*ASEBA*
A. Exposure to actual or threatened death, serious injury, or sexual violence in one (or more) of the following ways: 1. Directly experiencing the traumatic event(s). 2. Witnessing, in person, the event(s) as it occurred to others. 3. Learning that the traumatic event(s) occurred to a close family member or close friend. In cases of actual or threatened death of a family member or friend, the event(s) must have been violent or accidental. 4. Experiencing repeated or extreme exposure to aversive details of the traumatic event(s) (e.g., first responders collecting human remains; police officers repeatedly exposed to details of child abuse). • **Note:** Criterion A4 does not apply to exposure through electronic media, television, movies, or pictures, unless this exposure is work related. B. Presence of one (or more) of the following intrusion symptoms associated with the traumatic event(s), beginning after the traumatic event(s) occurred: 1. Recurrent, involuntary, and intrusive distressing memories of the traumatic event(s). • **Note:** In children older than 6 years, repetitive play may occur in which themes or aspects of the traumatic event(s) are expressed. 2. Recurrent distressing dreams in which the content and/or effect of the dream are related to the traumatic event(s). • **Note:** In children, there may be frightening dreams without recognizable content. 3. Dissociative reactions (e.g., flashbacks) in which the individual feels or acts as if the traumatic event(s) were recurring. (Such reactions may occur on a continuum, with the most extreme expression being a complete loss of awareness of present surroundings.) • **Note:** In children, trauma-specific reenactment may occur in play	Post-traumatic stress disorder (PTSD) is a disorder that may develop following exposure to an extremely threatening or horrific event or series of events. It is characterized by all of the following: (1) re-experiencing the traumatic event or events in the present in the form of vivid intrusive memories, flashbacks, or nightmares. These are typically accompanied by strong or overwhelming emotions, particularly fear or horror, and strong physical sensations; (2) avoidance of thoughts and memories of the event or events, or avoidance of activities, situations, or people reminiscent of the event or events; and (3) persistent perceptions of heightened current threat, for example as indicated by hypervigilance or an enhanced startle reaction to stimuli such as unexpected noises. The symptoms persist for at least several weeks and cause significant impairment in personal, family, social, educational, occupational, or other important areas of functioning.	**Ages 1.5–5 Years** **Stress Problems** • Concentration • Nausea • Nervous • Stomachaches • Stubborn • Mood changes • Sad **Ages 6–18** Not included

4. Intense or prolonged psychological distress at exposure to internal or external cues that symbolize or resemble an aspect of the traumatic event(s).
5. Marked physiological reactions to internal or external cues that symbolize or resemble an aspect of the traumatic event(s).

C. Persistent avoidance of stimuli associated with the traumatic event(s), beginning after the traumatic event(s) occurred, as evidenced by one or both of the following:

1. Avoidance of or efforts to avoid distressing memories, thoughts, or feelings about or closely associated with the traumatic event(s).
2. Avoidance of or efforts to avoid external reminders (people, places, conversations, activities, objects, situations) that arouse distressing memories, thoughts, or feelings about or closely associated with the traumatic event(s).

D. Negative alterations in cognitions and mood associated with the traumatic event(s), beginning or worsening after the traumatic event(s) occurred, as evidenced by two (or more) of the following:

1. Inability to remember an important aspect of the traumatic event(s) (typically due to dissociative amnesia and not to other factors such as head injury, alcohol, or drugs).
2. Persistent and exaggerated negative beliefs or expectations about oneself, others, or the world (e.g., "I am bad," "No one can be trusted," "The world is completely dangerous," "My whole nervous system is permanently ruined").
3. Persistent, distorted cognitions about the cause or consequences of the traumatic event(s) that lead the individual to blame himself/herself or others.

(Continued)

TABLE 14.1 (Continued)

DSM-5	*ICD-II*	*ASEBA*
4. Persistent negative emotional state (e.g., fear, horror, anger, guilt, or shame).		
5. Markedly diminished interest or participation in significant activities.		
6. Feelings of detachment or estrangement from others.		
7. Persistent inability to experience positive emotions (e.g., inability to experience happiness, satisfaction, or loving feelings).		
E. Marked alterations in arousal and reactivity associated with the traumatic event(s), beginning or worsening after the traumatic event(s) occurred, as evidenced by two (or more) of the following:		
1. Irritable behavior and angry outbursts (with little or no provocation) typically expressed as verbal or physical aggression toward people or objects.		
2. Reckless or self-destructive behavior.		
3. Hypervigilance.		
4. Exaggerated startle response.		
5. Problems with concentration.		
6. Sleep disturbance (e.g., difficulty falling or staying asleep or restless sleep).		
F. Duration of the disturbance (Criteria B, C, D, and E) is more than 1 month.		
G. The disturbance causes clinically significant distress or impairment in social, occupational, or other important areas of functioning.		
H. The disturbance is not attributable to the physiological effects of a substance (e.g., medication, alcohol) or another medical condition.		

trauma (e.g., places, people, feelings), negative alterations in cognition and mood (e.g., self-blame, mistrust of others), and increased physiological arousal, such as an exaggerated startle response (American Psychiatric Association, 2013). This particular diagnosis and its associated symptoms are significantly more common in children, adolescents, and adults who have experienced childhood maltreatment than individuals who have not been maltreated (Lansford et al., 2002; Scrafford, Grein, & Miller-Graff, 2018; Thompson et al., 2005).

Other mental health diagnoses and symptoms that are often identified as being more prevalent in individuals with a history of maltreatment include depression, anxiety, substance use (i.e., cannabis, alcohol, tobacco, and illicit drugs), suicidality, and oppositional defiant disorder (Hamburger, Leeb, & Swahn, 2008; Lansford et al., 2002; Lau et al., 2005; Oshri, Rogosch, Burnette, & Cicchetti, 2011; Scrafford et al., 2018; Vachon, Krueger, Rogosch, & Cicchetti, 2015). Furthermore, along with an increased risk of experiencing these disorders and symptoms, the age of onset may be earlier for maltreated children, such as using alcohol at earlier ages than their peers who also use alcohol but have not experienced maltreatment (Hamburger et al., 2008). In addition to specific diagnoses, researchers have found that maltreated children exhibit more general mental health symptoms and behavioral challenges (Flynn, Cicchetti, & Rogosch, 2014; Oh, Han, Choi, Lau, & Shum, 2019; Vachon et al., 2015).

FACTORS THAT INCREASE MALTREATED CHILDREN'S RISK FOR PSYCHOPATHOLOGY

With all the evidence available that maltreatment increases risk for developing a wide range of psychopathology, many researchers have attempted to identify those factors most responsible for this relationship. Figure 14.1 summarizes some of the most commonly studied factors in the literature. We begin our discussion with genetic factors.

Genetic factors (distal risk factors)

A handful of studies have identified specific genes that increase maltreated children's risk of developing multiple forms of psychopathology and behavioral challenges, including depression and substance dependence. One study of 362 maltreated and non-maltreated children found that youth who experienced maltreatment prior to age eight years and who had exhibited behavioral problems in preadolescence were at risk for developing marijuana dependence in adolescence if they had one or two copies of a particular gene haplotype (FK506 binding protein gene), which is involved in modulating stress responses. More specifically, maltreatment, an environmental exposure, only predicted adolescent marijuana dependence for individuals who had prior externalizing problems and who showed a particular expression of a gene (Handley, Rogosch, & Cicchetti, 2015). A similar finding was discovered when examining the impact of child abuse on adult depressive symptoms. Polymorphisms of the corticotrophin-releasing hormone type 1 receptor (CRHR1) gene, which influences physiological responses to stress, were associated with diminished effects of child sexual, physical, and emotional abuse on adult depressive symptoms (Bradley et al., 2008). Other researchers attempted to replicate this finding in two different samples of individuals who had been maltreated as children. This finding was confirmed in a prospective longitudinal cohort of women who were followed through age 40 years, but not in a cohort of men and women followed to age 32 years and which used a different measure of maltreatment (Polanczyk et al., 2009). Although interpreting these findings may seem complex and difficult, suffice to say that one's genetic constitution is at least partially responsible for the long-term outcomes stemming from the experience of child maltreatment.

Additional biomarkers (proximal vulnerability factors)

In addition to gene × environment interactions, several other studies have found evidence of maltreatment's impact on specific biological systems influencing their risk for psychopathology. One of these biological systems is the neuroendocrine system. This system has been covered in other chapters of this book, so we will provide only a brief overview. The hypothalamic–pituitary–adrenocortical (HPA) axis plays an important role in the regulation of stress hormones. Specifically, the experience of stress promotes the secretion of the corticotrophin-releasing factor (CRF), which in turn triggers the synthesis and release of adrenocorticotropin hormone (ACTH) by the pituitary gland. ACTH then stimulates the synthesis and release of glucocorticoids by the adrenal cortex. Abnormalities in the functioning of this system increases the risk for psychopathology, particularly depression and general internalizing symptoms. Childhood maltreatment is a particularly potent stressor that exerts an impact on the HPA axis. Several researchers have found evidence that maltreated children can exhibit both hypoactivity and hyperactivity of the HPA axis. One prospective longitudinal study with female participants who were followed from ages 6 to 30 years showed that sexually abused females initially showed higher levels of non-stress, morning cortisol compared to females who had not been sexually abused. However, beginning in adolescence, these abused females started to show lower levels of morning cortisol than their non-abused counterparts with significantly lower levels emerging by early adulthood (Trickett, Noll, Susman, Shenk, & Putnam, 2010). In other words, their cortisol levels when they were not under stress became attenuated over time. This has important implications for the development of internalizing psychopathology, as evidenced by one study, which demonstrated that children experiencing early physical and sexual abuse and high depressive or internalizing symptoms exhibited an attenuated diurnal decrease in cortisol (Cicchetti, Rogosch, Gunnar, & Toth 2010).

Individuals maltreated as children also show elevated levels of chronic inflammation in adulthood and adolescence, which may help to explain the link between maltreatment and various mental illnesses, including depression (Baumeister, Akhtar, Ciufolini, Pariante, & Mondelli, 2016; Danese, Pariante, Caspi, Taylor, & Poulton, 2007). Inflammation represents activation of a body's immune system, which is similar to our body's response to healing from injury and illness. However, maltreatment has been found to trigger an enduring systemic inflammatory response and trigger chronic hyperactivation of the immune system into adulthood. These elevated levels of inflammation in maltreated children have been associated with higher levels of internalizing symptoms. One specific study that followed 1,000 people from birth to 32 years of age found that depressed individuals with a history of childhood maltreatment were more likely to have elevated inflammation than individuals who were not depressed and were not maltreated as children. Furthermore, although depression and inflammation are positively associated with each other, researchers found that this association disappeared when maltreatment was taken into account (Danese et al., 2008). Thus, it appears that a history of childhood maltreatment was actually the reason for the link between depression and inflammation.

Cognitive changes and other individual factors

It is clear that the experience of maltreatment can lead to various changes in the functioning of key biological systems, which in turn impacts risk for psychopathology. Beyond biology, there are other ways that traumatic experiences can influence individuals and heighten their risk for developing mental illness. One study found that low self-worth mediated the relationship between childhood maltreatment and internalizing symptoms in a sample of adolescents. Specifically, adolescents who had experienced maltreatment were more likely to experience feelings of worthlessness, which in turn increased their risk for internalizing symptoms (Flynn et al., 2014). Other emotional and personality changes, such as difficulties regulating the expression of one's emotions and emotional impulses and a high level of emotional distress, have been found to be related to a greater degree of posttraumatic stress symptoms, behavioral problems, and cannabis abuse (Collishaw et al., 2007; Kim & Cicchetti, 2010; Oshri et al., 2013).

Interpersonal risk factors

People who interact with maltreated individuals may also increase the likelihood that maltreated individuals develop mental health problems. For example, people who were maltreated as children often experience victimization from others (i.e., bullying, intimate partner violence, sexual assault) later in childhood and adulthood (Stroem, Askvaag, & Wentzel-Larsen, 2019; Walker, Freud, Ellis, Fraine, & Wilson, 2019) and this partly helps to explain the relationship between maltreatment and mental health symptoms (Scrafford et al., 2018). Even experiences with others that are not characterized by victimization and violence can influence a maltreated individual's risk. For example, having a lower quality relationship with one's caregiver or lower levels of protective adult relationships, perceiving that one does not have tangible social support or does not belong to a social network, and being dissatisfied with one's friendships, have all been found to help explain the relationship between child maltreatment and depression, substance use, and psychiatric problems in adulthood (Alto, Handley, Rogosch, Cicchetti, & Toth, 2018; Seeds, Harkness, & Quilty, 2010).

Controversial issue: problematic development or a diagnosable disorder?

As can be gleaned from this chapter, child maltreatment may exert a profound negative effect on the development of an individual, including the development of emotion regulation, behavior regulation, cognitive abilities, and identity formation. As such, it should not be surprising that child maltreatment is a significant etiological factor in the development of myriad diagnosable mental health conditions, including mood, disruptive behavior (e.g., conduct disorder), substance use, eating and personality disorders, among others. At the current time, however, there is considerable debate within the trauma and child maltreatment fields as to whether a new diagnosis should be recognized, one that specifically denotes that the cause of significant emotional and behavioral concerns is related to ongoing trauma in childhood. Different from a diagnosis of Posttraumatic Stress Disorder (PTSD), which includes a very specific set of symptoms and has been recognized as a diagnosable condition since 1980, this new diagnosis would include diagnostic criteria across domains of interpersonal functioning, emotion regulation, and maladaptive cognitions, and specifically requires that the presumed etiology of these concerns should be a history of severe and prolonged trauma exposure in childhood, such as chronic maltreatment. Proponents argue that such a disorder, variably named "Complex PTSD" or "Developmental Trauma Disorder," will emphasize the role of trauma and maltreatment in the development of an individual's psychiatric concerns, spur research on the long-term impact of chronic trauma and maltreatment, and potentially lead to new breakthroughs in treatment. In addition, recognition of such a disorder may decrease the need to diagnose comorbid conditions, reducing the number of diagnoses assigned to a given patient. Some research supports that such a symptom profile is distinct from other diagnoses already in use; however, these studies also suggest that significant overlap of Complex PTSD symptoms with those of other currently available diagnoses is possible, particularly Borderline Personality Disorder (BPD) (see Chapter 13 of Jowett, Karatzias, Shevlin, & Albert, 2020). Such findings have led others to argue that a new diagnosis is not warranted. In addition, critics express concern that interventions already well-established for diagnoses such as PTSD and BPD will be ignored by practitioners in favor of new interventions explicitly marketed to treat Complex PTSD, although these new interventions are not yet sufficiently studied to determine their effectiveness. Instead, opponents of the new diagnosis argue for utilizing already well-established diagnoses and interventions, and recognizing that patients may present with problems in any number of developmental areas as a result of prolonged child maltreatment. Do you think there a need for a new diagnosis that explicitly recognizes a person's emotional and behavioral difficulties are the result of chronic trauma in childhood?

RESILIENCE/CONTEXTUAL PROTECTIVE FACTORS

We have spent a lot of time discussing the risk of maltreated individuals developing psychopathology and all of the factors that increase their risk of going down an unhealthy developmental pathway. However, as stated in other chapters, it is important to remember that not all people with a similar experience (e.g., maltreatment) go on to develop adverse outcomes such as psychopathology. This refers to the developmental psychopathology concept of multifinality, or the idea that there are many different outcomes that can result from the same experience, and even maltreated children can achieve positive adaptation and resilient outcomes despite this threat to their normal development. A list of such factors is displayed in Figure 11.1. Similar to our discussion of risk for psychopathology, we will review multiple categories of factors that can contribute to the absence of psychopathology.

Individual factors

In the same way that genetics can put maltreated children at greater risk of exhibiting psychopathology, they can also protect these individuals. A landmark study that used a cohort of over 1,000 children followed from birth into adulthood found that a specific polymorphism in the gene that encodes monoamine oxidase A (MAOA)—an enzyme that metabolizes neurotransmitters such as norepinephrine, dopamine, and serotonin—moderated the impact of maltreatment on the development of antisocial behavior in adult males. Specifically, the impact of maltreatment on adult antisocial behavior was significantly reduced in males who had high levels of MAOA activity compared to males with low MAOA activity (Caspi et al., 2002). Also at an individual level, factors such as having positive self-esteem and greater control over one's emotions predicted resilient functioning in maltreated children who were studied over the course of three years (Cicchetti & Rogosch, 1997).

Interpersonal factors

Although maltreated children's relationships may be harmful, these connections with other people can also be protective as well. Many studies in the literature have found that various forms of social support can contribute to resilient outcomes. One study found that the absence of psychopathology in adults who had experienced severe, repeated physical and/or sexual abuse was related to the presence of having at least one parent rated as very caring, quality adolescent peer relationships, a stable relationship history in adulthood, and high-quality adult love and friend relationships (Collishaw et al., 2007). Similar studies looking at maltreated populations have shown family and/or friend support to be associated with less symptoms of depression and anxiety (Ezzell, Swenson, & Brondino, 2000; Musliner & Singer, 2014). For studies that looked at both maltreated and non-maltreated individuals, perceived support from family and/or friends has been found to provide a buffer against the impact of childhood abuse/neglect on outcomes as diverse as depression in adult women (Powers, Ressler, & Bradley, 2008) to behavioral problems in Chinese college students (Oh et al., 2019). In these studies, maltreated individuals who had higher levels of perceived support were less likely to experience mental health problems. Other studies have examined different forms of social support as a mediator of the relationship between maltreatment and psychopathology and found that parent and peer relationship quality and peer social acceptance can help to explain the connection between maltreatment and depressive symptoms. Specifically, maltreatment was associated with lower levels of relationship quality or acceptance, which in turn predicted higher levels of depressive symptoms (Alto et al., 2018; Ju & Lee, 2018).

Despite available evidence that relationships can be protective, it is also important to note some limitations of these relationships. For example, one study did not find evidence that social support mediated the relationship between maltreatment and depressive symptoms (Negriff, Cederbaum, & Lee, 2019). Additionally, a review on social support in maltreated children noted that family support generally acts as buffer for individuals with lower, but not higher, levels of maltreatment, which suggests that social support may not be sufficient for protecting against psychopathology and other adverse outcomes among those with more severe maltreatment histories (Wright & Folger, 2017). Additionally, when maltreated and non-maltreated populations are included in studies, it appears that relationships with caring adults, including the parent–child relationship, may be more of a factor in contributing to the resilience of non-maltreated children who have experienced other types of adversity than maltreated children (Cicchetti & Rogosch, 1997).

Prevention and Intervention

It is probably not surprising to hear that the general consensus is that the best way to address the problem of child maltreatment is to prevent its occurrence. If successful, such approaches serve to prevent a multitude of potentially adverse consequences to the child, as well as to the family and society in general. The design of such prevention programs often starts by identifying the particular risk factors that most signal the potential for abuse and/or neglect to occur and designing practices to mitigate that risk. For instance, Family Connects (www.familyconnect.org) is a program developed in North Carolina that involves a registered nurse visiting with the mothers of newborns a handful of times in the first months of the baby's life to foster an effective understanding of infant physical and emotional needs, develop sound parenting practices, and assess for needs and connect the mother with necessary community services. The goals of Family Connects include reducing parental mental illness and stress, preventing misunderstandings of infant cues that might lead to physical abuse (i.e., shaking), reduce other forms of violence in the family, and improve health care decision-making. Clinical trials suggest that the Family Connects program results in fewer visits to hospital emergency departments, greater connection with community resources, more positive and less violent parenting behaviors, and lower rates of mental illness among mothers (Dodge, Goodman, Murphy, O'Donnell, & Sato, 2013; Dodge, Goodman, Murphy, O'Donnell, Sato, & Guptill, 2014). This family-visiting approach to prevention is widely accepted in the field and other well-respected programs are employed throughout the United States and around the world. For instance, the Nurse–Family Partnership (NFP) utilizes a similar format, but sessions may begin prenatally to help ensure adequate prenatal care and continue throughout the first two years of a child's life (www.nursefamilypartnership.org). SafeCare is another home-visiting program with a broader focus, including components that cover topics as diverse as improving health outcomes, eliminating household hazards and increasing supervision of young children, and improving parent and child interactions, among children up to 5 years (www.safecare.publichealth.gsu.edu).

Another form of physical abuse prevention in common use involves training parents to eliminate physical forms of discipline. Oftentimes this occurs after the parent has already been investigated for physical abuse with the goal of preventing future contact with the child welfare system. One such program, Parent–Child Interaction Therapy

(PCIT; www.pcit.org), is delivered in a one-on-one format with the parent where a trained clinician teaches the parent a number of non-violent behavior management skills. After discussing these skills with the parent, the clinician then provides live, in-the-moment coaching to the parent as he or she interacts with the child. PCIT has been demonstrated to decrease child behavioral problems (Thomas, Abell, Webb, Avdagic, & Zimmer-Gembeck, 2017) as well as reduce a parent's use of physical discipline and recidivism with the child welfare system when compared to standard services (Chaffin et al., 2004). Other programs are available that essentially teach the same types of parenting skills and have been marketed to child welfare services. The Incredible Years (www.incredibleyears.com) is one such program that occurs in a group format, but does not provide direct coaching to the parent. Instead, parents role-play various scenarios with other parents in the group and watch video clips demonstrating the use of the techniques with children. Other tested programs include interventions such as the Positive Parenting Program (Triple P; www.triplep.net) and, for children younger than five years, the Attachment and Biobehavioral Catch-up program (ABC; www.abcintervention.org). There are literally dozens of programs available that focus specifically on parenting; however, many of these programs have not been evaluated for effectiveness and some do not teach the same parenting skills as those with significant empirical evidence of effectiveness. Before implementing or receiving training in a parent-training program, it is important to thoroughly examine the quantity and quality of the scientific research on that particular approach.

After maltreatment has occurred, mental health intervention may be necessary. In previous eras of clinical practice it was not uncommon to hear people refer to "treating sexual abuse" or "treating trauma." While these phrases are still around, there is a general consensus that such terms are misleading and may result in the delivery of ineffective practices. The reason is quite simple: trauma and abuse are events that occurred in the past and cannot be "treated." Rather, clinicians are tasked with treating the sequelae, or lasting effects, of abuse and neglect. As demonstrated in this chapter, any number of emotional or behavioral problems may occur as a result of maltreatment. As such, there is no panacea or one-size-fits-all treatment. Effective intervention must begin with an appropriate assessment that both determines the most pressing presenting issues to target for intervention and obtains a thorough trauma history to comprehensively identify the child's experiences. Depending on the presenting concern, any number of treatments may be indicated, as reviewed in other chapters of this volume. For example, PCIT, reviewed above, has been shown to be particularly effective in reducing behavioral problems among maltreated children. One unique presenting concern among trauma-exposed children, such as those experiencing sexual or physical abuse, is PTSD. At the current time, the gold standard treatment for PTSD among youth is Trauma-Focused Cognitive-Behavioral Therapy (TF-CBT; www.tfcbt.org). This intervention teaches children a number of coping skills before having them develop a factual narrative, to the best of their memory and ability, about the abuse they experienced. Thus, TF-CBT teaches children how to cope with reminders and reactions related to their traumatic experience and provides gradual desensitization to memories and other stimuli associated with the trauma. A large body of evidence shows that TF-CBT is superior to rapport-focused play therapy and supportive counseling for the treatment of PTSD, and improves other studied outcomes, such as depression, anxiety, and behavioral problems (Morina, Koerssen, & Pollet, 2016).

Future Research Directions

In the light of this existing body of work, there are at three important directions for future research that will accelerate our understanding of how child maltreatment leads to psychiatric disorders and the ways in which we can optimize interventions, both existing and new, to treat a broader range of these disorders more effectively and efficiently. One direction for future research involves addressing a long-standing methodological challenge when evaluating the risk for psychiatric disorders in *prospective cohort studies* of child maltreatment. Prospective cohort studies, where maltreated and comparison conditions are first established and then assessed repeatedly over time to evaluate differential rates in the onset of specific health outcomes, are the ideal methodology for research with the child maltreatment population (Widom, Raphael, & DuMont, 2004). However, often unbeknownst to researchers, many members of comparison conditions are exposed to child maltreatment either prior to study entry or during longitudinal follow-up. This methodological phenomenon is known as *contamination* and it can bias results obtained in prospective cohort studies in ways that can affect both the statistical significance and effect size magnitude of risk estimates (Shenk, Noll, Peugh, Griffin, & Bensman, 2016).

For example, Scott, Smith, and Ellis (2010) conducted a study where official case records were used to create confirmed child maltreatment and comparison conditions to determine the risk for past year and lifetime rates of psychiatric disorders at young adulthood. As a result of a careful and multimethod assessment, they discovered that 14.4% of the comparison condition reported experiencing maltreatment at some point prior to adulthood even though there was no official record of it, providing a prevalence estimate of contamination in this study. When this contamination was removed from the statistical analysis, effect size estimates for confirmed child maltreatment increased in magnitude for any past-year and any lifetime history of a psychiatric disorder, with the risk for several individual disorders subsequently reaching statistical significance. These results suggest that contamination can make it harder to detect statistically significant results within a single study as well as reproduce effect size estimates across independent studies of child maltreatment, leading to replication and reproducibility failures (Open Science Collaboration, 2015). Research on the optimal ways of controlling contamination and its impact on risk estimates in prospective cohort studies is underway. For now, using a multimethod approach of both official case records and self-report instruments to screen for the presence of child maltreatment in comparison conditions at study entry and at each subsequent data collection assessment appears to be the ideal approach for detecting and controlling contamination in prospective child maltreatment research. Doing so has the potential to strengthen causal inferences about the risk child maltreatment creates for subsequent health, especially psychiatric disorders.

A second direction for future research involves the identification of mechanistic pathways affected by child maltreatment that lead to a diverse range of psychiatric disorders. These mechanisms are called *transdiagnostic mechanisms* (Nolen-Hoeksema & Watkins, 2011) and they serve a critical role in modern classifications of psychiatric disorders because they identify the etiological pathways to multiple and often comorbid psychiatric disorders as well as the most critical targets for interventions designed to treat broad dimensions of mental health, instead of individual disorders. Examples of transdiagnostic mechanisms include emotion regulation, physiological systems mediating stress responses, family communication, and neural processes (McEwen, 2007). While child maltreatment researchers have wisely adopted mediation models as a way to identify transdiagnostic mechanisms, this research has been limited by a reliance on simple mediation models that test only one transdiagnostic mechanism at a time, as opposed to multiple mediation models that test several mechanisms simultaneously. The reason evaluating one transdiagnostic mechanism at a time is a limitation is because child maltreatment leads to sustained change across multiple transdiagnostic mechanisms simultaneously, including stress physiology, behavior, and family function. Examining only one of these mechanisms at a time can erroneously attribute causation to that mechanism simply through the omission of other relevant mechanisms. Such an approach also makes it difficult to prioritize critical targets for intervention with the child maltreatment population. For example, Shenk, Putnam, Rausch, Peugh, and Noll (2014) examined a model that evaluated simultaneous change across physiological, hormonal, and avoidance behavior mechanisms following child maltreatment and discovered that only the avoidance behavior mechanism predicted more severe posttraumatic stress disorder (PTSD) symptoms one year later. These results suggest that targeting avoidance behavior, say with exposure and response prevention as found in an intervention like TF-CBT, is a higher priority target in the treatment of PTSD. By adopting a framework where several different mechanisms are tested simultaneously in mediation models, future child maltreatment research will be able to identify the mechanisms causing a variety of psychiatric disorders that ultimately become the critical targets for existing or new interventions.

A third direction for future research pertains to the optimization of behavioral interventions for the purposes of treating a wider range of psychiatric disorders common to the broader child maltreatment population. Well-conducted research demonstrates that child maltreatment creates a sustained risk for multiple psychiatric disorders, accounting for 27–50% of all such disorders in adulthood (Kessler et al., 2010; Li, D'Arcy, & Meng, 2016). This research suggests that the risk created by child maltreatment is not specific to any one disorder and that behavioral interventions need to be capable of addressing a variety of psychiatric disorders at the times and places services are accessed. However, behavioral interventions for psychiatric disorders in the child maltreatment population have been developed with the purpose of generating empirically supported treatments for specific disorders. While this approach has many strengths, it makes it difficult to treat a range of disorders common to the broader child maltreatment population. For example, cognitive-behavioral therapies (CBTs) with an explicit trauma focus are the recommended, first-line mental health intervention for the treatment of PTSD in the child maltreatment population (Cohen et al., 2010). Yet, independent meta-analyses (Kowalik, Weller, Venter, & Drachman, 2011; Macdonald et al., 2016; Silverman et al., 2008) show that while CBTs exert moderate effects on PTSD, they have much smaller effects on mood, anxiety, and disruptive behavior disorders—mental health disorders that are as common as PTSD in this population (Lewis et al., 2019). This has led to a common concern among practitioners that CBTs may not be effective in treating the full range of psychiatric disorders seen in the community.

There are two approaches that can address this challenge in future research. One, instead of requiring samples meet specified PTSD eligibility criteria, and therefore evaluate the effects of a treatment for PTSD, future research can apply existing CBTs to the treatment of other psychiatric disorders common in the child maltreatment population. For example, evaluating the efficacy of TF-CBT for the treatment of other psychiatric disorders common to the broader child maltreatment population, such as major depressive disorder, has the potential not only to widen the target population of this intervention, but also to improve treatment response rates for those with a child maltreatment history receiving standard cognitive-behavioral therapy. Two, research on the individual components that make up many of the interventions delivered with the child maltreatment population can create a scientific evidence base for the effectiveness of each of these components as well as their ideal combination for improving treatment effects beyond existing interventions. Research on the effects of multiple components would allow for the development of novel interventions that can more precisely target and engage transdiagnostic mechanisms leading to multiple psychiatric disorders common in the child maltreatment population. This would increase both the effectiveness and efficiency of treatments for the full range of psychiatric disorders. Together, these approaches to future treatment development research will have significant potential in driving down the lifelong public health costs attributable to child maltreatment through its sustained impact on psychiatric disorders.

Chapter Summary

As demonstrated throughout this chapter, child maltreatment is difficult to adequately define, but the negative impact it may cause on the development of the person is without question. Any number of developmental capacities may be compromised as a result of childhood physical abuse, sexual abuse, and neglect, among other forms of maltreatment, and potentially contribute to the development of any number of presenting mental health concerns, like those we discussed in Parts II and III of this book. Research over the past half century has clearly identified a number of risk factors for the occurrence of maltreatment, leading to the development and testing of multiple prevention approaches. Similarly, treatment research has identified a number of effective interventions, depending on the specific presenting issue, which we also reviewed in previous chapters. In the coming years it is expected that we will learn an even greater deal about how to prevent and intervene in cases of maltreatment and, thus, improve the development and well-being of children and adolescents, and reduce the social and economic impact of maltreatment on society.

Further Reading

1 Caspi, A., McClay, J., Moffitt, T. E., Mill, J., Martin, J., Craig, I. W., & Poulton, R. (2002). Role of genotype in the cycle of violence in maltreated children. *Science*, *297*(5582), 851–854.

2 Cicchetti, D., & Toth, S. L. (1995). A developmental psychopathology perspective on child abuse and neglect. *Journal of the American Academy of Child and Adolescent Psychiatry*, *34*, 541–565.

3 Stoltenborgh, M., van IJzendoorn, M. H., Euser, E. M., & Bakermans-Kranenburg, M. J. (2011). A global perspective on child sexual abuse: Meta-analysis of prevalence around the world. *Child Maltreatment*, *16*, 79–101.

Discussion/Essay Questions

1. Child maltreatment is a pervasive social problem that results in considerable cost to the legal, educational, child welfare, and healthcare systems, as well as other services commonly provided by governmental agencies. Prevention programs are well-validated, and research suggests broad-scale implementation of such programs have the potential to save billions of dollars in the future. However, funding these programs now will be expensive and are likely to require raising taxes. Should taxes be raised to fund child maltreatment prevention programs? If so, who should shoulder the burden of paying higher taxes? If not, discuss alternative options or opinions to addressing the problem of child maltreatment.
2. Sexual abuse is by far the most prominently recognized form of child maltreatment, receiving the bulk of media attention, particularly given recent high-profile cases (e.g., priests within the Catholic Church, Jerry Sandusky at Penn State, Larry Nassar with the USA gymnastics team, troop leaders in the Boy Scouts). As reviewed here, however, there is evidence that other forms of maltreatment (e.g., physical abuse, neglect) are equally, if not more, prevalent as sexual abuse and can result in similar negative outcomes. Why do you think sexual abuse creates more outrage amongst the public than other forms of maltreatment? Would it change your opinion to learn that the vast majority of sexual abuse is perpetrated by a family member within their home and that such cases are much less likely to be reported by the media?
3. The advent of technology has created multiple problems for law enforcement, child welfare, and other professionals serving maltreated children. A current challenge is how to address the issue of an underage child recording or taking sexually explicit pictures of him- or herself using a smart phone and sending the image(s) to another individual. In this situation, the child has both produced and distributed child pornography and the individual who received it is in possession of child pornography. Many prosecutors are hesitant to press charges against the child who is technically viewed as the victim, but it becomes difficult legal grounds to charge the one in possession of the image and not charge the one who produced and distributed the image. Mental health and child welfare professionals are being increasingly called upon to treat or otherwise provide services to the child, but in the twenty-first century, digital sharing of one's personal lives is commonplace and it can be difficult for an 11-year-old child, for instance, to consider the long-term ramifications of his or her actions now. How would you go about addressing this issue?

Glossary

Act of commission is when an individual performs a specific act.

Act of omission is when an individual fails to act.

Child maltreatment is an act of commission (i.e., an individual performs a specific act) or omission (i.e., an individual fails to act) toward a child that causes harm or creates the potential of harm that exceeds a defined threshold (e.g., serious, substantial).

Child maltreatment investigation is an investigation by an appointed authoritative body (e.g., law enforcement, child welfare) for the purposes of determining whether a child was the victim of abuse or neglect. Such investigations often include interviewing the child and any witnesses, and may include interviewing the alleged perpetrator, collection of physical evidence, and medical evaluation.

Child protection agency ia a public or private agency tasked with investigating allegations of child maltreatment and/or providing services to children and families impacted by child maltreatment or who are at risk for child maltreatment.

Contamination is a process where two supposedly distinct groups are, in actuality, not as distinct as originally believed as a result of one group possessing traits believed to only occur in the other group. In child maltreatment research, this occurs when a comparison group is believed to include only non-maltreated children, but unknown to the researchers, a proportion of the children in the group have experienced maltreatment.

Neglect concerns acts of omission that result in a child not receiving sufficient care. These acts may be subdivided into the type of care not received by the child, such as physical (e.g., food, clothing, shelter), psychological or emotional (e.g., nurturance, love), medical, and educational, among others.

Physical abuse is a physical act of commission where pain is intentionally inflicted upon a child and results in pain and/or injury that exceeds a predetermined threshold. In some jurisdictions that have banned physical punishment of children, all forms of intentionally striking a child are deemed physically abusive.

Polyvictimization is exposure to multiple forms of interpersonal trauma.

Posttraumatic Stress Disorder (PTSD) is a disorder that can develop following exposure to a traumatic event that includes four symptom categories: intrusion, avoidance, negative alterations in cognition/mood, and hyperarousal.

Prospective cohort study is an important research design in child maltreatment research where a group of interest (i.e., maltreated children) is recruited for a study alongside a comparison group (i.e., non-maltreated children) and both groups are repeatedly assessed at various points in time to determine differences in development.

Psychological abuse is a non-physical act of commission that serves to ridicule, intimidate, exploit, or otherwise spurn and degrade a child and causes impairment or disruption in functioning that exceeds a predetermined threshold. Also commonly referred to as emotional abuse and verbal abuse.

Sexual abuse is an act of commission where one engages or attempts to engage in sexual behavior with a child through physical or non-physical coercion, or with a child being younger than a pre-determined age of consent to engage in sexual behavior.

Substantiate is a legal decision made by an authoritative agency investigating an allegation of child maltreatment where the evidence collected suggests that the maltreatment in question did, indeed, occur. The standard that must be met to substantiate an allegation differs between jurisdictions.

Transdiagnostic mechanism is a deficient capability or skill that is identified as an etiological factor in the development of multiple psychiatric diagnoses. Examples include difficulties with emotion regulation, behavior regulation, cognitive ability, and social skills.

References

Alto, M., Handley, E., Rogosch, F., Cicchetti, D., & Toth, S. (2018). Maternal relationship quality and peer social acceptance as mediators between child maltreatment and adolescent depressive symptoms: Gender differences. *Journal of Adolescence*, *63*, 19–28.

American Psychiatric Association (2013). *Diagnostic and Statistical Manual of Mental Health Disorders* (5th ed.). Washington, DC.

Annerbäck, E.-M., Wingren, G., Svedin, C. G., & Gustafsson, P. A. (2010). Prevalence and characteristics of child physical abuse in Sweden: Findings from a population-based youth survey. *Acta Pædiatrica*, *99*, 1229–1236.

Bradley, R. G., Binder, E. B., Epstein, M. P., Tang, Y., Nair, H. P., Liu, W., & Ressler, K. J. (2008). Influence of child abuse on adult depression: Moderation by the corticotropin-releasing hormone receptor gene. *Archives of General Psychiatry*, *65*(2), 190–200.

Caspi, A., McClay, J., Moffitt, T. E., Mill, J., Martin, J., Craig, I. W., & Poulton, R. (2002). Role of genotype in the cycle of violence in maltreated children. *Science*, *297*(5582), 851–854.

Center for Disease Control and Prevention (n.d.). Defining child maltreatment. Retrieved from: https://vetoviolence.cdc.gov/defining-child-maltreatment.

Chaffin, M., Silovsky, J. F., Funderburk, B., Valle, L. A., Brestan, E. V., Balachova, T., & Bonner, B. L. (2004). Parent–child interaction therapy with physically abusive parents: Efficacy for reducing future abuse reports. *Journal of Consulting and Clinical Psychology*, *72*, 500–510.

Child Welfare Information Gateway. (2019). What is child abuse and neglect? Retrieved from: https://www.acf.hhs.gov/cb/faq.

Cicchetti, D. (2013). Annual research review: Resilient functioning in maltreated children—Past, present, and future perspectives. *Journal of Child Psychology and Psychiatry*, *54*, 402–422.

Cicchetti, D., & Rogosch, F. (1997). The role of self-organization in the promotion of resilience in maltreated children. *Development and Psychopathology*, *9*, 797–814.

Cicchetti, D., Rogosch, F. A., Gunnar, M. R., & Toth, S. L. (2010). The differential impacts of early physical and sexual abuse and internalizing problems on daytime cortisol rhythm in school-aged children. *Child Development*, *81*, 252–269.

Cohen, J. A., Bukstein, O., Walter, H., Benson, S. R., Chrisman, A., Farchione, T. R., & Medicus, J. (2010). Practice parameter for the assessment and treatment of children and adolescents with posttraumatic stress disorder. *Journal of the American Academy of Child & Adolescent Psychiatry*, *49*, 414–430.

Collishaw, S., Pickles, A., Messer, J., Rutter, M., Shearer, C., & Maughan, B. (2007). Resilience to adult psychopathology following childhood maltreatment: Evidence from a community sample. *Child Abuse & Neglect*, *31*, 211–229.

Danese, A., Moffitt, T. E., Pariante, C. M., Ambler, A., Poulton, R., & Caspi, A. (2008). Elevated inflammation levels in depressed adults with a history of childhood maltreatment. *Archives of General Psychiatry*, *65*, 409–414.

Danese, A., Pariante, C. M., Caspi, A., Taylor, A., & Poulton, R. (2007). Childhood maltreatment predicts adult inflammation in a life-course study. *Proceedings of the National Academy of Sciences*, *104*, 1319–1324.

Dodge, K. A., Goodman, W. B., Murphy, R. A., O'Donnell, K., & Sato, J. (2013). Randomized controlled trial of universal postnatal nurse home visiting: Impact of emergency care. *Pediatrics*, *132*, S140–S146.

Dodge, K. A., Goodman, W. B., Murphy, R. A., O'Donnell, K., Sato, J., & Guptill, S. (2014). Implementation and randomized controlled trial evaluation of universal postnatal nurse home visiting. *American Journal of Public Health*, *104*, S136–S143.

Elgar, F. J., Donnelly, P. D., Michaelson, V., Gariepy, G., Riehm, K. E., Walsh, S. D., & Pickett, W. (2018). Corporal punishment bans and physical fighting in adolescents: An ecological study of 88 countries. *BMJ Open, 8*.

Ezzell, C. E., Swenson, C. C., & Brondino, M. J. (2000). The relationship of social support to physically abused children's adjustment. *Child Abuse and Neglect, 24*, 641–651.

Fang, X., Brown, D. S., Florence, C. S., & Mercy, J. A. (2012). The economic burden of child maltreatment in the United State and implications for prevention. *Child Abuse and Neglect, 36*, 156–165.

Fang, X., Fry, D. A., Brown, D. S., Mercy, J. A., Dunne, M. P., Butchart, A. R., & Swales, D. M. (2015). The burden of child maltreatment in the East Asia and Pacific region. *Child Abuse and Neglect, 42*, 146–162.

Finkelhor, D., Turner, H. A., Hamby, S., & Ormrod, R. (2011, October). Polyvictimization: Children's exposure to multiple types of violence, crime, and abuse. *Juvenile Justice Bulletin*. Washington, DC: U.S. Department of Justice, Office of Juvenile Justice and Delinquency Prevention.

Finkelhor, D., Turner, H. A., Shattuck, A., & Hamby, S. L. (2015). Prevalence of childhood exposure to violence, crime, and abuse: Results from the National Survey of Children's Exposure to Violence. *JAMA Pediatrics, 169*, 746–754.

Flynn, M., Cicchetti, D., & Rogosch, F. (2014). The prospective contribution of childhood maltreatment to low self-worth, low relationship quality, and symptomatology across adolescence: A developmental-organizational perspective. *Developmental Psychology, 50*, 2165–2175.

Gershoff, E. T., & Grogan-Kaylor, A. (2016). Spanking and child outcomes: Old controversies and new meta-analyses. *Journal of Family Psychology, 30*, 453–469.

Hamburger, M. E., Leeb, R. T., & Swahn, M. H. (2008). Childhood maltreatment and early alcohol use among high-risk adolescents. *Journal of Studies on Alcohol and Drugs, 69*, 291–295.

Handley, E. D., Rogosch, F. A., & Cicchetti, D. (2015). Developmental pathways from child maltreatment to adolescent marijuana dependence: Examining moderation by FK506 binding protein 5 gene (FKBP5). *Development and Psychopathology, 27*, 1489–1502.

Hindley, N., Ramchandani, P. G., & Jones, D. P. H. (2006). Risk factors for recurrence of maltreatment: A systematic review. *Archives of Disease in Childhood, 91*, 744–752.

Hussey, J. M., Chang, J. J., & Kotch, J. B. (2006). Child maltreatment in the United States: Prevalence, risk factors, and adolescent health consequences. *Pediatrics, 118*, 933–942.

Jowett, S., Karatzias, T., Shevlin, M., & Albert, I. (2020). Differentiating symptom profiles of ICD-11 PTSD, complex PTSD, and borderline personality disorder: A latent class analysis in a multiply traumatized sample. *Personality Disorders, 11*, 36–45.

Ju, S., & Lee, Y. (2018). Developmental trajectories and longitudinal mediation effects of self-esteem, peer attachment, child maltreatment and depression on early adolescents. *Child Abuse and Neglect, 76*, 353–363.

Kessler, R. C., McLaughlin, K. A., Green, J. G., Gruber, M. J., Sampson, N. A., Zaslavsky, A. M., & Williams, D. R. (2010). Childhood adversities and adult psychopathology in the WHO World Mental Health Surveys. *British Journal of Psychiatry, 197*, 378–385.

Kilpatrick, D. G., & Saunders, B. E. (1997). *Prevalence and consequences of child victimization: Results from the National Survey of Adolescents, final report*. Washington, DC: U.S. Department of Justice, Office of Justice Programs.

Kim, J., & Cicchetti, D. (2010). Longitudinal pathways linking child maltreatment, emotion regulation, peer relations, and psychopathology. *Journal of Child Psychology and Psychiatry, 51*(6), 706–716.

Kowalik, J., Weller, J., Venter, J., & Drachman, D. (2011). Cognitive behavioral therapy for the treatment of pediatric posttraumatic stress disorder: A review and meta-analysis. *Journal of Behavior Therapy and Experimental Psychiatry*, *42*, 405–413.

Lansford, J. E., Dodge, K. A., Pettit, G. S., Bates, J. E., Crozier, J., & Kaplow, J. (2002). A 12-year prospective study of the long-term effects of early child physical maltreatment on psychological, behavioral, and academic problems in adolescence. *Archives of Pediatrics & Adolescent Medicine*, *156*, 824–830.

Lau, J. T. F., Kim, J. H., Tsui, H.-Y., Cheung, A., Lau, M., & Yu, A. (2005). The relationship between physical maltreatment and substance use among adolescents: A survey of 95,788 adolescents in Hong Kong. *Journal of Adolescent Health*, *37*, 110–119.

Letourneau, E. J., Brown, D. S., Fang, X., Hassan, A., & Mercy, J. A. (2018). The economic burden of child sexual abuse in the United States. *Child Abuse and Neglect*, *79*, 413–422.

Lewis, S. J., Arseneault, L., Caspi, A., Fisher, H. L., Matthews, T., Moffitt, T. E., & Danese, A. (2019). The epidemiology of trauma and post-traumatic stress disorder in a representative cohort of young people in England and Wales. *Lancet Psychiatry*, *6*, 247–256.

Li, M., D'Arcy, C., & Meng, X. (2016). Maltreatment in childhood substantially increases the risk of adult depression and anxiety in prospective cohort studies: Systematic review, meta-analysis, and proportional attributable fractions. *Psychological Medicine*, *46*, 717–730.

Macdonald, G., Livingstone, N., Hanratty, J., McCartan, C., Cotmore, R., Cary, M., & Churchill, R. (2016). The effectiveness, acceptability and cost-effectiveness of psychosocial interventions for maltreated children and adolescents: An evidence synthesis. *Health Technology Assessment*, *20*, 1–508.

May-Chahal, C., & Cawson, P. (2005). Measuring child maltreatment in the United Kingdom: A study of the prevalence of child abuse and neglect. *Child Abuse and Neglect*, *29*, 969–984.

McEwen, B. S. (2007). Physiology and neurobiology of stress and adaptation: Central role of the brain. *Physiological Reviews*, *87*, 873–904.

McLaughlin K. A., Green J. G., Gruber M. J., Sampson, N. A., Zaslavsky, A. M., & Kessler, R. C. (2012). Childhood adversities and first onset of psychiatric disorders in a national sample of US adolescents. *Archives of General Psychiatry*, *69*, 1151–1160.

Morina, N., Koerssen, R., & Pollet, T. V. (2016). Interventions for children and adolescents with posttraumatic stress disorder: A meta-analysis of comparative outcome studies. *Clinical Psychology Review*, *47*, 41–54.

Musliner, K. L., & Singer, J. B. (2014). Emotional support and adult depression in survivors of childhood sexual abuse. *Child Abuse & Neglect*, *38*, 1331–1340.

Negriff, S., Cederbaum, J. A., & Lee, D. S. (2019). Does social support mediate the association between maltreatment experiences and depressive symptoms in adolescence? *Child Maltreatment*, *24*, 203–212.

Nolen-Hoeksema, S., & Watkins, E. R. (2011). A heuristic for developing transdiagnostic models of psychopathology: Explaining multifinality and divergent trajectories. *Perspectives on Psychological Science*, *6*, 589–609.

Oh, A., Han, M., Choi, Y., Lau, S., & Shum, M. S. W. (2019). Exploring relationship among child maltreatment experience in childhood and behavior problems as young adults: Role of social support among college students in Hong Kong. *International Social Work*, *62*(2), 1011–1024.

Open Science Collaboration (2015). Estimating the reproducibility of psychological science. *Science*, *349*(6251), aac4716.

Oshri, A., Rogosch, F. A., Burnette, M. L., & Cicchetti, D. (2011). Developmental pathways to adolescent cannabis abuse and dependence: Child maltreatment, emerging personality, and internalizing versus externalizing psychopathology. *Psychology of Addictive Behaviors*, *25*(4), 634.

Oshri, A., Rogosch, F. A., & Cicchetti, D. (2013). Child maltreatment and mediating influences of childhood personality types on the development of adolescent psychopathology. *Journal of Clinical Child & Adolescent Psychology*, *42*, 287–301.

Polanczyk, G., Caspi, A., Williams, B., Price, T. S., Danese, A., Sugden, K., & Moffitt, T. E. (2009). Protective effect of CRHR1 gene variants on the development of adult depression following childhood maltreatment: Replication and extension. *Archives of General Psychiatry*, *66*, 978–985.

Powers, A., Ressler, K. J., & Bradley, R. G. (2008). The protective role of friendship on the effects of childhood abuse and depression. *Depression and Anxiety*, *26*, 46–53.

Scott, K. M., Smith, D. R., & Ellis, P. M. (2010). Prospectively ascertained child maltreatment and its association with DSM-IV mental disorders in young adults. *Archives of General Psychiatry*, *67*, 712–719.

Scrafford, K. E., Grein, K., & Miller-Graff, L. E. (2018). Legacies of childhood victimization: Indirect effects on adult mental health through re-victimization. *Journal of Child & Adolescent Trauma*, *11*, 317–326.

Sedlak, A.J., Mettenburg, J., Basena, M., Petta, I., McPherson, K., Greene, A., & Li, S. (2010). *Fourth National Incidence Study of Child Abuse and Neglect (NIS–4): Report to Congress, Executive Summary*. Washington, DC: U.S. Department of Health and Human Services, Administration for Children and Families.

Seeds, P. M., Harkness, K. L., & Quilty, L. C. (2010). Parental maltreatment, bullying, and adolescent depression: Evidence for the mediating role of perceived social support. *Journal of Clinical Child & Adolescent Psychology*, *39*, 681–692.

Shenk, C. E., Noll, J. G., Peugh, J. L., Griffin, A. M., & Bensman, H. E. (2016). Contamination in the prospective study of child maltreatment and female adolescent health. *Journal of Pediatric Psychology*, *41*, 37–45.

Shenk, C. E., Putnam, F. W., Rausch, J. R., Peugh, J. L., & Noll, J. G. (2014). A longitudinal study of several potential mediators of the relationship between child maltreatment and posttraumatic stress disorder symptoms. *Development and Psychopathology*, *26*(1), 81– 91.

Silverman, W. K., Ortiz, C. D., Viswesvaran, C., Burns, B. J., Kolko, D. J., Putnam, F. W., & Amaya-Jackson, L. (2008). Evidence-based psychosocial treatments for children and adolescents exposed to traumatic events. *Journal of Clinical Child & Adolescent Psychology*, *37*(1), 156–183.

Smith, T. W., Davern, M., Freese, J., & Morgan, S. (2018). General Social Surveys, 1972–2018. *GSS Data Explorer*. Chicago, IL: NORC at the University of Chicago. Data accessed from the GSS Data Explorer website at: gssdataexplorer.norc.org.

Stoltenborgh, M., van IJzendoorn, M. H., Euser, E. M., & Bakermans-Kranenburg, M. J. (2011). A global perspective on child sexual abuse: Meta-analysis of prevalence around the world. *Child Maltreatment*, *16*, 79–101.

Stroem, I. F., Aakvaag, H. F., & Wentzel-Larsen, T. (2019). Characteristics of different types of childhood violence and the risk of revictimization. *Violence Against Women*, *25*(14), 1696–1716.

Thomas, R., Abell, B., Webb, H. J., Avdagic, E., & Zimmer-Gembeck, M. J. (2017). Parent– child interaction therapy: A meta-analysis. *Pediatrics*, *140*, e20170352.

Thompson, K. M., Crosby, R. D., Wonderlich, S. A., Mitchell, J. E., Redlin, J., Demuth, G., & Haseltine, B. (2005). Psychopathology and sexual trauma in childhood and adulthood. *Journal of Traumatic Stress*, *16*, 35–38.

Trickett, P. K., Noll, J. G., Susman, E. J., Shenk, C. E., & Putnam, F. W. (2010). Attenuation of cortisol across development for victims of sexual abuse. *Development and Psychopathology*, *22*, 165–175.

U.S. Department of Health & Human Services, Administration for Children and Families, Administration on Children, Youth and Families, Children's Bureau (2019). Child Maltreatment 2017. Available from: https://www.acf.hhs.gov/

cb/research-data-technology/statistics-research/child-maltreatment.

Vachon, D., Krueger, R. F., Rogosch, F., & Cicchetti, D. (2015). Assessment of the harmful psychiatric and behavioral effects of different forms of child maltreatment. *JAMA Psychiatry*, *72*, 1135–1142.

Valentino, K., Nuttall, A. K., Comas, M., Borkowski, J. G., & Akai, C. E. (2012). Intergenerational continuity of child abuse among adolescent mothers: Authoritarian parenting, community violence, and race. *Child Maltreatment*, *17*, 172–181.

Walker, H. E., Freud, J. S., Ellis, R. A., Fraine, S. M., & Wilson, L. C. (2019). The prevalence of sexual revictimization: A meta-analytic review. *Trauma, Violence, & Abuse*, *20*, 67–80.

Widom, C. S., Raphael, K. G., & DuMont, K. A. (2004). The case for prospective longitudinal studies in child maltreatment research: Commentary on Dube, Williamson, Thompson, Felitti, and Anda (2004). *Child Abuse & Neglect*, *28*, 715–722.

Wright, M. O., & Folger, S. F. (2017). Creating a safe haven following child maltreatment: The benefits and limits of social support. In D. M. Teti (Ed.), *Parenting and family processes in child maltreatment and intervention* (pp. 23–34). New York, NY: Springer.

Chapter 15

Divorce, Separation, and Loss

Amanda Venta and Jesse Walker

Chapter Overview

In this chapter, we focus on some of the most difficult events in a child's life—divorce, separation, or loss of parents. While none of these events determine psychopathology, we discuss models and research describing why some children experience difficulty adjusting to these events. In conjunction, we review the *adjustment disorder* categories appropriate for children with difficulty adapting to major events. The bulk of this chapter will be devoted to research on divorce and separation, with a smaller section reviewing research on parental loss. Both research bases are small in comparison to existing literature on the etiology of childhood psychiatric disorders, so the developmental psychopathology models described are sparse.

Definition, Diagnosis, and Clinical Features

As we define divorce, separation, and loss, it will be important to keep in mind what you have already learned about attachment theory and the invaluable presence of a child's attachment figures across development (Chapter 4). For this chapter, we will define separation as the decision of a married couple to live separately. In many cases, a separation is a step that precedes divorce—the formal, legal separation of assets and dissolution of a marriage—though some individuals separate briefly, with the aim of reuniting. Loss refers to the death of a parent during childhood and we will focus on experiences of loss that affect a caregiver.

Many individuals experience these difficult events and subsequent grief. While typical loss reactions are painful, they are time-limited and

Developmental Psychopathology, First Edition. Edited by Amanda Venta, Carla Sharp, Jack M. Fletcher, and Peter Fonagy.

functioning will return to baseline after some time (Neria & Litz, 2004). However, a diagnosis may be warranted when significant behavioral or emotional symptoms emerge and then persist. Currently, the DSM-5 allows for the diagnosis of an *adjustment disorder* if a stressor, like divorce or loss, causes difficulties that exceed a typical reaction (American Psychiatric Association, 2013). Adjustment disorders can be diagnosed when emotional or behavioral symptoms emerge within 3 months of the stressor, are clinically significant, and cause significant impairment in the individual's functioning. Table 15.1 shows specific diagnostic criteria for adjustment disorders.

Researchers have argued for additional diagnostic categories to capture adjustment difficulties specific to parental loss. The DSM-5 has included a new possible diagnosis, *persistent complex bereavement disorder*, in need of additional research. The diagnostic criteria would include experiencing death of a loved one, followed by at least 6 months (or 12 for

TABLE 15.1 Adjustment Disorders as Defined by the DSM-5 and ICD-11

DSM 5	*ICD-11*
A. The development of emotional or behavioral symptoms in response to an identifiable stressor(s) occurring within 3 months of the onset of the stressor(s). B. These symptoms or behaviors are clinically significant, as evidenced by one or both of the following: • Marked distress that is out of proportion to the severity or intensity of the stressor, taking into account the external context and the cultural factors that might influence symptom severity and presentation. • Significant impairment in social, occupational, or other important areas of functioning. C. The stress-related disturbance does not meet the criteria for another mental disorder and is not merely an exacerbation of a preexisting mental disorder. D. The symptoms do not represent normal bereavement. E. Once the stressor (or its consequences) has terminated, the symptoms do not persist for more than an additional 6 months.	Adjustment disorder is a maladaptive reaction to an identifiable psychosocial stressor or multiple stressors (e.g., divorce, illness or disability, socioeconomic problems, conflicts at home or work) that usually emerge within a month of the stressor. The disorder is characterized by: • Preoccupation with the stressor or its consequences, including excessive worry, recurrent and distressing thoughts about the stressor, or constant rumination about its implications. • Failure to adapt to the stressor that causes significant impairment in personal, family, social, educational, occupational or other important areas of functioning. The symptoms are not of sufficient specificity or severity to justify the diagnosis of another Mental and Behavioral Disorder and typically resolve within 6 months, unless the stressor persists for a longer duration.

Source: Adapted from the DSM-5 (APA, 2013), ICD-11 (WHO, 2018). ASEBA items were not included due to the absence of a scale representing adjustment disorders.

adults) of persistent yearning or longing, sorrow or crying, preoccupation with them, and preoccupation with circumstances of the death. Additional symptoms related to reactive distress and social/identity disruption are also required (see Table 15.1; APA, 2013). While researchers continue to study whether this diagnostic classification is reliable and valid, research on *complicated grief* and *prolonged grief* shows that the process can take on a qualitatively different structure from typical bereavement, depression, and anxiety (Tay et al., 2015), or a protracted course (Kaplow et al., 2012) warranting a unique diagnostic category.

Divorce and separation

Prevalence

Divorce is quite common, affecting an estimated 3.2 per 1,000 people in 2014 (reflecting a decline from 4.0 per 1,000 people in 2000; CDC/NCHS National Vital Statistics System; see CDC/National Center for Health Statistics (US) 2015). In the United States, an estimated 10.9% of people (15 years and over) identify as divorced and 2.2% identify as separated (U.S. Census Bureau, 2010–2014 American Community Survey 5-Year Estimates). Researchers estimate approximately half of all marriages in the United States end in divorce (Weaver & Schofield, 2015) and half of American children experience divorce (Lansford, 2009). Estimates of what percentage of children will experience serious, long-term impairment vary widely.

PREVALENCE BY GENDER AGE

General trends demonstrate that divorce has more deleterious effects on younger children, with some researchers positing that parental divorce prior to age 6 poses a particular risk of subsequent emotional and behavioral difficulties (Rogers, 2004). This idea is refuted by some researchers, suggesting that the manifestation of adjustment difficulties experienced by children, rather than the magnitude of those difficulties, changes across development (Lansford, 2009).

PREVALENCE BY SOCIOECONOMIC STATUS (SES), RACE, AND ETHNICITY

A large *meta-analytic study* showed the effects of parental divorce on later psychosocial functioning of African Americans are smaller than the effects for European Americans (Amato & Kieth, 1991). Other studies have shown that decline in family income following divorce may be a risk factor for adjustment difficulties, and that this decline is smaller for African Americans, suggesting that the effects of parental divorce on African American children are mitigated by the smaller decline in income (Lansford, 2009).

Developmental Continuities and Discontinuities (Course)

Consequences of parental separation last into adulthood. For instance, researchers have linked parental divorce in childhood to lower occupational success, less relational satisfaction, and more health complications (Troxel & Matthews, 2004). These impairments have correlates in earlier developmental stages, with academic difficulties noted among children whose parents divorce. Occupational impairment noted in adults may reflect the same underlying impairment expressed differently across developmental stages. This notion is suggestive of homotypic continuity and a chronic course associated with adjustment difficulties related to divorce in childhood. However, researchers have documented a waning course for adjustment difficulties where the first two years after divorce reflect a "crisis period" characterized by intense emotional and behavioral issues and resolution of most difficulties after the two-year period (Rogers, 2004). Still others note a "sleeper influence" in which difficulties lay dormant until adulthood when social and emotional difficulties manifest (Rogers, 2004). It is not known whether these possibilities—long term, homotypic continuity; brief crisis period; or delayed sleeper presentation—reflect truly different trajectories of adjustment or are artifacts of varied methodologies across studies.

A Developmental Psychopathology Model of Child Adjustment After Divorce or Separation

Parental divorce affects many aspects of a child's life, including physical proximity and degree of closeness to caregivers, and can substantially affect parents' socioeconomic standing, emotional states, and behavior. Not surprisingly, the risk of adjustment problems is nearly doubled in children whose parents divorced (Clarke-Stewart & Brentano, 2006; Størksen, Røysamb, Holmen, & Tambs, 2006), with increased risk for *internalizing*, *externalizing*, and academic problems (Lansford et al., 2006). However, not all children of divorce will experience persistent psychological difficulties, and, in some cases, adjustment difficulties reflect an exacerbation of problems already present prior to divorce (Kelly, 2000) or selection biases (Weaver & Schofield, 2015). In Figure 15.1, we organized factors that contribute to (or protect from) significant difficulties following divorce.

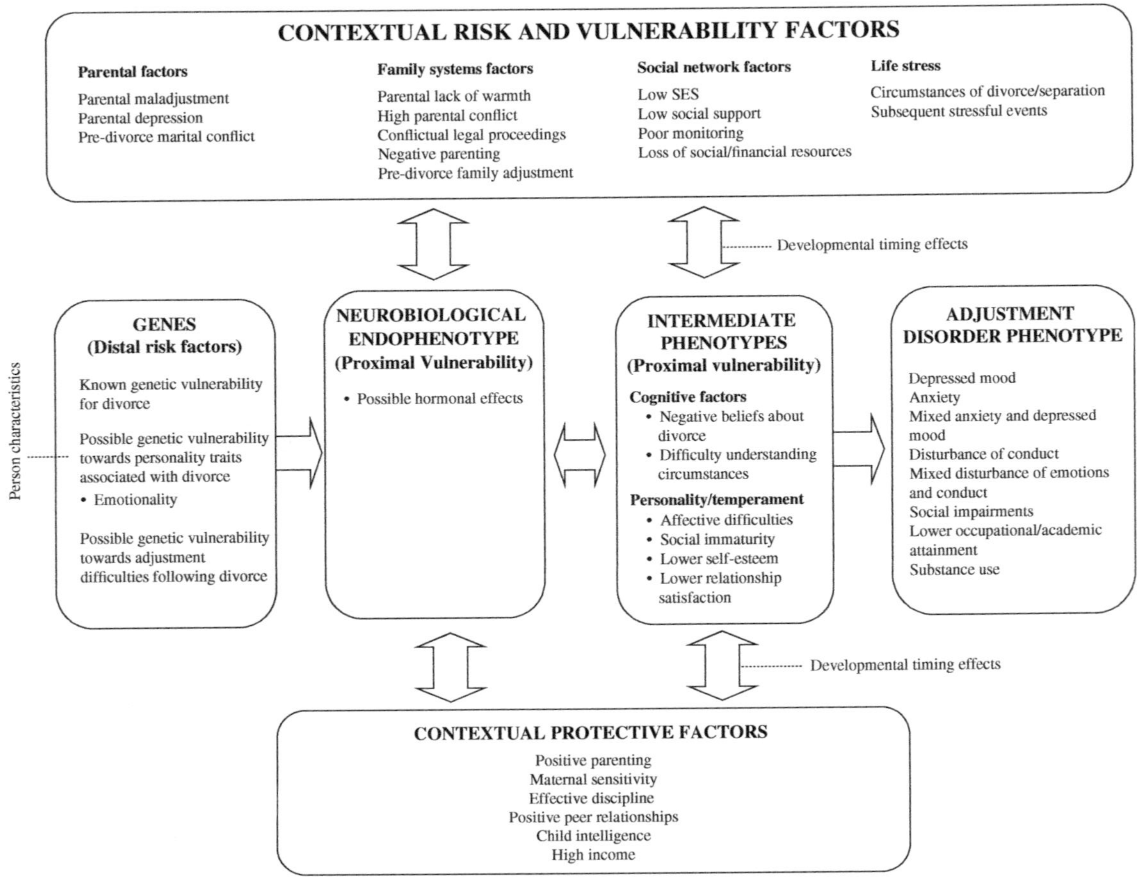

FIGURE 15.1 A Developmental Psychopathology Model of Childhood Effects Following Divorce/Separation

GENETIC (DISTAL RISK) AND NEUROBIOLOGICAL FACTORS (PROXIMAL VULNERABILITY FACTORS)

Few studies have examined genetic effects in relation to risk for divorce (in adults) or maladjustment to divorce (in children). Twin studies suggest some genetic role in divorce risk as monozygotic twins are 250% more at risk of divorce if the co-twin has divorced (Lykken, 2002) and concordance rates regarding divorce are larger in monozygotic twins than in dizygotic ones (McGue & Lykken,1992). Other studies have been careful to point out that an apparent genetic propensity toward divorce may reflect a genetic vulnerability to personality traits associated with divorce (Lansford, 2009). Some extensions of this view suggest psychological, social, and academic/occupational consequences of divorce may stem from inherited genetic propensity toward these personality traits, rather than reflecting divorce effects (see D'Onofrio et al., 2007). Several studies have sought to disentangle genetic and environmental contributions to adjustment difficulties following divorce using the Children of Twins Design. Most recently, D'Onofrio and colleagues (2007) examined 4,800 children of twins (and their biological cousins) to determine whether difficulties experienced by adult offspring of divorced parents were causally related to divorce. Findings suggest substance use difficulties in offspring of divorced parents are causally linked to divorce, whereas common genetic vulnerabilities are likely to underlie internalizing symptoms (D'Onofrio et al., 2007). This study, and several others (D'Onofrio et al., 2005, 2006), suggests adjustment difficulties after divorce are likely to reflect interplay of genetic and environmental factors. Few studies have tested neurobiological factors of a child's vulnerability for divorce adjustment difficulties. In fact, to our knowledge, no structural or functional brain imaging studies have examined child adjustment to divorce.

TEMPERAMENT

A study by Hetherington (1989) revealed the first links between child temperament and divorce adjustment, as infants with difficult temperaments experienced poorer adjustment at age 10 in the case of their parents divorcing. In a later study of 648 children assessed between 1 and 10 years of age and again 8 years later, Kasen and colleagues (1996) found significant links between early temperament and subsequent adjustment. Their findings suggested that, for some children, changes in family structure may overwhelm coping abilities with affective difficulties, leading to subsequent behavioral issues, whereas for others, the challenges of a new family structure may enhance development towards mature social skills in children previously characterized as immature.

COGNITIVE FACTORS

Child intelligence

Weaver and Schofield (2015) suggest more intelligent children may better understand the circumstances, and potential benefits, of their parents' divorce. Likewise, cognitive development may protect children from blaming themselves or polarizing their parents (Leon, 2003). In their study of 5- to 15-year-old children from divorced families, Weaver and Schofield (2015) demonstrated that the effects of divorce on child behavior problems were weaker in more intelligent children (Katz & Gottman, 1997).

Beliefs about divorce

Several studies have noted increased self-blame among children from divorced parents, with Goodman and Pickens (2001) identifying this pattern into adulthood. In a longitudinal study of 121 children of divorcing parents (ages 6–12), about 33% of children reported self-blame regarding divorce 6 months after, with 20% still endorsing this belief one year after. In this study, self-blame was associated with varied psychological and behavioral impairments. A child who believes they are to blame for their family's separation may experience negative emotions and behaviors. Indeed, a study conducted by Rotenberg, Kim, and Herman-Stahl (1998) linked high self-blame for stressful events with increased negative emotions and adjustment difficulties.

CONTEXTUAL RISK FACTORS

High conflict

A dominant view in the study of divorce effects has been that parental conflict, rather than parental divorce, is the important predictor of childhood outcomes and that children from conflict-ridden homes would experience poor outcomes regardless of parents' marital status (Maccoby & Martin, 1983). Based on this premise, divorces characterized by a greater intensity or duration of conflict will have a larger deleterious effect on children—a view highly supported in divorce research (Lansford, 2009). Many children whose parents have high levels of pre-divorce conflict will fare better after divorce (Amato, Loomis, & Booth, 1995). Many studies have shown *high-conflict divorces* lead to significant, broad, and negative consequences for children (see Bing, Nelson, & Wesolowski, 2009), including signs of attachment disorganization (Leon, 2003). Conflict also continues to affect children throughout divorce proceedings.

Adjustment of parents

Parent psychosocial functioning is an important confounding variable in studies examining the effect of conflictual family environments or high-conflict divorce on child outcomes. Parents with psychopathology are likely to select a partner with psychopathology (Maes et al., 1998) and psychopathology increases conflict and risk of divorce (Merikangas, 1984; Lansford, 2009). Similarly, stress of divorce proceedings, a subsequent decline in income and parenting support, and other consequences can increase parental maladjustment including psychopathology. Across studies of depressed families, maternal depressive symptoms are associated with increased child behavior problems (Whiteside & Becker, 2000) and maternal strain and lack of support have been linked with increased negativity and behavior problems (Pett, Wampold, Turner, & Vaughan-Cole, 1999).

Negative parenting

Numerous negative consequences for parenting have been linked to divorce, including difficulties providing supervision, consistent discipline, and warmth/affection (Lansford, 2009). This is sometimes called "diminished parenting" because it reflects a negative change from pre-divorce functioning (Rogers, 2004), though many of these problems have been documented in families years prior to divorce (Amato & Booth, 1996). Based on a large meta-analytic study, Amato and Gilbreth (1999) concluded that while frequency of contact with resident fathers was not related to child outcomes, feelings of closeness and an *authoritative* parenting style were. An extension of this meta-analysis in 2013 confirmed frequency of contact and financial support were not associated with child outcomes whereas overall father involvement was (Adamsons & Johnson, 2013).

Contextual Protective Factors

Positive parenting

Certainly, the absence of aforementioned risk factors in the parent–child relationship has been linked to better outcomes for children with divorced parents, but some positive parenting behaviors have also been identified as specific protective factors. Strengths of the parent–child relationship prior to a divorce are thought to augment a child's coping resources and, after a divorce, parental variables can buffer stress, leading to fewer emotional and behavioral problems (Wolchik, Wilcox, Tein, & Sandler, 2000). In a 15-year longitudinal study conducted by Weaver and Schofield (2015), pre-divorce maternal sensitivity protected against emergence of internalizing and externalizing symptoms (see Figure 15.2).

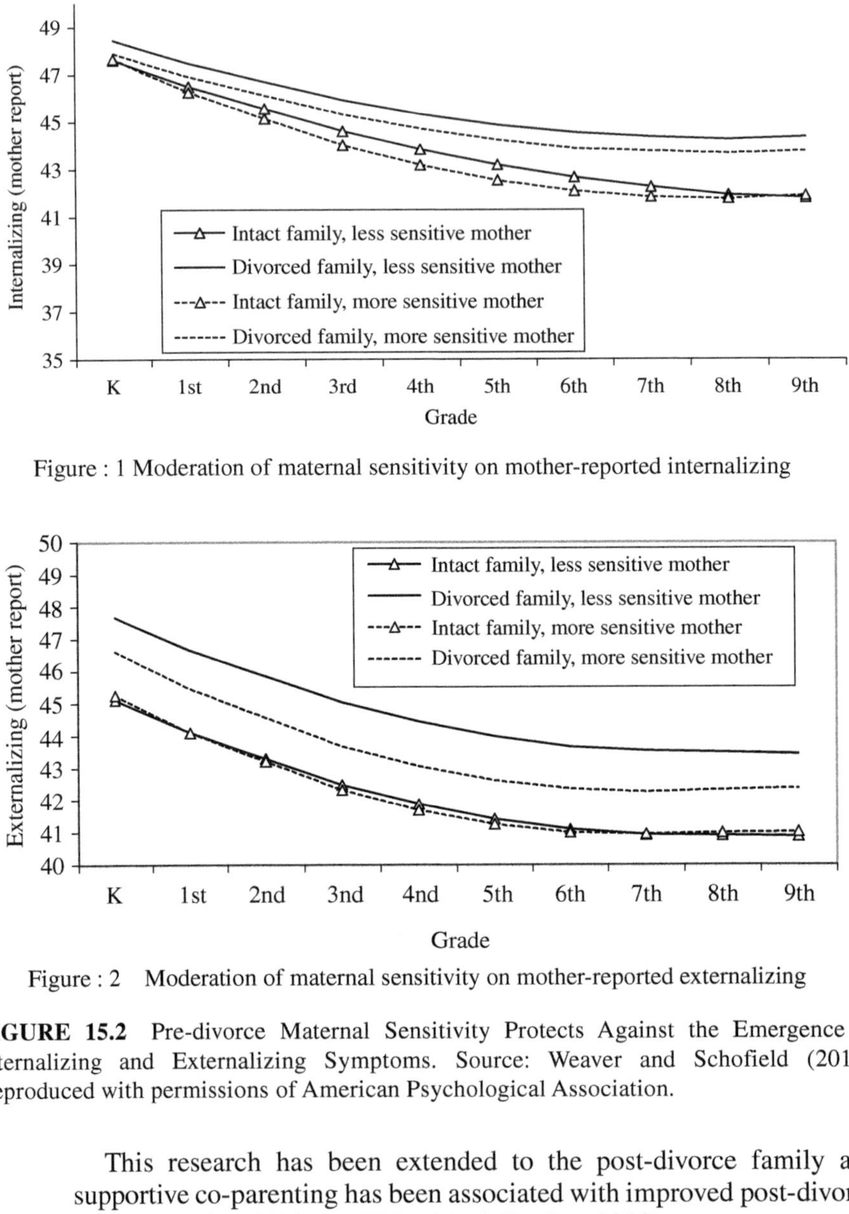

FIGURE 15.2 Pre-divorce Maternal Sensitivity Protects Against the Emergence of Internalizing and Externalizing Symptoms. Source: Weaver and Schofield (2015). Reproduced with permissions of American Psychological Association.

This research has been extended to the post-divorce family and supportive co-parenting has been associated with improved post-divorce adjustment for children (Whiteside & Becker, 2000).

Income

Studies have shown child adjustment to divorce is partially explained by decreases in income following divorce, such that post-divorce household income decline relates to increased behavioral problems (Weaver & Schofield, 2015). Moreover, maladjustment in children of divorced parents has been linked to lower parental income (Hodges et al., 1979). This research base is strengthened by research showing differences between child outcomes from divorced versus non-divorced parents were insignificant after controlling for family income, though some evidence of worse outcomes associated with divorce remained (Guidubaldi, Cleminshaw, Perry, & Mclaughlin, 1983).

Pre-divorce family adjustment

Many models of child outcomes from divorce show pre-divorce functioning is an important variable. While adjustment problems in response to divorce may increase in previously well-adjusted children, long-term functioning of well-adjusted children tends to be better (Chase-Lansdale, Cherlin, & Kiernan, 1995). Moreover, studies that control for pre-divorce child adjustment find smaller differences between children from divorced versus non-divorced families (Cherlin et al., 1991; Lansford, 2009).

GENE–ENVIRONMENT INTERPLAY

Like the D'Onofrio et al. (2007) study, several other studies have shown that difficulties experienced by adult offspring of divorced parents can reflect both environmental and genetic effects. While D'Onofrio et al. (2007) related substance use difficulties to divorce whereas internalizing symptoms were linked to general genetic vulnerabilities, an earlier study linked divorce causally to emotional symptoms, academic difficulties, depressive symptoms, and suicidal ideation, but pointed to early substance use as a genetically based difficulty (D'Onofrio et al., 2006). These contradictory findings reflect a young and sparse research base in need of more investigation of gene–environment interplay.

Using a different method, O'Connor and colleagues (2000) found evidence of a gene–environment interaction with regard to adjustment difficulties after divorce. Specifically, this study followed 398 adoptive and biological families over the course of a child's life from ages 1 to 12. Results revealed biological and adopted children who experienced parental divorce were at increased risk of experiencing behavioral and substance related difficulties, but biological children were also at increased risk of developing academic and social difficulties. The authors suggest while behavioral and substance use difficulties reflect environmentally driven processes, social and academic impairments likely reflected a *passive genotype-environment correlation*, where biological parents pass on genetic vulnerability and expose children to environmental experiences (i.e., divorce) that produce varied adjustment difficulties.

DEVELOPMENTAL TIMING EFFECTS: THE INTERPLAY NORMAL AND ABNORMAL DEVELOPMENT

Some research suggests younger children have more problems following divorce than older children (Allison & Furstenberg, 1989), perhaps because they are less able to understand or because attachment security is threatened earlier in development (Leon, 2003). Some findings suggest divorce may have prominent effects on outcomes most relevant to the child's developmental stage at the time of divorce, but this hypothesis requires a broader conceptualization of outcomes, including developmentally salient constructs like academic achievement or romantic relationship emergence (Lansford, 2009). Lansford and colleagues (2006) sought to address developmental timing effects regarding divorce consequences by examining trajectories of internalizing, externalizing, and academic problems in children from kindergarten through grade 10 as a function of parental divorce. Their study showed early divorce (i.e., elementary school) was more related to internalizing and externalizing problems than later divorce, whereas the latter was more related to academic problems. Additionally, researchers have suggested the interaction of risk and protective factors changes across development. Leon (2003) suggests that while positive parenting may be protective for young children, variables like parental monitoring and involvement may become more important in older children.

Interventions for Children of Divorced Parents

Interventions for children of divorced parents generally focus on fostering adaptive coping skills and resilience or on enhancing parental behaviors known to predict positive trajectories for children. Here, we will focus on the latter—group-based, child-focused programs that reflect the bulk of current research. Still, given parent behavior can act as a risk and protective factor for adjustment difficulties following divorce, it is important to note parenting programs have also received empirical support. For instance, the Family Transitions Triple P program (Stallman & Sanders, 2007) builds upon well-researched interventions based on *parent-management training* by targeting parenting challenges faced during divorce transition. At post-treatment and one-year follow-up, parents that participate in this program report decreased parental distress and increased successful co-parenting (Stallman & Sanders, 2014).

Many divorce intervention programs target children and include *psychoeducation* about divorce, cognitive-behavioral interventions to address maladaptive thoughts about divorce, and training to enhance coping skills (Pelleboer-Gunnink et al., 2015). Typically, these interventions use a group format to increase social support and, though the length varies, length does not seem related to effectiveness (Lee, Picard, & Blain,

CoD-CoD Program Outline

Module 1: Feelings and Divorce

- Introduction to the Program
- The Challenge of Divorce
    - Divorce stressors
- Normalizing Divorce Experiences
- Recognizing Feelings
- How CoD-CoD can Help
    - Stressful situations
    - Difficult Feelings
    - Hiding Feelings

Module 2: Inside Tools

- Cognitive Restructuring
    - Divorce Appraisals
    - Doom and Gloom Thinking
- Events, Thoughts, Feelings & Actions
- Relaxation
- Using Distraction Coping
- Divorce Related Information

Module 3: Tools for Communication

- Identifying Uncontrollable Problems
- 4-Steps to Good Communication
- Starting a Helping Conversation
- Starting a Supportive Conversation
- How to Resolve Conflict Positively

Module 4: Problem-Solving

- Problem-Solving Training
- Choosing Coping Strategies

Module 5: Integrating Program skills

- Using Problem-Focused Coping
- Summary of CoD-CoD Coping Skills
- Opportunity to Apply CoD-CoD Skills
- Practicing skills in the Real World

FIGURE 15.3 Children of Divorce-Coping with Divorce Program Outline. Source: CoD-CoD Program Outline. Retreived from: http://familytransitions-ptw.com/CoDCoD/parents/index.html. © 2020, Family Transitions. Reproduced with permissions.

1994). While generally these programs have proven effective in reducing adjustment difficulties (Pelleboer-Gunnink et al., 2015; Haine et al., 2003), modest effect sizes are common (Lee, Picard, & Blain, 1994). Recent explorations of online coping skills interventions, like the Children of Divorce Coping with Divorce online prevention program (Boring et al., 2015), have demonstrated promise in increasing coping ability and decreasing mental health problems for most children at rates comparable to group-based programs (though a small subset seemed to be negatively affected by the intervention). The online program contains five modules described in Figure 15.3, which can be tried for free through the program preview: http://familytransitions-ptw.com/CoDCoD/parents/index.html.

Many of the modules use *cognitive-behavioral* techniques. For example, Module 2 asks a child to "Imagine this scenario. Brian is a 15-year-old kid whose parents divorced about 12 months ago. After the divorce, his family didn't have as much money and had to move to another neighborhood and change schools. He hates his new school and doesn't have any friends there. Brian used to talk to his Mom about things, but she's lately been depressed. He feels alone and doesn't think things will get better. Think about the hurtful thoughts Brian might be thinking." The hurtful thoughts are compared to common cognitive distortions and the child is coached to think of "hopeful thoughts" instead. While more research is needed to test online program utility, they may play an important role in providing services to a population that might not otherwise receive help.

Parental loss

Prevalence of Loss Difficulties

While less common than parental divorce or separation, parental loss to death also affects a large group of children and can lead to increased depressive symptoms, anxiety, withdrawal, social impairment, and academic issues (see Ayers et al., 2014). Approximately 10% of children who experience parental loss will develop clinically significant symptoms (Melhem et al., 2011), with 21% continuing to experience symptoms of internalizing and externalizing behavior two years later (Worden, 1996).

PREVALENCE BY GENDER AND AGE

Several studies have documented higher prevalence of internalizing symptoms among girls than boys. Likewise, the trajectory of internalizing distress is stable for girls, whereas symptoms tend to decline over 3–4 years for boys (Schmiege et al., 2006). In a longitudinal study, girls demonstrated higher levels of cognitive vulnerability, which explained a higher level of symptoms at follow-up (Little et al., 2009).

Few studies have also suggested gender differences regarding course of adjustment difficulties. Schmiege and colleagues (2006) assessed the effect of an intervention on internalizing and externalizing symptoms for 244 children who had experienced the death of a parent and reported that girls benefitted from the intervention more than a control group, whereas boys in the intervention and control conditions demonstrated comparable symptom decreases across a two-year period. Many theoretical models of adjustment in response to parental loss suggest age at time of parental death is a significant predictor of outcome trajectories. This research is mixed, however, so we will reserve discussion of that topic for Section 15.7.4 on Developmental Timing Effects.

PREVALENCE BY SOCIOECONOMIC STATUS (SES), RACE, AND ETHNICITY

Broad claims have been made that socioeconomic status does not moderate bereavement effects (Stroebe, Folkman, Hansson, & Schut, 2006), but recent studies suggest low socioeconomic status places youth at a higher risk of internalizing symptoms (Stikkelbroek et al., 2015). Likewise, other studies suggest poverty before and resulting from parental death may negatively impact outcomes (Kaplow et al., 2010). Though little research has examined race and ethnicity in the context of parental loss, several studies suggest minority children (McClatchey, Vonk, Lee, & Bride, 2014), specifically African American children (McClatchey, Vonk, & Palardy, 2009), are more vulnerable to severe adjustment difficulties following parental loss.

A *Brief* Developmental Psychopathology Model of Child Adjustment After Loss

Existing research on factors related to adjustment difficulties following parental loss is limited; a review of literature regarding genetic and neurobiological risk factors of bereavement difficulties yields few studies. Thus, we will focus on risk and protective factors often noted in theoretical models of adjustment difficulties related to bereavement (Stroebe et al., 2006), namely individual cognitive and contextual factors.

Certainly, circumstances of parental loss can have substantial implications for adjustment difficulties a child is likely to experience. When the loss is traumatic, survivors typically experience increased difficulties, particularly with regard to trauma symptoms. Similar findings are reported among children who lost a loved one to suicide (Cerel, Fristad, Weller, & Weller, 1999). Research is mixed regarding whether expected or unexpected deaths are associated with increased psychological impairment, suggesting other factors that are likely to moderate this relation.

Cognitive Factors

Control beliefs

Theoretical models of bereavement posit parental loss may lead a child to believe life is uncontrollable. When loss co-occurs with uncontrollable consequences, like a decrease in family financial stability, children may develop cognitions that life is uncontrollable. Wolchik and colleagues (2008) posit this may lead a child to believe they cannot handle problems effectively (i.e., *coping efficacy*), maintaining grief. Wolchik et al. (2008) found low coping efficacy partially explained a child's experience of grief from the loss of a parent. Moreover, children with supportive caregivers following parental loss experienced higher beliefs of coping efficacy and less grief. Wolchik and colleagues (2008) posit a supportive caregiver who maintains consistent routines and monitoring communicates a sense of controllability and, thus, protects from beliefs of low coping efficacy. A child who believes the world is (at least partially) controllable and has strong coping efficacy will engage in adaptive coping that can mitigate grief reactions (Wolchik et al., 2008; Sandler, 2001).

Fear of abandonment

Think what a child might learn from the death of a parent. A simple, distressing lesson may be that our parents will not always be present to protect us. From this perspective, a child might develop a fear they may lose their other caregivers, producing fears they will be left without anyone to meet basic attachment and daily living needs. Increased fears of abandonment have been linked to increased bereavement difficulties several times. However, some evidence suggests having a supportive surviving caregiver can mitigate these fears, reducing ultimate grief symptoms (Wolchik et al., 2008). In a longitudinal study, Wolchik and colleagues (2006) documented that fear of abandonment *mediated* the relation between stressors associated with parental loss and psychological symptoms.

Threat appraisal

Researchers have also posited that parental loss can contribute to misinterpretations of threat when children encounter difficult future situations. Wolchik and colleagues (2006) suggest that beliefs of uncontrollability and poor coping efficacy can affect children by contributing to increased threat appraisals. Research suggests bereaved children who perceive a threat as stable and/or global are at increased risk of anxiety and depression symptoms more than a year later (Little et al., 2009). A study conducted in college students who had lost a parent prior to age 16 demonstrated increased salivary *cortisol* levels in response to an experimental stressor (Luecken, 1998), suggesting that threat appraisals, in conjunction with broader stress-reactivity systems, are affected in bereaved children at a neurobiological level with long-term consequences.

CONTEXTUAL RISK FACTORS

Caregiver mental health and negative life events

Certainly, death of a spouse can have serious consequences for adult family members, including precipitating a prolonged period of adjustment difficulties or onset of a depressive episode. Declining mental health among a surviving caregiver has been linked to child mental health and, in a study of bereaved children, Kalter and colleagues (2003) reported that parental adjustment was the best predictor of child adjustment. Luecken and Roubinov (2012) speculate that this link may be driven by impaired parenting associated with caregiver maladjustment and an overburdening of the child. Further, several studies have shown death of a parent puts a child at risk of experiencing additional negative life events. Specifically, before and after a parent's death, the family may experience financial strain, reduced contact with sources of social support, and change in residences (Wolchik et al., 2008). These subsequent negative life events exacerbate grief (Sandler, 2001) and produce aforementioned self-system beliefs that contribute to greater adjustment difficulty.

Contextual Protective Factors

Positive parenting

Parental warmth and consistent limit setting are associated with fewer adjustment difficulties for children who have experienced parental loss. Specifically, being open to the child's emotional experience (Raveis, Siegel, & Karus, 1999), being warm (Tein, Sandler, MacKinnon, & Wolchik, 2004), and continuing to maintain effective discipline have all been tied to improved outcomes for children.

Effective discipline

Prior research shows consistent discipline can protect children from developing adjustment problems to divorce (Wolchik, Wilcox, Tein, & Sandler, 2000) and suggests effective discipline may be more critical for families where a death may have created a sense of uncontrollability. Though research on effective discipline in the context of parental loss is small, bereavement programs commonly address effective discipline and have linked improvements to improved overall functioning (Hagan et al., 2012).

Developmental Timing Effects: The Interplay of Normal and Abnormal Development

Sandler, Wolchik, and Ayers (2008) arranged many of the risk and protective factors reviewed in this section into their Contextual Framework on Adaptation Following Bereavement (Figure 15.4).

They describe adaptation to the death of a loved one as an interactive, developmental process in which individual and contextual risk and protective factors interact across time. Adaptation to bereavement is a cumulative process, in which risk and protective factors contribute to resilience.

Sandler et al. (2008) further posit that the interaction of risk and protective factors is subject to developmental influences, such that the child's experience of bereavement at one stage has a "cascading" effect on future development. Goldman (1994) further posited that children experience new grief with each transition between developmental stages and, thus, children who experience parental loss early will suffer worse consequences. Finally, most theories of adaptation to parental loss suggest that the psychological impact is worse when parental loss is out-of-sync with the individual's current developmental stage. For instance, it is developmentally expected that although an adult child will experience the loss of their elderly parents, the form of parental loss will have less adjustment difficulties than when death occurs at earlier developmental stages (Stroebe et al., 2006).

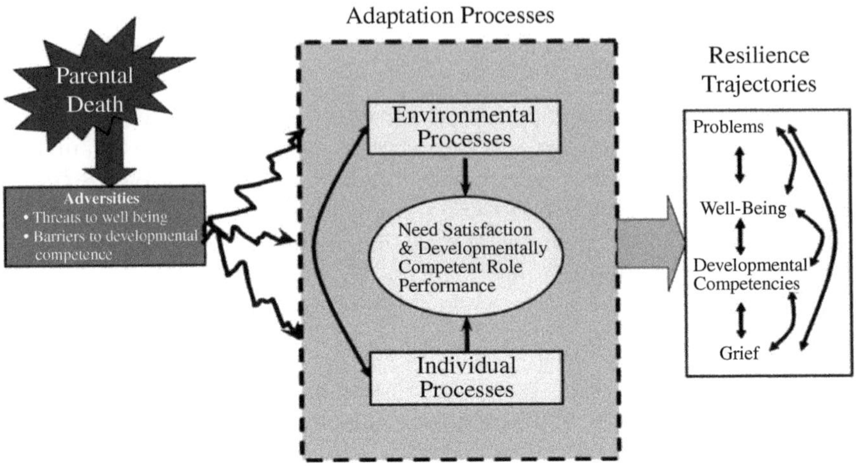

FIGURE 15.4 Sandler et al.'s (2008) Contextual Framework on Adaptation Following Bereavement Reproduced with permission of Taylor & Francis from Sandler et al., 2008.

Interventions for Bereaved Children

Few interventions have been developed for children who have experienced parental loss and fewer have been subjected to empirical research. The Family Bereavement Program has been the subject of a randomized trial and its utility has been examined longitudinally (Sandler et al., 2003). In a group-based setting, this intervention works with parents to address risk factors and with children to address coping skills and emotional awareness. After completion, caregivers demonstrate increased positive parenting with continued evidence 11 months later. Both parents and children experienced decreased psychological symptoms, and children demonstrated increased coping skills and control beliefs at post-treatment and follow-up (Sandler et al., 2003). Other studies have demonstrated positive intervention effects in a six-year follow-up with neurobiological evidence of individual differences in intervention participants (Sandler et al., 2010; Luecken et al., 2010; Hagan et al., 2012).

Chapter Summary

In this chapter we discussed two important events: parental divorce/separation and parental loss. Both are expected to produce psychological symptoms; however, some children's reactions to these events are severe (compared to the typical response) or of excessive duration.

In those cases, adjustment difficulties may represent an adjustment disorder warranting additional intervention. Across both divorce/separation and loss, contextual risk factors play a role in predicting whether a child will experience pronounced adjustment difficulties. It is no surprise that interventions reviewed in this chapter are quite similar, whether designed for children who have lost a parent or are struggling with parental divorce.

Further Reading

Lansford, J. E. (2009). Parental divorce and children's adjustment. *Perspectives on Psychological Science*, 4(2), 140–152.

Sandler, I. N., Ayers, T. S., Wolchik, S. A., Tein, J. Y., Kwok, O. M., Haine, R. A., & Weyer, J. L. (2003). The family bereavement program: Efficacy evaluation of a theory-based prevention program for parentally bereaved children and adolescents. *Journal of Consulting and Clinical Psychology*, 71(3), 587.

Sandler, I. N., Wolchik, S. A., & Ayers, T. S. (2008). Resilience rather than recovery: A contextual framework on adaptation following bereavement. *Death Studies*, 32(1), 59–73.

Weaver, J. M., & Schofield, T. J. (2015). Mediation and moderation of divorce effects on children's behavior problems. *Journal of Family Psychology*, 29(1), 39.

Discussion/Essay Questions

1. Compare and contrast the contextual risk and protective factors for adjustment difficulties related to separation/divorce and loss.
2. Interventions for childhood bereavement and divorce are similar. Describe the similarities and explain why you believe similar interventions may be effective in both contexts.
3. Do you believe that evidence supports including persistent complex bereavement disorder in the DSM? Why or why not?

Glossary

Adjustment disorder is a DSM-5 diagnosed maladaptive reaction that typically emerges within one month of a significant life-stressor, such as illness, family or partnership problems, job-related issues, or financial difficulties, including a failure to adapt and preoccupation with the stressor or its consequences.

Authoritative is a parenting style characterized by high responsiveness to a child's emotional needs while setting high standards and consistently enforcing boundaries.

Cognitive-behavioral is a short-term, goal-oriented therapeutic technique aimed to change the patterns of thinking and behavior behind one's difficulties.

Complicated grief is a mental health condition in which problems related to the circumstances, consequences, or context of a loss or by an internal problem with the adaptation process prolong grief and cause significant distress or impairment.

Coping efficacy is one's belief that they have the capacity to handle their problems effectively.

Cortisol is the primary stress hormone released during times of stress to enhance and curb specific bodily functions in preparation for fight-or-flight.

Externalizing is outward behavior that is reflective of negatively acting on one's environment, characterized by impulsive, disruptive, conduct, substance use, and other addictive symptoms.

High-conflict divorces are divorces characterized by ongoing hostility, drawn-out or frequent court actions, custody battles, domestic violence, and/or abuse.

Internalizing is inward behavior that is reflective of keeping problems to oneself and often characterized by anxiety, depressive, and somatic symptoms.

Mediate is when a specific variable explains the relation between a predictor and criterion variable.

Meta-analytic study is a scientific study that combines the results of multiple specific studies.

Parent-management training includes treatment programs aimed to change parenting behaviors and teach parents positive reinforcement methods to improve child behavior problems.

Passive genotype–environment correlation is when biological parents pass on genetic vulnerability and expose children to environmental experiences that ultimately produce varied adjustment difficulties.

Persistent complex bereavement disorder is a DSM-5 bereavement-specific diagnosis characterized by prolonged and impairing grief.

Prolonged grief is mourning that it is marked by a pervasive yearning for the deceased.

Psychoeducation is an evidence-based therapeutic intervention that provides information and support to better understand and cope with symptoms or illness.

References

Adamsons, K., & Johnson, S. K. (2013). An updated and expanded meta-analysis of nonresident fathering and child well-being. *Journal of Family Psychology*, 27(4), 589.

Allison, P. D., & Furstenberg, F. F. (1989). How marital dissolution affects children: Variations by age and sex. *Developmental Psychology*, 25(4), 540.

Amato, P. R., & Booth, A. (1996). A prospective study of divorce and parent–child relationships. *Journal of Marriage and the Family*, 58(2), 356–365.

Amato, P. R., & Gilbreth, J. G. (1999). Nonresident fathers and children's well-being: A meta-analysis. *Journal of Marriage and the Family*, 61(3), 557–573.

Amato, P. R., & Keith, B. (1991). Parental divorce and adult well-being: A meta-analysis. *Journal of Marriage and the Family*, 54, 43–58.

Amato, P. R., Loomis, L. S., & Booth, A. (1995). Parental divorce, marital conflict, and offspring well-being during early adulthood. *Social Forces*, 73(3), 895–915.

American Psychiatric Association (2013). Diagnostic and statistical manual of mental disorders (5th ed.). Retrieved from: https://doi.org/10.1176/appi.books.9780890425596.

Ayers, T. S., Wolchik, S. A., Sandler, I. N., Twohey, J. L., Weyer, J. L., Padgett-Jones, S., & Kriege, G. (2014). The Family Bereavement Program: Description of a theory-based prevention program for parentally-bereaved children and adolescents. *Omega: Journal of Death and Dying*, 69(4), 293–314.

Bing, N. M., Nelson III, W. M., & Wesolowski, K. L. (2009). Comparing the effects of amount of conflict on children's adjustment following parental divorce. *Journal of Divorce & Remarriage*, 50(3), 159–171.

Boring, J. L., Sandler, I. N., Tein, J. Y., Horan, J. J., & Vélez, C. E. (2015). Children of divorce–coping with divorce: A randomized control trial of an online prevention program for youth experiencing parental divorce. *Journal of Consulting and Clinical Psychology*, 83(5), 999.

CDC/National Center for Health Statistics (US) (2015). *Vital Statistics of the United States*. United States Bureau of the Census, Washington, DC.

Cerel, J., Fristad, M. A., Weller, E. B., & Weller, R. A. (1999). Suicide-bereaved children and adolescents: A controlled longitudinal examination. *Journal of the American Academy of Child & Adolescent Psychiatry*, 38(6), 672–679.

Chase-Lansdale, P. L., Cherlin, A. J., & Kiernan, K. E. (1995). The long-term effects of parental divorce on the mental health of young adults: A developmental perspective. *Child Development*, 66(6), 1614–1634.

Cherlin, A. J., Furstenberg, F. F., Chase-Lansdale, L., Kiernan, K. E., Robins, P. K., Morrison, D. R., & Teitler, J. O. (1991). Longitudinal studies of effects of divorce on children in Great Britain and the United States. *Science*, 252(5011), 1386–1389.

Clarke-Stewart, A., & Brentano, C. (2006). *Divorce: Causes and consequences*. New Haven, CT: Yale University Press.

D'Onofrio, B. M., Turkheimer, E., Emery, R. E., Maes, H. H., Silberg, J., & Eaves, L. J. (2007). A children of twins study of parental divorce and offspring psychopathology. *Journal of Child Psychology and Psychiatry*, 48(7), 667–675.

D'Onofrio, B. M., Turkheimer, E., Emery, R. E., Slutske, W. S., Heath, A. C., Madden, P. A., & Martin, N. G. (2005). A genetically informed study of marital instability and its association with offspring psychopathology. *Journal of Abnormal Psychology*, 114(4), 570.

D'Onofrio, B. M., Turkheimer, E., Emery, R. E., Slutske, W. S., Heath, A. C., Madden, P. A., & Martin, N. G. (2006). A genetically informed study of the processes underlying the association between parental marital instability and offspring adjustment. *Developmental Psychology*, 42(3), 486.

Goldman, L. (1994). *Life & loss: A guide to help grieving children*. Philadelphia, PA, USA: Accelerated Development.

Goodman, C., & Pickens, J. (2001). Self-blame and self-esteem in college-aged children from divorced families. *Journal of Divorce & Remarriage*, 34(3–4), 119–135.

Guidubaldi, J., Cleminshaw, H. K., Perry, J. D., & Mcloughlin, C. S. (1983). The impact of parental divorce on children: Report of the nationwide NASP study. *School Psychology Review*, 12(3), 300–323.

Hagan, M. J., Tein, J. Y., Sandler, I. N., Wolchik, S. A., Ayers, T. S., & Luecken, L. J. (2012). Strengthening effective parenting practices over the long term: Effects of a preventive intervention for parentally bereaved families. *Journal of Clinical Child & Adolescent Psychology*, 41(2), 177–188.

Hetherington, E. M. (1989). Coping with family transitions: Winners, losers, *and survivors. Child Development*, 60, 1–14.

Hetherington, E. M., & Kelly, J. (2002). *For better or for worse: Divorce reconsidered*. New York, NY: W. W. Norton & Co.

Hodges, W. F., Wechsler, R. C., & Ballantine, C. (1979). Divorce and the preschool child: Cumulative stress. *Journal of Divorce*, 3(1), 55–67.

Kalter, N., Lohnes, K. L., Chasin, J., Cain, A. C., Dunning, S., & Rowan, J. (2003). The adjustment of parentally bereaved children: I. Factors associated with short-term adjustment. *OMEGA–Journal of Death and Dying*, 46(1), 15–34.

Kaplow, J. B., Layne, C. M., Pynoos, R. S., Cohen, J. A., & Lieberman, A. (2012). DSM-V diagnostic criteria for bereavement-related disorders in children and adolescents: Developmental considerations. *Psychiatry*, 75(3), 243–266.

Kaplow, J. B., Saunders, J., Angold, A., & Costello, E. J. (2010). Psychiatric symptoms in bereaved versus nonbereaved youth and young adults: A longitudinal epidemiological study. *Journal of the American Academy of Child & Adolescent Psychiatry*, 49(11), 1145–1154.

Kasen, S., Cohen, P., Brook, J. S., & Hartmark, C. (1996). A multiple-risk interaction model: Effects of temperament and divorce on psychiatric disorders in children. *Journal of Abnormal Child Psychology*, 24(2), 121–150.

Katz, L. F., & Gottman, J. M. (1997). Buffering children from marital conflict and dissolution. *Journal of Clinical Child Psychology*, 26(2), 157–171.

Kelly, J. B. (2000). Children's adjustment in conflicted marriage and divorce: A decade review of research. *Journal of the American Academy of Child & Adolescent Psychiatry*, 39(8), 963–973.

Lansford, J. E. (2009). Parental divorce and children's adjustment. *Perspectives on Psychological Science*, 4(2), 140–152.

Lansford, J. E., Malone, P. S., Castellino, D. R., Dodge, K. A., Pettit, G. S., & Bates, J. E. (2006). Trajectories of internalizing, externalizing, and grades for children who have and have not experienced their parents' divorce or separation. *Journal of Family Psychology*, 20(2), 292.

Lee, C. M., Picard, M., & Blain, M. D. (1994). A methodological and substantive review of intervention outcome studies for families undergoing divorce. *Journal of Family Psychology*, 8(1), 3.

Leon, K. (2003). Risk and protective factors in young children's adjustment to parental divorce: A review of the research. *Family Relations*, 52(3), 258–270.

Little, M., Sandler, I. N., Wolchik, S. A., Tein, J. Y., & Ayers, T. S. (2009). Comparing cognitive, relational and stress mechanisms underlying gender differences in recovery from bereavement-related internalizing problems. *Journal of Clinical Child & Adolescent Psychology*, 38(4), 486–500.

Luecken, L. J. (1998). Childhood attachment and loss experiences affect adult cardiovascular and cortisol function. *Psychosomatic Medicine*, 60(6), 765–772.

Luecken, L. J., Hagan, M. J., Sandler, I. N., Tein, J. Y., Ayers, T. S., & Wolchik, S. A. (2010). Cortisol levels six-years after participation in the Family Bereavement Program. *Psychoneuroendocrinology*, 35(5), 785–789.

Luecken, L. J., & Roubinov, D. S. (2012). Pathways to lifespan health following childhood parental death. *Social and Personality Psychology Compass*, 6(3), 243–257.

Lykken, D. T. (2002). How relationships begin and end: A genetic perspective. In A. L. Vangelisti, H. T. Reis, M. A. Fitzpatrick, A. L. Vangelisti, H. T. Reis, & M. A. Fitzpatrick (Eds.), *Stability and change in relationships* (pp. 83–102). New York, NY: Cambridge University Press. doi: 10.1017/CBO9780511499876.006.

Maccoby, E. E., & Martin, J. A. (1983). Socialization in the context of the family: Parent–child interaction. *Handbook of child psychology: formerly Carmichael's Manual of child psychology*. New York, NY: John Wiley & Sons, Inc.

Maes, H. M., Neale, M. C., Kendler, K. S., Hewitt, J. K., Silberg, J. L., Foley, D. L., & Eaves, L. J. (1998). Assortive mating for major psychiatric diagnoses in two population-based samples. *Psychological Medicine*, 28(6), 1389–1401. doi: 10.1017/S0033291798007326.

McClatchey, I. S., Vonk, M. E., Lee, J., & Bride, B. (2014). Traumatic and complicated grief among children: One or two constructs? *Death Studies*, 38(2), 69–78.

McClatchy, I. S., Vonk, M. E., & Palardy, G. (2009). The prevalence of childhood traumatic grief—A comparison of violent/sudden and expected loss. *OMEGA–Journal of Death and Dying*, 59(4), 305–323.

McGue, M., & Lykken, D. T. (1992). Genetic influence on risk of divorce. *Psychological Science*, 3(6), 368–373.

Melhem, N. M., Porta, G., Shamseddeen, W., Payne, M. W., & Brent, D. A. (2011). Grief in children and adolescents bereaved by sudden parental death. *Archives of General Psychiatry*, 68(9), 911–919.

Merikangas, K. R. (1984). Divorce and assortative mating among depressed patients. *American Journal of Psychiatry*, 141(1), 74–76.

Neria, Y., & Litz, B. T. (2004). Bereavement by traumatic means: The complex synergy of trauma and grief. *Journal of Loss and Trauma*, 9(1), 73–87.

O'Connor, T. G., Caspi, A., DeFries, J. C., & Plomin, R. (2000). Are associations between parental divorce and children's adjustment genetically mediated? An adoption study. *Developmental Psychology*, 36(4), 429.

Pelleboer-Gunnink, H. A., Van der Valk, I. E., Branje, S. J., Van Doorn, M. D., & Deković, M. (2015). Effectiveness and moderators of the preventive intervention kids in divorce situations: A randomized controlled trial. *Journal of Family Psychology*, 29(5), 799.

Pett, M. A., Wampold, B. E., Turner, C. W., & Vaughan-Cole, B. (1999). Paths of influence of divorce on preschool children's psychosocial adjustment. *Journal of Family Psychology*, 13(2), 145–164. doi: 10.1037/0893-3200.13.2.145.

Raveis, V. H., Siegel, K., & Karus, D. (1999). Children's psychological distress following the death of a parent. *Journal of Youth and Adolescence*, 28(2), 165–180.

Rogers, K. N. (2004). A theoretical review of risk and protective factors related to post-divorce adjustment in young children. *Journal of Divorce & Remarriage*, 40(3–4), 135–147.

Rotenberg, K. J., Kim, L. S., & Herman-Stahl, M. (1998). The role of primary and secondary appraisals in the negative emotions and psychological maladjustment of children of divorce. *Journal of Divorce & Remarriage*, 29(1–2), 43–66.

Sandler, I. N. (2001). Quality and ecology of adversity as common mechanisms of risk and resilience. *American Journal of Community Psychology*, 29, 19–61.

Sandler, I. N., Ayers, T. S., Wolchik, S. A., Tein, J. Y., Kwok, O. M., Haine, R. A., & Weyer, J. L. (2003). The family bereavement program: Efficacy evaluation of a theory-based prevention program for parentally bereaved children and adolescents. *Journal of Consulting and Clinical Psychology*, 71(3), 587.

Sandler, I. N., Ma, Y., Tein, J. Y., Ayers, T. S., Wolchik, S., Kennedy, C., & Millsap, R. (2010). Long-term effects of the family bereavement program on multiple indicators of grief in parentally bereaved children and adolescents. *Journal of Consulting and Clinical Psychology*, 78(2), 131.

Sandler, I. N., Wolchik, S. A., & Ayers, T. S. (2008). Resilience rather than recovery: A contextual framework on adaptation following bereavement. *Death Studies*, 32(1), 59–73.

Schmiege, S. J., Khoo, S. T., Sandler, I. N., Ayers, T. S., & Wolchik, S. A. (2006). Symptoms of internalizing and externalizing problems: Modeling recovery curves after the death of a parent. *American Journal of Preventive Medicine*, 31(6), 152–160.

Stallman, H. M., & Sanders, M. R. (2007). Family Transitions Triple P: The theoretical basis and development of a program for parents going through divorce. *Journal of Divorce & Remarriage*, 47(3–4), 133–153.

Stallman, H. M., & Sanders, M. R. (2014). A randomized controlled trial of Family Transitions Triple P: A group-administered parenting program to minimize the adverse effects of parental divorce on children. *Journal of Divorce & Remarriage*, 55(1), 33–48.

Stikkelbroek, Y., Bodden, D. H., Reitz, E., Vollebergh, W. A., & Baar, A. L. (2015). Mental health of adolescents before and after the death of a parent or sibling. *European Child & Adolescent Psychiatry*, doi: 10.1007/s00787-015-0695-3.

Størksen, I., Røysamb, E., Holmen, T. L., & Tambs, K. (2006). Adolescent adjustment and well-being: Effects of parental divorce and distress. *Scandinavian Journal of Psychology*, 47(1), 75–84.

Stroebe, M. S., Folkman, S., Hansson, R. O., & Schut, H. (2006). The prediction of bereavement outcome: Development of an integrative risk factor framework. *Social Science & Medicine*, 63(9), 2440–2451.

Tay, A. K., Rees, S., Chen, J., Kareth, M., & Silove, D. (2015). Factorial structure of complicated grief: Associations with loss-related traumatic events and psychosocial impacts of mass conflict amongst west papuan refugees. *Social Psychiatry and Psychiatric Epidemiology*, 51(3), 395–406. doi:10.1007/s00127-015-1099-x.

Tein, J., Sandler, I. N., MacKinnon, D. P., & Wolchik, S. A. (2004). How did it work? Who did it work for? Mediation in the context of a moderated prevention effect for children of divorce. *Journal of Consulting and Clinical Psychology*, 72(4), 617–624. doi: 10.1037/0022-006X.72.4.617.

Troxel, W. M., & Matthews, K. A. (2004). What are the costs of marital conflict and dissolution to children's physical health? *Clinical Child and Family Psychology Review*, 7(1), 29–57.

U.S. Census Bureau (2015). 2010–2014 American Community Survey 5-Year Estimates. Retrieved from: https://www.census.gov/programs-surveys/acs/technical-documentation/table-and-geography-changes/2014/5-year.html.

Weaver, J. M., & Schofield, T. J. (2015). Mediation and moderation of divorce effects on children's behavior problems. *Journal of Family Psychology*, 29(1), 39.

Whiteside, M. F., & Becker, B. J. (2000). Parental factors and the young child's post-divorce adjustment: A meta-analysis with implications for parenting arrangements. *Journal of Family Psychology*, 14(1), 5.

Wolchik, S. A., Ma, Y., Tein, J. Y., Sandler, I. N., & Ayers, T. S. (2008). Parentally bereaved children's grief: Self-system beliefs as mediators of the relations between grief and stressors and caregiver–child relationship quality. *Death Studies*, 32(7), 597–620.

Wolchik, S. A., Tein, J. Y., Sandler, I. N., & Ayers, T. S. (2006). Stressors, quality of the child–caregiver relationship, and children's mental health problems after parental death: The mediating role of self-system beliefs. *Journal of Abnormal Child Psychology*, 34(2), 212–229.

Wolchik, S. A., Wilcox, K. L., Tein, J. Y., & Sandler, I. N. (2000). Maternal acceptance and consistency of discipline as buffers of divorce stressors on children's psychological adjustment problems. *Journal of Abnormal Child Psychology*, 28(1), 87–102.

Worden, J. W. (1996). *Children and grief: When a parent dies*. New York, NY: Guilford Press.

World Health Organization (2018). International classification of diseases for mortality and morbidity statistics (11th rev.). Retrieved from: https://icd.who.int/browse11/l-m/en.

Chapter 16

Quo Vadis

Amanda Venta, Carla Sharp, and Peter Fonagy

Chapter Overview

In this chapter, we first look back over what we have covered, revisiting the foundations we established in Part I and reviewing the skills we practiced and knowledge we gained in Parts II, III, and IV. We then turn our attention to the future of developmental psychopathology, asking "quo vadis" or "where are you going?"

Where Have We Been?

We began this textbook probably in the same way that you have begun many of your other psychology courses. We discussed the roots of our diagnostic system, the DSM, and the traditional, categorical approaches to classification. For our purposes, the most fatal flaw of traditional systems like the categorical DSM-based diagnostic system is that they create artificial categories of disorder that are not supported by data. Factor analytic research has shown this most acutely: when analysing all symptoms of all disorders, the diagnostic categories described in Section II of the DSM-5 rarely emerge. What we find instead are dimensions of psychopathology (for example, the internalizing, externalizing, and psychotic spectra) that explain correlations among symptoms. Disorder and non-disorder are not as neatly distinguishable as suggested by categorical diagnostic systems.

The discussion of dimensionality in Chapter 1 set the stage for the introduction of an alternative system to understanding psychopathology

Developmental Psychopathology, First Edition. Edited by Amanda Venta, Carla Sharp, Jack M. Fletcher, and Peter Fonagy.

in Chapter 2—the developmental psychopathology approach. We introduced you to a discipline and approach to science that we carried through the remaining chapters of this volume. We highlighted multiple important principles of the developmental psychopathology approach that all rely on the idea of a continuum between typical and atypical behaviour. For instance, you learned about homotypic and heterotypic continuity and how psychopathology may change shape over the course of development. You learned about equifinality and multifinality and how risk factors may lead to different or similar outcomes depending on interactions with developmental timing effects. You learned about multiple levels of analyses and how risk factors influence each other transactionally over time. Together, these characteristics of the developmental psychopathology approach can be organized into a framework that can be visually represented, and which we provide in broad terms again here for reference (Figure 16.1). You will by now be used to seeing this framework!

With the introduction of the developmental psychopathology approach, we were ready to introduce you to various manifestations of psychopathology. First, given the basic principle of typical–atypical continuity espoused in the developmental psychopathology approach, we had to introduce you to normal development to provide a context for the understanding of atypical behavior. We devoted Chapter 3 to ensuring that you have a good basic understanding of typical development, realizing that we look to typical developmental milestones to understand the development of psychopathology. For instance, in adolescence, we expect to see the beginnings of identity consolidation. It is against the backdrop of this expectation that we must interpret the development of, for instance, personality disorder. In those introductory chapters you also took an in-depth look at the research on attachment theory, a contextual variable that is highly predictive of a child's well-being, and a variable that was returned to time and time again in the subsequent chapters.

With this foundation, Part II highlighted the problems that typically emerge in childhood, providing a developmental psychopathology model for each diagnostic category we cover. It is somewhat unfortunate that we are still organizing problems according to DSM-based categories. We made the decision to do so, however, because this organization is familiar to most scholars and clinicians, and most research is conducted with this organizational structure in mind. We hope that in future years we can reorganize a volume such as this according to perhaps dimensional spectra (internalizing–externalizing–psychoticism) or even the RDoC dimensions that we referred to in Chapter 1. Likewise, in Part III we took the same approach, focusing on the problems that typically emerge during adolescence. Each of those chapters organized existing research along multiple levels of analysis—as the developmental psychopathology approach encourages— covering how a child's genes, brains, bodies, families, and environments predict whether they will demonstrate risk or resilience for psychopathology. While we included contextual factors in

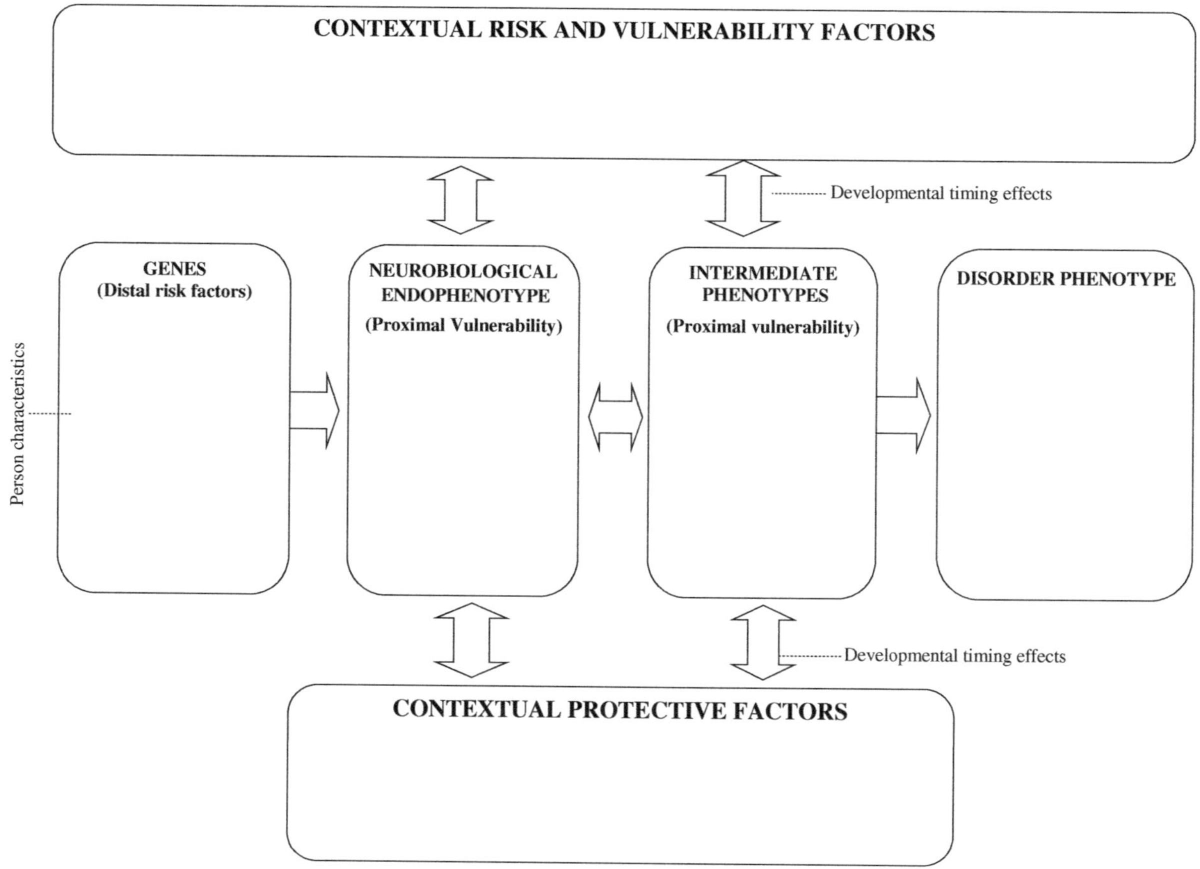

FIGURE 16.1 Developmental Psychopathology Framework

every model we presented in Parts II and III, we emphasized the importance of the child's context even more in Part IV, which covered maltreatment, divorce, and loss—events that can occur in a child's context and which play a strong role in predicting a child's developmental trajectory. The problems we discussed in Part IV are transdiagnostic and exemplify the developmental psychopathology approach perhaps best, because they break out of the confines of a categorical diagnostic approach.

Across the textbook, we hope you have seen how the principles of developmental psychopathology prove true in the mental health research we presented. Autism spectrum disorders, as you saw, tend to demonstrate homotypic continuity, while there is evidence of heterotypic continuity when we think about behavior problems changing shape across the lifespan. Individual factors, like beliefs and attitudes, play a strong role in risk for depression, but those individual factors may indeed come from familial, genetic, and brain-based sources. These are just a few examples of the principles of developmental psychopathology in action. Ultimately, we acknowledge that a developmental psychopathology approach is more complex than a traditional, categorical system of understanding mental disorders—but it does a better job of representing the best, cutting-edge science we have and perhaps cuts nature a little closer to its bones.

Where Are We Going?

Consistent with the developmental psychopathology approach, in recent years we have seen a developing consensus on the shared *etiology*, genetic manifestation, and transdiagnostic factors in the treatment of mental disorder. In some ways, the developmental psychopathology approach was ahead of its time. Indeed, there is accumulating evidence that might support the construction of a unified model of psychopathology that addresses diagnostic difficulties arising from comorbidity and differing severity of disorders as well as psychometric, genetic, and neuroscientific evidence suggestive of a general factor model of psychopathology. Think back across the chapters in this book—did you notice that some risk and protective factors came up again and again across disorders? Indeed, we have covered contextual, individual, biological, and genetic risk factors as well as protective factors that act *transdiagnostically*, or across disorders.

The General Psychopathology Factor: A Singular Model of Psychopathology

Why might we need a singular model for psychopathology? Mental disorder is traditionally divided into numerous diagnostic categories ostensibly associated with independent disease entities and, indeed, as we mentioned, most of this textbook has been arranged in that way. In this section, as we ask where developmental psychopathology is going, we are intending to make the case for a unified model of mental illness that may be termed *general psychopathology*. Accumulating evidence is mostly *factorial*, but is nonetheless proving increasingly troublesome for the currently dominant categorical models of mental disorder (Caspi & Moffitt, 2018; Lahey, Krueger, Rathouz, Waldman, & Zald, 2017; Smith, Atkinson, Davis, Riley, & Oltmanns, 2020).

Perhaps the most acutely felt source of dissatisfaction with diagnostic taxonomies arises from the high frequency of comorbidity (Kessler, Chiu, Demler, Merikangas, & Walters, 2005; Merikangas et al., 2010), as repeatedly demonstrated in large-scale surveys in the United States (Kessler et al., 2005; Kessler et al., 2011) and the U.K. (Bebbington et al., 2009; Farrell et al., 2003). Indeed, comorbidity appears to be very common in both clinical and community samples (e.g., Barlow, Sauer-Zavala, Carl, Bullis, & Ellard, 2014; Cummings, Caporino, & Kendall, 2014; Ormel et al., 2015). Comorbidity transcends diagnoses and overlap is observed between most symptoms known to be associated with mental disorder (e.g. Budde et al., 2018). If disorders were reconceptualized as indicators of latent transdiagnostic spectra, comorbidity would no longer be a problem. Indeed, if disorders share phenotypic and genotypic variance, comorbidity seems an inappropriate term that could be readily replaced by the phrase "frequent co-occurrence" (Goldberg, 2015).

A second, equally problematic area is the concept of *severity*. For example, Zimmerman and colleagues (Zimmerman, Morgan, & Stanton, 2018) demonstrate that the concept of severity has no reliable generally agreed referent, either across diagnostic categories or, at closer scrutiny, even within disorders such as depression. Severity is used to refer to the number of symptoms, intensity of symptoms, frequency or persistence of symptoms, impact of symptoms on quality of life, and likelihood of permanent disability or death. In brief, the current system of classification for mental disorders fails because it is unable to identify mutually exclusive and exhaustive categories and it fails to yield an empirically valid dimension of severity that is superior to clinical intuition. A single general category would remove the first problem and offer an elegant dimensional solution for the second.

Evidence for a singular model for psychopathology also derives from recent work in *factor analysis*, a well-established yet rapidly developing statistical method for depicting covariation (Wright, 2017). The *bifactor model* assumes that all variables have common variance contributing to a single factor independent of covariance accounted for by clusters of such variables (spectral level factors). The *p factor* (*p*) is thus a statistical summary of the variance common to symptoms, across diagnoses and spectral clusters. Caspi and Moffitt (2018) explain: "latent variable analysis posits that the positive correlations between symptoms (as well as disorders) arise from a g-like causal factor," where g refers to the concept of general intelligence. Replicated across numerous samples, *p* appears to capture an underlying propensity for any kind of psychopathology (Lahey et al., 2017; Smith et al., 2020).

GENETIC EVIDENCE

Behaviour genetic studies on families and twins tend to show that genetic risk is not specific to particular disorders, rather it is largely a transdiagnostic vulnerability (Franic, Dolan, Borsboom, van Beijsterveldt, & Boomsma, 2014; Lahey, Van Hulle, Singh, Waldman, & Rathouz, 2011; Pettersson, Anckarsater, Gillberg, & Lichtenstein, 2013; Pettersson, Larsson, & Lichtenstein, 2016). Findings from twin studies indicate a balanced influence between genetic and environmental effects on *p* scores (Harden et al., 2019; Rosenstrom et al., 2019; Waldman, Poore, van Hulle, Rathouz, & Lahey, 2016). The notion of a general vulnerability to psychopathology, regardless of diagnosis, is also supported by family studies that show a general rising of risk of mental disorder with increased relatedness given a diagnosis of severe mental disorder in a *proband* (e.g., Song et al., 2015). Molecular genetic studies confirm that phenotypic similarity can be accounted for by concordance at the molecular level (Cross-Disorder Group of the Psychiatric Genomics Consortium, 2013; Lee et al., 2013). A genome-wide association study of 25 brain disorders and 17 mental disorders from over 1 million participants reveals that mental disorders shared common variance risks (Brainstorm Consortium et al., 2018). This was less evident for brain disorders, normally considered neurological, which appear more distinct from each other.

NEUROBIOLOGICAL MODELS

A singular model of mental disorder most commonly invokes dysfunction of the prefrontal cortex (PFC) (Macdonald, Goines, Novacek, & Walker, 2016). There is evidence from meta-analytic studies of reduced grey matter volume in the PFC and limbic regions of individuals with mental disorder (Wise et al., 2016). Other findings of structural anomalies associated with *p* include grey matter in the cerebellum (Moberget et al., 2019; Romer et al., 2017), which has a role in coordinating thought and affect, and in white matter integrity in the body of the corpus callosum (Hinton et al., 2019; Riem et al., 2019). This finding may explain why a number of disorders are associated with anomalies of the corpus callosum (Phillips, Hewedi, Eissa, & Moustafa, 2015). These anomalies are likely to correspond to one or more neuro-behavioural processes that mediate the association between brain and psychological function across disorders; irregular cortical connectivity might be an endophenotype of general psychopathology (Caspi et al., 2014).

COGNITIVE FUNCTIONS

If we think in terms of brain activity, rather than biology, neuroscience consistently implicates two related areas of functioning across most mental health disorders. The first is *emotion dysregulation*. In general, poorly managed feelings interfere with purposeful activity (Beauchaine, 2015). In contrast, a person who regulates their emotion well can direct their attention to what they need to do to cope, can use their attention to focus but also to distract themselves if focusing is unlikely to help, and can reassess risks as the results of their actions unfold (Gross, 2014). Emotion dysregulation has been shown to be a feature of almost every diagnostic condition known to psychiatry (Beauchaine & Cicchetti, 2019) including: substance abuse (Weiss, Williams, & Connolly, 2015), eating disorder (Seidel et al., 2018; Svaldi, Griepenstroh, Tuschen-Caffier, & Ehring, 2012), depression (Lopez, Luby, Belden, & Barch, 2018), anxiety (Kircanski et al., 2018), PTSD (Fitzgerald, DiGangi, & Phan, 2018), ADHD (Steinberg & Drabick, 2015), conduct disorder (Beauchaine, Gatzke-Kopp, & Mead, 2007), borderline personality disorder (Herpertz, Schneider, Schmahl, & Bertsch, 2018; van Zutphen et al., 2018), and psychotic disorders (Kring & Caponigro, 2010; Nook et al., 2018). Just think about all the times that emotion regulation has come up in your reading of previous chapters!

The second general area of function that has been consistently associated with mental health disorder is *executive function* (McTeague et al., 2017). Executive function is the capacity to control thought (i.e., memory, attention, action) and generally direct information in the appropriate direction as relevant to any specific task. The quality of executive functions—cognitive processes that are deemed to be essential for healthy functioning—are thought to affect *p*. These executive functions include self-regulation, decision-making, sequencing of actions, planning, prioritizing, and navigating new tasks (Banich, 2009). Individuals with a high *p* score—signifying high persistent psychological distress—are oversensitive to difficult social interactions and they find it difficult to interpret the reasons for others' actions reliably and put potentially upsetting memories of experiences out of their mind. This leaves them vulnerable to emotional storms.

CONTINUITY AND DISCONTINUITY IN *P*

Researchers still do not understand very well what *p* is and there are many open questions and conflicting data about how *p* relates to mental disorder across the lifespan. Many believe that *p* reflects a vulnerability to psychopathology, as Caspi et al. (2014) suggest. If that were true, then we would expect it to show moderate-to-strong *homotypic differential stability*. In other words, individual differences in the propensity to develop mental health problems would be stable over time. We would also expect *p* and specific factors to show heterotypic associations in later childhood and adolescence. Across studies, the extent of heterotypic continuity (prediction across rather than within specific spectral factors) is relatively small (Castellanos-Ryan et al., 2016; McElroy, Belsky, Carragher, Fearon, & Patalay, 2018; McElroy, Shevlin, & Murphy, 2017; Snyder, Young, & Hankin, 2017). Surprisingly, longitudinal studies do not suggest that *p* becomes more specific across development (i.e., general vulnerability for psychopathology, *p*, in childhood does not seem to become specific to depression or anxiety in adolescence and adulthood, which would be called the increased specificity model). Likewise, longitudinal studies do not suggest a cascade model in which general vulnerability, *p*, creates increasing or snowballing problems across development (Greene & Eaton, 2017). Taken together, these findings show that the bulk of the variance in psychopathology, as it unfolds across development, may be largely attributable to an overarching mental disorder factor that is shared among symptoms that are currently assumed by clinicians to be manifestations of individual diagnostic domains. This is particularly true for internalizing problems: the phenotypic stability of diagnoses such as depression or anxiety may be owed to stability in general psychopathology. The stability coefficients hint that change over time may be greatest at the level of the general factor, *p*. Of course, it is possible that both cascade and increased specificity models are correct, but through the developmental processes one cancels out the other. In any case, there is little evidence to suggest that people with higher *p* scores will move in and out of various problems. The predictable sequence of emergence of specific diagnoses with development (for example, early fears in early childhood, increase in oppositional defiant disorder across middle childhood, the emergence of depression in adolescence, and personality disorders in young adulthood) is poorly explained by *p*. We may presume that the developmental salience of particular social experiences explains this sequence (Hankin et al., 2016)—that individuals may have the same difficulties from childhood to adulthood but that the environment around them changes and makes certain types of problems more prominent depending on their age—but there is no generally accepted model for the predictable developmental sequence of individual syndromes.

CLINICAL IMPLICATIONS

No one would suggest that we have sufficient evidence to advance a coherent singular biological model of mental disorder. What seems clear is that evidence from clinical, psychometric, developmental, genetic, and neuroscience domains suggest that substantial transdiagnostic overlap should be part of our understanding of what mental disorder is. The bifactor model neatly bypasses the controversy and makes the classical question of whether categories such as neuroses should be segregated into anxiety and depression obsolete (Norton & Paulus, 2016).

There is a practical reason for this emphasis on *p*. Although it is helpful for clinicians to shape their thinking in terms of diagnostic categories, and some (but not all) patients find it useful to have a diagnosis as a way of making sense of their distress, in reality there has been very little success in finding treatments that are highly tailored to a particular diagnosis. Pharmaceutical therapies are mostly focused around specific symptoms and the co-occurrence of symptoms in severe disorders accounts for the high prevalence of *polypharmacy* (prescribing a number of medications to the same person; Medhekar et al., 2019), relatively more common in groups at greatest social disadvantage (dosReis, Zhang, Qato, Camelo Castillo, & Reeves, 2020). The current trend for transdiagnostic approaches to psychological therapies may also link to the recognition that young people presenting with multiple problems will be best served by approaches that are relevant to a wide range of presenting problems (Hofmann & Hayes, 2019).

There are, in summary, several lines of research that suggest turning away from considering the diagnostic entities listed in DSM and instead turning towards considering mental disorders to be problems of living that are powerfully imbued with genetic influence but evolve into complex structures shaped by biological and social influences reflecting a range of loosely coupled mechanisms. The idea is also in keeping with a broader movement in mental health to shift towards thinking of mental health as a dimensional spectrum, rather than in terms of discrete disease units—as you might remember from Chapter 1.

However, the emphasis on *p* leaves us with another, larger problem that will also shape work in developmental psychopathology in the near future: what is *p*, other than a clever statistical construct derived through factor analyses? Perhaps the *p*-factor is best understood as a resilience index, such that individuals with high levels of *p* have low resilience. This idea is very much consistent with the developmental psychopathology approach that we discussed in Chapter 2 when we talked about how the complex transactions of risk and protective factors in interaction with developmental timing effects differentially affect outcomes. Low resilience in our proposed model is derived from an inability to make use of social learning. Specifically, research has shown that those with higher levels of psychopathology struggle to learn from caregivers, peers, teachers, and even therapists. The problem in making use of the social environment to learn about yourself, others, and the world may stem from the fact that individuals thus afflicted do not trust that the knowledge transmitted from others is in their best interest. We have termed this "epistemic mistrust." Imagine, for instance, an 11-year-old whose mother asks her to help tidy up the living room because guests will arrive soon. If the child has epistemic trust, she will likely agree with her mother's request, trusting that her mom is teaching her the norms for when guests come to visit. The knowledge imparted from mom is therefore seen as useful and relevant to her, personally. However, if the child has epistemic mistrust, she might refuse on the basis of thinking that her mom just wants to impress the neighbors and is using her for that purpose. In this case, the knowledge is seen as irrelevant at best, and malignant at worst. We think that epistemic mistrust may come about in cases where a child had continuously felt misunderstood or unrecognized, thereby obliterating any openness to learn from others.

The developmental psychopathology approach recommended dimensionalization of psychopathology nearly 40 years ago and we are very happy to see this labor now bearing fruit. Our interpretation of *p* is one of many, and we predict that most of the attention in psychopathology research moving forward will be focused on further elucidating the meaning of *p*, alongside alternative dimensional structures for psychopathology. Accordingly, our treatment approaches will focus on addressing the common factor *p*, shared by all psychopathology. In this regard, we welcome the move away from manualized treatments that focus on discreet disorders and look forward to the development and evaluation of more transdiagnostic treatment approaches. As developmental psychopathologists, we will always argue most strongly in favor of not losing sight of development in this pursuit.

Glossary

Bifactor model assumes that all variables have common variance contributing to a single factor independent of covariance accounted for by clusters of such variables (spectral level factors).

Emotion dysregulation refers to poorly managed feelings that can interfere with purposeful activity.

Etiology refers to the cause of a disorder.

Executive function is the capacity to control thought (i.e., memory, attention, action) and generally direct information in the appropriate direction as relevant to any specific task.

Factor analysis (or *factorial*) is a well-established statistical method for depicting covariation.

Homotypic differential stability means that individual differences in the propensity to develop mental health problems will be stable over time.

P factor (*p*) is a statistical summary of the variance common to symptoms, across diagnoses and spectral clusters.

Polypharmacy refers to prescribing a number of medications to the same person.

Proband refers to the person who serves as the starting point in a genetic study.

Transdiagnostically means cutting across diagnostic categories.

References

Banich, M. T. (2009). Executive function: The search for an integrated account. Current Directions in Psychological Science, 18(2), 89–94. doi: 10.1111/j.1467-8721.2009.01615.x.

Barlow, D. H., Sauer-Zavala, S., Carl, J. R., Bullis, J. R., & Ellard, K. K. (2014). The nature, diagnosis, and treatment of neuroticism. Clinical Psychological Science, 2(3), 344–365.doi:10.1177/2167702613505532.

Beauchaine, T. P. (2015). Future directions in emotion dysregulation and youth psychopathology. Journal of Clinical Child and Adolescent Psychology, 44(5), 875–896. doi: 10.1080/15374416.2015.1038827.

Beauchaine, T. P., & Cicchetti, D. E. (2019). Emotion dysregulation. Development and Psychopathology, 31(3). doi: 10.1017/S0954579419000415.

Beauchaine, T. P., Gatzke-Kopp, L., & Mead, H. K. (2007). Polyvagal theory and developmental psychopathology: Emotion dysregulation and conduct problems from preschool to adolescence. Biological Psychology, 74(2), 174–184. doi: 10.1016/j.biopsycho.2005.08.008.

Bebbington, P. E., Cooper, C., Minot, S., Brugha, T. S., Jenkins, R., Meltzer, H., & Dennis, M. (2009). Suicide attempts, gender, and sexual abuse: Data from the 2000 British Psychiatric Morbidity Survey. American Journal of Psychiatry, 166(10), 1135–1140. doi: 10.1176/appi.ajp.2009.09030310.

Brainstorm Consortium, Anttila, V., Bulik-Sullivan, B., Finucane, H. K., Walters, R. K., Bras, J., & Murray, R. (2018). Analysis of shared heritability in common disorders of the brain. Science, 360(6395). doi: 10.1126/science.aap8757.

Budde, M., Anderson-Schmidt, H., Gade, K., Reich-Erkelenz, D., Adorjan, K., Kalman, J. L., & Heilbronner, U. (2018). A longitudinal approach to biological psychiatric research: The PsyCourse study. *American Journal of Medical Genetics Part B: Neuropsychiatric Genetics*. doi: 10.1002/ajmg.b.32639.

Caspi, A., Houts, R. M., Belsky, D. W., Goldman-Mellor, S. J., Harrington, H., Israel, S., & Moffitt, T. E. (2014). The *p* factor: One general psychopathology factor in the structure of psychiatric disorders? Clinical Psychological Science, 2(2), 119–137. doi: 10.1177/2167702613497473.

Caspi, A., & Moffitt, T. E. (2018). All for one and one for all: Mental disorders in one dimension. American Journal of Psychiatry, 175(9), 831–844. doi: 10.1176/appi.ajp.2018.17121383.

Castellanos-Ryan, N., Briere, F. N., O'Leary-Barrett, M., Banaschewski, T., Bokde, A., Bromberg, U., & Consortium, I. (2016). The structure of psychopathology in adolescence and its common personality and cognitive correlates. Journal of Abnormal Psychology, 125(8), 1039–1052. doi: 10.1037/abn0000193.

Cross-Disorder Group of the Psychiatric Genomics Consortium (2013). Identification of risk loci with shared effects on five major psychiatric disorders: A genome-wide analysis. Lancet, 381(9875), 1371–1379. doi: 10.1016/S0140-6736(12)62129-1.

Cummings, C. M., Caporino, N. E., & Kendall, P. C. (2014). Comorbidity of anxiety and depression in children and adolescents: 20 years after. Psychological Bulletin, 140(3), 816–845. doi: 10.1037/a0034733.

dosReis, S., Zhang, C., Qato, D. M., Camelo Castillo, W., & Reeves, G. (2020). Family adverse experiences and psychotropic polypharmacy among US youth: 2009–2015. *Pediatrics*. doi: 10.1542/peds.2019-2705.

Farrell, M., Howes, S., Bebbington, P., Brugha, T., Jenkins, R., Lewis, G., & Meltzer, H. (2003). Nicotine, alcohol and drug dependence, and psychiatric comorbidity—Results of a national household survey. International

Review of Psychiatry, 15(1–2), 50–56. doi: 10.1080/09540260210000045949.

Fitzgerald, J. M., DiGangi, J. A., & Phan, K. L. (2018). Functional neuroanatomy of emotion and its regulation in PTSD. Harvard Review of Psychiatry, 26(3), 116–128. doi: 10.1097/HRP.0000000000000185.

Franic, S., Dolan, C. V., Borsboom, D., van Beijsterveldt, C. E., & Boomsma, D. I. (2014). Three-and-a-half-factor model? The genetic and environmental structure of the CBCL/6-18 internalizing grouping. Behavior Genetics, 44(3), 254–268. doi: 10.1007/s10519-013-9628-4.

Goldberg, D. (2015). Psychopathology and classification in psychiatry. Social Psychiatry and Psychiatric Epidemiology, 50(1), 1–5. doi: 10.1007/s00127-014-0924-y.

Greene, A. L., & Eaton, N. R. (2017). The temporal stability of the bifactor model of comorbidity: An examination of moderated continuity pathways. Comprehensive Psychiatry, 72, 74–82. doi: 10.1016/j.comppsych.2016.09.010.

Gross, J. J. (2014). Emotion regulation: Conceptual and empirical foundations. In J. J. Gross (Ed.), *Handbook of emotion regulation* (2nd ed., pp. 3–20). New York, NY: Guilford Press.

Hankin, B. L., Snyder, H. R., Gulley, L. D., Schweizer, T. H., Bijttebier, P., Nelis, S., & Vasey, M. W. (2016). Understanding comorbidity among internalizing problems: Integrating latent structural models of psychopathology and risk mechanisms. Development and Psychopathology, 28(4 pt.1), 987–1012. doi: 10.1017/S0954579416000663.

Harden, K. P., Engelhardt, L. E., Mann, F. D., Patterson, M. W., Grotzinger, A. D., Savicki, S. L., & Church, J. A. (2019). Genetic associations between executive functions and a general factor of psychopathology. *Journal of the American Academy of Child & Adolescent Psychiatry.*

Herpertz, S. C., Schneider, I., Schmahl, C., & Bertsch, K. (2018). Neurobiological mechanisms mediating emotion dysregulation as targets of change in borderline personality disorder. Psychopathology, 51(2), 96–104. doi: 10.1159/000488357.

Hinton, K. E., Lahey, B. B., Villalta-Gil, V., Meyer, F. A. C., Burgess, L. L., Chodes, L. K., & Zald, D. H. (2019). White matter microstructure correlates of general and specific second-order factors of psychopathology. NeuroImage. Clinical, 22, 101705. doi: 10.1016/j.nicl.2019.101705.

Hofmann, S. G., & Hayes, S. C. (2019). The future of intervention science: Process-based therapy. Clinical Psychological Science, 7(1), 37–50. doi: 10.1177/2167702618772296.

Kessler, R. C., Chiu, W. T., Demler, O., Merikangas, K. R., & Walters, E. E. (2005). Prevalence, severity, and comorbidity of 12-month DSM-IV disorders in the National Comorbidity Survey Replication. Archives of General Psychiatry, 62(6), 617–627. doi: 10.1001/archpsyc.62.6.617.

Kessler, R. C., Ormel, J., Petukhova, M., McLaughlin, K. A., Green, J. G., Russo, L. J., & Ustun, T. B. (2011). Development of lifetime comorbidity in the World Health Organization world mental health surveys. Archives of General Psychiatry, 68(1), 90–100. doi: 10.1001/archgenpsychiatry.2010.180.

Kircanski, K., White, L. K., Tseng, W. L., Wiggins, J. L., Frank, H. R., Sequeira, S., & Brotman, M. A. (2018). A latent variable approach to differentiating neural mechanisms of irritability and anxiety in youth. JAMA Psychiatry, 75(6), 631–639. doi: 10.1001/jamapsychiatry.2018.0468.

Kring, A. M., & Caponigro, J. M. (2010). Emotion in schizophrenia: Where feeling meets thinking. Current Directions in Psychological Science, 19(4), 255–259. doi: 10.1177/0963721410377599.

Lahey, B. B., Krueger, R. F., Rathouz, P. J., Waldman, I. D., & Zald, D. H. (2017). Validity and utility of the general factor of psychopathology. World Psychiatry, 16(2), 142–144. doi: 10.1002/wps.20410.

Lahey, B. B., Van Hulle, C. A., Singh, A. L., Waldman, I. D., & Rathouz, P. J. (2011). Higher-order genetic and environmental structure of prevalent forms of child and adolescent psychopathology. Archives of General Psychiatry, 68(2), 181–189. doi: 10.1001/archgenpsychiatry.2010.192.

Lee, S. H., Ripke, S., Neale, B. M., Faraone, S. V., Purcell, S. M., Perlis, R. H., & International Inflammatory Bowel Disease Genetics (2013). Genetic relationship between five psychiatric disorders estimated from genome-wide SNPs. Nature Genetics, 45(9), 984–994. doi: 10.1038/ng.2711.

Lopez, K. C., Luby, J. L., Belden, A. C., & Barch, D. M. (2018). Emotion dysregulation and functional connectivity in children with and without a history of major depressive disorder. Cognitive, Affective & Behavioral Neuroscience, 18(2), 232–248. doi: 10.3758/s13415-018-0564-x.

Macdonald, A. N., Goines, K. B., Novacek, D. M., & Walker, E. F. (2016). Prefrontal mechanisms of comorbidity from a transdiagnostic and ontogenic perspective. Development and Psychopathology, 28(4 pt.1), 1147–1175. doi: 10.1017/S0954579416000742.

McElroy, E., Belsky, J., Carragher, N., Fearon, P., & Patalay, P. (2018). Developmental stability of general and specific factors of psychopathology from early childhood to adolescence: Dynamic mutualism or *p*-differentiation? Journal of Child Psychology and Psychiatry, 59(6), 667–675. doi: 10.1111/jcpp.12849.

McElroy, E., Shevlin, M., & Murphy, J. (2017). Internalizing and externalizing disorders in childhood and adolescence: A latent transition analysis using ALSPAC data. Comprehensive Psychiatry, 75, 75–84. doi: 10.1016/j.comppsych.2017.03.003.

McTeague, L. M., Huemer, J., Carreon, D. M., Jiang, Y., Eickhoff, S. B., & Etkin, A. (2017). Identification of common neural circuit disruptions in cognitive control across psychiatric disorders. American Journal of Psychiatry, 174(7), 676–685. doi: 10.1176/appi.ajp.2017.16040400.

Medhekar, R., Fujimoto, K., Aparasu, R. R., Bhatara, V. S., Johnson, M. L., Alonzo, J. P., & Chen, H. (2019). Physician care coordination and the use of psychotropic polypharmacy in the management of pediatric mental disorders. Journal of Management Care Special Pharmacy, 25(1), 29–38. doi: 10.18553/jmcp.2019.25.1.029.

Merikangas, K. R., He, J. P., Burstein, M., Swanson, S. A., Avenevoli, S., Cui, L., & Swendsen, J. (2010). Lifetime prevalence of mental disorders in U.S. adolescents: Results from the National Comorbidity Survey Replication—Adolescent Supplement (NCS-A). Journal of the American Academy of Child and Adolescent Psychiatry, 49(10), 980–989. doi: 10.1016/j.jaac.2010.05.017.

Moberget, T., Alnaes, D., Kaufmann, T., Doan, N. T., Cordova-Palomera, A., Norbom, L. B., & Westlye, L. T. (2019). Cerebellar gray matter volume is associated with cognitive function and psychopathology in adolescence. Biological Psychiatry, 86(1), 65–75. doi: 10.1016/j.biopsych.2019.01.019.

Nook, E. C., Dodell-Feder, D., Germine, L. T., Hooley, J. M., DeLisi, L. E., & Hooker, C. I. (2018). Weak dorsolateral prefrontal response to social criticism predicts worsened mood and symptoms following social conflict in people at familial risk for schizophrenia. NeuroImage. Clinical, 18, 40–50. doi: 10.1016/j.nicl.2018.01.004.

Norton, P. J., & Paulus, D. J. (2016). Toward a unified treatment for emotional disorders: Update on the science and practice. Behavior Therapy, 47(6), 854–868. doi: 10.1016/j.beth.2015.07.002.

Ormel, J., Raven, D., van Oort, F., Hartman, C. A., Reijneveld, S. A., Veenstra, R., & Oldehinkel, A. J. (2015). Mental health in Dutch adolescents: A TRAILS report on prevalence, severity, age of onset, continuity and co-morbidity of DSM disorders. Psychological Medicine, 45(2), 345–360. doi: 10.1017/S0033291714001469.

Pettersson, E., Anckarsater, H., Gillberg, C., & Lichtenstein, P. (2013). Different neurodevelopmental symptoms have a common genetic etiology. Journal of Child Psychology and Psychiatry, 54(12), 1356–1365. doi: 10.1111/jcpp.12113.

Pettersson, E., Larsson, H., & Lichtenstein, P. (2016). Common psychiatric disorders share the same genetic origin: A multivariate sibling study of the Swedish population. Molecular Psychiatry, 21(5), 717–721. doi: 10.1038/mp.2015.116.

Phillips, J. R., Hewedi, D. H., Eissa, A. M., & Moustafa, A. A. (2015). The cerebellum and psychiatric disorders. Front Public Health, 3, 66. doi: 10.3389/fpubh.2015.00066.

Riem, M. M. E., van Hoof, M. J., Garrett, A. S., Rombouts, S., van der Wee, N. J. A., van, I. M. H., & Vermeiren, R. (2019). General psychopathology factor and unresolved-disorganized attachment uniquely correlated to white matter integrity using diffusion tensor imaging. Behavioural Brain Research, 359, 1–8. doi: 10.1016/j.bbr.2018.10.014.

Romer, A. L., Knodt, A. R., Houts, R., Brigidi, B. D., Moffitt, T. E., Caspi, A., & Hariri, A. R. (2017). Structural alterations within cerebellar circuitry are associated with general liability for common mental disorders. *Molecular Psychiatry*. doi: 10.1038/mp.2017.57.

Rosenstrom, T., Czajkowski, N. O., Ystrom, E., Krueger, R. F., Aggen, S. H., Gillespie, N. A., & Torvik, F. A. (2019). Genetically informative mediation modeling applied to stressors and personality-disorder traits in etiology of alcohol use disorder. Behavior Genetics, 49(1), 11–23. doi: 10.1007/s10519-018-9941-z.

Seidel, M., King, J. A., Ritschel, F., Boehm, I., Geisler, D., Bernardoni, F., & Ehrlich, S. (2018). Processing and regulation of negative emotions in anorexia nervosa: An fMRI study. NeuroImage. Clinical, 18, 1–8. doi: 10.1016/j.nicl.2017.12.035.

Smith, G. T., Atkinson, E. A., Davis, H. A., Riley, E. N., & Oltmanns, J. R. (2020). The general factor of psychopathology. *Annual Review of Clinical Psychology*. doi: 10.1146/annurev-clinpsy-071119-115848.

Snyder, H. R., Young, J. F., & Hankin, B. L. (2017). Strong homotypic continuity in common psychopathology-, internalizing-, and externalizing-specific factors over time in adolescents. Clinical Psychological Science, 5(1), 98–110. doi: 10.1177/2167702616651076.

Song, J., Bergen, S. E., Kuja-Halkola, R., Larsson, H., Landen, M., & Lichtenstein, P. (2015). Bipolar disorder and its relation to major psychiatric disorders: A family-based study in the Swedish population. Bipolar Disorders, 17(2), 184–193. doi: 10.1111/bdi.12242.

Steinberg, E. A., & Drabick, D. A. (2015). A developmental psychopathology perspective on ADHD and comorbid conditions: The role of emotion regulation. Child Psychiatry and Human Development, 46(6), 951–966. doi: 10.1007/s10578-015-0534-2.

Svaldi, J., Griepenstroh, J., Tuschen-Caffier, B., & Ehring, T. (2012). Emotion regulation deficits in eating disorders: A marker of eating pathology or general psychopathology? Psychiatry Research, 197(1–2), 103–111. doi: 10.1016/j.psychres.2011.11.009.

van Zutphen, L., Siep, N., Jacob, G. A., Domes, G., Sprenger, A., Willenborg, B., & Arntz, A. (2018). Always on guard: Emotion regulation in women with borderline personality disorder compared to nonpatient controls and patients with cluster-C personality disorder. Journal of Psychiatry and Neuroscience, 43(1), 37–47. doi: 10.1503/jpn.170008.

Waldman, I. D., Poore, H. E., van Hulle, C., Rathouz, P. J., & Lahey, B. B. (2016). External validity of a hierarchical dimensional model of child and adolescent psychopathology: Tests using confirmatory factor analyses and multivariate behavior genetic analyses. Journal of Abnormal Psychology, 125(8), 1053–1066. doi: 10.1037/abn0000183.

Weiss, N. H., Williams, D. C., & Connolly, K. M. (2015). A preliminary examination of negative affect, emotion dysregulation, and risky behaviors among military veterans in residential substance abuse treatment.

Military Behavioral Health, 3(4), 212–218. doi: 10.1080/21635781.2015.1038405.

Wise, T., Radua, J., Via, E., Cardoner, N., Abe, O., Adams, T. M., & Arnone, D. (2016). Common and distinct patterns of grey-matter volume alteration in major depression and bipolar disorder: Evidence from voxel-based meta-analysis. *Molecular Psychiatry*. doi: 10.1038/mp.2016.72.

Wright, A. G. C. (2017). The current state and future of factor analysis in personality disorder research. Personality Disorders: Theory, Research, and Treatment, 8(1), 14–25. doi: 10.1037/per0000216.

Zimmerman, M., Morgan, T. A., & Stanton, K. (2018). The severity of psychiatric disorders. World Psychiatry, 17(3), 258–275. doi: 10.1002/wps.20569.

Index

Please note that page references to Figures will be followed by the letter 'f', to Tables by the letter 't'

Developmental Psychopathology, First Edition. Edited by Amanda Venta, Carla Sharp, Peter Fonagy, and Jack M. Fletcher.